Pro MySQL

MICHAEL KRUCKENBERG AND JAY PIPES

Lead Editors: Jason Gilmore, Matthew Moodie
Technical Reviewer: Chad Russell
Editorial Board: Steve Anglin, Dan Appleman, Ewan Buckingham, Gary Cornell, Tony Davis, Jason Gilmore, Jonathan Hassell, Chris Mills, Dominic Shakeshaft, Jim Sumser
Associate Publisher: Grace Wong
Project Manager: Kylie Johnston
Copy Edit Manager: Nicole LeClerc
Copy Editors: Marilyn Smith, Susannah Pfalzer
Assistant Production Director: Kari Brooks-Copony
Production Editor: Linda Marousek
Compositor, Artist, and Interior Designer: Diana Van Winkle, Van Winkle Design Group
Proofreader: Patrick Vincent, Write Ideas Editorial Consulting
Indexer: Ann Rogers
Cover Designer: Kurt Krames
Manufacturing Manager: Tom Debolski

Distributed to the book trade worldwide by Springer-Verlag New York, Inc., 233 Spring Street, 6th Floor, New York, NY 10013. Phone 1-800-SPRINGER, fax 201-348-4505, e-mail orders-ny@springer-sbm.com, or visit http://www.springeronline.com.

For information on translations, please contact Apress directly at 2560 Ninth Street, Suite 219, Berkeley, CA 94710. Phone 510-549-5930, fax 510-549-5939, e-mail info@apress.com, or visit http://www.apress.com.

The information in this book is distributed on an "as is" basis, without warranty. Although every precaution has been taken in the preparation of this work, neither the author(s) nor Apress shall have any liability to any person or entity with respect to any loss or damage caused or alleged to be caused directly or indirectly by the information contained in this work.

The source code for this book is available to readers at http://www.apress.com in the Downloads section.

Contents at a Glance

PART 1 ■■■ Design and Development

PART 2 ■■■ Administration

Contents

PART 1 ■■■ Design and Development

PART 2 ■■■ Administration

Foreword

I get a lot of requests to review books—at least one a month. I've made a point of telling publishers that I will be happy to try, but then explain to them that I complete only every other request. I stay fairly busy working on MySQL and directing its development. If the book puts me to sleep in the first chapter, I know I will never make it through. Even on the best of occasions, I normally read only perhaps three-quarters of the book before I need to get back to coding.

One reason I rarely finish books that I am reviewing is that I don't believe that technical books need to be dry. I think that any topic can be made interesting. I read very few technical books from cover to cover for this reason. To write a good technical book that someone will enjoy does not mean that you have to be funny. (I once read a JDBC book that made mention of different rock lyrics every other paragraph in an attempt to be hip; I obviously never completed it.) I could never finish a book that covered the basics of MySQL and rehashed the material of the dozens of other MySQL books written.

Now, writing a foreword for a book is even harder than reviewing a book for me. Not only do I have to read the book, but I know that I am so late in the review process that I can't point out factual errors. Let's start right here by giving some credit to the authors of this book. Pointing out any errors in this book would just be me being nitpicky. This book covers the 5.0 release of the MySQL Server, and getting a book right on 5.0 is pretty hard, since we are at a code freeze for release right now; 5.0 is done and we are getting ready to ship. Software being what it is, that doesn't mean a few changes don't occur. Getting a book this close is an incredible feat, and nothing you read here will lead you astray.

MySQL use is continuing to grow. I first started hacking on MySQL in graduate school while I worked on medical projects. The database I was using at the time ran out of steam, and I needed something that was fast enough to store the data I was mining. I had MySQL up and running the same morning I found it, and had data being logged into it by that afternoon. Now, years later, I'm one of the few dozen programmers who work on it full time. Success was not only due to the fact that the database was easy to install and free, but was because it was well-written software. MySQL's install base is about six million today, with forty thousand downloads a day occurring from our web site alone. This means, in the world of the Internet and Open Source, that we probably dramatically underestimate our usage.

Two linked observations occur to me nowadays about MySQL's place in the software ecosystem: it's spreading fast, and not enough people know it deeply enough to truly be called MySQL experts.

Once a month in Seattle, I go to my favorite bar and sit down with MySQL users and discuss whatever they want to talk about. Some months we discuss obscure issues like B-tree fragmentation, and other months we talk about the latest and greatest in RAID controller cards. We never discuss beer, honest. There are many large companies in Seattle, from classical companies like actuaries to more modern ones like online merchants. MySQL users run the gamut. They realize that MySQL plays some part in their diverse IT infrastructure, and their DBAs and CTOs show up to talk about what they are doing and how they are making use of MySQL. We also get a few people each meeting who are trying to learn about MySQL and are looking for resources to do so.

Even with more people learning about MySQL every day, there are simply not enough MySQL experts to go around. There are employers and projects who need more experts. As enterprise growth with MySQL has increased, I've seen an increase in the number of questions concerning how MySQL works. How does it store its indexes? How can I benchmark my application with my database? What is the best storage engine for my application? These questions and similar ones really push what MySQL experts need to know. If you are a DBA today, you really need to know more about how your database runs and how you integrate it into your environment.

There have been a number of poorly written books on MySQL over the years. Reading this book brings a smile to my face, since I can see that some great writers are now putting their efforts into changing this. This bodes well for people on all sides of the database world.

Brian Aker

Director of Architecture, MySQL AB

About the Authors

MICHAEL KRUCKENBERG started his career with web technologies more than ten years ago. His first major undertaking was bringing a small mail-order company online (using MySQL). After hopping around a bit during the 1990s Internet boom and spending time in the Internet startup world, Mike put his feet down at his current gig, senior programmer at Tufts University. He is now the technical manager for the Apache/Perl/MySQL-driven Tufts University Sciences Knowledgebase (TUSK), a content repository for faculty and students. Mike likes to spend his elusive free time with his wife and kids on New England adventures, has a healthy addiction to music, and likes to dabble in the arts (photography, video, and literature). You can read the latest about Mike at `http://mike.kruckenberg.com` and can always get in touch with him at `mike@kruckenberg.com`.

For the past ten years, **JAY PIPES** has worked with all kinds of companies, large and small, to identify the value of the information they collect and help them build software that best addresses the needs of their businesses. From e-commerce to work-order management systems, Jay has been involved in projects with both Microsoft and open-source technologies. Passionate about programming and all things technical, Jay now runs his own consulting business, based in Columbus, Ohio. When not being bothered by his two cats, two dogs, and a constantly ringing phone, he can be found, headphones pulled across his ears, happily coding away at home. He welcomes any suggestions regarding this book (or any other subject, for that matter), and you can read about Jay's current adventures at `http://jpipes.com`. You can always contact him at `jay@jpipes.com`.

About the Technical Reviewer

CHAD RUSSELL is currently a software engineer/project manager for CDI IT Solutions, specifically with LiquidMedium web-based software. He is also the founder of Russell Information Technologies, Inc. (RIT), an open-source enterprise software startup. Chad currently resides in Jacksonville, Florida, with his wife Kim. Chad has worked on numerous enterprise-level projects over the past six years, primarily developing and integrating PHP and MySQL web-based applications. He is currently busy with RIT and providing IT consulting. Chad is very active in his church, where he has been a member for 23 years. His hobbies include music (playing bass guitar), writing, fishing, programming, and finding new business opportunities. His key to success: Matthew 6:33.

Acknowledgments

I grew up in a tiny town in North Dakota, where it was not unusual to see tumbleweeds roll through the middle of town, and movies always came six months later than the posters said they would. Despite being a bit behind the times, the town's two-year college and library both prioritized acquisition of a few of the early personal computers, and made them available to reckless kids who would otherwise be putting coins on the train tracks or riding dirt bikes through the alleys looking for trouble. It was in that library and the iconic "Old Main" building of the technical college that I first got a taste for the power of writing instructions and letting the computer do the work. It's easy to trace my computing addiction back to those early years. Thanks to the folks in small-town North Dakota for putting at my fingertips the tools that would eventually lead to a career in technology and my having the confidence to agree to tackle this book. I would like to thank all the friends, family members, employees, employers, and co-workers who supported my interest in learning new technologies.

More specifically, I'd like to thank my older brother, Pete, who is a mentor extraordinaire and a source of career and personal inspiration. Our history of conversations is a big part of where I am and where I'm going. I also owe a lot to my father, Marlyn, who has always been an example of working hard and not letting sleep take precedence over opportunity. Thanks for letting Pete and me convince you that having a TRS-80 at home would revitalize your in-home business.

This book wouldn't be much without Jay, who wrote about everything I couldn't (or didn't want to), including taking the book into the depths of the MySQL code. Your writing, and suggestions for my writing, made a huge difference in the direction and outcome of the book.

I must also thank the Apress team, who are all superstars and have an incredible (although it's the only one I've seen) process for helping authors get their thoughts into print. Working with Jason, Kylie, Chad, Matt, Marilyn, Linda, and Susannah has been a great experience. Thanks for your contributions to the book, which wouldn't be nearly as good without your efforts.

To my kids, Johanna and Ezra, thanks for learning to get breakfast yourself so I could sleep a few more minutes in the morning after countless late nights. You have both been patient while dad spends evenings and weekends hunkered over the laptop.

And last, to Heidi, you have been more supportive than I could have imagined. Thanks for pulling double-duty during this longer-than-expected process, and for making it easy for me to feel good about spending yet another evening writing.

Michael Kruckenberg

I once sat through a technical interview a number of years ago for a position I eventually received. My interviewer, Ron Kyle, drilled me on a battery of programming questions, and I answered each to the best of my knowledge. After hearing my answers to the technical questions, Ron turned to me and asked with a sly smile on his mug, "In the United States Senate, what is the purpose of *cloture*?"

I remember turning a bit pale-faced at the time. Ron had noticed on my résumé that I had been a political science major in university. It just so happened that Ron had held a politics and military history teaching position at West Point while in the United States Army. He had decided to test whether I actually remembered anything from my classes in college. I don't remember whether I answered correctly (cloture is a method by which a filibuster can be ended through a 60% vote of senators), but Ron's question made a lasting impression on me.

The technical acumen of a person is not the entire measure of one's ability to contribute to a project. A team of people devoted to a project brings a wide range of skills, passions, knowledge, and differences to the table; it is the mark of a good team to recognize and celebrate those differences.

Though the members of the remarkable team of which Ron and I were each a part have long since gone our separate ways, I look back fondly at the work we accomplished and the extraordinary mixture of talent and diversity manifested there. So, Ron, I'd like to thank you for showing me the human side of technology and reminding me that our differences provide our work with strength and flexibility.

I would also like to thank the brilliant and patient team at Apress. First and foremost, Jason Gilmore, our editor, and the Apress team, thank you for the opportunity to write about a subject which so thrills me, and secondly for providing a consistent and supportive foundation on which to create both Mike's and my first major text. Kylie Johnston, our project manager, thank you for your unending patience in dealing with our often sidetracked schedule; your efforts are much appreciated. Chad Russell, our excellent technical reviewer, thank you for your diligence in examining our code and scripts with as much attention as you paid to your own book.

Marilyn Smith, your attention to detail during our copyedit stage saved me unknown embarrassment for my flagrant violations of English grammar rules. And finally, Linda Marousek, thank you for your work during the production stages of the book.

To my co-author, Mike, I know that both of us have been through a roller coaster in this, our first book. I thank you for your wonderful input and your technical and writing skills. I couldn't have asked for a more complementary author in this endeavor. I feel our long hours and many conversations have created something greater than the sum of its two parts. Thank you ever so much.

Last, but far from least, thank you to Julie for persevering through countless nights of me working until 4 a.m. scrambling to complete a chapter; you've been my biggest and most unsung supporter.

Jay Pipes

Introduction

Data, in all varieties, continues to be the cornerstone from which modern organizations and businesses derive their information capital. Whether putting items in an online shopping cart for checkout or tracking terabytes of purchase history to find shopping trends, having a database to store and retrieve data has become a necessity. From the individual to the small nonprofit organization, the small business to the large corporation, retrieving stored information at the right time and in the right format is helping people make more informed business decisions. The demand for larger amounts of data, stored in more user-friendly formats and using faster database tools, continues to grow.

About MySQL and MySQL AB

While the demand for tools to store, retrieve, and mine data has grown, MySQL AB has been hard at work building the database to handle these ever-increasing needs. When initially released, MySQL focused on speed and simplicity, intentionally sacrificing some of the more advanced features of proprietary relational database management systems for better performance. For many years, MySQL focused on performance and stability, but as it rose in the market, the database fell under criticism for its lack of advanced features, including things like foreign keys, row-level locking, stored procedures, views, triggers, and clustering.

As MySQL has matured, these features have been added to the database server, after ensuring that such functionality does not come at the cost of performance and ease of use. The combination of simplicity, speed, and a full feature set makes MySQL a compelling option when considering how to meet the data demands of your application or organization.

We believe MySQL can play a central part in helping you better meet your data storage and retrieval needs. We are excited to be writing about MySQL, because it's an exciting movement as well as exciting software, which continues to demonstrate its value to a wide array of organizations. We are both passionate about MySQL as a company and MySQL as a database platform. MySQL AB has set the bar for how open-source technology companies can and *should* embrace the community of developers who have long been locked into the traditional patent-based software paradigm. The MySQL database server platform is a shining example of what can happen when truly brilliant minds are brought together under the umbrella of a company that values diversity, community input, and the contributions of the world community.

As we've written this book, it's painfully clear that MySQL is constantly moving forward. Performance enhancement, stability, and new features continue to take the source code and interface to the next level. While this can make writing a book a challenge, it is a sign of the health of the MySQL community and the active development happening at MySQL AB. As we're writing, there is a lot of talk starting about MySQL 5.1 and things like multimaster replication, foreign keys for all storage engines, new backup mechanisms, and more. We look forward to the future of MySQL and the changes it will require to the chapters in this book.

As you read this book, going from general subjects like determining business requirements all the way into the gritty details of subjects like clustering, we hope you will find your interaction with the database as rewarding and exciting as we've found our work with MySQL.

Who This Book Is For

This book is for the individual who has used MySQL at some level and is interested in exploring advanced MySQL topics. You'll find coverage of techniques and technologies that aren't included in introductory or general-usage MySQL books. If you have a passion for learning new technologies, this book is for you.

We assume that readers have worked with relational databases, are familiar with general database concepts, have some experience with MySQL, have written database queries, and have used command-line tools. We do not cover basic SQL, but we do explore how to use joins, subqueries, and derived tables to retrieve information efficiently.

If you aren't familiar with SQL, general database concepts, or MySQL, you might find *Beginning MySQL Database Design and Optimization: From Novice to Professional*, by John Stephens and Chad Russell (Apress, 2004), a helpful place to start.

How This Book Is Structured

The first part of the book covers issues in design and development of your MySQL applications. The second part of the book examines topics in the database administration and maintenance arena. Here are brief summaries of the contents of each chapter:

Chapter 1, Analyzing Business Requirements: Before getting into the nitty-gritty of MySQL, we'll first take a look at the software development process in general, as well as specifics that apply to almost all database-driven applications. From the unique perspective of each development team role, we'll graze over topics such as requirements gathering, use cases, and putting together a project plan. Next, we'll dive into a discussion on object and data modeling, covering UML and entity-relationship diagramming. We'll look at the strength of MySQL and its versions. Finally, we'll talk a bit about your development environment in general and the target audience of your project's software.

Chapter 2, Index Concepts: Here, we'll examine how MySQL's different indexes work. We'll start with a detailed discussion on index concepts, breaking down how they help the database quickly locate information in the database. You'll learn how the database server manages disk and memory-based data access, and how indexes and other data structures aid in this retrieval process. From B-tree indexing to hash-based lookups, we'll thoroughly explore how indexing algorithms work with varying table sizes and data types.

Chapter 3, Transaction Processing: In this chapter, we'll start with a detailed discussion of transaction theory. We'll go over what the ACID test is and how transactions serve to protect the integrity of your data. After the theory, we'll jump right into some examples where transactions can be used in common business scenarios, and you'll work through exercises designed to highlight how transactions are used. We'll then dig into how the MySQL database server enforces transactions and what happens in the event of a failure when transactions are not used. We'll end with a look at how locking, logging, and checkpointing come into play with transactions in general. This will provide a foundation on transaction processing concepts that we'll build on with our internal examination of the InnoDB storage engine in Chapter 5.

Chapter 4, MySQL System Architecture: Things start to get really interesting in Chapter 4, where we'll present an in-depth examination of the MySQL system internals—something you won't find in other texts. You'll learn how the various subsystems interrelate inside the server architecture and how to find what you need in the developer's documentation. We'll even walk you through the code execution of a simple SELECT statement.

Chapter 5, Storage Engines and Data Types: Your choice of storage engines in MySQL largely depends on the type of application you will run on the database and the data types you intend to store in your tables. In Chapter 5, we'll take a look at each of MySQL's storage engines, their various abilities, and where you will want to employ them. We'll focus predominantly on the InnoDB and MyISAM engines, detailing the record and index formats of each. After looking into the storage engines, we'll examine MySQL's data types and how best to use each of them. We'll discuss the differences between seemingly common data types and explain which data types to use for common storage requirements and typical data elements.

Chapter 6, Benchmarking and Profiling: Profiling your database system is an essential part of the ongoing development process. In this chapter, you'll learn a number of techniques to monitor the performance of your database queries. You'll learn how to identify key bottlenecks in the system, both in your SQL code and on the hardware in general. In the section on benchmarking, you'll work on using open-source tools to determine the limits of your application on your deployment hardware. We'll have you benchmarking real-world scenarios, walking you through setting up a benchmarking framework and running profiles on your own hardware to give you a feel for how to profile and benchmark your own code.

Chapter 7, Essential SQL: Your SQL code is the workhorse of your database application. Learning how to write effective queries is a critical component of designing high-performance systems, and we'll use this chapter to both review the SQL language in general and also provide some insight into the difference in set-based programming versus procedural or object-oriented programming. We'll focus on the fundamentals here, and ask you to reexamine what you already know about SQL. Most of the chapter will be centered around how to retrieve the information you need efficiently and effectively through the various joins that MySQL provides. Extensive coverage of the subqueries and derived tables will lead up to the more advanced SQL topics covered in Chapter 8.

Chapter 8, SQL Scenarios: The fundamentals you learned in Chapter 7 will provide the foundation for this chapter, which contains a collection of database development and administrative scenarios. Here, you will learn how to push the limits of the SQL language and explore alternate ways to accomplish complex database applications tasks. We'll step through exercises that show how slight variations in similar SQL statements can have performance impacts for your applications. Among other topics, you'll learn how to manage tree structures in SQL using set-based techniques; how to handle duplicate, orphaned, and random data in MySQL; and how to perform distance and radius calculations on GIS data using only your MySQL database server.

Chapter 9, Stored Procedures: This chapter will show you how to harness the power of storing groups of SQL statements and logic using MySQL and stored procedures compliant with the SQL:2003 standard. We'll look at concepts surrounding stored procedure technology and how stored procedures fit into the process of designing and building your application. Then we'll delve into the details of MySQL's implementation and how to build stored procedures using the SQL:2003 syntax.

Chapter 10, Functions: Following on the tails of stored procedures are stored functions. Stored functions allow you to encapsulate sets of SQL statements into a single function call, which can be used in any SQL statement. Unlike previous versions of MySQL, where you were required to write C code, with MySQL 5.0, stored functions are created dynamically in the database with SQL statements. This chapter will look at some of the differences between stored functions, stored procedures, triggers, and views. Then we'll cover the details of MySQL's function implementation, using examples to demonstrate creating and managing functions in your database. Finally, we'll look at the performance implications of using stored functions.

Chapter 11, Cursors: Long supported in other commercial database servers, cursors have now found their way into MySQL. We'll start this chapter with an examination of how cursors have been implemented in MySQL, and then move on to examples of how they are used. Then we'll take a look at the pros and cons of using cursors, and situations where they can be used effectively.

Chapter 12, Views: This chapter details MySQL's implementation of views, which provide a mechanism to join columns from multiple tables into one virtual table, or limit access to certain columns and/or rows of a single table. We'll review how views can help or hinder your use of the database, and go through the syntax to create and manage MySQL's views. You'll also learn how using views affects the performance of queries, and how to manage permissions for views.

Chapter 13, Triggers: With MySQL 5.0 comes support for triggers. The ability to trigger actions based on events in a table can provide a great deal of relief to application programmers and database programmers, but the power must be used wisely. This chapter will step through how triggers are created and used in MySQL, giving examples of various situations where triggers are particularly useful.

Chapter 14, MySQL Installation and Configuration: MySQL can be installed, configured, and put to use in a matter of minutes, or the process can consume days. It all depends on whether you use a prebuilt installation or want to dig into the fine details of building and configuring the database on your own. This chapter will review the available release formats and how to get up and running with each one. Once you're up and running with the database, we'll go through some post-installation steps and configuration options you may consider before using the database. Before we leave the chapter, we will go through the procedures for upgrading and uninstalling a MySQL installation.

Chapter 15, User Administration: Proper administration of user accounts and permissions is an important skill to have under your belt. This chapter will go through the simple process of creating users and granting permissions, from the most limited to global. As we go over granting permissions, we'll talk about some of the implications in providing user accounts and how they impact the security of your data and database.

Chapter 16, Security: Protecting your data, and the server it lives on, is a critical piece of administering a database. One of the first steps in securing the database is to review your data and determine the risk associated with the information in your database. In this chapter, we'll start with a discussion and examples of setting up a security policy. Next, we'll present a quick list of critical MySQL security issues you should address immediately. We'll then go through an example of implementing a security plan. Finally, we'll look into seven major areas that deserve attention when attempting to secure your database.

Chapter 17, Backup and Restoration: In this chapter, we'll discuss the reasons for backing up data, how to make sure your backup mechanism matches the expectations for restoring data, and what to consider when creating your backup and recovery plan. We'll then look at all the major tools for backing up and restoring MySQL data, including specific examples of the syntax used to create point-in-time snapshots of your data and restore your database with those snapshots.

Chapter 18, Replication: The MySQL database server software includes everything to perform near real-time replication to one or more servers. Replication can help with a wide variety of database demands, but it doesn't solve every problem with database load. This chapter will go into detail on a variety of scenarios where database replication will and will not help your database or application. We will also cover the commands to establish and manage both the master and slave database servers, and configuration options to tweak the behavior of your replication setup.

Chapter 19, Cluster: MySQL Cluster is the combination of MySQL and an in-memory storage engine, NDB Cluster, which spreads data redundantly across storage nodes. Using clustering provides scalability, high availability, and high-performance interactions with the database, but isn't always the right answer. In this chapter, we will give an overview of cluster concepts, and then go through MySQL's implementation of clustering technology. We'll review commands for setting up and maintaining a cluster environment.

Chapter 20, Troubleshooting: In this chapter, we'll take a look at some of the most commonly experienced problems with MySQL and provide pointers on how to fix or find solutions as problems arise. For example, you'll find tips on identifying and repairing corrupt tables, determining why `mysqld` won't start on your system, and identifying the query that's bringing the database to its knees.

Chapter 21, MySQL Data Dictionary: The standardized `INFORMATION_SCHEMA` virtual database is supported in MySQL 5. In this final chapter, we'll cover how to replace the MySQL `SHOW` commands with the more flexible and standardized `INFORMATION_SCHEMA` views. We'll walk through each of the available views in the virtual database and finish with some practical examples that demonstrate the power of this new functionality.

Downloading the Code

You can download the code for this book by navigating to the publisher's web site at `http://www.apress.com/` and proceeding to the Download section. Additionally, some of the Doxygen-generated code analysis and internals documentation covered in Chapter 4 is available at `http://jpipes.com/mysqldox/`.

Contacting the Authors

We appreciate your questions, comments, and suggestions regarding this book. Feel free to e-mail Michael Kruckenberg at mike@kruckenberg.com and Jay Pipes at jay@jpipes.com.

PART 1

###

Design and
Development

CHAPTER 1

■ ■ ■

Analyzing Business Requirements

Are you a network administrator whose days are filled with an incessant stream of work orders related to database configuration and maintenance? Or are you a lone applications programmer who has created small to medium-sized database systems for a number of business clients? Perhaps you're an in-house programming team member at a large business that's contemplating a new ERP system, or maybe "just" a port of an older legacy application framework to a Unix-based environment?

Whatever your current employment or daily activities, we're going to hazard a guess that you've picked up this book because you are striving to do whatever it is that you do faster and more efficiently. Regardless of your technical acumen, there are common roles and practices in application (and database) development that apply to most technical projects. From the smallest one-man contractor business to the largest enterprises, applications are designed by people with different skill sets and focuses, each of which contributes in a particular way to the outcome of the project.

A project's success can often be attributed to the legwork done at the onset of the venture. By the same token, the maintenance of existing applications is easier to handle when the team managing the application is aware of the initial designer's intentions and choices. This chapter details best-practice elements common in most successful project beginnings. However, most of these concepts are dually critical to application maintenance and refactoring.

Although this book covers how to use MySQL in building and deploying applications, this first chapter predominantly covers topics that are not specific to MySQL. The material in this chapter provides general insight into the software development cycle, and these topics should be foremost in your thoughts when designing efficient, scalable database applications. In particular, we'll discuss the following topics:

- The project, including functional requirements and the group dynamic

- Models, which are the foundations of solid applications

- Database alternatives and how MySQL stacks up

- Your environment: hosting companies, controlled platforms, and advice

The Project

Entire books have been written on the software development process, and this chapter will not attempt to elaborate on the intricacies of it. We will look at the software development process largely from the database designer's perspective, but we encourage you to explore other texts that detail the entire development process more thoroughly. Unlike some other books on this topic, however, we intend to walk you through the concepts of the development process by examining the different roles played by project team members and highlighting the key actions performed by the project team. Although this book predominantly focuses on the roles of the database designer, database administrator, and application developer, we'll look at other team roles here to give you the whole picture.

Common Team Roles

Taking the time to understand the roles that team members play greatly influences the outcome of a project because it allows work to be allotted based on each member's skill set and the type of work to be completed. Not only does thoughtful delegation speed development and improve quality, but understanding how each role in a project team interacts is crucial to the effective coordination between various parties.

Even if you are a single contractor starting a new project, it is important to understand the differences between common project roles. Not only will other people likely need to maintain your applications, but understanding project roles can help to properly divide up your own workload. As a single contractor, one of the most difficult tasks is envisioning yourself as many different project players all rolled up into one. Without realizing the different parts to a project team, lone technicians often fall into the trap of viewing the entire project in terms of the subject area of which they are most interested or skilled. Learning to appreciate the common roles of database application projects can help ensure your project's well-rounded and complete design. We will cover the following roles:

- Customer

- Business analyst

- Database designer

- Database administrator

- Application developer

- Interface designer

- Project manager

The Customer

Of all the members involved in a project, perhaps the most untapped resource during the development cycle is the *customer* (sometimes the customer is called the *business functional expert*, BFE, or *subject matter expert*, SME). The customer is usually a key source of insight into two things: how the business process currently works and how the end user is likely to react to proposed changes in that business process.

Customers have a wealth of information on end-user habits and daily work activity, and this information should not be undervalued. It is critical to remember that the customer, not the developer, will be using the application that you create.

Most business customers will have a vested interest in the shape and direction that a project takes. Often called *stakeholders*, customers are foremost concerned with addressing the needs of the business, which typically involve efficiency gains or enhancements to current business processes.

The Business Analyst

Serving as a liaison between the end user and the developers and designers, the *business analyst* is responsible for identifying the key problem domain that the project seeks to address. Customers are consulted, meetings and functional requirement specifications are hammered out, and eventually, a project scope is determined.

The project scope should be the driver for all application decisions. It should define the limitations the customer has placed on the breadth of the project, illustrate the functional areas of the problem domain that the application should handle, and identify key business rules to which the application should adhere.

As a business analyst, you serve as the point of contact for the customer as well as the development team. Often, a business analyst working on IT projects must have the ability to translate complex technical issues into language that most business users will understand and appreciate.

When developing the project scope documentation, a business analyst will focus on three distinct areas:

- Defining problem domains with the customer

- Developing functional requirements

- Defining application scenarios

Problem Domains

Each project ultimately begins with defining a problem domain. This represents the real-world scope of the problem that the project attempts to solve. Often, problem domains start as vague, amorphous ideas about a particular business situation, such as "Our intranet site is slow and useless." As a business analyst, you must often coax and prod business users into providing a more detailed view of their needs, such as "Our intranet site needs more advanced reporting, and response speed for downloading shared documents must be less than two seconds."

Working with the customer at this level, you will begin to form a set of *expectations* about what the end goal of the project should be. It is critical that you document these expectations in your project scope document, so that over the course of the project, the project team can refer to these expectations when questions arise as to how a particular application piece should perform. Also, getting the expectations in writing helps to reinforce the boundaries of the project and to prevent what is euphemistically termed *scope creep*—the growth in the range of an application's expected functionality over the course of the project.

■**Note** Throughout the course of this book, we will come back to this theme of well-documented policy and procedures. We feel that a cornerstone of professional development practices is written documentation of all levels of the development cycle. By having procedures, policies, and expectations contained in a document repository, a project team gains the ability to most effectively track and manage changes to a project's scope and design.

Good business analysts ask the customer questions that drive to the root of the problem, *without* having the customer provide any details as to what solution they envision. Customers commonly think in terms of the end interface that they want to see on the screen. Analysts must instead strive to address what the customer sees as the main problems or inefficiencies of the business process that could be improved through the project, and leave the work of designing end-user interfaces and program design to the interface designers and application developers.

Let's work through an example to illustrate the work of the business analyst. Suppose your project is to design an e-commerce application for a local toy store. The project team is composed of your IT team and the business users, who range from the toy store's corporate officers to the customer service representatives who will use your eventual application.

From the customer, you learn that the company currently keeps track of its sales using a point-of-sale (POS) system located at the store. Each POS system is linked to an inventory application in the company's warehouse. Currently, the company's web site has only a phone number and address information to help toy buyers locate the store; however, the company expects that the online e-commerce application will allow clients to be able to purchase any toy in the store that is in stock.

This is a rough outline of the customer's problem domain and expectations. From here, you will work toward developing a clearer picture of how the application will handle the customer's needs by listing the *functional requirements*.

Functional Requirements

As you interview subject matter experts, a rough idea of what the application will be required to do starts to emerge. This list of proposed system abilities is called the *functional requirements list*. Each item on the requirements list should be a representation of what goals the application should be able to accomplish.

Two examples of broad functional requirements for the toy store e-commerce application example might be:

- The application should provide a web-based interface for clients (buyers) to search through the toy store's catalog of products.

- The application should provide the ability to purchase products.

As a business analyst, you whittle these broad functional requirements into smaller, more detailed lists. Focus on business rules along with the requirements. Refining these two vague requirements, we might come up with the following:

- The online store catalog must have categories that the buyer can browse.

- The categories can have one or more subcategories, each containing products that the buyer can click to see more details about the product.

- The buyer can add products to a shopping cart.
- The shopping cart should display products that the buyer has added to it and allow the buyer to enter payment information.
- The buyer should be able to submit payment information and get a purchase receipt.

Notice how the level of detail gets finer as we iterate through the requirements list. This iterative process is crucial in the early stages of the requirement gathering, and you will find that new requirements emerge as you work with the customer to hammer out more details. For instance, as you start to detail the ability of the payment process, you may find that the customers should be able to select a delivery method to ship the products they have ordered.

A good list of functional requirements will serve as the *project boundary*, and it will be critical to providing a basic structure to the development process.

Application Scenarios (Use Cases)

It is the job of the analyst to extract from the customer a set of *scenarios* (often called *use cases*). These scenarios, along with the functional requirements, provide the framework for the application's functionality, and represent what actual tasks the application is to help the end user complete. Typical examples of these use case scenarios might include:

- Customer places order online.
- System sends e-mail to all users in the administrator group.
- Support agent schedules a technician to complete a service order.
- Accounting manager closes accounting period and runs closeout batches.

While there are no requirements for how much detail use cases should contain, you should try to make them as simple as possible. Minute details only complicate the aim of use cases. They should focus on how the application adds value to the business process. The *actors* in the scenario must experience some tangible benefit from the system, and the use case should concentrate on providing descriptions of scenarios that might occur during the use case's action. For instance, consider the following use case based on our toy store example.

Customer Places Order Online:

Main Success Scenario:

> • *Customer, after finding items needed, enters customer information. System validates and records customer information and processes credit card information. A printable receipt of order is displayed.*

Alternate Scenarios:

> • *If credit card payment fails, alert customer to failure and reason, and prompt for correction. Repeat order process.*

> • *If payment processor is not responsive, alert customer of difficulties, store information for later processing, inform customer that credit card will be deducted later, and display receipt.*

> • *If system detects a purchased item is out of stock, alert customer and ask if customer would like to back-order the item, informing customer of length of wait until in stock. If back-order OK, store customer information and print back-order receipt, notifying customer that credit card will be billed on date of shipment.*

Clearly, this is a simplified view of what can be a very complicated business process. But, use cases are just that: a collection of real-world scenarios describing the system's goals. Once the use cases are compiled, they are used by the application developer and database designer as an outline to what the system *should* accomplish and the common alternate outcomes that may occur in the system.

■**Note** How to write use cases can be a fairly complex and scientific process, and entire volumes have been devoted to the topic. It is not our intention to detail the myriad software development practices here, only to highlight the benefits of use cases in the overall process of refining customer demands into a workable framework for developing database applications. Use cases are the first step in the long design process; they enable further design detail by focusing on the "big picture" as a set of related scenarios accomplishing customer goals. For further reading on use cases, see *Fast Track UML 2.0,* by Kendall Scott (Apress, 2004) and *Writing Effective Use Cases, by* Alistair Cockburn (Addison-Wesley, 2001).

The Database Designer

At its heart, any software application is primarily concerned with the manipulation, display, and storage of data. Graphical data, textual data, statistical data—the application must be the interpreter and controller of all this information. The relational database has become the primary tool of the application in doing the work of retrieving and storing this data.

It is the primary responsibility of the *database designer* (also called the *database architect*) to determine the grouping and relationships between these various pieces of information. As a database designer, you must find ways to organize this data in the most efficient and logical (from a database's perspective) manner possible. Your key concerns will be related to the following concepts:

- Efficiency

- Data integrity

- Scalability

Efficiency

In terms of efficiency, you will be asked to determine the optimal storage types for both data elements (fields) and groupings of data (tables). The choices made in the early stages of database design often affect an application's long-term performance and stability. Proper choices depend on your ability to translate the information you will receive from the business analyst regarding customer data, and particularly end-user expectations, such as the frequency of reporting, the frequency of changes to data, and so forth.

In terms of efficiency, the relationships between data groups will be a foremost concern. An ill-conceived relational design can wreak havoc on both application performance and design, and so you need to take care in determining how to tie groups of related data together. That said, it is common for the database designer to want to adhere tightly to a certain level of normalization. This can sometimes lead to circumstances that may have been more efficiently solved in a different manner. You will often encounter situations where there are multiple ways to structure information in the database design. You should try to work out the advantages and drawbacks of each approach during the design phase.

■**Note** We assume that you are familiar with the concept of database normalization. If not, consider picking up a copy of Jon Stephens and Chad Russell's *Beginning MySQL Database Design and Optimization* (Apress, 2004). You will find an in-depth discussion of normalization forms in Chapter 3 of that book.

A common example of this situation is the storage of hierarchical data (such as menu items of category listings). Most database designers will tend to favor a solution that has menu items stored in a table with a self-referencing, nullable key representing a parent menu item. When retrieving menu items from the database, the application developer is faced with a tricky dilemma: without knowing the number of levels deep the menu items go, a SQL statement must be issued for each nesting level, or application code must build the menu after retrieving the entire set of menu items in a single SQL call. The application developer may come to the design table with a method of serializing menu item data into a single string, reducing the number of times a database retrieval is needed or significantly reducing the amount of application code needed to present the menu. The structure of the menu items table, however, would no longer be normalized to the degree desired by the database designer. It behooves both parties to investigate the pros and cons of each method of storing the specific information. Depending on customer requirements, either way may have significant advantages over the other.

■**Tip** On the topic of retrieving and storing hierarchical data in SQL, check out Chapter 8 for an in-depth discussion of an alternative technique called the nested set model.

Data Integrity

Imagine the following common scenario: A customer places an order containing a number of line items through a database application that your team has designed. The application code that is responsible for recording the order to your database is responsible for performing the following three steps:

1. Generate a random 16-character order identifier.

2. Save the main order record.

3. For each line item, save the item information along with the order identifier, so that order items can be related to the main order record.

Let's suppose that the application code generates the order identifier correctly and moves on to adding the main order record. However, there is a bug in the routine that prevents the main order record from being saved to the database. Furthermore, the code doesn't throw an error that would stop the code from adding the line items in the next step. So, not knowing any better, the application creates three line item records in the database with the order identifier that the routine generated. You now have a messy situation on your hands: items are entered into the database for an order that doesn't exist. You have *inconsistent data*.

■**Note** The concept of inconsistent data is often described as *orphaned records* because the *parent*, or main record, is absent while the *child* records exist. We cover how to handle orphaned records and data inconsistencies in Chapter 8.

An application that generates inconsistent data is a maintenance nightmare. It requires a database administrator's constant attention and can produce inaccurate, unreliable reports. The most effective way to ensure that an application cannot store inconsistent data is to ensure that the database itself enforces relationships through foreign key constraints. While it is true that the application code could be fixed to prevent the adding of the child records without a parent record, the only way to ensure consistent data is to provide for the relation through the database.

Astute readers may correctly point out that the scenario outlined in this example could also have been prevented through the use of transactions (see Chapter 3, where we cover transaction processing, including topics related to data consistency and constraints). While this is true, transactions are not enforced at the table level of the database, and, like the application code in the example, a poorly written transaction could just as easily produce the same effect.

Unfortunately, inconsistent data is common in many MySQL-based database applications for two reasons:

- MySQL makes it painfully easy to create table structures that have no inherent referential integrity (MyISAM tables). This has been pointed out by many experts on database systems, and their complaints have been the major catalyst for an increased use of InnoDB table structures and features such as constraints in later versions of MySQL.[1]

- Because of the availability and easy installation of MySQL, programmers with little-to-no knowledge of database design have created a flurry of LAMP-based applications[2] based on poor database designs.

■**Caution** Foreign key constraints were introduced for the InnoDB storage engine in version 3.23.44, but InnoDB is not the default storage engine for most MySQL installations (only the Windows installer for version 4.1.5 and later sets the default storage engine to InnoDB). Therefore, it is easy for database schemas to be created with little or no relational integrity.

The database designer must strive to design a database architecture that protects the integrity of its data. Although it is possible to create applications that enforce referential integrity through application code, such a strategy is not as stable as integrity enforced through the database itself. As a database designer, you should work closely with application developers to create the best of both worlds: an application that has database-level integrity and application code that respects, and indeed flourishes using, the database's rules of relationships.

---

1. See `http://dev.mysql.com/doc/mysql/en/InnoDB_foreign_key_constraints.html` for more information about foreign key constraints.

2. LAMP is the combination of Linux/Apache/MySQL and PHP/Perl/Python.

Scalability

Scalability is the ability of an application database to perform at an optimal level after the volume of data storage and the frequency of data retrieval have increased severalfold. By focusing energy on making the database design as efficient as possible, you will naturally improve the scalability of the database, because efficiency gains complement scale.

Your data type choices for indexed fields affect the scalability of an application dramatically. As the volume of data increases, indexes—and how quickly they can locate the desired data—are relied on to provide adequate application performance. As a database designer, you must think *long-term*.

The Database Administrator

Picture it: the database designer pats himself on the back for creating a brilliantly efficient and scalable database architecture. "It will maintain itself," he says. And the database administrator laughs heartily.

No database—no matter how craftily designed or well implemented—exists in a vacuum. *Database administrators* know this all too well, and their knowledge of common maintenance tasks (like backups and user administration) and replication is an invaluable asset to the design team.

As a database administrator, you must work closely with the database designer and the business analyst to outline plans for the application's growth. The business analyst will provide a rough idea of the volume of customer data you can expect in a given time period. Through the database designer, you will see a clearer picture of the organization of this data across table structures. It is your job to accurately predict and plan for how this data should be handled in the short- and long-term. Given the limitations of the available hardware, you will make recommendations on how and how often the data should be backed up or consolidated. For example, if the database designer, at the behest of the application designer, has included tables for storing web site statistics, the database administrator would do well to analyze the expected web site traffic and provide a plan for consolidating the logged data at regular intervals into aggregate tables representing certain time periods.

For many projects, functional requirements or environmental limitations may call for a distributed database architecture, with local slave database servers synchronizing with a master database (replication). The database administrator must work closely to plan the implementation of such complex systems.

The Application Developer

As an *application developer*, your primary focus is coding the solution that accomplishes the given problem domain outlined in the project definition. The database is your tool for storing all the data that the problem domain involves. Your concerns lie largely in retrieving and manipulating the information, rather than in how this data is physically stored. Armed with one or more programming languages, you go about the arduous task of addressing each of the functional requirements of the project.

Working closely with the business analyst to ensure that application pieces meet requirements, you use the table blueprints created by the database designer to construct a solid framework for data access. Using the principles of tiered application design and object-oriented development, you work toward creating a single data access layer, which forms the "plumbing" that moves data in and out of the database to and from the application and presentation layers.

While data access components and libraries often look similar to the database schema to and from which they map information movement, this is by no means a necessity. Good data access frameworks must provide application programmers with a consistent and organized method for retrieving data.

A successful software project requires an application developer who can listen to and incorporate the concerns of other project team members into a cohesive application framework.

The Interface Designer

The team member with the most visible impact on a project's perceived success by the eventual customer is the *interface designer*, charged with the task of creating the look and feel of the application's interactive elements. Your work is the first and last the customer will see. Often a thankless job, designing interfaces requires a unique understanding of the customer's environment, effective color and word choice, and the skill to represent often complex tasks and data structures in a clear and simple manner.

A common occurrence in the software development process is to have interface designers work closely with business analysts to *prototype* application interfaces for customers during the process of defining use cases and functional requirements. Often, customers can more easily explain business processes when looking at a mock-up of an interface. They can envision what the application will eventually look like and imagine how users of the application will behave.

■**Caution** While having interface designers provide customers with prototypes is a common development practice, this can sometimes lead to negative consequences. Providing customers with interface prototypes too early in the design process can lead to mismatched expectations. The eventual interface may not look like the interface the customer saw prototyped, possibly leading to the dreaded, "That's not at all what I expected to see!" If you choose to provide interface prototypes to customers, be sure to show them revised prototypes when significant changes are made to the interface.

The Project Manager

Overseeing the completion of milestones and keeping the project team on track are the key responsibilities of the *project manager*. Project management is indeed an art form. Good project managers know how to resolve internal team disputes and to coordinate myriad daily tasks and assignments, while keeping an eye on the overall project scope, budget, and timeline.

Project managers often need good negotiation skills, as they manage the overall relationship between the team and the project's stakeholders. Often, a project manager is responsible for the fiscal health of the project, and works with stakeholders to produce and maintain a budget for the project. Good project managers make it a top priority to ensure that changes to the project scope are well documented and communicated to the project team in a consistent fashion.

Tip Commercial software like Microsoft Project (http://www.microsoft.com) or Macromedia's Sitespring (http://www.macromedia.com) and open-source tools like phpCollab (http://www.php-collab.org) can assist the project manager in developing a timeline, delegating tasks to various team members, tracking time, and estimating development costs. Additionally, tools like Fog Creek Software's FogBugz (http://www.fogcreek.com/FogBUGZ/) and open-source issue tracking software like phpBugTracker (http://phpbt.sourceforge.net) and Mantis (http://www.mantisbt.org/) provide platforms for managing the software development cycle and tracking bugs in the project source code.

Importance of Team Roles

As we detailed the common team roles, many of you realized that in real-life business situations, a project team is rarely composed of team members playing such succinct roles. More often, each team member is skilled in multiple technical arenas and contributes in overlapping ways.

We aren't suggesting that an ideal team is one that has every one of the roles we discussed here. We do, however, believe that project teams that recognize the *importance* of each role will be more likely to produce balanced, well-thought-out designs, because they will be forced to compromise on certain ideals.

From Concept to Model

Functional requirements, use case scenarios, and the project scope document are forged in order to illustrate and describe the *concepts* of the application domain. To move the project closer toward actual development, we must find ways to take these ideas and requirements and provide *models* from which the application developer and database designer are able to sculpt the eventual application.

This section covers the basic process of building models from this conceptual foundation. We take a look at the following areas:

- Developing textual object models

- Using modeling approaches

- Developing a database blueprint

Textual Object Models

Once the business analysts and application developers compile a working collection of use cases, the developers undertake the gritty work of hammering out the solution. Each use case scenario represents what the application *should* accomplish, and so application developers should set about determining the objects *acting* and *being acted upon* in the use cases. For each object, describe on paper how each object interacts with other objects in the system and what data elements each type (or *class*) of object may contain.

Identifying Classes and Data Members

As an application developer working through the use case and functional requirements of the toy store example, you might identify the different classes of objects like so:

- Customer (the buyer of the product)

- CustomerOrder (an object representing the purchase)

- CustomerOrderItem (a product purchased in a CustomerOrder)

- PaymentProcessor (a method for fulfilling CustomerOrder payment)

Examining each class further, you might conclude that the classes might act or be acted upon in the following ways:

- A Customer places a CustomerOrder

- A CustomerOrder is validated for accuracy

- A PaymentProcessor processes a CustomerOrder

Along the same lines, you find that your Customer, CustomerOrder, and CustomerOrderItem classes contain certain data elements.

The Customer object might contain the following elements:

- Customer ID (a unique customer identifier)

- Name (the customer's full name)

- Address (the customer's location)

For the CustomerOrder object, these elements may be necessary:

- Order ID (a unique order identifier)

- Customer ID (which customer placed the order?)

- Date Placed (the date the order was placed by the customer)

- Collection of Items Ordered

The CustomerOrderItem object might have these elements:

- Product SKU (a unique product identifier)

- Quantity (the number of this type of product ordered)

- Price (the cost of this product)

Work with the customer to determine what kind of information each class of object might contain. At this stage, it's not necessary to think in terms of proper database normalization; don't regard the object classes as database tables. Instead, think of the classes strictly in terms of the real-world objects they represent. The data elements (class members) may not all become database fields. Include *all* data members that may be useful for other objects to use in the life of the application, including calculated data members or complex data members. For instance, the CustomerOrder class might contain a calculated OrderTotal field, even if you don't plan to store the calculated field in the database table.

Identifying Methods

Once those class members are completed, you will want to write down the abilities of each object, in the form of class *methods*. These methods represent the various functions that the object can perform. The class methods may have one or more parameters, which may be passed from the *caller* of the object in order to provide the method with data it needs to perform the action. Here is a list of actions you might give to the sample Customer class. You'll notice a pattern of Get/Set pairs, representing a common object-oriented paradigm designed to provide structure and consistency to how an object's information is both retrieved and stored.

For the Customer object, the following methods might be appropriate:

- GetID (returns the customer's ID)

- SetID (takes an ID and makes it the customer object's identifier)

- GetName (returns the customer's full name)

- SetName (takes a string and sets the customer's full name)

- GetAddress (returns the customer's location)

- SetAddress (takes a string and sets the customer's location)

Avoid creating "superclasses" that encapsulate too much information. Usually, such classes should be broken down into smaller classes that closely map to a specific functionality or actor. Breaking down classes into small units allows for greater reuse and a conceptually clearer model.

Many experienced application developers will pass over the step of writing down on paper their text-based object models, and instead use their favorite modeling software application to map the object models directly from their functional requirements and use cases. Whether you choose to write down the models in a text format first is entirely up to you. The key point here is that you go through the exercise of separating the different objects and the elements of those objects in a descriptive manner.

Modeling Approaches

In order to most effectively communicate the concepts that have been developed by the business analyst and customer, application developers and database designers are tasked with graphically representing how the software system will function. *Object modeling* is this process of visually describing the actors, processes, and scenarios that make up your problem domain.

In this section, we will look at the two most common approaches to modeling database application objects:

- Unified Modeling Language (UML)

- Entity-relationship (E-R) approach

These two approaches are not mutually exclusive, and it is not unusual to see both techniques deployed in the development process.

Unified Modeling Language (UML)

The need to accurately model complex system concepts and functions has existed from the early days of software engineering. How do you represent all these interrelated actions and complexities in a way that developers and other team members can understand? By the same token, as software projects became more complex, and more people were involved in the creation of software, it became necessary to have a common way of expressing software system concepts, like object classes and object associations. Unified Modeling Language (UML) has become the de-facto standard in addressing this need.[3]

UML gives software developers a tool set for mapping out a conceptual model of their systems through a set of defined diagramming techniques. Each type of diagram in the UML toolbox addresses a different facet of the overall design process. This design process is separated by UML into separate domains:

- *Use Case Model*: Defines the interaction between the system and its real-world users. (Who uses the system and what are the goals that the system helps them achieve?)

- *Communication Model*: Defines the interaction between internal system objects. (How do system objects work together to achieve the system goals?)

- *State Model*: Describes the different conditions (*states*) that objects take on over a time span. (How will an object's properties change over the course of a system's workflow?)

- *Logical Model*: Provides the conceptual documentation of which objects make up the system. (How are actors in the system and the things they act upon related to each other?)

- *Component Model*: Defines how the actual software will be packaged and grouped into related *namespaces* or *components*. (How will the software code be organized?)

- *Physical or Deployment Model*: Communicates the hardware organization of the application. (How will actual hardware be organized to support the system?)

The business analyst and application developers will use the use case and communication model to draw up specialized diagrams pertaining to how the real-world actors interact with each other within the system. As those diagrams begin to take shape, the application developer, and possibly the database designer, will work with the state, logical, and component models to diagram how these real-world actors can be represented in the virtual world of the application code. Network and systems administrators will be primarily concerned with diagrams from the physical model, which outline how the various nodes in the network and hardware infrastructure will be organized.

A database designer will predominantly work with diagrams in the logical and state model domains. Much of the designer's work entails figuring out how a system of related objects will be represented in a structured database format, and how the *persistence* of an object's state can best be accomplished through the database (the subject that we're most interested in). Let's examine two UML diagramming formats you will use most commonly in your database work: the *class diagram* and the *deployment diagram*.

---

3. UML was developed from the work of Ivar Jacobson, James Rumbaugh, and Grady Booch. Its web site is http://www.uml.org/.

Class Diagrams

Of all the diagrams involved in the UML framework, the database designer will focus primarily on the class diagram. Class diagrams serve to illustrate the relationship (or association) between all or some of the objects within a software application. The diagram contains *class models* that detail the data elements (*attributes*) contained within each class of object and the actions that each object may perform (*operations*). The easiest way to learn about class diagrams is to look at one in action. Figure 1-1 shows a class diagram illustrating the simple objects described in our example use case for the toy store application.

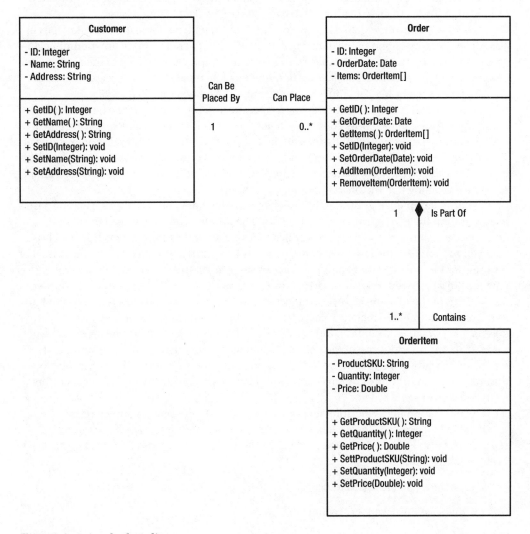

Figure 1-1. *A simple class diagram*

Three of the four classes we outlined earlier have been incorporated into Figure 1-1. Each class is represented by a rectangle divided into *compartments*. The top compartment contains the class name, and the bottom compartment has the class attributes and operations.

The name of each attribute and operation directly follows the plus sign (+) or minus sign (–) at the left edge of the rectangle. The plus and minus signs represent the scope of the attribute or operation, which is the ability of outside objects to use the specific attribute or operation. *Public* scope (represented by the plus sign) means that objects other than the instance of the class itself can use the attribute or operation. *Private* scope (represented by the minus sign) means that only the specific class instance may use the attribute or operation. In the example of Figure 1-1, notice that we have made all the attributes of each class private, and given each class public Get and Set operations to change those private attributes. This is a common programming practice used to ensure that all internal class variables are protected by a set of publicly available methods that can validate the data before it is set.

Following the attribute name is a colon, and then a data type. Typically, the data types in class diagrams correspond to the data types used in the software's primary programming language. It will be up to you as a database designer to interpret, with the help of the application developer and the business analyst, how to refine the data types shown in class diagrams to the data types used by MySQL. You'll learn more about data types in Chapter 5.

For operations, you will notice that data types are also present inside the parentheses following the operation's name. These data types represent function *arguments*. Data types after operation names represent the type of data *returned* by the function call. For example, in + SetAddress(String): void, a parameter (argument) of type String is passed to the function named SetAddress. Once SetAddress has completed its operation, it returns the special data type void (meaning that the operation returns nothing).

Of particular interest to the database designer are the lines connecting each class. These lines represent the *relationship* between classes. The numbers on each side of the lines describe the relationship between the elements. A single number 1 represents that the class on the *opposite end* of the line must contain exactly one reference to an object of the class that the number 1 is closest to. In Figure 1-1, you can see that an Order must contain exactly one reference to a Customer. This makes sense: an order can be placed by only a single customer. *Multiplicity*, or the relationship of one object to zero or more other objects, is represented by the minimum number of related objects, two dots, then the maximum number of related objects (or *, which represents an infinite number). Therefore, 0..* means that an instance of the class on the opposite end of the line can be related to zero up to an infinite number of objects on the side of the line where 0..* is located. In Figure 1-1, you see that 0..* is next to the Order class on the line between Customer and Order. This means that a Customer may be related to zero or more orders.

The phrases on the association lines are optional, and represent, in human terms, the relationship between the classes. Read them like so: *opposite class name + phrase + closest class name*. So, in Figure 1-1, the association line between Customer and Order can be phrased in either of these ways:

- Customer Can Place Order

- Order Can Be Placed By Customer

The phrases simply provide an alternate way of describing the relationship between the class objects.

Also notice the black diamond on the connecting line between OrderItem and Order in Figure 1-1. The diamond represents *aggregation*, and it means that objects of the class at the end of the line closest to the diamond are partly composed of objects from the other end of the line. In Figure 1-1, you can see that an Order is composed, partly, of a collection of OrderItem objects. The aggregation diamonds can either be solid or outlined. Solid diamonds represent *composite aggregation,* and mean that if an object of the aggregating type is deleted, all composite (contained) objects should be removed as well. This makes sense: why would you want to delete an order but not delete its order items at the same time?

Database designers should pay close attention to association lines and aggregation descriptions, as they often describe how database tables will be related to each other and how things like constraints and foreign keys will be established. Spend some time reviewing Figure 1-1 to get a feel for how class diagrams describe relationships between software system objects.

■**Tip** Pay special attention to the data type of operation arguments, because they often provide clues as to how the application developers will most likely query your database schema. If you know how the application will query for information, you can more effectively plan how your tables should be indexed. If you see an operation like + GetCustomerByName(String) : void, you can be fairly certain that the application plans to find customer records using the customer's name. This may be your first hint that an index on the Name field of the Customer table might be warranted.

One other common notation in class diagrams is *generalization.* Generalization indicates that a class hierarchy exists—that one class *inherits* the attributes and operations of another. You can see this notation in the class diagram describing the fourth class in our customer/order example, shown in Figure 1-2.

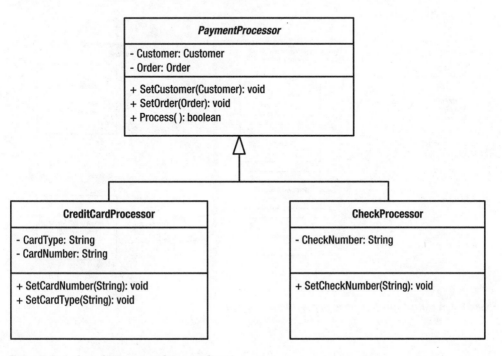

Figure 1-2. *A class diagram with generalization*

In Figure 1-2, notice that the `PaymentProcessor` class name is italicized. This denotes that the class is *abstract*, meaning that instances of the `PaymentProcessor` class will never actually be instantiated by the application. Instead, instances of the classes `CreditCardProcessor` and `CheckProcessor` will be instantiated. These two classes inherit the attributes and operations of the generalized abstract class, `PaymentProcessor`. The line with an outlined triangle on one end represents this inheritance, and the triangle always points to the class from which the other classes inherit.

So, how is the concept of generalization important to the database designer? Well, you need to figure out how best to store this nonstandard information. Do you use separate tables to store the separate information for credit card and check payments, or should you use just one table? What happens when the end user needs to process money-order payments? We'll look at how to answer these questions during the course of this book.

Throughout this book, we will use class diagrams to show the relationship between common application objects.

Deployment Diagrams

Class diagrams will help you understand the structure of the application's objects. As a database administrator, you also will want to know how the actual software will be deployed, and its interaction with hardware and other systems and databases. A deployment diagram does just that—it shows a static view of the hardware on which your system will run, along with the different software components that will run on that hardware.

Figure 1-3 shows a sample deployment diagram for an e-commerce project. In this simple example, the diagram has been shown at a project-level, not at enterprise-level. In other words, the diagram shows only the components of the e-commerce project, not the entire company's architecture.

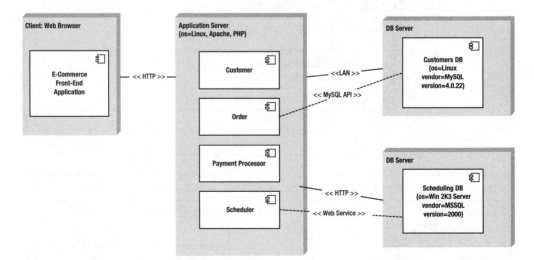

Figure 1-3. *A sample project-level deployment diagram*

In the deployment diagram, each three-dimensional rectangle represents a *node* in the deployment scenario. The node is an actual physical separation of a system's components; it represents a separate computer. In Figure 1-3, the leftmost node is the e-commerce client application, running through a web browser, which, in turn, transmits requests via HTTP to the application server housing application component packages. These packages communicate via the local Ethernet (LAN) to a local database server node and also to a remote database server via HTTP. In this sample scenario, a scheduling database running Microsoft SQL Server 2000 is being used by the Scheduling component on the application server to return scheduling information via a web service. Solid lines between nodes represent the physical communication medium, and dashed lines represent the software communication method used to communicate. A few details about the server software are included in the center and right node descriptions.

In this example, you can see we have a tiered application, with an application server housing components and classes of the application. Two database servers are present. We have our main MySQL database server containing our customer information database. Additionally, we've included a node for a legacy SQL Server database currently housing scheduling information, which is connected to the application server via a web services API. In large organizations, it is common to have this sort of arrangement of legacy software and services. When the organization decides to move the scheduling information out of the SQL Server database and onto the MySQL server, a new deployment diagram would outline the new model. As plans for the proposed integration occurred, it would be critical to have a deployment diagram outlining the physical and logical effects of the change.

On the project level, a deployment diagram serves to illustrate the overall communication methods among the application nodes. A database administrator can use a project-level deployment model to configure database and server software to maximize efficiency for the given communication protocols and methods.

Enterprise-level deployment diagrams give the database administrator a higher view of the application's role in the entire company's systems and hardware deployment. This type of deployment diagram is a static picture of an enterprise's entire database, application, and network. As a database administrator, you use these deployment diagrams to graphically represent the bird's-eye view of your enterprise's hardware infrastructure. In a sense, the diagram represents your strategy for most effectively structuring your production environment. On larger projects, you might create separate deployment diagrams for your development and testing environments, or you could choose to model your development environment in exactly the same way as your production environment.

■**Tip** Clearly, we've only touched the surface of UML here. We highly recommend that any database designer pick up a good book on UML and learn the intricacies of class diagramming. One such book is *Fast Track UML 2.0*, by Kendall Scott (Apress, 2004).

UML Modeling Software

As software projects grew and the languages used to describe the process of development became both more standardized and more complex, modeling software filled the growing need for automation and flexibility in the design process. Today, modeling software exists for all major platforms. While we surely don't intend to provide an exhaustive list here, we will highlight some of the major software to give you a feel:

- Computer Associates' AllFusion Component Modeler

- Microsoft Visio

- SmartDraw 7 Technical Edition

- ArgoUML (Tigris.org)

AllFusion Component Modeler

Designed with both Microsoft and Java development environments in mind, Computer Associates' AllFusion Component Modeler (`http://www.ca.com/`, where you can download a trial version) is tightly integrated with Microsoft .NET and CORBA frameworks, allowing models and code to be synchronized as changes are made through the development process. Also, Component Modeler is integrated with Computer Associates' ERwin Data Modeler, discussed in the next section, to allow for E-R data modeling construction from the UML diagrams created in the main workspace.

You can begin building your UML models by creating a new workspace, then adding a new class diagram to the workspace. Classes are constructed, along with attributes and operations, in the design space, and related to each other with relation connectors, as shown in the example in Figure 1-4.

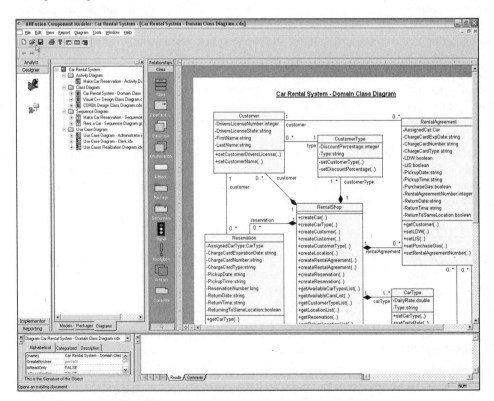

Figure 1-4. *AllFusion Component Modeler*

Visio

One of the most popular *diagramming* tools on the market, Microsoft Visio (http://
www.microsoft.com/office/visio/) comes in two flavors, Standard and Professional. Now
part of the Microsoft Office family, Visio can be relatively easy to learn, as it uses the same
look and feel as many other Office programs, as shown in Figure 1-5.

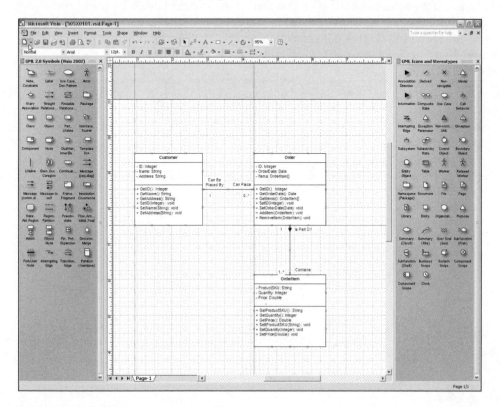

Figure 1-5. *Visio 2002*

To do serious UML modeling, you should install a UML 2.0 stencil, which has the modeling shapes in a handy template, enabling you to drag-and-drop class objects and relation
connectors onto the drawing board the same way most other modeling programs do.

Tip While the Visio Professional version ($499) comes with a greater variety of built-in stencils, Pavel
Hruby has created an excellent free Visio stencil for UML 2.0 that will work with the Standard ($199) version
as well. You can find it at http://www.phruby.com/stencildownload.html. (Interestingly, Pavel himself
recommends SmartDraw 7 on his own web site.)

SmartDraw 7 Technical Edition

At $149, SmartDraw 7 Technical Edition (http://www.smartdraw.com) is a pretty good bargain. While it runs only on Windows platforms, the interface is easy to use. SmartDraw comes with a plethora of symbols for UML diagramming and other charting and drawing functions, and makes it a snap to quickly generate good-looking UML diagrams, as shown in Figure 1-6. The web site also features a good deal of example and tutorial material that will certainly help the developer starting out in structured modeling. While it may not have some of the functionality of ArgoUML (discussed next)—code generation, reverse-engineering, and so on—SmartDraw is perfect for the designer who needs to hammer out a lot of class diagrams.

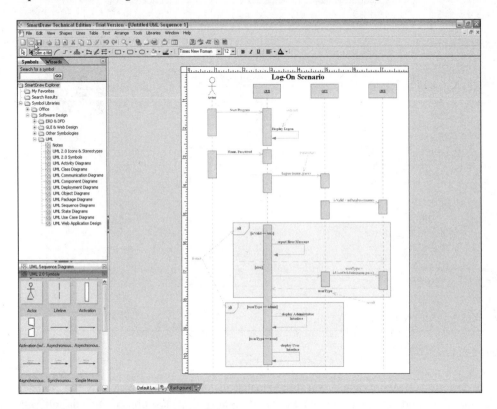

Figure 1-6. *SmartDraw 7 Technical Edition*

ArgoUML

In the open-source arena, ArgoUML (http://argouml.tigris.org/), shown in Figure 1-7, is among the leaders for UML modeling software. Running on a variety of platforms (Windows, Macintosh, and Unix), this Java-based modeling software is supported entirely by the open-source community. Though it currently supports UML 1.3 (not the newer 2.0), ArgoUML has some integrated CASE abilities, like code generation and reverse-engineering, that has made it quite popular, particularly in the Java development community. Like many high-priced modeling tools, ArgoUML has the ability to save models in an extensible XML Metadata Interchange (XMI) format, which has become the standard in the industry for allowing the open interchange of model structure and data between systems and repositories.

■**Note** CASE tools are software programs that automate parts of the development cycle. Code generation
—the ability of a program to translate a graphical model into the actual software code represented by the
model—is an example of CASE. Generally speaking, if the modeling software has some ability to interact,
change, or create the application code or underlying data structures, it is said to have some CASE capacity.

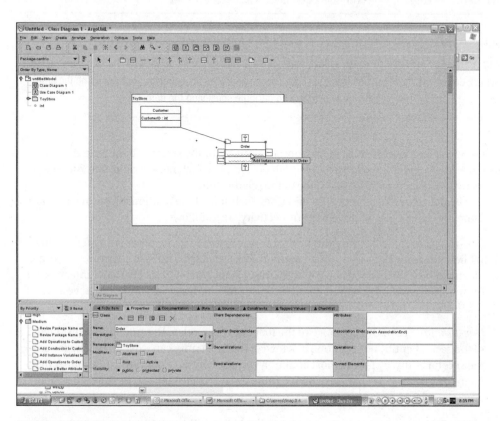

Figure 1-7. *ArgoUML in action*

Entity-Relationship Approach (E-R Diagramming)

While UML is a great tool for modeling complex software designs, it can often be a little overkill,
especially for small systems or inexperienced teams. Another approach, entity-relationship (E-R)
modeling, can complement a team's existing UML models by serving as a streamlined model to
help business users understand the system, or it can be a complete model for the system.

An entity is best described as a single unit of something—a noun or object. Similar to
the classes from a UML model, entities in E-R diagramming represent the objects in your
database system. They are the logical groupings of like data. E-R modeling is simply a way
to graphically express the relationships between the entities of our database system.

The first step in E-R modeling is to list the entities that compose the system. Similar to
what you do in the requirements gathering (use case) stage of the design, write down all the
entities for which you store information in the database. For each entity, write down a brief

description that will help business users understand its purpose in the system, as in the following example:

`Customer`	The user purchasing products from XYZ company
`CustomerOrder`	A set of one or more items purchased by the `Customer`
`CustomerOrderItem`	A product contained in a `CustomerOrder`

Tip You should not have separate entities that represent different time periods for the same object. For instance, don't write down entities like `2004Timesheets` and `2005Timesheets`. Instead, name the entity `Timesheets` and ensure that the entity contains an attribute specifying the date.

Once you've compiled a list of appropriate entities for the system, identify, in regular language, how each entity relates to the other entities. For each relationship, determine the connectivity and cardinality of each side of the relationship.

The *connectivity* of a relationship describes each side of the relationship as one or many. Therefore, the three types of relational connectivity are as follows:

One-to-one (1:1): Each entity can have only one instance of the other entity related to it. While 1:1 relationships aren't that common in normalized database structures, an example might be a situation where you want to separate a set of basic customer information from a set of extra information about the customer. In this case, you would have a 1:1 relationship between the main `Customer` entity and a `CustomerExtra` entity.

One-to-many (1:N): One instance of the first entity can relate to zero or more instances of the second entity, but only one instance of the first entity can exist for one instance of the second entity. By far the most common connectivity, an example of 1:N connectivity might be that an `Order` can have one or more `OrderItem` instances. The `OrderItem`, however, can exist on only a single `Order`.

Many-to-many (M:N): For one instance of the first entity, there can exist zero, one, or many instances of the second entity, and for every instance of the second entity, there can be zero, one, or many instances of the first entity. An example might be the relationship between a `Product` entity and a `ProductCategory` entity. A `Product` could belong to one or more `ProductCategory` instances, and a `ProductCategory` may have one or more `Product` instances tied to it.

Cardinality is the actual number of instances that can be related to each entity in the relationship. For instance, the cardinality of a `Car` entity relationship to a `Wheel` entity would be 1:4.

Next, for each entity, list the attributes that make up the entity. For each attribute, write a description of the attribute, so that business users will understand clearly what the attribute represents. Remember that attribute values should represent a single fact, a characteristic called *atomicity*. Breaking down complex information into its smallest components helps in data reuse and in data normalization

When working out the attributes for each entity, watch out for accidentally including concatenated, coded, or calculated values. For instance, a common mistake is to include an attribute such as `TotalCost` in a `CustomerOrderItem` entity. The total cost represents the product of two other attributes: `Price` and `Quantity`. The `TotalCost` attribute, therefore, is redundant data, and adds no value to the entity itself.[4]

You can think of an E-R diagram as a sort of stripped-down class diagram that focuses only on the attributes of a class and its relationship to other classes. Entities are represented in rectangles containing compartments with the entity's name and a list of its attributes.

E-R Diagramming Tools

As with UML, there are a number of software applications that you can use to create E-R diagrams. We'll look at the following here:

- Microsoft Access

- Computer Associates' AllFusion ERwin Data Modeler

- fabFORCE's DBDesigner4

Quick and Dirty: Using Access for E-R Diagramming

Microsoft Access is widely available to users, because of its relatively low cost and because it's included in some Microsoft Office packages. Using Access to do E-R diagramming is relatively simple. When you have opened a database, you first need to add your table objects, and then you can create a relationship. Here are the steps:

1. In the left panel of the Access window, click Tables.

2. Double-click Create Table in Design View.

3. In the grid, for each column in your table, enter the name of the column and select a data type. The data types will *not* be the same as in MySQL, but the end diagram will give you an idea of the type of data to be stored in your MySQL database.

4. In the field(s) containing your primary key, click the toolbar button with a key icon to mark the columns as the primary key.

5. When you're finished, click the Save button. Access will ask you for a name for the table. Enter a name and click OK.

6. Repeat steps 1 through 5 for each of your table objects. Don't forget to add a primary key to each table.

7. When you're finished adding all of your table objects, select Tools ➤ Relationships. Access displays the Show Table dialog box. Select all the tables you just created and click Add.

---

4. There is some disagreement in the modeling community as to whether calculated fields (attributes) should be included in E-R models. The proponents say that calculated attributes are as important to document as other attributes, as they commonly reflect what business users expect the entity to contain. Opponents say that calculated or derived data should not be in the database (as it is redundant), and therefore should not be included in the modeling process.

8. You will be presented with a "drawing canvas," which has a rectangle for each table with the attributes (fields) of the tables inside. Primary keys will be bold. By dragging a primary key field from one table to another, you can create relationships between the tables, represented by a line with a symbol on either end. Access uses the infinity symbol to represent "many" in relationships.

Figure 1-8 shows an E-R diagram in Access.

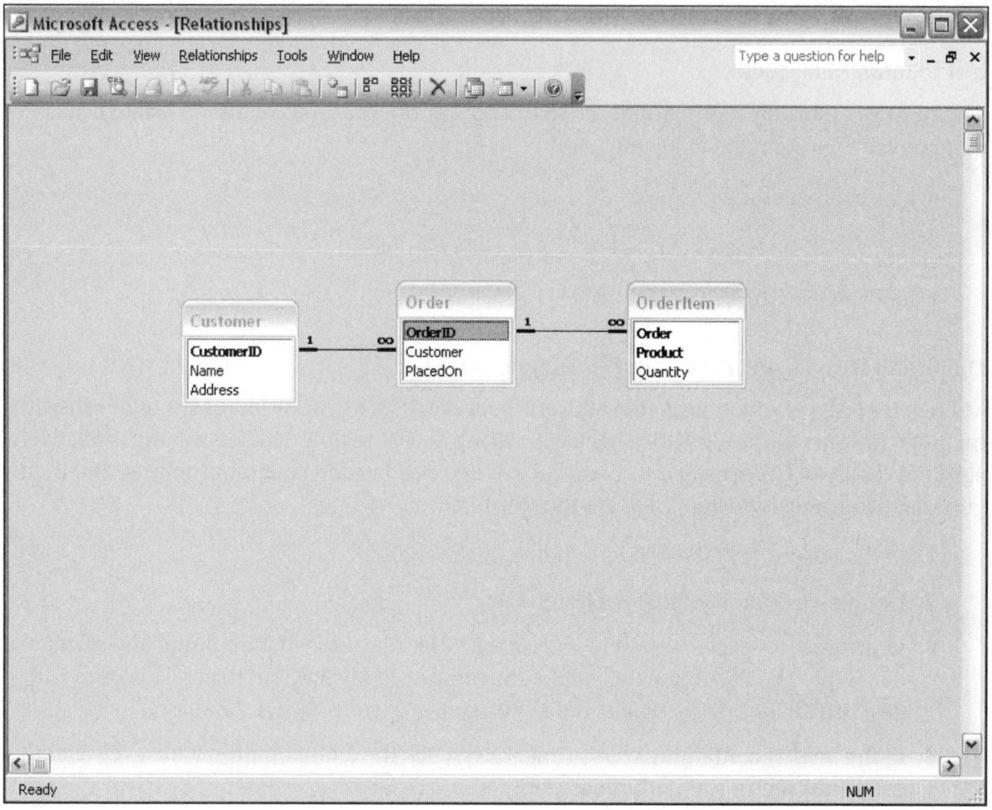

Figure 1-8. *Microsoft Access 2003 Relationships Designer*

AllFusion ERwin Data Modeler

Computer Associates' AllFusion ERwin Data Modeler (http://www.ca.com, where you can find a trial version) allows you to create entities by clicking the entity button on the top toolbar. Adding attributes is as easy as right-clicking the entity, selecting Attribute Properties, and filling in the dialog box for your attributes. Make sure you select Primary Key for your key attributes. The drawing area will show key attributes in the top compartment of the entity box and non-key attributes in the lower compartment. To create a relationship, simply click the appropriate relationship button on the top toolbar, and then click the two entities you wish to relate. Data Modeler does a decent job at showing the relationship by drawing a line between each entity, and also identifies foreign key fields in the child entity automatically.

If you are used to the Windows-type environment, you may find a few aspects of Data Modeler aggravating. In particular, the inability of the program to undo actions can be quite bothersome. Also, Data Modeler does not give you the option of selecting MySQL as your database format, so you can throw possible schema code generation out the window.

DBDesigner4

If you are looking for a free E-R diagramming tool that runs on most major platforms and is designed with MySQL in mind, fabFORCE's DBDesigner4 (`http://fabforce.net`) is a good match. The Java-based interface can sometimes be a bit slow to work with, but the interface is well organized and includes a comprehensive tool set that allows you to quickly build a graphical representation of your MySQL database.

You can choose storage engines when creating new table objects, along with data types for each attribute that correspond to MySQL's data types (see Chapter 5). Simply clicking the appropriate relationship connector button on the toolbar, and then the entities you wish to relate, draws a line showing the connectivity between the objects, as illustrated in Figure 1-9. You can easily add comments to each entity, the drawing surface in general, and the relationship connectors by double-clicking the objects and typing the comment.

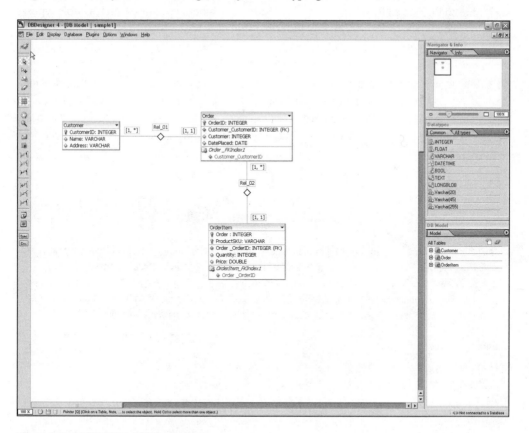

Figure 1-9. *fabFORCE's DBDesigner4*

When you are finished creating your diagram, you can have DBDesigner4 output the MySQL Data Definition Language (DDL) statements that will set up your database by selecting File ➤ Export ➤ SQL Create Script. You can copy the created script to the clipboard or save it to a file. Additionally, the schema and model are stored in an XML format, making the model (somewhat) portable to other software applications.

A Database Blueprint (Baseline Model)

Once you have completed the first iteration of conceptual models—using UML, E-R modeling, or a combination of both—the next step is to create your first database *blueprint*, sometimes called the *baseline model*. Remember that software design should be a dynamic process. Use cases, models, and diagrams should be refined through an iterative approach. As business rules are developed into the models, you will find that relationships you have created between objects may change, or you may feel a different arrangement of data pieces may work more effectively. Don't be afraid to change models and experiment with scenarios throughout the process. Each iteration generally helps to expand your knowledge of the subject domain and refine the solution.

The baseline database model is your first draft of the eventual database schema, and as such, should include all the things that your production schema will need: tables, table types, columns, data types, relationships, and indexes.

■**Tip** Determine a naming convention for your tables and other database objects *before* you start creating the database schema. We cannot stress enough the importance of maintaining consistency in naming your objects. Over the course of a typical application's lifetime, many people work on the database and the code that uses it. Sticking to a naming convention and documenting the convention saves everyone time and prevents headaches.

DATABASE NAMING CONVENTIONS

The actual naming convention you use for database objects is far less important than the consistency with which you apply it. That said, there are numerous methods of naming database objects, all of which have their advocates. Your team should come up with a convention that (hopefully) everyone likes, and stick to it.

Naming conventions generally can be divided into two categories: those that prefix object names with an object or data type identifier and those that do not. Side by side, the two styles might look like this:

Object	Prefix	No Prefix
Database	`db_Sales`	`Sales`
Table	`tbl_Customer`	`Customer`
Field (column)	`int_CustID`	`CustomerID`
Index	`idx_Customer_FirstName_LastName`	`FirstNameLastName` (or left unnamed)

Since database schemas change over time, prefixing column names with the data type (like `int_` for integer or `str_` for character data) can cause unnecessary work for programmers and database administrators alike. Consider a system that contains thousands of stored procedures or script blocks that reference a table `tbl_OrderItem`, which has a column of integer data named `int_Quantity`. Now, suppose that the business rules change and the management decides you should be able to enter fractional quantities for some items. The data type of the column is changed to be a double. Here, you have a sticky situation: either change the name of the column name to reflect the new data type (which requires significant time to change all the scripts or procedures which reference the column) or leave the column name alone and have a mismatch of prefix with actual data type. Neither situation is favorable, and the problem could have been prevented by not using the prefix in the column name to begin with. Having been through this scenario ourselves a few times, we see no tangible benefit to object prefixing compared with the substantial drawbacks it entails.

Conventions for the single or plural form (`Customer` table or `Customers` table, for example) or case of names are a matter of preference. As in the programming world, some folks prefer all lower case (`tbl_customer`), and others use camel or Pascal-cased naming (`orderItem` or `OrderItem`).

Working through your E-R diagrams or other models, begin to create the schema to the database. Some modeling programs may actually be able to perform the creation of your database schema based on models you have built. This can be an excellent timesaver, but when the program finishes creating the initial schema, take the time to go through each table to examine the schema closely.

Use what you will learn in Chapter 5 to adjust the storage engine and data types of your tables and columns. After settling on data types for each of your columns, use your E-R diagram as a guide in creating the primary keys for your tables. Next, ensure that the relationships in your models are translated into your database schema in the form of foreign keys and constraints.

Finally, create an index plan for tables based on your knowledge of the types of queries that will be run against your database. While index placement can and should be adjusted throughout the lifetime of an application (see Chapter 2), you have to start somewhere, right? Look through your class diagrams for operations that likely will query the database for information. Note the parameters for those operations, or the attributes for the class, and add indexes where they seem most appropriate.

Another helpful step that some designers and administrators take during baseline modeling is to populate the tables with some sample data that closely models the data a production model would contain. Populating a sample data set can help you more accurately predict storage requirements. Once you've inserted a sample data set, you can do a quick `show table status from` *your_database_name* to find the average row lengths of your tables (sizes are in bytes, so divide by 1,024 to get kilobytes). Taking the product of the average row length of a table and the number of records you can expect given a certain time period (see your use cases and modeling) can give you a rough estimate of storage requirements and growth over a month.

Check the `Index_length` value for each table as well, to get an idea of the index size in comparison to the table size. Determine the percentage of the table's size that an index takes up by dividing the `Data_length` column by the `Index_length` column. In your storage growth model, you can assume that as the table grows by a certain percentage per month, so will the index size.

Database Selection

It may seem a bit odd to have a section called "Database Selection" in a book titled *Pro MySQL*. We do, however, want you to be aware of the alternatives to MySQL, both on Linux and non-Linux platforms, and be familiar with some of the differences across vendors. If you are already familiar with the alternatives to and the strengths of MySQL, feel free to skip ahead to the next section.

Surveying the Landscape

Here, we're going to take a look at the alternative database management systems available on the market to give you an idea of the industry's landscape. In the enterprise database arena, there is a marked competition among relatively few vendors. Each vendor's product line has its own unique set of capabilities and strengths; each company has spent significant resources identifying its key market and audience. We will take a look at the following products:

- Microsoft SQL Server

- Oracle

- PostgreSQL

- MySQL

SQL Server

Microsoft SQL Server (http://www.microsoft.com/sql/), currently in version 8 (commonly called SQL Server 2000), is a popular database server software from our friends up in Redmond, Washington. Actually adapted from the original Sybase SQL Server code to be optimized for the NTFS file systems and Windows NT kernel, SQL Server has been around for quite some time. It has a robust administrative and client tool set, with newer versions boasting tighter and tighter integration with Microsoft operating systems and server software applications.

SQL Server 2000 natively supports many of the features found only in MySQL's non-production versions, including support for stored procedures, triggers, views, constraints, temporary tables, and user-defined functions. Along with supporting ANSI-92 SQL, SQL Server also supports Transact-SQL, an enhanced version of SQL that adds functionality and support to the querying language.

Unlike MySQL, SQL Server does not have different storage engines supporting separate schema functionality and locking levels. Instead, constraint and key enforcement are available in all tables, and row-level locking is always available.

Through the Enterprise Manager and Query Analyzer, SQL Server users are able to accomplish most database chores easily, using interfaces designed very much like other common Windows server administrative GUIs. The Profiler tool and OLAP Analysis Services are both excellent bundled tools that come with both the Standard and Enterprise Editions of SQL Server 2000. Licensing starts at $4,999 per processor for the Standard Edition, and $18,999 per processor for the Enterprise Edition, which supports some very large database (VLDB) functionality, increased memory support, and other advanced features like indexed partitioned views.

As we go to print, SQL Server 2005 has not yet been released publicly, though that software release is expected this year.

Oracle

Oracle (http://www.oracle.com) competes primarily in the large enterprise arena along with IBM's DB2, Microsoft SQL Server, and Sybase Adaptive Server. While SQL Server has gained some ground in the enterprise database market in the last decade, both DB2 and Adaptive Server have lost considerable market share, except for legacy customers and very large enterprises.

Oracle is generally considered to be less user-friendly than SQL Server, but with a less user-friendly interface comes much more configurability, especially with respect to hardware and tablespaces. PL/SQL (Procedural Language extensions for SQL), Oracle's enhanced version of SQL that can be used to write stored procedures for Oracle, is quite a bit more complicated yet more extensive than Microsoft's Transact-SQL.

Unlike SQL Server, Oracle can run on all major operating system/hardware platforms, including Unix variations and MVS mainframe environments. Oracle, like DB2, can scale to extreme enterprise levels, and it is designed to perform exceptionally well in a clustered environment. If you are in a position of evaluating database server software for companies requiring terabytes of data storage with extremely high transaction processing strength, Oracle will be a foremost contender. Though initial licensing costs matter little in the overall calculation of a database server's ongoing total costs of ownership, it is worth mentioning the licensing for Oracle Database 10*g* servers start at $15,000 per processor for the standard edition and $40,000 per processor for the enterprise edition. Unlike SQL Server, online analytical processing (OLAP) and other administrative tool sets are not bundled in the license.

PostgreSQL

In the world of open-source databases, PostgreSQL (http://www.postgresql.org) is "the other guy." With out-of-the-box database-level features rivaling that of Oracle and SQL Server—stored procedures, triggers, views, constraints, and clustering—many have wondered why this capable database has not gained the same level of popularity that MySQL has. Many features found only in either MySQL's InnoDB storage engine or the latest development versions of MySQL have been around in PostgreSQL for years. Yet the database server has been plagued by a reputation for being somewhat hard to work with and having a propensity to corrupt data files.

For the most part, developers choosing PostgreSQL over MySQL have done so based on the need for more advanced functionality not available in MySQL until later versions. It's worth mentioning that the PostgreSQL licensing model is substantially different from MySQL's model. It uses the Berkeley open-source licensing scheme, which allows the product to be packaged and distributed along with other commercial software as long as the license is packaged along with it.

Why Choose MySQL?

The original developers of MySQL wanted to provide a fast, stable database that was easy to use, with a feature set that met the most common needs of application developers. This goal has remained to this day, and additional feature requests are evaluated to ensure that they can be implemented without sacrificing the original requirements of speed, stability, and ease of use. These features have made MySQL the most popular open-source database in the world among novice users and enterprises alike.

The following are some reasons for choosing MySQL:

Speed: Well known for its extreme performance, MySQL has flourished in the small to medium-sized database arena because of the speed with which it executes queries. It does so through advanced join algorithms, in-memory temporary tables, query caching, and efficient B-tree indexing algorithms.[5]

Portability: Available on almost every platform and hardware combination you could think of, MySQL frees you from being tied to a specific operating system vendor. Unlike Microsoft's SQL Server, which can run on only Windows platforms, MySQL performs well on Unix, Windows, and Mac OS X platforms. One of the nicest things about this cross-platform portability is that you can have a local development machine running on a separate platform than your production machine. While we don't recommend running tests on a different platform than your production server, it is often cost-prohibitive to have a development environment available that is exactly like the production machine. MySQL gives you that flexibility.

Reliability: Because MySQL versions are released to a wide development community for testing before becoming production-ready, the core MySQL production versions are extremely reliable. Additionally, problems with corruption of data files are almost nonexistent in MySQL.

Flexibility: MySQL derives power from its ability to let the developer choose which storage engine is most appropriate for each table. From the super-fast MyISAM and MEMORY in-memory table types, to the transaction-safe InnoDB storage engine, MySQL gives developers great flexibility in how they choose to have the database server manage its data. Additionally, the wide array of configuration variables available in MySQL allow for fine-tuning of the database server. Configuration default settings (outlined in Chapter 14) meet most needs, but almost all aspects of the database server can be changed to achieve specific performance goals in a given environment.

Ease of use: Unlike some other commercial database vendors, installing and using MySQL on almost any platform is a cinch. MySQL has a number of administrative tools, both command-line and GUI, to accomplish all common administrative tasks. Client APIs are available in almost any language you might need, including the base C API, and wrapper APIs for PHP, Perl, Python, Java, C++, and more. MySQL also provides an excellent online manual and other resources.

Licensing: Licensing for MySQL products falls into two categories: Gnu General Public License (GPL) and commercial licensing. For developers of software that is distributed to a commercial community that *does not* get released with 100% open-source code and under a GPL or GPL-compatible license, a commercial license is required. For all other cases, the free GPL license is available.

---

5. MySQL and Oracle were neck and neck in *eWeek*'s 2002 database server performance benchmarks. You can read more about the tests at http://www.mysql.com/it-resources/benchmarks/eweek.html.

ABOUT MYSQL AB
MySQL AB is the company that manages and supports the MySQL database server and its related products, including MaxDB, MySQL's large-enterprise mySAP implementation. The company is dedicated to the principles of open-source software and has a mission to provide affordable, high-quality data management.   MySQL AB makes revenue through the commercial licensing of the MySQL database server and related products, from training and certification services, and through franchise and brand licensing. It is a "virtual company," employing around a hundred people internationally.

Your Environment

Many of you have experience writing or deploying database applications for small to medium-sized businesses. In that experience, you have probably run into some of the complications that go along with deploying software to shared hosting environments or even external dedicated server environments.

On Hosting Companies

The number one concern when dealing with hosting companies is control over environment. In most cut-rate hosting services and many full-service ones, you, as an application developer or database administrator, may not have root access to the server running your applications. This can often make installation of software difficult, and the configuration of certain MySQL settings sometimes impossible. Often, your user administration privileges and access levels will not allow you to execute some of the commands that will be detailed in this book, particularly those involved with backups and other administrative functions.

The best advice we can give to you if you are in a situation where you simply do not have access or full control over your production environment is to develop a relationship with the network and server administrators that *do* have that control. Set up a development and test environment on local machines that *you* have full control over and test your database and application code thoroughly on that local environment. If you find that a certain configuration setting makes a marked improvement in performance on your testing environment, contact the hosting company's server administrators and e-mail them documentation on the changes you need to make to configuration settings. Depending on the company's policies, they may or may not implement your request. Having the documentation ready for the hosting company, however, does help in demonstrating your knowledge of the changes to be made.

Commercial Web Software Development

If you are developing commercial software that may be installed in shared hosting environments, you must be especially sensitive to the version of MySQL that you tailor your application towards. As of the time of this writing, many hosting companies are still deploying MySQL 3.23 on shared web sites. This significantly limits your ability to use some of the more advanced features in this book that are available. Not only is the SQL you are able to write limited in certain ways (no SUBSELECT or UNION operations), but also the InnoDB storage engine, which allows for foreign key support and referential integrity, is not available except in the max version of 3.23. In fact, even in version 4.0.*x*, InnoDB support needed to be compiled during the installation, and many companies running 4.0.*x* servers still don't have InnoDB support enabled. Fortunately, the CREATE TABLE statement with TYPE=InnoDB degrades nicely to simply default to the MyISAM storage engine.

The bottom line is that if you are writing applications that will be installed on shared database servers with down-level versions of MySQL, you must be extremely careful in writing application code so that business rules and referential integrity are enforced through the application code. This situation of defaulting the storage engine to MyISAM has been a major complaint of MySQL in the past, and detractors have pointed out the relative ease of setting up a database that does not support referential integrity, one of the keys to "serious" enterprise-level database design.

One possible remedy to this situation is to section your commercial software into version-aware packages. If you are writing software that takes advantage of MySQL's performance and tuning capabilities and you want to enforce referential integrity of your data source whenever you can, consider spending part of your design time investigating how to build an installer or install script that checks for version and functionality dependencies during installation and installs a code package that is customized to take advantage of that version's capabilities. This may sound like a lot of extra work up front, but, especially if your application is data-centric, the benefits to such an approach would be great.

On Controlled Environments

If you can count on having full-server access rights and control over all levels of your deployment environment, then determining the version of MySQL on which to develop your application becomes more a matter of functionality and risk assessment.

Develop a capabilities list for your software design that represents those things that are critical, beneficial, and nice to have for your application to function at an acceptable level. Table 1-1 shows a list of capabilities, along with which versions of MySQL support them. Use Table 1-1 to determine which version of MySQL is right for your application. Remember that, in most cases, functionality not present in some version can be simulated through code.

In some cases, the functional requirements will dictate a specific storage engine rather than a MySQL version (though, to be sure, certain storage engines are available only in specific versions of MySQL). For instance, full-text indexing is currently supported only on MyISAM tables. Transaction-safe requirements currently dictate using the InnoDB or Berkeley DB storage engine. The new NDB Cluster storage engine is designed for clustered environments and is available from versions 4.1.2 (BitKeeper) and 4.1.3-max (Binary releases) of MySQL, supported only on non-Windows platforms.

Table 1-1. *Version Capabilities Overview*

Capability	v 3.23.x	v 4.0.x	v 4.1.x	v 5.0.x	v5.1	Comments
InnoDB storage engine	Available	Standard	Standard	Standard	Standard	Prior to 4.0.*x* versions, InnoDB support had to be compiled into the binary manually (after 3.23.34a) or the max version of 3.23 binary used.
Foreign key constraints	InnoDB	InnoDB	InnoDB	InnoDB	All	Starting with 5.1, foreign key constraints (referential integrity) will be available for all storage engines, not just InnoDB.
Query cache	N	Y	Y	Y	Y	Greatly increases performance of repetitive queries.
Character sets	Limited	Limited	Y	Y	Y	Starting with 4.0.*x*, character sets and collations are supported more fully, however, 4.1.*x* syntax is different and support is much more robust. See the MySQL manual for more information.
Subqueries	N	N	Y	Y	Y	Ability to have nested SELECT statements.
Unions	N	Y	Y	Y	Y	SQL to join two resultsets on a same-server request.
Support for OpenGIS spatial types	N	N	Y	Y	Y	Geographical data support.
Stored procedures	N	N	N	Y	Y	See Chapter 9 for details on MySQL stored procedure support.
Views	N	N	N	Y	Y	See Chapter 12 for details on MySQL view support.
Triggers	N	N	N	Y	Y	See Chapter 13 for details on MySQL trigger support.
Cursors	N	N	N	Y	Y	Read-only server-side cursor support.

Summary

In this chapter, we've made a whirlwind pass over topics that describe the software development process, and in particular those aspects of the process most significant to the design of database applications. You've seen how different roles in the project team interplay with each other to give roundness and depth to the project's design. From the all-important customer hammering out design requirements with the business analyst, to the modeling work of the database designer and application developer, we've presented a rough sketch of a typical development cycle.

Outlining the concepts of object modeling, we took a look at how UML can help you visualize the relationships between the classes interacting in your system, and how E-R data modeling helps you formalize the data-centric world of the database. Your baseline model has started to take shape, and the beginnings of a working schema have emerged.

In the chapters ahead, the material will become much more focused. We'll look at specific topics in the development of our database and the administration and maintenance of the application. As you encounter new information, be sure to revisit this chapter. You will find that as you gain knowledge in these focus areas, you'll have a new perspective on some of the more general material we have just presented.

CHAPTER 2

■■■

Index Concepts

Many novice database programmers are aware that indexes exist to speed the retrieval of data, yet many don't understand how an index's structure can affect the efficiency of data retrieval. This chapter will provide you with a good understanding of what's going on behind the scenes when you issue queries against your database tables.

Armed with this knowledge of the patterns by which the server looks for and stores your data, you will make smarter choices in designing your schema, as well as save time when optimizing and evaluating the SQL code running against the server. Instead of needing to run endless EXPLAIN commands on a variety of different SQL statements, or creating and testing every combination of index on a table, you'll be able to make an informed decision from the outset of your query building and index design. If the performance of your system begins to slow down, you'll know what changes may remedy the situation.

MySQL's storage engines use different strategies for storing and retrieving your data. Knowing about these differences will help you to decide which storage engine to use in your schemata. (Chapter 5 covers the MySQL storage engines.)

In order to understand what is happening inside the server, we'll begin by covering some basic concepts regarding data access and storage. Understanding how the database server reads data to and from the hard disk and into memory will help you understand certain key MySQL subsystems, in particular the key cache and storage engine abstraction layer (discussed in Chapter 4).

In this chapter, we'll work through the following key areas:

- Data storage: the hard disk, memory, and pages

- How indexes affect data access

- Clustered versus non-clustered data page and index organization

- Index layouts

- Compression

- General index strategies

Data Storage

Data storage involves physical storage media and logical organization of the data. Here, we'll look at three essential elements: the hard disk, memory, and pages. These concepts are fundamental to any database server storage and retrieval system. For example, the notion of persistent versus volatile data storage is central to transaction processing (the subject of Chapter 3).

The Hard Disk: Persistent Data Storage

Database management systems need to persist data across restarts of the server. This means that persistent media must be used to store the data. This persistent media is commonly called the *hard disk* or *secondary storage*.

A hard disk is composed of a *spindle*, which rotates a set of disk *platters*, at a certain speed (commonly 7,500 rpm or 15,000 rpm). Each disk platter is striped with a number of *tracks*. These tracks are markers for the disk drive to move a data reader to. This data reader is called the *arm assembly*, and contains *disk heads*, which move to and from the outside of the platters toward the spindle, reading a *sector* of the disk at a time. See Figure 2-1 for a visual depiction of this structure.

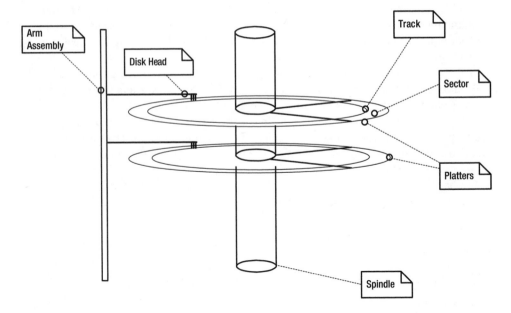

Figure 2-1. *The hard disk*

On the hard disk, data is arranged in *blocks*. These data blocks can be managed as either a fixed or variable size, but they always represent a multiple of the fixed size of the sector on disk. The cost of accessing a block of data on a hard disk is the sum of the time it takes for the arm assembly to perform the following steps:

1. Move the disk head to the correct track on the platter.
2. Wait for the spindle to rotate to the sector that must be read.
3. Transfer the data from the start of the sector to the end of the sector.

Of the total time taken to access or write data to the disk, the first and second operations are the most costly. All of this happens remarkably quickly. The exact speed mostly depends on the speed at which the spindle rotates, which governs the time the assembly must wait for the sector to be reached. This is why disks with higher rotations per minute will read and write data faster.

Memory: Volatile Data Storage

The problem with the hard disk is that because of the process of moving the arm assembly and finding the needed data on the disk, the performance of reading and writing data is slow. In order to increase the performance of data processing, a volatile storage medium is used: random access memory, or RAM.

Reading data from memory is instantaneous; no physical apparatus is needed to move an arm assembly or rotate a disk. However, memory is *volatile*. If the power is lost to the server, all data residing in memory is lost. In order to take advantage of both the speed of memory and the safety of persistent storage, computer programs use a process of transferring data from the hard disk into memory and vice versa. All modern operating systems perform this low-level activity and expose this functionality to computer programs through a standard set of function calls. This set of function calls is commonly called the *buffer management API*. Figure 2-2 shows the flow of data between persistent storage and memory.

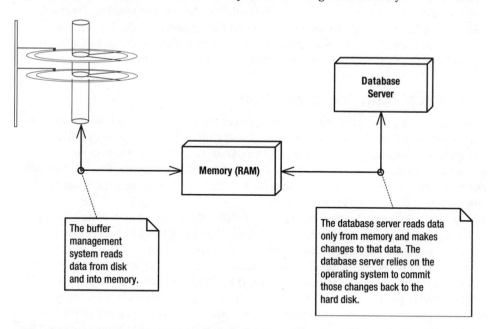

Figure 2-2. *Data flow from the hard disk to memory to the database server*

When MySQL reads information to a hard disk or other persistent media, for example a tape drive, the database server transfers the data from the hard disk into and out of memory. MySQL relies on the underlying operating system to handle this low-level activity through the operating system's buffer management library. You'll find details on how MySQL interacts with the operating system in Chapter 4.

The process of reading from and writing to a hard disk—when the arm assembly moves to a requested sector of a platter to read or write the information needed—is called *seeking*. The seeking speed depends on the time the arm assembly must wait for the spindle to rotate to the needed sector and the time it takes to move the disk head to the needed track on the platter.

If the database server can read a *contiguous* section of data from the hard disk, it performs what is called a *scan* operation. A scan operation can retrieve large amounts of data faster than multiple seeks to various locations on disk, because the arm assembly doesn't need to move more than once. In a scan operation, the arm assembly moves to the sector containing the first piece of data and reads all the data from the disk as the platter rotates to the end of the contiguous data.

Note The term *scan* can refer to both the operation of pulling sequential blocks of data from the hard disk and to the process of reading sequentially through in-memory records.

In order to take advantage of scan operations, the database server can ask the operating system to arrange data on the hard disk in a sequential order if it knows the data will be accessed sequentially. In this way, the seek time (time to move the disk head to the track) and wait time (time for the spindle to rotate to the sector start) can be minimized. When MySQL optimizes tables (using the OPTIMIZE TABLE command), it groups record and index data together to form contiguous blocks on disk. This process is commonly called *defragmenting*.

Pages: Logical Data Representation

As Figure 2-2 indicates, the buffer management system reads and writes data from the hard disk to the main memory. A block of data is read from disk and *allocated* in memory. This allocation is the process of moving data from disk into memory. Once in memory, the system keeps track of multiple data blocks in *pages*. The pages are managed atomically, meaning they are allocated and deallocated from memory as a single unit. The container for managing these various in-memory data pages is called the *buffer pool*.[1]

MySQL relies on the underlying operating system's buffer management, and also its own buffer management subsystem to handle the caching of different types of data. Different storage engines use different techniques to handle record and index data pages.

The MyISAM storage engine relies on the operating system buffer management in order to read table data into memory,[2] but uses a different internal subsystem, the key cache, to handle the buffering of index pages. The InnoDB storage engine employs its own cache of index and record data pages. Additionally, the query cache subsystem available in version 4.0.1 and later uses main memory to store actual resultsets for frequently issued queries. The query cache is specially designed to maintain a list of statistics about frequently used row data and provides a mechanism for invalidating that cache when changes to the underlying row

---

1. The InnoDB storage engine has a buffer pool also, which we cover in Chapter 5. Here, however, we are referring to the buffer pool kept by the operating system and hardware.

2. MyISAM does not use a paged format for reading record data, only for index data.

data pages occur. In Chapter 4, we'll examine the source code of the key cache and query cache, and we will examine the record and index data formats for the MyISAM and InnoDB storage engines in Chapter 5.

While data blocks pertain to the *physical* storage medium, we refer to pages as a *logical* representation of data. Pages typically represent a fixed-size logical group of related data. By "related," we mean that separate data pages contain record, index data, or metadata about a single table. When we speak about a page of data, keep in mind that this page is a logical representation of a group of data; the page itself may actually be represented on a physical storage medium as any number of contiguous blocks.

The database server is always fighting an internal battle of sorts. On the one hand, it needs to efficiently store table data so that retrieval of that information is quick. However, this goal is in contention with the fact that data is not static. Insertions and deletions will happen over time, sometimes frequently, and the database server must proactively plan for them to occur.

If the database server only needed to fetch data, it could pack as many records into a data page as possible, so that fewer seeks would be necessary to retrieve all the data. However, because the database server also needs to write data to a page, several issues arise. What if it must insert the new record in a *particular place* (for instance, when the data is ordered)? Then the database server would need to find the page where the record naturally fit, and move the last record into the next data page. This would trigger a reaction down the line, forcing the database server to load *every* data page, moving one record from each page to the page after, until reaching the last page. Similarly, what would happen if a record were removed? Should the server leave the missing record alone, or should it try to backfill the records from the latter data pages in order to defragment the hole? Maybe it wouldn't do this for just one record, but what if a hundred were removed?

These competing needs of the database server have prompted various strategies for alleviating this contention. Sometimes, these methods work well for highly dynamic sets of data. Sometimes, the methods are designed for more stable data sets. Other methods of managing the records in a data file are designed specifically for index data, where search algorithms are used to quickly locate one or more groups of data records. As we delve deeper into index theory, you will see some more examples of this internal battle going on inside the database server.

The strategy that MySQL's storage engines take to combat these competing needs takes shape in the *layout*, or *format*, in which the storage engine chooses to store record and index data. Pages of record or index data managed by MySQL's storage engines typically contain what is called a *header*, which is a small portion of the data page functioning as a sort of directory for the storage engine. The header has meta information about the data page, such as an identifier for the file that contains the page, an identifier for the actual page, the number of data records or index entries on the page, the amount of free space left on the page, and so on. Data records are laid out on the page in logical *slots*. Each record slot is marked with a record identifier, or RID. The exact size and format of this record identifier varies by storage engine. We'll take a closer look at those internals in Chapter 5.

How Indexes Affect Data Access

An index does more than simply speed up search operations. An index is a tool that offers the database server valuable services and information.

The speed or efficiency in which a database server can retrieve data from a file or collection of data pages depends in large part on the information the database server has about the data set contained within those data pages and files. For example, MySQL can more efficiently find data that is stored in fixed-length records, because there is no need to determine the record length at runtime. The MyISAM storage engine, as you'll see in Chapter 5, can format record data containing only fixed-length data types in a highly efficient manner. The storage engine is aware that the records are all the same length, so the MyISAM storage engine knows ahead of time where a record lies in the data file, making insertion and memory allocation operations easier. This type of meta information is available to help MySQL more efficiently manage its resources.

This meta information's purpose is identical to the purpose of an index: it provides information to the database server in order to more efficiently process requests. The more information the database server has about the data, the easier its job becomes. An index simply provides more information about the data set.

Computational Complexity and the Big "O" Notation

When the database server receives a request to perform a query, it breaks that request down into a logical procession of functions that it must perform in order to fulfill the query. When we talk about database server operations—particularly joins, sorting, and data retrieval—we're broadly referring to the functions that accomplish those basic sorting and data joining operations. Each of these functions, many of which are nested within others, relies on a well-defined set of instructions for solving a particular problem. These formulas are known as *algorithms*.

Some operations are quite simple; for instance, "access a data value based on a key." Others are quite complex; for example, "take two sets of data, and find the intersection of where each data set meets based on a given search criteria." The algorithm applied through the operation's function tries to be as efficient as possible. Efficiency for an algorithm can be thought of as the number of operations needed to accomplish the function. This is known as an algorithm's *computational complexity*.

Throughout this book, we'll look at different algorithms: search, sort, join, and access algorithms. In order for you to know how and when they are effective, it is helpful to understand some terminology involved in algorithm measurements. When comparing the efficiency of an algorithm, folks often refer to the big "O" notation. This indication takes into account the relative performance of the function as the size of the data it must analyze increases. We refer to this size of the data used in a function's operation as the algorithm *input*. We represent this input by the variable n when discussing an algorithm's level of efficiency. Listed from best to worst efficiency, here are some common orders of algorithm efficiency measurement:

- $O(1)$: Constant order
- $O(\log n)$: Logarithmic order
- $O(n)$: Linear order
- $O(n^X)$: Polynomial order
- $O(x^n)$: Exponential order

In computation complexity terminology, each of the O representations refers to the speed at which the function can perform an operation, given the number (n) of data elements involved in the operational data set. You will see the measurement referenced in terms of its *function*, often represented as $f(n) = measurement$.[3]

In fact, the order represents the worst possible case scenario for the algorithm. This means that while an algorithm *may not* take the amount of time to access a key that the O efficiency indicates, it *could*. In computer science, it's much easier to think in terms of the boundary in which the algorithm resides. Practically speaking, though, the O speed is not actually used to calculate the speed in which an index will retrieve a key (as that will vary across hardware and architectures), but instead to represent that *nature* of the algorithm's performance as the data set increases.

O(1) Order

O(1) means that the speed at which the algorithm performs an operation remains *constant* regardless of the number of data elements within the data set. If a data retrieval function deployed by an index has an order of O(1), the algorithm deployed by the function will find the key in the same number of operations, regardless of whether there are $n = 100,000$ keys or $n = 1,000,000$ keys in the index. Note that we don't say the index would perform the operation in the same amount of time, but in the same number of operations. Even if an algorithm has an order of O(1), two runs of the function on data sets could theoretically take different amounts of time, since the processor may be processing a number of operations in any given time period, which may affect the overall time of the function run.

Clearly, this is the highest level of efficiency an algorithm can achieve. You can think of accessing a value of an array at index x as a constant efficiency. The function always takes the same number of operations to complete the retrieval of the data at location array[x], regardless of the number of array elements. Similarly, a function that does absolutely nothing but return 0 would have an order of O(1).

O(*n*) Order

O(n) means that as the number of elements in the index increases, the retrieval speed increases at a *linear* rate. A function that must search through all the elements of an array to return values matching a required condition operates on a linear efficiency factor, since the function must perform the operations for every element of the array. This is a typical efficiency order for table scan functions that read data sequentially or for functions that use linked lists to read through arrays of data structures, since the linked list pointers allow for only sequential, as opposed to random, access.

You will sometimes see coefficients referenced in the efficiency representation. For instance, if we were to determine that an algorithm's efficiency can be calculated as three times the number of elements (inputs) in the data set, we write that $f(n) = O(3n)$. However, the coefficient 3 can be *ignored*. This is because the actual *calculation* of the efficiency is less important than the *pattern* of the algorithm's performance over time. We would instead simply say that the algorithm has a *linear* order, or pattern.

---

3. If you are interested in the mathematics involved in O factor calculations, head to
   http://en.wikipedia.org/wiki/Big_O_notation and follow some of the links there.

O(log n) Order

Between constant and linear efficiency factors, we have the logarithmic efficiency factors. Typical examples of logarithmic efficiency can be found in common binary search functions. In a binary search function, an ordered array of values is searched, and the function "skips" to the middle of the remaining array elements, essentially cutting the data set into two logical parts. The function examines the next value in the array "up" from the point to where the function skipped. If the value of that array element is greater than the supplied search value, the function ignores all array values above the point to where the function skipped and repeats the process for the previous portion of the array. Eventually, the function will either find a match in the underlying array or reach a point where there are no more elements to compare—in which case, the function returns no match. As it turns out, you can perform this division of the array (skipping) a maximum of log n times before you either find a match or run out of array elements. Thus, log n is the outer boundary of the function's algorithmic efficiency and is of a logarithmic order of complexity.

As you may or may not recall from school, logarithmic calculations are done on a specific *base*. In the case of a binary search, when we refer to the binary search having a log n efficiency, it is implied that the calculation is done with base 2, or $\log_2 n$. Again, the base is less important than the pattern, so we can simply say that a binary search algorithm has a logarithmic performance order.

O(n^x) and O(x^n) Orders

O(n^x) and O(x^n) algorithm efficiencies mean that as more elements are added to the input (index size), the index function will return the key less efficiently. The boundary, or worst-case scenario, for index retrieval is represented by the two equation variants, where x is an arbitrary constant. Depending on the number of keys in an index, either of these two algorithm efficiencies might return faster. If algorithm A has an efficiency factor of O(n^x) and algorithm B has an efficiency factor of O(x^n), algorithm A will be more efficient once the index has approximately x elements in the index. But, for either algorithm function, as the size of the index increases, the performance suffers dramatically.

Data Retrieval Methods

To illustrate how indexes affect data access, let's walk through the creation of a simple index for a set of records in a hypothetical data page. Imagine you have a data page consisting of product records for a toy store. The data set contains a collection of records including each product's unique identifier, name, unit price, weight, and description. Each record includes the record identifier, which represents the row of record data within the data page. In the real world, the product could indeed have a numeric identifier, or an alphanumeric identifier, known as a SKU. For now, let's assume that the product's unique identifier is an integer. Take a look at Table 2-1 for a view of the data we're going to use in this example.

Table 2-1. *A Simple Data Set of Product Information*

RID	Product ID	Name	Price	Weight	Description
1	1002	Teddy Bear	20.00	2.00	A big fluffy teddy bear.
2	1008	Playhouse	40.99	50.00	A big plastic playhouse with two entrances.
3	1034	Lego Construction Set	35.99	3.50	Lego construction set includes 300 pieces.
4	1058	Seesaw	189.50	80.00	Metal playground seesaw. Assembly required.
5	1000	Toy Airplane	215.00	20.00	Build-your-own balsa wood flyer.

Note that the data set is not ordered by any of the fields in our table, but by the order of the internal record identifier. This is important because your record sets are not always stored on disk in the order you might think they are. Many developers are under the impression that if they define a table with a primary key, the database server actually stores the records for that table in the order of the primary key. This is not necessarily the case. The database server will place records into various pages within a data file in a way that is efficient for the insertion and deletion of records, as well as the retrieval of records. Regardless of the primary key you've affixed to a table schema, the database server may distribute your records across multiple, nonsequential data pages, or in the case of the MyISAM storage engine, simply at the end of the single data file (see Chapter 5 for more details on MyISAM record storage). It does this to save space, perform an insertion of a record more efficiently, or simply because the cost of putting the record in an already in-memory data page is less than finding where the data record would "naturally" fit based on your primary key.

Also note that the records are composed of different types of data, including integer, fixed-point numeric, and character data of varying lengths. This means that a database server cannot rely on how large a single record will be. Because of the varying lengths of data records, the database server doesn't even know how many records will go into a fixed-size data page. At best, the server can make an educated guess based on an average row length to determine on average how many records can fit in a single data page.

Let's assume that we want to have the database server retrieve all the products that have a weight equal to two pounds. Reviewing the sample data set in Table 2-1, it's apparent that the database server has a dilemma. We haven't provided the server with much information that it might use to efficiently process our request. In fact, our server has only one way of finding the answer to our query. It must load all the product records into memory and loop through each one, comparing the value of the weight part of the record with the number two. If a match is found, the server must place that data record into an array to return to us. We might visualize the database server's request response as illustrated in Figure 2-3.

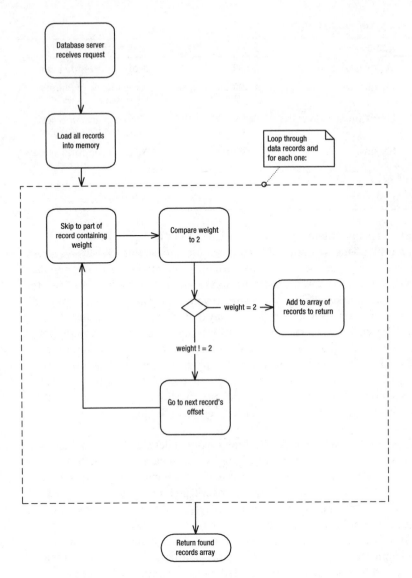

Figure 2-3. *Read all records into memory and compare weight.*

A number of major inefficiencies are involved in this scenario:

- Our database server is consuming a relatively large amount of memory in order to fulfill our request. Every data record must be loaded into memory in order to fulfill our query.

- Because there is no ordering of our data records by weight, the server has no method of eliminating records that don't meet our query's criteria. This is an important concept and worth repeating: *the order in which data is stored provides the server a mechanism for reducing the number of operations required to find needed data.* The server can use a number of more efficient search algorithms, such as a binary search, if it knows that the data is sorted by the criteria it needs to examine.

- For each record in the data set, the server must perform the step of skipping to the piece of the record that represents the weight of the product. It does this by using an *offset* provided to it by the table's meta information, or schema, which informs the server that the weight part of the record is at byte offset *x*. While this operation is not complicated, it adds to the overall complexity of the calculation being done inside the loop.

So, how can we provide our database server with a mechanism capable of addressing these problems? We need a system that eliminates the need to scan through all of our records, reduces the amount of memory required for the operation (loading all the record data), and avoids the need to find the weight part inside the whole record.

Binary Search

One way to solve the retrieval problems in our example would be to make a narrower set of data containing only the weight of the product, and have the record identifier *point* to where the rest of the record data could be found. We can presort this new set of weights and record pointers from smallest weight to the largest weight. With this new sorted structure, instead of loading the entire set of full records into memory, our database server could load the smaller, more streamlined set of weights and pointers. Table 2-2 shows this new, streamlined list of sorted product weights and record pointers.

Table 2-2. *A Sorted List of Product Weights*

RID	Weight
1	2.00
3	3.50
5	20.00
2	50.00
4	80.00

Because the data in the smaller set is sorted, the database server can employ a fast binary search algorithm on the data to eliminate records that do not meet the criteria. Figure 2-4 depicts this new situation.

A binary search algorithm is one method of efficiently processing a sorted list to determine rows that match a given value of the sorted criteria. It does so by "cutting" the set of data in half (thus the term *binary*) repeatedly, with each iteration comparing the supplied value with the value where the cut was made. If the supplied value is greater than the value at the cut, the lower half of the data set is ignored, thus eliminating the need to compare those values. The reverse happens when the skipped to value is less than the supplied search criteria. This comparison repeats until there are no more values to compare.

This seems more complicated than the first scenario, right? At first glance, it *does* seem more complex, but this scenario is actually significantly faster than the former, because it doesn't loop through as many elements. The binary search algorithm was able to eliminate the need to do a comparison on each of the records, and in doing so reduced the overall computational complexity of our request for the database server. Using the smaller set of sorted weight data, we are able to avoid needing to load all the record data into memory in order to compare the product weights to our search criteria.

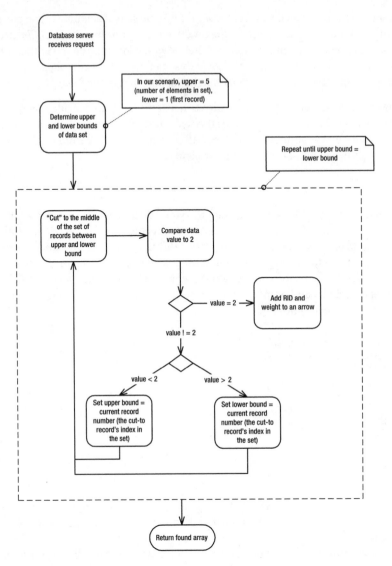

Figure 2-4. *A binary search algorithm speeds searches on a sorted list.*

■**Tip** When you look at code—either your own or other people's—examine the `for` and `while` loops closely to understand the number of elements actually being operated on, and what's going on *inside* those loops. A function or formula that may *seem* complicated and overly complex at first glance may be much more efficient than a simple-looking function because it uses a process of elimination to reduce the number of times a loop is executed. So, the bottom line is that you should pay attention to what's going on in looping code, and don't judge a book by its cover!

So, we've accomplished our mission! Well, not so fast. You may have already realized that we're missing a big part of the equation. Our new smaller data set, while providing a faster, more memory efficient search on weights, has returned only a set of weights and record pointers. But our request was for *all* the data associated with the record, not just the weights! An additional step is now required for a *lookup* of the actual record data. We can use that set of record pointers to retrieve the data in the page.

So, have we really made things more efficient? It seems we've added another layer of complexity and more calculations. Figure 2-5 shows the diagram of our scenario with this new step added. The changes are shown in bold.

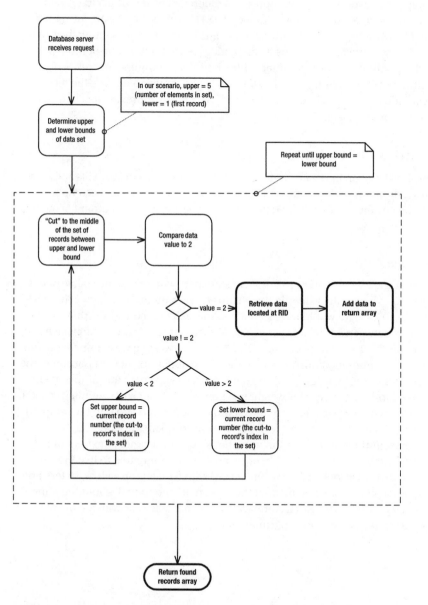

Figure 2-5. *Adding a lookup step to our binary search on a sorted list*

The Index Sequential Access Method

The scenario we've just outlined is a simplified, but conceptually accurate, depiction of how an actual index works. The reduced set of data, with only weights and record identifiers, would be an example of an index. The index provides the database server with a streamlined way of comparing values to a given search criteria. It streamlines operations by being *sorted*, so that the server doesn't need to load all the data into memory just to compare a small piece of the record's data.

The style of index we created is known as the *index sequential access method*, or ISAM. The MyISAM storage engine uses a more complex, but theoretically identical, strategy for structuring its record and index data. Records in the MyISAM storage engine are formatted as sequential records in a single data file with record identifier values representing the slot or offset within the file where the record can be located. Indexes are built on one or more fields of the row data, along with the record identifier value of the corresponding records. When the index is used to find records matching criteria, a *lookup* is performed to retrieve the record based on the record identifier value in the index record. We'll take a more detailed look at the MyISAM record and index format in Chapter 5.

Analysis of Index Operations

Now that we've explored how an index affects data retrieval, let's examine the benefits and some drawbacks to having the index perform our search operations. Have we actually accomplished our objectives of reducing the number of operations and cutting down on the amount of memory required?

Number of Operations

In the first scenario (Figure 2-3), all five records were loaded into memory, and so five operations were required to compare the values in the records to the supplied constant 2. In the second scenario (Figure 2-4), we would have skipped to the weight record at the third position, which is halfway between 5 (the number of elements in our set) and 1 (the first element). Seeing this value to be 20.00, we compare it to 2. The 2 value is lower, so we eliminate the top portion of our weight records, and jump to the middle of the remaining (lower) portion of the set and compare values. The 3.50 value is still greater than 2, so we repeat the jump and end up with only one remaining element. This weight just happens to match the supplied criteria, so we look up the record data associated with the record identifier and add it to the returned array of data records. Since there are no more data values to compare, we exit.

Just looking at the number of comparison operations, we can see that our streamlined set of weights and record identifiers took fewer operations: three compared to five. However, we still needed to do that extra lookup for the one record with a matching weight, so let's not jump to conclusions too early. If we assume that the lookup operation took about the same amount of processing power as the search comparison did, that leaves us with a score of 5 to 4, with our second method winning only marginally.

The Scan vs. Seek Choice: A Need for Statistics

Now consider that if two records had been returned, we would have had the same number of operations to perform in either scenario! Furthermore, if more than two records had met the criteria, it would have been more operationally efficient *not* to use our new index and simply scan through all the records.

This situation represents a classic problem in indexing. If the data set contains too many of the same value, the index becomes less useful, and can actually hurt performance. As we explained earlier, sequentially scanning through contiguous data pages on disk is faster than performing many seek operations to retrieve the same data from numerous points in the hard disk. The same concept applies to indexes of this nature. Because of the extra CPU effort needed to perform the lookup from the index record to the data record, it can sometimes be faster for MySQL to simply load all the records into memory and *scan through them*, comparing appropriate fields to any criteria passed in a query.

If there are many matches in an index for a given criterion, MySQL puts in extra effort to perform these record lookups for each match. Fortunately, MySQL keeps statistics about the uniqueness of values within an index, so that it may estimate (before actually performing a search) how many index records will match a given criterion. If it determines the estimated number of rows is higher than a certain percentage of the total number of records in the table, it chooses to instead scan through the records. We'll explore this topic again in great detail in Chapter 6, which covers benchmarking and profiling.

Index Selectivity

The *selectivity* of a data set's values represents the degree of uniqueness of the data values contained within an index. The selectivity (S) of an index (I), in mathematical terms, is the number of *distinct* values (d) contained in a data set, divided by the *total number of records* (n) in the data set: $S(I) = d/n$ (read "S of I equals d over n"). The selectivity will thus always be a number between 0 and 1. For a completely unique index, the selectivity is always equal to 1, since $d = n$.

So, to measure the selectivity of a potential index on the product table's weight value, we could perform the following to get the d value:

```
mysql> SELECT COUNT( DISTINCT weight) FROM products;
```

Then get the n value like so:

```
mysql> SELECT COUNT(*) FROM products;
```

Run these values through the formula $S(I) = d/n$ to determine the potential index's selectivity.

A high selectivity means that the data set contains mostly or entirely unique values. A data set with low selectivity contains groups of identical data values. For example, a data set containing just record identifiers and each person's gender would have an extremely low selectivity, as the only possible values for the data would be male and female. An index on the gender data would yield ineffective performance, as it would be more efficient to scan through all the records than to perform operations using a sorted index. We will refer to this dilemma as the *scan versus seek choice*.

This knowledge of the underlying index data set is known as *index statistics*. These statistics on an index's selectivity are invaluable to MySQL in *optimizing*, or determining the most efficient method of fulfilling, a request.

■**Tip** The first item to analyze when determining if an index will be helpful to the database server is to determine the selectivity of the underlying index data. To do so, get your hands on a sample of *real* data that will be contained in your table. If you don't have any data, ask a business analyst to make an educated guess as to the frequency with which similar values will be inserted into a particular field.

Index selectivity is not the only information that is useful to MySQL in analyzing an optimal path for operations. The database server keeps a number of statistics on both the index data set *and* the underlying record data in order to most effectively perform requested operations.

Amount of Memory

For simplicity's sake, let's assume each of our product records has an average size of 50 bytes. The size of the weight part of the data, however, is always 6 bytes. Additionally, let's assume that the size of the record identifier value is always 6 bytes. In either scenario, we need to use the same ~50 bytes of storage to return our single matched record. This being the same in either case, we can ignore the memory associated with the return in our comparison.

Here, unlike our comparison of operational efficiency, the outcome is more apparent. In the first scenario, total memory consumption for the operation would be 5×50 bytes, or 250 bytes. In our index operations, the total memory needed to load the index data is $5 \times (6 + 6) = 60$ bytes. This gives us a total savings of operation memory usage of 76%! Our index beat out our first situation quite handily, and we see a substantial savings in the amount of memory consumed for the search operation.

In reality, memory is usually allocated in fixed-size pages, as you learned earlier in this chapter. In our example, it would be unlikely that the tiny amount of row data would be more than the amount of data available in a single data page, so the use of the index would actually not result in any memory savings. Nevertheless, the concept is valid. The issue of memory consumption becomes crucial as more and more records are added to the table. In this case, the smaller record size of the index data entries mean more index records will fit in a single data page, thus reducing the number of pages the database server would need to read into memory.

Storage Space for Index Data Pages

Remember that in our original scenario, we needed to have storage space only *on disk* for the actual data records. In our second scenario, we needed additional room to store the index data—the weights and record pointers.

So, here, you see another classic trade-off that comes with the use of indexes. While you consume less memory to actually perform searches, you need more physical storage space for the extra index data entries. In addition, MySQL uses main memory to store the index data as well. Since main memory is limited, MySQL must balance which index data pages and which record data pages remain in memory.

The actual storage requirements for index data pages will vary depending on the size of the data types on which the index is based. The more fields (and the larger the fields) are indexed, the greater the need for data pages, and thus the greater the requirement for more storage.

To give you an example of the storage requirements of each storage engine in relation to a simple index, we populated two tables (one MyISAM and one InnoDB) with 90,000 records each. Each table had two CHAR(25) fields and two INT fields. The MyISAM table had just a PRIMARY KEY index on one of the CHAR(25) fields. Running the SHOW TABLE STATUS command revealed that the space needed for the data pages was 53,100,000 bytes and the space needed by the index data pages was 3,716,096 bytes. The InnoDB table also had a PRIMARY KEY index on one of the CHAR(25) fields, and another simple index on the other CHAR(25) field. The space used by the data pages was 7,913,472 bytes, while the index data pages consumed 10,010,624 bytes.

■Note To check the storage space needed for both data pages and index pages, use the SHOW TABLE ➡
STATUS command.

The statistics here are not meant to compare MyISAM with InnoDB, because the index organization is completely different for each storage engine. The statistics are meant to show the significant storage space required for *any* index.

Effects of Record Data Changes

What happens when we need to insert a new product into our table of products? If we left the index untouched, we would have out-of-date (often called *invalidated*) index data. Our index will need to have an additional record inserted for the new product's weight and record identifier. For each index placed on a table, MySQL must maintain both the record data *and* the index data. For this reason, indexes can slow performance of INSERT, UPDATE, and DELETE operations.

When considering indexes on tables that have mostly SELECT operations against them, and little updating, this performance consideration is minimal. However, for highly dynamic tables, you should carefully consider on which fields you place an index. This is especially true for transactional tables, where locking can occur, and for tables containing web site session data, which is highly volatile.

Clustered vs. Non-Clustered Data and Index Organization

Up until this point in the chapter, you've seen only the organization of data pages where the records in the data page are not sorted in any particular order. The index sequential access method, on which the MyISAM storage engine is built, orders index records but not data records, relying on the record identifier value to provide a pointer to where the actual data record is stored. This organization of data records to index pages is called a *non-clustered* organization, because the data is not stored on disk sorted by a keyed value.

■**Note** You will see the term *non-clustered index* used in this book and elsewhere. The actual term *non-clustered* refers to the *record* data being stored on disk in an unsorted order, with *index* records being stored in a sorted order. We will refer to this concept as a non-clustered organization of data and index pages.

The InnoDB storage engine uses an alternate organization known as *clustered index* organization. Each InnoDB table *must* contain a unique non-nullable primary key, and records are stored in data pages according to the order of this primary key. This primary key is known as the *clustering key*. If you do not specify a column as the primary key during the creation of an InnoDB table, the storage engine will automatically create one for you and manage it internally. This auto-created clustering key is a 6-byte integer, so if you have a smaller field on which a primary key would naturally make sense, it behooves you to specify it, to avoid wasting the extra space required for the clustering key.

Clearly, only one clustered index can exist on a data set at any given time. Data cannot be sorted on the same data page in two different ways simultaneously.

Under a clustered index organization, all *other* indexes built against the table are built on top of the clustered index keys. These non-primary indexes are called *secondary indexes*. Just as in the index sequential access method, where the record identifier value is paired with the index key value for each index record, the clustered index key is paired with the index key value for the secondary index records.

The primary advantage of clustered index organization is that the searches on the primary key are remarkably fast, because no lookup operation is required to jump from the index record to the data record. For searches on the clustering key, the index record *is* the data record—they are one and the same. For this reason, InnoDB tables make excellent choices for tables on which queries are primarily done on a primary key. We'll take a closer look at the InnoDB storage engine's strengths in Chapter 5.

It is critical to understand that secondary indexes built on a clustered index are *not* the same as non-clustered indexes built on the index sequential access method. Suppose we built two tables (used in the storage requirements examples presented in the preceding section), as shown in Listing 2-1.

Listing 2-1. *CREATE TABLE Statements for Similar MyISAM and InnoDB Tables*

```
CREATE TABLE http_auth_myisam (
  username CHAR(25) NOT NULL
, pass CHAR(25) NOT NULL
, uid INT NOT NULL
, gid INT NOT NULL
, PRIMARY KEY (username)
, INDEX pwd_idx (pass)) ENGINE=MyISAM;

CREATE TABLE http_auth_innodb (
  username CHAR(25) NOT NULL
, pass CHAR(25) NOT NULL
, uid INT NOT NULL
, gid INT NOT NULL
```

```
, PRIMARY KEY (username)
, INDEX pwd_idx (pass)) ENGINE=InnoDB;
```

Now, suppose we issued the following SELECT statement against http_auth_myisam:

```
SELECT username FROM http_auth_myisam WHERE pass = 'somepassword';
```

The pwd_idx index would indeed be used to find the needed records, but an index lookup would be required to read the username field from the data record. However, if the same statement were executed against the http_auth_innodb table, *no lookup would be required*. The secondary index pwd_idx on http_auth_innodb *already contains* the username data because it is the clustering key.

The concept of having the index record contain all the information needed in a query is called a *covering index*. In order to best use this technique, it's important to understand what pieces of data are contained in the varying index pages under each index organization. We'll show you how to determine if an index is covering your queries in Chapter 6, in the discussion of the EXPLAIN command.

Index Layouts

Just as the organization of an index and its corresponding record data pages can affect the performance of queries, so too can the layout (or structure) of an index. MySQL's storage engines make use of two common and tested index layouts: *B-tree* and *hash* layouts. In addition, the MyISAM storage engine provides the FULLTEXT index format and the R-tree index structure for spatial (geographic) data. Table 2-3 summarizes the types of index layout used in the MyISAM, MEMORY, and InnoDB storage engines.

Table 2-3. *MySQL Index Formats*

Storage Engine	B-Tree	R-Tree	Hash	FULLTEXT
MyISAM	All versions	Version 4.1+	No	All versions
MEMORY	Version 4.1+	No	All versions	No
InnoDB	All versions	No	Adaptive	No

Here, we'll cover each of these index layouts, including the InnoDB engine's adaptive version of the hash layout. You'll find additional information about the MySQL storage engines in Chapter 5.

The B-Tree Index Layout

One of the drawbacks of storing index records as a simple sorted list (as described in the earlier section about the index sequential access method) is that when insertions and deletions occur in the index data entries, large blocks of the index data must be reorganized in order to maintain the sorting and compactness of the index. Over time, this reorganization of data pages can result in a flurry of what is called *splitting*, or the process of redistributing index data entries across multiple data pages.

If you remember from our discussion on data storage at the beginning of the chapter, a data page is filled with both row data (records) and meta information contained in a data page header. Tree-based index layouts take a page (pun intended) out of this technique's book. A sort of *directory* is maintained about the index records—data entries—which allows data to be spread across a range of data pages in an *even* manner. The directory provides a clear path to find individual, or groups of, records.

As you know, a read request from disk is much more resource-intensive than a read request from memory. If you are operating on a large data set, spread across multiple pages, reading in those multiple data pages is an expensive operation. Tree structures alleviate this problem by dramatically reducing the number of disk accesses needed to *locate* on which data page a key entry can be found.

The tree is simply a collection of one or more data pages, called *nodes*. In order to find a record within the tree, the database server starts at the *root* node of the tree, which contains a set of *n* key values in sorted order. Each key contains not only the value of the key, but it also has a pointer to the node that contains the keys less than or equal to its own key value, but no greater than the key value of the preceding key.

The keys point to the data page on which records containing the key value can be found. The pages on which key values (index records) can be found are known as *leaf* nodes. Similarly, index data pages containing these index nodes that do not contain index records, but only pointers to where the index records are located, are called *non-leaf* nodes.

Figure 2-6 shows an example of the tree structure. Assume a data set that has 100 unique integer keys (from 1 to 100). You'll see a tree structure that has a non-leaf root node holding the pointers to the leaf pages containing the index records that have the key values 40 and 80. The shaded squares represent *pointers* to leaf pages, which contain index records with key values less than or equal to the associated keys in the root node. These leaf pages point to data pages storing the actual table records containing those key values.

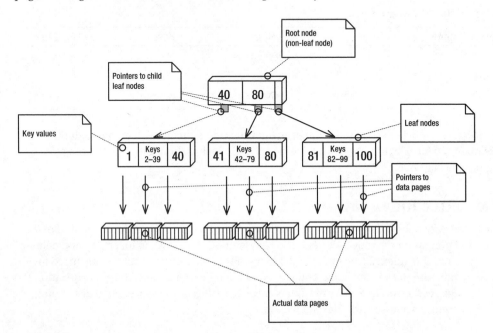

Figure 2-6. *A B-tree index on a non-clustered table*

To find records that have a key value of 50, the database server queries the root node until it finds a key value equal to or greater than 50, and then follows the pointer to the child leaf node. This leaf contains pointers to the data page(s) where the records matching key = 50 can be found.

Tree indexes have a few universal characteristics. The height (*h*) of the tree refers to the number of levels of leaf or non-leaf pages. Additionally, nodes can have a minimum and maximum number of keys associated with them. Traditionally, the minimum number of keys is called the *minimization factor* (*t*), and the maximum is sometimes called the *order*, or *branching factor* (*n*). A specialized type of tree index structure is known as *B-tree*, which commonly means "balanced tree."[4] B-tree structures are designed to spread key values evenly across the tree structure, adjusting the nodes within a tree structure to remain in accordance with a predefined branching factor whenever a key is inserted. Typically, a high branching factor is used (number of keys per node) in order to keep the height of the tree low. Keeping the height of the tree minimal reduces the overall number of disk accesses.

Generally, B-tree search operations have an efficiency of $O(\log_x n)$, where *x* equals the branching factor of the tree. (See the "Computational Complexity and the Big 'O' Notation" section earlier in this chapter for definitions of the O efficiencies.) This means that finding a specific entry in a table of even millions of records can take very few disk seeks. Additionally, because of the nature of B-tree indexes, they are particularly well suited for *range queries*. Because the nodes of the tree are ordered, with pointers to the index pages between a certain range of key values, queries containing any range operation (IN, BETWEEN, >, <, <=, =>, and LIKE) can use the index effectively.

The InnoDB and MyISAM storage engines make heavy use of B-tree indexes in order to speed queries. There are a few differences between the two implementations, however. One difference is where the index data pages are actually stored. MyISAM stores index data pages in a separate file (marked with an .MYI extension). InnoDB, by default, puts index data pages in the same files (called *segments*) as record data pages. This makes sense, as InnoDB tables use a clustered index organization. In a clustered index organization, the leaf node of the B-tree index *is the data page*, since data pages are sorted by the clustering key. All secondary indexes are built as normal B-tree indexes with leaf nodes containing pointers to the clustered index data pages.

As of version 4.1, the MEMORY storage engine supports the option of having a tree-based layout for indexes instead of the default hash-based layout.

You'll find more details about each of these storage engines in Chapter 5.

The R-Tree Index Layout

The MyISAM storage engine supports the R-tree index layout for indexing spatial data types. Spatial data types are geographical coordinates or three-dimensional data. Currently, MyISAM is the only storage engine that supports R-tree indexes, in versions of MySQL 4.1 and later. R-tree index layouts are based on the same tree structures as B-tree indexes, but they implement the comparison of values differently.

---

4. The name *balanced tree index* reflects the nature of the indexing algorithm. Whether the *B* in B-tree actually stands for balanced is debatable, since the creator of the algorithm was Rudolf Bayer (see http://www.nist.gov/dads/HTML/btree.html).

The Hash Index Layout

In computer lingo, a *hash* is simply a key/value pair. Consequently, a *hash table* is merely a collection of those key value pairs. A *hash function* is a method by which a supplied search key, *k*, can be mapped to a distinct set of *buckets*, where the values paired with the hash key are stored. We represent this hashing activity by saying $h(k) = \{1,m\}$, where *m* is the number of buckets and $\{1,m\}$ represents the set of buckets. In performing a hash, the hash function reduces the size of the key value to a smaller subset, which cuts down on memory usage and makes both searches *and* insertions into the hash table more efficient.

The InnoDB and MEMORY storage engines support hash index layouts, but only the MEMORY storage engine gives you control over whether a hash index should be used instead of a tree index. Each storage engine internally implements a hash function differently.

As an example, let's say you want to search the product table by name, and you know that product names are always unique. Since the value of each record's Name field could be up to 100 bytes long, we know that creating an index on all Name records, along with a record identifier, would be space- and memory-consuming. If we had 10,000 products, with a 6-byte record identifier and a 100-byte Name field, a simple list index would be 1,060,000 bytes. Additionally, we know that longer string comparisons in our binary search algorithm would be less efficient, since more bytes of data would need to be compared.

In a hash index layout, the storage engine's hash function would "consume" our 100-byte Name field and *convert* the string data into a smaller integer, which corresponds to a bucket in which the record identifier will be placed. For the purpose of this example, suppose the storage engine's particular hash function happens to produce an integer in the range of 0 to 32,768. See Figure 2-7 for an idea of what's going on. Don't worry about the implementation of the hash function. Just know that the conversion of string keys to an integer occurs *consistently* across requests for the hash function given a specific key.

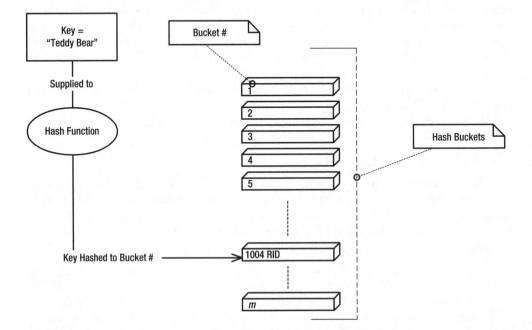

Figure 2-7. *A hash index layout pushes a key through a hash function into a bucket.*

If you think about the range of possible combinations of a 20-byte string, it's a little staggering: 2^160. Clearly, we'll never have that many products in our catalog. In fact, for the toy store, we'll probably have fewer than 32,768 products in our catalog, which makes our hash function pretty efficient; that is, it produces a range of values around the same number of unique values we expect to have in our product name field data, but with *substantially* less data storage required.

Figure 2-7 shows an example of *inserting* a key into our hash index, but what about *retrieving* a value from our hash index? Well, the process is almost identical. The value of the searched criteria is run through the same hash function, producing a hash bucket #. The bucket is checked for the existence of data, and if there is a record identifier, it is returned. This is the essence of what a hash index is. When searching for an equality condition, such as `WHERE key_value = searched_value`, hash indexes produce a constant $O(1)$ efficiency.[5]

However, in some situations, a hash index is not useful. Since the hash function produces a single hashed value for each supplied key, or set of keys in a multicolumn key scenario, lookups based on a range criteria are not efficient. For range searches, hash indexes actually produce a linear efficiency $O(n)$, as each of the search values in the range must be hashed and then compared to each tuple's key hash. Remember that there is no sort order to the hash table! Range queries, by their nature, rely on the underlying data set to be sorted. In the case of range queries, a B-tree index is much more efficient.

The InnoDB storage engine implements a special type of hash index layout called an *adaptive hash index*. You have no control over how and when InnoDB deploys these indexes. InnoDB monitors queries against its tables, and if it sees that a particular table could benefit from a hash index—for instance, if a foreign key is being queried repeatedly for single values—it creates one on the fly. In this way, the hash index is adaptive; InnoDB adapts to its environment.

The FULLTEXT Index Layout

Only the MyISAM storage engine supports `FULLTEXT` indexing. For large textual data with search requirements, this indexing algorithm uses a system of weight comparisons in determining which records match a set of search criteria. When data records are inserted into a table with a `FULLTEXT` index, the data in a column for which a `FULLTEXT` index is defined is analyzed against an existing "dictionary" of statistics for data in that particular column.

The index data is stored as a kind of normalized, condensed version of the actual text, with stopwords[6] removed and other words grouped together, along with how many times the word is contained in the overall expression. So, for long text values, you will have a number of entries into the index—one for each distinct word meeting the algorithm criteria. Each entry will contain a pointer to the data record, the distinct word, and the statistics (or weights) tied to the word. This means that the index size can grow to a decent size when large text values are frequently inserted. Fortunately, MyISAM uses an efficient packing mechanism when inserting key cache records, so that index size is controlled effectively.

---

5. The efficiency is generally the same for insertions, but this is not always the case, because of *collisions* in the hashing of key values. In these cases, where two keys become synonyms of each other, the efficiency is degraded. Different hashing techniques—such as linear probing, chaining, and quadratic probing—attempt to solve these inefficiencies.

6. The `FULLTEXT` stopword file can be controlled via configuration options. See `http://dev.mysql.com/doc/mysql/en/fulltext-fine-tuning.html` for more details.

When key values are searched, a complex process works its way through the index structure, determining which keys in the cache have words matching those in the query request, and attaches a weight to the record based on how many times the word is located. The statistical information contained with the keys speeds the search algorithm by eliminating outstanding keys.

Compression

Compression reduces a piece of data to a smaller size by eliminating bits of the data that are redundant or occur frequently in the data set, and thus can be mapped or encoded to a smaller representation of the same data. Compression algorithms can be either *lossless* or *lossy*. Lossless compression algorithms allow the compressed data to be uncompressed into the exact same form as before compression. Lossy compression algorithms encode data into smaller sizes, but on decoding, the data is not quite what it used to be. Lossy compression algorithms are typically used in sound and image data, where the decoded data can still be recognizable, even if it is not precisely the same as its original state.

One of the most common lossless compression algorithms is something called a *Huffman tree*, or *Huffman encoding*. Huffman trees work by analyzing a data set, or even a single piece of data, and determining at what frequency pieces of the data occur within the data set. For instance, in a typical group of English words, we know that certain letters appear with much more frequency than other letters. Vowels occur more frequently than consonants, and within vowels and consonants, certain letters occur more frequently than others. A Huffman tree is a representation of the frequency of each piece of data in a data set. A Huffman encoding function is then used to translate the tree into a compression algorithm, which strips down the data to a compressed format for storage. A decoding function allows data to be uncompressed when analyzed.

For example, let's say we had some string data like the following:

"EALKNLEKAKEALEALELKEAEALKEAAEE"

The total size of the string data, assuming an ASCII (single-byte, or technically, 7-bit) character set, would be 30 bytes. If we take a look at the actual string characters, we see that of the 30 total characters, there are only 5 distinct characters, with certain characters occurring more frequently than others, as follows:

Letter	Frequency
E	10
A	8
L	6
K	5
N	1

To represent the five different letters in our string, we will need a certain number of bits. In our case, 3 bits will do, which produce eight combinations (2^3=8). A Huffman tree is created by creating a node for each distinct value in the data set (the letters, in this example) and systematically building a binary tree—meaning that no node can have more than two children—from the nodes, from least frequent to most frequent data. See Figure 2-8 for an example.

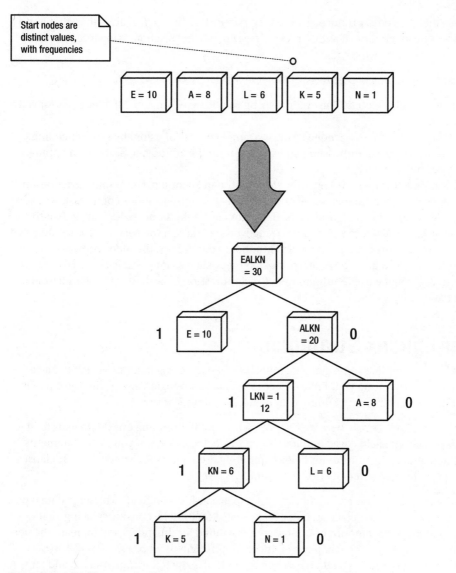

Figure 2-8. *A Huffman encoding tree*

The tree is then used to assign a bit value to each node, with nodes on the right side getting a 0 bit, and nodes on the left getting a 1 bit:

Letter	Frequency	Code
E	10	1
A	8	00
L	6	010
K	5	0111
N	1	0110

Notice that the codes produced by the Huffman tree do not *prefix* each other; that is, no entire code is the beginning of another code. If we encode the original string into a series of Huffman encoded bits, we get this:

`"10001001110110010101110001111000101000101010011110010001001111000011"`

Now we have a total of 68 bits. The original string was 30 bytes long, or 240 bits. So, we saved a total of 71.6%.

Decoding the Huffman encoded string is a simple matter of using the same encoding table as was used in the compression, and starting from the leftmost bits, simply mapping the bits back into characters.

This Huffman technique is known as *static* Huffman encoding. Numerous variations on Huffman encoding are available, some of which MySQL uses in its index compression strategies. Regardless of the exact algorithm used, the concept is the same: reduce the size of the data, and you can pack more entries into a single page of data. If the cost of the encoding algorithm is low enough to offset the increased number of operations, the index compression can lead to serious performance gains on certain data sets, such as long, similar data strings. The MyISAM storage engine uses Huffman trees for compression of both record and index data, as discussed in Chapter 5.

General Index Strategies

In this section, we outline some general strategies when choosing fields on which to place indexes and for structuring your tables. You can use these strategies, along with the guidelines for profiling in Chapter 6, when doing your own index optimization:

Analyze WHERE, ON, GROUP BY, *and* ORDER BY *clauses*: In determining on which fields to place indexes, examine fields used in the WHERE and JOIN (ON) clauses of your SQL statements. Additionally, having indexes for fields commonly used in GROUP BY and ORDER BY clauses can speed up aggregated queries considerably.

Minimize the size of indexed fields: Try not to place indexes on fields with large data types. If you absolutely must place an index on a VARCHAR(100) field, consider placing an index prefix to reduce the amount of storage space required for the index, and increase the performance of queries. You can place an index prefix on fields with CHAR, VARCHAR, BINARY, VARBINARY, BLOB, and TEXT data types. For example, use the following syntax to add an index to the product.name field with a prefix on 20 characters:

```
CREATE INDEX part_of_field ON product (name(20));
```

▮**Note** For indexes on TEXT and BLOB fields, you are required to specify an index prefix.

Pick fields with high data selectivity: Don't put indexes on fields where there is a low distribution of values across the index, such as fields representing gender or any Boolean values. Additionally, if the index contains a number of unique values, but the concentration of one or two values is high, an index may not be useful. For example, if you have a status field (having one of twenty possible values) on a customer_orders table, and 90% of the status field values contain 'Closed', the index may rarely be used by the optimizer.

Clustering key choice is important: Remember from our earlier discussion that one of the primary benefits of the clustered index organization is that it alleviates the need for a lookup to the actual data page using the record identifier. Again, this is because, for clustered indexes, the data page is the clustered index leaf page. Take advantage of this performance boon by carefully choosing your primary key for InnoDB tables. We'll take a closer look at how to do this shortly.

Consider indexing multiple fields if a covering index would occur: If you find that a number of queries would use an index to fulfill a join or WHERE condition entirely (meaning that no lookup would be required as all the information needed would be in the index records), consider indexing multiple fields to create a covering index. Of course, don't go overboard with the idea. Remember the costs associated with additional indexes: higher INSERT and UPDATE times and more storage space required.

Make sure column types match on join conditions: Ensure that when you have two tables joined, the ON condition compares fields with the same data type. MySQL may choose not to use an index if certain type conversions are necessary.

Ensure an index can be used: Be sure to write SQL code in a way that ensures the optimizer will be able to use an index on your tables. Remember to isolate, if possible, the indexed column on the left-hand side of a WHERE or ON condition. You'll see some examples of this strategy a little later in this chapter.

Keep index statistics current with the ANALYZE TABLE *command*: As we mentioned earlier in the discussion of the scan versus seek choice available to MySQL in optimizing queries, the statistics available to the storage engine help determine whether MySQL will use a particular index on a column. If the index statistics are outdated, chances are your indexes won't be properly utilized. Ensure that index statistics are kept up-to-date by periodically running an ANALYZE TABLE command on frequently updated tables.

Profile your queries: Learn more about using the EXPLAIN command, the slow query log, and various profiling tools in order to better understand the inner workings of your queries. The first place to start is Chapter 6 of this book, which covers benchmarking and profiling.

Now, let's look at some examples to clarify clustering key choices and making sure MySQL can use an index.

Clustering Key Selection

InnoDB's clustered indexes work well for both single value searches and range queries. You will often have the option of choosing a couple of different fields to be your primary key. For instance, assume a customer_orders table, containing an order_id column (of type INT), a customer_id field (foreign key containing an INT), and an order_created field of type DATETIME. You have a choice of creating the primary key as the order_id column *or* having a UNIQUE INDEX on order_created and customer_id form the primary key. There are cases to be made for both options.

Having the clustering key on the order_id field means that the clustering key would be small (4 bytes as opposed to 12 bytes). A small clustering key gives you the benefit that all of the secondary indexes will be small; remember that the clustering key is paired with secondary index keys. Searches based on a single order_id value *or* a range of order_id values would be lightning fast. But, more than likely, range queries issued against the orders database would be filtered based on the order_created date field. If the order_created/customer_id index were a secondary index, range queries would be fast, but would require an extra lookup to the data page to retrieve record data.

On the other hand, if the clustering key were put on a UNIQUE INDEX of order_created and customer_id, those range queries issued against the order_created field would be very fast. A secondary index on order_id would ensure that the more common single order_id searches performed admirably. But, there are some drawbacks. If queries need to be filtered by a single or range of customer_id values, the clustered index would be ineffective without a criterion supplied for the leftmost column of the clustering key (order_created). You could remedy the situation by adding a secondary index on customer_id, but then you would need to weigh the benefits of the index against additional CPU costs during INSERT and UPDATE operations. Finally, having a 12-byte clustering key means that all secondary indexes would be fatter, reducing the number of index data records InnoDB can fit in a single 16KB data page.

More than likely, the first choice (having the order_id as the clustering key) is the most sensible, but, as with all index optimization and placement, your situation will require testing and monitoring.

Query Structuring to Ensure Use of an Index

Structure your queries to make sure that MySQL will be able to use an index. Avoid wrapping functions around indexed columns, as in the following poor SQL query, which filters order from the last seven days:

```
SELECT * FROM customer_orders
WHERE TO_DAYS(order_created) - TO_DAYS(NOW()) <= 7;
```

Instead, rework the query to isolate the indexed column on the left side of the equation, as follows:

```
SELECT * FROM customer_orders
WHERE order_created >= DATE_SUB(NOW(), INTERVAL 7 DAY);
```

In the latter code, the function on the right of the equation is reduced by the optimizer to a constant value and compared, using the index on order_created, to that constant value.

The same applies for wildcard searches. If you use a LIKE expression, an index cannot be used if you begin the comparison value with a wildcard. The following SQL will never use an index, even if one exists on the email_address column:

```
SELECT * FROM customers
WHERE email_address LIKE '%aol.com';
```

If you absolutely need to perform queries like this, consider creating an additional column containing the reverse of the e-mail address and index that column. Then the code could be changed to use a wildcard *suffix*, which *can* be used by an index, like so:

```
SELECT * FROM customers
WHERE email_address_reversed LIKE CONCAT(REVERSE('aol.com'), '%');
```

Summary

In this chapter, we've rocketed through a number of fairly significant concepts and issues surrounding both data access fundamentals and what makes indexes tick.

Starting with an examination of physical storage media and then moving into the logical realm, we looked at how different pieces of the operating system and the database server's subsystems interact. We looked at the various sizes and shapes that data can take within the database server, and what mechanisms the server has to work with and manipulate data on disk and in memory.

Next, we dove into an exploration of how indexes affect both the retrieval of table data, and how certain trade-offs come hand in hand with their performance benefits. We discussed various index techniques and strategies, walking through the creation of a simple index structure to demonstrate the concepts. Then we went into detail about the physical layout options of an index and some of the more logical formatting techniques, like hashing and tree structures.

Finally, we finished with some general guidelines to keep in mind when you attempt the daunting task of placing indexes on your various tables.

Well, with that stuff out the way, let's dig into the world of transaction processing. In the next chapter, you'll apply some of the general data access concepts you learned in this chapter to an examination of the complexities of transaction-safe storage and logging processes. Ready? Okay, roll up your sleeves.

CHAPTER 3

■ ■ ■

Transaction Processing

In the past, the database community has complained about MySQL's perceived lack of transaction management. However, MySQL has supported transaction management, and indeed multiple-statement transaction management, since version 3.23, with the inclusion of the InnoDB storage engine. Many of the complaints about MySQL's transaction management have arisen due to a lack of understanding of MySQL's storage engine-specific implementation of it.

InnoDB's full support for all areas of transaction processing now places MySQL alongside some impressive company in terms of its ability to handle high-volume, mission-critical transactional systems. As you will see in this chapter and the coming chapters, your knowledge of transaction processing concepts and the ability of InnoDB to manage transactions will play an important part in how effectively MySQL can perform as a transactional database server for your applications.

One of our assumptions in writing this book is that you have an intermediate level of knowledge about using and administering MySQL databases. We assume that you have an understanding of how to perform most common actions against the database server and you have experience building applications, either web-based or otherwise, that run on the MySQL platform. You may or may not have experience using other database servers. That said, we do *not* assume you have the same level of knowledge regarding transactions and the processing of transactions using the MySQL database server. Why not? Well, there are several reasons for this.

First, transaction processing issues are admittedly some of the most difficult concepts for even experienced database administrators and designers to grasp. The topics related to ensuring the integrity of your data store on a fundamental server level are quite complex, and these topics don't easily fit into a nice, structured discussion that involves executing some SQL statements. The concepts are often obtuse and are unfamiliar territory for those of you who are accustomed to looking at some code listings in order to learn the essentials of a particular command. Discussions regarding transaction processing center around both the unknown and some situations that, in all practicality, may *never* happen on a production system. Transaction processing is, by its very nature, a safeguard against these unlikely but potentially disastrous occurrences. Human nature tends to cause us to ignore such possibilities, especially if the theory behind them is difficult to comprehend.

Second, performance drawbacks to using the transaction processing abilities of a MySQL (or any other) database server have turned off some would-be experimenters in favor of the less-secure, but much more palatable, world of non-transaction-safe databases. We will examine some of the performance impacts of transaction processing in this chapter. Armed with the knowledge of how transaction processing truly benefits certain application environments, you'll be able to make an informed decision about whether to implement transaction-safe features of MySQL in your own applications.

Lastly, as we've mentioned, MySQL has a unique implementation of transaction processing that relies on the InnoDB storage engine. Although InnoDB has been around since version 3.23, it is still not the default storage engine for MySQL (MyISAM is), and due to this, many developers have not implemented transaction processing in their applications. At the end of this chapter, we'll discuss the ramifications of having InnoDB fulfill transaction-processing requirements, as opposed to taking a storage-engine agnostic approach, and advise you how to determine the level of transaction processing you require.

As you may have guessed by the title, we'll be covering a broad range of topics in this chapter, all related to transaction processing. Our goal is to address the *concepts* of transaction processing, in a database-agnostic fashion. However, at certain points in the chapter, we'll discuss how MySQL handles particular aspects of transaction processing. This should give you the foundation from which you can evaluate InnoDB's *implementation* of transaction processing within MySQL, which we'll cover in detail in Chapter 5.

In this chapter, we'll cover these fundamental concepts regarding transaction processing:

- Transaction processing basics, including what constitutes a transaction and the components of the ACID test (the de-facto standard for judging a transaction processing system)

- How transaction processing systems ensure atomicity, consistency, and durability—three closely related ACID properties

- How transaction processing systems implement isolation (the other ACID property) through concurrency

- Guidelines for identifying your own transaction processing requirements—do you really need this stuff?

Transaction Processing Basics

A *transaction* is a set of events satisfying a specific *business requirement*. Defining a transaction in terms of a business function instead of in database-related terms may seem strange to you, but this definition will help you keep in mind the purpose of a transaction. At a fundamental level, the database server isn't concerned with how different operations are related; the *business* is concerned with these relationships.

To demonstrate, let's consider an example. In a banking environment, the archetypal example of a transaction is a customer transferring monies from one account to another. For instance, Jane Doe wants to transfer $100 from her checking account to her savings account. In the business world, we envision this action comprises two distinct, but related, operations:

1. Deduct the $100 from the balance of the checking account.

2. Increase the balance of the savings account by $100.

In reality, our database server has no way—and no reason—to regard the two operations as *related* in any way. It is the *business*—the bank in this case[1]—that views the two operations as a related operation: the single action of *transferring* monies. The database server executes the two operations distinctly, as the following SQL might illustrate:

```
mysql> UPDATE account SET balance = balance - 100
       WHERE customer = 'Jane Doe' AND account = 'checking';
mysql> UPDATE account SET balance = balance + 100
       WHERE customer = 'Jane Doe' AND account = 'savings';
```

Again, the database server has no way to know that these operations are logically related to the business user. We need a method, therefore, of informing the database server that these operations are indeed related. The logic involved in how the database server manages the information involved in grouping multiple operations as a single unit is called *transaction processing*.

As another example, suppose that our business analyst, after speaking with the management team, informs us that they would like the ability to *merge* an old customer account with a new customer account. Customers have been complaining that if they forget their old password and create a new account, they have no access to their old order history. To achieve this, we need a way to update the old account orders with the newest customer account information. A possible transaction might include the following steps:

1. Get the newest account number for customer Mark Smith.

2. Get all old account numbers also related to Mark Smith.

3. Move all the orders that exist under the old customer accounts to the new customer account.

4. Remove the old account records.

All of these steps, from a business perspective, are a related group of operations, and they are viewed as a single action. Therefore, this scenario is an excellent example of what a transaction is. Any time you are evaluating a business function requirement, and business users refer to a number of steps *by a single verb*—in this example, the verb *merge*—you can be positive that you are dealing with a transaction.

Transaction Failures

All this talk about related operations is somewhat trivial if everything goes as planned, right? The only thing that we really care about is a situation in which one step of the transaction *fails*.

In the case of our banking transaction, we would have a tricky customer service situation if our banking application crashed after deducting the amount from Jane's checking account but before the money was added to her savings account. We would have a pretty irate customer on our hands.

Likewise, in the scenario of our merged customer accounts, what would happen if something went wrong with the request to update the old order records, but the request to delete the old customer record went through? Then we would have some order records tied to a customer

---

1. And, indeed, Jane Doe would view the operations as a single unit as well.

record that didn't exist, and worse, we would have no way of knowing that those old order records should be related to the new customer record. Or consider what would happen if sometime during the loop Mark Smith created another new account? Then the "newest" customer ID would actually be an old customer ID, but our statements wouldn't know of the new changes. Clearly, a number of potential situations might cause problems for the integrity of our underlying data.

WHAT ABOUT FOREIGN KEY CONSTRAINTS?

Those of you familiar with foreign key constraints might argue that a constraint on the `customer_id` field of the `orders` table would have prevented the inconsistency from occurring in our account merge scenario. You would be correct, of course. However, foreign key constraints can ensure only a certain level of consistency, and they can be applied only against key fields. When the number of operations executed increases, and the complexity of those operations involves multiple tables, foreign key constraints can provide only so much protection against inconsistencies.

To expand, let's consider our banking transfer scenario. In this situation, foreign key constraints are of no use at all. They provide no level of consistency protection if a failure occurs after step 1 and before step 2. The database is left in an inconsistent state because the checking account has been debited but the savings account has not been credited. On the other hand, transactions provide a robust framework for protecting the consistency of the data store, regardless of whether the data being protected is in a parent-child relationship.

As any of you who work with database servers on a regular basis already know, things that you don't want to happen sometimes do happen. Power outages, disk crashes, that pesky developer who codes a faulty recursive loop—all of these occurrences should be seen as potential problems that can negatively affect the integrity of your data stores. We can view these potential problems in two main categories:

- *Hardware failure*: When a disk crashes, a processor fails, or RAM is corrupted, and so forth.

- *Software failure or conflicts*: An inconspicuous coding problem that causes memory or disk space to run out, or the failure of a specific software component running on the server, such as an HTTP request terminating unexpectedly halfway through execution.

In either of these cases, there is the potential that statements running inside a transaction could cause the database to be left in an inconsistent state. The transaction processing system inside the database is responsible for writing data to disk in a way that, in the event of a failure, the database can restore, or *recover*, its data to a state that is consistent with the state of the database *before* the transaction began.

The ACID Test

As we stated earlier, different database servers *implement* transaction processing logic in different ways. Regardless of the implementation of the transaction processing system, however, a database server must conform to a set of rules, called the ACID test for transaction compliancy, in order to be considered a fully *transaction-safe* system.

No, we're not talking about pH balances here. By ACID test, computer scientists are referring to the assessment of a database system's ability to treat groups of operations as a single unit, or as a *transaction*. ACID stands for:

- Atomicity

- Consistency

- Isolation

- Durability

These four characteristics are tightly related to each other, and if a processing system demonstrates the ability to maintain each of these four characteristics for every transaction, it is said to be ACID-compliant.

MySQL is not currently an ACID-compliant database server. However, InnoDB *is* an ACID-compliant storage engine. What does this mean? On a practical level, it means that if you require the database operations to be transaction-safe, you must use InnoDB tables to store your data. While it is possible to mix and match storage engines within a single database transaction issued against the database, the only data guaranteed to be protected in the transaction is data stored in the InnoDB tables.

■**Caution** Don't mix and match storage engines within a single transaction. You may get unexpected results if you do so and a failure occurs!

Here, we'll define each of these components of ACID. In the remainder of this chapter, we'll describe in depth how these properties are handled by transaction processing systems.

Atomicity

The transaction processing system must be able to execute the operations involved in a transaction as a *single unit of work*. The characteristic of *atomicity* refers to the indivisible nature of a transaction. Either all of the operations must complete or none of them should happen. If a failure occurs before the last operation in the transaction has succeeded, then all other operations must be undone.

Consistency

Closely related to the concept of atomic operations is the issue of *consistency*. The data store must always move from one consistent state to another. The term *consistent state* refers to both the logical state of the database and the physical state of the database.

Logical State

The *logical state* of the database is a representation of the business environment. In the banking transfer example, the logical state of the data store can be viewed in terms of Jane Doe's aggregated account balance; that is, the sum of her checking and savings accounts. If the balance of Jane's checking account is $1,000 and the balance of her savings account is $1,000, the logical state of the data store can be said to be $2,000. To maintain the logical state of the data store, this state must be consistent *before* and *after* the execution of the transaction. If a failure occurred after the deduction of her checking account and before the corresponding increase to her savings account, the transaction processing system must ensure that it returns the state of the data store to be consistent with its state before the failure occurred.

The consistency of the logical state is managed by both the transaction processing system and the rules and actions of the underlying application. Clearly, if a poorly coded transaction leaves the data store in an inconsistent logical state after the transaction has been committed to disk, it is the responsibility of the application code, not the transaction processing system.

Physical State

The *physical state* of the database refers to how database servers keep a copy of the data store in memory and a copy of the data store on disk. As we discussed in the previous chapter, the database server operates on data stored in local memory. When reading data, the server requests the needed data page from a buffer pool in memory. If the data page exists in memory, it uses that in-memory data. If not, it requests that the operating system read the page from secondary storage (disk storage) into memory, and then reads the data from the in-memory buffer pool. Similarly, when the database server needs to write data, it first accesses the in-memory data page and modifies that copy of the data, and then it relies on the operating system to *flush* the pages in the buffer pool to disk.

■**Note** *Flushing* data means that the database server has told the operating system to actually write the data page to *disk*, as opposed to change (write) the data page to memory and cache write requests until it is most efficient to execute a number of writes at once. In contrast, a *write* call lets the operating system decide when the data is actually written to disk.

Therefore, under normal circumstances, the *state* of the database server is different on disk than it is in memory. The most current state of the data contained in the database is always in memory, since the database server reads and writes only to the in-memory buffers. The state of the data on disk may be slightly older than (or inconsistent with) the state of the data in memory. Figure 3-1 depicts this behavior.

In order for a transaction processor to comply with the ACID test for consistency, it must provide mechanisms for ensuring that consistency of both the logical *and* physical state endures in the event of a failure. For the most part, the actions a transaction processor takes to ensure atomicity prevent inconsistencies in the logical state. The transaction processor relies on *recovery* and *logging* mechanisms to ensure consistency in the physical state in the event of a failure. These processes are closely related to the characteristic of durability, described shortly.

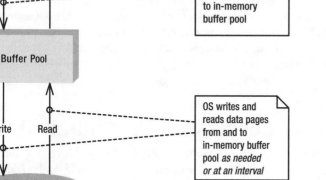

Figure 3-1. *Data flow between the disk and database server*

Isolation

Isolation refers to the containment of changes that occur during the transaction and the ability of other transactions to see the results of those changes. The concept of isolation is applicable only when using a database system that supports *concurrent* execution, which MySQL does. During concurrent execution, separate transactions may occur asynchronously, as opposed to in a serialized, or synchronous, manner.

For example, in the user account merge scenario, the transaction processing system must prevent other transactions from modifying the data store being operated on in the transaction; that is, the data rows in the customers and orders tables corresponding to Mark Smith. It must do this in order to avoid a situation where another process changes the same data rows that would be deleted from the customers table or updated in the orders table.

As you will see later in this chapter, transaction processing systems support different *levels* of isolation, from weak to strong isolation. All database servers accomplish isolation by *locking resources*. The resource could be a single row, an entire page of data, or whole files, and this lock granularity plays a role in isolation and concurrency issues.

Durability

A transaction is seen as *durable* if the changes made during the transaction's execution are made permanent once the transaction is *committed* to the database.

One thing to note, however, is that the durability requirement for a transaction processing system's ACID compliancy does not depend on the redundancy of the data store. If a disk drive fails, and there is no redundant, or backup, disk drive, this does not mean that the transaction processing system does not support durable transactions. Instead, durability from the transaction processing system's perspective is supported if a mechanism is available to ensure that there is a permanent record of the data changes made by the transaction once the transaction has been committed, even if the actual data pages have not been written to disk. Does this sound strange? Conceptually, it might sound complicated, but transaction processing systems overcome this obstacle through the use of transaction logging.

Ensuring Atomicity, Consistency, and Durability

Mechanisms built in to transaction processing systems to address the needs of one of the closely related characteristics of atomicity, consistency, and durability usually end up addressing the needs of all three. In this section, we'll take a look at some of these mechanisms, including the transaction wrapper and demarcation, MySQL's autocommit mode, logging, recovery, and checkpointing.

The Transaction Wrapper and Demarcation

When describing a transaction, the entire boundary of the transaction is referred to as the *transaction wrapper*. The transaction wrapper contains all the instructions that you want the database server to view as a single atomic unit. In order to inform your database server that a group of statements are intended to be viewed as a single transaction, you need a method of indicating to the server when a transaction begins and ends. These indicating marks are called *demarcation*, which defines the boundary of the transaction wrapper.

In MySQL, the demarcation of transactions is indicated through the commands START TRANSACTION and COMMIT. When a START TRANSACTION command is received, the server creates a transaction wrapper for the connection and puts incoming statements into the transaction wrapper until it receives a COMMIT statement marking the end of the transaction.[2] The database server can rely on the boundary of the transaction wrapper, and it views all internal statements as a single unit to be executed entirely or not at all.

■**Note** The START TRANSACTION command marks the start of a transaction. If you are using a version of MySQL before 4.0.11, you can use the older, deprecated command BEGIN or BEGIN WORK.

---

2. This is not quite true, since certain SQL commands, such as ALTER TABLE, will implicitly force MySQL to mark the end of a current transaction. But for now, let's just examine the basic process the database server is running through.

Regardless of the number of distinct actions that may compose the transaction, the database server must have the ability to *undo* changes that may have been made within the container if a certain condition (usually an error, but it could be any arbitrary condition) occurs. If something happens, you need to be able to undo actions that have occurred up to that point inside the transactional container. This ability to undo changes is called a *rollback* in transaction processing lingo. In MySQL, you inform the server that you wish to explicitly undo the statements executed inside a transaction using the ROLLBACK command. You roll back the changes made inside the transaction wrapper to a certain point in time.

■**Note** MySQL allows you to explicitly roll back the statements executed inside a transaction to the *beginning* of the transaction demarcation or to marks called *savepoints* (available as of version 4.0.14 and 4.1.1). If a savepoint is marked, a certain segment of the transaction's statements can be considered committed, even before the COMMIT terminating instruction is received. (There is some debate, however, as to the use of savepoints, since the concept seems to violate the concept of a transaction's atomicity.) To mark a savepoint during a set of transactional statements, issue a SAVEPOINT *identifier* command, where *identifier* is a name for the savepoint. To explicitly roll back to a savepoint, issue a ROLLBACK TO SAVEPOINT *identifier* command.

MySQL's Autocommit Mode

Be default, MySQL creates a transaction wrapper for each SQL statement that modifies data it receives across a user connection. This behavior is known as autocommit mode. In order to ensure that the data modification is actually committed to the underlying data store, MySQL actually flushes the data change to disk after each statement! MySQL is smart enough to recognize that the in-memory data changes are volatile, so in order to prevent data loss due to a power outage or crash, it actually tells the operating system to flush the data to disk as well as make changes to the in-memory buffers. Consider the following code from our previous bank transfer example:

```
mysql> UPDATE account SET balance = balance - 100
       WHERE customer = 'Jane Doe' AND account = 'checking';
mysql> UPDATE account SET balance = balance + 100
       WHERE customer = 'Jane Doe' AND account = 'savings';
```

This means that every UPDATE or DELETE statement that is received through your MySQL server session is wrapped in *implicit* START TRANSACTION and COMMIT commands. Consequently, MySQL actually converts this SQL code to the following execution:

```
mysql> START TRANSACTION;
mysql> UPDATE account SET balance = balance - 100
       WHERE customer = 'Jane Doe' AND account = 'checking';
mysql> COMMIT;
mysql> START TRANSACTION;
mysql> UPDATE account SET balance = balance + 100
       WHERE customer = 'Jane Doe' AND account = 'savings';
mysql> COMMIT;
```

Figure 3-2 shows how MySQL actually handles these statements while operating in its default autocommit mode.

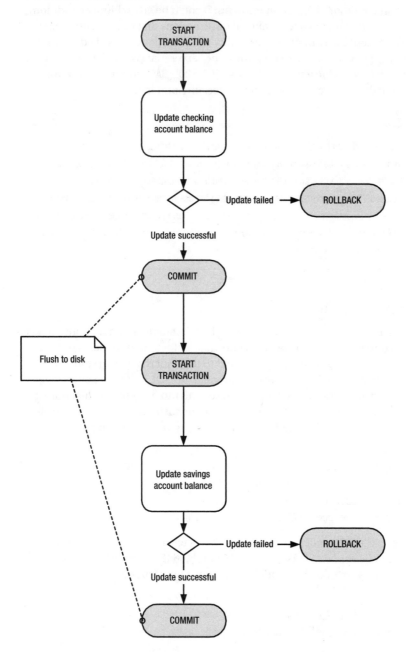

Figure 3-2. *Autocommit behavior*

This autocommit behavior is perfect for single statements, because MySQL is ensuring that the data modifications are indeed flushed to disk, and it maintains a consistent physical state to the data store. But what would happen in the scenario depicted in Figure 3-3?

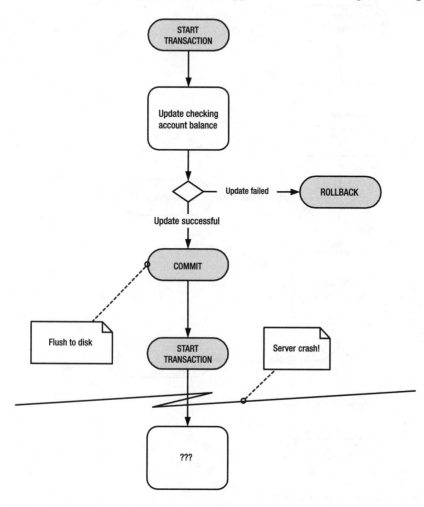

Figure 3-3. *Autocommit behavior with a failure between statements*

The result of MySQL's default behavior in a situation like the one shown in Figure 3-3 is disaster. The autocommit behavior has committed the first part of our transaction to disk, but the server crashed before the savings account was credited. In this way, the atomicity of the transaction is compromised. To avoid this problem, you need to tell the database server *not* to commit the changes until a final transaction COMMIT is encountered. What you need is a flow of events such as depicted in Figure 3-4.

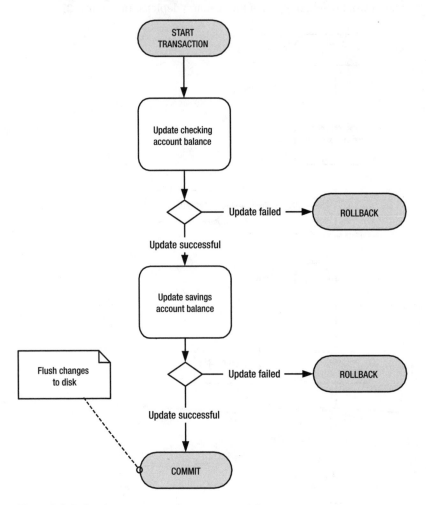

Figure 3-4. *Behavior necessary to ensure atomicity*

As you can see in Figure 3-4, the behavior you need causes a flush of the data changes to disk only after all statements in the transaction have succeeded, ensuring the atomicity of the transaction, as well as ensuring the consistency of the physical and logical state of the data store. If any statement fails, all changes made during the transaction are rolled back. The following SQL statements match the desired behavior:

```
mysql> START TRANSACTION;
mysql> UPDATE account SET balance = balance - 100
       WHERE customer = 'Jane Doe' AND account = 'checking';
mysql> UPDATE account SET balance = balance + 100
       WHERE customer = 'Jane Doe' AND account = 'savings';
mysql> COMMIT;
```

So, what would happen if we executed these statements against a MySQL database server running in the default autocommit mode? Well, fortunately, the START TRANSACTION command actually tells MySQL to disable its autocommit mode and view the statements within the START TRANSACTION and COMMIT commands as a single unit of work. However, if you prefer, you can explicitly tell MySQL not to use autocommit behavior by issuing the following command:

```
mysql> SET AUTOCOMMIT = 0;
```

An important point is that if you issue a START TRANSACTION and then a COMMIT, after the COMMIT is received, the database server reverts *back* to whatever autocommit mode it was in before the START TRANSACTION command was received. This means that if autocommit mode is enabled, the following code will issue three flushes to disk, since the default behavior of wrapping each modification statement in its own transaction will occur after the COMMIT is received.

```
mysql> START TRANSACTION;
mysql> UPDATE account SET balance = balance - 100
       WHERE customer = 'Jane Doe' AND account = 'checking';
mysql> UPDATE account SET balance = balance + 100
       WHERE customer = 'Jane Doe' AND account = 'savings';
mysql> COMMIT;
mysql> UPDATE account SET balance = balance - 100
       WHERE customer = 'Mark Smith' AND account = 'checking';
mysql> UPDATE account SET balance = balance + 100
       WHERE customer = 'Mark Smith' AND account = 'savings';
```

So, it is important to keep in mind whether or not MySQL is operating in autocommit mode.

IMPLICIT COMMIT COMMANDS

There are both implicit and explicit transaction processing commands. What we mean by *explicit* is that you actually send the specified command to the database server during a connection session. *Implicit* commands are commands that are executed by the database server without you actually sending the command during the user connection.

MySQL automatically issues an implicit COMMIT statement when you disconnect from the session or issue any of the following commands during the user session:

- ALTER TABLE
- BEGIN
- CREATE INDEX
- DROP DATABASE
- DROP TABLE
- RENAME TABLE
- TRUNCATE
- LOCK TABLES
- UNLOCK TABLES

Logging

As we mentioned, an inherent obstacle to ensuring the characteristics of atomicity, consistency, and durability exists because of the way a database server accesses and writes data. Since the database server operates on data that is in memory, there is a danger that if a failure occurs, the data in memory will be lost, leaving the disk copy of the data store in an inconsistent state. MySQL's autocommit mode combats this risk by flushing data changes to disk automatically. However, as you saw, from a transaction's perspective, if one part of the transaction were recorded to disk, and another change remained in memory at the time of the failure, the atomic nature of the transaction would be in jeopardy.

To remedy this problem, database servers use a mechanism called *logging* to record the changes being made to a database. In general, logs write data directly to disk instead of to memory.[3] As explained in the previous chapter, the database server uses the buffer pool of data pages to allow the operating system to cache write requests and fulfill those requests in a manner most efficient for the hardware. Since the database server does writes and reads to data pages in a random manner, the operating system caches the requested writes until it can write the data pages in a faster *serialized* manner.

Log records are written to disk in a serialized manner because, as you'll see, they are written in the order in which operations are executed. This means that log writing is an efficient process; it doesn't suffer from the usual inefficiencies of normal data page write operations.

MySQL has a number of logs that record various activities going on inside the database server. Many of these logs, particularly the binary log (which has replaced the old update log), function in a manner similar to what we will refer to as *transaction logs*. Transaction logs are log files dedicated to preserving the atomicity and consistency of transactions. In a practical sense, they are simply specialized versions of normal log files that contain specific information in order to allow the recovery process to determine what composes a transaction.

The central theory behind transaction logging is a concept called *write-ahead* logging. This theory maintains that changes to a data store must be made only after a record of those changes has been permanently recorded in a log file. The log file must contain the instructions that detail what data has changed and how it has changed. Once the record of the changes has been recorded in the log file, which resides in secondary storage, the database server is free to make the data modifications effected by those instructions. The benefit of write-ahead logging is that in-memory data page changes do not need to be flushed to disk immediately, since the log file contains instructions to re-create those changes.

The log file records contain the instructions for modifying the data pages, yet these records are not necessarily SQL commands. In fact, they are much more specific instructions detailing the exact change to be made to a particular data page on disk. The log record structure usually contains a header piece that has a timestamp for when the data change occurred. This timestamp is useful in the recovery process in identifying which instructions must be executed anew in order to return the database to a consistent state. Figure 3-5 shows a depiction of the logging process for our banking transaction.

In Figure 3-5, the dashed bubbles after the ROLLBACK commands indicate an alternative scenario where an in-memory buffer of log records is kept along with a log file on disk. In this scenario, if a rollback occurs, there is no need to record the transactions to the log file if the changes have not been made permanent on disk. InnoDB uses this type of log record buffer, which we'll look at in more detail in Chapter 5.

---

3. This is a bit of an oversimplification, but the concept is valid. We'll look at the implementation of logging in InnoDB in the next chapter, where you will see that the log is actually written to disk *and* memory.

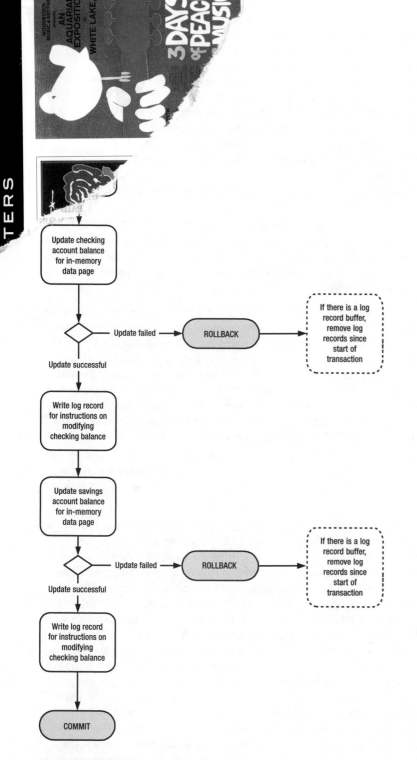

Figure 3-5. *Write-ahead logging*

Recovery

Clearly, the goal of write-ahead transaction logging is to provide a method of recording data changes *before* those changes are affected in memory. This is so that in the case of a failure, a *recovery* process can use these log records in order to reconstruct the database back to its consistent state before the failure occurred. In MySQL, this recovery process is run on startup, *before* any other action that may modify the state of the database.

Currently, MySQL implements a type of recovery process using the binary log, which contains records for each transaction that modified the data store, regardless of whether those modifications affected transaction-safe storage engines. InnoDB implements its own ACID-compliant recovery process as well, in order to ensure the atomicity of transactions run against InnoDB's transaction-safe tables.

Transaction logging enables a recovery process by supplying what are known as the REDO and the UNDO logs. These logs work as follows:

REDO log records: Log records belonging to transactions that have a COMMIT mark in the transaction log but do not exist in the data pages in secondary storage are committed to secondary storage during the first part of the recovery process. These records, representing data that had been in memory but not flushed to disk, are known as the REDO log records. REDO functionality is sometimes called *roll-forward recovery*.

UNDO log records: If log records in the log file do *not* have a COMMIT mark for that transaction in the log, then all data changes that had been made permanent by flushing to disk before the transaction commit had occurred are, in effect, rolled back. This situation can occur if the transaction contained a series of operations that were written to disk through a flush some time during the transaction's execution—through normal database operations and operating system timing—but a failure occurred before the executing connection closed properly, or before an explicit COMMIT was received and written as a log record. For UNDO functionality, the log records must contain both the old (original) value and the new value for the data being modified. UNDO functionality is sometimes called *roll-backward recovery*.

These logs are the glue between the old state of the database contained in secondary storage and the newest state that existed in memory before a failure, as Figure 3-6 indicates.

Checkpointing

So, we have a logging mechanism recording all the actions that are occurring on our database system, writing ahead of the changes to the data page buffer pool to ensure that we have a permanent record of the changes made to the system. During the recovery process, the log records are used to reconstruct the state of the data store to its most current state, meaning all data modifications that succeeded for transactions that had been marked with a COMMIT.

Indeed, there are points in time when a database's data is, at least partially, considered stable. The current data pages have been flushed to disk, even if modifications are going on in the background, with the log files picking up any changes before they actually occur in memory. These moments in time are called *checkpoints*, and they are actually written as special log records in the log file to indicate that all data pages in memory (buffers) at the time of the checkpoint have been flushed to disk (made permanent). In standard checkpointing, it is customary to include in the checkpoint record a list of transaction identifiers that are active (currently executing) at the time the checkpoint occurred. These checkpoints enable the recovery process to reduce the amount of transaction log records it needs to read and use to re-create the database, because they indicate that the state of the secondary storage at the checkpoint is current, except for any uncommitted transactions at the time of the checkpoint.

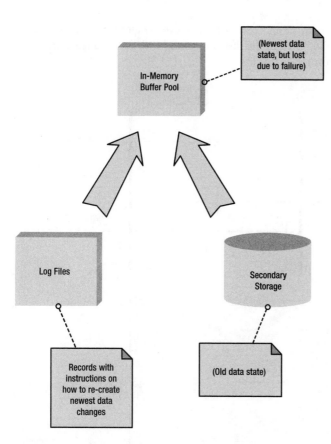

Figure 3-6. *Recovery process*

Figure 3-7 shows a theoretical depiction of a transaction log with a number of transactions and a checkpoint record. T*x* designates the transaction identifier, which is generated for a transaction by the transaction processing system during logging. You can see the START TRANSACTION and COMMIT log records for some of the transactions marked in bold. Change records are italicized. We've shaded the checkpoint record to highlight it.

T1 - START TRANSACTACTION
T1 - CHANGE DATA PAGE 40938
T2 - START TRANSACT
T1 - CHANGE DATA PAGE 40554
T2 - CHANGE DATA PAGE 42300
T1 - COMMIT
CHECKPOINT (ACTIVE: T2)
T3 - START TRANSACTION
T2 - CHANGE DATA PAGE 45184
T3 - CHANGE DATA PAGE 94844
T3 - CHANGE DATA PAGE 94876
T1 - COMMIT

Figure 3-7. *Sample pseudo log file*

Figure 3-8 depicts the pseudo transaction log shown in Figure 3-7 along a timeline. The checkpoint and a failure point are displayed in the timeline, along with each transaction, marked by start and (for some) commit time points.

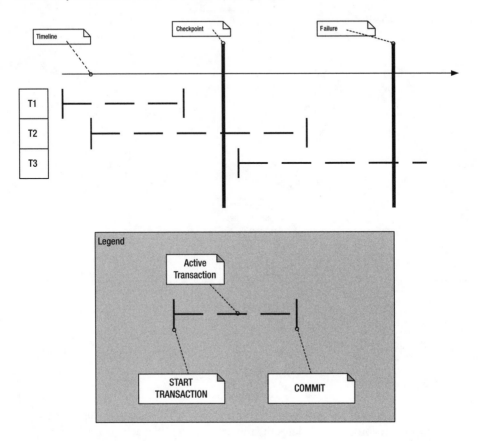

Figure 3-8. *Recovery timeline*

During the recovery process, the transaction processing system must UNDO some of the log record changes and REDO others. The following steps are taken in order to restore the database state to its most current version:

1. Start at the most recent checkpoint in the log file (for our purposes here, the only checkpoint shown). The recovery process first adds all active transactions recorded in the checkpoint record to a list of UNDO transactions. This means that in our scenario, the T2 transaction is added to the UNDO list.

2. Read each log record in order from the checkpoint. For each START TRANSACTION record encountered, put that transaction in the UNDO list as well. For any COMMIT records encountered, move that transaction out of the UNDO list and into the REDO list.

3. REDO all the actions contained in the REDO list, ensuring that these operations are made permanent.

4. UNDO all the operations in the UNDO list, including any statements contained in that transaction that occurred before the checkpoint.

In this manner, checkpointing allows the system to restore the database to a consistent state, but does not need to read through all the database modifications recorded in the entire log file. Only those records after the checkpoint, and possibly a few records from before the checkpoint if an UNDO list is necessary, are required for restoration.[4]

One other topic that is often mentioned in regard to checkpointing relates to how the actual log file itself is maintained. Because of the way checkpointing essentially makes a piece of the log file (the oldest piece) obsolete, most transaction logging systems deploy a method of reusing segments of the log file in order to keep the log file from growing out of control.

Steps are taken by the transaction processing system to ensure that no segments that would be critical in a restore situation are overwritten. In Chapter 5, we'll take an in-depth look at how InnoDB maintains the length of its transaction log and how it handles overflow situations where segments contain large transactions that cannot be truncated.

WHERE DOES THE MYSQL BINARY LOG COME INTO PLAY?

Some of you may be wondering how the MySQL binary log (binlog) comes into play during MySQL transaction processing. The binary log replaces the old update log, and as of version 5.0, the update log is not available in packaged binaries. The binary log is a significant improvement over the update log, and there is no functionality available in the update log that is not available in the binary log.

The binary log, similar to a transaction log, records every modification made to a MySQL table *regardless of the storage engine*. This means that changes to non-transaction-safe tables, as well as InnoDB-affected data changes, are recorded as entries in the binary log. In addition to all data modifications, the binary log will record some replication activities. It even records data modifications that *may* affect data, but when executed did not—for instance, a DELETE statement that found no rows to delete.

By enabling the binary log, you can significantly reduce the possibility of losing data on a production system. The binary log works in a manner similar to what we've described for a transaction log; however, the binary log does *not* ensure atomicity or consistency of your data. The binary log is *not* a write-ahead log. Records are entered into the binary log *after* changes to the in-memory copy of the data have been made. InnoDB uses its own write-ahead system (called a double-write buffer) to ensure consistency. We'll cover the InnoDB transaction system in Chapter 5.

However, the binary log does allow for checkpointing and plays a role in the recovery process, where the transaction processing system inside InnoDB uses the log file in order to ensure ACID compliancy. Remember that MySQL's autocommit mode means that all statements are implicitly wrapped in START TRANSACTION and COMMIT commands. This means that all modifications run against the server will be recorded in the binary log as a transaction and can be rolled forward and backward as such. The only thing missing is that multiple statements executed inside a START TRANSACTION and COMMIT will not be handled in a transaction-safe manner if they operate on non-transaction-safe tables.

Enabling the binary log functionality has a small performance impact (about 1%), which, in our opinion, is easily outweighed by the benefit it brings for enabling you to restore your database state up to immediately before a failure.[5]

Continued

---

4. This is a very simplified explanation of a very complex process. This describes a standard form of checkpointing. In MySQL, a more advanced version of the same idea is implemented in the InnoDB storage engine.

5. This, of course, hinges on you having a redundant secondary storage source, if the cause of failure is disk-related. See Chapter 17 for more on this issue.

> To enable the binary log in MySQL, simply start the `mysqld` process with the following command-line option:
>
> ```
> --log-bin[=filename]
> ```
>
> where `filename` is an optional filename for the log file. If no filename is given, MySQL will use the name of the server, plus `-bin`. Alternatively, you can enable the binary log through your configuration file, adding the following option under the `[mysqld]` section:
>
> ```
> log-bin
> ```
>
> See the MySQL manual (`http://dev.mysql.com/doc/mysql/en/binary-log.html`) for more details on the binary log.

Implementing Isolation and Concurrency

The concepts we've touched on so far have focused on ensuring the atomicity, consistency, and durability (A, C, and D) properties of the ACID test. We have not yet discussed the I in ACID, because the properties of isolation are less closely related to the other properties. Now, we will examine the unique mix of concepts related to isolation, focusing on the issue of concurrency.

Concurrency is the ability of the database server to fulfill many requests to retrieve or modify data at the same time. By *same time*, we don't necessarily mean that requests to modify data occur simultaneously, but rather that multiple transactions can stretch over an overlapping time frame. You saw a depiction of this overlapping nature of transactions in the earlier discussion of recovery and how logs work.

The ability of the transaction processor to provide protection of the resources being used by transactions executing in the same time interval is known as *isolation*. The isolation refers to a boundary, either weak or strong, that exists to prevent other transactions from interfering with, or using, the data involved in an executing transaction. Here, we'll take a closer look at locking resources, isolation levels, and multiversion concurrency control (MVCC).

Locking Resources

When a transaction attempts to either read or write a piece of data, it must acquire a lock on that piece of data, which we'll refer to for now as a *resource*. This lock is simply information that informs all the other processes running in the database server that the process running this transaction intends to do something with the resource. Exactly what the process intends to do with the resource determines the type of lock placed on the resource.

Lock Granularity

The *granularity* of a lock determines the size, or extent, of the resource being locked. In database server terms, there are three basic levels of lock granularity when we're dealing with actual table data:

- *Table-level locks* place a lock on the entire set of table data.

- *Page-level locks* place a lock on the specific data page where the requested data can be found.

- *Row-level locks* lock only the specific row of data within the data page where the requested data can be found.

The different storage engines in MySQL support varying levels of lock granularity, which affect how resources are managed for concurrent requests for the same data. We'll examine the differences between the storage engines in Chapter 5.

■**Note** Currently, the MyISAM storage engine supports only table-level lock granularity. Although MyISAM does not support row-level locking, concurrent insertions into a table are possible, as you'll learn in Chapter 5. InnoDB supports table and row-level lock granularity. InnoDB's row-level locking is critical because of its transaction processing ability and its use of multiversion concurrency control, which we'll look at a little later in this chapter.

The database server combines the lock granularity along with the type (or intent) of the lock in order to determine whether to allow other processes access to a resource while a lock is placed on the resource.[6] Let's examine the two basic types of locks: shared and exclusive.

Shared (Read) Locks

Shared, or *read*, locks inform the database server that other processes requesting data from the specified resource, at whichever granularity, do not need to wait for the lock to release in order to obtain data from within the resource. In other words, the resource is shared among all processes that need access to it. This makes sense when the process is simply reading from the resource, as opposed to writing to the resource. As long as the data contained in the resource is not being modified, any number of processes can access the data.

Locks are managed using a sort of counter system. The counter simply records how many processes have requested a lock on the resource. When a shared lock on a resource is requested, the lock counter is incremented. When the process is finished retrieving data from the resource, the lock is released, and the counter is decremented.

Exclusive (Write) Locks

On the flip side of the coin, when a process needs to modify the data contained in the resource, or write to the resource, a different type of lock intent is used: an *exclusive*, or *write*, lock. This informs the database server that the process intends to change the resource, and any other processes that need access to the resource must wait until these changes have been made.

When an exclusive lock intent is received, the database server must look at the counter maintained in the lock. If the counter is greater than zero, the database server modifies the state

---

6. Although it is possible to control the type of lock placed on a resource, if you don't specify a lock type, MySQL's storage engines will choose the most appropriate lock level for you.

of the lock and does not allow any other read locks to access the resource; instead, it tells these processes to wait until the writing process has finished. If the counter is greater than zero, the state of the lock is changed, preventing any new processes from accessing the resource, and the database server makes the write process wait until all read requests have finished accessing the resource and decrementing the internal counter. When the counter reaches zero, the database server lets the write request proceed.

SEMAPHORES AND MUTEXES

This lock structure, consisting of a state and a counter for acquired locks, is commonly known as a *semaphore*. A specialized version of a semaphore, known as a *mutex*, for *mutually exclusive*, is a simpler Boolean type of semaphore (known as a binary semaphore).

Mutexes typically just describe to the program whether a resource, or critical section of memory, is available for a process to modify. Additionally, a mutex structure usually contains some sort of owner identifier, informing the system which process owns, or controls, the resource. Semaphore and mutex lock structures are used internally by the database server and the operating system to control access to critical sections of the program that may be shared among running threads or processes. These lock structures need to control access to database resources. Any resource (or variable) shared by multiple processes can be controlled.

Isolation Levels

ANSI/ISO SQL-92 specifications define four distinct levels of isolation. The level of isolation refers to the strength of the protection against certain consequences of concurrently executing transactions. These consequences are known as *anomalies*, in transaction processing lingo, and we'll cover the three types of anomalies as we take a look at each supported isolation level:

- READ UNCOMMITTED: Weak protection

- READ COMMITTED: Better protection

- REPEATABLE READ: Good protection

- SERIALIZABLE: Zero anomalies

READ UNCOMMITTED

At the READ UNCOMMITTED isolation level, there really isn't much protection at all. Other transactions may see changes to data that have occurred within an uncommitted transaction. Clearly, this isn't a good thing, since the other transactions may rely on information that may eventually be rolled back. This anomaly, or phenomenon, is known as a *dirty read*. Dirty reads are reads that cannot be relied on.

READ COMMITTED

The next isolation level, READ COMMITTED, eliminates the possibility of dirty reads by ensuring that other transactions cannot view the results of changes made during a transaction until the transaction processing system has committed the entire transaction. This ensures that dirty reads are not possible. However, at this isolation level, another anomaly is possible: a *nonrepeatable read*, which is a phenomenon where a transaction may read data from a resource that may not be available, or may be a different value, after a concurrently executing transaction commits. This is also known as an *inconsistent read*.

For instance, let's say transaction A starts and begins a modification on the customers table. Before the transaction commits, transaction B starts and reads a record from the customers table for customer ID 1002. The data returned by this statement may be modified or deleted by statements executing under transaction A. This means that if transaction B relies on the data read from the customers table during its own execution, it may be relying on a read request that could not be repeated once transaction A commits.

REPEATABLE READ

The REPEATABLE READ isolation level resolves the anomaly of nonrepeatable reads by placing a special lock on the resources used by the transaction so that other transactions must wait for the first transaction to complete before reading data from those resources used by the first transaction.

In our scenario from the previous section, a REPEATABLE READ isolation level would prevent transaction B from reading the customers table—or the row in the customers table, depending on the lock granularity—that is being used by transaction A. In this way, the transaction processing system ensures that nonrepeatable reads are avoided.

However, even with this level of isolation, a third phenomenon can occur, called *phantom reads*. A phantom read is possible when transaction A submits a read request for a group of data. The data is used in the transaction, and then another read request for a similar group of data is submitted later in the transaction. Transaction B, meanwhile, has added records to the resource read in transaction A, so on the second read request in transaction A, more records were returned than on the first request. For example, let's say that transaction A issues the following statements:

```
mysql> START TRANSACTION;
mysql> SELECT * FROM customers WHERE create_date > '2005-05-01';
```

Then the transaction does some sort of operations on this customer data, such as summing the number of orders placed by these customers. While it is doing this, transaction B starts and inserts new customer records into the table. Transaction A completes whatever operations it was performing, and then issues the following statements:

```
mysql> SELECT * FROM customers WHERE create_date > '2005-05-01';
mysql> COMMIT;
```

intending to print a summary of the customers data that was operated on during the transaction—for before and after snapshots. Yet, unfortunately, transaction B has inserted new customer records during transaction A's execution, so the after snapshot contains more records than the before snapshot. These additional records weren't *locked* during the first SELECT in transaction A because, of course, they didn't exist yet. These new records are called *phantoms*.

The REPEATABLE READ isolation level does not prevent phantom rows from occurring. In order to prevent this anomaly, the SERIALIZABLE isolation level exists.

SERIALIZABLE

The SERIALIZABLE isolation level is the strongest protection against the read anomalies we've described. At the SERIALIZABLE level, no phantom reads are allowed, because the transaction processing system locks the resource so that records cannot be appended to the tables being operated on in another transaction.

Note Phantom reads are prevented from occurring by InnoDB's next-key-locking technique.

INNODB DEFAULT ISOLATION MODE AND OTHER DATABASE VENDORS

InnoDB operates, by default, in the REPEATABLE READ isolation mode. This means that all transactions are guaranteed to be free of dirty reads and nonrepeatable reads. InnoDB's next-key-locking technique prevents phantom reads; however, a SERIALIZABLE isolation level is offered "just in case."

InnoDB differs from other database vendors in its default isolation level and its supported isolation levels. You should be aware of some of the differences, in case you routinely deal with other database vendors:

- Microsoft SQL Server operates in READ COMMITTED mode, by default, and supports all ANSI standard isolation levels.

- Oracle also operates in READ COMMITTED mode by default, but does not support REPEATABLE READ or READ UNCOMMITTED. A SERIALIZABLE mode is supported, as well as a READ ONLY nonstandard mode.

- PostgreSQL operates in REPEATABLE READ mode by default and supports only the additional SERIALIZABLE mode.

Locking and Isolation Levels in MySQL: Some Examples

MySQL, through InnoDB's transaction processing system, provides you the ability to specify certain types of locks on a resource during a user session. Because it is much easier to see how these concepts interrelate when you work through some examples, that's what you'll do in this section. These examples will give you an idea of the differences between the lock types and how concurrently executing transactions can be affected by a variety of commands.

We'll use the following table during this exercise:

```
mysql> CREATE TABLE numbers (my_number INT NOT NULL PRIMARY KEY) ENGINE=InnoDB;
```

We recommend that you follow along as we walk through these examples. Go ahead and open a connection and execute this CREATE TABLE statement in your test database.

■**Note** In order for these examples to work, you must be running a version of MySQL with InnoDB compiled into the binary. You can use `SHOW VARIABLES LIKE 'have_innodb'` to check if a particular MySQL instance has the InnoDB engine installed. The possible values are NO, YES, and DISABLED. If the DISABLED option shows, you can modify the `my.cnf` file to remove the `skip-innodb` option in order to enable it. If the NO value shows, you must install a version of MySQL that has the InnoDB storage engine compiled into it. See Chapter 14 for more information MySQL installation and configuration.

Next, add some sample data to your table:

```
mysql> INSERT INTO numbers VALUES (1), (2), (3), (4), (5);
```

Now, open a second connection to the MySQL server. This second connection will be used to emulate a concurrent execution scenario. We'll call the first connection window you opened Connection 1, and the second one Connection 2.

Autocommit and Concurrent Transactions

First, let's see how the autocommit behavior influences concurrent transactions. In Connection 1, execute the following statements:

```
mysql> SET AUTOCOMMIT = 0;
mysql> INSERT INTO numbers VALUES (6);
mysql> SELECT MAX(my_number) FROM numbers;
```

You should see the following resultset in the first connection window:

```
mysql> SELECT * FROM numbers;
+-----------+
| my_number |
+-----------+
|         1 |
|         2 |
|         3 |
|         4 |
|         5 |
|         6 |
+-----------+
6 rows in set (0.03 sec)
```

Now, execute the same statement in Connection 2, and you should see a different result:

```
mysql> SELECT * FROM numbers;
+-----------+
| my_number |
+-----------+
|         1 |
|         2 |
|         3 |
|         4 |
|         5 |
+-----------+
5 rows in set (0.00 sec)
```

This shows that by setting the AUTOCOMMIT setting to 0 in Connection 1, you have essentially issued a START TRANSACTION statement. What else do you see? Well, Connection 2 cannot see the new row that has been added by Connection 1's transaction. This is because of InnoDB's default isolation level, which enforces consistent reads as well as eliminates phantom reads by the use of next-key-locking technique.

Isolation Level Effects

Now, let's see how changing the isolation level on the transaction affects things. First, commit Connection 1's transaction:

```
mysql> COMMIT;
```

You will notice that Connection 2 now shows the new values:

```
mysql> SELECT * FROM numbers;
+-----------+
| my_number |
+-----------+
|         1 |
|         2 |
|         3 |
|         4 |
|         5 |
|         6 |
+-----------+
6 rows in set (0.01 sec)
```

This is exactly what you would expect.

Returning to Connection 1, change the *global* isolation level by issuing the following command (again, make sure you're in Connection 1):

```
mysql> SET GLOBAL TRANSACTION ISOLATION LEVEL READ UNCOMMITTED;
```

MySQL gives you the ability to set the transaction isolation level for either the current session or globally. Global isolation level sets the level for all *new* sessions connecting to the MySQL server *after* the setting is changed.

Note You will need to be logged in to the server as a user with the SUPER privilege in order to change the global isolation level.

Next, execute a new INSERT statement in an explicit transaction in Connection 1:

```
mysql> START TRANSACTION;
mysql> INSERT INTO numbers VALUES (7);
mysql> SELECT * FROM numbers;
+-----------+
| my_number |
+-----------+
|         1 |
|         2 |
|         3 |
|         4 |
|         5 |
|         6 |
|         7 |
+-----------+
7 rows in set (0.00 sec)
```

You can see the new row in Connection 1. Now switch to Connection 2 and exit, since the new isolation level will be available only for *new* sessions. Open a new session and issue the same SELECT statement:

```
mysql> SELECT * FROM numbers;
+-----------+
| my_number |
+-----------+
|         1 |
|         2 |
|         3 |
|         4 |
|         5 |
|         6 |
|         7 |
+-----------+
7 rows in set (0.00 sec)
```

As you can see, the READ UNCOMMITED isolation level weakened the protection against the new data, allowing the new connection to see the result of an as-of-yet-uncommitted transaction in Connection 1.

Let's go ahead and ROLLBACK our transaction in Connection 1, causing the INSERT to be undone:

```
mysql> ROLLBACK;
Query OK, 0 rows affected (0.08 sec)
mysql> SELECT * FROM numbers;
+-----------+
| my_number |
+-----------+
|         1 |
|         2 |
|         3 |
|         4 |
|         5 |
|         6 |
+-----------+
6 rows in set (0.00 sec)
```

As you can see, our new record is gone in Connection 1. Let's check Connection 2:

```
mysql> SELECT * FROM numbers;
+-----------+
| my_number |
+-----------+
|         1 |
|         2 |
|         3 |
|         4 |
|         5 |
|         6 |
+-----------+
6 rows in set (0.00 sec)
```

Sure enough, it's gone in that session, too. This is a great example of the danger of the READ UNCOMMITTED isolation level, and why, in practice, it is rarely used on production systems. If Connection 2 had been relying on the data in that seventh record to be current, it would have been out of luck. Being out of luck on a mission-critical production system is, of course, out of the question.

Next, let's demonstrate the difference between the READ COMMITTED and REPEATABLE READ isolation levels. It is very important that you follow the steps to re-create these effects exactly as we explain them; otherwise, you'll be left scratching your head a bit. You may want to exit from your open connections and give yourself a fresh start with a new Connection 1. If you've been following along, your numbers table in the test schema should contain six records, in order. If not, go ahead and make the necessary changes to have this as your starting point.

In Connection 1, set the isolation level to READ COMMITTED and start a new transaction:

```
mysql> SET GLOBAL TRANSACTION ISOLATION LEVEL READ COMMITTED;
Query OK, 0 rows affected (0.00 sec)
mysql> START TRANSACTION;
Query OK, 0 rows affected (0.00 sec)
```

Now, in a new Connection 2, start another connection and issue the following statement:

```
SELECT MAX(my_number) FROM numbers
```

You should see the following:

```
mysql> START TRANSACTION;
Query OK, 0 rows affected (0.00 sec)
mysql> SELECT MAX(my_number) FROM numbers;
+----------------+
| MAX(my_number) |
+----------------+
|              6 |
+----------------+
1 row in set (0.00 sec)
```

Now, switch back to Connection 1 and insert a new record into the numbers table, and then COMMIT that transaction (again, in Connection 1):

```
mysql> INSERT INTO numbers VALUES (7);
Query OK, 1 row affected (0.03 sec)
mysql> COMMIT;
Query OK, 0 rows affected (0.06 sec)
```

Next, switch to Connection 2 and run the same SELECT statement again:

```
SELECT MAX(my_number) FROM numbers
mysql> SELECT MAX(my_number) FROM numbers;
+----------------+
| MAX(my_number) |
+----------------+
|              7 |
+----------------+
1 row in set (0.00 sec)
```

As the READ COMMITTED name indicates, our statement has indeed returned the newly inserted record from the transaction committed in Connection 1, even though we have not yet committed our transaction in Connection 2. Now, let's see how the same experiment works when the isolation level is set to REPEATABLE READ. First, let's commit our second transaction in Connection 2, reset our numbers table to its original state, and then exit Connection 2's session:

```
mysql> COMMIT;
Query OK, 0 rows affected (0.00 sec)
mysql> DELETE FROM numbers WHERE my_number = 7;
Query OK, 1 row affected (0.11 sec)
mysql> exit;
Bye
```

```
mysql> SET GLOBAL TRANSACTION ISOLATION LEVEL REPEATABLE READ;
Query OK, 0 rows affected (0.00 sec)
mysql> START TRANSACTION;
Query OK, 0 rows affected (0.00 sec)
```

Then, in Connection 2, start a new session and a new transaction, with a SELECT from the numbers table:

```
mysql> START TRANSACTION;
Query OK, 0 rows affected (0.00 sec)
mysql> SELECT MAX(my_number) FROM numbers;
+----------------+
| MAX(my_number) |
+----------------+
|              6 |
+----------------+
1 row in set (0.00 sec)
```

Everything is the same so far. Now, switch back to Connection 1, add a new record to the numbers table, and then COMMIT the transaction:

```
mysql> INSERT INTO numbers VALUES (7);
Query OK, 1 row affected (0.02 sec)
mysql> COMMIT;
Query OK, 0 rows affected (0.06 sec)
```

Switch back to Connection 2 and rerun the SELECT statement:

```
mysql> SELECT MAX(my_number) FROM numbers;
+----------------+
| MAX(my_number) |
+----------------+
|              6 |
+----------------+
1 row in set (0.00 sec)
```

Aha! Even though the first transaction has been committed, our second transaction does not see the changes. Why? Because identical reads within a transaction with the isolation level set to REPEATABLE READ must be *consistent* (thus, *repeatable*). InnoDB accomplishes this feat by taking a snapshot of the data returned in the first SELECT MAX(my_number) FROM numbers statement and ensuring that this snapshot was used in the next SELECT statement.

■**Tip** If you ever need to see the global isolation level, here's an easy method: SELECT @@tx_isolation;.

FOR UPDATE and LOCK IN SHARE MODE Command Clauses

In addition to offering the global transaction isolation level, MySQL lets you specify how the transaction processing system in InnoDB should treat *individual* statements within a transaction.

The LOCK IN SHARE MODE clause, appended to a SELECT statement, informs InnoDB that it should prevent other transactions from updating or deleting any rows that are affected by the SELECT statement until the transaction containing the LOCK IN SHARE MODE statement has finished. Additionally, that transaction must wait until any currently executing (uncommitted) transaction that may update or delete those SELECTed data rows has committed, and will check that the data rows still exist before proceeding with the transaction. Here is an example of a transaction that uses the LOCK IN SHARE MODE to prevent other transactions from deleting of modifying the parent key data before it commits:

```
mysql> START TRANSACTION;
mysql> SELECT child.* FROM child JOIN parent ON child.parent_id = parent.id
       WHERE parent.id = 4 LOCK IN SHARE MODE;
mysql> // Do Some processing here on child record…
mysql> COMMIT;
```

You can use the FOR UPDATE clause of the SELECT statement when you want to alert InnoDB that the transaction intends to eventually update the needed row, and that other transactions must wait until this transaction is finished before updating the data that is included in the result of the SELECT statement. This is useful for ensuring that the data you read inside a transaction that you will later use for an update of, say, a summary table, is reliable for the duration of the transaction.

Deadlocks

If two or more transactions happen to want to update the same resource at the same time, they end up waiting for each other to commit in order to complete their own update. This behavior is known as a *deadlock*, and it usually occurs on high-volume transactional systems, where numerous concurrent connections are actively updating similar data records.

InnoDB has some built-in safeguards to resolve deadlocks and contention among connections. Let's create a deadlock in our system so you can see what happens when InnoDB is stuck between transactions needing access to the same resource.

Continuing with our previous example, execute this code in Connection 1:

```
mysql> START TRANSACTION;
mysql> SELECT * FROM numbers WHERE my_number = 5 FOR UPDATE;
+-----------+
| my_number |
+-----------+
|         5 |
+-----------+
1 rows in set (0.00 sec)
```

(We've removed some of the zero resultsets returned by the first two statements for brevity.)

Now, exit from your session in Connection 2, start a new session and transaction, and try to update the record:

```
mysql> START TRANSACTION;
Query OK, 0 rows affected (0.00 sec)
mysql> UPDATE numbers SET my_number = 12 WHERE my_number = 5;
```

The MySQL client doesn't return anything. It just seems to hang! A deadlock has occurred, since Connection 2 is waiting for Connection 1's transaction to commit in order to update its record.

After a short while (50 seconds by default), you'll see the following in the Connection 2 window:

```
ERROR 1205 (HY000): Lock wait timeout exceeded; try restarting transaction
mysql>
```

What happened? Well, InnoDB sets a timeout on the lock acquired by Connection 2's transaction, and this timeout has expired, meaning the transaction is aborted.

Now that you've seen some examples of MySQL's isolation-related features, let's look at another isolation feature provided by the InnoDB storage engine.

Multiversion Concurrency Control

The InnoDB storage engine deploys a special method of increasing consistent, nonlocking concurrent access to the same resource, called *multiversion concurrency control* (MVCC). InnoDB uses row-level lock granularity, so a resource is a specific row of data in an InnoDB table.

■Note MVCC is deployed by both PostgreSQL and Oracle, as well as InnoDB. This differs from other database vendors, such as Microsoft SQL Server, which use standard row-level locking and a type of lock escalation system.

MVCC improves the throughput of concurrency by allowing reads of a resource, *even while locking the resource for a write request.* It does so by keeping a snapshot of the record data available to read requests. The data records are tied to a version, which identifies when the data record was created, called a *create version ID*, and when it was deleted, if at all, called a *delete version ID*.[7] These identifiers are internally counted version numbers that InnoDB tracks, but they can be seen as a timestamp for our purposes here. The *system version ID* is an increasing value that corresponds to a serialized execution timeline, which the database server increments as transactions are executed against it.[8]

---

7. To get technical, the deletion of a record is actually called the *expiration* in MVCC lingo.

8. Actually, this version number is tied to the log sequence number, but essentially, this is the same thing.

As modifications are made to the row data, a separate version of the row data is maintained, resulting in a set of row data that may match any particular query. Only one record of this set will actually be returned or used by InnoDB during a transaction's execution. Which of the records is returned depends on a number of conditions.

Depending on which statement is received during a transaction's request, InnoDB's MVCC logic kicks in differently:[9]

SELECT: When it receives a SELECT statement with a read request for a specific resource (row or set of rows), the database server scans through the set of available data records matching the WHERE criteria and looks at each record version information. It returns the record in the set that passes all of the following criteria:

- The create version ID must be less than or equal to the system version ID. This criterion ensures that the data record returned was created before the currently executing transaction began.

- If the delete version ID is not null, then it must be greater than the system version ID. This criterion makes it impossible to return records that were deleted before the currently executing transaction began.

- The create version ID cannot be in the list of actively running transactions. Here, MVCC is ensuring that the row data being returned hasn't been created or modified by any uncommitted transactions.

INSERT: For INSERT operations, a new record is added to the table, and the system version ID is used as the create version ID. The delete version ID is, of course, left null.

DELETE: For DELETE operations, instead of removing the record, the delete version ID of the record is set to the system version ID.

UPDATE: Here is where things get interesting, and how the whole process comes together. On an UPDATE, InnoDB, instead of modifying the existing data row, adds a new row record to the table, with a create version ID equal to the system version ID. For the old row data record, its delete version ID is set to that same system version ID. In this way, the set of related row data records is maintained, and this set can be retrieved by the criteria selection process used in the SELECT statement row retrieval.

As you would expect, all this extra maintenance demands a higher processing power than the simplified locking system involved in standard row-level or table-level locking. That processing power comes at a performance cost. However, on very high concurrency systems, the benefit of reducing the chance of deadlocks and lock wait times is significant.

Fortunately, MySQL gives you different storage engines from which to choose. We'll take a look at those options in Chapter 5. But now you have the fundamental knowledge with which to make an informed decision.

---

9. The summary of MVCC record operations was adapted from *High Performance MySQL*, by Jeremy Zawodny and Derek Balling (O'Reilly, 2004), which has an excellent summary of MVCC.

Identifying Your Transaction Control Requirements

So, what does all this stuff mean to you anyway? How do you go about deciding whether transaction processing requirements should play an active part in your application design? Indeed, even if you decide that you should employ some of the transaction processing benefits of MySQL and InnoDB, how do you decide which levels of transaction control, and specifically isolation, you should use?

Basically, you'll need to consider your comfort level and also user actions to determine your transaction needs.

A saying in the database administration world is "Your paranoia is only as deep as your pockets." The usual context of the phrase refers to how much money a business is willing to invest to ensure that it doesn't lose data due to a system failure. It costs real money to deploy redundant backup systems to protect the data store, and so a company's level of risk is inversely proportional to the amount of money spent on RAID configurations, redundant power supplies, and so on.

In a sense, this is a good way to think about your need for transaction processing. If you simply cannot tolerate, either personally or from a business perspective, the possibility of your data store becoming inconsistent, you should invest time, and thus money, in implementing transaction-safe capabilities in your application. Of course, ensuring that every single execution of business transactions is secured via ACID-compliant, transaction-safe tables and processing takes a level of commitment from the development team.

Whatever comfort level you and your business users settle on should be the result of honest, thoughtful discourse between the development team and the stakeholders of the application (the actual business). This discourse *must* occur *before* application design begins, for two reasons:

- The design of an application and its code base is profoundly affected by the decision to ensure transaction safety. Client code, business logic, and the core layout of a system's components will be markedly different due to the restraints of an ACID-compliant application requirement. Consider, for instance, a decision to use procedure calls against a *remote* server in the application's design. This decision may be influenced by your team's preliminary assessment that the transaction processing system coupled with the higher connection cost of the remote server would be unacceptable, and therefore, a local procedure call might be preferable.

- Changing application code to ensure transaction safety once an application has been designed without transaction processing is extremely costly. The time and effort taken by the design team in order to rethink existing application logic and code can be avoided by dedicating sufficient time to the discussion of transaction processing before the application is designed.

When discussing the transactional needs of a business application, you must analyze the use cases provided to you by a business analyst and the business functional expert. These use cases will provide clues about the business's transaction needs. For instance, if you encounter a number of use cases that describe actions taken by an end user using a single verb—like our user account *merge* scenario earlier in this chapter—this provides a hint that the business entity views the action in terms of a transaction.

Whether or not strong transaction processing is necessary is up to the comfort level of the business. In order to determine the comfort level of the business, it is up to your design team, including the business analyst, to properly explain the advantages and disadvantages transaction processing incurs. Lay the scenario out in clear terms for the business users: "If we implement X level of security, you can be assured that Y will never happen; however, this will impact the project schedule by Z number of weeks, because we must make certain application design changes."

■**Tip** As we go to print, there are some rumors of changes to transaction processing in MySQL 5.1. Though little information has surfaced, it seems there will be some support for using MySQL to manage distributed transactions (across remote machines or multiple databases) using the X/Open model (or XA). We encourage you to check mailing lists and the MySQL web site for more information about this emerging functionality.

Summary

We covered a lot of ground in this chapter. Although we walked through some exercises specific to the MySQL database server, the vast majority of the fundamentals covered here are applicable to most database servers. This fundamental knowledge will help you evaluate MySQL's ability to provide true transaction-safe capability to your applications, and give you insight on the benefits and drawbacks of transaction processing.

We covered the ACID test, and went over how this acronym refers to a measure of how a database server's transaction processing system works to ensure the viability of transactions executed against it. Some of the diagrams in the earlier part of the chapter gave you a visual picture of how a failure can affect a transactional system, and how the recovery and logging systems of the database server work to alleviate the trouble caused by failures.

The topic of transaction isolation is closely related to issues of concurrency. You learned how locking systems work to shield multiple processes from interfering with a certain resource and saw how the different granularities of locks, and type of lock, affect concurrency issues.

From there, we dove into some practical examples of concurrency concerns, by executing different schedules of transactions using multiple user connections. These examples helped you to see the real-life effects of isolation levels and locking concepts. We also took a look at how deadlocks occur and why. Our discussion of multiversion concurrency control (MVCC) showed you how the InnoDB storage engine manages to provide data isolation to concurrently executing transactions through a system of row-level version tracking.

Finally, we addressed the question of whether all this transactional ability is really necessary. We gave you some tips on how to determine the comfort level of your own team and the business.

In the upcoming chapters, we'll build on the basic knowledge you've picked up in this and the previous chapters. In Chapter 4, we'll look inside MySQL's database server and analyze how the different parts of the server work together.

CHAPTER 4

■■■

MySQL System Architecture

In this chapter, we're going to take a look at MySQL internals. It will be a fun, informative examination of how all the different pieces and parts of the MySQL server operate together. MySQL's implementation is a fascinating mix of technology that is truly a remarkable achievement—an achievement born from the sweat and inspiration of numerous developers over many years.

One of the joys of open-source technology is just that: it's open source! On a system as large as MySQL,[1] taking a look at the source code gives you a true understanding of the dilemmas faced by the developers over the course of the software evolution. In this chapter, we'll investigate the source code of the server itself, so put on your hard hat. We encourage you to take a look at the source code, even if you have no intention of making any changes. You will gain an appreciation of the enormity of the tasks undertaken by the development team at MySQL AB, as well as gain a much deeper understanding of how the software works, and thus how you can optimize your programs to best utilize MySQL's strengths and avoid its weaknesses.

The information presented in this chapter comes from an analysis of both the internal system documentation and the actual source code for the MySQL database server system. Because MySQL is an evolving code repository, since press time, some of the design features explained here have likely changed and will continue to do so over time. If you look at the source code from one version to the next, you'll notice variations in the implementations of subsystems and how they interrelate; however, much of the way in which the system generally functions has persisted over the evolution of the software.

Even if you're not a C programming guru, you should be able to follow most of what we'll cover here. The focus will be less on the code itself and more on the structure and flow of operations within the server, and how the different code libraries interact with each other. Our intention is to provide a basic road map from which you can navigate the source code and documentation yourself. However, there are a few sections of this chapter that require a significant knowledge of C and C++ programming, and are meant for more advanced readers. If you don't have a whole lot of experience in C programming, just do your best to follow along, and don't worry about it too much!

---

1. At the time of this writing, the MySQL server consists of roughly 500,000 lines of source code.

In this discussion, we'll cover the following topics:

- How to access the MySQL source code and documentation

- An overview of the MySQL architecture and base function library

- The process, thread, and resource management subsystem

- The storage engine abstraction subsystem

- The caching and memory management subsystem

- The network and connection management subsystem

- The security and access control subsystem

- The log management subsystem

- The query parsing and execution subsystem

- The query cache

- The execution of a typical query

The MySQL Source Code and Documentation

Since we're going to be looking at the MySQL server source code, you'll want to download a copy of the latest MySQL source code so that you can follow along, as well as embark on your own code review adventures. The source code used in this chapter comes from a copy of the source code for version 5.0.2. To download a copy of the source code, head over to MySQL's download site (http://dev.mysql.com/downloads/mysql/5.0.html) and download the version of interest to you.

■**Caution** The source distribution we used for this chapter's analysis came from the 5.0.2-alpha source tree. Bear in mind that MySQL is an *evolving* piece of software, and as such, various implementation details discussed in this chapter may change over time. *Always* obtain the proper source versions of development documentation before you assume anything is the case for a particular version of MySQL.

The Source Code

The source code is organized into a shallow directory tree containing the major libraries of the MySQL server and its different extensions.

Top-Level Directories

Table 4-1 shows all the major top-level directories, with a brief description of the files contained in each directory and the general purpose of those files. As we progress through the chapter, we'll break down the information in this table into smaller groups that relate to each subsystem, but you may use this larger table as a reference.

Table 4-1. *Main Top-Level Directories in the Source Tree*

Directory	Contents
/bdb	The Berkeley DB storage engine handler implementation files
/BUILD	Program compilation files
/client	The mysql command tool (client program) implementation files
/data	The mysql database (system database) schema, data, and index files
/dbug	Debugging utility code
/Docs	The documentation, both internal developer documents and the MySQL online manual
/heap	The MEMORY storage engine handler implementation files
/include	Core system header files and type definitions
/innobase	The InnoDB storage engine handler implementation files
/isam	The old ISAM storage engine handler implementation files
/libmysql	The MySQL C client API (all C source and header files)
/libmysqld	The MySQL server core library (C, C++, and some header files)
/libmysqltest	A simple program to test MySQL
/merge	The old Merge storage engine handler implementation files
/myisam	The MyISAM storage engine handler implementation files
/myisammrg	The MyISAM Merge storage engine handler implementation files
/mysys	The core function library, with basic low-level functions
/regex	The regular expression function library
/scripts	Shell scripts for common utilities
/share	Internationalized error messages
/sql	The meat of the server's implementation, with core classes and implementations for all major server and client activity
/sql-bench	MySQL benchmarking shell scripts
/strings	Lower-level string-handling functions
/support-files	Preconfigured MySQL configuration files (such as my-huge.cnf)
/tests	Test programs and scripts
/vio	Network/socket utility functions, virtual I/O, SSL, and so on
/zlib	Compression function source files

You can take some time now to dig through the source code a bit, for fun, but you will most likely find yourself quickly lost in the maze of classes, structs, and C functions that compose the source distribution. The first place you will want to go is the documentation for the distribution, located in the /Docs directory. Then follow along with us as we discuss the key subsystems and where you can discover the core files that correspond to the different system functionality.

C AND C++ PROGRAMMING TERMS

We'll be referring to a number of C and C++ programming paradigms in this chapter. C source code files are those files in the distribution that end in `.c`. C++ source files end in `.cc`, or on some Windows systems, `.cpp`. Both C and C++ source files can include (using the `#include` directive) *header* files, identified by an `.h` extension. In C and C++, it is customary to *define* the functions and variables used in the source files in a header file. Typically, the header file is named the same as the source file, but with an `.h` extension, but this is not always the case. One of the first tasks you'll attempt when looking at the source code of a system is identifying *where* the variables and functions are defined. Sometimes, this task involves looking through a vast hierarchy of header files in order to find where a variable or function is officially defined.

Undoubtedly, you're familiar with what variables and functions are, so we won't go into much depth about that. In C and C++ programming, however, some other data types and terms are frequently used. Most notably, we'll be using the following terms in this chapter:

- Struct

- Class

- Member variable

- Member method

A *struct* is essentially a container for a bunch of data. A typical definition for a *struct* might look something like this:

```
typedef struct st_heapinfo /* Struct from heap_info */
{
  ulong records; /* Records in database */
  ulong deleted; /* Deleted records in database */
  ulong max_records;
  ulong data_length;
  ulong index_length;
  uint reclength; /* Length of one record */
  int errkey;
  ulonglong auto_increment;
} HEAPINFO;
```

This particular definition came from /include/heap.h. It defines a `struct` (st_heapinfo) as having a number of member variables of various data types (such as `records`, `max_records`) and `typedef`s (aliases) the word `HEAPINFO` to represent the st_heapinfo struct. Comments in C code are marked with the `//` or `/* … */` characters.

A *class*, on the other hand, is a C++ object-oriented structure that is similar to a C struct, but can also have *member methods*, as well as *member variables*. The member methods are functions of the class, and they can be called through an *instance* of the class.

Doxygen for Source Code Analysis

A recommended way to analyze the source code is to use a tool like Doxygen (`http://www.stack.nl/ ~dimitri/doxygen/index.html`), which enables you to get the code structure from a source distribution. This tool can be extremely useful for navigating through functions in a large source distribution like MySQL, where a single execution can call hundreds of class members and functions. The documented output enables you to see where the classes or structs are defined and where they are implemented.

Doxygen provides the ability to configure the output of the documentation produced by the program, and it even allows for UML inheritance and collaboration diagrams to be produced. It can show the class hierarchies in the source code and provide links to where functions are defined and implemented.

On Unix machines, download the source code from the Doxygen web site, and then follow the manual instructions for installation (also available online at the web site). To produce graphical output, you'll want to first download and install the Graph visualization toolkit from `http://www.graphviz.org/`. After installing Doxygen, you can use the following command to create a default configuration file for Doxygen to process:

```
# doxygen -g -s /path/to/newconfig.file
```

The option `/path/to/newconfig.file` should be the directory in which you want to eventually produce your Doxygen documentation. After Doxygen has created the configuration file for you, simply open the configuration file in your favorite editor and edit the sections you need. Usually, you will need to modify only the `OUTPUT_DIRECTORY`, `INPUT`, and `PROJECT_NAME` settings. Once you've edited the configuration file, simply execute the following:

```
# doxygen </path/to/config-file>
```

For your convenience, a version of the MySQL 5.0.2 Doxygen output is available at `http://www.jpipes.com/mysqldox/`.

The MySQL Documentation

The internal system documentation is available to you if you download the source code of MySQL. It is in the `Docs` directory of the source tree, available in the `internals.texi` TEXI document.

The TEXI documentation covers the following topics in detail:

- Coding guidelines

- The optimizer (highly recommended reading)

- Important algorithms and structures

- Charsets and related issues

- How MySQL performs different `SELECT` operations (very useful information)

- How MySQL transforms queries

- Communication protocol

- Replication

- The MyISAM record structure

- The .MYI file structure

- The InnoDB record structure

- The InnoDB page structure

Although the documentation is extremely helpful in researching certain key elements of the server (particularly the query optimizer), it is worth noting that the internal documentation does not directly address how the different subsystems interact with each other. To determine this interaction, it is necessary to examine the source code itself and the comments of the developers.[2]

■**Caution** Even the most recent `internals.texi` documentation has a number of bad hyperlinks, references, and incorrect filenames and paths, so do your homework before you take everything for granted. The `internals.texi` documentation may not be as up-to-date as your MySQL server version!

TEXI and texi2html Viewing

TEXI is the GNU standard documentation format. A number of utilities can convert the TEXI source documentation to other, perhaps more readable or portable, formats. For those of you using Emacs or some variant of it, that editor supports a TEXI major mode for easy reading.

If you prefer an HTML version, you can use the free Perl-based utility `texi2html`, which can generate a highly configurable HTML output of a TEXI source document. `texi2html` is available for download from `https://texi2html.cvshome.org/`. Once you've downloaded this utility, you can install it, like so:

```
# tar -xzvf texi2html-1.76.tar.gz
# cd texi2html-1.6
# ./configure
# make install
```

Here, we've untarred the latest (as of this writing) `texi2html` version and installed the software on our Linux system. Next, we want to generate an HTML version of the `internals.texi` document available in our source download:

```
# cd /path/to/mysql-5.0.2-alpha/
# texi2html Docs/internals.texi
```

After installation, you'll notice a new HTML document in the /Docs directory of your source tree called `internals.html`. You can now navigate the internal documentation via a web browser. For your convenience, this HTML document is also available at `http://www.jpipes.com/mysqldox/`.

---

2. Whether the developers chose to purposefully omit a discussion on the subsystem's communication in order to allow for changes in that communication is up for debate.

MySQL Architecture Overview

MySQL's architecture consists of a web of interrelated function sets, which work together to fulfill the various needs of the database server. A number of authors[3] have implied that these function sets are indeed components, or entirely encapsulated packages; however, there is little evidence in the source code that this is the case.

Indeed, the architecture includes separate function libraries, composed of functions that handle similar tasks, but there is not, in the traditional object-oriented programming sense, a full component-level separation of functionality. By this, we mean that you will be disappointed if you go into the source code looking for classes called `BufferManager` or `QueryManager`. They don't exist. We bring this point up because some developers, particularly ones with Java backgrounds, write code containing a number of "manager" objects, which fulfill the requests of client objects in a very object-centric approach. In MySQL, this simply isn't the case.

In some cases—notably in the source code for the query cache and log management subsystems—a more object-oriented *approach* is taken to the code. However, in most cases, system functionality is run through the various function libraries (which pass along a core set of structs) and classes (which do the dirty work of code execution), as opposed to an encapsulated approach, where components manage their internal execution and provide an API for other components to use the component. This is due, in part, to the fact that the system architecture is made up of both C and C++ source files, as well as a number of Perl and shell scripts that serve as utilities. C and C++ have different functional capabilities; C++ is a fully object-oriented language, and C is more procedural. In the MySQL system architecture, certain libraries have been written entirely in C, making an object-oriented component type architecture nearly impossible. For sure, the architecture of the server subsystems has a lot to do with performance and portability concerns as well.

■**Note** As MySQL is an evolving piece of software, you will notice variations in both coding and naming style and consistency. For example, if you compare the source files for the older MyISAM handler files with the newer query cache source files, you'll notice a marked difference in naming conventions, commenting by the developers, and function-naming standards. Additionally, as we go to print, there have been rumors that significant changes to the directory structure and source layout will occur in MySQL 5.1.

Furthermore, if you analyze the source code and internal documentation, you will find little mention of components or packages.[4] Instead, you will find references to various task-related functionality. For instance, the internals TEXI document refers to "The Optimizer," but you will find no component or package in the source code called Optimizer. Instead, as the internals TEXI document states, "The Optimizer is a set of routines which decide what execution path the RDBMS should take for queries." For simplicity's sake, we

---

3. For examples, see *MySQL: The Complete Reference*, by Vikram Vaswani (McGraw-Hill/Osborne) and `http://wiki.cs.uiuc.edu/cs427/High-Level+Component+Diagram+of+the+MySQL+Architecture`.

4. The function init_server_components() in /sql/mysqld.cpp is the odd exception. Really, though, this method runs through starting a few of the functional subsystems and initializes the storage handlers and core buffers.

will refer to each related set of functionality by the term *subsystem*, rather than *component*, as it seems to more accurately reflect the organization of the various function libraries.

Each subsystem is designed to both accept information from and feed data into the other subsystems of the server. In order to do this in a standard way, these subsystems expose this functionality through a well-defined *function application programming interface (API)*.[5] As requests and data funnel through the server's pipeline, the subsystems pass information between each other via these clearly defined functions and data structures. As we examine each of the major subsystems, we'll take a look at some of these data structures and methods.

MySQL Server Subsystem Organization

The overall organization of the MySQL server architecture is a layered, but not particularly hierarchical, structure. We make the distinction here that the subsystems in the MySQL server architecture are quite independent of each other.

In a hierarchical organization, subsystems depend on each other in order to function, as components *derive* from a tree-like set of classes. While there are indeed tree-like organizations of classes within some of the subsystems—notably in the SQL parsing and optimization subsystem—the subsystems themselves do not follow a hierarchical arrangement.

A base function library and a select group of subsystems handle lower-level responsibilities. These libraries and subsystems serve to support the abstraction of the storage engine systems, which feed data to requesting client programs. Figure 4-1 shows a general depiction of this layering, with different subsystems identified. We'll cover each of the subsystems separately in this chapter.

Note that client programs interact with an *abstracted* API for the storage engines. This enables client connections to issue statements that are storage-engine agnostic, meaning the client does not need to know which storage engine is handling the data request. No special client functions are required to return InnoDB records versus MyISAM records. This arrangement enables MySQL to extend its functionality to different storage requirements and media. We'll take a closer look at the storage engine implementation in the "Storage Engine Abstraction" section later in this chapter, and discuss the different storage engines in detail in the next chapter.

---

5. This abstraction generally leads to a loose *coupling*, or dependence, of related function sets to each other. In general, MySQL's components are loosely coupled, with a few exceptions.

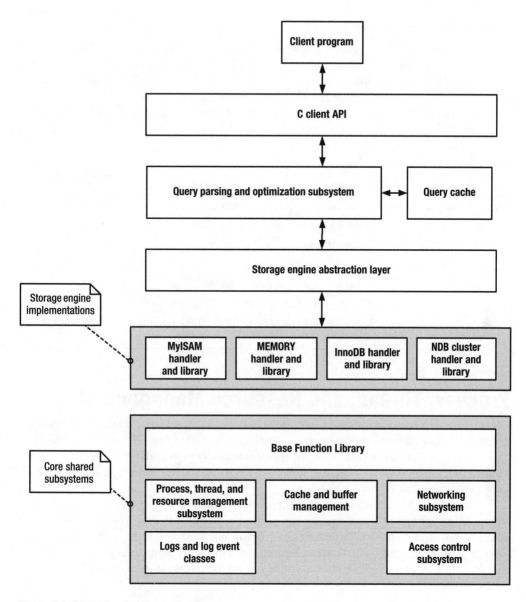

Figure 4-1. *MySQL subsystem overview*

Base Function Library

All of MySQL's subsystems share the use of a base library of common functions. Many of these functions exist to shield the subsystem (and the developers) from needing to operate directly with the operating system, main memory, or the physical hardware itself.[6] Additionally, the base function library enables code reuse and portability. Most of the functions in this base library are found in the C source files of the /mysys and /strings directories. Table 4-2 shows a sampling of core files and locations for this base library.

Table 4-2. *Some Core Function Files*

File	Contents
/mysys/array.c	Dynamic array functions and definitions
/mysys/hash.c/.h	Hash table functions and definitions
/mysys/mf_qsort.c	Quicksort algorithms and functions
/mysys/string.c	Dynamic string functions
/mysys/my_alloc.c	Some memory allocation routines
/mysys/mf_pack.c	Filename and directory path packing routines
/strings/*	Low-level string and memory manipulation functions, and some data type definitions

Process, Thread, and Resource Management

One of the lowest levels of the system architecture deals with the management of the various processes that are responsible for various activities on the server. MySQL happens to be a thread-based server architecture, which differs dramatically from database servers that operate on a process-based system architecture, such as Oracle and Microsoft SQL Server. We'll explain the difference in just a minute.

The library of functions that handles these various threads of execution is designed so that all the various executing threads can access key shared *resources*. These resources— whether they are simple variables maintained for the entire server system or other resources like files and certain data caches—must be monitored to avoid having multiple executing threads conflict with each other or overwriting critical data. This function library handles the coordination of the many threads and resources.

Thread-Based vs. Process-Based Design

A *process* can be described as an executing set of instructions the operating system has allocated an address space in which to conduct its operations. The operating system grants the process control over various resources, like files and devices. The operations conducted by the process have been given a certain priority by the operating system, and, over the course of its execution, the process maintains a given state (sleeping, running, and so on).

---

6. Certain components and libraries, however, will still interact directly with the operating system or hardware where performance or other benefits may be realized.

A *thread* can be thought of as a sort of lightweight process, which, although not given its own address space in memory, does execute a series of operations and does maintain its own state. A thread has a mechanism to save and restore its resources when it changes state, and it has access to the resources of its parent process. A *multithreaded* environment is one in which a process can create, or *spawn*, any number of threads to handle—sometimes synchronously[7] —its needed operations.

Some database servers have multiple processes handling multiple requests. However, MySQL uses multiple threads to accomplish its activities. This strategy has a number of different advantages, most notably in the arena of performance and memory use:

- It is less costly to create or destroy threads than processes. Because the threads use the parent process's address space, there is no need to allocate additional address space for a new thread.

- Switching between threads is a relatively inexpensive operation because threads are running in the same address space.

- There is little overhead involved in shared resources, since threads automatically have access to the parent's resources.

■**Tip** Since each instance of a MySQL database server—that is, each execution of the `mysqd` server daemon—executes in its own address space, it is possible to simulate a multiprocess server by creating multiple instances of MySQL. Each instance will run in its own process and have a set of its own threads to use in its execution. This arrangement is useful when you need to have separate configurations for different instances, such as in a shared hosting environment, with different companies running different, separately configured and secured MySQL servers on the same machine.

Implementation Through a Library of Related Functions

A set of functions handles the creation of a myriad threads responsible for running the various parts of the server application. These functions are optimized to take advantage of the ability of the underlying operating system resource and process management systems. The process, thread, and resource management subsystem is in charge of creating, monitoring, and destroying threads. Specifically, threads are created by the server to manage the following main areas:

- A thread is created to handle each new user connection. This is a special thread we'll cover in detail later in the upcoming "User Connection Threads and THD Objects" section. It is responsible for carrying out both query execution and user authentication, although, as you will see, it passes this responsibility to other classes designed especially to handle those events.

- A global (instance-wide) thread is responsible for creating and managing each user connection thread. This thread can be considered a sort of user connection manager thread.

---

7. This depends on the available hardware; for instance, whether the system supports symmetric multi-processing.

- A single thread handles all DELAYED INSERT requests separately.

- Another thread handles table flushes when requested by the system or a user connection.

- Replication requires separate threads for handling the synchronization of master and slave servers.

- A thread is created to handle shutdown events.

- Another thread handles signals, or alarms, inside the system.

- Another thread handles maintenance tasks.

- A thread handles incoming connection requests, either TCP/IP or Named Pipes.

The system is responsible for regulating the use of shared resources through an internal locking system. This locking system ensures that resources shared by all threads are properly managed to ensure the atomicity of data. Locks on resources that are shared among multiple threads, sometimes called *critical sections*, are managed using mutex structures.

MySQL uses the POSIX threads library. When this library is not available or not suited to the operating system, MySQL *emulates* POSIX threads by *wrapping* an operating system's available process or resource management library in a standard set of POSIX function definitions. For instance, Windows uses its own common resource management functions and definitions. Windows threads are known as *handles*, and so MySQL wraps, or redefines, a HANDLE struct to match a POSIX thread definition. Likewise, for locking shared resources, Windows uses functions like InitializeCriticalSection() and EnterCriticalSection(). MySQL wraps these function definitions to match a POSIX-style API: pthread_mutex_init() and pthread_mutex_lock().

On server initialization, the function init_thread_environment() (in /sql/mysqld.cc) is called. This function creates a series of lock structures, called *mutexes*, to protect the resources used by the various threads executing in the server process. Each of these locks protects a specific resource or group of resources. When a thread needs to modify or read from the resource or resource group, a call is made to lock the resource, using pthread_mutex_lock(). The thread modifies the resource, and then the resource is unlocked using pthread_mutex_unlock(). In our walk-through of a typical query execution at the end of this chapter, you'll see an example of how the code locks and unlocks these critical resources (see Listing 4-10).

Additionally, the functions exposed by this subsystem are used by specific threads in order to allocate resources inside each thread. This is referred to as *thread-specific data* (TSD). Table 4-3 lists a sampling of files for thread and process management.

Table 4-3. *Some Thread and Process Management Subsystem Files*

File	Contents
/include/my_pthread.h	Wrapping definitions for threads and thread locking (mutexes)
/mysys/my_pthread.c	Emulation and degradation of thread management for nonsupporting systems
/mysys/thr_lock.c and /mysys/thr_lock.h	Functions for reading, writing, and checking status of thread locks
/sql/mysqld.cc	Functions like create_new_thread(), which creates a new user connection thread, and close_connection(), which removes (either destroys or sends to a pool) that user connection

User Connection Threads and THD Objects

For each user connection, a special type of thread, encapsulated in a class named THD, is responsible for handling the execution of queries and access control duties. Given its importance, you might think that it's almost ubiquitously found in the source code, and indeed it is. THD is defined in the /sql/sql_class.h file and implemented in the /sql/sql_class.cc file. The class represents everything occurring during a user's connection, from access control through returning a resultset, if appropriate. The following are just some of the class members of THD (some of them should look quite familiar to you):

- last_insert_id
- limit_found_rows
- query
- query_length
- row_count
- session_tx_isolation
- thread_id
- user

This is just a sampling of the member variables available in the substantial THD class. You'll notice on your own inspection of the class definition that THD houses all the functions and variables you would expect to find to maintain the state of a user connection and the statement being executed on that connection. We'll take a more in-depth look at the different parts of the THD class as we look further into how the different subsystems make use of this base class throughout this chapter.

The create_new_thread() function found in /sql/mysqld.cc spawns a new thread and creates a new user thread *object* (THD) for each incoming connection.[8] This function is called by the managing thread created by the server process to handle all incoming user connections. For each new thread, two global counters are incremented: one for the total number of threads created and one for the number of open threads. In this way, the server keeps track of the number of user connections created since the server started and the number of user connections that are currently open. Again, in our examination of a typical query execution at the end of this chapter, you'll see the actual source code that handles this user thread-spawning process.

Storage Engine Abstraction

The storage engine abstraction subsystem enables MySQL to use different handlers of the table data within the system architecture. Each storage engine implements the handler superclass defined in /sql/handler.h. This file indicates the standard API that the query parsing and execution subsystem will call when it needs to store or retrieve data from the engine.

---

8. This is slightly simplified, as there is a process that checks to see if an existing thread can be reused (pooling).

Not all storage engines implement the entire handler API; some implement only a small fraction of it. Much of the bulk of each handler's implementation details is concerned with converting data, schema, and index information into the format needed by MySQL's internal record format (in-memory record format).

■**Note** For more information about the internal format for record storage, see the internals.texi document included with the MySQL internal system documentation, in the Docs directory of the source tree.

Key Classes and Files for Handlers

When investigating the storage engine subsystem, a number of files are important. First, the definition of the handler class is in /sql/handler.h. All the storage engines implement their own subclass of handler, meaning each subclass inherits all the functionality of the handler superclass. In this way, each storage engine's handler subclass follows the same API. This enables client programs to operate on the data contained in the storage engine's tables in an identical manner, even though the implementation of the storage engines—how and where they actually store their data—is quite different.

The handler subclass for each storage engine begins with ha_ followed by the name of the storage engine. The definition of the subclass and its member variables and methods are available in the /sql directory of the source tree and are named after the handler subclass. The files that actually implement the handler class of the storage engine differ for each storage engine, but they can all be found in the directory named for the storage engine:

- The MyISAM storage engine handler subclass is ha_myisam, and it is defined in /sql/ha_myisam.h. Implementation files are in the /myisam directory.

- The MyISAM MERGE storage engine handler subclass is ha_myisammrg, and it is defined in /sql/ha_myisammrg.h. Implementation files are in the /myisammrg directory.

- The InnoDB storage engine handler subclass is ha_innodb, and it is defined in /sql/ha_innodb.h. Implementation files are in the /innobase directory.

- The MEMORY storage engine handler subclass is ha_heap, and it is defined in /sql/ha_heap.h. Implementation files are in the /heap directory.

- The NDB Cluster handler subclass is ha_ndbcluster, and it is defined in /sql/ha_ndbcluster.h. Unlike the other storage engines, which are implemented in a separate directory, the Cluster handler is implemented entirely in /sql/ha_ndbcluster.cc.

The Handler API

The storage engine handler subclasses must implement a base interface API defined in the handler superclass. This API is how the server interacts with the storage engine.

Listing 4-1 shows a stripped-out version (for brevity) of the handler class definition. Its member methods are the API of which we speak. We've highlighted the member method names to make it easier for you to pick them out. Out intention here is to give you a feel for the base class of each storage engine's implementation.

Listing 4-1. *handler Class Definition (Abridged)*

```
class handler // ...
{
protected:
  struct st_table *table;        /* The table definition */

  virtual int index_init(uint idx) { active_index=idx; return 0; }
  virtual int index_end() { active_index=MAX_KEY; return 0; }
  // omitted ...
  virtual int rnd_init(bool scan) =0;
  virtual int rnd_end() { return 0; }

public:

  handler (TABLE *table_arg) {}
  virtual ~handler(void) {}
  // omitted ...
  void update_auto_increment();
  // omitted ...
  virtual bool has_transactions(){ return 0;}
  // omitted ...
  // omitted ...
  virtual int open(const char *name, int mode, uint test_if_locked)=0;
  virtual int close(void)=0;
  virtual int write_row(byte * buf) { return  HA_ERR_WRONG_COMMAND; }
  virtual int update_row(const byte * old_data, byte * new_data) {}
  virtual int delete_row(const byte * buf) {}
  virtual int index_read(byte * buf, const byte * key,
            uint key_len, enum ha_rkey_function find_flag) {}
  virtual int index_read_idx(byte * buf, uint index, const byte * key,
               uint key_len, enum ha_rkey_function find_flag);
  virtual int index_next(byte * buf) {}
  virtual int index_prev(byte * buf) {}
  virtual int index_first(byte * buf) {}
  virtual int index_last(byte * buf) {}
  // omitted ...
  virtual int rnd_next(byte *buf)=0;
  virtual int rnd_pos(byte * buf, byte *pos)=0;
  virtual int read_first_row(byte *buf, uint primary_key);
  // omitted ...
  virtual void position(const byte *record)=0;
  virtual void info(uint)=0;
  // omitted ...
  virtual int start_stmt(THD *thd) {return 0;}
  // omitted ...
  virtual ulonglong get_auto_increment();
  virtual void restore_auto_increment();
  virtual void update_create_info(HA_CREATE_INFO *create_info) {}
```

```
/* admin commands - called from mysql_admin_table */
virtual int check(THD* thd, HA_CHECK_OPT* check_opt) {}
virtual int backup(THD* thd, HA_CHECK_OPT* check_opt) {}
virtual int restore(THD* thd, HA_CHECK_OPT* check_opt) {}
virtual int repair(THD* thd, HA_CHECK_OPT* check_opt) {}
virtual int optimize(THD* thd, HA_CHECK_OPT* check_opt) {}
virtual int analyze(THD* thd, HA_CHECK_OPT* check_opt) {}
virtual int assign_to_keycache(THD* thd, HA_CHECK_OPT* check_opt) {}
virtual int preload_keys(THD* thd, HA_CHECK_OPT* check_opt) {}
/* end of the list of admin commands */

// omitted ...
virtual int add_index(TABLE *table_arg, KEY *key_info, uint num_of_keys) {}
virtual int drop_index(TABLE *table_arg, uint *key_num, uint num_of_keys) {}
// omitted ...
virtual int rename_table(const char *from, const char *to);
virtual int delete_table(const char *name);
virtual int create(const char *name, TABLE *form, HA_CREATE_INFO *info)=0;
// omitted ...
};
```

You should recognize most of the member methods. They correspond to features you may associate with your experience using MySQL. Different storage engines implement some or all of these member methods. In cases where a storage engine does not implement a specific feature, the member method is simply left alone as a placeholder for possible future development. For instance, certain administrative commands, like OPTIMIZE or ANALYZE, require that the storage engine implement a specialized way of optimizing or analyzing the contents of a particular table for that storage engine. Therefore, the handler class provides placeholder member methods (**optimize()** and **analyze()**) for the subclass to implement, *if it wants to.*

The member variable table is extremely important for the handler, as it stores a pointer to an st_table struct. This struct contains information about the table, its fields, and some meta information. This member variable, and four member methods, are in a *protected* area of the handler class, which means that only classes that inherit from the handler class—specifically, the storage engine handler subclasses—can use or see those member variables and methods.

Remember that not all the storage engines actually implement each of handler's member methods. The handler class definition provides default return values or functional equivalents, which we've omitted here for brevity. However, certain member methods must be implemented by the specific storage engine subclass to make the handler at least useful. The following are some of these methods:

- rnd_init(): This method is responsible for preparing the handler for a scan of the table data.

- rnd_next(): This method reads the next row of table data into a buffer, which is passed to the function. The data passed into the buffer must be in a format consistent with the internal MySQL record format.

- `open()`: This method is in charge of opening the underlying table and preparing it for use.

- `info()`: This method fills a number of member variables of the handler by querying the table for information, such as how many records are in the table.

- `update_row()`: This member method replaces old row data with new row data in the underlying data block.

- `create ()`: This method is responsible for creating and storing the schema for a table definition in whatever format used by the storage engine. For instance, MyISAM's `ha_myisam::create()` member method implementation writes the `.frm` file containing the table schema information.

We'll cover the details of storage engine implementations in the next chapter.

■**Note** For some light reading on how to create your *own* storage engine and handler implementations, check out John David Duncan's article at `http://dev.mysql.com/tech-resources/articles/ creating-new-storage-engine.html`.

Caching and Memory Management Subsystem

MySQL has a separate subsystem devoted to the caching and retrieval of different types of data used by all the threads executing within the server process. These data caches, sometimes called *buffers*, enable MySQL to reduce the number of requests for disk-based I/O (an expensive operation) in return for using data already stored in memory (in buffers).

The subsystem makes use of a number of different types of caches, including the record, key, table, hostname, privilege, and other caches. The differences between the caches are in the type of data they store and why they store it. Let's briefly take a look at each cache.

Record Cache

The record cache isn't a buffer for just *any* record. Rather, the record cache is really just a set of function calls that mostly read or write data *sequentially* from a collection of files. For this reason, the record cache is used primarily during table scan operations. However, because of its ability to both read *and* write data, the record cache is also used for sequential writing, such as in some log writing operations.

The core implementation of the record cache can be found in `/mysys/io_cache.c` and `/sql/records.cc`; however, you'll need to do some digging around before anything makes much sense. This is because the key struct used in the record cache is called `st_io_cache`, aliased as `IO_CACHE`. This structure can be found in `/mysys/my_sys.h`, along with some very important macros, all named starting with `my_b_`. They are defined immediately after the `IO_CACHE` structure, and these macros are one of the most interesting implementation details in MySQL.

The IO_CACHE structure is essentially a structure containing a built-in buffer, which can be filled with record data structures.[9] However, this buffer is a fixed size, and so it can store only so many records. Functions throughout the MySQL system can use an IO_CACHE object to retrieve the data they need, using the my_b_ functions (like my_b_read(), which reads from the IO_CACHE internal buffer of records). But there's a problem.

What happens when somebody wants the "next" record, and IO_CACHE's buffer is full? Does the calling program or function need to switch from using the IO_CACHE's buffer to something else that can read the needed records from disk? No, the caller of my_b_read() does not. These macros, in combination with IO_CACHE, are sort of a built-in switching mechanism for other parts of the MySQL server to freely read data from a record cache, but not worry about whether or not the data actually exists in memory. Does this sound strange? Take a look at the definition for the my_b_read macro, shown in Listing 4-2.

Listing 4-2. *my_b_read Macro*

```
#define my_b_read(info,Buffer,Count) \
  ((info)->read_pos + (Count) <= (info)->read_end ? \
  (memcpy(Buffer,(info)->read_pos,(size_t) (Count)), \
  ((info)->read_pos+=(Count)),0) : \
  (*(info)->read_function)((info),Buffer,Count))
```

Let's break it down to help you see the beauty in its simplicity. The info parameter is an IO_CACHE object. The Buffer parameter is a reference to some output storage used by the caller of my_b_read(). You can consider the Count parameter to be the number of records that need to be read.

The macro is simply a ternary operator (that ? : thing). my_b_read() simply looks to see whether the request would read a record from before the end of the internal record buffer ((info)->read_pos + (Count) <= (info)->read_end). If so, the function copies (memcpy) the needed records from the IO_CACHE record buffer into the Buffer output parameter. If not, it calls the IO_CACHE read_function. This read function can be any of the read functions defined in /mysys/mf_iocache.c, which are specialized for the type of disk-based file read needed (such as sequential, random, and so on).

Key Cache

The implementation of the key cache is complex, but fortunately, a good amount of documentation is available. This cache is a repository for frequently used B-tree index data blocks for all MyISAM tables and the now-deprecated ISAM tables. So, the key cache stores key data for MyISAM and ISAM tables.

---

9. Actually, IO_CACHE is a generic buffer cache, and it can contain different data types, not just records.

The primary source code for key cache function definitions and implementation can be found in /include/keycache.h and mysys/mf_keycache.c. The KEY_CACHE struct contains a number of linked lists of accessed index data blocks. These blocks are a fixed size, and they represent a single block of data read from an .MYI file.

Tip As of version 4.1 you can change the key cache's block size by changing the key_cache_block_size configuration variable. However, this configuration variable is still not entirely implemented, as you cannot currently change the size of an index block, which is set when the .MYI file is created. See http://dev.mysql.com/doc/mysql/en/key-cache-block-size.html for more details.

These blocks are kept in memory (inside a KEY_CACHE struct instance), and the KEY_CACHE keeps track of how "warm"[10] the index data is—for instance, how frequently the index data block is requested. After a time, cold index blocks are purged from the internal buffers. This is a sort of least recently used (LRU) strategy, but the key cache is smart enough to retain blocks that contain index data for the root B-tree levels.

The number of blocks available inside the KEY_CACHE's internal list of used blocks is controlled by the key_buffer_size configuration variable, which is set in multiples of the key cache block size.

The key cache is created the first time a MyISAM table is opened. The multi_key_cache_search() function (found in /mysys/mf_keycaches.c) is called during the storage engine's mi_open() function call.

When a user connection attempts to access index (key) data from the MyISAM table, the table's key cache is first checked to determine whether the needed index block is available in the key cache. If it is, the key cache returns the needed block from its internal buffers. If not, the block is read from the relevant .MYI file into the key cache for storage in memory. Subsequent requests for that index block will then come from the key cache, until that block is purged from the key cache because it is not used frequently enough.

Likewise, when changes to the key data are needed, the key cache first writes the changes to the internally buffered index block and marks it as dirty. If this dirty block is selected by the key cache for purging—meaning that it will be replaced by a more recently requested index block—that block is flushed to disk before being replaced. If the block is not dirty, it's simply thrown away in favor of the new block. Figure 4-2 shows the flow request between user connections and the key cache for requests involving MyISAM tables, along with the relevant function calls in /mysys/mf_keycache.c.

---

10. There is actually a BLOCK_TEMPERATURE variable, which places the block into warm or hot lists of blocks (enum BLOCK_TEMPERATURE { BLOCK_COLD, BLOCK_WARM , BLOCK_HOT }).

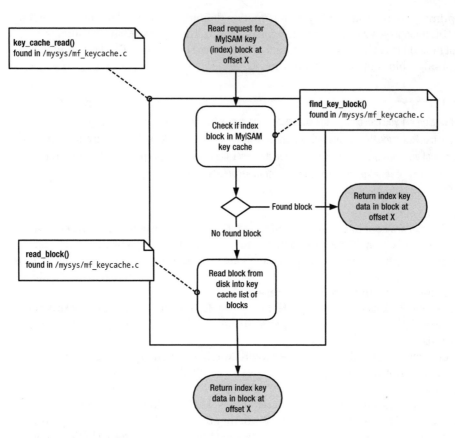

Figure 4-2. *The key cache*

You can monitor the server's usage of the key cache by reviewing the following server statistical variables:

- Key_blocks_used: This variable stores the number of index blocks currently contained in the key cache. This should be high, as the more blocks in the key cache, the less the server is using disk-based I/O to examine the index data.

- Key_read_requests: This variable stores the total number of times a request for index blocks has been received by the key cache, regardless of whether the key cache actually needed to read the block from disk.

- Key_reads: This variable stores the number of disk-based reads the key cache performed in order to get the requested index block.

- Key_write_requests: This variable stores the total number of times a write request was received by the key cache, regardless of whether the modifications (writes) of the key data were to disk. Remember that the key cache writes changes to the actual .MYI file only when the index block is deemed too cold to stay in the cache *and* it has been marked dirty by a modification.

- Key_writes: This variable stores the number of actual writes to disk.

Experts have recommended that the Key_reads to Key_read_requests and Key_writes to Key_write_requests should have, at a minimum, a 1:50–1:100 ratio.[11] If the ratio is lower than that, consider increasing the size of key_buffer_size and monitoring for improvements. You can review these variables by executing the following:

```
mysql> SHOW STATUS LIKE 'Key_%';
```

Table Cache

The table cache is implemented in /sql/sql_base.cc. This cache stores a special kind of structure that represents a MySQL table in a simple HASH structure. This hash, defined as a global variable called open_cache, stores a set of st_table structures, which are defined in /sql/table.h and /sql/table.cc.

Note For the implementation of the HASH struct, see /include/hash.h and /mysys/hash.c.

The st_table struct is a core data structure that represents the actual database table in memory. Listing 4-3 shows a small portion of the struct definition to give you an idea of what is contained in st_table.

Listing 4-3. *st_table Struct (Abridged)*

```
struct st_table {
  handler *file;
  Field **field;            /* Pointer to fields */
  Field_blob **blob_field;    /* Pointer to blob fields */
  /* hash of field names (contains pointers to elements of field array) */
  HASH name_hash;
  byte *record[2];    /* Pointer to records */
  byte *default_values;      /* Default values for INSERT */
  byte *insert_values;        /* used by INSERT ... UPDATE */
  uint fields;    /* field count */
  uint reclength;    /* Recordlength */
// omitted…
  struct st_table *next,*prev;
};
```

The st_table struct fulfills a variety of purposes, but its primary focus is to provide other objects (like the user connection THD objects and the handler objects) with a mechanism to find out meta information about the table's structure. You can see that some of st_table's member variables look familiar: fields, records, default values for inserts, a length of records, and a count of the number of fields. All these member variables provide the THD and other consuming classes with information about the structure of the underlying table source.

---

11. Jeremy Zawodny and Derrek Bailing, *High Performance MySQL* (O'Reilly, 2004), p 242.

This struct also serves to provide a method of linking the storage engine to the table, so that the THD objects may call on the storage engine to execute requests involving the table. Thus, one of the member variables (*file) of the st_table struct is a pointer to the storage engine (handler subclass), which handles the actual reading and writing of records in the table and indexes associated with it. Note that the developers named the member variable for the handler as file, bringing us to an important point: the handler represents a link for this in-memory table structure to the physical storage managed by the storage engine (handler). This is why you will sometimes hear some folks refer to the number of open *file descriptors* in the system. The handler class pointer represents this physical file-based link.

The st_table struct is implemented as a linked list, allowing for the creation of a list of used tables during executions of statements involving multiple tables, facilitating their navigation using the next and prev pointers. The table cache is a hash structure of these st_table structs. Each of these structs represents an in-memory representation of a table schema. If the handler member variable of the st_table is an ha_myisam (MyISAM's storage engine handler subclass), that means that the .frm file has been read from disk and its information dumped into the st_table struct. The task of initializing the st_table struct with the information from the .frm file is relatively expensive, and so MySQL caches these st_table structs in the table cache for use by the THD objects executing queries.

■**Note** Remember that the key cache stores index blocks from the .MYI files, and the table cache stores st_table structs representing the .frm files. Both caches serve to minimize the amount of disk-based activity needed to open, read, and close those files.

It is very important to understand that the table cache does not share cached st_table structs *between* user connection threads. The reason for this is that if a number of concurrently executing threads are executing statements against a table whose schema may change, it would be possible for one thread to change the schema (the .frm file) while another thread is relying on that schema. To avoid these issues, MySQL ensures that each concurrent thread has its own set of st_table structs in the table cache. This feature has confounded some MySQL users in the past when they issue a request like the following:

```
mysql> SHOW STATUS LIKE 'Open_%';
```

and see a result like this:

```
+---------------+-------+
| Variable_name | Value |
+---------------+-------+
| Open_tables   | 200   |
| Open_files    | 315   |
| Open_streams  | 0     |
| Opened_tables | 216   |
+---------------+-------+
4 rows in set (0.03 sec)
```

knowing that they have only ten tables in their database.

The reason for the apparently mismatched open table numbers is that MySQL opens a new `st_table` struct for each concurrent connection. For each opened table, MySQL actually needs two file descriptors (pointers to files on disk): one for the `.frm` file and another for the `.MYD` file. The `.MYI` file is shared among all threads, using the key cache. But just like the key cache, the table cache has only a certain amount of space, meaning that a certain number of `st_table` structs will fit in there. The default is 64, but this is modifiable using the `table_cache` configuration variable. As with the key cache, MySQL provides some monitoring variables for you to use in assessing whether the size of your table cache is sufficient:

- `Open_tables`: This variable stores the number of table schemas opened by all storage engines for all concurrent threads.

- `Open_files`: This variable stores the number of actual file descriptors currently opened by the server, for all storage engines.

- `Open_streams`: This will be zero unless logging is enabled for the server.

- `Opened_tables`: This variable stores the total number of table schemas that have been opened since the server started, across all concurrent threads.

If the `Opened_tables` status variable is substantially higher than the `Open_tables` status variable, you may want to increase the `table_cache` configuration variable. However, be aware of some of the limitations presented by your operating system for file descriptor use. See the MySQL manual for some gotchas: `http://dev.mysql.com/doc/mysql/en/table-cache.html`.

■**Caution** There is some evidence in the MySQL source code comments that the table cache is being redesigned. For future versions of MySQL, check the changelog to see if this is indeed the case. See the code comments in the `sql/sql_cache.cc` for more details.

Hostname Cache

The hostname cache serves to facilitate the quick lookup of hostnames. This cache is particularly useful on servers that have slow DNS servers, resulting in time-consuming repeated lookups. Its implementation is available in `/sql/hostname.cc`, with the following globally available variable declaration:

```
static hash_filo *hostname_cache;
```

As is implied by its name, `hostname_cache` is a first-in/last-out (FILO) hash structure. `/sql/hostname.cc` contains a number of functions that initialize, add to, and remove items from the cache. `hostname_cache_init()`, `add_hostname()`, and `ip_to_hostname()` are some of the functions you'll find in this file.

Privilege Cache

MySQL keeps a cache of the privilege (grant) information for user accounts in a separate cache. This cache is commonly called an *ACL*, for *access control list*. The definition and implementation of the ACL can be found in `/sql/sql_acl.h` and `/sql/sql_acl.cc`. These files define a number of key classes and structs used throughout the user access and grant management system, which we'll cover in the "Access and Grant Management" section later in this chapter.

The privilege cache is implemented in a similar fashion to the hostname cache, as a FILO hash (see /sql/sql_acl.cc):

```
static hash_filo *acl_cache;
```

acl_cache is initialized in the acl_init() function, which is responsible for reading the contents of the mysql user and grant tables (mysql.user, mysql.db, mysql.tables_priv, and mysql.columns_priv) and loading the record data into the acl_cache hash. The most interesting part of the function is the sorting process that takes place. The sorting of the entries as they are inserted into the cache is important, as explained in Chapter 15. You may want to take a look at acl_init() after you've read that chapter.

Other Caches

MySQL employs other caches internally for specialized uses in query execution and optimization. For instance, the heap table cache is used when SELECT...GROUP BY or DISTINCT statements find all the rows in a MEMORY storage engine table. The join buffer cache is used when one or more tables in a SELECT statement cannot be joined in anything other than a FULL JOIN, meaning that all the rows in the table must be joined to the results of all other joined table results. This operation is expensive, and so a buffer (cache) is created to speed the returning of result sets. We'll cover JOIN queries in great detail in Chapter 7.

Network Management and Communication

The network management and communication system is a low-level subsystem that handles the work of sending and receiving network packets containing MySQL connection requests and commands across a variety of platforms. The subsystem makes the various communication protocols, such as TCP/IP or Named Pipes, transparent for the connection thread. In this way, it releases the query engine from the responsibility of interpreting the various protocol packet headers in different ways. All the query engine needs to know is that it will receive from the network and connection management subsystem a standard data structure that complies with an API.

The network and connection management function library can be found in the files listed in Table 4-4.

Table 4-4. *Network and Connection Management Subsystem Files*

File	Contents
/sql/net_pkg.cc	The client/server network layer API and protocol for communications between the client and server
/include/mysql_com.h	Definitions for common structs used in the communication between the client and server
/include/my_net.h	Addresses some portability and thread-safe issues for various networking functions

The main struct used in client/server communications is the st_net struct, aliased as NET. This struct is defined in /include/mysql_com.h. The definition for NET is shown in Listing 4-4.

Listing 4-4. *st_net Struct Definition*

```
typedef struct st_net {
  Vio* vio;
  unsigned char *buff,*buff_end,*write_pos,*read_pos;
  my_socket fd;     /* For Perl DBI/dbd */
  unsigned long max_packet,max_packet_size;
  unsigned int pkt_nr,compress_pkt_nr;
  unsigned int write_timeout, read_timeout, retry_count;
  int fcntl;
  my_bool compress;
  /*
    The following variable is set if we are doing several queries in one
    command ( as in LOAD TABLE ... FROM MASTER ),
    and do not want to confuse the client with OK at the wrong time
  */
  unsigned long remain_in_buf,length, buf_length, where_b;
  unsigned int *return_status;
  unsigned char reading_or_writing;
  char save_char;
  my_bool no_send_ok;  /* For SPs and other things that do multiple stmts */
  my_bool no_send_eof; /* For SPs' first version read-only cursors */
  /*
    Pointer to query object in query cache, do not equal NULL (0) for
    queries in cache that have not stored its results yet
  */
  char last_error[MYSQL_ERRMSG_SIZE], sqlstate[SQLSTATE_LENGTH+1];
  unsigned int last_errno;
  unsigned char error;
  gptr query_cache_query;
  my_bool report_error; /* We should report error (we have unreported error) */
  my_bool return_errno;
} NET;
```

The NET struct is used in client/server communications as a handler for the communication protocol. The buff member variable of NET is filled with a packet by either the server or client. These packets, like all packets used in communications protocols, follow a rigid format, containing a fixed header and the packet data.

Different packet types are sent for the various legs of the trip between the client and server. The legs of the trip correspond to the diagram in Figure 4-3, which shows the communication between the client and server.

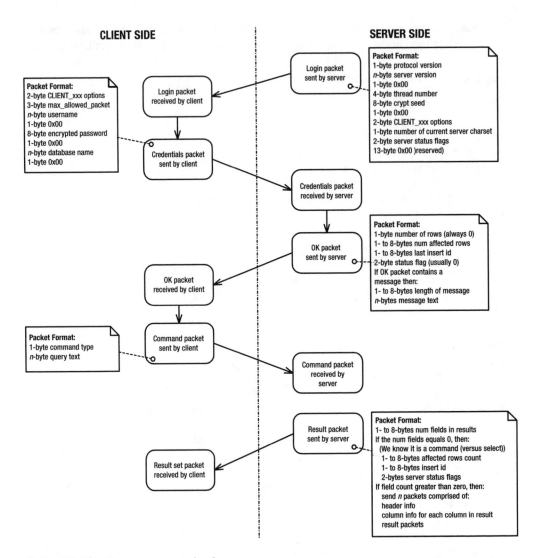

Figure 4-3. *Client/server communication*

In Figure 4-3, we've included some basic notation of the packet formats used by the various legs of the communication trip. Most are self-explanatory. The result packets have a standard header, described in the protocol, which the client uses to obtain information about how many result packets will be received to get all the information back from the server.

The following functions actually move the packets into the NET buffer:

- my_net_write(): This function stores a packet to be sent in the NET->buff member variable.

- net_flush(): This function sends the packet stored in the NET->buff member variable.

- `net_write_command()`: This function sends a command packet (1 byte; see Figure 4-3) from the client to the server.

- `my_net_read()`: This function reads a packet in the `NET` struct.

These functions can be found in the `/sql/net_serv.cc` source file. They are used by the various client and server communication functions (like `mysql_real_connect()`, found in `/libmysql/libmysql.c` in the C client API). Table 4-5 lists some other functions that operate with the `NET` struct and send packets to and from the server.

Table 4-5. *Some Functions That Send and Receive Network Packets*

Function	File	Purpose
`mysql_real_connect()`	`/libmysql/client.c`	Connects to the `mysqld` server. Look for the `CLI_MYSQL_REAL_CONNECT` function, which handles the connection from the client to the server.
`mysql_real_query()`	`/libmysql/client.c`	Sends a query to the server and reads the OK packet or columns header returned from the server. The packet returned depends on whether the query was a command or a resultset returning `SHOW` or `SELECT`.
`mysql_store_result()`	`/libmysql/client.c`	Takes a resultset sent from the server entirely into client-side memory by reading all sent packets definitions
various	`/include/mysql.h`	Contains some useful definitions of the structs used by the client API, namely `MYSQL` and `MYSQL_RES`, which represent the MySQL client session and results returned in it.

■**Note** The `internals.texi` documentation thoroughly explains the client/server communications protocol. Some of the file references, however, are a little out-of-date for version 5.0.2's source distribution. The directories and filenames in Table 4-5 are correct, however, and should enable you to investigate this subsystem yourself.

Access and Grant Management

A separate set of functions exists solely for the purpose of checking the validity of incoming connection requests and privilege queries. The access and grant management subsystem defines all the GRANTs needed to execute a given command (see Chapter 15) and has a set of functions that query and modify the in-memory versions of the grant tables, as well as some utility functions for password generation and the like. The bulk of the subsystem is contained in the `/sql/sql_acl.cc` file of the source tree. Definitions are available in `/sql/sql_acl.h`, and the implementation is in `/sql/sql_acl.cc`. You will find all the actual GRANT constants defined at the top of `/sql/sql_acl.h`, as shown in Listing 4-5.

Listing 4-5. *Constants Defined in sql_acl.h*

```
#define SELECT_ACL      (1L << 0)
#define INSERT_ACL      (1L << 1)
#define UPDATE_ACL      (1L << 2)
#define DELETE_ACL      (1L << 3)
#define CREATE_ACL      (1L << 4)
#define DROP_ACL      (1L << 5)
#define RELOAD_ACL      (1L << 6)
#define SHUTDOWN_ACL      (1L << 7)
#define PROCESS_ACL      (1L << 8)
#define FILE_ACL      (1L << 9)
#define GRANT_ACL      (1L << 10)
#define REFERENCES_ACL      (1L << 11)
#define INDEX_ACL      (1L << 12)
#define ALTER_ACL      (1L << 13)
#define SHOW_DB_ACL      (1L << 14)
#define SUPER_ACL      (1L << 15)
#define CREATE_TMP_ACL      (1L << 16)
#define LOCK_TABLES_ACL      (1L << 17)
#define EXECUTE_ACL      (1L << 18)
#define REPL_SLAVE_ACL      (1L << 19)
#define REPL_CLIENT_ACL      (1L << 20)
#define CREATE_VIEW_ACL      (1L << 21)
#define SHOW_VIEW_ACL      (1L << 22)
```

These constants are used in the ACL functions to compare user and hostname privileges. The << operator is bit-shifting a long integer one byte to the left and defining the named constant as the resulting power of 2. In the source code, these constants are compared using Boolean operators in order to determine if the user has appropriate privileges to access a resource. If a user is requesting access to a resource that requires more than one privilege, these constants are ANDed together and compared to the user's own access integer, which represents all the privileges the user has been granted.

We won't go into too much depth here, because Chapter 15 covers the ACL in detail, but Table 4-6 shows a list of functions in this library.

Table 4-6. *Selected Functions in the Access Control Subsystem*

Function	Purpose
acl_get()	Returns the privileges available for a user, host, and database combination (database privileges).
check_grant()	Determines whether a user thread THD's user has appropriate permissions on all tables used by the requested statement on the thread.
check_grant_column()	Same as check_grant(), but on a specific column.
check_grant_all_columns()	Checks all columns needed in a user thread's field list.
mysql_create_user()	Creates one or a list of users; called when a command received over a user thread creates users, such as GRANT ALL ON *.* ➡ TO 'jpipes'@'localhost', 'mkruck'@'localhost'.

Feel free to roam around the access control function library and get a feel for these core functions that handle the security between the client and server.

Log Management

In one of the more fully encapsulated subsystems, the log management subsystem implements an inheritance design whereby a variety of *log event* subclasses are consumed by a *log* class. Similar to the strategy deployed for storage engine abstraction, this strategy allows the MySQL developers to add different logs and log events as needed, without breaking the subsystem's core functionality.

The main log class, MYSQL_LOG, is shown in Listing 4-6 (we've stripped out some material for brevity and highlighted the member variables and methods).

Listing 4-6. *MYSQL_LOG Class Definition*

```
class MYSQL_LOG
 {
 private:
  /* LOCK_log and LOCK_index are inited by init_pthread_objects() */
  pthread_mutex_t LOCK_log, LOCK_index;
  // ... omitted
  IO_CACHE log_file;
  // ... omitted
  volatile enum_log_type log_type;
  // ... omitted
 public:
  MYSQL_LOG();
  ~MYSQL_LOG();
  // ... omitted
  void set_max_size(ulong max_size_arg);
  void signal_update();
  void wait_for_update(THD* thd, bool master_or_slave);
  void set_need_start_event() { need_start_event = 1; }
  void init(enum_log_type log_type_arg,
        enum cache_type io_cache_type_arg,
        bool no_auto_events_arg, ulong max_size);
  void init_pthread_objects();
  void cleanup();
  bool open(const char *log_name,enum_log_type log_type,
        const char *new_name, const char *index_file_name_arg,
        enum cache_type io_cache_type_arg,
        bool no_auto_events_arg, ulong max_size,
          bool null_created);
  void new_file(bool need_lock= 1);
  bool write(THD *thd, enum enum_server_command command,
        const char *format,...);
  bool write(THD *thd, const char *query, uint query_length,
        time_t query_start=0);
```

```
    bool write(Log_event* event_info); // binary log write
    bool write(THD *thd, IO_CACHE *cache, bool commit_or_rollback);
    /*
      v stands for vector
      invoked as appendv(buf1,len1,buf2,len2,...,bufn,lenn,0)
    */
    bool appendv(const char* buf,uint len,...);
    bool append(Log_event* ev);
    // ... omitted
    int purge_logs(const char *to_log, bool included,
                   bool need_mutex, bool need_update_threads,
                   ulonglong *decrease_log_space);
    int purge_logs_before_date(time_t purge_time);
    // ... omitted
    void close(uint exiting);
    // ... omitted
    void report_pos_in_innodb();
    // iterating through the log index file
    int find_log_pos(LOG_INFO* linfo, const char* log_name,
           bool need_mutex);
    int find_next_log(LOG_INFO* linfo, bool need_mutex);
    int get_current_log(LOG_INFO* linfo);
    // ... omitted
};
```

This is a fairly standard definition for a logging class. You'll notice the various member methods correspond to things that the log must do: open, append stuff, purge records from itself, and find positions inside itself. Note that the log_file member variable is of type IO_CACHE. You may recall from our earlier discussion of the record cache that the IO_CACHE can be used for writing as well as reading. This is an example of how the MYSQL_LOG class uses the IO_CACHE structure for exactly that.

Three global variables of type MYSQL_LOG are created in /sql/mysql_priv.h to contain the three logs available in global scope:

```
extern MYSQL_LOG mysql_log,mysql_slow_log,mysql_bin_log;
```

During server startup, a function called init_server_components(), found in /sql/mysqld.cc, actually initializes any needed logs based on the server's configuration. For instance, if the server is running with the binary log enabled, then the mysql_bin_log global MYSQL_LOG instance is initialized and opened. It is also checked for consistency and used in recovery, if necessary. The function open_log(), also found in /sql/mysqld.cc, does the job of actually opening a log file and constructing a MYSQL_LOG object.

Also notice that a number of the member methods accept arguments of type `Log_event`, namely `write()` and `append()`. The `Log_event` class represents an event that is written to a `MYSQL_LOG` object. `Log_event` is a base (abstract) class, just like `handler` is for the storage engines, and a number of subclasses derive from it. Each of the subclasses corresponds to a specific event and contains information on *how* the event should be recorded (written) to the logs. Here are some of the `Log_event` subclasses:

- `Query_log_event`: This subclass logs when SQL queries are executed.

- `Load_log_event`: This subclass logs when the logs are loaded.

- `Intvar_log_event`: This subclass logs special variables, such as `auto_increment` values.

- `User_var_log_event`: This subclass logs when a user variable is set. This event is recorded *before* the `Query_log_event`, which actually sets the variable.

The log management subsystem can be found in the source files listed in Table 4-7. The definitions for the main log class (`MYSQL_LOG`) can be found in `/sql/sql_class.h`, so don't look for a `log.h` file. There isn't one. Developer's comments note that there are plans to move log-specific definitions into their own header file at some later date.

Table 4-7. *Log Management Source Files*

File	Contents
`/sql/sql_class.h`	The definition of the `MYSQL_LOG` class
`/sql/log_event.h`	Definitions of the various `Log_event` class and subclasses
`/sql/log_event.cc`	The implementation of `Log_event` subclasses
`/sql/log.cc`	The implementation of the `MYSQL_LOG` class
`/sql/ha_innodb.h`	The InnoDB-specific log implementation (covered in the next chapter)

Note that this separation of the logging subsystem allows for a variety of system activities—from startup, to multistatement transactions, to auto-increment value changes—to be logged via the subclass implementations of the `Log_event::write()` method. For instance, the `Intvar_log_event` subclass handles the logging of `AUTO_INCREMENT` values and partly implements its logging in the `Intvar_log_event::write()` method.

Query Parsing, Optimization, and Execution

You can consider the query parsing, optimization, and execution subsystem to be the brains behind the MySQL database server. It is responsible for taking the commands brought in on the user's thread and deconstructing the requested statements into a variety of data structures that the database server then uses to determine the best path to execute the requested statement.

Parsing

This process of deconstruction is called *parsing*, and the end result is sometimes referred to as an *abstract syntax tree*. MySQL's parser was actually generated from a program called Bison.[12] Bison generates the parser using a tool called YACC, which stands for Yet Another Compiler Compiler. YACC accepts a stream of rules. These rules consist of a regular expression and a snippet of C code designed to handle any matches made by the regular expression. YACC then produces an executable that can take an input stream and "cut it up" by matching on regular expressions. It then executes the C code paired with each regular expression in the order in which it matches the regular expression.[13] Bison is a complex program that uses the YACC compiler to generate a parser for a specific set of symbols, which form the *lexicon* of the parsable language.

Tip If you're interested in more information about YACC, Bison, and Lex, see `http://dinosaur.compilertools.net/`.

The MySQL query engine uses this Bison-generated parser to do the grunt work of cutting up the incoming command. This step of parsing not only standardizes the query into a tree-like request for tables and joins, but it also acts as an in-code representation of what the request needs in order to be fulfilled. This in-code representation of a query is a struct called Lex. Its definition is available in `/sql/sql_lex.h`. Each user thread object (THD) has a Lex member variable, which stores the *state* of the parsing.

As parsing of the query begins, the Lex struct fills out, so that as the parsing process executes, the Lex struct is filled with an increasing amount of information about the items used in the query. The Lex struct contains member variables to store lists of tables used by the query, fields used in the query, joins needed by the query, and so on. As the parser operates over the query statements and determines which items are needed by the query, the Lex struct is updated to reflect the needed items. So, on completion of the parsing, the Lex struct contains a sort of road map to get at the data. This road map includes the various objects of interest to the query. Some of Lex's notable member variables include the following:

- `table_list` and `group_list` are lists of tables used in the FROM and GROUP BY clauses.

- `top_join_list` is a list of tables for the top-level join.

- `order_list` is a list of tables in the ORDER BY clause.

- `where` and `having` are variables of type Item that correspond to the WHERE and HAVING clauses.

- `select_limit` and `offset_limit` are used in the LIMIT clause.

---

12. Bison was originally written by Richard Stallman.

13. The order of matching a regular expression is not necessarily the order in which a particular word appears in the input stream.

■**Tip** At the top of `/sql/sql_lex.h`, you will see an enumeration of all of the different SQL commands that may be issued across a user connection. This enumeration is used throughout the parsing and execution process to describe the activity occurring.

In order to properly understand what's stored in the `Lex` struct, you'll need to investigate the definitions of classes and structs defined in the files listed in Table 4-8. Each of these files represents the core units of the SQL query execution engine.

Table 4-8. *Core Classes Used in SQL Query Execution and Parsing*

File	Contents
`/sql/field.h` and `/sql/field.cc`	Definition and implementation of the `Field` class
`/sql/item.h` and `/sql/item.cc`	Definition and implementation of the `Item` class
`/sql/item_XXX.h` and `/sql/item_XXX.cc`	Definition and implementation of the specialized `Item_` classes used to represent various objects in database; for instance, `Item_row` and `Item_subselect`
`/sql/sql_class.h` and `/sql/sql_class.cc`	Definition and implementation of the various generic classes and `THD`

The different `Item_XXX` files implement the various components of the SQL language: its operators, expressions, functions, rows, fields, and so on.

At its source, the parser uses a table of symbols that correspond to the parts of a query or command. This symbol table can be found in `/sql/lex.h`, `/sql/lex_symbol.h`, and `/sql/lex_hash.h`. The symbols are really just the keywords supported by MySQL, including ANSI standard SQL and all of the extended functions usable in MySQL queries. These symbols make up the lexicon of the query engine; the symbols are the query engine's alphabet of sorts.

Don't confuse the files in `/sql/lex*` with the `Lex` class. They're not the same. The `/sql/lex*` files contain the symbol tables that act as tokens for the parser to deconstruct the incoming SQL statement into machine-readable structures, which are then passed on to the optimization processes.

You may view the MySQL-generated parser in `/sql/sql_yacc.cc`. Have fun. It's obscenely complex. The meat of the parser begins on line 11676 of that file, where the yyn variable is checked and a gigantic `switch` statement begins. The yyn variable represents the currently parsed symbol number. Looking at the source file for the parser will probably result in a mind melt. For fun, we've listed some of the files that implement the parsing functionality in Table 4-9.

Table 4-9. *Parsing and Lexical Generation Implementation Files*

File	Contents
/sql/lex.h	The base symbol table for parsing.
/sql/lex_symbol.h	Some more type definitions for the symbol table.
/sql/lex_hash.h	A mapping of symbols to functions.
/sql/sql_lex.h	The definition of the Lex class and other parsing structs.
/sql/sql_lex.cc	The implementation of the Lex class.
/sql/sql_yacc.h	Definitions used in the parser.
/sql/sql_yacc.cc	The Bison-generated parser implementation
/sql/sql_parse.cc	Ties in all the different pieces and parts of the parser, along with a huge library of functions used in the query parsing and execution stages.

Optimization

Much of the optimization of the query engine comes from the ability of this subsystem to "explain away" parts of a query, and to find the most efficient way of organizing how and in which order separate data sets are retrieved and merged or filtered. We'll go into the details of the optimization process in Chapters 6 and 7, so stay tuned. Table 4-10 shows a list of the main files used in the optimization system.

Table 4-10. *Files Used in the Optimization System*

File	Contents
/sql/sql_select.h	Definitions for classes and structs used in the SELECT statements, and thus, classes used in the optimization process
/sql/sql_select.cc	The implementation of the SELECT statement and optimization system
/sql/opt_range.h and /sql/opt_range.cc	The definition and implementation of range query optimization routines
/sql/opt_sum.cc	The implementation of aggregation optimization (MIN/MAX/GROUP BY)

For the most part, optimization of SQL queries is needed only for SELECT statements, so it is natural that most of the optimization work is done in /sql/sql_select.cc. This file uses the structs defined in /sql/sql_select.h. This header file contains the definitions for some of the most widely used classes and structs in the optimization process: JOIN, JOIN_TAB, and JOIN_CACHE. The bulk of the optimization work is done in the JOIN::optimize() member method. This complex member method makes heavy use of the Lex struct available in the user thread (THD) and the corresponding road map into the SQL request it contains.

JOIN::optimize() focuses its effort on "optimizing away" parts of the query execution by eliminating redundant WHERE conditions and manipulating the FROM and JOIN table lists into the smoothest possible order of tables. It executes a series of subroutines that attempt to optimize each and every piece of the JOIN conditions and WHERE clause.

Execution

Once the path for execution has been optimized as much as possible, the SQL commands must be executed by the *statement execution unit*. The statement execution unit is the function responsible for handling the execution of the appropriate SQL command. For instance, the statement execution unit for the SQL INSERT commands is `mysql_insert()`, which is found in `/sql/sql_insert.cc`. Similarly, the SELECT statement execution unit is `mysql_select()`, housed in `/sql/sql_select.cc`. These base functions all have a pointer to a THD object as their first parameter. This pointer is used to send the packets of result data back to the client. Take a look at the execution units to get a feel for how they operate.

The Query Cache

The query cache is not a subsystem, per se, but a wholly separate set of classes that actually do function as a component. Its implementation and documentation are noticeably different from other subsystems, and its design follows a cleaner, more component-oriented approach than most of the rest of the system code.[14] We'll take a few moments to look at its implementation and where you can view the source and explore it for yourself.

The purpose of the query cache is not just to cache the SQL commands executed on the server, but also to store the actual results of those commands. This special ability is, as far as we know, unique to MySQL. Its addition to the MySQL source distribution, as of version 4.0.1, greatly improves MySQL's already impressive performance. We'll take a look at how the query cache can be used. Right now, we'll focus on the internals.

The query cache is a single class, `Query_cache`, defined in `/sql/sql_cache.h` and implemented in `/sql/sql_cache.cc`. It is composed of the following:

- Memory pool, which is a cache of memory blocks (`cache` member variable) used to store the results of queries

- Hash table of queries (`queries` member variable)

- Hash table of tables (`tables` member variable)

- Linked lists of all the blocks used for storing queries, tables, and the root block

The memory pool (`cache` member variable) contains a directory of both the allocated (used) memory blocks and the free blocks, as well as all the actual blocks of data. In the source documentation, you'll see this directory structure referred to as *memory bins*, which accurately reflects the directory's hash-based structure.

A memory block is a specially defined allocation of the query cache's resources. It is not an index block or a block on disk. Each memory block follows the same basic structure. It has a header, represented by the `Query_cache_block` struct, shown in Listing 4-7 (some sections are omitted for brevity).

---

14. This may be due to a different developer or developers working on the code than in other parts of the source code, or simply a change of approach over time taken by the development team.

Listing 4-7. *Query_cache_block Struct Definition (Abridged)*

```
struct Query_cache_block
{
    enum block_type {FREE, QUERY, RESULT, RES_CONT, RES_BEG,
            RES_INCOMPLETE, TABLE, INCOMPLETE};
    ulong length;                  // length of all block
    ulong used;                    // length of data
    // ... omitted
    Query_cache_block *pnext,*pprev,    // physical next/previous block
            *next,*prev;           // logical next/previous block
    block_type type;
    TABLE_COUNTER_TYPE n_tables;        // number of tables in query
    // ... omitted
};
```

As you can see, it's a simple header struct that contains a block type (type), which is one of the enum values defined as block_type. Additionally, there is a length of the whole block and the length of the block used for data. Other than that, this struct is a simple doubly linked list of other Query_cache_block structs. In this way, the Query_cache.cache contains a chain of these Query_cache_block structs, each containing different types of data.

When user thread (THD) objects attempt to fulfill a statement request, the Query_cache is first asked to see if it contains an identical query as the one in the THD. If it does, the Query_cache uses the send_result_to_client() member method to return the result in its memory pool to the client THD. If not, it tries to register the new query using the store_query() member method.

The rest of the Query_cache implementation, found in /sql/sql_cache.cc, is concerned with managing the freshness of the memory pool and invalidating stored blocks when a modification is made to the underlying data source. This invalidation process happens when an UPDATE or DELETE statement occurs on the tables connected to the query result stored in the block. Because a list of tables is associated with each query result block (look for the Query_cache_result struct in /sql/sql_cache.h), it is a trivial matter for the Query_cache to look up which blocks are invalidated by a change to a specific table's data.

A Typical Query Execution

In this section, we're going to explore the code execution of a typical user connection that issues a typical SELECT statement against the database server. This should give you a good picture of how the different subsystems work with each other to complete a request. The code snippets we'll walk through will be trimmed down, stripped editions of the actual source code. We'll highlight the sections of the code to which you should pay the closest attention.

For this exercise, we assume that the issued statement is a simple SELECT * FROM ➥ some_table WHERE field_x = 200, where some_table is a MyISAM table. This is important, because, as you'll see, the MyISAM storage engine will actually execute the code for the request through the storage engine abstraction layer.

We'll begin our journey at the starting point of the MySQL server, in the main() routine of /sql/mysqld.cc, as shown in Listing 4-8.

Listing 4-8. */sql/mysqld.cc main()*

```
int main(int argc, char **argv)
{
  init_common_variables(MYSQL_CONFIG_NAME,
                  argc, argv, load_default_groups);
  init_ssl();
  server_init();
  init_server_components();
  start_signal_handler();                  // Creates pidfile
  acl_init((THD *)0, opt_noacl);
  init_slave();
  create_shutdown_thread();
  create_maintenance_thread();
  handle_connections_sockets(0);
  DBUG_PRINT("quit",("Exiting main thread"));
  exit(0);
}
```

This is where the main server process execution begins. We've highlighted some of the more interesting sections. init_common_variables() works with the command-line arguments used on executing mysqld or mysqld_safe, along with the MySQL configuration files. We've gone over some of what init_server_components() and acl_init() do in this chapter. Basically, init_server_components() makes sure the MYSQL_LOG objects are online and working, and acl_init() gets the access control system up and running, including getting the privilege cache into memory. When we discussed the thread and resource management subsystem, we mentioned that a separate thread is created to handle maintenance tasks and also to handle shutdown events. create_maintenance_thread() and create_shutdown_thread() accomplish getting these threads up and running.

The handle_connections_sockets() function is where things start to really get going. Remember from our discussion of the thread and resource management subsystem that a thread is created for each incoming connection request, and that a separate thread is in charge of monitoring those connection threads?[15] Well, this is where it happens. Let's take a look in Listing 4-9.

---

15. A thread might be taken from the connection thread pool, instead of being created.

Listing 4-9. */sql/mysqld.cc handle_connections_sockets()*

```
handle_connections_sockets(arg attribute((unused)))
{
  if (ip_sock != INVALID_SOCKET)
  {
    FD_SET(ip_sock,&clientFDs);
    DBUG_PRINT("general",("Waiting for connections."));
    while (!abort_loop)
    {
        new_sock = accept(sock, my_reinterpret_cast(struct sockaddr *)
            (&cAddr), &length);
        thd= new THD;
        if (sock == unix_sock)
            thd->host=(char*) my_localhost;
        create_new_thread(thd);
    }
  }
}
```

The basic idea is that the mysql.sock socket is tapped for listening, and listening begins on the socket. While the listening is occurring on the port, if a connection request is received, a new THD struct is created and passed to the create_new_thread() function. The if (sock==unix_sock) checks to see if the socket is a Unix socket. If so, it defaults the THD->host member variable to be localhost. Let's check out what create_new_thread() does, in Listing 4-10.

Listing 4-10. */sql/mysqld.cc create_new_thread()*

```
static void create_new_thread(THD *thd)
{
  DBUG_ENTER("create_new_thread");
  /* don't allow too many connections */
  if (thread_count - delayed_insert_threads >= max_connections+1 || abort_loop)
  {
    DBUG_PRINT("error",("Too many connections"));
    close_connection(thd, ER_CON_COUNT_ERROR, 1);
    delete thd;
    DBUG_VOID_RETURN;
  }
  pthread_mutex_lock(&LOCK_thread_count);
  if (cached_thread_count > wake_thread)
  {
    start_cached_thread(thd);
  }
  else
  {
```

```
    thread_count++;
    thread_created++;
    if (thread_count-delayed_insert_threads > max_used_connections)
      max_used_connections=thread_count-delayed_insert_threads;
    DBUG_PRINT("info",(("creating thread %d"), thd->thread_id));
    pthread_create(&thd->real_id,&connection_attrib, \
handle_one_connection, (void*) thd))
      (void) pthread_mutex_unlock(&LOCK_thread_count);
  }
  DBUG_PRINT("info",("Thread created"));
}
```

In this function, we've highlighted some important activity. You see firsthand how the resource subsystem locks the LOCK_thread_count resource using pthread_mutex_lock(). This is crucial, since the thread_count and thread_created variables are modified (incremented) during the function's execution. thread_count and thread_created are global variables shared by all threads executing in the server process. The lock created by pthread_mutex_lock() prevents any other threads from modifying their contents while create_new_thread() executes. This is a great example of the work of the resource management subsystem.

Secondly, we highlighted start_cached_thread() to show you where the connection thread pooling mechanism kicks in. Lastly, and most important, pthread_create(), part of the thread function library, creates a new thread with the THD->real_id member variable and passes a function pointer for the handle_one_connection() function, which handles the creation of a single connection. This function is implemented in the parsing library, in /sql/sql_parse.cc, as shown in Listing 4-11.

Listing 4-11. */sql/sql_parse.cc handle_one_connection()*

```
handle_one_connection(THD *thd)
{
  while (!net->error && net->vio != 0 && !(thd->killed == THD::KILL_CONNECTION))
  {
    if (do_command(thd))
      break;
  }
}
```

We've removed most of this function's code for brevity. The rest of the function focuses on initializing the THD struct for the session. We highlighted two parts of the code listing within the function definition. First, we've made the net->error check bold to highlight the fact that the THD->net member variable struct is being used in the loop condition. This must mean that do_command() must be sending and receiving packets, right? net is simply a pointer to the THD->net member variable, which is the main structure for handling client/server communications, as we noted in the earlier section on the network subsystem. So, the main thing going on in handle_one_connection() is the call to do_command(), which we'll look at next in Listing 4-12.

Listing 4-12. /sql/sql_parse.cc do_command()

```
bool do_command(THD *thd)
{
  char *packet;
  ulong packet_length;
  NET *net;
  enum enum_server_command command;
  packet=0;
  net_new_transaction(net);
  packet_length=my_net_read(net);
  packet=(char*) net->read_pos;
  command = (enum enum_server_command) (uchar) packet[0];
  DBUG_RETURN(dispatch_command(command,thd, packet+1, (uint) packet_length));
}
```

Now we're really getting somewhere, eh? We've highlighted a bunch of items in do_command()
to remind you of topics we covered earlier in the chapter.

First, remember that packets are sent using the network subsystem's communication protocol. net_new_transaction() starts off the communication by initiating that first packet from the
server to the client (see Figure 4-3 for a refresher). The client uses the passed net struct and fills
the net's buffers with the packet sent back to the server. The call to my_net_read() returns the
length of the client's packet and fills the net->read_pos buffer with the packet string, which is
assigned to the packet variable. Voilá, the network subsystem in all its glory!

Second, we've highlighted the command variable. This variable is passed to the dispatch_
command() routine along with the THD pointer, the packet variable (containing our SQL statement), and the length of the statement. We've left the DBUG_RETURN() call in there to remind
you that do_command() returns 0 when the command requests succeed to the caller, handle_
one_connection(), which, as you'll recall, uses this return value to break out of the connection
wait loop in case the request failed.

Let's now take a look at dispatch_command(), in Listing 4-13.

Listing 4-13. /sql/sql_parse.cc dispatch_command()

```
bool dispatch_command(enum enum_server_command command, THD *thd,
              char* packet, uint packet_length)
{
  switch (command) {
      // ... omitted
  case COM_TABLE_DUMP:
  case COM_CHANGE_USER:
      // ... omitted
  case COM_QUERY:
  {
    if (alloc_query(thd, packet, packet_length))
      break;                    // fatal error is set
    mysql_log.write(thd,command,"%s",thd->query);
    mysql_parse(thd,thd->query, thd->query_length); .
```

```
  }
  // ... omitted
}
```

Just as the name of the function implies, all we're doing here is dispatching the query to the appropriate handler. In the `switch` statement, we get `case`'d into the `COM_QUERY` block, since we're executing a standard SQL query over the connection. The `alloc_query()` call simply pulls the packet string into the `THD->query` member variable and allocates some memory for use by the thread. Next, we use the `mysql_log` global `MYSQL_LOG` object to record our query, as is, in the log file using the log's `write()` member method. This is the General Query Log (see Chapter 6) simply recording the query which we've requested.

Finally, we come to the call to `mysql_parse()`. This is sort of a misnomer, because besides parsing the query, `mysql_parse()` actually executes the query as well, as shown in Listing 4-14.

Listing 4-14. */sql/sql_parse.cc mysql_parse()*

```
void mysql_parse(THD *thd, char *inBuf, uint length)
{
  if (query_cache_send_result_to_client(thd, inBuf, length) <= 0)
  {
    LEX *lex= thd->lex;
    yyparse((void *)thd);
    mysql_execute_command(thd);
    query_cache_end_of_result(thd);
  }
  DBUG_VOID_RETURN;
}
```

Here, the server first checks to see if the query cache contains an identical query request that it may use the results from instead of actually executing the command. If there is no hit on the query cache, then the THD is passed to `yyparse()` (the Bison-generated parser for MySQL) for parsing. This function fills the `THD->Lex` struct with the optimized road map we discussed earlier in the section about the query parsing subsystem. Once that is done, we go ahead and execute the command with `mysql_execute_command()`, which we'll look at in a second. Notice, though, that after the query is executed, the `query_cache_end_of_result()` function awaits. This function simply lets the query cache know that the user connection thread handler (thd) is finished processing any results. We'll see in a moment how the query cache actually stores the returned resultset.

Listing 4-15 shows the `mysql_execute_command()`.

Listing 4-15. */sql/sql_parse.cc mysql_execute_command()*

```
bool mysql_execute_command(THD *thd)
{
  all_tables= lex->query_tables;
  statistic_increment(thd->status_var.com_stat[lex->sql_command],
              &LOCK_status);
  switch (lex->sql_command) {
```

```
  case SQLCOM_SELECT:
  {

    select_result *result=lex->result;
    check_table_access(thd,
                    lex->exchange ? SELECT_ACL | FILE_ACL :
                    SELECT_ACL,
                    all_tables, 0);
    open_and_lock_tables(thd, all_tables);
    query_cache_store_query(thd, all_tables);
    res= handle_select(thd, lex, result);
    break;

  }
  case SQLCOM_PREPARE:
  case SQLCOM_EXECUTE:
// ...
  default:                      /* Impossible */
    send_ok(thd);
    break;

  }
}
```

In mysql_execute_command(), we see a number of interesting things going on. First, we highlighted the call to statistic_increment() to show you an example of how the server updates certain statistics. Here, the statistic is the com_stat variable for SELECT statements. Secondly, you see the access control subsystem interplay with the execution subsystem in the check_table_access() call. This checks that the user executing the query through THD has privileges to the list of tables used by the query.

Of special interest is the open_and_lock_tables() routine. We won't go into the code for it here, but this function establishes the table cache for the user connection thread and places any locks needed for any of the tables. Then we see query_cache_store_query(). Here, the query cache is storing the query text used in the request in its internal HASH of queries. And finally, there is the call to handle_select(), which is where we see the first major sign of the storage engine abstraction layer. handle_select() is implemented in /sql/sql_select.cc, as shown in Listing 4-16.

Listing 4-16. /sql/sql_select.cc handle_select()

```
bool handle_select(THD *thd, LEX *lex, select_result *result)
{
    res= mysql_select(thd, &select_lex->ref_pointer_array,
                (TABLE_LIST*) select_lex->table_list.first,
                select_lex->with_wild, select_lex->item_list,
                select_lex->where,
                select_lex->order_list.elements +
                select_lex->group_list.elements,
                (ORDER*) select_lex->order_list.first,
                (ORDER*) select_lex->group_list.first,
```

```
                select_lex->having,
                (ORDER*) lex->proc_list.first,
                select_lex->options | thd->options,
                result, unit, select_lex);
  DBUG_RETURN(res);
}
```

As you can see in Listing 4-17, handle_select() is nothing more than a wrapper for the statement execution unit, mysql_select(), also in the same file.

Listing 4-17. */sql/sql_select.cc mysql_select()*

```
bool mysql_select(THD *thd, Item ***rref_pointer_array,
        TABLE_LIST *tables, uint wild_num, List<Item> &fields,
        COND *conds, uint og_num,  ORDER *order, ORDER *group,
        Item *having, ORDER *proc_param, ulong select_options,
        select_result *result, SELECT_LEX_UNIT *unit,
        SELECT_LEX *select_lex)
{

  JOIN *join;
  join= new JOIN(thd, fields, select_options, result);
  join->prepare(rref_pointer_array, tables, wild_num,
              conds, og_num, order, group, having, proc_param,
              select_lex, unit));
  join->optimize();
  join->exec();
}
```

Well, it seems that mysql_select() has shrugged the responsibility of executing the SELECT statement off onto the shoulders of a JOIN object. We've highlighted the code sections in Listing 4-17 to show you where the optimization process occurs.

Now, let's move on to the JOIN::exec() implementation, in Listing 4-18.

Listing 4-18. */sql/sql_select.cc JOIN:exec()*

```
void JOIN::exec()
{
    error= do_select(curr_join, curr_fields_list, NULL, procedure);
    thd->limit_found_rows= curr_join->send_records;
    thd->examined_row_count= curr_join->examined_rows;
}
```

Oh, heck, it seems that we've run into another wrapper. JOIN::exec() simply calls the do_select() routine to do its dirty work. However, we do acknowledge that once do_select() returns, we have some information about record counts to populate some of the THD member variables. Let's take a look at do_select() in Listing 4-19. Maybe that function will be the answer.

Listing 4-19. */sql/sql_select.cc do_select()*

```
static int do_select(JOIN *join,List<Item> *fields,TABLE \
 *table,Procedure *procedure)
{
  JOIN_TAB *join_tab;
  sub_select(join,join_tab,0);
  join->result->send_eof())
}
```

This looks a little more promising. We see that `join` object's `result` member variable sends an end-of-file (EOF) marker after a call to another function called `sub_select()`, so we must be getting closer. From this behavior, it looks as though the `sub_select()` function should fill the `result` member variable of the `join` object with some records. Let's see whether we're right, in Listing 4-20.

Listing 4-20. */sql/sql_select.cc sub_select ()*

```
static int sub_select(JOIN *join,JOIN_TAB *join_tab,bool end_of_records)
{
    join_init_read_record(join_tab);
    READ_RECORD *info= &join_tab->read_record;

    join->thd->row_count= 0;
    do
    {
       join->examined_rows++;
       join->thd->row_count++;
    } while (info->read_record(info)));
  }
  return 0;
}
```

The key to the `sub_select()`[16] function is the do…while loop, which loops until a `READ_RECORD` struct variable (`info`) finishes calling its `read_record()` member method. Do you remember the record cache we covered earlier in this chapter? Does the `read_record()` function look familiar? You'll find out in a minute.

■Note The `READ_RECORD` struct is defined in `/sql/structs.h`. It represents a record in the MySQL internal format.

---

16. We've admittedly taken a few liberties in describing the `sub_select()` function here. The real `sub_select()` function is quite a bit more complicated than this. Some very advanced and complex C++ paradigms, such as recursion through function pointers, are used in the real `sub_select()` function. Additionally, we removed much of the logic involved in the JOIN operations, since, in our example, this wasn't needed. In short, we kept it simple, but the concept of the function is still the same.

But first, the join_init_read_record() function, shown in Listing 4-21, is our link (finally!) to the storage engine abstraction subsystem. The function initializes the records available in the JOIN_TAB structure and populates the read_record member variable with a READ_RECORD object. Doesn't look like much when we look at the implementation of join_init_read_ records(), does it?

Listing 4-21. */sql/sql_select.cc join_init_read_record()*

```
static int join_init_read_record(JOIN_TAB *tab)
{
  init_read_record(&tab->read_record, tab->join->thd, tab->table,
          tab->select,1,1);
  return (*tab->read_record.read_record)(&tab->read_record);
}
```

It seems that this simply calls the init_read_record() function, and then returns the record number read into the read_record member variable of tab. That's exactly what it is doing, so where do the storage engines and the record cache come into play? We thought you would never ask. Take a look at init_read_record() in Listing 4-22. It is found in /sql/records.cc (sound familiar?).

Listing 4-22. */sql/records.cc init_read_record ()*

```
void init_read_record(READ_RECORD *info,THD *thd, TABLE *table,
            SQL_SELECT *select,
            int use_record_cache, bool print_error)
{
    info->read_record=rr_sequential;
    table->file->ha_rnd_init(1);
}
```

Two important things are happening here. First, the info pointer to a READ_RECORD variable (passed in the arguments of init_read_records()) has had its read_record member variable changed to rr_sequential. rr_sequential is a function pointer, and setting this means that subsequent calls to info->read_record() will be translated into rr_sequential(READ_RECORD ➥ *info), which uses the record cache to retrieve data. We'll look at that function in a second. For now, just remember that all those calls to read_record() in the while loop of Listing 4-21 will hit the record cache from now on. First, however, notice the call to ha_rnd_init().

Whenever you see ha_ in front of a function, you know immediately that you're dealing with a table handler method (a storage engine function). A first guess might be that this function is used to scan a segment of records from disk for a storage engine. So, let's check out ha_rnd_init(), shown in Listing 4-23, which can be found in /sql/handler.h. Why just the header file? Well, the handler class is really just an interface for the storage engine's subclasses to implement. We can see from the class definition that a skeleton method is defined.

Listing 4-23. */sql/handler.h handler::ha_rnd_init()*

```
int ha_rnd_init(bool scan)
  {
    DBUG_ENTER("ha_rnd_init");
    DBUG_ASSERT(inited==NONE || (inited==RND && scan));
    inited=RND;
    DBUG_RETURN(rnd_init(scan));
  }
```

Since we are querying on a MyISAM table, we'll look for the *virtual* method declaration for rnd_init() in the ha_myisam handler class, as shown in Listing 4-24. This can be found in the /sql/ha_myisam.cc file.

Listing 4-24. */sql/ha_myisam.cc ha_myisam::rnd_init()*

```
int ha_myisam::rnd_init(bool scan)
{
  if (scan)
    return mi_scan_init(file);
// …
}
```

Sure enough, as we suspected, the rnd_init method involves a scan of the table's records. We're sure you've gotten tired of us saying this by now, but yes, the mi_scan_init() function is implemented in yet another file: /myisam/mi_scan.c, shown in Listing 4-25.

Listing 4-25. */myisam/mi_scan.c mi_scan_init()*

```
int mi_scan_init(register MI_INFO *info)
{
  info->nextpos=info->s->pack.header_length; /* Read first record */
// …
}
```

Unbelievable—all this work just to read in a record to a READ_RECORD struct! Fortunately, we're almost done. Listing 4-26 shows the rr_sequential() function of the record cache library.

Listing 4-26. */sql/records.cc rr_sequential()*

```
static int rr_sequential(READ_RECORD *info)
{
  while ((tmp=info->file->rnd_next(info->record)))
  {
    if (tmp == HA_ERR_END_OF_FILE)
      tmp= -1;
  }
  return tmp;
}
```

This function is now called whenever the `info` struct in `sub_select()` calls its `read_record()` member method. It, in turn, calls another MyISAM handler method, `rnd_next()`, which simply moves the current record pointer into the needed `READ_RECORD` struct. Behind the scenes, `rnd_next` simply maps to the `mi_scan()` function implemented in the same file we saw earlier, as shown in Listing 4-27.

Listing 4-27. */myisam/mi_scan.c mi_scan()*

```
int mi_scan(MI_INFO *info, byte *buf)
{
// …
  info->update&= (HA_STATE_CHANGED | HA_STATE_ROW_CHANGED);
  DBUG_RETURN ((*info->s->read_rnd)(info,buf,info->nextpos,1));
}
```

In this way, the record cache acts more like a wrapper library to the handlers than it does a cache. But what we've left out of the preceding code is much of the implementation of the shared `IO_CACHE` object, which we touched on in the section on caching earlier in this chapter. You should go back to `records.cc` and take a look at the record cache implementation now that you know a little more about how the handler subclasses interact with the main parsing and execution system. This advice applies for just about any of the sections we covered in this chapter. Feel free to go through this code execution over and over again, even branching out to discover, for instance, how an `INSERT` command is actually executed in the storage engine.

Summary

We've certainly covered a great deal of ground in this chapter. Hopefully, you haven't thrown the book away in frustration as you worked your way through the source code. We know it can be a difficult task, but take your time and read as much of the documentation as you can. It really helps.

So, what have we covered in this chapter? Well, we started off with some instructions on how to get your hands on the source code, and configure and retrieve the documentation in various formats. Then we outlined the general organization of the server's subsystems.

Each of the core subsystems was covered, including thread management, logging, storage engine abstraction, and more. We intended to give you an adequate road map from which to start investigating the source code yourself, to get an even deeper understanding of what's behind the scenes. Trust us, the more you dig in there, the more you'll be amazed at the skill of the MySQL development team to "keep it all together." There's a *lot* of code in there.

We finished up with a bit of a code odyssey, which took us from server initialization all the way through to the retrieval of data records from the storage engine. Were you surprised at just how many steps we took to travel such a relatively short distance?

We hope this chapter has been a fun little excursion into the world of database server internals. The next chapter will cover some additional advanced topics, including implementation details on the storage engines themselves and the differences between them. You'll learn the strengths and weaknesses of each of the storage engines, to gain a better understanding of when to use them.

CHAPTER 5

■ ■ ■

Storage Engines
and Data Types

In this chapter, we'll delve into an aspect of MySQL that sets it apart from other relational database management systems: its ability to use entirely different storage mechanisms for various data within a single database. These mechanisms are known as *storage engines*, and each one has different strengths, restrictions, and uses. We'll examine these storage engines in depth, suggesting how each one can best be utilized for common data storage and access requirements.

After discussing each storage engine, we'll review the various types of information that can be stored in your database tables. We'll look at how each data type can play a role in your system, and then provide guidelines on which data types to apply to your table columns. In some cases, you'll see how your choice of storage engine, and indeed your choice of primary and secondary keys, will influence which type of data you store in each table.

In our discussion of storage engines and data types, we'll cover the following topics:

- Storage engine considerations

- The MyISAM storage engine

- The InnoDB storage engine

- The MERGE storage engine

- The MEMORY storage engine

- The ARCHIVE storage engine

- The CSV storage engine

- The FEDERATED storage engine

- The NDB Cluster storage engine

- Guidelines for choosing a storage engine

- Considerations for choosing data types

Storage Engine Considerations

The MySQL storage engines exist to provide flexibility to database designers, and also to allow for the server to take advantage of different types of storage media. Database designers can choose the appropriate storage engines based on their application's needs. As with all software, to provide specific functionality in an implementation, certain trade-offs, either in performance or flexibility, are required. The implementations of MySQL's storage engines are no exception—each one comes with a distinct set of benefits and drawbacks.

■**Note** Storage engines used to be called *table types* (or table handlers). In the MySQL documentation, you will see both terms used. They mean the same thing, although the preferred description is *storage engine*.

As we discuss each of the available storage engines in depth, keep in mind the following questions:

- What type of data will you eventually be storing in your MySQL databases?

- Is the data constantly changing?

- Is the data mostly logs (INSERTs)?

- Are your end users constantly making requests for aggregated data and other reports?

- For mission-critical data, will there be a need for foreign key constraints or multiple-statement transaction control?

The answers to these questions will affect the storage engine and data types most appropriate for your particular application.

■**Tip** In order to specify a storage engine, use the CREATE TABLE (…) ENGINE=*EngineType* option, where *EngineType* is one of the following: MYISAM, MEMORY, MERGE, INNODB, FEDERATED, ARCHIVE, or CSV.

The MyISAM Storage Engine

ISAM stands for *indexed sequential access method*. The MyISAM storage engine, an improved version of the original but now deprecated ISAM storage engine, allows for fast retrieval of its data through a non-clustered index and data organization. (See Chapter 2 to learn about non-clustered index organization and the index sequential access method.)

MyISAM is the default storage engine for all versions of MySQL. However, the Windows installer version of MySQL 4.1 and later offers to make InnoDB the default storage engine when you install it.

The MyISAM storage engine offers very fast and reliable data storage suitable for a variety of common application requirements. Although it does not currently have the transaction processing or relational integrity capacity of the InnoDB engine, it more than makes up for these deficiencies in its speed and in the flexibility of its storage formats. We'll cover those storage formats here, and take a detailed look at the locking strategy that MyISAM deploys in order to provide consistency to table data while keeping performance a priority.

MyISAM File and Directory Layout

All of MySQL's storage engines use one or more files to handle operations within data sets structured under the storage engine's architecture. The `data_dir` directory contains one subdirectory for each schema housed on the server. The MyISAM storage engine creates a separate file for each table's row data, index data, and metadata:

- *table_name*.frm contains the meta information about the MyISAM table definition.

- *table_name*.MYD contains the table row data.

- *table_name*.MYI contains the index data.

Because MyISAM tables are organized in this way, it is possible to move a MyISAM table from one server to another simply by moving these three files (this is *not* the case with InnoDB tables). When the MySQL server starts, and a MyISAM table is first accessed, the server reads the *table_name*.frm data into memory as a hash entry in the table cache (see Chapter 4 for more information about the table cache for MyISAM tables).

■**Note** *Files* are *not* the same as *file descriptors*. A *file* is a collection of data records and data pages into a logical unit. A *file descriptor* is an integer that corresponds to a file or device opened by a specific process. The file descriptor contains a *mode*, which informs the system whether the process opened the file in an attempt to read or write to the file, and where the first offset (base address) of the underlying file can be found. This offset does not need to be the zero-position address. If the file descriptor's mode was append, this offset may be the address at the end of the file where data may first be written.

As we noted in Chapter 2, the MyISAM storage engine manages only *index* data, not record data, in pages. As *sequential access* implies, MyISAM stores records one after the other in a single file (the .MYD file). The MyISAM record cache (discussed in Chapter 4) reads records through an IO_CACHE structure into main memory record by record, as opposed to a larger-sized page at a time. In contrast, the InnoDB storage engine loads and manages record data in memory as entire 16KB pages.

Additionally, since the MyISAM engine does not store the record data on disk in a paged format (as the InnoDB engine does), there is no wasted "fill factor" space (free space available for inserting new records) between records in the .MYD file. Practically speaking, this means that the actual data portion of a MyISAM table will likely be smaller than an identical table managed by InnoDB. This fact, however, should *not* be a factor in how you choose your storage engines, as the differences between the storage engines in functional capability are much more significant than this slight difference in size requirements of the data files.

For managing index data, MyISAM uses a 1KB page (internally, the developers refer to this index page as an *index block*). If you remember from our coverage of the MyISAM key cache in Chapter 4, we noted that the index blocks were read from disk (the .MYI file) if the block was not found in the key cache (see Figure 4-2). In this way, the MyISAM and InnoDB engine's treatment of index data using fixed-size pages is similar. (The InnoDB storage engine uses a clustered index and data organization, so the 16KB data pages are actually the index leaf pages.)

MyISAM Record Formats

When analyzing a table creation statement (CREATE TABLE or ALTER TABLE), MyISAM determines whether the data to be stored in each row of the table will be a static (*fixed*) length or if the length of each row's data might vary from row to row (*dynamic*). The physical format of the .MYD file and the records contained within the file depend on this distinction. In addition to the fixed and dynamic record formats, the MyISAM storage engine supports a compressed row format. We'll cover each of these record formats in the following sections.

■**Note** The MyISAM record formats are implemented in the following source files: /myisam/mi_sta➥ trec.c (for fixed records), /myisam/mi_dynrec.c (for dynamic records), and /myisam/mi_packrec.c (for compressed records).

Fixed Record Format

When the record format is of a fixed length, the .MYD file will contain each MyISAM record in sequential order, with a NULL byte (0x00) between each record. Each record contains a bitmap record header. By *bitmap*, we're not referring to the graphic. A bitmap in programming is a set of single bits, arranged in segments of eight (to align them into a byte structure), where each bit in the byte is a *flag* that represents some status or Boolean value. For instance, the bitmap 1111 0101 in binary, or 0xF5 in hexadecimal, would have the second and fourth bits turned off (set to 0) and all other bits turned on (set to 1). Remember that a byte is composed of a low-order and a high-order byte, and is read right to left. Therefore, the first bit is the rightmost bit.

The MyISAM bitmap record header for fixed-length records is composed of the following bits, in this order:

- One bit representing whether the record has been deleted (0 means the row is deleted).

- One bit for each field in the MyISAM table that can be NULL. If the record contains a NULL value in the field, the bit is equal to 1, else 0.

- One or more "filler" bits set to 1 up to the byte mark.

The total size of the record header bitmap subsequently depends on the number of nullable fields the table contains. If the table contains zero to seven nullable fields, the header bitmap will be 1 byte; eight to fifteen nullable fields, it will be 2 bytes; and so on. Therefore, although it is advisable to have as few NULL fields as possible in your schema design, there will be no practical effect on the size of the .MYD file unless your table contains more than *seven* nullable fields.

After each record header, the values of the record's fields, in order of the columns defined in the table creation, will follow, consuming as much space as the data type requires.

Since it can rely on the length of the row data being static for fixed-format records, the MyISAM table cache (see Chapter 4) will contain information about the maximum length of each row of data. With this information available, when row data is sequentially read (*scanned*) by the separate MyISAM access requests, there is no need to calculate the next record's offset in the record buffer. Instead, it will always be x bytes forward in the buffer, where x is the maximum row length plus the size of the header bitmap. Additionally, when *seeking* for a specific data record through the key cache, the MyISAM engine can very quickly locate the needed row data by simply multiplying the sum of the record length and header bitmap size by the row's internal record number (which starts at zero). This allows for faster access to tables with fixed-length records, but can lead to increased actual storage space on disk.

■**Note** You can force MySQL to apply a specific row format using the ROW_FORMAT option in your CREATE ➥ TABLE statement.

Dynamic Record Format

When a MyISAM table contains variably sized data types (VARCHAR, TEXT, BLOB, and so on), the format of the records in the .MYD file is known as *dynamic*. Similar to the fixed-length record storage, each dynamically sized record contains a record header, and records are laid out in the .MYD file in sequential order, one after the next. That is where the similarities end, however.

The header for a dynamically sized record is composed of more elements, including the following:

- A 2-byte record header start element indicates the beginning of the record header. This is necessary because, unlike the fixed-length record format, the storage engine cannot rely on record headers being at a static offset in the .MYD file.

- One or more bytes that store the actual length (in bytes) of the record.

- One or more bytes that store the unused length (in bytes) of the record. MyISAM leaves space in each record to allow for the data to expand a certain amount without needing to move records around within the .MYD file. This part of the record header indicates how much unused space exists from the end of the actual data stored in the record to the beginning of the next record.

- A bitmap similar to the one used for fixed-length record, indicating NULL fields and whether the record has been deleted.

- An *overflow pointer* that points to a location in the .MYD file if the record has been updated and now contains more data than existed in the original record length. The overflow location is simply the address of another record storing the rest of the record data.

After this record header, the actual data is stored, followed by the unused space until the next record's record header. Unlike the fixed-record format, however, the dynamic record format does not consume the full field size when a NULL value is inserted. Instead, it stores only a single NULL value (0x00) instead of one or more NULL values up to the size of the same nullable field in a fixed-length record.

A significant difference between the static-length row format and this dynamic-length row format is the behavior associated with updating a record. For a static-length row record, updating the data does not have any effect on the structure of the record, because the length of the data being inserted is the same as the data being deleted.[1] For a varying-length row record, if the updating of the row data causes the length of the record to be greater than it was before, a *link* is inserted into the row pointing to another record where the remainder of the data can be found (the overflow pointer). The reason for this linking is to avoid needing to facilitate the rearrangement of multiple buffers of row records in order to accommodate the new record. The link serves as a placeholder for the new information, and the link will point to an address location that is available to the engine at the time of the update. This fragmentation of the record data can be corrected by running an OPTIMIZE TABLE command, or by running #> myisamchk -r.

MINIMIZE MYISAM TABLE FRAGMENTATION

Because of the fragmentation that can occur, if you are using MyISAM tables for data that is frequently updated or deleted, you should avoid using variably sized data types and instead use fixed-length fields. If this is not possible, consider separating a large table definition containing both fixed and variably sized fields into two tables: one containing the fixed-length data and the other containing the variably sized data. This strategy is particularly effective if the variably sized fields are not frequently updated compared to the fixed-size data.

For instance, suppose you had a MyISAM table named Customer, which had some fixed-length fields like last_action (of type DATETIME) and status (of type TINYINT), along with some variably sized fields for storing address and location data. If the address data and location data are updated infrequently compared to the data in the last_action and status fields, it might be a good idea to separate the one table into a CustomerMain table and a CustomerExtra table, with the latter containing the variably sized fields. This way, you can minimize the table fragmentation and allow the main record data to take advantage of the speedier MyISAM fixed-size record format.

For data of types TEXT and BLOB, this behavior does not occur for the in-memory record, since for these data types, the in-memory record structure contains only a pointer to where the actual TEXT or BLOB data is stored. This pointer is a fixed size, and so no additional reordering or linking is required.

Compressed Record Format

An additional flavor of MyISAM allows you to specify that the entire contents of a specified table are read-only, and the records should be compressed on insertion to save disk space. Each data record is compressed separately and uncompressed when read.

To compress a MyISAM table, use the myisampack utility on the .MYI index data file:

```
#> myisampack [options] tablename.MYI
```

---

1. Remember that an UPDATE is really a DELETE of the existing data and an INSERT of the new data.

MyISAM uses Huffman encoding (see Chapter 2) to compress data, along with a technique where fields with few distinct values are compressed to an ENUM format. Typical compression ratios are between 40% and 70% of the original size. The myisampack utility can, among other things, combine multiple large MyISAM tables into a single compressed table (suitable for CD distribution for instance). For more information about the myisampack utility, visit http://dev.mysql.com/doc/mysql/en/myisampack.html.

The .MYI File Structure

The .MYI file contains the disk copy of *all* MyISAM B-tree and R-tree indexes built on a single MyISAM table. The file consists of a header section and the index records.

■**Note** The developer's documentation (/Docs/internals.texi) contains a very thorough examination of the structures composing the header and index records. We'll cover these basic structures from a bird's-eye view. We encourage you to take a look at the TEXI documentation for more technical details.

The .MYI File Header Section

The .MYI header section contains a blueprint of the index structure, and is used in navigating through the tree. There are two main structures contained in the header section, as well as three other sections that repeat for the various indexes attached to the MyISAM table:

- A single state structure contains meta information about the indexes in the file. Some notable elements include the number of indexes, type of index (B-tree or R-tree), number of key parts in each index, number of index records, and number of records marked for deletion.

- A single base structure contains information about the table itself and some additional offset information, including the start address (offset) of the first index record, length of each index block (index data page in the key cache), length of a record in the base table or an average row length for dynamic records, and index packing (compression) information.

- For each index defined on the table, a keydef struct is inserted in the header section, containing information about the size of the key, whether it can contain NULL values, and so on.

- For each column in the index, a keyseg struct defines what data type the key part contains, where the column is located in the index record, and the size of the column's data type.

- The end of the header section contains a recinfo struct for each column in the indexes, containing (somewhat redundant) information about the data types in the indexes. An extra recinfo struct contains information about removal of key fields on an index.

Note You can find the definition for these data structures in /myisam/myisamdef.h. Additionally, /myisam/ mi_open.c contains functions that write the respective header section elements to the .MYI file. Each section has its own function; for instance, the recinfo struct is written to file in the mi_recinfo_write() function.

The .MYI File Index Records

After the header section, the MyISAM index blocks compose the remainder of the .MYI file. The index blocks are 1KB on-disk pages of data, representing the B-tree leaf and non-leaf nodes. A single index block contains only key values pertaining to one index in the table. The header section (detailed in the previous section) contains information about how the MyISAM storage engine should find the root node of each index by supplying the offset for the root node's index block in the keydef elements.

Each index block contains the following:

- A single 2-byte block header. The first bit of the 16 bits in the header indicates whether the block is a leaf node (0 for leaf; 1 for non-leaf). The remaining 15 bits contain the total length of bytes used in the block (nonfree space).

- Following the header, index keys and record identifiers are laid out in a balanced organization (the B-tree format). With each key is stored the key value (of a length equal to the data type of the indexed field) and a 4-byte record pointer.

- The remainder of the index block is junk bytes (filler bytes), which become used as the B-tree index "fills out" with inserts. This is the "fill factor" for MyISAM B-tree index pages, and typically represents between 65% and 80% of the data used within the index block under normal operations, to allow for split-free growth along with the insertions.

Tip Running #> myisamchk -rq on a MyISAM table will cause the fill factor to rise to close to 100%, as it fills the index blocks as compactly as possible, which may be advisable on static or infrequently modified MyISAM tables.

MyISAM Table-Level Locking

To ensure the integrity of its data, the MyISAM storage engine supports only a single type of locking level: *table-level* locking. Much has been made of this "deficiency," but for many applications, this level of locking, and its specific implementation in the MyISAM storage engine, works quite well and can be effective even in very high concurrency scenarios.

MyISAM issues one of three separate types of locks on its resources (data records), depending on the request issued to it by the connecting thread:

- READ LOCAL: If the thread issues a SELECT statement against the in-memory copy of the data records, MyISAM asks for a READ LOCAL lock on the data. This type of lock *does not* prevent INSERTs into the table, as long as the data will be appended to the end of the data file. If the INSERT would push data into the middle of the data file, then the INSERT statement would need to wait until the READ LOCAL lock was released by the SELECT statement's thread.

- READ: If the actual .MYD data file is used to get information for the requesting client (for instance, the myisamchk utility), as opposed to the in-memory cache of the table data, a lock of type READ (sometimes called a *shared* lock) is issued. While a READ lock is placed on the resource, all UPDATE, INSERT, and DELETE statements are blocked from executing against the table's data.

- WRITE: A WRITE lock (sometimes called an *exclusive* lock) is placed on the table resource whenever an UPDATE or DELETE request is received, or if an INSERT is received that would fill an existing space in the data file that had previously been removed via a DELETE request.

So, with the READ LOCAL lock type, MyISAM tables can *write* data to the table without blocking simultaneous *reads* of the table's data. You may wonder, given your understanding of data isolation levels, how this is possible. MyISAM recognizes that INSERT operations occurring on a table in which the primary key is an auto-incrementing number can write the new key data at the end of the index file, as opposed to reading into the index file to find an appropriate place to insert new data. Because the insertion of new keys will always occur at the end of the index file for this type of table, there is no need to hold up SELECT statements that have requested keys or data from anywhere else in the table.

For this reason, MyISAM makes an excellent choice for tables that primarily accomplish logging activity. For instance, it's ideal for a table containing web site traffic data, where you may want to issue queries against a part of the traffic data, while continuing to insert thousands of new records a minute.

MyISAM Index Choices

Although the actual *data* is not stored in the order of the table's primary key, MyISAM *does* maintain a list of pointers (think of them as internal record numbers) to those data records within its indexes. This *key cache* contains a linked list of pointers referencing address spaces inside the .MYD file where the actual data rows are stored. Regardless of the number of indexes attached to the MyISAM table, all indexes are implemented using this non-clustered organization (see Chapter 2).

You can have up to 64 separate indexes on a MyISAM table (32 in versions prior to 4.1.2). MyISAM supports three indexing options through which it can retrieve data from its key cache: B-tree, R-tree, and FULLTEXT.

B-Tree Indexes

In order to quickly locate information within the non-clustered index buffers, MyISAM uses a B-tree search algorithm. Therefore, keys are inserted into the index based on the key's logical location in the index tree. If the key has a string data type and can be compressed using prefix compression, it will be. Alternatively, you can manually specify that compression should happen on INSERT by using the PACK_KEYS=1 option in the CREATE TABLE or CREATE INDEX statement. This can be useful for integer keys where you have a data set with most, if not all, key values using just the low-byte value (see the earlier section on the MyISAM fixed-record format). Packing the keys will strip the nonunique high-byte part of the integer value to allow for higher density indexing.

■**Note** The MyISAM key buffer system can be found in the /myisam/mi_key.c and /myisam/mi_keycache.c files. The B-tree algorithm is implemented in /myisam/mi_search.c. Table scans on MyISAM are implemented in /myisam/mi_scan.c.

R-Tree Indexes

For those of you who require the ability to work with spatial data types (geographical coordinates or three-dimensional shapes), the MyISAM storage engine supports R-tree indexing for that spatial data. Currently, MyISAM is the only storage engine that supports R-tree analysis. Effectively, the implementation of R-tree indexing on the MyISAM storage engine is a kind of extension to its existing key cache organization. It used the same informational structures as the B-tree indexes, but implements the comparison of values in a different way (the spatial way).

■**Note** The R-tree algorithm is implemented in the /myisam/rt_* files. Notably, rt_mbr.c contains the implementation for how key values are compared. By the way, mbr stands for minimum bounding rectangle.

FULLTEXT Indexes

MyISAM is currently the only storage engine supporting the FULLTEXT index option. A FULLTEXT index can be defined on any CHAR, VARCHAR, or TEXT field of a MyISAM table. When a record is inserted into a MyISAM table containing a FULLTEXT index, the data for the indexed fields is analyzed and split into "words." For each word, an index entry is created, with the following elements:

- The word itself

- The number of times the word is found in the text being inserted

- A floating-point weight value designed to express the importance of this word in *relation to the entire string of data*

- The record identifier of the record, used as a pointer into the .MYD file

When a query is run against the index, the index entries are queried and, by default, returned in an order based on the weight value in the index entries. To query a FULLTEXT index, use the MATCH … AGAINST construct, as follows:

```
SELECT * FROM some_table
WHERE MATCH(fulltext_field1, fulltext_field2) AGAINST ('some search string');
```

In order to see the weighting of the index in your query results, simply use the MATCH construct in the SELECT clause, like so:

```
SELECT some_field, MATCH (fulltext_field1, fulltext_field2)
AGAINST ('some search string') FROM some_table;
```

Tip You can make numerous tweaks to your FULLTEXT indexes, such as changing the minimum word length, altering the stopword file, and running queries in Boolean mode. http://dev.mysql.com/doc/mysql/en/fulltext-search.html has more information about various FULLTEXT options. In addition, Peter Gulutzan's article, "The Full-Text Stuff That We Didn't Put in the Manual" (http://dev.mysql.com/tech-resources/articles/full-text-revealed.html) has some excellent material.

MyISAM Limitations

Despite MyISAM's various strengths, it does have a few downsides, primarily its lack of foreign key constraints and multiple-statement transaction safety.

Despite plans to include it, there is currently no way of making the MyISAM storage engine *enforce* a foreign key constraint. Though the FOREIGN KEY clause in your CREATE TABLE statement is parsed by the DDL compiler, nothing is actually stored or done to protect foreign key relational integrity.

The protection of foreign key constraints is a principle of sound database design, yet some in the database community have come out against foreign key constraints because of performance reasons. The MySQL development team is determined to keep performance as a top priority, and has indicated that the MyISAM storage engine may support foreign key constraints in the future, but only if doing so would not seriously impact the performance of the engine.

Unfortunately, at the time of this writing, if you are designing an application that has foreign key dependency support as a top priority, your storage engine choice is limited to InnoDB.[2] As with other things, enforcing relational integrity for foreign keys comes with a performance cost in InnoDB. However, we should stress that for *most* applications, this performance difference will be negligible, partly due to InnoDB's row-level locking scheme, discussed in the next section.

MyISAM also does not give you the ability to ensure the atomicity, consistency, and durability of multiple statements executed with a transaction. The ACID test (see Chapter 3) cannot be applied to statement sets run against MyISAM tables. Although it is possible to mix and match storage engines in the database, if you have a transaction executing against both InnoDB tables (which *do* support transaction control) and MyISAM tables, you can be assured only that the statements executed against the InnoDB tables will be written to disk and recovered in the event of a crash.

---

2. Technically, you could also use the BDB storage engine, but there are few to no advantages to using this earlier transaction-safe engine over InnoDB.

The InnoDB Storage Engine

The InnoDB storage engine[3] addresses some of the drawbacks to the MyISAM storage engine. Namely, it provides enforcement of foreign key constraints and full ACID-compliant transaction processing abilities (see Chapter 3).

Much of InnoDB's power is derived from its implementation of *row-level* locking through multiversion concurrency control (MVCC). Through MVCC, InnoDB has support for a number of transaction isolation levels, giving you control over how your transactions are processed. In the following sections, we'll examine these transaction-processing capabilities, as well as InnoDB's doublewrite log system, file and record formats, and buffers.

Enforcement of Foreign Key Relationships

InnoDB enforces the referential integrity of foreign key relationships at the database level. When a CREATE TABLE statement is issued with the FOREIGN KEY … REFERENCES clause, the parent table (REFERENCES table) is checked to verify the existence of a key when a record in the child table is inserted.

A common example of this parent-child relationship, as we discussed in Chapter 1, is the Customer to CustomerOrder to CustomerOrderItem scenario. A customer can place zero or more orders. An order can contain one or more order details. In order to enforce the relationship, we would issue the statements in Listing 5-1. Note that the *parent* tables must be created first, before any foreign keys reference them, and the parent tables must have a unique index containing the columns referenced in the FOREIGN KEY clause. Additionally, all data types must be identical on both sides of the relationship.

Listing 5-1. *Creating an InnoDB Table with a Foreign Key Constraint*

```
mysql> CREATE TABLE customer (
    > id INT NOT NULL AUTO_INCREMENT,
    > name VARCHAR(30) NOT NULL,
    > address VARCHAR(100) NOT NULL,
    > PRIMARY KEY (id)) ENGINE = INNODB;
mysql> CREATE TABLE customer_order (
    > id INT NOT NULL AUTO_INCREMENT,
    > customer INT NOT NULL,
    > date_ordered INT NOT NULL,
    > PRIMARY KEY (id),
    > FOREIGN KEY (customer) REFERENCES customer (id)) ENGINE = INNODB;
mysql> CREATE TABLE customer_order_item (
    > id INT NOT NULL AUTO_INCREMENT,
    > order INT NOT NULL,
    > product VARCHAR(30) NOT NULL,
    > PRIMARY KEY (id),
    > FOREIGN KEY (order) REFERENCES customer_order (id)) ENGINE = INNODB;
```

---

3. InnoDB was originally developed by Heikki Tuuri and is now developed and maintained by Innobase Oy (http://www.innodb.com/).

■**Tip** You can use the ON UPDATE CASCADE and ON UPDATE DELETE options in order to force InnoDB to automatically handle updates and deletes on the *parent* record. Refer to the manual for detailed instructions on these options. See http://dev.mysql.com/doc/mysql/en/create-table.html and also http://dev.mysql.com/doc/mysql/en/ansi-diff-foreign-keys.html.

InnoDB Row-Level Locking

Although InnoDB *does* implement table-level locking (you can order it to use table-level locks using the LOCK TABLES statement), the default lock granularity is at the row level. While table-level lock granularity is more efficient from a memory perspective, a row-level lock is crucial for applications that have a high read and write rate where updates to the data are common.

You might wonder how table-level locking could be more efficient, since it locks a larger block of records. During table-level locking, MyISAM places a lock on the table information structure that is shared by threads reading and writing. The lock is applied to this single shared resource and is held for a relatively short period of time (usually nanoseconds). In row-level locking, an array of locks must be maintained for the rows active in transactions. So, while on the surface, table-level locking may seem inefficient because it holds on to a large logical block, the implementation of row-level locking is more CPU- and memory-intensive because of the number of locks that must be tracked.

InnoDB's implementation of row-level locking uses an internal table that contains lock information for the keys. This internal format is a memory-efficient, compressed hash lookup of the primary keys in the table. (This is, by the way, the reason you cannot have an InnoDB table without a PRIMARY KEY assigned to it; see the discussion of clustered versus non-clustered data and index organization in Chapter 2 for details.)

That said, there are situations in which the level of lock granularity becomes more of a player than the resources needed to maintain the actual locks. For systems where there are a large number of concurrent users issuing both UPDATE and SELECT statements on the same data—typically in a mixed OLTP/OLAP[4] environment—situations arise where there are too many requests for write locks, which inhibit, or block, the read requests until the write has completed. For table-level lock granularity, these read requests must wait until the write request has released the table-level lock in order to read *any* of the data records in the table.

Row-level locking solves this dilemma by allowing update requests to only block read (or other write) requests to the data records that are affected by the update. Other read requests—ones that do not need to be read from the segment being written by the write request—are not held up. InnoDB implements this granularity of locking. This is one of the reasons that the InnoDB storage engine is an excellent candidate for systems having high read and write requests.

Like MyISAM, InnoDB implements a mechanism to allow insertions that occur at the end of the data file—which, in the case of InnoDB, is always the end of the clustered index—to happen concurrently without issuing any exclusive locks on the table.

---

4. OLTP stands for online transaction processing, and these systems typically have high write requests. OLAP stands for online analytical processing, and these systems typically have high read requests.

ACID-Compliant Multistatement Transaction Control

If you have an absolute requirement that certain sets of statements run against your database tables must be completed inside an ACID-compliant transaction, InnoDB is your storage engine of choice. As noted earlier, InnoDB accomplishes transaction control through MVCC.

The default isolation level in which InnoDB runs multistatement transactions is REPEATABLE READ and, for most situations, this isolation level is sufficient.[5] However, in certain circumstances, you may need a higher level of isolation. In these cases, InnoDB offers a SERIALIZABLE isolation level that can be set using the SET TRANSACTION ISOLATION LEVEL statement *before* issuing any commands in the connection thread. See Chapter 2 for a detailed discussion of isolation levels and MVCC, to determine situations where you may need to set a specific isolation level.

The InnoDB File and Directory Layout

The InnoDB storage engine file organization is different from the MyISAM arrangement. While the MySQL server maintains an .frm file for each InnoDB table, similar to MyISAM tables, InnoDB also keeps its own store of meta information about InnoDB tables. Because of this, it is *not* currently possible to simply transfer InnoDB databases from one server to another by copying the table files.

By default, the storage engine manages *all* InnoDB tables in what's called a *tablespace*, which is modeled after the Oracle concept of the same name. The tablespace is composed of multiple files, which can grow to the size limitation of the operating system. These files are named based on what is in your configuration file. By default, these files begin with ibdata and then a number. In your my.cnf file (discussed in Chapter 14), you will see a section similar to the following:

```
innodb_data_home_dir = /usr/local/var/
innodb_data_file_path = ibdata1:2000M;ibdata2:10M:autoextend
```

The ibdata files contain both the table *and* index data for all InnoDB tables. These ibdata files will be in innodb_data_home_dir, while the .frm file will be in the schema's directory under the main MySQL data_dir directory. All the ibdata files are concatenated by InnoDB to form the InnoDB tablespace. The tablespace can contain any number of files, and the autoextend functionality ensures that the tablespace files can grow with the database. This also means that file system size limitations (for instance, 2GB on most Linux distributions) can be overcome, since the tablespace can contain multiple files, unlike with the MyISAM .MYD storage.

---

5. A few folks will insist that this isolation level is indeed *more* than sufficient for normal default operations. Oracle and SQL Server both default to the READ COMMITTED isolation level. See the InnoDB manual for a discussion on its isolation levels: http://dev.mysql.com/doc/mysql/en/innodb-transaction-model.html and follow the links to the various subsections.

Within the tablespace, two internal files (called *segments*) maintain each InnoDB table (these segments aren't visible to you, however). One segment is used for the clustered index data pages, and another segment is used for any secondary indexes built on that clustering key. The reason this is done this way is so that records may be added sequentially in large blocks, to both the data and secondary index pages of the table.

To implement InnoDB's transaction processing system, a series of log files will also be created. In your my.cnf file, you will find something like the following two lines:

```
innodb_log_group_home_dir = /usr/local/var/
innodb_log_arch_dir = /usr/local/var/
```

These are the directories where the main log files and archive log files are stored. The default naming convention for these log files is ib_logfile and then a number representing the log segment. You will have a number of log files equal to the innodb_log_files_in_group configuration variable (with a default of two log files). We'll take a closer look at the log system a little later in the chapter, in the "InnoDB Doublewrite Buffer and Log Format" section.

Optionally, as of version 4.1.1, you can elect to have InnoDB organize its files in a per-table format, similar to the MyISAM file organization. To enable this file layout, insert the innodb_file_per_table configuration option under the mysqld section of your my.cnf file. Keep in mind, however, that enabling this option does not remove the ibdata files, nor allow you to transfer InnoDB schema to another machine by simply copying the .ibd files, as you can with the MyISAM storage engine's files.

■**Note** Currently, the tables cannot be manually assigned to the multiple ibdata files. Therefore, it is *not* possible to have InnoDB store separate tables on separate disks or devices.

InnoDB Data Page Organization

The InnoDB storage engine stores (both on disk and in-memory) record and index data in 16KB pages. These pages are organized within the ibdata files as *extents* of 64 *consecutive* pages. The reason InnoDB does this is to allocate large spaces of memory and disk space at once, to ensure that data is as sequential on the hard disk as possible. This is a proactive stance at maintaining as defragmented a system as possible.

Each extent stores data related to a single index, with one exception. One extent contains a *page directory*, or catalog, which contains the master list of data pages as a linked tree of pointers to all extents in the tablespace.

Clustered Index Page Format

Since the storage engine uses a clustered index organization, the leaf pages of the index contain the actual record data. Secondary B-tree indexes are built on the clustered index data pages.

A clustered index data page in the InnoDB storage engine is a complex beast. It consists of seven distinct elements:

- *Fil header*: This 34-byte header contains the directory information about the page within the segment. Important directory information includes an identifier for the page, the previous and next page's identifiers,[6] and the log serial number (LSN) for the latest log record for the page. We'll discuss the importance of the log serial number in the upcoming section on the InnoDB log format.

- *Page header*: This 50-byte header contains meta information about the data page itself. Important elements of this section include pointers to the first record on the page, the first free record, and the last inserted record. Also of interest are an identifier for the index to which the data page belongs and the number of records on the page.

- *Infimum and Supremum records*: These are two fixed-size records placed in the header. These records are used to prevent the next-previous link relationship to go beyond the index bounds and as a space to put dummy lock information.

- *User records*: After the Infimum and Supremum records come one or more user records. The format of the user record is detailed in the next section.

- *Free space*: After the user records is free space available for InnoDB to insert new records. This is the "fill factor" space for InnoDB, which attempts to keep data pages at 15/16 filled.

- *Page directory*: Following the free space, the page directory contains a variably sized set of pointers to each record, paired with the record's clustering key. In this way, queries can use the page directory's smaller size to do very fast lookups and range queries for records on the page.

- *Fil trailer*: Finally, this section contains a checksum of the page's data, along with the page log sequence number, for use in error-checking the contents of the page.

InnoDB Record Format

InnoDB records have a very different format from MyISAM records. The record is composed of three parts:

- One- or two-byte field start offsets contain the position of the next field in the record, relative to the start address of the record. There will be *n* field offsets, where *n* is the number of fields in the table. The field offsets will be 1 byte if the total record size is 127 bytes or less; otherwise, each field offset will be 2 bytes long.

---

6. The next and previous page identifiers provide a mechanism for InnoDB to perform fast range query and scan operations by providing a linking relationship between the index data pages. This linking relationship is a major difference between the implementation of the B-tree index structure in InnoDB versus MyISAM. This type of B-tree algorithm is commonly called a B+ tree (B-plus tree) and is useful for clustered data organizations.

- A fixed-size 48-bit (6-byte) "extra bytes" information section contains meta information about the record. This meta information includes the following important elements:

    - One bit denoting if the record is deleted. In this case, a value of 1 means the record is deleted (the opposite of MyISAM).

    - Ten bits detailing the number of fields in the record.

    - Thirteen bits identifying the record within the data page (the *heap* number).

    - One bit telling InnoDB whether the field offsets mentioned previously are 1 or 2 bytes long.

    - Sixteen-bit (2-byte) pointer to the next-key record in the page.

- The field contents compose the remainder of the record, with no NULL value separating the field contents, because the field offsets enable the storage engine to navigate to the beginning of each field.

The most important aspect of the InnoDB record structure is the two parts of the "extra bytes" section that contain the 13-bit *heap number* and the 16-bit *next-key pointer*.

Remember that InnoDB tables follow a clustered data organization where the data page is clustered, or ordered, based on the primary key value. Would it then surprise you to know that InnoDB does not actually store records in the order of the primary key?

"But wait!" you say. "How is it possible that a clustered data organization can be built on index pages without those records being laid out in primary key order?" The answer lies in the storage engine's use of next-key pointers in the data records.

The designers of InnoDB knew that maintaining clustered index data pages in sort order of the primary key would be a performance problem. When records were inserted, the storage engine would need to find where the record "fit" into the appropriate data page, then move records around within the file in order to sort correctly. Updating a record would likewise cause problems. Additionally, the designers knew that inserting records on a *heap* structure (with no regard to the order of the records) would be faster, since multiple insertions could be serialized to go into contiguous blocks on the data page. Therefore, the developers came up with a mechanism whereby records can be inserted into the data page in no particular order (a heap), but be affixed with a pointer to the record that had the next primary key value.

The InnoDB storage engine inserts a record wherever the first available free space is located. It gets this free record space address from the page header section. To determine the next-key pointer, it uses the small, condensed page directory trailing section of the data page to locate the appropriate place to insert the primary key value for the inserted record. In this way, only the small page directory set of key values and pointers must be rearranged. Note also that the next-key pointers are a one-way (forward-only) list.

■**Note** The InnoDB page and record source code files are in the /innobase/page/ and /innobase/rem/ directories of your source distribution. rem stands for record manager.

Internal InnoDB Buffers

InnoDB caches information in two major internal buffers:

- *Buffer pool*: This buffer contains cached index data pages (both leaf and non-leaf). The `innodb_buffer_pool_size` configuration variable controls the size of this buffer.

- *Log buffer*: This buffer contains cached log records. The `innodb_log_buffer_size` configuration variable controls the size of the log buffer.

■**Note** It is unfortunate that InnoDB currently does not have the ability to change the configuration variables associated with the internal buffers on the fly. A restart of the `mysqld` process is required in order to facilitate the changes, which considering InnoDB was designed for always-on, high-availability systems, may be a significant downside. We hope that, in the future, these values will be modifiable through SQL commands.

In addition to these two main buffers, InnoDB also keeps a separate cache of memory for its internal data dictionary about the table and index structures in the tablespace.

InnoDB Doublewrite Buffer and Log Format

In order to ensure the ACID properties of transaction control, InnoDB uses a write-ahead logging system called a *doublewrite buffer system*. Remember from Chapters 2 and 3 that there is a difference between a *write* and a *flush* of data. A *write* simply changes the in-memory copy of a piece of data. A *flush* commits those writes to disk.

The doublewrite buffer refers to the dual-write process that occurs when InnoDB records changes issued under a transaction, as illustrated in Figure 5-1. Because of the principles of write-ahead logging, InnoDB must ensure that any statement that modifies the in-memory data set is first recorded on disk (in a log) before a COMMIT is issued for the entire transaction. This ensures that, in the case of a disk failure or software crash, the changes can be re-created from the log records. However, the designers of InnoDB realized that if a transaction were rolled back before a COMMIT was received, the statements on log records representing those changes would not need to be reissued during a recovery. So, InnoDB inserts transactional statements as log records into the log buffer (described in the previous section), while simultaneously executing the modifications those statements make against the in-memory copy of the record data available in the buffer pool. This dual-buffer write explains the doublewrite buffer terminology.

When a COMMIT is received for a transaction, by default, InnoDB flushes to disk (to the ib_logfile files) the log records in the log buffer representing the transaction in question. The reason we say "by default" is that you can tell InnoDB to only flush the transaction log files to disk every second, approximately. You can tell InnoDB to flush to disk based on the operating system process scheduling (around one second) by setting `innodb_flush_log_at_trx_commit` to 0. This practice is not, however, recommended for mission-critical applications.

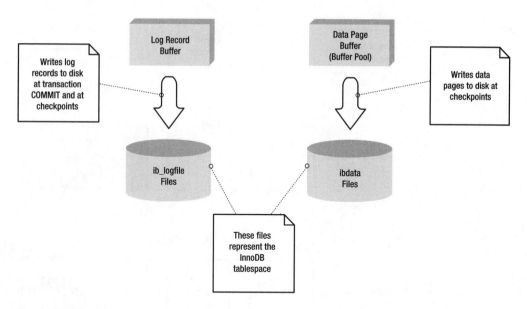

Figure 5-1. *The doublewrite buffer process*

■**Caution** Regardless of whether `innodb_flush_log_at_trx_commit` is set to 1, if the operating system on which the MySQL server is running does not have a reliable flushing mechanism, *or* if the disk drives attempt to fool the operating system into thinking a flush has occurred when, in fact, it hasn't, InnoDB may lose data. This is *not* a fault of the storage engine, but rather of the operating system or hardware. For more information about this problem, see Peter Zaitsev's (one of the InnoDB developers) article at `http://www.livejournal.com/users/peter_zaitsev/12639.html`.

InnoDB log files contain a fixed number of log records.[7] Because the log files cannot grow to an infinite size, and because log records are going to continue to be inserted into the log, there must be a way of overwriting log records that have been flushed to disk, and therefore are redundant.

InnoDB's log record flushing system is circular in this way: it overwrites log records from the beginning of the log record with newer log records if the log file's file size limit is reached. Figure 5-2 depicts a sample log file with a maximum of 14 log records.

■**Caution** Because of InnoDB's process of overwriting logs, you must ensure that you provide enough room in your log file to cover the data changes made between backups. See Chapter 17 for more information about these administrative precautions.

---

7. The number of records depends on the number of log files set in the `innodb_log_files_in_group` configuration setting and the actual size of the file set with `innodb_log_file_size`.

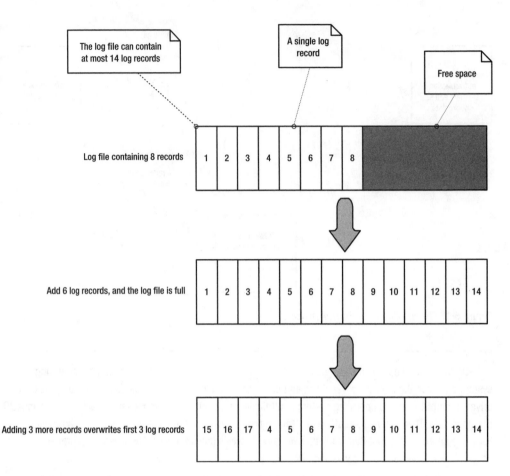

Figure 5-2. *InnoDB's log file overwrites itself from the beginning of the file when it's full.*

The actual log record format is itself quite compact. It contains a log serial number (LSN), which is an 8-byte file and byte offset for the particular log record. Along with the LSN is a compressed form of the data modifications made by the statement.

In the case when the buffer pool exceeds its limits, InnoDB is forced to flush data pages to disk in order to remove the least recently used data pages. But, before it does so, InnoDB uses the LSN element of the page header section of the data page to check that the LSN of the page header is less than the last log record in the log file. If it's not, then InnoDB writes the log file records before flushing the data pages.

The Checkpointing and Recovery Processes

As we explained in Chapter 3, transaction processing systems employ a checkpointing process to mark in a log file that all data pages that have had changes made to records have been flushed to disk. We explained that this checkpoint mark contained a list of open transaction numbers at the time that the checkpoint was made. In the InnoDB checkpointing process, the checkpoint contains a linked list of data pages that may still be dirty because of pending transactions.

A separate background thread spawned specifically to handle the InnoDB checkpointing process wakes on a timed interval to flush changed data pages in the buffer pool to the ibdata files. However, InnoDB may not actually flush any data pages at this interval. This is due to the fact that InnoDB is a *fuzzy checkpointer*, meaning that it will *not* flush data changes in memory as long as *all* of the following conditions exist:

- Either the log buffer or buffer pool is not filled beyond a certain percentage of its total size limit

- Log file writes have not fallen behind data page writes (a separate thread handles each)

- No data pages have a page header LSN the same as a log record about to be overwritten by the log writer

After a crash, the InnoDB recovery process automatically kicks in on startup. InnoDB uses the LSN values in the log record to bring the data store to a consistent state based on the last checkpoint record's LSN.

Other Storage Engines

Although MyISAM and InnoDB are the most commonly used storage engines, MySQL also offers other storage engines that are more specialized. In the following sections, we'll cover the MERGE, MEMORY, ARCHIVE, CSV, FEDERATED, and NDB Cluster choices.

The MERGE Storage Engine

If you have a situation where, for performance or space reasons, you need to cut large blocks of similar data into smaller blocks, the MERGE storage engine can virtually combine identical MyISAM tables into an aggregated virtual table. A MERGE table must be created with an identical table definition to the MyISAM tables for which it offers a combined view. To create a MERGE table from multiple MyISAM tables, follow the CREATE TABLE statement with the ENGINE=MERGE UNION=(*table_list*) construct, as shown in Listing 5-2 for a fictional set of tables.[8]

Listing 5-2. *Creating a MERGE Table from Two Identical Tables*

```
mysql> CREATE TABLE t1 (
    ->     a INT NOT NULL AUTO_INCREMENT PRIMARY KEY,
    ->     message CHAR(20));
mysql> CREATE TABLE t2 (
    ->     a INT NOT NULL AUTO_INCREMENT PRIMARY KEY,
    ->     message CHAR(20));
mysql> INSERT INTO t1 (message) VALUES ('Testing'),('table'),('t1');
mysql> INSERT INTO t2 (message) VALUES ('Testing'),('table'),('t2');
mysql> CREATE TABLE total (
    ->     a INT NOT NULL AUTO_INCREMENT,
    ->     message CHAR(20), INDEX(a))
    ->     ENGINE=MERGE UNION=(t1,t2);
```

---

8. The example in Listing 5-2 is adapted from the MySQL manual.

Note that column definitions for all three tables (the original tables and the MERGE table) are identical. Instead of a `PRIMARY KEY` being defined in the MERGE table, a normal index is used on the column a.

The most common example of MERGE storage engine usage is in archival and logging schemes. For instance, suppose we have a MyISAM table that stores the web site traffic information from our online toy store. It is a fairly simple log table, which looks something like Listing 5-3.

Listing 5-3. *A Simple MyISAM Web Traffic Log Table*

```
mysql> CREATE TABLE traffic_log (
    > id INT UNSIGNED NOT NULL AUTO_INCREMENT,
    > refer_site VARCHAR(255) NOT NULL,
    > requested_uri VARCHAR(255) NOT NULL,
    > hit_date TIMESTAMP NOT NULL,
    > user_agent VARCHAR(255) NOT NULL,
    > PRIMARY KEY (id),
    > INDEX (hit_date, refer_site(30))) ENGINE=MYISAM;
```

Although this table is simple, it could quickly fill up with a lot of information over the course of a month's average web traffic to our store. Let's imagine that, in the first month of tracking, our `traffic_log` table logged 250,000 hits. MyISAM is buzzing along, inserting records at light speed because of its ability to do thousands of writes per second on an incrementing numeric primary key. But this growth rate will eventually make the table unwieldy, consuming a massive amount of disk space or, worse, using up all the available space for the data file. So, we decide to make some slight changes to the application code that inserts the log records. Instead of one giant table, we create monthly tables, named `traffic_log_`*yymm*, where *y* and *m* are the year and month, respectively. We create the tables for the year up front and change the application code to insert into the appropriate month's table based on the log record's timestamp.

A couple month's into our new system's lifetime, we make a bold move and compress older logs using the `myisampack` utility (discussed earlier, in the section about the MyISAM compressed record format). Then we seem to be getting more and more requests to provide reporting for a number of months of data at a time. Manually `UNION`ing table results together has started to get a bit annoying.

So, we decide to investigate the MERGE storage engine option. We define a MERGE table as in Listing 5-4.

Listing 5-4. *Creating a MERGE Table from Monthly Log Tables*

```
mysql> CREATE TABLE traffic_log_05 (
    > id INT UNSIGNED NOT NULL AUTO_INCREMENT,
    > refer_site VARCHAR(255) NOT NULL,
    > requested_uri VARCHAR(255) NOT NULL,
    > hit_date TIMESTAMP NOT NULL,
    > user_agent VARCHAR(255) NOT NULL,
    > INDEX (id),
    > INDEX (hit_date, refer_site(30)))
    > ENGINE=MERGE
    > UNION=( traffic_log_0501, traffic_log_0502, … , traffic_log_0512)
    > INSERT_METHOD=NO;
```

This creates a table that aggregates the data for the entire year of 2005. Setting the INSERT_METHOD to NO is good because our application is inserting records into one of the underlying tables anyway. We create indexes on id and on hit_date and refer_site because most of the requests from the sales team have been for reports grouped by week and by referring site. We put a limit of 30 characters for the index on refer_site because, after analyzing the data, the majority of the data is variable at or below 30 characters. Note that we did not define a PRIMARY KEY index for the MERGE table; doing so would produce an error since the MERGE storage engine cannot enforce primary key constraints over all its UNIONed underlying tables.

We now have a method of accessing the varying log tables using a single table interface, as shown in Listing 5-5.

Listing 5-5. *Aggregated Results from the MERGE Table*

```
mysql> SELECT LEFT(refer_site, 30) AS 'Referer', COUNT(*) AS 'Referrals'
    > FROM traffic_log_05
    > WHERE hit_date BETWEEN '2005-01-01' AND '2005-01-10'
    > GROUP BY LEFT(refer_site, 30)
    > HAVING 'Referrals' > 1000
    > ORDER BY 'Referrals' DESC
    > LIMIT 5;
```

This would return the top five highest referring sites (limited to 30 characters), in the first ten days of January 2005, with the number of referrals greater than a thousand. The MERGE engine, internally, will access the traffic_log_0501 table, but, now, we don't need to use different table names in order to access the information. All we need to do is supply our WHERE condition value to the name of the MERGE table—in this case: traffic_log_05. Furthermore, we could create a separate MERGE table, traffic_log (replacing your original table), which houses all records for our web site traffic.

Be aware that MERGE tables have some important limitations. You cannot use the REPLACE command on a MERGE table, and UNIQUE INDEX constraints are not enforced across the entire combined data set. For more information, see the MySQL manual at http://dev.mysql.com/doc/mysql/en/MERGE_table_problems.html.

When you're considering using a MERGE table, also investigate using views, available only in MySQL 5.0, instead. They provide much more flexibility than the MERGE storage engine. See Chapter 12 for a detailed discussion of views.

The MEMORY Storage Engine

The MEMORY storage engine,[9] as its name aptly implies, stores its entire contents, both data and index records, in memory. The trick with MEMORY tables, however, is that the data in the table is lost when the server is restarted. Therefore, data stored in MEMORY tables should be data that can be easily re-created on startup by using application scripts, such as lookup sets, or data that represents a time period of temporary data, like daily stock prices.

When you create a MEMORY table, one file is created under the /data_dir/schema_name/ directory named *table_name*.frm. This file contains the definition of the table.

---

9. Prior to MySQL 4.1, the MEMORY storage engine was called the HEAP table type.

To automatically re-create data in MEMORY tables, you should use the `--init-file=file` startup option. The `file` specified should contain the SQL statements used to populate the MEMORY tables from a persistent table. You do not need to issue a `CREATE TABLE` statement in the file, because the table definition is persistent across restarts.

For instance, if you wanted to increase the speed of queries asking for information on zip code radius searching (a topic we will cover in Chapter 8), you might have an InnoDB table `zips` for persistent, transaction-safe storage, coupled with a MEMORY table `zips_mem`, which contains the zip codes entirely in memory. While the InnoDB `zips` table might contain a lot of information about each zip code—population statistics, square mileage, and so on—the `zips_mem` table would contain only the information needed to do radius calculations (longitude and latitude of the zip code's centroid). In the startup file, you could have the following SQL statement, which would populate the MEMORY table:

```
INSERT INTO zips_mem SELECT zip, latitude, longitude FROM zips;
```

The downside is that any changes to the zip code information would need to be replicated against the `zips_mem` table to ensure consistency. This is why static lookups are ideally suited for MEMORY tables. After all, how often do the latitude and longitudes of zip codes change?

As you learned in Chapter 2, certain data sets and patterns can be searched more efficiently using different index algorithms. Starting with version 4.1, you can specify either a hash (the default) or B-tree index be created on a MEMORY table. Do so with the `USING algorithm` clause, where `algorithm` is the index algorithm, in your `CREATE TABLE` statement. For example, Listing 5-6 demonstrates how to implement a B-tree algorithm on a MEMORY table where you expect a lot of range queries to be issued against a temporal data type. This query pattern is often best implemented with a B-tree algorithm, versus the default hash algorithm.

Listing 5-6. *Making a MEMORY Table Use a B-Tree Index*

```
mysql> CREATE TABLE daily_stock_prices (
    > symbol VARCHAR(8) NOT NULL,
    > high DECIMAL(6,2) NOT NULL,
    > low DECIMAL(6,2) NOT NULL,
    > date DATE NOT NULL,
    > INDEX USING BTREE (date, resource)) ENGINE = MEMORY;
```

The ARCHIVE Storage Engine

New in MySQL 4.1.3 is the ARCHIVE storage engine. Its purpose is to compress large volumes of data into a smaller size. While this storage engine should not be used for regular data access (normal operations), it is excellent for storing log or archive information that is taking up too much regular space on disk.

The ARCHIVE storage engine is not available on default installations of MySQL. In order to create an ARCHIVE table, you will need to build MySQL with the `--with-archive-storage-⬥ engine` option.

No indexes are allowed when creating an ARCHIVE table; indeed, the *only* access method for retrieving records is through a table scan. Typically, you would want to convert stale log data tables into ARCHIVE tables. On the rare occasion that analysis is needed, you could create a temporary MyISAM table by selecting the entire data set and create indexes on the MyISAM table.

The CSV Storage Engine

As of version 4.1.4, MySQL introduced the CSV storage engine. The CSV storage engine is not available on default installations of MySQL. In order to create a CSV table, you will need to build MySQL with the `--with-csv-storage-engine` option.

Although this is not the most useful of all the storage engines, it can have its advantages. The CSV engine stores table meta information, like all storage engines, in an `.frm` file in the database directory. However, for the actual data file, the CSV engine creates a file with the table name and a `.CSV` extension. This is handy in that the table data can be easily copied from the database directory and transferred to a client, like Microsoft Excel, to open the table in spreadsheet format.

Practically speaking, however, there is little use to the CSV storage engine given two facts. First, no indexing is available for the storage engine, making the use of it in normal operations somewhat implausible. Second, the `INTO OUTFILE` extension clause of the `SELECT` statement negates some of the benefits we mentioned. In order to output a section of an existing table into a CSV format, you could just as easily run the following statement:

```
mysql> SELECT * INTO OUTFILE '/home/user1/my_table.csv'
    > FIELDS TERMINATED BY ',' ENCLOSED BY '"'
    > FROM my_table;
```

This would dump the file to the server's location of `/home/user1/my_table.csv`. If you wanted to place the output file onto the local client (say, if you were connecting remotely), you could execute the following from a shell prompt:

```
mysql -t -e "SELECT * FROM my_schema.my_table" | tr "\011" "," > my_file.csv
```

This would pipe tabbed results (the `-t` option) from MySQL to the `tr` program, which would translate the tab character (`\011`) to a comma character and dump the results to a CSV file on the local computer.

The FEDERATED Storage Engine

If any of you are coming from a Microsoft SQL Server background and have wondered whether MySQL implements anything like the concept of linked servers in SQL Server, look no further. Starting in version 5.0.3, you can use the FEDERATED storage engine to access databases located *on remote servers* in the same way you would on the local server.

The FEDERATED storage engine is not available on default installations of MySQL. In order to create a FEDERATED table, you will need to build a version of MySQL 5.0.3 or later with the `--with-federated-storage-engine` option.

On the local server, only an `.frm` file is created when a table with `ENGINE=FEDERATED` is created. Naturally, the data file is stored on the remote server, and thus there is no actual data file stored on the local server.

When accessing records from a FEDERATED table, MySQL uses the `mysql` client API to request resultsets from the remote server. If any results are returned, the FEDERATED storage engine converts the results to the format used by the underlying remote server's storage engine. So, if an InnoDB table on the remote server were accessed on the local server via a FEDERATED table, the local FEDERATED storage engine would create an InnoDB handler for the request and issue the requested statements to the remote server, which would execute and return any resultset needed in the standard client format. The FEDERATED storage engine would then convert the returned results into the internal format of the needed table handler (in this case, InnoDB), and use that handler to return the results through the handler's own API.

The NDB Cluster Storage Engine

The MySQL Cluster (NDB) is not really a storage engine, in that it delegates the responsibility of storage to the actual storage engines used in the databases that it manages. Once a cluster of database nodes is created, NDB controls the partitioning of data across the nodes to provide redundancy of data and performance benefits. We discuss clustering and NDB in detail in Chapter 19.

Guidelines for Choosing a Storage Engine

At this point, you might be wondering how to go about determining which storage engine is a good match for your application databases. MySQL gives you the ability to mix and match storage engines to provide the maximum flexibility when designing your schema. However, there are some caveats and some exceptions to keep in mind when making your choices.

Take time to investigate which index algorithms best fit the type of data you wish to store. As different storage engines provide different index algorithms, you may get a significant performance increase by using one over another. In the case of InnoDB, the storage engine will actually pick a B-tree or hash index algorithm based on its assessment of your data set. This takes away some of the control you might have by using a combination of MEMORY and MyISAM tables for storage; however, it might be the best fit overall. When it comes to requirements for FULLTEXT or spatial indexing, your only choice currently is MyISAM. Look for implementation of these other indexing algorithms to appear in other storage engines in the future.

Here, we present some general guidelines for choosing an appropriate storage engine for your various tables.

> *Use MyISAM for logging.* For logging purposes, the MyISAM storage engine is the best choice. Its ability to serve concurrent read requests and INSERT operations is ideal for log tables where data is naturally inserted at the end of the data file, and UPDATE and DELETE operations are rare.

> *Use MyISAM for* SELECT COUNT(*) *queries.* If you have an application that relies on multiple SELECT COUNT(*) FROM *table* queries, use the MyISAM storage engine for those tables. MyISAM's index statistics make this type of query almost instantaneous. InnoDB's performance degrades rapidly on larger data sets because it must do a scan of the index data to find the number of rows in a table. There are plans to improve InnoDB's performance of this type of query in the near future.

> *Use InnoDB for transaction processing.* When your application needs to ensure a specific level of isolation across read requests over multiple statements, use the InnoDB storage engine. Before deciding to use InnoDB, however, be sure that the transactions issued by your application code are indeed necessary. It is a mistake to start a multistatement transaction for statements that can be reduced to a single SQL request.

Use InnoDB for enforcing foreign key constraints. If the data you are storing has relationships between a master and child table (foreign keys), and it is absolutely imperative that the relationship be enforced, use InnoDB tables for both the master and child tables. Consider using the ON UPDATE CASCADE and ON UPDATE DELETE options to enforce any business rules. These options can cut down significantly on application code that would normally be required to handle enforcing business rules.

Use InnoDB for web site session data. If you store web application sessions in your database, as opposed to a file-based storage, consider using InnoDB for your storage engine. The reason for this is that typical web application sessions are UPDATE-intensive. New sessions are created, modified, and destroyed in a continual cycle as new HTTP requests are received and their sessions mapped and remapped to the database table. InnoDB's row-level locking enables fast, concurrent access for both read and write requests. Why not use a MEMORY table instead, since it is fast for reads and writes, including DELETE operations? Well, the reason is that MEMORY tables cannot support TEXT or BLOB data because the hashing algorithm used in the storage engine cannot include the TEXT and BLOB pointers. Web session data is typically stored in TEXT columns, often as a serialized array of values.

You should not assume that an initial choice of a storage engine will be appropriate throughout the life of your applications. Over time, not only will your storage and memory requirements change, but the selectivity and the data types of your tables may change. If you feel that changing a table's storage engine would have an impact, first create a test environment and make the changes there. Use the information in Chapter 6 to benchmark both schema and determine if the application would perform better with the changes.

Data Type Choices

As you know, MySQL offers various data types that you can apply to your table columns. Here, we cover the different data types in terms of some common recommendations for their use and knowledge areas we feel are often misunderstood.

■**Tip** If you're unsure about a specific data type, or simply want a reference check, consider picking up a copy of Jon Stephens and Chad Russell's excellent *Beginning MySQL Database Design and Optimization* (Apress, 2004).

Numeric Data Considerations

MySQL provides an array of numeric data types in different sizes and flavors. Choose numeric column types based on the size of the storage you need and whether you need precise or imprecise storage.

For currency data, use the DECIMAL column type, and specify the precision and scale in the column specification. *Do not use the* DOUBLE *column type to store currency data.* The DOUBLE column type is not precise, but approximate. If you are doing calculations involving currency data, you may be surprised at some of the results of your queries.

For instance, assume you defined a field product_price as DECIMAL(9,4) NOT NULL, and populate a data record with the value 99.99:

```
mysql> CREATE TABLE product (id INT NOT NULL, product_price DECIMAL(9,4) NOT NULL);
mysql> INSERT INTO product (id, product_price) VALUES (1, 99.99);
```

Next, you go to select the data records where product_price is equal to 99.99:

```
mysql> SELECT * FROM product WHERE product_price = 99.99;
```

Everything works as expected:

```
+----+---------------+
| id | product_price |
+----+---------------+
|  1 |       99.9900 |
+----+---------------+
1 row in set (0.00 sec)
```

However, you may be surprised to learn that the following query:

```
mysql> SELECT * FROM product WHERE 100 - product_price = .01;
```

yields different results depending on the data type definition:

```
mysql> SELECT * FROM product WHERE 100 - product_price = .01;
+----+---------------+
| id | product_price |
+----+---------------+
|  1 | 99.9900       |
+----+---------------+
1 row in set (0.03 sec)

mysql> ALTER TABLE product CHANGE COLUMN product_price product_price DOUBLE;
Query OK, 1 row affected (0.10 sec)
Records: 1  Duplicates: 0  Warnings: 0

mysql> SELECT * FROM product WHERE 100 - product_price = .01;
Empty set (0.00 sec)
```

As you can see, the same query produces different results depending on the precision of the data type. The DOUBLE column type cannot be relied on to produce accurate results across all hardware architectures, whereas the DECIMAL type can. But calculations involving DECIMAL data can yield unexpected results due to the underlying architecture's handling of floating-point arithmetic. Always test floating-point calculations thoroughly in application code and when upgrading MySQL versions. We have noticed differences in the way precision arithmetic is handled even across minor version changes. See http://dev.mysql.com/doc/mysql/en/problems-with-float.html for details about floating-point arithmetic issues.

String Data Considerations

As with all data types, don't go overboard when choosing the length of string fields. Be conservative, especially when deciding on the length of character columns that will be frequently indexed. For those columns that should be indexed because they frequently appear in WHERE conditions, consider using an INDEX prefix to limit the amount of actual string data stored in the index rows.

Character fields are frequently used in the storage of address data. When determining how these character columns should be structured, first consider the maximum number of characters that can be stored in the specific data field. For example, if your data set includes *only* United States zip codes, use a CHAR(5) column type. Don't make the field have a length of 10 just because you may need to store the zip+4 format data for some of the records. Instead, consider having *two* fields, one CHAR(5) to store the main, non-nullable zip code, and another nullable field for storing the +4 extension. If you are dealing with international postal addresses, investigate the maximum characters needed to store the postal code; usually, a CHAR(8) will do nicely.

■**Tip** Store spaces that naturally occur in a postal code. The benefit of removing the single space character is almost nonexistent compared to the pain of needing to remove and restore the space for display and storage purposes.

Also consider how the data will actually be searched, and ensure that separate search fields are given their own column. For instance, if your application allows end users to search for customer records based on a street address, consider using separate fields for the street number and the street name. Searches, and indexes, can then be isolated on the needed field, and thus made more efficient. Also, following rules for good database normalization, don't have separate fields for different address lines. Instead of having two fields of type VARCHAR(50) named address_1 and address_2, have a single field address, defined as VARCHAR(100). Address information can be inserted into the single field with line breaks if needed.

For applications where search speed is critical, consider replacing city and region (state) fields with a single numeric lookup value. Because they are denser, numeric indexes will have faster search speeds. You can provide a lookup system defined something like this:

```
mysql> CREATE TABLE region (
    > id INT NOT NULL AUTO_INCREMENT PRIMARY KEY
    > , region_name VARCHAR(30) NOT NULL
    > , country CHAR(2) NOT NULL);
mysql> CREATE TABLE location (
    > id INT NOT NULL AUTO_INCREMENT PRIMARY KEY
    > , region INT NOT NULL
    > , city VARCHAR(30) NOT NULL
    > , INDEX (region, city));
```

You would populate your region and location tables with the data for all cities in your coverage area. Your customer table would then need only store the 4-byte pointer to the parent location record. Let's assume you have a region with an ID of 23, which represents the state of California, in the United States. In order to find the names of customers in this region living in the city Santa Clara, you would do something like this:

```
mysql> SELECT c.name FROM location l
    > INNER JOIN customer c ON l.id = c.location
    > WHERE l.region = 23 AND l.city = 'Santa Clara';
```

This search would be able to use the index on location to find the records it needs. If you had placed the city and region information in the customer table, an index on those two fields would have needed to contain many more entries, presuming that there would be many more customer entries than location entries.

Again, indexes on numeric columns will usually be faster than character data columns of the same length, so think about converting data from a character format into a normalized lookup table with a numeric key.

Temporal Data Considerations

If you need to store only the date part of your temporal data, use the DATE column type. Don't use an INT or TIMESTAMP column type if you don't need that level of granularity. MySQL stores all the temporal data types as integers internally. The only real difference between the variations is how the data is formatted for display. So use the smallest data type (sound familiar?) that you can.

Use the TIMESTAMP column type if you have audit needs for some tables. Timestamps are an easy, efficient, and reliable method of determining when applications make changes to a record. Just remember that the first column defined as a TIMESTAMP column in the CREATE ➥ TABLE statement will be used for the create time of the record. The columns *after* that field can be updated to the current system time by updating the column equal to NULL. For instance, suppose you define your orders table like so:

```
mysql> CREATE TABLE orders (
    > id INT NOT NULL AUTO_INCREMENT PRIMARY KEY
    > , customer INT NOT NULL
    > , update_time TIMESTAMP NOT NULL
    > , create_time TIMESTAMP NOT NULL);
```

If you insert a record into the orders table, explicitly set the create_time field; otherwise, it will be entered as a 0. The update_time, being the first TIMESTAMP column defined, will automatically be set to the current timestamp:

```
mysql> INSERT INTO orders (customer, create_time) VALUES (3, NOW());
```

When you do a SELECT from the table, you will notice that the first TIMESTAMP is set to the Unix timestamp value of the current time. The second TIMESTAMP field will be 0.

```
mysql> SELECT * FROM orders;
+----+----------+----------------+----------------+
| id | customer | update_time    | create_time    |
+----+----------+----------------+----------------+
| 1  |        3 | 20050122190832 | 20050122190832 |
+----+----------+----------------+----------------+
1 row in set (0.00 sec)
```

When updating the order record later on, the update_time will automatically get updated with the current system timestamp, while the create_time will stay the same:

```
mysql> UPDATE orders SET customer = 4 WHERE id = 1;
```

Selecting from the table then yields the following:

```
mysql> SELECT * FROM orders;
+----+----------+----------------+----------------+
| id | customer | update _time   | create_time    |
+----+----------+----------------+----------------+
| 1  |        3 | 20050122192244 | 20050122190832 |
+----+----------+----------------+----------------+
1 row in set (0.00 sec)
```

So, in this way, you have a good way of telling not only when records have been updated, but also which records have *not* been updated:

```
mysql> SELECT COUNT(*) FROM orders WHERE update_time = create_time;
```

Tip Starting with version 4.1.2, you can tell MySQL how to handle the automatic updates of individual TIMESTAMP columns, instead of needing to explicitly set the TIMESTAMP to its own value during INSERT statements. See http://dev.mysql.com/doc/mysql/en/timestamp-4-1.html for more information and suggestions.

Spatial Data Considerations

The Spatial Data Extensions for MySQL will become more and more useful as more of the OpenGIS specification is implemented, and, in particular, when MySQL implements the ability to load geographic information system (GIS) data through the LOAD DATA INFILE command directly from well-known text (WKT) or well-known binary (WKB) values. Until then, using spatial types may be a little cumbersome, but you can still reap some benefits. As far as the actual data types go, the MySQL online manual provides a good lesson on how the myriad geometry types behave.

SET and ENUM Data Considerations

Now we come to a topic about which people have differing opinions. Some folks love the SET and ENUM column types, citing the time and effort saved in not having to do certain joins. Others dismiss these data types as poor excuses for not understanding how to normalize your database.

These data types are sometimes referred to as *inline tables* or *array* column types, which can be a bit of a misnomer. In actuality, both SET and ENUM are internally stored as integers. The shared meta information struct for the table handler contains the string values for the numeric index stored in the field for the data record, and these string values are mapped to the results array when returned to the client.

The SET column type differs from the ENUM column type only in the fact that multiple values can be assigned to the field, in the way a flag typically is. Values can be ANDed and ORed together when inserting in order to set the values for the flag. The FIND_IN_SET function can be used in a WHERE clause and functionally is the same as bitwise ANDing the column value. To demonstrate, the following two WHERE clauses are identical, assuming that the SET definition is option_flags SET('Red','White','Blue') NOT NULL:

```
mysql> SELECT * FROM my_table WHERE FIND_IN_SET('White', option_flags);
mysql> SELECT * FROM my_table WHERE option_flags & 2;
```

For both ENUM and SET column types, remember that you can always retrieve the underlying numeric value (versus the string mapping) by appending a +0 to your SELECT statement:

```
mysql> SELECT option_flags+0 FROM my_table;
```

Boolean Values

For Boolean values, you will notice that there is no corresponding MySQL data type. To mimic the functionality of Boolean data, you have a few different options:

- You can define the column as a TINYINT, and populate the field data with either 0 or 1. This option takes a single byte of storage per record if defined as NOT NULL.

- You may set the column as a CHAR(1) and choose a single character value to put into the field; 'Y'/'N' or '0'/'1' or 'T'/'F', for example. This option also takes a single byte of storage per record if defined as NOT NULL.

- An option offered in the MySQL documentation is to use a CHAR(0) NOT NULL column specification. This specification uses only a single bit (as opposed to a full byte), but the values inserted into the records can only be NULL[10] or '' (a null string).

Of these choices, one of the first two is probably the best route. One reason is that you will have the flexibility to add more values over time if needed—say, because your is_active Boolean field turned into a status lookup field. Also, the NULL and '' values are difficult to keep separate, and application code might easily fall into interpreting the two values distinctly.

We hope that, in the future, the BIT data type will be a full-fledged MySQL data type as it is in other databases, without the somewhat ungraceful current definition.

---

10. Yes, you did read that correctly. The column *must* be defined as NOT NULL, but can have NULL values inserted into data records for the field.

STORING DATA OUTSIDE THE DATABASE

Before you store data in a database table, first evaluate if a database is indeed the correct choice of storage. For certain data, particularly image data, the file system is the best choice—storing binary image data in a database adds an unnecessary level of complexity. The same rule applies to storing HTML or large text values in the database. Instead, store a file path to the HTML or text data.

There are, of course, exceptions to this rule. One would be if image data needed to be replicated across multiple servers, in which case, you would store the image data as a BLOB and have slave servers replicate the data for retrieval. Another would be if there were security restrictions on the files you want to display to a user. Say, for instance, you need to provide medical documents to doctors around the country through a web site. You don't want to simply put the PDF documents on a web server, as doctors may forward a link to one another, and trying to secure each web directory containing separate documents with an .htaccess file would be tedious. Instead, it would be better to write the PDF to the database as a BLOB field and provide a link in your secure application that would download the BLOB data and display it.

Some General Data Type Guidelines

Your choice of not only which data types you use for your field definitions, but the size and precision you specify for those data types can have a huge impact on database performance and maintainability. Here are some tips on choosing data types:

Use an auto-incrementing primary key value for MyISAM tables that require many reads and writes. As shown earlier, the MyISAM storage engine READ LOCAL table locks do not hinder SELECT statements, nor do they impact INSERT statements, as long as MySQL can append the new records to the end of the .MYD data file.

Be minimalistic. Don't automatically make your auto-incrementing primary key a BIGINT if that's not required. Determine the realistic limits of your storage requirements and remember that, if necessary, you can resize data types later. Similarly, for DECIMAL fields, don't waste space and speed by specifying a precision and scale greater than you need. This is especially true for your primary keys. Making them as small as possible will enable more records to fit into a single block in the key cache, which means fewer reads and faster results.

Use CHAR with MyISAM; VARCHAR with InnoDB. For your MyISAM tables, you can see a performance benefit by using fixed-width CHAR fields for string data instead of VARCHAR fields, especially if only a few columns would actually benefit from the VARCHAR specification. The InnoDB storage engine internally treats CHAR and VARCHAR fields the same way. This means that you will see a benefit from having VARCHAR columns in your InnoDB tables, because more data records will fit in a single index data page.

■**Note** From time to time, you will notice MySQL silently change column specifications upon table creation. For character data, MySQL will automatically convert requests for CHAR data types to VARCHAR data types when the length of the CHAR field is greater than or equal to four and there is already a variable length column in the table definition. If you see column specifications change silently, head to http://dev.mysql.com/doc/mysql/en/Silent_column_changes.html to see why the change was made.

Don't use NULL *if you can avoid it.* NULLs complicate the query optimization process and increase storage requirements, so avoid them if you can. Sometimes, if you have a majority of fields that are NOT NULL and a minority that are NULL, it makes sense to create a separate table for the nullable data. This is especially true if the NOT NULL fields are a fixed width, as MyISAM tables can use a faster scan operation algorithm when the row format is fixed length. However, as we noted in our coverage of the MyISAM record format, you will see no difference unless you have more than seven NULL fields in the table definition.

Use DECIMAL *for money data, with* UNSIGNED *if it will always be greater than zero.* For instance, if you want to store a column that will contain prices for items, and those items will never go above $1,000.00, you should use DECIMAL(6,2) UNSIGNED, which accounts for the maximum scale and precision necessary without wasting any space.

Consider replacing ENUM *column types with separate lookup tables.* Not only does this encourage proper database normalization, but it also eases changes to the lookup table values. Changing ENUM values once they are defined is notoriously awkward. Similarly, consider replacing SET columns with a lookup table for the SET values and a relationship (N-M) table to join lookup keys with records. Instead of using bitwise logic for search conditions, you would look for the existence or absence of values in the relational table.

If you are really unsure about whether a data type you have chosen for a table is appropriate, you can ask MySQL to help you with your decision. The ANALYSE() procedure returns suggestions for an appropriate column definition, based on a query over existing data, as shown in Listing 5-7. Use an actual data set with ANALYSE(), so that your results are as realistic as possible.

Listing 5-7. *Using PROCEDURE ANALYSE() to Find Data Type Suggestions*

```
mysql> SELECT * FROM http_auth_idb PROCEDURE ANALYSE() \G
*************************** 1. row ***************************
        Field_name: test.http_auth_idb.username
         Min_value: aaafunknufcnhmiosugnsbkqp
         Max_value: yyyxjvnmrmsmrhadwpwkbvbdd
        Min_length: 25
        Max_length: 25
  Empties_or_zeros: 0
             Nulls: 0
```

```
        Avg_value_or_avg_length: 25.0000
                        Std: NULL
          Optimal_fieldtype: CHAR(25) NOT NULL
*************************** 2. row ***************************
                Field_name: test.http_auth_idb.pass
                 Min_value: aaafdgtvorivxgobgkjsvauto
                 Max_value: yyyllrpnmuphxyiffifxhrfcq
                Min_length: 25
                Max_length: 25
         Empties_or_zeros: 0
                     Nulls: 0
        Avg_value_or_avg_length: 25.0000
                        Std: NULL
          Optimal_fieldtype: CHAR(25) NOT NULL
*************************** 3. row ***************************
                Field_name: test.http_auth_idb.uid
                 Min_value: 1
                 Max_value: 90000
                Min_length: 1
                Max_length: 5
         Empties_or_zeros: 0
                     Nulls: 0
        Avg_value_or_avg_length: 45000.5000
                        Std: 54335.7692
          Optimal_fieldtype: MEDIUMINT(5) UNSIGNED NOT NULL
*************************** 4. row ***************************
                Field_name: test.http_auth_idb.gid
                 Min_value: 1210
                 Max_value: 2147446891
                Min_length: 4
                Max_length: 10
         Empties_or_zeros: 0
                     Nulls: 0
        Avg_value_or_avg_length: 1073661145.4308
                        Std: 0.0000
          Optimal_fieldtype: INT(10) UNSIGNED NOT NULL
4 rows in set (1.53 sec)
```

As you can see, the ANALYSE() procedure gives suggestions on an optimal field type based on its assessment of the values contained within the columns and the minimum and maximum lengths of those values. Be aware that ANALYSE() tends to recommend ENUM values quite often, but we suggest using separate lookup tables instead. ANALYSE() is most useful for quickly determining if a NULL field can be NOT NULL (see the Nulls column in the output), and for determining the average, minimum, and maximum values for textual data.

Summary

In this chapter, we've covered information that will come in handy as you develop an understanding of how to implement your database applications in MySQL. Our discussion on storage engines focused on the main differences in the way transactions, storage, and indexing are implemented across the range of available options. We gave you some recommendations in choosing your storage engines, so that you can learn from the experience of others before making any major mistakes.

We also examined the various data types available to you as you define the schema of your database. We looked at the strengths and peculiarities of each type of data, and then provided some suggestions to guide you in your database creation.

In the next chapter, you will learn some techniques for benchmarking and profiling your database applications. These skills will be vital to our exploration of SQL and index optimization in the following chapters.

CHAPTER 6

■■■

Benchmarking and Profiling

This book departs from novice or intermediate texts in that we focus on using and developing for MySQL from a *professional* angle. We don't think the difference between a normal user and a professional user lies in the ability to recite every available function in MySQL's SQL extensions, nor in the capacity to administer large databases or high-volume applications.

Rather, we think the difference between a novice user and a professional is twofold. First, the professional has the desire to understand *why* and *how* something works. Merely knowing the steps to accomplish an activity is not enough. Second, the professional approaches a problem with an understanding that the circumstances that created the problem can and will change over time, leading to variations in the problem's environment, and consequently, a need for different solutions. The professional developer or administrator focuses on understanding how things work, and sets about to build a framework that can react to and adjust for changes in the environment.

The subject of benchmarking and profiling of database-driven applications addresses the core of this professional outlook. It is part of the foundation on which the professional's framework for understanding is built. As a professional developer, understanding how and why benchmarking is useful, and how profiling can save you and your company time and money, is critical.

As the size of an application grows, the need for a reliable method of measuring the application's performance also grows. Likewise, as more and more users start to query the database application, the need for a standardized framework for identifying bottlenecks also increases. Benchmarking and profiling tools fill this void. They create the framework on which your ability to identify problems and compare various solutions depends. Any reader who has been on a team scrambling to figure out why a certain application or web page is not performing correctly understands just how painful *not* having this framework in place can be.

Yes, setting up a framework for benchmarking your applications takes time and effort. It's not something that just happens by flipping a switch. Likewise, effectively profiling an application requires the developer and administrator to take a proactive stance. Waiting for an application to experience problems is *not* professional, but, alas, is usually the status quo, even for large applications. Above all, we want you to take from this chapter not only knowledge of how to establish benchmarks and a profiling system, but also a true understanding of the importance of each.

In this chapter, we don't assume you have any knowledge of these topics. Why? Well, one reason is that most novice and intermediate books on MySQL don't cover them. Another reason is that the vast majority of programmers and administrators we've met over the years (including ourselves at various points) have resorted to the old trial-and-error method of identifying bottlenecks and comparing changes to application code.

In this chapter, we'll cover the following topics:

- Benefits of benchmarking

- Guidelines for conducting benchmarks

- Tools for benchmarking

- Benefits of profiling

- Guidelines for profiling

- Tools for profiling

What Can Benchmarking Do for You?

Benchmark tests allow you to measure your application's performance, both in execution speed and memory consumption. Before we demonstrate how to set up a reliable benchmarking framework, let's first examine what the results of benchmark tests can show you about your application's performance and in what situations running benchmarks can be useful. Here is a brief list of what benchmark tests can help you do:

- Make simple performance comparisons

- Determine load limits

- Test your application's ability to deal with change

- Find potential problem areas

BENCHMARKING, PROFILING—WHAT'S THE DIFFERENCE?

No doubt, you've all heard the terms *benchmarking* and *profiling* bandied about the technology schoolyard numerous times over the years. But what do these terms mean, and what's the difference between them?

Benchmarking is the practice of creating a set of performance results for a given set of tests. These tests represent the performance of an entire application or a piece of the application. The performance results are used as an indicator of how well the application or application piece performed given a specific configuration. These benchmark test results are used in comparisons between the application changes to determine the effects, if any, of that change.

Profiling, on the other hand, is a method of diagnosing the performance bottlenecks of an application. Like benchmark tests, profilers produce resultsets that can be analyzed in order to determine the pieces of an application that are problematic, either in their performance (time to complete) or their resource usage (memory allocation and utilization). But, unlike benchmark tools, which typically test the *theoretical limits* of the application, profilers show you a snapshot of what is *actually occurring* on your system.

Taken together, benchmarking and profiling tools provide a platform that can pinpoint the problem areas of your application. Benchmark tools provide you the ability to compare changes in your application, and profilers enable you to diagnose problems as they occur.

Conducting Simple Performance Comparisons

Suppose you are in the beginning phases of designing a toy store e-commerce application. You've mapped out a basic schema for the database and think you have a real winner on your hands. For the product table, you've determined that you will key the table based on the company's internal SKU, which happens to be a 50-character alphanumeric identifier. As you start to add more tables to the database schema, you begin to notice that many of the tables you're adding have foreign key references to this product SKU. Now, you start to question whether the 50-character field is a good choice, considering the large number of joined tables you're likely to have in the application's SQL code.

You think to yourself, "I wonder if this large character identifier will slow down things compared to having a trimmer, say, integer identifier?" Common sense tells you that it will, of course, but you don't have any way of determining *how* much slower the character identifier will perform. Will the performance impact be negligible? What if it isn't? Will you redesign the application to use a smaller key once it is in production?

But you don't need to just guess at the ramifications of your schema design. You can *benchmark test it and prove it*! You can determine that using a smaller integer key would result in an improvement of x% over the larger character key.

The results of the benchmark tests alone may not determine whether or not you decide to use an alphanumeric key. You may decide that the benefit of having a natural key, as opposed to a generated key, is worth the performance impact. But, when you have the results of your benchmarks in front of you, you're making an *informed* decision, not just a guess. The benchmark test results show you *specifically* what the impact of your design choices will be.

Here are some examples of how you can use benchmark tests in performance comparisons:

- A coworker complained that when you moved from MySQL 4.0.18 to MySQL 4.1, the performance of a specific query decreased dramatically. You can use a benchmark test against both versions of MySQL to test the claim.

- A client complained that the script you created to import products into the database from spreadsheets does not have the ability to "undo" itself if an error occurs halfway through. You want to understand how adding transactions to the script will affect its performance.

- You want to know whether replacing the normal B-tree index on your `product.name` `varchar(150)` field with a full-text index will increase search speeds on the product name once you have 100,000 products loaded into the database.

- How will the performance of a `SELECT` query against three of your tables be affected by having 10 concurrent client connections compared with 20, 30, or 100 client connections?

Determining Load Limits

Benchmarks also allow you to determine the limitations of your database server under load. By *load*, we simply mean a heavy level of activity from clients requesting data from your application. As you'll see in the "Benchmarking Tools" section later in this chapter, the benchmarking tools you will use allow you to test the limits, measured in the number of queries performed per second, given a supplied number of concurrent connections. This ability to provide insight into the stress level under which your hardware and application will most likely fail is an invaluable tool in assessing both your hardware and software configuration.

Determining load limits is particularly of interest to web application developers. You want to know *before a failure occurs* when you are approaching a problematic volume level for the web server and database server. A number of web application benchmarking tools, commonly called *load generators*, measure these limits effectively. Load generators fall into two general categories:

Contrived load generator: This type of load generator makes no attempt to simulate actual web traffic to a server. Contrived load generators use a sort of brute-force methodology to push concurrent requests for a specific resource through the pipeline. In this way, contrived load generation is helpful in determining a particular web page's limitations, but these results are often *theoretical*, because, as we all know, few web sites receive traffic to only a single web page or resource. Later in this chapter, we'll take a look at the most common contrived load generator available to open-source web application developers: ApacheBench.

Realistic load generator: On the flip side of the coin, realistic load generators attempt to determine load limitations based on actual traffic patterns. Typically, these tools will use actual web server log files in order to simulate typical user sessions on the site. These realistic load generation tools can be very useful in determining the limitations of the overall system, not just a specific piece of one, because the entire application is put through the ropes. An example of a benchmarking tool with the capability to do realistic load generation is httperf, which is covered later in this chapter.

Testing an Application's Ability to Deal with Change

To continue our online store application example, suppose that after running a few early benchmark tests, you determine that the benefits of having a natural key on the product SKU outweigh the performance impact you found—let's say, you discovered an 8% performance degradation. However, in these early benchmark tests, you used a test data set of 10,000 products and 100,000 orders.

While this might be a realistic set of test data for the first six months into production, it might be significantly less than the size of those tables in a year or two. Your benchmark framework will show you how your application will perform with a larger database size, and in doing so, will help you to be realistic about when your hardware or application design may need to be refactored.

Similarly, if you are developing commercial-grade software, it is imperative that you know how your database design will perform under varying database sizes and hardware configurations. Larger customers may often *demand* to see performance metrics that match closely their projected database size and traffic. Your benchmarking framework will allow you to provide answers to your clients' questions.

Finding Potential Problem Areas

Finally, benchmark tests give you the ability to identify potential problems on a broad scale. More than likely, a benchmark test result won't show you what's wrong with that faulty loop you just coded. However, the test can be very useful for determining which general parts of an application or database design are the weakest.

For example, let's say you run a set of benchmark tests for the main pages in your toy store application. The results show that of all the pages, the page responsible for displaying the order history has the worst performance; that is, the least number of concurrent requests for the order history page could be performed by the benchmark. This shows you the *area* of the application that could be a potential problem. The benchmark test results won't show you the specific code blocks of the order history page that take the most resources, but the benchmark points you in the direction of the problem. Without the benchmark test results, you would be forced to wait until the customer service department started receiving complaints about slow application response on the order history page.

As you'll see later in this chapter, profiling tools enable you to see which specific blocks of code are problematic in a particular web page or application screen.

General Benchmarking Guidelines

We've compiled a list of general guidelines to consider as you develop your benchmarking framework. This list highlights strategies you should adopt in order to most effectively diagnose the health and growth prospects of your application code:

- Set real performance standards.

- Be proactive.

- Isolate the changed variables.

- Use real data sets.

- Make small changes and then rerun benchmarks.

- Turn off unnecessary programs and the query cache.

- Repeat tests to determine averages.

- Save benchmark results.

Let's take a closer look at each of these guidelines.

Setting Real Performance Standards

Have you ever been on the receiving end of the following statement by a fellow employee or customer? "Your application is really slow today." (We bet just reading it makes some of you cringe. Hey, we've all been there at some point or another.) You might respond with something to the effect of, "What does 'really slow' mean, ma'am?"

As much as you may not want to admit it, this situation is *not* the customer's fault. The problem has arisen due to the fact that the customer's *perception* of the application's performance is that there has been a slowdown compared with the *usual* level of performance. Unfortunately for you, there isn't anything written down anywhere that states *exactly* what the usual performance of the application is.

Not having a clear understanding of the acceptable performance standards of an application can have a number of ramifications. Working with the project stakeholders to determine performance standards helps involve the end users at an early stage of the development and gives the impression that your team cares about their perceptions of the application's performance and what an acceptable response time should be. As any project manager can tell you, setting expectations is one of the most critical components of a successful project. From a performance perspective, you should endeavor to set at least the following acceptable standards for your application:

Response times: You should know what the stakeholders and end users consider an acceptable response time for most application pieces from the outset of the project. For each application piece, work with business experts, and perhaps conduct surveys, to determine the threshold for how fast your application should return results to the user. For instance, for an e-commerce application, you would want to establish acceptable performance metrics for your shopping cart process: adding items to the cart, submitting an order, and so on. The more specific you can be, the better. If a certain process will undoubtedly take more time than others, as might be the case with an accounting data export, be sure to include *realistic* acceptable standards for those pieces.

Concurrency standards: Determining predicted levels of concurrency for a fledging project can sometimes be difficult. However, there is definite value to recording the stakeholders' expectation of how many users should be able to concurrently use the application under a normal traffic volume. For instance, if the company expects the toy store to be able to handle 50 customers simultaneously, then benchmark tests must test against those expectations.

Acceptable deviation: No system's traffic and load are static. Fluctuations in concurrency and request volumes naturally occur on all major applications, and it is important to set expectations with the stakeholders as to a normal deviation from acceptable standards. Typically, this is done by providing for a set interval during which performance standards may fluctuate a certain percentage. For instance, you might say that having performance degrade 10% over the course of an hour falls within acceptable performance standards. If the performance decrease lasts longer than this limit, or if the performance drops by 30%, then acceptable standards have not been met.

Use these performance indicators in constructing your baselines for benchmark testing. When you run entire application benchmarks, you will be able to confirm that the current database performance meets the acceptable standards set by you and your stakeholders. Furthermore, you can determine how the growth of your database and an increase in traffic to the site might threaten these goals.

The main objective here is to have these goals *in writing*. This is critical to ensuring that expectations are met. Additionally, having the performance standards on record allows your team to evaluate its work with a real set of guidelines. Without a record of acceptable standards and benchmark tests, you'll just be guessing that you've met the client's requirements.

Being Proactive

Being proactive goes to the heart of what we consider to be a professional outlook on application development and database administration. Your goal is to identify problems *before* they occur. Being *reactive* results in lost productivity and poor customer experience, and can significantly mar your development team's reputation. There is nothing worse than working in an IT department that is constantly "fighting fires." The rest of your company will come to view the team as inexperienced, and reach the conclusion that you didn't design the application properly in the first place.

Don't let reactive attitudes tarnish your project team. Take up the fight from the start by including benchmark testing as an integral part of your development process. By harnessing the power of your benchmarking framework, you can predict problems well before they rear their ugly heads.

Suppose early benchmark tests on your existing hardware have shown your e-commerce platform's performance will degrade rapidly once 50 concurrent users are consistently querying the database. Knowing that this limit will eventually be reached, you can run benchmarks against other hardware configurations or even different configurations of the MySQL server variables to determine if changes will make a substantial impact. You can then turn to the management team and show, certifiably, that without an expenditure of, say, $3,000 for new hardware, the web site will fall below the acceptable performance standards.

The management team will appreciate your ability to solve performance problems *before* they occur and provide real test results as opposed to a guess.

Isolating Changed Variables

When testing application code, or configurations of hardware or software, always isolate the variable you wish to test. This is an important scientific principle: in order to show a correlation between one variable and a test result, you must ensure that *all other things remain equal*.

You must ensure that the tests are run in an identical fashion, with no other changes to the test other than those tested for. In real terms, this means that when you run a benchmark to test that your integer product key is faster than your character product key, the only difference between the two benchmarks should be the product table's key field data type. If you make other changes to the schema, or run the tests against different data sets, you dilute the test result, and you cannot reliably state that the difference in the benchmark results is due to the change in the product key's data type.

Likewise, if you are testing to determine the impact of a SQL statement's performance given a twentyfold increase in the data set's size, the only difference between the two benchmarks should be the number of rows being operated upon.

Because it takes time to set up and to run benchmarks, you'll often be tempted to take shortcuts. Let's say you have a suspicion that if you increase the key_buffer_size, query_cache_size, and sort_buffer_size server system variables in your my.cnf file, you'll get a big performance increase. So, you run the test with and without those variable changes, and find you're absolutely right! The test showed a performance increase of 4% over the previous run. You've guessed correctly that your changes would increase throughput and performance, but, sadly, you're operating on false assumptions. You've assumed, because the test came back with an overall increase in performance, that increasing all three system variable values each improves the performance of the application. What if the changes to the sort_buffer_size and query_cache_size increased throughput by 5%, but the change in the key_buffer_size variable decreased performance by 1%? You wouldn't know this was the case. So, the bottom line is that you should try to isolate a single changed variable in your tests.

Using Real Data Sets

To get the most accurate results from your benchmark tests, try to use data sets from actual database tables, or at least data sets that represent a realistic picture of the data to be stored in your future tables. If you don't have actual production tables to use in your testing, you can use a data generator to produce sample data sets. We'll demonstrate a simple generation tool (the gen-data program that accompanies Super Smack) a little later in this chapter, but you may find that writing your own homegrown data set generation script will produce test sets that best meet your needs.

When trying to create or collect realistic test data sets, consider key selectivity, text columns, and the number of rows.

Key Selectivity

Try to ensure that fields in your tables on which indexes will be built contain a distribution of key values that accurately depicts the real application. For instance, assume you have an orders table with a char(1) field called status containing one of ten possible values, say, the letters A through J to represent the various stages that order can be in during its lifetime. You know that once the orders table is filled with production data, more than 70% of the status field values will be in the J stage, which represents a closed, completed order.

Suppose you run benchmark tests for an order-report SQL statement that summarizes the orders filtered by their status, and this statement uses an index on the status field. If your test data set uses an equal distribution of values in the status column—perhaps because you used a data generation program that randomly chose the status value—your test will likely be skewed. In the real-world database, the likelihood that the optimizer would choose an index on the status column might be much less than in your test scenario. So, when you generate data sets for use in testing, make sure you investigate the selectivity of indexed fields to ensure the generated data set approximates the real-world distribution as closely as possible.

Text Columns

When you are dealing with larger text columns, especially ones with varying lengths, try to put a realistic distribution of text lengths into your data sets. This will provide a much more accurate depiction of how your database will perform in real-world scenarios.

If you load a test data set with similarly sized rows, the performance of the benchmark may not accurately reflect a true production scenario, where a table's data pages contain varying numbers of rows because of varying length text fields. For instance, let's say you have a table in your e-commerce database that stores customer product reviews. Clearly, these reviews can vary in length substantially. It would be imprudent to run benchmarks against a data set you've generated with 100,000 records, each row containing a text field with 1,000 bytes of character data. It's simply not a realistic depiction of the data that would actually fill the table.

Number of Rows

If you actually have millions of orders completed in your e-commerce application, but run benchmarks against a data set of only 100,000 records, your benchmarks will not represent the reality of the application, so they will be essentially useless to you. The benchmark run against 100,000 records may depict a scenario in which the server was able to cache in memory most or all of the order records. The same benchmark performed against two million order records may yield dramatically lower load limits because the server was not able to cache all the records.

Making Small Changes and Rerunning Benchmarks

The idea of making only small changes follows nicely from our recommendation of always isolating a single variable during testing. When you do change a variable in a test case, make small changes if you are adjusting settings. If you want to see the effects on the application's load limits given a change in the max_user_connections setting, adjust the setting in small increments and rerun the test, noting the effects. "Small" is, of course, relative, and will depend on the specific setting you're changing. The important thing is to continue making similar adjustments in subsequent tests.

For instance, you might run a baseline test for the existing max_user_connections value. Then, on the next tests, you increase the value of the max_user_connections value by 20 each time, noting the increase or decrease in the queries per second and concurrency thresholds in each run. Usually, your end goal will be to determine the optimal setting for the max_user_connections, given your hardware configuration, application design, and database size.

By plotting the results of your benchmark tests and keeping changes at a small, even pace, you will be able to more finely analyze where the optimal setting of the tested variable should be.

Turning Off Unnecessary Programs and the Query Cache

When running benchmark tests against your development server to determine the difference in performance between two methods or SQL blocks, make sure you turn off any unnecessary programs during testing, because they might interfere or obscure a test's results. For instance, if you run a test for one block of code, and, during the test for a comparison block of code a cron job is running in the background, the test results might be skewed, depending on how much processing power is being used by the job.

Typically, you should make sure only necessary services are running. Make sure that any backup jobs are disabled and won't run during the testing. Remember that the whole purpose is to isolate the test environment as much as possible.

Additionally, we like to turn off the query cache when we run certain performance comparisons. We want to ensure that one benchmark run isn't benefiting from the caching of resultsets inserted into the query cache during a previous run. To disable the query cache, you can simply set the query_cache_size variable to 0 before the run:

```
mysql> SET GLOBALS query_cache_size = 0;
```

Just remember to turn it back on when you need it!

Repeating Tests to Determine Averages

Always repeat your benchmark tests a number of times. You'll sometimes find that the test results come back with slightly different numbers each time. Even if you've shut down all nonessential processes on the testing server and eliminated the possibility that other programs or scripts may interfere with the performance tests, you still may find some discrepancies from test to test. So, in order to get an accurate benchmark result, it's often best to take a series of the same benchmark, and then average the results across all test runs.

Saving Benchmark Results

Always save the results of your benchmarks for future analysis and as baselines for future benchmark tests. Remember that when you do performance comparisons, you want a baseline test to compare the change to. Having a set of saved benchmarks also allows you to maintain a record of the changes you made to your hardware, application configuration, and so on, which can be a valuable asset in tracking where and when problems may have occurred.

Benchmarking Tools

Now that we've taken a look at how benchmarking can help you and some specific strategies for benchmarking, let's get our hands dirty. We're going to show you a set of tools that, taken together, can provide the start of your benchmarking framework. Each of these tools has its own strengths, and you will find a use for each of them in different scenarios. We'll investigate the following tools:

- MySQL benchmarking suite
- MySQL Super Smack
- MyBench
- ApacheBench
- httperf

MySQL's Benchmarking Suite

MySQL comes with its own suite of benchmarking tools, available in the source distribution under the /sql-bench directory. This suite of benchmarking shell and Perl scripts is useful for testing differences between installed versions of MySQL and testing differences between MySQL running on different hardware. You can also use MySQL's benchmarking tools to compare MySQL with other database server systems, like Oracle, PostgreSQL, and Microsoft SQL Server.

■Tip Of course, many benchmark tests have already been run. You can find some of these tests in the source distribution in the /sql-bench/Results directory. Additionally, you can find other non-MySQL-generated benchmarks at http://www.mysql.com/it-resources/benchmarks/.

In addition to the benchmarking scripts, the crash-me script available in the /sql-bench directory provides a handy way to test the feature set of various database servers. This script is also available on MySQL's web site: http://dev.mysql.com/tech-resources/features.html.

However, there is one major flaw with the current benchmark tests: they run in a serial manner, meaning statements are issued one after the next in a brute-force manner. This means that if you want to test differences between hardware with multiple processes, you will need to use a different benchmarking toolset, such as MyBench or Super Smack, in order to get reliable results. Also note that this suite of tools is *not* useful for testing your own specific applications, because the tools test only a specific set of generic SQL statements and operations.

Running All the Benchmarks

Running the MySQL benchmark suite of tests is a trivial matter, although the tests themselves can take quite a while to execute. To execute the full suite of tests, simply run the following:

```
#> cd /path/to/mysqlsrc/sql-bench
#> ./run-all-tests [options]
```

Quite a few parameters may be passed to the run-all-tests script. The most notable of these are outlined in Table 6-1.

Table 6-1. *Parameters for Use with MySQL Benchmarking Test Scripts*

Option	Description
--server='server name'	Specifies which database server the benchmarks should be run against. Possible values include 'MySQL', 'MS-SQL', 'Oracle', 'DB2', 'mSQL', 'Pg', 'Solid', 'Sybase', 'Adabas', 'AdabasD', 'Access', 'Empress', and 'Informix'.
--log	Stores the results of the tests in a directory specified by the --dir option (defaults to /sql-bench/output). Result files are named in a format RUN-*xxx*, where *xxx* is the platform tested; for instance, /sql-bench/output/RUN-mysql-Linux_2.6.10_1.766_FC3_i686. If this looks like a formatted version of #> uname -a, that's because it is.
--dir	Directory for logging output (see --log).
--use-old-result	Overwrites any existing logged result output (see --log).
--comment	A convenient way to insert a comment into the result file indicating the hardware and database server configuration tested.
--fast	Lets the benchmark framework use non-ANSI-standard SQL commands if such commands can make the querying faster.
--host='host'	Very useful option when running the benchmark test from a remote location. 'Host' should be the host address of the remote server where the database is located; for instance 'www.xyzcorp.com'.
--small-test	Really handy for doing a short, simple test to ensure a new MySQL installation works properly on the server you just installed it on. Instead of running an exhaustive benchmark, this forces the suite to verify only that the operations succeeded.
--user	User login.
--password	User password.

So, if you wanted to run all the tests against the MySQL database server, logging to an output file and simply verifying that the benchmark tests worked, you would execute the following from the /sql-bench directory:

```
#> ./run-all-tests --small-test --log
```

Viewing the Test Results

When the benchmark tests are finished, the script states:

```
Test finished.  You can find the result in:
output/RUN-mysql-Linux_2.6.10_1.766_FC3_i686
```

To view the result file, issue the following command:

```
#> cat output/RUN-mysql-Linux_2.6.10_1.766_FC3_i686
```

The result file contains a summary of all the tests run, including any parameters that were supplied to the benchmark script. Listing 6-1 shows a small sample of the result file.

Listing 6-1. *Sample Excerpt from RUN-mysql-Linux_2.6.10_1.766_FC3_i686*

```
... omitted
alter-table: Total time:  2 wallclock secs ( 0.03 usr  0.01 sys +  0.00 cusr  0.00 \
  csys =  0.04 CPU)
ATIS: Total time:  6 wallclock secs ( 1.61 usr  0.29 sys +  0.00 cusr  0.00 \
  csys =  1.90 CPU)
big-tables: Total time:  0 wallclock secs ( 0.14 usr  0.05 sys +  0.00 cusr  0.00 \
  csys =  0.19 CPU)
connect: Total time:  2 wallclock secs ( 0.58 usr  0.16 sys +  0.00 cusr  0.00 \
  csys =  0.74 CPU)
create: Total time:  1 wallclock secs ( 0.08 usr  0.01 sys +  0.00 cusr  0.00 \
  csys =  0.09 CPU)
insert: Total time:  9 wallclock secs ( 3.32 usr  0.68 sys +  0.00 cusr  0.00 \
  csys =  4.00 CPU)
select: Total time: 14 wallclock secs ( 5.22 usr  0.63 sys +  0.00 cusr  0.00 \
  csys =  5.85 CPU)
... omitted
```

As you can see, the result file contains a summary of how long each test took to execute, in "wallclock" seconds. The numbers in parentheses, to the right of the wallclock seconds, show the amount of time taken by the script for some housekeeping functionality; they represent the part of the total seconds that should be disregarded by the benchmark as simply overhead of running the script.

In addition to the main RUN-*xxx* output file, you will also find in the /sql-bench/output directory nine other files that contain detailed information about each of the tests run in the benchmark. We'll take a look at the format of those detailed files in the next section (Listing 6-2).

Running a Specific Test

The MySQL benchmarking suite gives you the ability to run one specific test against the database server, in case you are concerned about the performance comparison of only a particular set of operations. For instance, if you just wanted to run benchmarks to compare connection operation performance, you could execute the following:

```
#> ./test-connect
```

This will start the benchmarking process that runs a series of loops to compare the connection process and various SQL statements. You should see the script informing you of various tasks it is completing. Listing 6-2 shows an excerpt of the test run.

Listing 6-2. *Excerpt from ./test-connect*

```
Testing server 'MySQL 5.0.2 alpha' at 2005-03-07  1:12:54

Testing the speed of connecting to the server and sending of data
Connect tests are done 10000 times and other tests 100000 times

Testing connection/disconnect
Time to connect (10000): 13 wallclock secs \
 ( 8.32 usr  1.03 sys +  0.00 cusr  0.00 csys =  9.35 CPU)

Test connect/simple select/disconnect
Time for connect+select_simple (10000): 17 wallclock secs \
 ( 9.18 usr  1.24 sys +  0.00 cusr  0.00 csys = 10.42 CPU)

Test simple select
Time for select_simple (100000): 10 wallclock secs \
 ( 2.40 usr  1.55 sys +  0.00 cusr  0.00 csys =  3.95 CPU)
… omitted

Total time: 167 wallclock secs \
 (58.90 usr 17.03 sys +  0.00 cusr  0.00 csys = 75.93 CPU)
```

As you can see, the test output shows a detailed picture of the benchmarks performed.

You can use these output files to analyze the effects of changes you make to the MySQL server configuration. Take a baseline benchmark script, like the one in Listing 6-2, and save it. Then, after making the change to the configuration file you want to test—for instance, changing the key_buffer_size value—rerun the same test and compare the output results to see if, and by how much, the performance of your benchmark tests have changed.

MySQL Super Smack

Super Smack is a powerful, customizable benchmarking tool that provides load limitations, in terms of queries per second, of the benchmark tests it is supplied. Super Smack works by processing a custom configuration file (called a *smack file*), which houses instructions on how to process one or more series of queries (called *query barrels* in smack lingo). These configuration files are the heart of Super Smack's power, as they give you the ability to customize the processing of your SQL queries, the creation of your test data, and other variables.

Before you use Super Smack, you need to download and install it, since it does not come with MySQL. Go to http://vegan.net/tony/supersmack and download the latest version of Super Smack from Tony Bourke's web site.[1] Use the following to install Super Smack, after

---

1. Super Smack was originally developed by Sasha Pachev, formerly of MySQL AB. Tony Bourke now maintains the source code and makes it available on his web site (http://vegan.net/tony/).

changing to the directory where you just downloaded the tar file to (we've downloaded version 1.2 here; there may be a newer version of the software when you reach the web site):

```
#> tar -xzf super-smack-1.2.tar.gz
#> cd super-smack-1.2
#> ./configure –with-mysql
#> make install
```

Running Super Smack

Make sure you're logged in as a root user when you install Super Smack. Then, to get an idea of what the output of a sample smack run is, execute the following:

```
#> super-smack -d mysql smacks/select-key.smack 10 100
```

This command fires off the super-smack executable, telling it to use MySQL (-d mysql), passing it the smack configuration file located in smack/select-key.smack, and telling it to use 10 concurrent clients and to repeat the tests in the smack file 100 times for each client.

You should see something very similar to Listing 6-3. The connect times and q_per_s values may be different on your own machine.

Listing 6-3. *Executing Super Smack for the First Time*

```
Error running query select count(*) from http_auth: \
Table 'test.http_auth' doesn't exist
Creating table 'http_auth'
Populating data file '/var/smack-data/words.dat' \
with # command 'gen-data -n 90000 -f %12-12s%n,%25-25s,%n,%d'
Loading data from file '/var/smack-data/words.dat' into table 'http_auth'
Table http_auth is now ready for the test
Query Barrel Report for client smacker1
connect: max=4ms  min=0ms avg= 1ms from 10 clients
Query_type      num_queries     max_time      min_time        q_per_s
select_index    2000            0             0               4983.79
```

Let's walk through what's going on here. Going from the top of Listing 6-3, you see that when Super Smack started the benchmark test found in smack/select-key.smack, it tried to execute a query against a table (http_auth) that didn't exist. So, Super Smack created the http_auth table. We'll explain how Super Smack knew how to create the table in just a minute. Moving on, the next two lines tell you that Super Smack created a test data file (/var/smack-data/words.dat) and loaded the test data into the http_auth table.

■**Tip** As of this writing, Super Smack can also benchmark against the PostgreSQL database server (using the -d pg option). See the file TUTORIAL located in the /super-smack directory for some details on specifying PostgreSQL parameters in the smack files.

Finally, under the line `Query Barrel Report for client smacker1`, you see the output of the benchmark test (highlighted in Listing 6-3). The first highlighted line shows a breakdown of the times taken to connect for the clients we requested. The number of clients should match the number from your command line. The following lines contain the output results of each type of query contained in the smack file. In this case, there was only one query type, called `select_index`. In our run, Super Smack executed 2,000 queries for the `select_index` query type. The corresponding output line in Listing 6-3 shows that the minimum and maximum times for the queries were all under 1 millisecond (thus, 0), and that 4,982.79 queries were executed per second (`q_per_s`). This last statistic, `q_per_s`, is what you are most interested in, since this statistic gives you the best number to compare with later benchmarks.

■Tip Remember to rerun your benchmark tests and average the results of the tests to get the most accurate benchmark results. If you rerun the smack file in Listing 6-3, even with the same parameters, you'll notice the resulting `q_per_s` value will be slightly different almost every time, which demonstrates the need for multiple test runs.

To see how Super Smack can help you analyze some useful data, let's run the following slight variation on our previous shell execution. As you can see, we've changed only the number of concurrent clients, from 10 to 20.

```
#> super-smack -d mysql smacks/select-key.smack 20 100
Query Barrel Report for client smacker1
connect: max=206ms  min=0ms avg= 18ms from 20 clients
Query_type        num_queries     max_time        min_time         q_per_s
select_index      4000            0               0                5054.71
```

Here, you see that increasing the number of concurrent clients actually *increased* the performance of the benchmark test. You can continue to increment the number of clients by a small amount (increments of ten in this example) and compare the `q_per_s` value to your previous runs. When you start to see the value of `q_per_s` decrease or level off, you know that you've hit your peak performance for this benchmark test configuration.

In this way, you perform a process of *determining an optimal condition*. In this scenario, the condition is the number of concurrent clients (the variable you're changing in each iteration of the benchmark). With each iteration, you come closer to determining the optimal value of a specific variable in your scenario. In our case, we determined that for the queries being executed in the `select-key.smack` benchmark, the optimal number of concurrent client connections would be around 30—that's where this particular laptop peaked in queries per second. Pretty neat, huh?

But, you might ask, how is this kind of benchmarking applicable to a real-world example? Clearly, `select-key.smack` doesn't represent much of anything (just a simple `SELECT` statement, as you'll see in a moment). The real power of Super Smack lies in the customizable nature of the smack configuration files.

Building Smack Files

You can build your own smack files to represent either your whole application or pieces of the application. Let's take an in-depth look at the components of the `select-key.smack` file, and you'll get a feel for just how powerful this tool can be. Do a simple `#> cat smacks/select-key.smack` to display the smack configuration file you used in the preliminary benchmark tests. You can follow along as we walk through the pieces of this file.

■**Tip** When creating your own smack files, it's easiest to use a copy of the sample smack files included with Super Smack. Just do `#> cp smacks/select-key.smack smacks/mynew.smack` to make a new copy. Then modify the `mynew.smack` file.

Configuration smack files are composed of sections, formatted in a way that resembles C syntax. These sections define the following parts of the benchmark test:

- *Client configuration*: Defines a named client for the smack program (you can view this as a client connection to the database).

- *Table configuration*: Names and defines a table to be used in the benchmark tests.

- *Dictionary configuration*: Names and describes a source for data that can be used in generating test data.

- *Query definition*: Names one or more SQL statements to be run during the test and defines what those SQL statements should do, how often they should be executed, and what parameters and variables should be included in the statements.

- *Main*: The execution component of Super Smack.

Going from the top of the smack file to the bottom, let's take a look at the code.

First Client Configuration Section

Listing 6-4 shows the first part of `select-key.smack`.

Listing 6-4. *Client Configuration in select-key.smack*

```
// this is will be used in the table section
client "admin"
{
 user "root";
 host "localhost";
 db "test";
 pass "";
 socket "/var/lib/mysql/mysql.sock"; // this only applies to MySQL and is
// ignored for PostgreSQL
}
```

This is pretty straightforward. This section of the smack file is naming a new client for the benchmark called admin and assigning some connection properties for the client. You can create any number of named client components, which can represent various connections to the various databases. We'll take a look at the second client configuration in the select-key.smack file soon. But first, let's examine the next configuration section in the file.

Table Configuration Section

Listing 6-5 shows the first defined table section.

Listing 6-5. *Table Section Definition in select-key.smack*

```
// ensure the table exists and meets the conditions
table "http_auth"
{
  client "admin"; // connect with this client
 // if the table is not found or does not pass the checks, create it
 // with the following, dropping the old one if needed
  create "create table http_auth
    (username char(25) not null primary key,
     pass char(25),
     uid integer not null,
     gid integer not null
    )";
  min_rows "90000"; // the table must have at least that many rows
  data_file "words.dat"; // if the table is empty, load the data from this file
  gen_data_file "gen-data -n 90000 -f %12-12s%n,%25-25s,%n,%d";
// if the file above does not exist, generate it with the above shell command
// you can replace this command with anything that prints comma-delimited
// data to stdout, just make sure you have the right number of columns
}
```

Here, you see we're naming a new table configuration section, for a table called http_auth, and defining a create statement for the table, in case the table does not exist in the database. Which database will the table be created in? The database used by the client specified in the table configuration section (in this case the client admin, which we defined in Listing 6-4).

The lines after the create definition are used by Super Smack to populate the http_auth table with data, if the table has less than the min_rows value (here, 90,000 rows). The data_file value specifies a file containing comma-delimited data to fill the http_auth table. If this file does not exist in the /var/smack-data directory, Super Smack will use the command given in the gen_data_file value in order to create the data file needed.

In this case, you can see that Super Smack is executing the following command in order to generate the words.dat file:

```
#> gen-data -n 90000 -f %12-12s%n,%25-25s,%n,%d
```

gen-data is a program that comes bundled with Super Smack. It enables you to generate random data files using a simple command-line syntax similar to C's fprintf() function. The -n [rows] command-line option tells gen-data to create 90,000 rows in this case, and the -f option is followed by a formatting string that can take the tokens listed in Table 6-2. The formatting string then outputs randomized data to the file in the data_file value, delimited by whichever delimiter is used in the format string. In this case, a comma was used to delimit fields in the data rows.

Table 6-2. *Super Smack gen-data -f Option Formatting Tokens*

Token	Used For	Comments
%[*min*][-][*max*]s	String fields	Prints strings of lengths between the *min* and *max* values. For example, %10-25s creates a character field between 10 and 25 characters long. For fixed-length character fields, simply set min equal to the maximum number of characters.
%n	Row numbers	Puts an integer value in the field with the value of the row number. Use this to simulate an auto-increment column.
%d	Integer fields	Creates a random integer number. The version of gen-data that comes with Super Smack 1.2 *does not* allow you to specify the length of the numeric data produced, so %07d does *not* generate a seven-digit number, but a random integer of a random length of characters. In our tests, gen-data simply generated 7-, 8-, 9-, and 10-character length positive integers.

You can optionally choose to substitute your own scripts or executables in place of the simple gen-data program. For instance, if you had a Perl script /tests/create-test-data.pl, which created custom test tables, you could change the table configuration section's gen-data-file value as follows:

```
gen-data-file "perl /tests/create-test-data.pl"
```

POPULATING TEST SETS WITH GEN-DATA

gen-data is a neat little tool that you can use in your scripts to generate randomized data. gen-data prints its output to the standard output (stdout) by default, but you can redirect that output to your own scripts or another file. Running gen-data in a console, you might see the following results:

```
#> gen-data -n 12 -f %10-10s,%n,%d,%10-40s
ilcpsklryv,1,1025202362,pjnbpbwllsrehfmxr
kecwitrsgl,2,1656478042,xvtjmxypunbqfgxmuvg
fajclfvenh,3,1141616124,huorjosamibdnjdbeyhkbsomb
ltouujdrbw,4,927612902,rcgbflqpottpegrwvgajcrgwdlpgitydvhedt
usippyvxsu,5,150122846,vfenodqasajoyomgsqcpjlhbmdahyvi
uemkssdsld,6,1784639529,esnnngpesdntrrvysuipywatpfoelthrowhf
exlwdysvsp,7,87755422,kfblfdfultbwpiqhiymmy
alcyeasvxg,8,2113903881,itknygyvjxnspubqjppj
brlhugesmm,9,1065103348,jjlkrmgbnwvftyveolprfdcajiuywtvg
fjrwwaakwy,10,1896306640,xnxpypjgtlhf
teetxbafkr,11,105575579,sfvrenlebjtccg
jvrsdowiix,12,653448036,dxdiixpervseavnwypdinwdrlacv
```

You can use a redirect to output the results to a file, as in this example:

```
#> gen-data -n 12 -f %10-10s,%n,%d,%10-40s > /test-data/table1.dat
```

A number of enhancements could be made to gen-data, particularly in the creation of more random data samples. You'll find that rerunning the gen-data script produces the same results under the same session. Additionally, the formatting options are quite limited, especially for the delimiters it's capable of producing. We tested using the standard \t character escape, which produces just a "t" character when the format string was left unquoted, and a literal "\t" when quoted. Using ";" as a delimiter, you must remember to use double quotes around the format string, as your console will interpret the string as multiple commands to execute.

Regardless of these limitations, gen-data is an excellent tool for quick generation, especially of text data. Perhaps there will be some improvements to it in the future, but for now, it seems that the author provided a simple tool under the assumption that developers would generally prefer to write their own scripts for their own custom needs.

As an alternative to gen-data, you can always use a simple SQL statement to dump existing data into delimited files, which Super Smack can use in benchmarking. To do so, execute the following:

```
SELECT field1, field2, field3 INTO OUTFILE "/test-data/test.csv"
FIELDS TERMINATED BY ','
OPTIONALLY ENCLOSED BY '"'
LINES TERMINATED BY "\n"
FROM table1
```

You should substitute your own directory for our /test-data/ directory in the code. Ensure that the mysql user has write permissions for the directory as well.

Remember that Super Smack looks for the data file in the /var/smack-data directory by default (you can configure it to look somewhere else during installation by using the --datadir configure option). So, copy your test file over to that directory before running a smack file that looks for it:

```
#> cp /test-data/test.csv /var/smack-data/test.csv
```

Dictionary Configuration Section

The next configuration section is to configure the dictionary, which is named word in select-key.smack, as shown in Listing 6-6.

Listing 6-6. *Dictionary Configuration Section in select-key.smack*

```
//define a dictionary
dictionary "word"
{
  type "rand"; // words are retrieved in random order
  source_type "file"; // words come from a file
  source "words.dat"; // file location
  delim ","; // take the part of the line before,
  file_size_equiv "45000"; // if the file is greater than this
//divive the real file size by this value obtaining N and take every Nth
//line skipping others. This is needed to be able to target a wide key
// range without using up too much memory with test keys
}
```

This structure defines a `dictionary` object named `word`, which Super Smack can use in order to find rows in a `table` object. You'll see how the `dictionary` object is used in just a moment. For now, let's look at the various options a dictionary section has. The variables are not as straightforward as you might hope.

The `source_type` variable is where to find or generate the dictionary entries; that is, where to find data to put into the array of entries that can be retrieved by Super Smack from the dictionary. The `source_type` can be one of the following:

- `"file"`: If `source_type = "file"`, the `source` value will be interpreted as a file path relative to the data directory for Super Smack. By default, this directory is `/var/smack-data`, but it can be changed with the `./configure --with-datadir=DIR` option during installation. Super Smack will load the dictionary with entries consisting of the *first* field in the row. This means that if the `source` file is a comma-delimited data set (like the one generated by `gen-data`), only the first character field (up to the comma) will be used as an entry. The rest of the row is discarded.

- `"list"`: When `source_type = "list"`, the `source` value must consist of a list of comma-separated values that will represent the entries in the dictionary. For instance, `source = "cat,dog,owl,bird"` with a `source_type` of `"list"` produces four entries in the dictionary for the four animals.

- `"template"`: If the `"template"` value is used for the `source_type` variable, the `source` variable must contain a valid `printf()`[2] format string, which will be used to generate the needed dictionary entries when the dictionary is called by a `query` object. When the `type` variable is also set to `"unique"`, the entries will be fed to the template defined in the `source` variable, along with an incremented integer ID of the entry generated by the dictionary. So, if you had set up the `source` template value as `"%05d"`, the generated entries would be five-digit auto-incremented integers.

The `type` variable tells Super Smack how to initialize the dictionary from the `source` variable. It can be any of the following:

- `"rand"`: The entries in the dictionary will be created by accessing entries in the `source` value or file in a random order. If the `source_type` is `"file"`, to load the dictionary, rows will be selected from the file randomly, and the characters in the row up to the delimiter (`delim`) will be used as the dictionary entry. If you used the same generated file in *populating* your table, you're guaranteed of finding a matching entry in your table.

- `"seq"`: Super Smack will read entries from the dictionary file in sequential order, for as many rows as the benchmark dictates (as you'll see in a minute). Again, you're guaranteed to find a match if you used the same generated file to populate the table.

- `"unique"`: Super Smack will generate fields in a unique manner similar to the way `gen-data` creates field values. You're not guaranteed that the uniquely generated field will match any values in your table. Use this `type` setting with the `"template"` `source_type` variable.

---

2. If you're unfamiliar with `printf()` C function, simply do a `#> man sprintf` from your console for instructions on its usage.

Query Definition Section

The next section in select-key.smack shows the query object definition being tested in the benchmark. The query object defines the SQL statements you will run for the benchmark. Listing 6-7 shows the definition.

Listing 6-7. *Query Object Definition in select-key.smack*

```
query "select_by_username"
{
  query "select * from http_auth where username = '$word'";
// $word will be substitute with the read from the 'word' dictionary
  type "select_index";
// query stats will be grouped by type
  has_result_set "y";
// the query is expected to return a result set
  parsed "y";
// the query string should be first processed by super-smack to do
// dictionary substitution
}
```

First, the query variable is set to a string housing a SQL statement. In this case, it's a simple SELECT statement against the http_auth table defined earlier, with a WHERE expression on the username field. We'll explain how the '$word' parameter gets filled in just a second. The type variable is simply a grouping for the final performance results output. Remember the output from Super Smack shown earlier in Listing 6-3? The query_type column corresponds to the type variable in the various query object definitions in your smack files. Here, in select-key.smack, there is only a single query object, so you see just one value in the query_type column of the output result. If you had more than one query, having distinct type values, you would see multiple rows in the output result representing the different query types. You can see an example of this in update-key.smack, the other sample smack file, which we encourage you to investigate.

The has_result_set value (either "y" or "n") is fairly self-explanatory and simply informs Super Smack that the query will return a resultset. The parsed variable value (again, either "y" or "n") is a little more interesting. It relates to the dictionary object definition we covered earlier. If the parsed variable is set to "y", Super Smack will fill any placeholders of the style $xxx with a dictionary entry corresponding to xxx. Here, the placeholder $word in the query object's SQL statement will be replaced with an entry from the "word" dictionary, which was previously defined in the file.

You can define any number of named dictionaries, similar to the way we defined the "word" dictionary in this example. For each dictionary, you may refer to dictionary entries in your queries using the name of the dictionary. For instance, if you had defined two dictionary objects, one called "username" and one called "password", which you had populated with usernames and passwords, you could have a query statement like the following:

```
query "userpass_select"
{
  query "SELECT * FROM http_auth WHERE username='$username' AND pass='$password'";
  has_result_set = "y";
  parsed = "y";
}
```

Second Client Configuration Section

In Listing 6-8, you see the next object definition, another `client` object. This time, it does the actual querying against the `http_auth` table.

Listing 6-8. *Second Client Object Definition in select-key.smack*

```
client "smacker1"
{
 user "test"; // connect as this user
 pass ""; // use this password
 host "localhost"; // connect to this host
 db "test"; // switch to this database
 socket "/var/lib/mysql/mysql.sock"; // this only applies to MySQL and is
// ignored for PostgreSQL
 query_barrel "2 select_by_username"; // on each round,
// run select_by_username query 2 times
}
```

This client is responsible for the brunt of the benchmark queries. As you can see, "smacker1" is a `client` object with the normal client variables you saw earlier, but with an extra variable called query_barrel.[3]

A *query barrel*, in smack terms, is simply a series of named queries run for the `client` object. The query barrel contains a string in the form of "n query_object_name [...]", where n is the number of "shots" of the query defined in query_object_name that should be "fired" for each invocation of this client. In this case, the "select_by_username" query object is shot twice for each client during firing of the benchmark smack file. If you investigate the other sample smack file, update-➥ key.smack, you'll see that Super Smack fires one shot for an "update_by_username" query object and one shot for a "select_by_username" query object in its own "smacker1" client object.

Main Section

Listing 6-9 shows the final main execution object for the select-key.smack file.

Listing 6-9. *Main Execution Object in select-key.smack*

```
main
{
  smacker1.init(); // initialize the client
  smacker1.set_num_rounds($2); // second arg on the command line defines
// the number of rounds for each client
  smacker1.create_threads($1);
// first argument on the command line defines how many client instances
// to fork. Anything after this will be done once for each client until
// you collect the threads
  smacker1.connect();
```

---

3. Super Smack uses a gun metaphor to symbolize what's going on in the benchmark runs. super-smack is the gun, which fires benchmark test bullets from its query barrels. Each query barrel can contain a number of shots.

```
// you must connect after you fork
  smacker1.unload_query_barrel(); // for each client fire the query barrel
// it will now do the number of rounds specified by set_num_rounds()
// on each round, query_barrel of the client is executed
  smacker1.collect_threads();
// the master thread waits for the children, each child reports the stats
// the stats are printed
  smacker1.disconnect();
// the children now disconnect and exit
}
```

This object describes the steps that Super Smack takes to actually run the benchmark using all the objects you've previously defined in the smack file.

■**Note** It doesn't matter in which order you define objects in your smack files, with one exception. You must define the main executable object *last.*

The client "smacker1", which you've seen defined in Listing 6-8, is initialized (loaded into memory), and then the next two functions, set_num_rounds() and create_threads(), use arguments passed in on the command line to configure the test for the number of iterations you passed through and spawn the number of clients you've requested. The $1 and $2 represent the command-line arguments passed to Super Smack *after* the name of the smack file (those of you familiar with shell scripting will recognize the nomenclature here). In our earlier sample run of Super Smack, we executed the following:

```
#> super-smack -d mysql smacks/select-key.smack 10 100
```

The 10 would be put into the $1 variable, and 100 goes into the $2 variable.

Next, the smacker1 client connects to the database defined in its db variable, passing the authentication information it also contains. The client's query_barrel variable is fired, using the unload_query_barrel() function, and finally some cleanup work is done with the collect_threads() and disconnect() functions. Super Smack then displays the results of the benchmark test to stdout.

When you're doing your own benchmarking with Super Smack, you'll most likely want to change the client, dictionary, table, and query objects to correspond to the SQL code you want to test. The main object definition will not need to be changed, unless you want to start tinkering with the C++ super-smack code.

■**Caution** For each concurrent client you specify for Super Smack to create, it creates a *persistent* connection to the MySQL server. For this reason, unless you want to take a crack at modifying the source code, it's not possible to simulate nonpersistent connections. This constraint, however, is not a problem if you are using Super Smack simply to compare the performance results of various query incarnations. If, however, you wish to truly simulate a web application environment (and thus, nonpersistent connections) you should use either ApacheBench or httperf to benchmark the entire web application.

MyBench

Although Super Smack is a very powerful benchmarking program, it can be difficult to bench-mark a complex set of logical instructions. As you've seen, Super Smack's configuration files are fairly limited in what they can test: basically, just straight SQL statements. If you need to test some complicated logic—for instance, when you need to benchmark a script that processes a number of statements inside a transaction, and you need to rely on SQL inline variables (`@variable...`)—you will need to use a more flexible benchmarking system.

Jeremy Zawodny, coauthor of *High Performance MySQL* (O'Reilly, 2004) has created a Perl module called MyBench (`http://jeremy.zawodny.com/mysql/mybench/`), which allows you to benchmark logic that is a little more complex. The module enables you to write your own Perl functions, which are fed to the MyBench benchmarking framework using a callback. The framework handles the chore of spawning the client threads and executing your function, which can contain any arbitrary logic that connects to a database, executes Perl and SQL code, and so on.

■**Tip** For server and configuration tuning, and in-depth coverage of Jeremy Zawodny's various utility tools like MyBench and mytop, consider picking up a copy of *High Performance MySQL* (O'Reilly, 2004), by Jeremy Zawodny and Derek Bailing. The book is fairly focused on techniques to improve the performance of your hardware and MySQL configuration, the material is thoughtful, and the book is an excellent tuning reference.

The sample Perl script, called `bench_example`, which comes bundled with the software, provides an example on which you can base your own benchmark tests. Installation of the module follows the standard GNU make process. Instructions are available in the tarball you can download from the MyBench site.

■**Caution** Because MyBench is not compiled (it's a Perl module), it can be more resource-intensive than running Super Smack. So, when you run benchmarks using MyBench, it's helpful to run them on a machine separate from your database, if that database is on a production machine. MyBench can use the standard Perl DBI module to connect to remote machines in your benchmark scripts.

ApacheBench (ab)

A good percentage of developers and administrators reading this text will be using MySQL for web-based applications. Therefore, we found it prudent to cover two web application stress-testing tools: ApacheBench (described here) and httperf (described in the next section).

ApacheBench (ab) comes installed on almost any Unix/Linux distribution with the Apache web server installed. It is a contrived load generator, and therefore provides a brute-force method of determining how many requests for a particular web resource a server can handle.

As an example, let's run a benchmark comparing the performance of two simple scripts, finduser1.php (shown in Listing 6-10) and finduser2.php (shown in Listing 6-11), which select records from the http_auth table we populated earlier in the section about Super Smack. The http_auth table contains 90,000 records and has a primary key index on username, which is a char(25) field. Each username has exactly 25 characters. For the tests, we've turned off the query cache, so that it won't skew any results. We know that the number of records that match both queries is exactly 146 rows in our generated table. However, here we're going to do some simple benchmarks to determine which method of retrieving the same information is faster.

Note If you're not familiar with the REGEXP function, head over to http://dev.mysql.com/doc/mysql/en/regexp.html. You'll see that the SQL statements in the two scripts in Listings 6-10 and 6-11 produce identical results.

Listing 6-10. *finduser1.php*

```php
<?php
// finduser1.php
$conn = mysql_connect("localhost","test","") or die (mysql_error());

mysql_select_db("test", $conn) or die ("Can't use database 'test'");

$result = mysql_query("SELECT * FROM http_auth WHERE username LIKE 'ud%'");

if ($result)
 echo "found: " . mysql_num_rows($result);
else
 echo mysql_error();
?>
```

Listing 6-11. finduser2.php

```php
<?php
// finduser2.php
$conn = mysql_connect("localhost","test","") or die (mysql_error());

mysql_select_db("test", $conn) or die ("Can't use database 'test'");

$result = mysql_query("SELECT * FROM http_auth WHERE username REGEXP '^ud'");

if ($result)
 echo "found: " . mysql_num_rows($result);
else
 echo mysql_error();
?>
```

You can call ApacheBench from the command line, in a fashion similar to calling Super Smack. Listing 6-12 shows an example of calling ApacheBench to benchmark a simple script and its output. The resultset shows the performance of the finduser1.php script from Listing 6-10.

Listing 6-12. *Running ApacheBench and the Output Results for finduser1.php*

```
# ab -n 100 -c 10 http://127.0.0.1/finduser1.php
Document Path:          /finduser1.php
Document Length:        84 bytes

Concurrency Level:      10
Time taken for tests:   1.797687 seconds
Complete requests:      1000
Failed requests:        0
Write errors:           0
Total transferred:      277000 bytes
HTML transferred:       84000 bytes
Requests per second:    556.27 [#/sec] (mean)
Time per request:       17.977 [ms] (mean)
Time per request:       1.798 [ms] (mean, across all concurrent requests)
Transfer rate:          150.19 [Kbytes/sec] received

Connection Times (ms)
              min  mean[+/-sd] median   max
Connect:        0    0   0.3      0       3
Processing:     1   15  62.2      6     705
Waiting:        1   11  43.7      5     643
Total:          1   15  62.3      6     708

Percentage of the requests served within a certain time (ms)
   50%      6
   66%      9
   75%     10
   80%     11
   90%     15
   95%     22
   98%     91
   99%     210
  100%     708 (longest request)
```

As you can see, ApacheBench outputs the results of its stress testing in terms of the number of requests per second it was able to sustain (along with the min and max requests), given a number of concurrent connections (the -c command-line option) and the number of requests per concurrent connection (the -n option).

We provided a high enough number of iterations and clients to make the means accurate and reduce the chances of an outlier skewing the results. The output from ApacheBench shows a number of other statistics, most notably the percentage of requests that completed within a certain time in milliseconds. As you can see, for finduser1.php, 80% of the requests completed in

11 milliseconds or less. You can use these numbers to determine whether, given a certain amount of traffic to a page (in number of requests and number of concurrent clients), you are falling within your acceptable response times in your benchmarking plan.

To compare the performance of finduser1.php with finduser2.php, we want to execute the same benchmark command, but on the finduser2.php script instead. In order to ensure that we were operating in the same environment as the first test, we did a quick reboot of our system and ran the tests. Listing 6-13 shows the results for finduser2.php.

Listing 6-13. *Results for finduser2.php (REGEXP)*

```
# ab -n 100 -c 10 http://127.0.0.1/finduser2.php
Document Path:          /finduser1.php
Document Length:        10 bytes

Concurrency Level:      10
Time taken for tests:   5.848457 seconds
Complete requests:      1000
Failed requests:        0
Write errors:           0
Total transferred:      203000 bytes
HTML transferred:       10000 bytes
Requests per second:    170.99 [#/sec] (mean)
Time per request:       58.485 [ms] (mean)
Time per request:       5.848 [ms] (mean, across all concurrent requests)
Transfer rate:          33.86 [Kbytes/sec] received

Connection Times (ms)
              min  mean[+/-sd] median   max
Connect:        0    0   0.6      0       7
Processing:     3   57 148.3     30    1410
Waiting:        2   56 144.6     29    1330
Total:          3   57 148.5     30    1413

Percentage of the requests served within a certain time (ms)
  50%     30
  66%     38
  75%     51
  80%     56
  90%     73
  95%    109
  98%    412
  99%   1355
 100%   1413 (longest request)
```

As you can see, ApacheBench reported a substantial performance decrease from the first run: 556.27 requests per second compared to 170.99 requests per second, making finduser1.php more than 325% faster. In this way, ApacheBench enabled us to get *real* numbers in order to compare our two methods.

Clearly, in this case, we could have just as easily used Super Smack to run the benchmark comparisons, since we're changing only a simple SQL statement; the PHP code does very little. However, the example is meant only as a demonstration. The power of ApacheBench (and httperf, described next) is that you can use a single benchmarking platform to test both MySQL-specific code and PHP code. PHP applications are a mixture of both, and having a benchmark tool that can test and isolate the performance of both of them together is a valuable part of your benchmarking framework.

The ApacheBench benchmark has told us only that the REGEXP method fared poorly compared with the simple LIKE clause. The benchmark hasn't provided any insight into *why* the REGEXP scenario performed poorly. For that, we'll need to use some profiling tools in order to dig down into the root of the issue, which we'll do in a moment. But the benchmarking framework has given us two important things: real percentile orders of differentiation between two comparative methods of achieving the same thing, and knowledge of how many requests per second the web server can perform given this particular PHP script.

If we had supplied ApacheBench with a page in an actual application, we would have some numbers on the load limits our actual server could maintain. However, the load limits reflect a scenario in which users are requesting only a single page of our application in a brute-force way. If we want a more realistic tool for assessing a web application's load limitations, we should turn to httperf.

httperf

Developed by David Mosberger of HP Research Labs, httperf is an HTTP load generator with a great deal of features, including the ability to read Apache log files, generate sessions in order to simulate user behavior, and generate realistic user-browsing patterns based on a simple scripting format. You can obtain httperf from `http://www.hpl.hp.com/personal/David_Mosberger/httperf.html`. After installing httperf using a standard GNU make installation, go through the man pages thoroughly to investigate the myriad options available to you.

Running httperf is similar to running ApacheBench: you call the httperf program and specify a number of connections (`--num-conn`) and the number of calls per connection (`--num-calls`). Listing 6-14 shows the output of httperf running a benchmark against the same `finduser2.php` script (Listing 6-11) we used in the previous section.

Listing 6-14. *Output from httperf*

```
# httperf --server=localhost --uri=/finduser2.php --num-conns=10 --num-calls=100
Maximum connect burst length: 1

Total: connections 10 requests 18 replies 8 test-duration 2.477 s

Connection rate: 4.0 conn/s (247.7 ms/conn, <=1 concurrent connections)
Connection time [ms]: min 237.2 avg 308.8 max 582.7 median 240.5 stddev 119.9
Connection time [ms]: connect 0.3
Connection length [replies/conn]: 1.000

Request rate: 7.3 req/s (137.6 ms/req)
Request size [B]: 73.0
```

```
Reply rate [replies/s]: min 0.0 avg 0.0 max 0.0 stddev 0.0 (0 samples)
Reply time [ms]: response 303.8 transfer 0.0
Reply size [B]: header 193.0 content 10.0 footer 0.0 (total 203.0)
Reply status: 1xx=0 2xx=8 3xx=0 4xx=0 5xx=0

CPU time [s]: user 0.06 system 0.44 (user 2.3% system 18.0% total 20.3%)
Net I/O: 1.2 KB/s (0.0*10^6 bps)

Errors: total 10 client-timo 0 socket-timo 0 connrefused 0 connreset 10
Errors: fd-unavail 0 addrunavail 0 ftab-full 0 other 0
```

As you've seen in our benchmarking examples, these tools can provide you with some excellent numbers in comparing the differences between approaches and show valuable information regarding which areas of your application struggle compared with others. However, benchmarks won't allow you to diagnose exactly what it is about your SQL or application code scripts that are causing a performance breakdown. For example, benchmark test results fell short in identifying *why* the REGEXP scenario performed so poorly. This is where profilers and profiling techniques enter the picture.

What Can Profiling Do for You?

Profilers and diagnostic techniques enable you to procure information about memory consumption, response times, locking, and process counts from the engines that execute your SQL scripts and application code.

PROFILERS VS. DIAGNOSTIC TECHNIQUES

When we speak about the topic of profiling, it's useful to differentiate between a *profiler* and a *profiling technique*. A *profiler* is a full-blown application that is responsible for conducting what are called *traces* on application code passed through the profiler. These traces contain information about the breakdown of function calls within the application code block analyzed in the trace. Most profilers commonly contain the functionality of *debuggers* in addition to their profiling ability, which enables you to detect errors in the application code as they occur and sometimes even lets you step through the code itself. Additionally, profiler traces come in two different formats: *human-readable* and *machine-readable*. Human-readable traces are nice because you can easily read the output of the profiler. However, machine-readable trace output is much more extensible, as it can be read into analysis and graphing programs, which can use the information contained in the trace file because it's in a standardized format. Many profilers today include the ability to produce both types of trace output.

Diagnostic techniques, on the other hand, are not programs per se, but methods you can deploy, either manually or in an automated fashion, in order to grab information about the application code while it is being executed. You can use this information, sometimes called a *dump* or a *trace*, in diagnosing problems on the server as they occur.

From a MySQL perspective, you're interested in determining how many threads are executing against the server, what these threads are doing, and how efficiently your server is processing these requests. You should already be familiar with many of MySQL's status variables, which provide insight into the various caches and statistics that MySQL keeps available. However, aside from this information, you also want to see the statements that threads are actually running against the server as they occur. You want to see just how many resources are being consumed by the threads. You want to see if one particular type of query is consistently producing a bottleneck—for instance, locking tables for an extended period of time, which can create a domino effect of other threads waiting for a locked resource to be freed. Additionally, you want to be able to determine *how* MySQL is attempting to execute SQL statement requests, and perhaps get some insight into *why* MySQL chooses a particular path of execution.

From a web application's perspective, you want to know much the same kind of information. Which, if any, of your application blocks is taking the most time to execute? For a page request, it would be nice to see if one particular function call is demanding the vast majority of processing power. If you make changes to the code, how does the performance change?

Anyone can guess as to why an application is performing poorly. You can go on any Internet forum, enter a post about your particular situation, and you'll get 100 different responses, all claiming their answer is accurate. But, the fact is, until they or you run some sort of diagnostic routines or a profiler against your application while it is executing, everyone's answer is simply a guess. Guessing just doesn't cut it in the professional world. Using a profiler and diagnostic techniques, you can find out for yourself what specific parts of an application aren't up to snuff, and take corrective action based on your findings.

General Profiling Guidelines

There's a principle in diagnosing and identifying problems in application code that is worth repeating here before we get into the profiling tools you'll be using. When you see the results of a profiler trace, you'll be presented with information that will show you an application block broken down into how many times a function (or SQL statement) was called, and how long the function call took to complete. It is extremely easy to fall into the trap of *overoptimizing* a piece of application code, simply because you have the diagnostic tools that show you what's going on in your code. This is especially true for PHP programmers who see the function call stack for their pages and want to optimize every single function call in their application.

Basically, the rule of thumb is to start with the block of code that is taking the longest time to execute or is consuming the most resources. Spend your time identifying and fixing those parts of your application code that will have noticeable impact for your users. Don't waste your precious time optimizing a function call that executes in 4 milliseconds just to get the time down to 2 milliseconds. It's just not worth it, unless that function is called so often that it makes a difference to your users. Your time is much better spent going after the big fish.

That said, if you *do* identify a way to make your code faster, by all means document it and use that knowledge in your future coding. If time permits, perhaps think about refactoring older code bases with your newfound knowledge. But always take into account the value of your time in doing so versus the benefits, in real time, to the user.

Profiling Tools

Your first question might be, "Is there a MySQL profiler?" The flat answer is no, there isn't. Although MySQL provides some tools that enable you to do profiling (to a certain extent) of the SQL statements being run against the server, MySQL does not currently come bundled with a profiler program able to generate storable trace files.

If you are coming from a Microsoft SQL Server background and have experience using the SQL Server Profiler, you will still be able to use your basic knowledge of how traces and profiling work, but unfortunately, MySQL has no similar tool. There are some third-party vendors who make some purported profilers, but these merely display the binary log file data generated by MySQL and are not hooked in to MySQL's process management directly.

Here, we will go over some tools that you can use to simulate a true profiler environment, so that you can diagnose issues effectively. These tools will prove invaluable to you as you tackle the often-difficult problem of figuring out what is going on in your systems. We'll cover the following tools of the trade:

- The SHOW FULL PROCESSLIST and SHOW STATUS commands

- The EXPLAIN command

- The slow query and general query logs

- Mytop

- The Zend Advanced PHP Debugger extension

The SHOW FULL PROCESSLIST Command

The first tool in any MySQL administrator's tool belt is the SHOW FULL PROCESSLIST command. SHOW FULL PROCESSLIST returns the threads that are active in the MySQL server as a snapshot of the connection resources used by MySQL at the time the SHOW FULL PROCESSLIST command was executed. Table 6-3 lists the fields returned by the command.

Table 6-3. *Fields Returned from SHOW FULL PROCESSLIST*

Field	Comment
Id	ID of the user connection thread
User	Authenticated user
Host	Authenticating host
db	Name of database or NULL for requests not executing database-specific requests (like SHOW FULL PROCESSLIST)
Command	Usually either Query or Sleep, corresponding to whether the thread is actually performing something at the moment
Time	The amount of time in seconds the thread has been in this particular state (shown in the next field)
State	The status of the thread's execution (discussed in the following text)
Info	The SQL statement executing, if you ran your SHOW FULL PROCESSLIST at the time when a thread was actually executing a query, or some other pertinent information

Other than the actual query text, which appears in the Info column during a thread's query execution,[4] the State field is what you're interested in. The following are the major states:

Sending data: This state appears when a thread is processing rows of a SELECT statement in order to return the result to the client. Usually, this is a normal state to see returned, especially on a busy server. The Info field will display the actual query being executed.

Copying to tmp table: This state appears after the Sending data state when the server needs to create an in-memory temporary table to hold part of the result set being processed. This usually is a fairly quick operation seen when doing ORDER BY or GROUP BY clauses on a set of tables. If you see this state a lot and the state persists for a relatively long time, it might mean you need to adjust some queries or rethink a table design, or it may mean nothing at all, and the server is perfectly healthy. Always monitor things over an extended period of time in order to get the best idea of how often certain patterns emerge.

Copying to tmp table on disk: This state appears when the server needs to create a temporary table for sorting or grouping data, but, because of the size of the resultset, the server must use space on disk, as opposed to in memory, to create the temporary storage area. Remember from Chapter 4 that the buffer system can seamlessly switch from in-memory to on-disk storage. This state indicates that this operation has occurred. If you see this state appearing frequently in your profiling of a production application, we advise you to investigate whether you have enough memory dedicated to the MySQL server; if so, make some adjustments to the tmp_table_size system variable and run a few benchmarks to see if you see fewer Copying to tmp table on disk states popping up. Remember that you should make small changes incrementally when adjusting server variables, and test, test, test.

Writing to net: This state means the server is actually writing the contents of the result into the network packets. It would be rare to see this status pop up, if at all, since it usually happens *very* quickly. If you see this repeatedly cropping up, it usually means your server is getting overloaded or you're in the middle of a stress-testing benchmark.

Updating: The thread is actively updating rows you've requested in an UPDATE statement. Typically, you will see this state only on UPDATE statements affecting a large number of rows.

Locked: Perhaps the most important state of all, the Locked state tells you that the thread is waiting for another thread to finish doing its work, because it needs to UPDATE (or SELECT ➥ FOR UPDATE) a resource that the other thread is using. If you see a lot of Locked states occurring, it can be a sign of trouble, as it means that many threads are vying for the same resources. Using InnoDB tables for frequently updated tables can solve many of these problems (see Chapter 5) because of the finer-grained locking mechanism it uses (MVCC). However, poor application coding or database design can sometimes lead to frequent locking and, worse, deadlocking, when processes are waiting for *each other* to release the same resource.

---

4. By execution, we mean the query parsing, optimization, and execution, including returning the result-set and writing to the network packets.

Listing 6-15 shows an example of SHOW FULL PROCESSLIST identifying a thread in the Locked state, along with a thread in the Copying to tmp table state. (We've formatted the output to fit on the page.) As you can see, thread 71184 is waiting for the thread 65689 to finishing copying data in the SELECT statement into a temporary table. Thread 65689 is copying to a temporary table because of the GROUP BY and ORDER BY clauses. Thread 71184 is requesting an UPDATE to the Location table, but because that table is used in a JOIN in thread 65689's SELECT statement, it must wait, and is therefore locked.

■**Tip** You can use the mysqladmin tool to produce a process list similar to the one displayed by SHOW ➥ FULL PROCESSLIST. To do so, execute #> mysqladmin processlist.

Listing 6-15. *SHOW FULL PROCESSLIST Results*

```
mysql> SHOW FULL PROCESSLIST;
+--------+--------+-----------+--------+---------+------+----------------------+-----
| Id     | User   | Host      | db     | Command | Time | State                | Info
+--------+--------+-----------+--------+---------+------+----------------------+-----
|     43 | job_db | localhost | job_db | Sleep   |   69 |                      | NULL
|  65378 | job_db | localhost | job_db | Sleep   |   23 |                      | NULL
|  65689 | job_db | localhost | job_db | Query   |    1 | Copying to tmp table |
SELECT e.Code, e.Name
FROM Job j
INNER JOIN Location l
ON j.Location = l.Code
INNER JOIN Employer e
ON j.Employer = e.Code
WHERE l.State = "NY"
AND j.ExpiresOn >= "2005-03-09"
GROUP BY  e.Code, e.Name
ORDER BY e.Sort ASC |
|  65713 | job_db | localhost | job_db | Sleep   |   60 |                      | NULL
|  65715 | job_db | localhost | job_db | Sleep   |   22 |                      | NULL
--- omitted ---
|  70815 | job_db | localhost | job_db | Sleep   |   12 |                      | NULL
|  70822 | job_db | localhost | job_db | Sleep   |   86 |                      | NULL
|  70824 | job_db | localhost | job_db | Sleep   |   62 |                      | NULL
|  70826 | root   | localhost | NULL   | Query   |    0 | NULL                 | \
SHOW FULL PROCESSLIST
|  70920 | job_db | localhost | job_db | Sleep   |   17 |                      | NULL
|  70999 | job_db | localhost | job_db | Sleep   |   34 |                      | NULL
--- omitted ---
|  71176 | job_db | localhost | job_db | Sleep   |   39 |                      | NULL
|  71182 | job_db | localhost | job_db | Sleep   |    4 |                      | NULL
|  71183 | job_db | localhost | job_db | Sleep   |   17 |                      | NULL
|  71184 | job_db | localhost | job_db | Query   |    0 | Locked               |
```

```
UPDATE Job
SET   TotalViews = TotalViews + 1
WHERE Location = 55900
AND Position = 147
| 71185 | job_db | localhost | job_db | Sleep  | 6   |                        | NULL
+-------+--------+-----------+--------+---------+------+----------------------+-----
57 rows in set (0.00 sec)
```

■**Note** You must be logged in to MySQL as a user with the SUPER privilege in order to execute the
SHOW FULL PROCESSLIST command.

Running SHOW FULL PROCESSLIST is great for seeing a snapshot of the server at any given
time, but it can be a bit of a pain to repeatedly execute the query from a client. The mytop utility, discussed shortly, takes away this annoyance, as you can set up mytop to reexecute the
SHOW FULL PROCESSLIST command at regular intervals.

The SHOW STATUS Command

Another use of the SHOW command is to output the status and system variables maintained
by MySQL. With the SHOW STATUS command, you can see the statistics that MySQL keeps on
various activities. The status variables are all incrementing counters that track the number of
times certain events occurred in the system. You can use a LIKE expression to limit the results
returned. For instance, if you execute the command shown in Listing 6-16, you see the status
counters for the various query cache statistics.

Listing 6-16. *SHOW STATUS Command Example*

```
mysql> SHOW STATUS LIKE 'Qcache%';
+-------------------------+----------+
| Variable_name           | Value    |
+-------------------------+----------+
| Qcache_queries_in_cache | 8725     |
| Qcache_inserts          | 567803   |
| Qcache_hits             | 1507192  |
| Qcache_lowmem_prunes    | 49267    |
| Qcache_not_cached       | 703224   |
| Qcache_free_memory      | 14660152 |
| Qcache_free_blocks      | 5572     |
| Qcache_total_blocks     | 23059    |
+-------------------------+----------+
8 rows in set (0.00 sec)
```

Monitoring certain status counters is a good way to track specific resource and performance measurements in real time and while you perform benchmarking. Taking before and
after snapshots of the status counters you're interested in during benchmarking can show

you if MySQL is using particular caches effectively. Throughout the course of this book, as the topics dictate, we cover most of the status counters and their various meanings, and provide some insight into how to interpret changes in their values over time.

The EXPLAIN Command

The EXPLAIN command tells you how MySQL intends to execute a particular SQL statement. When you see a particular SQL query appear to take up a significant amount of resources or cause frequent locking in your system, EXPLAIN can help you determine if MySQL has been able to choose an optimal pattern for data access. Let's take a look at the EXPLAIN results from the SQL commands in the earlier finduser1.php and finduser2.php scripts (Listings 6-10 and 6-11) we load tested with ApacheBench. First, Listing 6-17 shows the EXPLAIN output from our LIKE expression in finduser1.php.

Listing 6-17. *EXPLAIN for finduser1.php*

```
mysql> EXPLAIN SELECT * FROM test.http_auth WHERE username LIKE 'ud%' \G
*************************** 1. row ***************************
           id: 1
  select_type: SIMPLE
        table: http_auth
         type: range
possible_keys: PRIMARY
          key: PRIMARY
      key_len: 25
          ref: NULL
         rows: 128
        Extra: Using where
1 row in set (0.46 sec)
```

Although this is a simple example, the output from EXPLAIN has a lot of valuable information. Each row in the output describes an access strategy for a table or index used in the SELECT statement. The output contains the following fields:

id: A simple identifier for the SELECT statement. This can be greater than zero if there is a UNION or subquery.

select_type: Describes the type of SELECT being performed. This can be any of the following values:

- SIMPLE: Normal, non-UNION, non-subquery SELECT statement

- PRIMARY: Topmost (outer) SELECT in a UNION statement

- UNION: Second or later SELECT in a UNION statement

- DEPENDENT UNION: Second or later SELECT in a UNION statement that is dependent on the results of an outer SELECT statement

- UNION RESULT: The result of a UNION

- SUBQUERY: The first SELECT in a subquery

- DEPENDENT SUBQUERY: The first SELECT in a SUBQUERY that is dependent on the result of an outer query

- DERIVED: Subquery in the FROM clause

table: The name of the table used in the access strategy described by the row in the EXPLAIN result.

type: A description of the access strategy deployed by MySQL to get at the data in the table or index in this row. The possible values are system, const, eq_ref, ref, ref_or_null, index_merge, unique_subquery, index_subquery, range, index, and ALL. We go into detail about all the different access types in the next chapter, so stay tuned for an in-depth discussion on their values.

possible_keys: Lists the available indexes (or NULL if there are none available) that MySQL had to choose from in evaluating the access strategy for the table that the row describes.

key: Shows the actual key chosen to perform the data access (or NULL if there wasn't one available). Typically, when diagnosing a slow query, this is the first place you'll look, because you want to make sure that MySQL is using an appropriate index. Sometimes, you'll find that MySQL uses an index you didn't expect it to use.

key_len: The length, in bytes, of the key chosen. This number is often very useful in diagnosing whether a key's length is hindering a SELECT statement's performance. Stay tuned for Chapter 7, which has more on this piece of information.

ref: Shows the columns within the key chosen that will be used to access data in the table, or a constant, if the join has been optimized away with a single constant value. For instance, SELECT * FROM x INNER JOIN y ON x.1 = y.1 WHERE x.1 = 5 will be optimized away so that the constant 5 will be used instead of a comparison of key values in the JOIN between x and y. You'll find more on the topic of JOIN optimization in Chapter 7.

rows: Shows the number of rows that MySQL *expects* to find, based on the statistics it keeps on the table or index (key) chosen to be used and any preliminary calculations it has done based on your WHERE clause. This is a calculation MySQL does based on its knowledge of the distribution of key values in your indexes. The freshness of these statistics is determined by how often an ANALYZE TABLE command is run on the table, and, internally, how often MySQL updates its index statistics. In Chapter 7, you'll learn just how MySQL uses these key distribution statistics in determining which possible JOIN strategy to deploy for your SELECT statement.

Extra: This column contains extra information pertaining to this particular row's access strategy. Again, we'll go over all the possible things you'll see in the Extra field in our next chapter. For now, just think of it as any additional information that MySQL thinks you might find helpful in understanding how it's optimizing the SELECT statement you executed.

In the example in Listing 6-17, we see that MySQL has chosen to use the PRIMARY index on the http_auth table. It just so happens that the PRIMARY index is the only index on the table that contains the username field, so it decides to use this index. In this case, the access pattern is a range type, which makes sense since we're looking for usernames that begin with *ud* (LIKE 'ud%').

Based on its key distribution statistics, MySQL hints that there will be approximately 128 rows in the output (which isn't far off the actual number of 146 rows returned). In the Extra column, MySQL kindly informs us that it is using the WHERE clause on the index in order to find the rows it needs.

Now, let's compare that EXPLAIN output to the EXPLAIN on our second SELECT statement using the REGEXP construct (from finduser2.php). Listing 6-18 shows the results.

Listing 6-18. *EXPLAIN Output from SELECT Statement in finduser2.php*

```
mysql> EXPLAIN SELECT * FROM test.http_auth WHERE username REGEXP '^ud' \G
*************************** 1. row ***************************
           id: 1
  select_type: SIMPLE
        table: http_auth
         type: ALL
possible_keys: NULL
          key: NULL
      key_len: NULL
          ref: NULL
         rows: 90000
        Extra: Using where
1 row in set (0.31 sec)
```

You should immediately notice the stark difference, which should explain the performance nightmare from the benchmark described earlier in this chapter. The possible_keys column is NULL, which indicates that MySQL was not able to use an index to find the rows in http_auth. Therefore, instead of 128 in the rows column, you see 90000. Even though the result of both SELECT statements is identical, MySQL did not use an index on the second statement. MySQL simply cannot use an index when the REGEXP construct is used in a WHERE condition.

This example should give you an idea of the power available to you in the EXPLAIN statement. We'll be using EXPLAIN extensively throughout the next two chapters to show you how various SQL statements and JOIN constructs can be optimized and to help you identify ways in which indexes can be most effectively used in your application. EXPLAIN's output gives you an insider's diagnostic view into how MySQL is determining a pathway to execute your SQL code.

The Slow Query Log

MySQL uses the slow query log to record any query whose execution time exceeds the long_query_time configuration variable. This log can be very helpful when used in conjunction with the bundled Perl script mysqldumpslow, which simply groups and sorts the logged queries into a more readable format. Before you can use this utility, however, you must enable the slow query log in your configuration file. Insert the following lines into /etc/my.cnf (or some other MySQL configuration file):

```
log-slow-queries
long_query_time=2
```

Here, we've told MySQL to consider all queries taking two seconds and longer to execute as a slow query. You can optionally provide a filename for the log-slow-queries argument. By default, the log is stored in /var/log/systemname-slow.log. If you do change the log to a spe-cific filename, remember that when you execute mysqldumpslow, you'll need to provide that filename. Once you've made the changes, you should restart mysqld to have the changes take effect. Then your queries will be logged if they exceed the long_query_time.

■Note Prior to MySQL version 4.1, you should also include the log-long-format configuration option in your configuration file. This automatically logs any queries that aren't using any indexes at all, even if the query time does not exceed long_query_time. Identifying and fixing queries that are not using indexes is an easy way to increase the throughput and performance of your database system. The slow query log with this option turned on provides an easy way to find out which tables don't have any indexes, or any appropri-ate indexes, built on them. Version 4.1 and after have this option enabled by default. You can turn it off manually by using the log-short-format option in your configuration file.

Listing 6-19 shows the output of mysqldumpslow on the machine we tested our ApacheBench scripts against.

Listing 6-19. *Output from mysqldumpslow*

```
#> mysqldumpslow
Reading mysql slow query log from /var/log/mysql/slow-queries.log
Count: 1148  Time=5.74s (6585s)  \
Lock=0.00s (1s)  Rows=146.0 (167608), [test]@localhost
  SELECT * FROM http_auth WHERE username REGEXP 'S'

Count: 1  Time=3.00s (3s)  \
Lock=0.00s (0s)  Rows=90000.0 (90000), root[root]@localhost
  select * from http_auth
```

As you can see, mysqldumpslow groups the slow queries into buckets, along with some statistics on each, including an average time to execute, the amount of time the query was waiting for another query to release a lock, and the number of rows found by the query. We also did a SELECT * FROM http_auth, which returned 90,000 rows and took three seconds, subsequently getting logged to the slow query log.

In order to group queries effectively, mysqldumpslow converts any parameters passed to the queries into either 'S' for string or N for number. This means that in order to actually see the query parameters passed to the SQL statements, you must look at the log file itself. Alternatively, you can use the -a option to force mysqldumpslow to not replace the actual parameters with 'S' and N. Just remember that doing so will force many groupings of similar queries.

The slow query log can be very useful in identifying poorly performing queries, but on a large production system, the log can get quite large and contain many queries that may have performed poorly for only that one time. Make sure you don't jump to conclusions about any particular query in the log; investigate the circumstances surrounding its inclusion in the log. Was the server just started, and the query cache empty? Was an import or export process that caused long table locks running? You can use mysqldumpslow's various optional arguments, listed in Table 6-4, to help narrow down and sort your slow query list more effectively.

Table 6-4. *mysqldumpslow Command-Line Options*

Option	Purpose
-s=[t,at,l,al,r,ar]	Sort the results based on time, total time, lock time, total lock time, rows, total rows
-r	Reverse sort order (list smallest values first)
-t=n	Show only the top *n* queries (based on sort value)
-g=string	Include only queries from the include "*string*" (grep option)
-l	Include the lock time in the total time numbers
-a	Don't abstract the parameter values passed to the query into 'S' or N

For example, the -g=string option is very useful for finding slow queries run on a particular table. For instance, to find queries in the log using the REGEXP construct, execute #> mysqldumpslow -g="REGEXP".

The General Query Log

Another log that can be useful in determining exactly what's going on inside your system is the general query log, which records most common interactions with the database, including connection attempts, database selection (the USE statement), and all queries. If you want to see a realistic picture of the activity occurring on your database system, this is the log you should use.

Remember that the binary log records only statements that change the database; it does not record SELECT statements, which, on some systems, comprise 90% or more of the total queries run on the database. Just like the slow query log, the general query log must first be enabled in your configuration file. Use the following line in your /etc/my.cnf file:

log=/var/log/mysql/localhost.general.log

Here, we've set up our log file under the /var/log/mysql directory with the name general.log. You can put the general log anywhere you wish; just ensure that the mysql user has appropriate write permissions or ownership for the directory or file.

Once you've restarted the MySQL server, all queries executed against the database server will be written to the general query log file.

■Note There is a substantial difference between the way records are written to the general query log versus the binary log. Commands are recorded in the general query log in *the order they are received by the server*. Commands are recorded in the binary log in *the order in which they are executed by the server*. This variance exists because of the different purposes of the two logs. While the general query log serves as an information repository for investigating the activity on the server, the binary log's primary purpose is to provide an accurate recovery method for the server. Because of this, the binary log must write records in execution order so that the recovery process can rely on the database's state being restored properly.

Let's examine what the general query log looks like. Listing 6-20 shows an excerpt from our general query log during our ApacheBench benchmark tests from earlier in this chapter.

Listing 6-20. *Excerpt from the General Query Log*

```
# head -n 40 /var/log/mysql/mysqld.log
/usr/local/libexec/mysqld, Version: 4.1.10-log. started with:
Tcp port: 3306  Unix socket: /var/lib/mysql/mysql.sock
Time                 Id Command    Argument
050309 16:56:19       1 Connect    root@localhost on
050309 16:56:36       1 Quit
050309 16:56:52       2 Connect    test@localhost as anonymous on
                      3 Connect    test@localhost as anonymous on
                      4 Connect    test@localhost as anonymous on
                      5 Connect    test@localhost as anonymous on
                      6 Connect    test@localhost as anonymous on
                      7 Connect    test@localhost as anonymous on
                      8 Connect    test@localhost as anonymous on
                      9 Connect    test@localhost as anonymous on
                      2 Init DB    test
                      2 Query      SELECT * FROM http_auth WHERE username LIKE 'ud%'
                      3 Init DB    test
                      3 Query      SELECT * FROM http_auth WHERE username LIKE 'ud%'
                      4 Init DB    test
                      4 Query      SELECT * FROM http_auth WHERE username LIKE 'ud%'
                      5 Init DB    test
                      5 Query      SELECT * FROM http_auth WHERE username LIKE 'ud%'
                      6 Init DB    test
                      6 Query      SELECT * FROM http_auth WHERE username LIKE 'ud%'
                      7 Init DB    test
                      7 Query      SELECT * FROM http_auth WHERE username LIKE 'ud%'
                      8 Init DB    test
                      8 Query      SELECT * FROM http_auth WHERE username LIKE 'ud%'
                      9 Init DB    test
                      9 Query      SELECT * FROM http_auth WHERE username LIKE 'ud%'
                     10 Connect    test@localhost as anonymous on
                     10 Init DB    test
                     10 Query      SELECT * FROM http_auth WHERE username LIKE 'ud%'
050309 16:56:53      11 Connect    test@localhost as anonymous on
                     11 Init DB    test
                     11 Query      SELECT * FROM http_auth WHERE username LIKE 'ud%'
                      2 Quit
                      9 Quit
                      7 Quit
                      5 Quit
                      8 Quit
```

Using the head command, we've shown the first 40 lines of the general query log. The left-most column is the date the activity occurred, followed by a timestamp, and then the ID of the thread within the log. The ID does *not* correspond to any system or MySQL process ID. The Command column will display the self-explanatory "Connect", "Init DB", "Query", or "Quit" value. Finally, the Argument column will display the query itself, the user authentication information, or the database being selected.

The general query log can be a very useful tool in taking a look at exactly what's going on in your system, especially if you are new to an application or are unsure of which queries are typically being executed against the system.

Mytop

If you spent some time experimenting with SHOW FULL PROCESSLIST and the SHOW STATUS commands described earlier, you probably found that you were repeatedly executing the commands to see changes in the resultsets. For those of you familiar with the Unix/Linux top utility (and even those who aren't), Jeremy Zawodny has created a nifty little Perl script that emulates the top utility for the MySQL environment. The mytop script works just like the top utility, allowing you to set delays on automatic refreshing of the console, sorting of the resultset, and so on. Its benefit is that it summarizes the SHOW FULL PROCESSLIST and various SHOW STATUS statements.

In order to use mytop, you'll first need to install the Term::ReadKey Perl module from http://www.cpan.org/modules/by-module/Term/. It's a standard CPAN installation. Just follow the instructions after untarring the download. Then head over to http://jeremy.zawodny.com/mysql/mytop/ and download the latest version. Follow the installation instructions and read the manual (man mytop) to get an idea of the myriad options and interactive prompts available to you.

Mytop has three main views:

- Thread view (default, interactive key t) shows the results of SHOW FULL PROCESSLIST.

- Command view (interactive key c) shows accumulated and relative totals of various commands, or command groups. For instance, SELECT, INSERT, and UPDATE are commands, and various administrative commands sometimes get grouped together, like the SET command (regardless of which SET is changing). This view can be useful for getting a breakdown of which types of queries are being executed on your system, giving you an overall picture.

- Status view (interactive key S) shows various status variables.

The Zend Advanced PHP Debugger Extension

If you're doing any substantive work in PHP, at some point, you'll want to examine the inner workings of your PHP applications. In most database-driven PHP applications, you will want to profile the application to determine where the bottlenecks are. Without a profiler, diagnosing why a certain PHP page is performing slowly is just guesswork, and that guesswork can involve long, tedious hours of trial-and-error debugging. How do you know if the bottleneck in your page stems from a long-running MySQL query or a poorly coded looping structure? How can you determine if there is a specific function or object call that is consuming the vast majority of the page's resources?

With the Zend Advanced PHP Debugger (APD) extension, help is at hand. Zend extensions are a little different from normal PHP extensions, in that they interact with the Zend Engine itself. The Zend Engine is the parsing and execution engine that translates PHP code into what's called Zend OpCodes (for operation codes). Zend extensions have the ability to interact, or hook into, this engine, which parses and executes the PHP code.

■**Caution** Don't install APD on a production machine. Install it in a development or testing environment. The installation requires a source version of PHP (not the binary), which may conflict with some production concerns.

APD makes it possible to see the actual function call traces for your pages, with information on execution time and memory consumption. It can display the *call tree*, which is the tree organization of all subroutines executing on the page.

Setting Up APD

Although it takes a little time to set up APD, we think the reward for your efforts is substantial. The basic installation of APD is not particularly complicated. However, there are a number of shared libraries that, depending on your version of Linux or another operating system, may need to be updated. Make sure you have the latest versions of gcc and libtools installed on the server on which you'll be installing APD.

If you are running PHP 5, you'll want to download and install the latest version of APD. You can do so using PEAR's install process:

```
#> pear install apd
```

For those of you running earlier versions of PHP, or if there is a problem with the installation process through PEAR, you'll want to download the tarball designed for your version of PHP from the PECL repository: http://pecl.php.net/package/apd/.

Before you install the APD extension, however, you need to do a couple of things. First, you must have installed the source version of PHP (you will need the phpize program in order to install APD). phpize is available only in source versions of PHP. Second, while you don't need to provide any special PHP configuration options during installation (because APD is a Zend extension, not a loaded normal PHP extension), you *do* need to ensure that the CGI version of PHP is available. On most modern systems, this is the default.

After installing an up-to-date source version of PHP, install APD:

```
#> tar -xzf apd-0.9.1.tgz
#> cd apd-0.9.1
apd-0.9.1 #> phpize
apd-0.9.1 #> ./configure
apd-0.9.1 #> make
apd-0.9.1 #> make install
```

After the installation is completed, you will see a printout of the location of the APD shared library. Take a quick note of this location. Once APD is installed, you will need to change the `php.ini` configuration file, adding the following lines:

```
zend_extension = /absolute/path/to/apd.so
apd.dumpdir = /absolute/path/to/tracedir
apd.statement_trace = 0
```

Next, you'll want to create the `trace` directory for the APD trace files. On our system, we created the `apd.dumpdir` at /var/apddumps, but you can set it up anywhere. You want to create the directory and allow the public to write to it (because APD will be running in the public domain):

```
#> mkdir /var/apddumps
#> chmod 0766 /var/apddumps
```

Finally, restart the Apache server process to have your changes go into effect. On our system, we ran the following:

```
#> /etc/init.d/httpd restart
```

Profiling PHP Applications with APD

With APD set up, you're ready to see how it works. Listing 6-21 shows the script we'll profile in this example: `finduser3.php`, a modification of our earlier script that prints user information to the screen. We've used a variety of PHP functions for the demonstration, including a call to `sleep()` for one second every twentieth iteration in the loop.

■**Note** If this demonstration doesn't work for you, there is more than likely a conflict between libraries in your system and APD's extension library. To determine if you have problems with loading the APD extension, simply execute #> tail -n 20 /var/log/httpd/error_log and look for errors on the Apache process startup (your Apache log file may be in a different location). The errors should point you in the right direction to fix any dependency issues that arise, or point out any typo errors in your php.ini file from your recent changes.

Listing 6-21. *finduser3.php*

```php
<?php
apd_set_pprof_trace();
$conn = mysql_connect("localhost","test","") or die (mysql_error());
mysql_select_db("test", $conn) or die ("Can't use database 'test'");
$result = mysql_query("SELECT * FROM http_auth WHERE username REGEXP '^ud'");

if ($result) {
  echo '<pre>';
  echo "UserName\tPassword\tUID\tGID\n";
  $num_rows = mysql_num_rows($result);
```

```
  for ($i=0;$i<$num_rows;++$i) {
    mysql_data_seek($result, $i);
    if ($i % 20 == 0)
      sleep(1);
    $row = mysql_fetch_row($result);
    printf("%s\t%s\t%d\t%d\n", $row[0], $row[1], $row[2], $row[4]);
  }
  echo '</pre>';
}
?>
```

We've highlighted the apd_set_pprof_trace() function. This must be called at the top of the script in order to tell APD to trace the PHP page. The traces are dumped into pprof.*XXXXX* files in your apd.dumpdir location, where *XXXXX* is the process ID of the web page you trace. When we run the finduser3.php page through a web browser, nothing is displayed, which tells us the trace completed successfully. However, we can check the apd.dumpdir for files beginning with pprof. To display the pprof trace file, use the pprofp script available in your APD source directory (where you installed APD) and pass along one or more of the command-line options listed in Table 6-5.

Table 6-5. *pprofp Command-Line Options*

Option	Description
-a	Sort by alphabetic name of function
-l	Sort by number of calls to the function
-r	Sort by real time spent in function
-R	Sort by real time spent in function and all its child functions
-s	Sort by system time spent in function
-S	Sort by system time spent in function and all its child functions
-u	Sort by user time spent in function
-U	Sort by user time spent in function and all its child functions
-v	Sort by average amount of time spent in function (across all requests to function)
-z	Sort by total time spent in function (default)
-c	Display real time elapsed alongside call tree
-i	Suppress reporting for PHP built-in functions
-m	Display file/line number locations in trace
-O [n]	Display *n* number of functions (default = 15)
-t	Display compressed call tree
-T	Display uncompressed call tree

Listing 6-22 shows the output of pprofp when we asked it to sort our traced functions by the real time that was spent in the function. The trace file on our system, which resulted from browsing to finduser3.php, just happened to be called /var/apddumps/pprof.15698 on our system.

Listing 6-22. *APD Trace Output Using pprofp*

```
# ./pprofp -r /var/apddumps/pprof.15698
Content-type: text/html
X-Powered-By: PHP/4.3.10


Trace for /var/www/html/finduser3.php
Total Elapsed Time = 8.28
Total System Time  = 0.00
Total User Time    = 0.00


          Real          User          System          secs/   cumm
%Time (excl/cumm)  (excl/cumm)   (excl/cumm) Calls    call   s/call  Memory Usage Name
--------------------------------------------------------------------------------------
96.7 8.01 8.01 0.00 0.00   0.00 0.00     8  1.0012    1.0012        0 sleep
2.9 0.24 0.24  0.00 0.00   0.00 0.00     1  0.2400    0.2400        0 mysql_query
0.2 0.02 0.02  0.00 0.00   0.00 0.00     1  0.0200    0.0200        0 mysql_connect
0.1 0.01 0.01  0.00 0.00   0.00 0.00   146  0.0001    0.0001        0 mysql_data_seek
0.0 0.00 0.00  0.00 0.00   0.00 0.00   146  0.0000    0.0000        0 printf
0.0 0.00 0.00  0.00 0.00   0.00 0.00   146  0.0000    0.0000        0 mysql_fetch_row
0.0 0.00 0.00  0.00 0.00   0.00 0.00     1  0.0000    0.0000        0 mysql_num_rows
0.0 0.00 0.00  0.00 0.00   0.00 0.00     1  0.0000    0.0000        0 mysql_select_db
0.0 0.00 0.00  0.00 0.00   0.00 0.00     1  0.0000    0.0000        0 main
```

As you can see, APD supplies some very detailed and valuable information about the state of the page processing, which functions were used, how often they were called, and how much of a percentage of total processing time each function consumed. Here, you see that the sleep() function took the longest time, which makes sense because it causes the page to stop processing for one second at each call. Other than the sleep() command, only mysql_query(), mysql_connect(), and mysql_data_seek() had nonzero values.

Although this is a simple example, the power of APD is unquestionable when analyzing large, complex scripts. Its ability to pinpoint the bottleneck functions in your page requests relies on the pprofp script's numerous sorting and output options, which allow you to drill down into the call tree. Take some time to play around with APD, and be sure to add it to your toolbox of diagnostic tools.

> ■**Tip** For those of you interested in the internals of PHP, writing extensions, and using the APD profiler, consider George Schlossnagle's *Advanced PHP Programming* (Sams Publishing, 2004). This book provides extensive coverage of how the Zend Engine works and how to effectively diagnose misbehaving PHP code.

Summary

In this chapter, we stressed the importance of benchmarking and profiling techniques for the professional developer and administrator. You've learned how setting up a benchmarking framework can enable you to perform comprehensive (or even just quick) performance comparisons of your design features and help you to expose general bottlenecks in your MySQL applications. You've seen how profiling tools and techniques can help you avoid the guesswork of application debugging and diagnostic work.

In our discussion of benchmarking, we focused on general strategies you can use to make your framework as reliable as possible. The guidelines presented in this chapter and the tools we covered should give you an excellent base to work through the examples and code presented in the next few chapters. As we cover various aspects of the MySQL query optimization and execution process, remember that you can fall back on your established benchmarking framework in order to test the theories we outline next. The same goes for the concepts and tools of profiling.

We hope you come away from this chapter with the confidence that you can test your MySQL applications much more effectively. The profilers and the diagnostic techniques we covered in this chapter should become your mainstay as a professional developer. Figuring out performance bottlenecks should no longer be guesswork or a mystery.

In the upcoming chapters, we're going to dive into the SQL language, covering JOIN and optimization strategies deployed by MySQL in Chapter 7. We'll be focusing on real-world application problems and how to restructure problematic SQL code. In Chapter 8, we'll take it to the next step, describing how you can structure your SQL code, database, and index strategies for various performance-critical applications. You'll be asked to use the information and tools you learned about here in these next chapters, so keep them handy!

CHAPTER 7

■ ■ ■

Essential SQL

In this chapter, we'll focus on SQL code construction. Although this is an advanced book, we've named this chapter "Essential SQL" because we consider your understanding of the topics we cover here to be fundamental in how professionals approach tasks using the SQL language.

When you compare the SQL coding of beginning database developers to that of more experienced coders, you often find the starkest differences in the area of join usage. Experienced SQL developers can often accomplish in a single SQL statement what less experienced coders require multiple SQL statements to do. This is because experienced SQL programmers think about solving data problems in a set-based manner, as opposed to a procedural manner.

Even some competent software programmers—writing in a variety of procedural and object-oriented languages—still have not mastered the art of set-based programming because it requires a fundamental shift in thinking about the problem domain. Instead of approaching a problem from the standpoint of arrays and loops, professional SQL developers understand that this paradigm is inefficient in the world of retrieving data from a SQL store. Using joins appropriately, these developers reduce the problem domain to a single multitable statement, which accomplishes the same thing much more efficiently than a procedural approach. In this chapter, we'll explore this set-based approach to solving problems. Our discussion will start with an examination of joins in general, and then, more specifically, which types of joins MySQL supports. After studying topics related to joins, we'll move on to a few other related issues.

In this chapter, we'll cover the following topics:

- Some general SQL style issues

- MySQL join types

- Access types in EXPLAIN results

- Hints that may be useful for joins

- Subqueries and derived tables

In the next chapter, we'll focus more on situation-specific topics, such as how to deal with hierarchical data and how to squeeze every ounce of performance from your queries.

SQL Style

Before we go into the specifics of coding, let's take a moment to consider some style issues. We will first look at the two main categories of SQL styles, and then at some ways to ensure your code is readable and maintainable.

Theta Style vs. ANSI Style

Most of you will have seen SQL written in a variety of styles, falling into two major categories: theta style and ANSI style. Theta style is an older, and more obscure, nomenclature that looks similar to the following, which represents a simple join between two tables (Product and CustomerOrderItem):

```
SELECT coi.order_id, p.product_id, p.name, p.description
FROM CustomerOrderItem coi, Product p
WHERE coi.product_id = p.product_id
AND coi.order_id = 84463;
```

This statement produces identical results to the following ANSI-style join:

```
SELECT coi.order_id, p.product_id, p.name, p.description
FROM CustomerOrderItem coi
INNER JOIN Product p ON coi.product_id = p.product_id
WHERE coi.order_id = 84463;
```

For all of the examples in the next two chapters, we will be using the ANSI style. We hope that you will consider using an ANSI approach to your SQL code for the following main reasons:

- MySQL fully supports ANSI-style SQL. In contrast, MySQL supports only a small subset of the theta style. Notably, MySQL does not support outer joins with the theta style. While there is nothing preventing you from using both styles in your SQL code, we *highly discourage this practice*. It makes your code less maintainable and harder to decipher for other developers.

- We feel ANSI style encourages cleaner and more supportable code than theta style. Instead of using commas and needing to figure out which style of join is involved in each of the table relationships in your multitable SQL statements, the ANSI style forces you to be specific about your joins. This not only enhances the readability of your SQL code, but it also speeds up your own development by enabling you to easily see what you were attempting to do with the code.

Code Formatting

Make liberal use of indentations, line breaks, and comments in your SQL code. There are few things more frustrating than needing to decipher a 1KB complex SQL string that is written on a single line with no comments from the developer on why certain joins, hints, and such were used. In our opinion, there are no valid reasons for not inserting line breaks and proper indentations in your SQL code. It's simply bad practice.

Separate related clauses on separate lines, and use indentations to make your code more readable. Take a look at the following SQL code, imagining it stored in a file or in a script block:

```
SELECT os.description as "Status", sm.name as "ShippingMethod", COUNT(*) as "Orders"
FROM CustomerOrder o JOIN OrderStatus os ON o.status = os.order_status_id JOIN
ShippingMethod sm ON o.shipping_method = sm.shipping_method_id WHERE o.ordered_on
BETWEEN '2005-04-10' AND '2005-04-23' AND sm.max_order_total < 25.00 GROUP BY
os.description, sm.description ORDER BY "Orders" DESC;
```

Let's reproduce this code, but this time with line breaks and indentations:

```
SELECT
    os.description as "Status"
    , sm.name as "ShippingMethod"
    , COUNT(*) as "NumOrders"
FROM CustomerOrder o
    JOIN OrderStatus os
        ON o.status = os.order_status_id
    JOIN ShippingMethod sm
        ON o.shipping_method = sm.shipping_method_id
WHERE o.ordered_on BETWEEN '2005-04-10' AND '2005-04-23'
    AND sm.max_order_total < 25.00
GROUP BY os.description, sm.description
ORDER BY "NumOrders" DESC;
```

Which is easier to decipher at a glance? If you're wondering why we've put each column on a separate line, it is because this style allows for easy changes over time and easier readability. You'll find that as your applications develop, you'll often receive requests to add another element to the returned results. Laying out your columns on separate lines allows you to easily add columns to the SELECT clause. It also enables you to easily add comments to the code.

Specific and Consistent Coding

The INNER keyword is technically optional for inner joins, but we feel including the word INNER makes your code easier for other developers to more quickly discern what you are trying to do in the code.

Likewise, when running SQL statements on more than one table, make liberal use of table aliasing. Not only is this useful for schemas where you have identically named columns, but it also helps for code readability and maintenance. The earlier examples of theta and ANSI style show proper usage of aliasing in the SELECT clause.

When working with outer joins (both the LEFT JOIN and RIGHT JOIN types), stick to one or the other in your code. They serve identical purposes, and either can be rewritten to the other "side" by switching the order of the related tables in the ON clause. In general, the LEFT JOIN has become the industry standard, so we suggest avoiding the use of RIGHT JOIN entirely.

TEAM ENVIRONMENTS

When working in a team environment, it is imperative that your team develop a written coding style standard and that everyone follow the basic guidelines outlined in your standards document. When developing your style guide, work with everyone on the team to put together a style that is agreeable to everyone. Normally, you'll need to compromise on some things, but working toward that compromise makes it more likely that the team will actually follow the standard, as opposed to just paying lip service to it. So, take the time and effort to develop the standards; the payoff is well worth it.

Also important when working with a team of developers is the use of a code repository such as CVS or Subversion. Remember that just because it's SQL code doesn't mean it shouldn't be assigned the same level of importance as regular application code!

Additionally, if you are building an application supporting MySQL version 5.0 or higher, we strongly suggest you consider using stored procedures to organize your SQL code. Stored procedures make the development of large and complex applications easier by giving you the ability to put complex SQL scripts into callable routines. Check out Chapter 9 for an in-depth discussion on this new feature.

MySQL Joins

For our discussion on joins, we'll use a sample schema that includes some tables in our fictional toy store e-commerce application, which we've used in the examples in previous chapters. Figure 7-1 shows the E-R diagram for all the tables.

In Figure 7-1, we've indicated primary keys using bold print, and foreign key relationships using italics. If you're unsure about how to read the diagram, refer to Chapter 1, where E-R diagramming is explained. Take some time to review the diagram, and understand the business rules implied through it. For instance, looking at the relationship between Product, Category, and Product2Category, you might say that an existing business rule denotes "A Product must belong to one or more Category elements. Likewise, a Category can contain one or more Product elements. Additionally, a Category may have a single parent Category, thus making it a child of that Category."

The following are some items to note about our sample schema:

- We haven't shown the data types for columns because we're focusing on the relationships between the entities, not necessarily their makeup. When necessary, we'll talk about specific data type concerns in your SQL code.

- Assume all fields are NOT NULL unless noted.

- For the table representing a many-to-many relationship, we've used the number 2 between the related tables to indicate this more fully: Product2Category.

- This schema is clearly not intended to represent an optimal or full e-commerce database application. For brevity, we've omitted a number of columns, tables, and relationships that would be present in a real-world schema. The table structures shown are designed for our examples, nothing more.

- For our CustomerOrderItem table, which represents the products contained in the customer's order, we've created redundant price and weight columns. We've done this for the purpose of some examples, and to demonstrate that this table stores a *historical* view of the price and weight of the products when the order was made. If this were not done, price changes in the main product record would be reflected in past order details, where a different purchase price may have been used. In a real-world schema, you would use this technique for the customer's address information as well, which may change over the course of time. You might store the shipping address in the `CustomerOrder` table to represent the actual address used in the shipment.

- The `ShippingMethod` table has four fields—`min_order_weight`, `max_order_weight`, `min_order_total`, and `max_order_total`—which may seem odd. These fields represent criteria that will be used to identify which shipping method can be used for a `CustomerOrder`. We'll take a closer look at these fields in our later examples covering range queries.

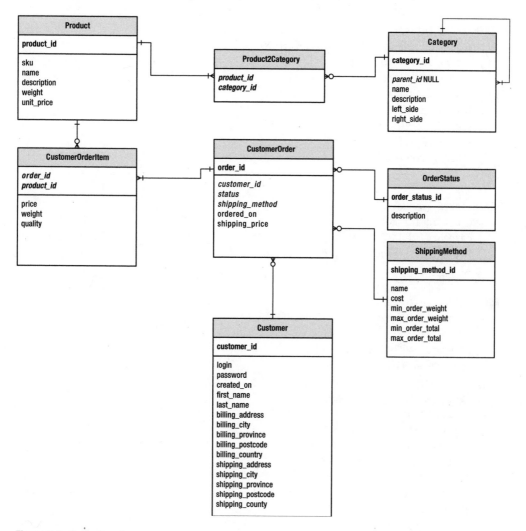

Figure 7-1. *Sample schema*

Listing 7-1 contains the create script for the sample schema.

Listing 7-1. *Create Script for the Sample Schema*

```
CREATE TABLE Product (
    product_id  INT NOT NULL AUTO_INCREMENT
    , sku    VARCHAR(35) NOT NULL
    , name  VARCHAR(150) NOT NULL
    , description TEXT NOT NULL
    , weight DECIMAL(7,2) NOT NULL
    , unit_price DECIMAL(9,2) NOT NULL
    , PRIMARY KEY (product_id)
);

CREATE TABLE Category (
    category_id INT NOT NULL AUTO_INCREMENT
    , parent_id INT NULL
    , name VARCHAR(100) NOT NULL
    , description TEXT
    , left_side INT NOT NULL
    , right_side INT NOT NULL
    , PRIMARY KEY (category_id)
    , INDEX (parent_id)
);

CREATE TABLE Product2Category (
    product_id INT NOT NULL
    , category_id INT NOT NULL
    , PRIMARY KEY (product_id, category_id)
);

CREATE TABLE Customer (
    customer_id INT NOT NULL AUTO_INCREMENT
    , login VARCHAR(32) NOT NULL
    , password VARCHAR(32) NOT NULL
    , created_on DATE NOT NULL
    , first_name VARCHAR(30) NOT NULL
    , last_name VARCHAR(30) NOT NULL
    , billing_address VARCHAR(100) NOT NULL
    , billing_city VARCHAR(35) NOT NULL
    , billing_province CHAR(2) NOT NULL
    , billing_postcode VARCHAR(8) NOT NULL
    , billing_country CHAR(2) NOT NULL
    , shipping_address VARCHAR(100) NOT NULL
    , shipping_city VARCHAR(35) NOT NULL
    , shipping_province CHAR(2) NOT NULL
```

```
    , shipping_postcode VARCHAR(8) NOT NULL
    , shipping_country CHAR(2) NOT NULL
    , PRIMARY KEY (customer_id)
    , INDEX (login, password)
);

CREATE TABLE OrderStatus (
    order_status_id CHAR(1) NOT NULL
    , description VARCHAR(150) NOT NULL
    , PRIMARY KEY (order_status_id)
);

CREATE TABLE ShippingMethod (
    shipping_method_id INT NOT NULL AUTO_INCREMENT
    , name VARCHAR(100) NOT NULL
    , cost DECIMAL(5,2) NOT NULL
    , min_order_weight DECIMAL(9,2) NOT NULL
    , max_order_weight DECIMAL(9,2) NOT NULL
    , min_order_total DECIMAL(9,2) NOT NULL
    , max_order_total DECIMAL(9,2) NOT NULL
    , PRIMARY KEY (shipping_method_id)
);

CREATE TABLE CustomerOrder (
    order_id INT NOT NULL AUTO_INCREMENT
    , customer_id INT NOT NULL
    , status CHAR(2) NOT NULL
    , shipping_method INT NOT NULL
    , ordered_on DATE NOT NULL
    , shipping_price DECIMAL(5,2) NOT NULL
    , PRIMARY KEY (order_id)
    , INDEX (customer_id)
);

CREATE TABLE CustomerOrderItem (
    order_id INT NOT NULL
    , product_id INT NOT NULL
    , price DECIMAL(9,2) NOT NULL
    , weight DECIMAL(7,2) NOT NULL
    , quantity INT NOT NULL
    , PRIMARY KEY (order_id, product_id)
);
```

We've populated our sample schema with some data using the code found in the /ch07/insert.sql file available from the Downloads section of the Apress web site (http://www.apress.com). Admittedly, our sample data is less than original.

Joins are the "glue" that allow you to connect two or more sets of data through one or more key values, thus enabling relationships to be constructed in your SELECT statements. MySQL supports a variety of standard and not-so-standard join types:

- Inner join

- Outer join

- Cross join

- Union join

Here, we will discuss each type, as well as natural joins and the USING keyword. Although this information may be review for some readers, we encourage you to read the material, even if it serves solely as a simple reminder of the fundamentals.

The Inner Join

The most basic and common join type is the inner join. You use this type of join when you want to relate two sets of data where values in the ON clause columns match in both tables. The columns are most often, but not always, key columns representing a primary key and foreign key relationship. For instance, consider the following English language request: "I need to know the name and SKU for each product purchased by John Doe on December 7, 2004, along with the price and weight of the product at the time he purchased it."

Based on our E-R diagram, we know that in order to get all the column data in the request—product's name, SKU, price, and weight at the time of the order—we'll need to query a number of different tables, if the only thing we can use to filter the data is the order date (CustomerOrder.ordered_on) and John Doe's name (Customer.first_name and Customer.last_name). The sets of data we'll need to deal with involve the Customer, CustomerOrder, CustomerOrderItem, and Product tables. We want to know where these sets of data intersect, thus we'll need to use inner joins. Specifically, we'll need to find the intersection of the following sets of data:

- Product (to know the name and SKU of the product); alias: p

- CustomerOrderItem (to relate the order and to get the weight and price); alias: coi

- CustomerOrder (to relate the customer and filter based on the order date); alias: co

- Customer (to filter for John Doe); alias: c

Although this is a fairly simple example, breaking down English-language[1] requests into a list of the sets of data needed or used by the request can be an extremely helpful practice. It encourages you to think in terms of the sets of data being operated on, and serves as an exercise in breaking down complex requests into smaller, simpler pieces. As you work on more

---

1. We say "English-language request" here to indicate that the request is coming from a nontechnical and non-SQL point of view. Clearly, any human language could be substituted.

advanced SQL statements—using derived tables, UNION constructs, and the like—you'll find that deconstructing the request in this manner can isolate problem areas in data-access patterns and help in identifying where indexes may provide key performance benefits.

Building complex SQL statements usually follows a fairly straightforward process. First, include the SELECT clause with the columns you wish to include in your result output, using an alias for the set of data from which the column is being obtained:

```
SELECT p.name, p.sku, coi.price, coi.weight
```

Next, retrieve the data set you believe will have the least number of rows in it. In this case, since we expect to find a single Customer record for John Doe, we start our FROM clause with that set of data:

```
FROM Customer c
```

Now, in order to intersect each of our data sets, we do an INNER JOIN on the key relationships from one data set to the next, until we've "chained" them all together along their key relationships:

```
INNER JOIN CustomerOrder co
  ON c.customer_id = co.customer_id
INNER JOIN CustomerOrderItem coi
  ON co.order_id = coi.order_id
INNER JOIN Product p
  ON coi.product_id = p.product_id
```

Finally, we add our WHERE clause to filter the appropriate values from our Customer and CustomerOrder sets based on the criteria in our request:

```
WHERE c.last_name = 'Doe'
AND c.first_name = 'John'
AND co.ordered_on = '2004-12-07';
```

Listing 7-2 shows the final SQL built from these data sets, along with the result.

Listing 7-2. *Example of a Multiple Inner Join*

```
mysql> SELECT p.name, p.sku, coi.price, coi.weight
    -> FROM Customer c
    ->   INNER JOIN CustomerOrder co
    ->     ON c.customer_id = co.customer_id
    ->   INNER JOIN CustomerOrderItem coi
    ->     ON co.order_id = coi.order_id
    ->   INNER JOIN Product p
    ->     ON coi.product_id = p.product_id
    -> WHERE c.last_name = 'Doe'
    -> AND c.first_name = 'John'
    -> AND co.ordered_on = '2004-12-07';
```

```
+-------------+--------+-------+--------+
| name        | sku    | price | weight |
+-------------+--------+-------+--------+
| Soccer Ball | SPT001 | 23.70 |   1.25 |
+-------------+--------+-------+--------+
1 row in set (0.00 sec)
```

This technique, which we'll call *top-down SQL*, is just one method of building complex SQL statements. Throughout this chapter, we'll take a look at other techniques you can use to generate complex SQL statements for other types of joins.

The Outer Join

While an inner join returns only rows where a key value in data set A appears as a key in data set B, an outer join is used in situations when you want to return all the elements of data set A, regardless of whether the key value exists in data set B. An outer join is designated in MySQL using the LEFT JOIN syntax, with the ON clause specifying the key values on which MySQL should perform the join relationship. As we noted earlier in this chapter, the RIGHT JOIN is identical to the LEFT JOIN, but includes all elements from the data set on the right side of the ON condition.

In an outer join, rows in data set B with matching key values to data set A will be returned just as an inner join; however, columns for data set B will be filled with NULL for those rows in data set A where no matching key was found in data set B.

Outer joins can or must be used in a number of situations. Here, we'll go over a few examples to illustrate outer joins:

- Aggregating data where not all keys are present

- Handling valid NULL column keys

- Finding nonexisting keys in relationships

Aggregating Data Where Not All Keys Are Present

Many times, you'll run into situations where you need to aggregate data (using the GROUP BY clause), but find your SQL results are missing records that you know are in the database. The most common cause of this is the incorrect use of an INNER JOIN in the aggregating SQL.

For instance, let's take the following request, received from our friends in the sales department: "Please provide a report showing how many orders contained each product in our catalog, and how many items of each were purchased." Your first attempt might look like Listing 7-3.

Listing 7-3. *First Report Attempt with an Inner Join*

```
mysql> SELECT p.name, COUNT(*) as "# Orders", SUM(coi.quantity)"Total Qty"
    -> FROM Product p
    ->    INNER JOIN CustomerOrderItem coi
    ->      ON p.product_id = coi.product_id
    -> GROUP BY p.name;
```

```
+-----------------------------+-----------+-----------+
| name                        | # Orders  | Total Qty |
+-----------------------------+-----------+-----------+
| Action Figure - Football    |        1  |        1  |
| Action Figure - Gladiator   |        1  |        1  |
| Action Figure - Tennis      |        1  |        1  |
| Doll                        |        1  |        2  |
| Soccer Ball                 |        1  |        1  |
| Tennis Balls                |        3  |       57  |
| Tennis Racket               |        1  |        1  |
| Video Game - Football       |        1  |        1  |
+-----------------------------+-----------+-----------+
8 rows in set (0.00 sec)
```

This looks about right, but then you notice that the list does not include all the products in the product catalog. The problem is that you've used an intersection of the data sets—an INNER JOIN—meaning that only the products that had been purchased by a customer were included in the final result. Instead, what you need is all the products in the catalog, along with a count and total quantity for each. So, you need to rewrite the query using an outer join. Listing 7-4 shows the rewritten query and its results.

Listing 7-4. *Second Report Attempt with an Outer Join*

```
mysql> SELECT p.name, COUNT(*) as "# Orders", SUM(coi.quantity)"Total Qty"
    -> FROM Product p
    ->    LEFT JOIN CustomerOrderItem coi
    ->      ON p.product_id = coi.product_id
    -> GROUP BY p.name;
+-----------------------------+-----------+-----------+
| name                        | # Orders  | Total Qty |
+-----------------------------+-----------+-----------+
| Action Figure - Football    |        1  |        1  |
| Action Figure - Gladiator   |        1  |        1  |
| Action Figure - Tennis      |        1  |        1  |
| Doll                        |        1  |        2  |
| Soccer Ball                 |        1  |        1  |
| Tennis Balls                |        3  |       57  |
| Tennis Racket               |        1  |        1  |
| Video Game - Car Racing     |        1  |     NULL  |
| Video Game - Football       |        1  |        1  |
| Video Game - Soccer         |        1  |     NULL  |
+-----------------------------+-----------+-----------+
10 rows in set (0.00 sec)
```

You're getting closer. Now, you have all ten products in the catalog, as well as some data returned in the rows for the two products no customer has yet purchased. You'll notice two interesting things.

First, the Total Qty field—SUM(coi.quantity)—has NULL values for the two unmatched rows in the product data set. This is the behavior of an outer join; columns from unmatched rows of the second data set are filled with NULL values. The SUM() SQL function treats NULL values as unknown, therefore summing unknown values always results in unknown, or NULL. This is a critical point to remember when doing aggregating reports. If you know that NULL values may be returned from a statement, use the IFNULL() function to "zero out" any NULL values if appropriate. You'll see this strategy in practice in Listing 7-5.

Second, given the behavior of SUM(), you would assume that the COUNT() function would also return NULL since there were no matching rows. This is not necessarily the case, and is the cause of numerous reporting errors. The COUNT() function works as follows with NULL values:

- COUNT(*): Simply returns the number of rows in the resultset matching the GROUP BY columns.

- COUNT(*table.column*): Returns the number of rows having non-NULL values found in *table*.

Notice the difference in the aggregated data values in our corrected Listing 7-5.

Listing 7-5. *Corrected Output Using COUNT(table.column) and IFNULL()*

```
mysql> SELECT
    ->    p.name
    ->    , COUNT(coi.order_id) as "# Orders"
    ->    , SUM(IFNULL(coi.quantity,0)) as "Total Qty"
    -> FROM Product p
    ->    LEFT JOIN CustomerOrderItem coi
    ->      ON p.product_id = coi.product_id
    -> GROUP BY p.name;
+------------------------------+----------+-----------+
| name                         | # Orders | Total Qty |
+------------------------------+----------+-----------+
| Action Figure - Football     |        1 |         1 |
| Action Figure - Gladiator    |        1 |         1 |
| Action Figure - Tennis       |        1 |         1 |
| Doll                         |        1 |         2 |
| Soccer Ball                  |        1 |         1 |
| Tennis Balls                 |        3 |        57 |
| Tennis Racket                |        1 |         1 |
| Video Game - Car Racing      |        0 |         0 |
| Video Game - Football        |        1 |         1 |
| Video Game - Soccer          |        0 |         0 |
+------------------------------+----------+-----------+
10 rows in set (0.01 sec)
```

This demonstration should serve to highlight the importance of always verifying that the results you get are indeed accurate and reflect the original request.

Handling Valid NULL Column Keys

In certain rare situations, it is necessary to have a foreign key column that contains NULL values, such as in hierarchical data sets. Luckily, we have just such a structure in our sample schema, all contained in the Category table. The Category.parent_id column contains either a NULL value when the row contains a "root" category (one with no parent) or the parent category's category_id value. Imagine the following request: "List all categories along with the name of their parent category."

Once again, an inner join fails to fulfill this request, because it cannot account for NULL values in the matching condition. Listing 7-6 shows a listing of all the categories and then an attempted inner join to get the parent category names. You should immediately notice the dilemma (observe the number of rows returned).

Listing 7-6. *Inner Join Fails to Get All Categories*

```
mysql> SELECT name, category_id, parent_id FROM Category;
+--------------------------+-------------+-----------+
| name                     | category_id | parent_id |
+--------------------------+-------------+-----------+
| All                      |           1 |      NULL |
| Action Figures           |           2 |         1 |
| Sport Action Figures     |           3 |         2 |
| Tennis Action Figures    |           4 |         3 |
| Football Action Figures  |           5 |         3 |
| Historical Action Figures|           6 |         2 |
| Video Games              |           7 |         1 |
| Racing Video Games       |           8 |         7 |
| Sports Video Games       |           9 |         7 |
| Shooting Video Games     |          10 |         7 |
| Sports Gear              |          11 |         1 |
| Soccer Equipment         |          12 |        11 |
| Tennis Equipment         |          13 |        11 |
| Dolls                    |          14 |         1 |
+--------------------------+-------------+-----------+
14 rows in set (0.05 sec)

mysql> SELECT c.name, pc.name AS "parent"
    -> FROM Category c
    ->    INNER JOIN Category pc
    ->    ON c.parent_id = pc.category_id;
```

```
+--------------------------+----------------------+
| name                     | parent               |
+--------------------------+----------------------+
| Action Figures           | All                  |
| Sport Action Figures     | Action Figures       |
| Tennis Action Figures    | Sport Action Figures |
| Football Action Figures  | Sport Action Figures |
| Historical Action Figures| Action Figures       |
| Video Games              | All                  |
| Racing Video Games       | Video Games          |
| Sports Video Games       | Video Games          |
| Shooting Video Games     | Video Games          |
| Sports Gear              | All                  |
| Soccer Equipment         | Sports Gear          |
| Tennis Equipment         | Sports Gear          |
| Dolls                    | All                  |
+--------------------------+----------------------+
13 rows in set (0.03 sec)
```

Notice that the root category that serves as the parent for the topmost parent categories is not included in the lower resultset. This is because the NULL parent_id column value for the root category—the one without a parent category—finds no matching value in the inner join from the Category table to itself, known as a *self join*. In order to show all the categories, we need to employ an outer join to get all the categories in the first data set, and then we'll use the IFNULL() function to indicate that categories without a parent are root categories. Listing 7-7 shows the updated version.

Listing 7-7. *Updated Category Listing*

```
mysql> SELECT
    ->    c.name
    ->    , IFNULL(pc.name, "Root Category") as "parent"
    -> FROM Category c
    ->    LEFT JOIN Category pc
    ->      ON c.parent_id = pc.category_id;
+--------------------------+----------------------+
| name                     | parent               |
+--------------------------+----------------------+
| All                      | Root Category        |
| Action Figures           | All                  |
| Sport Action Figures     | Action Figures       |
| Tennis Action Figures    | Sport Action Figures |
| Football Action Figures  | Sport Action Figures |
| Historical Action Figures| Action Figures       |
| Video Games              | All                  |
| Racing Video Games       | Video Games          |
| Sports Video Games       | Video Games          |
| Shooting Video Games     | Video Games          |
```

```
| Sports Gear               | All                   |
| Soccer Equipment          | Sports Gear           |
| Tennis Equipment          | Sports Gear           |
| Dolls                     | All                   |
+---------------------------+-----------------------+
14 rows in set (0.05 sec)
```

As you can see, now all the categories are included. However, one question still remains: What if there are more than two levels to this category tree? Currently, our category tree has only two levels: one root level and one subcategory level for some root-level categories. What if a subcategory had one or more child categories? We will consider this situation in the next chapter, where we will discuss how to deal with hierarchical data using the nested set model.

Finding Nonexisting Keys in Relationships

In some cases, you'll want to find the records in one data set that *don't* appear in a foreign key relationship. You can accomplish this task in a number of ways, but the most efficient method is to use an outer join. Consider the following request, again received from our illustrious sales department: "We'd like a list of all of the customers in our database who have signed up at our online store, but who have not ordered anything from our catalog."

This kind of request typifies a situation where beginner developers often get into trouble and overcomplicate things. Novices will often approach this problem using a procedural method: get a list of all customer ID values, loop through the list of customer IDs, and for each one, check if the customer ID value is in the CustomerOrder table; if not, add the ID to a list of values to return. This kind of approach might result in something like the PHP code shown in Listing 7-8.

Listing 7-8. *Inefficient PHP Code to Find Customers Without Orders*

```php
<?php
$conn = mysql_connect("localhost","test","") or die (mysql_error());
mysql_select_db("ToyStore", $conn) or die ("Can't use database 'ToyStore'");

$customers = mysql_query("SELECT customer_id, first_name, last_name
                          FROM Customer");
$customers_without_orders = array();
if ($customers) {
    while ($customer = mysql_fetch_row($customers)) {
        $orders = mysql_query("SELECT COUNT(*) FROM
                               CustomerOrder WHERE customer_id = " . $customer[0]);
        $order = mysql_fetch_row($orders);
        $has_orders = $order[0];
        if ($has_orders) {
            array_push($customers_without_orders, $customer);
        }
    }
}
?>
```

This kind of code exemplifies the procedural mindset, which goes against the grain of proper set-based SQL coding. All of the code in Listing 7-8 could be reduced to the outer join statement shown in Listing 7-9 (along with the result of the query).

Listing 7-9. *Proper Set-Based Approach Using an Outer Join*

```
mysql> SELECT
    ->    c.customer_id
    ->    , c.first_name
    ->    , c.last_name
    -> FROM Customer c
    ->    LEFT JOIN CustomerOrder co
    ->      ON c.customer_id = co.customer_id
    -> WHERE co.customer_id IS NULL;
+-------------+------------+-----------+
| customer_id | first_name | last_name |
+-------------+------------+-----------+
|           4 | Homer      | Simpson   |
+-------------+------------+-----------+
1 row in set (0.06 sec)
```

The key to the statement in Listing 7-9 is the WHERE co.customer_id IS NULL clause, which tells MySQL to find the rows in the outer-joined result that have no matching foreign key.

Understanding the ON Clause in Outer Joins

Let's test your understanding of outer joins so far. In English, what does Listing 7-10 accomplish?

Listing 7-10. *Another Example of an Outer Join*

```
mysql> SELECT os.description, COUNT(co.order_id) AS "NumOrders"
    -> FROM OrderStatus os
    ->    LEFT JOIN CustomerOrder co
    ->      ON os.order_status_id = co.status
    -> GROUP BY os.description;
```

If you answered something like, "It will show all order statuses, along with a count for the number of orders in each status, or zero if no orders are in that status," you would be correct, as Listing 7-11 indicates.

Listing 7-11. *Result of Query in Listing 7-10*

```
+-------------+-----------+
| description | NumOrders |
+-------------+-----------+
| Cancelled   |         1 |
| Closed      |         0 |
| Completed   |         2 |
| In Progress |         1 |
| Shipped     |         2 |
+-------------+-----------+
5 rows in set (0.00 sec)
```

If you got that correct, pat yourself on the back. Now answer the following. Given your knowledge of outer joins thus far, how many rows would you expect the adaptation of the first statement shown in Listing 7-12 to produce?

Listing 7-12. *Slight Adaptation of the Query in Listing 7-10*

```
mysql> SELECT os.description, COUNT(co.order_id) AS "NumOrders"
    -> FROM OrderStatus os
    ->   LEFT JOIN CustomerOrder co
    ->     ON os.order_status_id = co.status
    -> WHERE co.ordered_on = '2004-12-07'
    -> GROUP BY os.description;
```

As you can see, we've added a WHERE clause on the CustomerOrder.ordered_on column. Most readers will arrive at the conclusion that the results of the SQL in Listing 7-12 should still have five rows in it, because the LEFT JOIN should include all the OrderStatus rows, along with a count of the orders in each status placed on December 7, 2004. If you arrived at this conclusion, you would, unfortunately, be mistaken, but don't be discouraged. The behavior demonstrated in this example is one of the most common mistakes involving outer joins. The actual result returned is shown in Listing 7-13.

Listing 7-13. *Result from SQL in Listing 7-12*

```
+-------------+-----------+
| description | NumOrders |
+-------------+-----------+
| Completed   |         1 |
+-------------+-----------+
1 row in set (0.00 sec)
```

Now, why does the resultset contain only a single row if the outer join is supposed to include all the rows in the OrderStatus table? The reason stems from the fact that conditions present in the WHERE clause of a SQL statement filter the resultset *produced* by the outer join. In this case, the resultset produced by the outer join can be viewed as all the CustomerOrder rows, along with a status description matching the status key and NULLed out rows for any statuses with no matching orders.

When the WHERE condition is executed (after the rows from OrderStatus are LEFT JOINed with the CustomerOrder table), MySQL filters out all rows in the resulting set that do not have an ordered_on date of December 7, 2004. Since the WHERE filter was executed after the two tables were joined, any rows without an ordered_on date equal to '2004-12-07' were removed from the returned resultset. This eliminated any of the NULLed out rows for statuses having no matching orders, since NULL ≠ '2004-12-07'.

So, the question remains, how do we fulfill a request like this: "Show all order statuses, and the number of orders in each status, for orders placed on December 7, 2004."

The SQL in Listing 7-12 indeed filters the date properly, but, unfortunately, it also filters out all the nonmatching order statuses from the outer join. To remedy the situation, we must use the ON clause to limit the compared data set of the right side of the outer join before the outer join occurs. Listing 7-14 shows the correct SQL to fulfill the request.

Listing 7-14. *Corrected SQL Demonstrating the Outer Join ON Clause Filter*

```
mysql> SELECT os.description, COUNT(co.order_id) AS "NumOrders"
    -> FROM OrderStatus os
    ->    LEFT JOIN CustomerOrder co
    ->      ON os.order_status_id = co.status
    ->      AND co.ordered_on = '2004-12-07'
    -> GROUP BY os.description;
+-------------+-----------+
| description | NumOrders |
+-------------+-----------+
| Cancelled   |         0 |
| Closed      |         0 |
| Completed   |         1 |
| In Progress |         0 |
| Shipped     |         0 |
+-------------+-----------+
5 rows in set (0.00 sec)
```

If you are doing any sort of reporting work in MySQL, understanding this critical difference between seemingly similar SQL statements can help you avoid some very frustrating SQL debugging work. Make sure you understand when to use a filter in the ON clause of an outer join and when to use a WHERE clause filter.

■Tip Remember that the WHERE clause will filter the results *after* the outer join is processed, whereas the ON condition of the outer join will filter the second data set in the outer join *before* the join is processed.

The Cross Join (Cartesian Product)

A cross join, sometimes called a Cartesian product, unlike the other types of joins we've covered so far, does not attempt to relate the two sets of data based on some key values. Instead, it creates a result based on all possible row combinations in both sets of joined data. Thus, the number of rows returned from a cross join is $N \times M$, where N is the number of rows in data set A and M is the number of rows in data set B. Clearly, the number of rows in a cross join can quickly get out of hand!

Most often, cross joins are done by mistake because the developer forgets to include an ON condition, which will force MySQL to use a cross join across the two data sets by default. However, in some rare circumstances, the cross join can come in handy.

For example, let's say we've received a request from our product development department: "We wish to see a breakdown of our products at various pricing levels so that we can compare our prices against a study of market-average prices for similar products. Please show each of our products, along with the current price, and varying price levels, in 5% changes, differing 25% from the existing level." To handle this request, we might create a temporary table for storing the percentage differences in price, as shown in Listing 7-15.

Listing 7-15. *Temporary Storage for Percentage Differences*

```
mysql> CREATE TABLE Percentages (percent_difference DECIMAL(5,2) NOT NULL);
Query OK, 0 rows affected (0.94 sec)

mysql> INSERT INTO Percentages VALUES (-.25), (-.20), (-.15), (-.10), (-.05), (.00)
    -> , (.05), (.10), (.15), (.20), (.25);
Query OK, 11 rows affected (0.14 sec)
Records: 11  Duplicates: 0  Warnings: 0
```

Using a cross join, we can show the product prices at these various pricing levels, as shown in Listing 7-16 (for brevity, we've filtered for a single product only).

Listing 7-16. *Example of a Cross Join*

```
mysql>  SELECT
    ->    p.name as "Product"
    ->  , CONCAT((pct.percent_difference * 100), '%') as "% Difference"
    ->  , ROUND((pct.percent_difference + 1) * p.unit_price, 2) as "Price"
    ->  FROM Product p
    ->    CROSS JOIN Percentages pct
    ->  WHERE p.product_id = 2
    ->  ORDER BY pct.percent_difference;
```

```
+-------------------------------+---------------+---------+
| Product                       | % Difference  | Price   |
+-------------------------------+---------------+---------+
| Action Figure - Football      | -25.00%       |  8.96   |
| Action Figure - Football      | -20.00%       |  9.56   |
| Action Figure - Football      | -15.00%       | 10.16   |
| Action Figure - Football      | -10.00%       | 10.76   |
| Action Figure - Football      | -5.00%        | 11.35   |
| Action Figure - Football      | 0.00%         | 11.95   |
| Action Figure - Football      | 5.00%         | 12.55   |
| Action Figure - Football      | 10.00%        | 13.15   |
| Action Figure - Football      | 15.00%        | 13.74   |
| Action Figure - Football      | 20.00%        | 14.34   |
| Action Figure - Football      | 25.00%        | 14.94   |
+-------------------------------+---------------+---------+
11 rows in set (0.00 sec)
```

We've highlighted the CROSS JOIN and WHERE clauses. Notice that there is no ON clause attached to the cross join. This is because there is no relation between the two data sets. In this case, the WHERE clause filters the first data set (Product) to a single row (product_id = 2). The second data set is all rows from the Percentages table.

While you won't find too many uses for cross joins in your code, they can occasionally be useful in this type of analysis, where you want to cross a static (fixed number of rows) table with another table.

The Union Join

MySQL version 4.0 and higher supports the UNION join type. If you use a lot of complex OR statements in your application code, and you are using a version of MySQL prior to 5.0, our advice is to get familiar with UNIONs. We'll explain why in the next chapter, where we show you how to optimize complex OR clauses in your WHERE condition using UNION joins.

The basic point of a UNION query is to combine the results of two different, but structurally similar, data sets. By default, MySQL forces the row uniqueness of the eventual returned result. This may sounds strange, so we'll show you by example.

For this example, let's assume that we have archived our 2004 store data into a set of identically named tables, appended with the number 2004. We've just received this request: "We need a report showing the orders received in December 2004 and January 2005 only. Provide the total quantity purchased for any product purchased in those time frames."

To accomplish this task, we will need to produce one resultset from two similar sets of tables: one from the 2004 data tables and one from the current tables. Let's first start with the current data, and obtain our first data set, shown in Listing 7-17.

Listing 7-17. *Current Year's Data Set*

```
mysql> SELECT
    ->    p.name as "Product"
    ->    , "2005 - January" as "Date"
    ->    , SUM(coi.quantity) as "Total Purchased"
    -> FROM CustomerOrder co
    ->    INNER JOIN CustomerOrderItem coi
    ->      ON co.order_id = coi.order_id
    ->    INNER JOIN Product p
    ->      ON coi.product_id = p.product_id
    -> WHERE co.ordered_on BETWEEN '2005-01-01' AND '2005-01-31'
    -> GROUP BY p.name;
+---------------------------+----------------+-----------------+
| Product                   | Date           | Total Purchased |
+---------------------------+----------------+-----------------+
| Action Figure - Football  | 2005 - January |               1 |
| Action Figure - Gladiator | 2005 - January |               1 |
| Doll                      | 2005 - January |               2 |
| Tennis Balls              | 2005 - January |              42 |
| Tennis Racket             | 2005 - January |               1 |
| Video Game - Football     | 2005 - January |               1 |
+---------------------------+----------------+-----------------+
6 rows in set (0.00 sec)
```

Notice we include the static column Date, set to the value of "2005 - January". We do this so that the rows of our next resultset (from 2004) will be distinguishable from the current data rows. Next, let's put together our 2004 data in a similar fashion, as shown in Listing 7-18. We've included CREATE TABLE statements for you to create the 2004 archive tables.

Listing 7-18. *Creating 2004 Summary Data and Selecting December's Data*

```
mysql> CREATE TABLE CustomerOrder2004
    -> SELECT * FROM CustomerOrder
    -> WHERE ordered_on BETWEEN '2004-01-01' AND '2004-12-31';
Query OK, 2 rows affected (0.62 sec)
Records: 2  Duplicates: 0  Warnings: 0

mysql> CREATE TABLE CustomerOrderItem2004
    -> SELECT coi.*
    -> FROM CustomerOrder co
    ->   INNER JOIN CustomerOrderItem coi
    ->     ON co.order_id = coi.order_id
    -> WHERE co.ordered_on BETWEEN '2004-01-01' AND '2004-12-31';
Query OK, 3 rows affected (0.00 sec)
Records: 3  Duplicates: 0  Warnings: 0
```

```
mysql> SELECT
    -> p.name as "Product"
    -> , "2004 - December" as "Date"
    -> , SUM(coi.quantity) as "Total Purchased"
    -> FROM CustomerOrder2004 co
    -> INNER JOIN CustomerOrderItem2004 coi
    ->   ON co.order_id = coi.order_id
    -> INNER JOIN Product p
    ->   ON coi.product_id = p.product_id
    -> WHERE co.ordered_on BETWEEN '2004-12-01' AND '2004-12-31'
    -> GROUP BY p.name;
+-----------------------+------------------+------------------+
| Product               | Date             | Total Purchased  |
+-----------------------+------------------+------------------+
| Action Figure - Tennis | 2004 - December | 1                |
| Soccer Ball           | 2004 - December  | 1                |
| Tennis Balls          | 2004 - December  | 15               |
+-----------------------+------------------+------------------+
3 rows in set (0.00 sec)
```

Once we're satisfied with our second result, we finalize the query, adding the UNION keyword between the two separate queries, as in Listing 7-19.

Listing 7-19. *UNION Query Merging Two Previous Resultsets*

```
mysql> (
    -> SELECT
    ->   p.name as "Product"
    ->   , "2005 - January" as "Date"
    ->   , SUM(coi.quantity) as "Total Purchased"
    -> FROM CustomerOrder co
    ->   INNER JOIN CustomerOrderItem coi
    ->     ON co.order_id = coi.order_id
    ->   INNER JOIN Product p
    ->     ON coi.product_id = p.product_id
    -> WHERE co.ordered_on BETWEEN '2005-01-01' AND '2005-01-31'
    -> GROUP BY p.name
    -> )
    -> UNION
    -> (
    -> SELECT
    ->   p.name as "Product"
    ->   , "2004 - December" as "Date"
    ->   , SUM(coi.quantity) as "Total Purchased"
    -> FROM CustomerOrder2004 co
    ->   INNER JOIN CustomerOrderItem2004 coi
    ->     ON co.order_id = coi.order_id
    ->   INNER JOIN Product2004 p
```

```
->      ON coi.product_id = p.product_id
-> WHERE co.ordered_on BETWEEN '2004-12-01' AND '2004-12-31'
-> GROUP BY p.name
-> );
```

```
+--------------------------+-----------------+-----------------+
| Product                  | Date            | Total Purchased |
+--------------------------+-----------------+-----------------+
| Action Figure - Football | 2005 - January  |               1 |
| Action Figure - Gladiator| 2005 - January  |               1 |
| Doll                     | 2005 - January  |               2 |
| Tennis Balls             | 2005 - January  |              42 |
| Tennis Racket            | 2005 - January  |               1 |
| Video Game - Football    | 2005 - January  |               1 |
| Action Figure - Tennis   | 2004 - December |               1 |
| Soccer Ball              | 2004 - December |               1 |
| Tennis Balls             | 2004 - December |              15 |
+--------------------------+-----------------+-----------------+
9 rows in set (0.09 sec)
```

Here, the parentheses are optional, but we feel they help to distinguish the two component resultsets. Furthermore, when using the ORDER BY or LIMIT clause in your UNION statements, the parentheses are required in order to tell MySQL that you wish the ORDER BY or LIMIT to operate on the entire merged resultset.

As you can see, the two various results are merged together into a single result. Now, what would happen if we had not included the static Date column? Listing 7-20 shows the result of removing this column.

Listing 7-20. *Removing the Static Date Column*

```
mysql> (
    -> SELECT
    ->   p.name as "Product"
    ->   , SUM(coi.quantity) as "Total Purchased"
    -> FROM CustomerOrder co
    ->   INNER JOIN CustomerOrderItem coi
    ->     ON co.order_id = coi.order_id
    ->   INNER JOIN Product p
    ->     ON coi.product_id = p.product_id
    -> WHERE co.ordered_on BETWEEN '2005-01-01' AND '2005-01-31'
    -> GROUP BY p.name
    -> )
    -> UNION
    -> (
    -> SELECT
    ->   p.name as "Product"
    ->   , SUM(coi.quantity) as "Total Purchased"
    -> FROM CustomerOrder2004 co
    ->   INNER JOIN CustomerOrderItem2004 coi
```

```
    ->       ON co.order_id = coi.order_id
    ->    INNER JOIN Product2004 p
    ->       ON coi.product_id = p.product_id
    -> WHERE co.ordered_on BETWEEN '2004-12-01' AND '2004-12-31'
    -> GROUP BY p.name
    -> );
+--------------------------+------------------+
| Product                  | Total Purchased  |
+--------------------------+------------------+
| Action Figure - Football |                1 |
| Action Figure - Gladiator|                1 |
| Doll                     |                2 |
| Tennis Balls             |               42 |
| Tennis Racket            |                1 |
| Video Game - Football    |                1 |
| Action Figure - Tennis   |                1 |
| Soccer Ball              |                1 |
| Tennis Balls             |               15 |
+--------------------------+------------------+
9 rows in set (0.00 sec)
```

As you can see, you can't tell which row for the Tennis Balls product refers to the 2005 data and which belongs to the 2004 data. Furthermore, if the two Total Purchased columns for those rows had been the same, one of the rows would have been eliminated from the resultset, unless the UNION ALL keywords were used in the statement.

■Tip By default, UNIONs operate in the UNION DISTINCT behavior, which eliminates any duplicate rows from the return. You may override this behavior by using the UNION ALL keywords. If you know with certainty that the UNIONed results will naturally contain no duplicates, you can realize a small performance gain using the UNION ALL variation.

In practice, if you have a properly normalized database, there should be few situations, if any, where you would use a UNION join. If you do find yourself using UNION for more than optimizing OR conditions or aggregating log or archive data, you may need to reexamine your schema to see if some normalization should occur. For example, take a look at the E-R diagram shown in Figure 7-2.

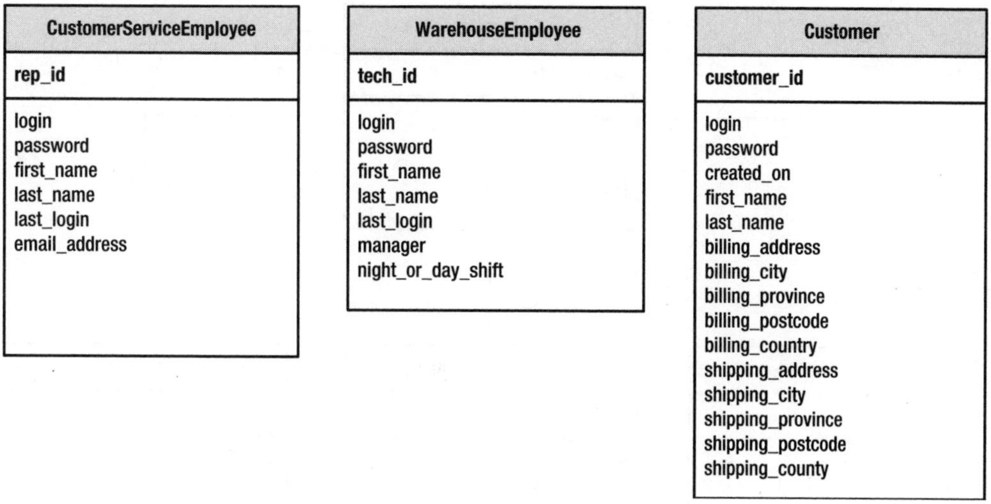

CustomerServiceEmployee
rep_id
login
password
first_name
last_name
last_login
email_address

WarehouseEmployee
tech_id
login
password
first_name
last_name
last_login
manager
night_or_day_shift

Customer
customer_id
login
password
created_on
first_name
last_name
billing_address
billing_city
billing_province
billing_postcode
billing_country
shipping_address
shipping_city
shipping_province
shipping_postcode
shipping_county

Figure 7-2. *Account schema that isn't normalized*

Each of the entities you see in Figure 7-2 represents a different type of user in the application. In order to get a list of all the names, logins, and passwords of all the users in this system, you would need to perform a UNION query similar to the one shown in Listing 7-21. (Note the required use of parentheses around the statements because of the ORDER BY clause.)

Listing 7-21. *UNION Query to Find System User Information*

```
(
SELECT first_name, last_name, login, password
FROM CustomerServiceEmployee
UNION
SELECT first_name, last_name, login, password
FROM WarehouseEmployee
UNION
SELECT first_name, last_name, login, password
FROM Customer
) ORDER BY last_name, first_name;
```

However, if the schema were properly normalized, to a form similar to Figure 7-3, the UNION would not be necessary, and instead could be a simple SELECT from a single table, Account, like so:

```
SELECT first_name, last_name, login, password FROM Account;
```

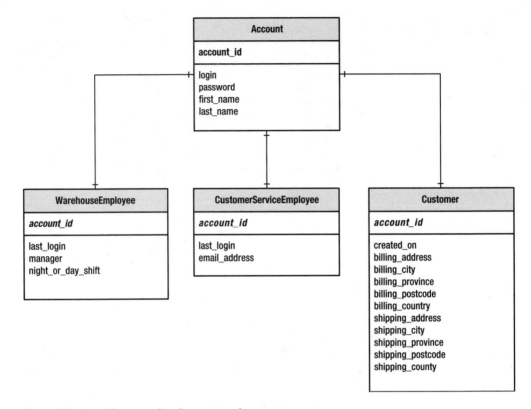

Figure 7-3. *Properly normalized account schema*

The point here is that if you find yourself dealing with UNIONs a lot, it may be time to take a closer look at your schema and get back to basics. The Account table in Figure 7-3 houses the attributes common to all system users, thus accomplishing the normalization step of removing redundant data columns. Similarly, the two types of employee data—WarehouseEmployee and CustomerServiceEmployee—have been stripped of their redundant Account data and contain only attributes specific to each entity.

Although this brief discussion on proper normalization may come across as common sense to many of you who have experience using relational database management systems, we almost guarantee that in the course of your IT travels, you will run across this type of situation. Why? In the world of object-oriented programming, it is natural, and sometimes encouraged, to create multiple classes for related objects. Sometimes these related objects correspond to a naturally normalized relational database model; other times they don't. In the latter case, object-oriented programmers with little database experience tend to "translate" their object model quite literally into the database schema. This is an all-too-common occurrence and is why you will often see schemas like the one shown in Figure 7-2.

The Natural Join

A natural join, in the MySQL world, is not a different type of join, but rather a different way of expressing either an inner join or outer join on tables that have identically named columns. For example, the two statements shown in Listing 7-22 are identical, given our sample schema.

Listing 7-22. *Example of a Natural Join*

```
mysql> SELECT p2c.category_id
    -> FROM Product p
    -> NATURAL JOIN Product2Category p2c
    -> WHERE p.product_id = 2;
+-------------+
| category_id |
+-------------+
|           2 |
+-------------+
1 row in set (0.11 sec)

mysql> SELECT p2c.category_id
    -> FROM Product p
    -> INNER JOIN Product2Category p2c ON p.product_id = p2c.product_id
    -> WHERE p.product_id = 2;
+-------------+
| category_id |
+-------------+
|           2 |
+-------------+
1 row in set (0.00 sec)
```

Likewise, using NATURAL LEFT JOIN would do an outer join based on any identically named columns in both tables.

We generally discourage the use of NATURAL JOIN, because it leads to less specificity in your SQL code.

The USING Keyword

Just like NATURAL JOIN, the USING keyword is simply an alternate way of expressing the ON condition for some joins. Instead of ON tableA.column1 = tableB.column1, you could write USING (column1). Listing 7-23 shows an example that uses the USING keyword.

Listing 7-23. *Example of the USING Keyword*

```
mysql> SELECT p2c.category_id
    -> FROM Product p
    -> INNER JOIN Product2Category p2c USING (product_id)
    -> WHERE p.product_id = 2;
+-------------+
| category_id |
+-------------+
|           2 |
+-------------+
1 row in set (0.00 sec)
```

The use of USING is primarily related to style preference. If you're concerned about portability issues, however, you may want to stay away from this nonstandard syntax. If not, just decide which style of syntax you want to adopt, and adhere to that single style.

EXPLAIN and Access Types

The access strategy MySQL chooses for your SELECT statements is based on a complex set of decisions made by the join optimizer, which is part of the query parsing, optimization, and execution subsystem (see Chapter 4). The EXPLAIN command, introduced in Chapter 6, helps you in analyzing the access strategy MySQL chooses in order fulfill your SELECT requests. This will provide you the information you need to determine if MySQL has indeed chosen an optimal path for joining your various data sets or if your query requires some additional tweaking.

The EXPLAIN statement's type column[2] shows the access type MySQL is using for the query. In order of most efficient access to least efficient, the following are the values that may appear in the type column of your EXPLAIN results:

- system

- const

- eq_ref

- ref

- ref_or_null

- index_merge (new in MySQL 5.0.0)

- unique_subquery

- index_subquery

- range

- index

- ALL

The system value refers to a special type of access strategy that MySQL can deploy when the SELECT statement is requesting data from a MySQL system (in-memory) table and the table has only one row of data. In the following sections, we'll look at the meaning of each of the other values.

---

2. The MySQL online documentation refers to the type column as the *join type*. This is a bit of a misnomer, as this column actually refers to the access type, since no actual joins may be present in the SELECT statement. We encourage you to investigate the internals.texi developer's documentation, where this same clarification is made.

The const Access Type

The const access type is shown when the table for which the row in the EXPLAIN result is describing meets one of the following conditions:

- The table has either zero or one row in it.

- The table has a *unique, non-nullable* key for which a WHERE condition containing a *single* value for each column in the key is present.

If the table and any expression on it meet either of these conditions, that means that, at most, one value can be retrieved for the columns needed in the SELECT statement from this table. Because of this, MySQL will replace any of the data set's columns used in the SELECT statement with the single row's data before any query execution is begun. This is a form of constant propagation, a technique that the optimizer uses when it can substitute a constant value for variables or join conditions in the query.

Listing 7-24 shows an EXPLAIN with the const access type. You can see that because the join's ON condition provides a single value for the Customer primary key, MySQL is able to use a const access type.

Note In the examples here, we use the \G switch from the mysql client utility in order to output wide display results in rows, rather than in columns.

Listing 7-24. *Example of the const Access Type*

```
mysql> EXPLAIN
    -> SELECT * FROM Customer
    -> WHERE customer_id = 1 \G
*************************** 1. row ***************************
           id: 1
  select_type: SIMPLE
        table: Customer
         type: const
possible_keys: PRIMARY
          key: PRIMARY
      key_len: 4
          ref: const
         rows: 1
        Extra:
1 row in set (0.01 sec)
```

As mentioned, MySQL performs a lookup for constant conditions on a unique key before the query execution begins. In this way, if it finds that no rows match the WHERE expression, it will stop the processing of the query, and in the Extra column, EXPLAIN will output Impossible ➥ WHERE noticed after reading const tables.

The eq_ref Access Type

When the eq_ref access type appears, it means that a *single* row is read from this table for each combination of rows returned from previous data set retrieval. When all parts of a key are used by a join and the key is *unique and non-nullable*, then an eq_ref access can be performed. Interestingly, the join condition value can be an expression that uses columns from tables that are read before this table or a constant.

For example, Listing 7-25 shows a SELECT statement used to retrieve the orders details for any orders having the product with an ID of 2. The result returned from the access of table co (using the index access type discussed shortly) is matched using the eq_ref access type to the PRIMARY key columns in CustomerOrderItem (coi). Even though CustomerOrderItem's primary key has two parts, the eq_ref is possible because the second part of the key (product_id) is eliminated through the WHERE expression containing a constant. We've highlighted the ref column of the EXPLAIN output to show this more clearly.

Listing 7-25. *Example of the eq_ref Access Type*

```
mysql> EXPLAIN
    -> SELECT coi.*
    -> FROM CustomerOrder co
    ->  INNER JOIN CustomerOrderItem coi
    ->   ON co.order_id = coi.order_id
    -> WHERE coi.product_id = 2 \G
*************************** 1. row ***************************
           id: 1
  select_type: SIMPLE
        table: co
         type: index
possible_keys: PRIMARY
          key: PRIMARY
      key_len: 4
          ref: NULL
         rows: 6
        Extra: Using index
*************************** 2. row ***************************
           id: 1
  select_type: SIMPLE
        table: coi
         type: eq_ref
possible_keys: PRIMARY
          key: PRIMARY
      key_len: 8
          ref: ToyStore.co.order_id,const
         rows: 1
        Extra:
2 rows in set (0.01 sec)
```

The ref Access Type

The ref access type is identical to the eq_ref access type, except that one or more rows that match rows returned from previous table retrieval will be read from the current table. This access type is performed when either of the following occurs:

- The join condition uses only the leftmost part of a multicolumn key.

- The key is not unique but does *not* contain NULLs.

To continue our eq_ref example from Listing 7-25, Listing 7-26 shows the effect of removing the constant part of our WHERE expression, leaving MySQL to use only the leftmost part of the CustomerOrderItem table's primary key (order_id).

Listing 7-26. *Example of the ref Access Type*

```
mysql> EXPLAIN
    -> SELECT coi.*
    -> FROM CustomerOrder co
    ->  INNER JOIN CustomerOrderItem coi
    ->   ON co.order_id = coi.order_id \G
*************************** 1. row ***************************
           id: 1
  select_type: SIMPLE
        table: co
         type: index
possible_keys: PRIMARY
          key: PRIMARY
      key_len: 4
          ref: NULL
         rows: 6
        Extra: Using index
*************************** 2. row ***************************
           id: 1
  select_type: SIMPLE
        table: coi
         type: ref
possible_keys: PRIMARY
          key: PRIMARY
      key_len: 4
          ref: ToyStore.co.order_id
         rows: 1
        Extra:
2 rows in set (0.01 sec)
```

The ref_or_null Access Type

The ref_or_null access type is used in an identical fashion to the ref access type, but when the key can contain NULL values and a WHERE expression indicates an OR key_column IS NULL condition. Listing 7-27 shows an example of the ref_or_null access strategy used when doing a WHERE on Category.parent_id, which can contain NULLs for root categories. Here, we've used a USE INDEX hint to force MySQL to use the ref_or_null access pattern. If we did not do this, MySQL would choose to perform the access strategy differently, because there are other, more efficient ways of processing this SELECT statement. You'll learn more about USE INDEX and other hints in the "Join Hints" section later in this chapter.

Listing 7-27. *Example of the ref_or_null Access Type*

```
mysql> EXPLAIN
    -> SELECT *
    -> FROM Product p
    ->   INNER JOIN Product2Category p2c
    ->     ON p.product_id = p2c.category_id
    ->   INNER JOIN Category c USE INDEX (parent_id)
    ->     ON p2c.category_id = c.category_id
    -> WHERE c.parent_id = 2
    -> OR c.parent_id IS NULL \G
*************************** 1. row ***************************
           id: 1
  select_type: SIMPLE
        table: c
         type: ref_or_null
possible_keys: parent_id
          key: parent_id
      key_len: 5
          ref: const
         rows: 2
        Extra: Using where
*************************** 2. row ***************************
           id: 1
  select_type: SIMPLE
        table: p
         type: eq_ref
possible_keys: PRIMARY
          key: PRIMARY
      key_len: 4
          ref: ToyStore.c.category_id
         rows: 2
        Extra:
*************************** 3. row ***************************
           id: 1
  select_type: SIMPLE
        table: p2c
         type: index
```

```
possible_keys: NULL
          key: PRIMARY
      key_len: 8
          ref: NULL
         rows: 10
        Extra: Using where; Using index
3 rows in set (0.28 sec)
```

The index_merge Access Type

Up until MySQL 5.0.0, the following rule always applied to your queries: For each table referenced in your SELECT statement, only one index could be used to retrieve the selected table columns.

With the release of version MySQL 5.0.0, a new type of access strategy is enabled, called an *Index Merge*. In some cases, this type can enable data retrieval using more than one index for a single referenced table in your queries. In an Index Merge access, multiple executions of ref, ref_or_null, or range accesses are used to retrieve key values matching various WHERE conditions, and the results of these various retrievals are combined together to form a single data set.

You'll learn about the Index Merge ability in the next chapter, when we discuss dealing with OR conditions.

The unique_subquery Access Type

A *subquery* is simply a child query that returns a set of values using an IN clause in the WHERE condition. When MySQL knows the subquery will return a list of unique values, because a unique, non-nullable index is used in the subquery's SELECT statement, then the unique_subquery access type may appear in the EXPLAIN result. Listing 7-28 shows an example of this.

Listing 7-28. *Example of the unique_subquery Access Type*

```
mysql> EXPLAIN
    -> SELECT * FROM CustomerOrder co
    -> WHERE co.status IN (
    ->    SELECT order_status_id
    ->    FROM OrderStatus os
    ->    WHERE os.description LIKE 'C%'
    -> ) \G
*************************** 1. row ***************************
           id: 1
  select_type: PRIMARY
        table: co
         type: ALL
possible_keys: NULL
          key: NULL
      key_len: NULL
          ref: NULL
         rows: 6
        Extra: Using where
```

```
*************************** 2. row ***************************
           id: 2
  select_type: DEPENDENT SUBQUERY
        table: os
         type: unique_subquery
possible_keys: PRIMARY
          key: PRIMARY
      key_len: 2
          ref: func
         rows: 1
        Extra: Using index; Using where
2 rows in set (0.02 sec)
```

During a `unique_subquery` access, MySQL is actually executing the subquery first, so that the values returned from the subquery can replace the subquery in the IN clause of the parent query. In this way, a subquery access is more like an optimization process than a true data retrieval. To be sure, data (or rather, key) values are being returned from the subquery; however, these values are immediately transformed into a set of constant values in the IN clause.

You may have noticed that the example in Listing 7-28 can be rewritten in a more set-based manner by using a simple inner join. We'll discuss this point later in the chapter, in the "Subqueries and Derived Tables" section.

The index_subquery Access Type

The `index_subquery` access type is identical to the `unique_subquery` access type, only in this case, MySQL has determined that the values returned by the subquery will not be unique. Listing 7-29 indicates this behavior.

Listing 7-29. *Example of the index_subquery Access Type*

```
mysql> EXPLAIN
    -> SELECT * FROM CustomerOrderItem coi
    -> WHERE coi.product_id IN (
    ->   SELECT product_id
    ->   FROM Product2Category p2c
    ->   WHERE p2c.category_id BETWEEN 1 AND 5
    -> ) \G
*************************** 1. row ***************************
           id: 1
  select_type: PRIMARY
        table: coi
         type: ALL
possible_keys: NULL
          key: NULL
      key_len: NULL
          ref: NULL
         rows: 10
        Extra: Using where
```

```
*************************** 2. row ***************************
           id: 2
  select_type: DEPENDENT SUBQUERY
        table: p2c
         type: index_subquery
possible_keys: PRIMARY
          key: PRIMARY
      key_len: 4
          ref: func
         rows: 1
        Extra: Using index; Using where
2 rows in set (0.00 sec)
```

This query returns all order details for any products that are assigned to categories 1 through 5. MySQL knows, because of the two-column primary key on product_id and category_id, that more than one category_id can be found in the subquery's WHERE expression (BETWEEN 1 AND 5). Again, this particular query is performed before the primary query's execution, and its results are dumped as constants into the IN clause of the primary query's WHERE condition.

Not all subqueries will be reduced to a list of values before a primary query is executed. These subqueries, known as *correlated subqueries*, depend on the values in the primary table, and are thus executed for each value returned in the primary data set. We'll look at this difference in the "Correlated Subqueries" section later in this chapter.

The range Access Type

The range access type will be used when your SELECT statements involve WHERE clauses (or ON conditions) that use any of the following operators: >, >=, <, <=, IN, LIKE, or BETWEEN.

For the LIKE operator, a range operation can be used only if the first character of the comparison expression is not a wildcard; therefore, WHERE column1 LIKE 'cat%' will use the range access type, but WHERE column1 LIKE '%cat' will not.

Listings 7-30 and 7-31 show two examples of the range access type being deployed against our sample schema. We've shown a couple different operators that cause MySQL to apply the range access strategy.

Listing 7-30. *Example of the range Access Type with the BETWEEN Operator*

```
mysql> EXPLAIN
    -> SELECT *
    -> FROM Product p
    -> WHERE product_id BETWEEN 1 AND 3 \G
*************************** 1. row ***************************
           id: 1
  select_type: SIMPLE
        table: p
         type: range
possible_keys: PRIMARY
          key: PRIMARY
      key_len: 4
```

```
        ref: NULL
       rows: 3
      Extra: Using where
1 row in set (0.00 sec)
```

Listing 7-31. *Example of the range Access Type with the IN Operator*

```
mysql> EXPLAIN
    -> SELECT *
    -> FROM Customer c
    -> WHERE customer_id IN (2,3) \G
*************************** 1. row ***************************
           id: 1
  select_type: SIMPLE
        table: c
         type: range
possible_keys: PRIMARY
          key: PRIMARY
      key_len: 4
          ref: NULL
         rows: 2
        Extra: Using where
1 row in set (0.00 sec)
```

Remember that the range access type, and indeed all access types above the ALL access type, require that an index be available containing the key columns used in WHERE or ON conditions. To demonstrate this, Listing 7-32 shows a SELECT on our CustomerOrder table based on a range of order dates. It just so happens that CustomerOrder does not have an index on the ordered_on column, so MySQL can use only the ALL access type, since no WHERE or ON condition exists containing columns found in the table's indexes (its primary key on order_id and an index on the foreign key of customer_id).

Listing 7-32. *No Usable Index, Even with a range Type Query*

```
mysql> EXPLAIN
    -> SELECT *
    -> FROM CustomerOrder co
    -> WHERE ordered_on >= '2005-01-01' \G
*************************** 1. row ***************************
           id: 1
  select_type: SIMPLE
        table: co
         type: ALL
possible_keys: NULL
          key: NULL
      key_len: NULL
          ref: NULL
         rows: 6
```

```
        Extra: Using where
1 row in set (0.00 sec)
```

As you can see, no possible keys (indexes) were available for the range access strategy to be applied. Let's see what happens if we add an index on the ordered_on column, as shown in Listing 7-33.

Listing 7-33. *Adding an Index on CustomerOrder*

```
mysql> ALTER TABLE CustomerOrder ADD INDEX (ordered_on);
Query OK, 6 rows affected (0.35 sec)
Records: 6  Duplicates: 0  Warnings: 0

mysql> EXPLAIN
    -> SELECT *
    -> FROM CustomerOrder co
    -> WHERE ordered_on >= '2005-01-01' \G
*************************** 1. row ***************************
           id: 1
  select_type: SIMPLE
        table: co
         type: ALL
possible_keys: ordered_on
          key: NULL
      key_len: NULL
          ref: NULL
         rows: 6
        Extra: Using where
1 row in set (0.00 sec)
```

Well, it seems MySQL didn't choose the range access strategy even when the index was added on ordered_on. Why did this happen? The answer has to do with some of the concepts you learned in Chapter 2 regarding how MySQL accesses data.

When MySQL does an evaluation of how to perform a SELECT query, it weighs each of the strategies for accessing the various tables contained in your request using an optimization formula. Each access strategy is assigned a sort of sliding performance scale that is compared to a number of statistics. The following are two of the most important statistics:

- The selectivity of an index. This number tells MySQL the relative *distribution* of values within the index tree, and helps it determine how many keys in an index will likely match the WHERE or ON condition in your query. This predicted number of matching key values is output in the rows column of the EXPLAIN output.

- The relative speed of doing sequential reads for data on disk versus reading an index's keys and accessing table data using random seeks from the index row pointers to the actual data location. If MySQL determines that a WHERE or ON condition will retrieve a large number of keys, it may decide that it will be faster to simply read through the data on disk sequentially (perform a scan) than do lookup seeks for each matching key found in the sorted index.

MySQL uses a threshold value to determine whether repeated seek operations will be faster than a sequential read. The threshold value depends on the two statistics listed here, as well as other storage engine-specific values.

In the case of Listing 7-33, MySQL determined that six matches would be found in the index on ordered_on. Since the number of rows in CustomerOrder is small, MySQL determined it would be faster to simply do a sequential scan of the table data (the ALL access type) than to perform lookups from the matched keys in the index on ordered_on. Let's see what happens if we limit the WHERE expression to a smaller range of possible values, as in Listing 7-34.

Listing 7-34. *A Smaller Possible Range of Values*

```
mysql> EXPLAIN
    -> SELECT *
    -> FROM CustomerOrder co
    -> WHERE ordered_on >= '2005-04-01' \G
*************************** 1. row ***************************
           id: 1
  select_type: SIMPLE
        table: co
         type: range
possible_keys: ordered_on
          key: ordered_on
      key_len: 3
          ref: NULL
         rows: 1
        Extra: Using where
1 row in set (0.01 sec)
```

As you can tell from Listing 7-34, this time, MySQL chose to use the range access strategy, performing lookups from the ordered_on index for matched key values on the WHERE expression. Keep this behavior in mind when analyzing the effectiveness of your indexes and your SQL statements. If you notice that a particular index is not being used effectively, it may be a case of the index having too little diversity of key values (poor key distribution), or it may be that the WHERE condition is simply too broad for the index to be effective.

Tip When running benchmarking and profiling tests on your database, ensure that your test data set is representative of your real database. If you are testing queries that run against a production database, but are using only a subset of the production data, MySQL may choose different access strategies for your test data than your production data.

The index Access Type

Indexes are supposed to improve the retrieval speed for data access, right? So why would the index access strategy be so low on MySQL's list of possible access strategies? The index access type is a bit confusing. It should be more appropriately named "index_scan." This access type refers to the strategy deployed by MySQL when it does a sequential scan of all the key entries in an index.

This access type is usually seen only when both of the following two conditions exist:

- No WHERE clause is specified *or* the table in question does not have an index that would speed up data retrieval (see the preceding discussion of the range access type).

- All *columns* used in the SELECT statement for this table are available in the index. This is called a *covering index*.

To see an example, let's go back to Listing 7-33, where we continued to see MySQL use an ALL access type, even though an index was available on columns in the WHERE condition. The ALL access type indicates that a sequential scan of the table data is occurring. The reason the table data is being sequentially scanned is because of the SELECT *, which means that all table columns in CustomerOrder are used in the SELECT statement. Watch what happens if we change the statement to read SELECT ordered_on, so that the only column used in the SELECT statement is available in the index on ordered_on, and we remove the WHERE clause to force a scan, as shown in Listing 7-35.

Listing 7-35. *Example of the index Access Type*

```
mysql> EXPLAIN
    -> SELECT ordered_on
    -> FROM CustomerOrder co \G
*************************** 1. row ***************************
           id: 1
  select_type: SIMPLE
        table: co
         type: index
possible_keys: NULL
          key: ordered_on
      key_len: 3
          ref: NULL
         rows: 6
        Extra: Using index
1 row in set (0.00 sec)
```

Notice that in the Extra column of the EXPLAIN output, you see Using index. This is MySQL informing you that it was able to use the index data pages to retrieve all the information it needed for this table. You will always see Using index when the index access type is shown; this is because the index access type is used only when a covering index is available. Generally, having Using index in the Extra column is a very good thing. It means that MySQL was able to use the smaller index pages to retrieve all the data.

Seeing the index access type, however, is not often a good thing. It means that all values of the index are being read. The only thing that makes the index access type better than the ALL table scan access type is the fact that index data pages contain more records, and thus the scan usually happens faster than a scan through the actual table data pages.

The ALL Access Type

The ALL access type, as mentioned in the previous section, refers to a sequential scan of the table's data. This access type is used if either of the following conditions exists:

- No WHERE or ON condition is specified for any columns in any of the table's keys.

- Index key distribution is poor, making a sequential scan more efficient than numerous index lookups.

You've already seen a number of examples that contained the ALL access type, and by now, you will have realized that most of our attention has been focused on avoiding this type of access strategy. You can avoid using the ALL access strategy by paying attention to the EXPLAIN output of your SQL statements and ensuring that indexes exist on columns that many WHERE and ON conditions will reference.

Join Hints

For most of the queries you write, MySQL's join optimization system will pick the most efficient access path and join order for the various tables involved in your SELECT statements. For those other cases, MySQL enables you to influence the join optimization process through the use of join hints. Join hints can be helpful in a number of situations. Here, we'll discuss the following MySQL hints:

- STRAIGHT_JOIN

- USE INDEX

- FORCE INDEX

- IGNORE INDEX

▨Caution If MySQL isn't choosing an efficient access strategy, usually there is a very good reason for it. Before deciding to use a join hint, you should investigate the causes of an inefficient join strategy. Additionally, always take note of queries in which you place join hints of any type. You will often find that when a database's size and index distribution change, your join hints will be forcing MySQL to use a less-than-optimal access strategy. So, do yourself a favor, and regularly check that join hints are performing up to expectations.

The STRAIGHT_JOIN Hint

Occasionally, you will notice that MySQL chooses to access the tables in a multitable join statement in an order that you feel is inefficient or unnatural. You can ask MySQL to access tables in the order you tell it to by using the STRAIGHT_JOIN hint. Using this hint, MySQL will access tables in order from left to right in the SELECT statement, meaning the first table in the FROM clause will be accessed first, then its values joined to the first joined table, and so on.

Listing 7-36 shows an example of using the STRAIGHT_JOIN hint. In the first SQL statement, the EXPLAIN output shows that MySQL chose to access the three tables used in the SELECT statement in an order different from the order coded; in fact, the order is backwards from the order given in the SELECT statement.

Listing 7-36. *A Join Order Different from the Written SELECT*

```
mysql> EXPLAIN
    -> SELECT *
    -> FROM Category c
    ->  INNER JOIN Product2Category p2c
    ->   ON c.category_id = p2c.category_id
    ->  INNER JOIN Product p
    ->   ON p2c.product_id = p.product_id
    -> WHERE c.name LIKE 'Video%' \G
*************************** 1. row ***************************
           id: 1
  select_type: SIMPLE
        table: p
         type: ALL
possible_keys: PRIMARY
          key: NULL
      key_len: NULL
          ref: NULL
         rows: 10
        Extra:
*************************** 2. row ***************************
           id: 1
  select_type: SIMPLE
        table: p2c
         type: ref
possible_keys: PRIMARY
          key: PRIMARY
      key_len: 4
          ref: ToyStore.p.product_id
         rows: 2
        Extra: Using index
*************************** 3. row ***************************
           id: 1
  select_type: SIMPLE
        table: c
         type: eq_ref
possible_keys: PRIMARY
          key: PRIMARY
      key_len: 4
          ref: ToyStore.p2c.category_id
         rows: 1
        Extra: Using where
3 rows in set (0.00 sec)
```

If you felt that a more efficient join order would be to use the order given in the SELECT statement, you would use the STRAIGHT_JOIN hint, as shown in Listing 7-37.

Listing 7-37. *Example of the STRAIGHT_JOIN Hint*

```
mysql> EXPLAIN
    -> SELECT *
    -> FROM Category c
    ->  STRAIGHT_JOIN Product2Category p2c
    ->  STRAIGHT_JOIN Product p
    -> WHERE c.name LIKE 'Video%'
    -> AND c.category_id = p2c.category_id
    -> AND p2c.product_id = p.product_id \G
*************************** 1. row ***************************
           id: 1
  select_type: SIMPLE
        table: c
         type: ALL
possible_keys: PRIMARY
          key: NULL
      key_len: NULL
          ref: NULL
         rows: 14
        Extra: Using where
*************************** 2. row ***************************
           id: 1
  select_type: SIMPLE
        table: p2c
         type: index
possible_keys: PRIMARY
          key: PRIMARY
      key_len: 8
          ref: NULL
         rows: 8
        Extra: Using where; Using index
*************************** 3. row ***************************
           id: 1
  select_type: SIMPLE
        table: p
         type: eq_ref
possible_keys: PRIMARY
          key: PRIMARY
      key_len: 4
          ref: ToyStore.p2c.product_id
         rows: 1
        Extra:
3 rows in set (0.00 sec)
```

As you can see, MySQL dutifully follows your desired join order. The access pattern it comes up with, in this case, is suboptimal compared with the original, MySQL-chosen access path. Where in the original EXPLAIN from Listing 7-36, you see MySQL using ref and eq_ref access types for the joins to Product2Category and Category, in the STRAIGHT_JOIN EXPLAIN (Listing 7-37), you see MySQL has reverted to using an index scan on Product2Category and an eq_ref to access Product.

In this case, the STRAIGHT_JOIN made things worse. In most cases, MySQL will indeed choose the most optimal pattern for accessing tables in your SELECT statements. However, if you encounter a situation in which you suspect a different order would produce speedier results, you can use this technique to test your theories.

Caution If you do find a situation in which you suspect changing the join order would speed up a query, make sure that MySQL is using up-to-date statistics on your table before making any changes. After you run a baseline EXPLAIN to see MySQL's chosen access strategy for your query, run an ANALYZE TABLE against the table, and then check your EXPLAIN again to see if MySQL changed the join order or access strategy. ANALYZE TABLE will update the statistics on key distribution that MySQL uses to decide an access strategy. Remember that running ANALYZE TABLE will place a read lock on your table, so carefully choose when you run this statement on large tables.

The USE INDEX and FORCE INDEX Hints

You've noticed a particularly slow query, and run an EXPLAIN on it. In the EXPLAIN result, you see that for a particular table, MySQL has a choice of more than one index that contain columns on which your WHERE or ON condition depends. It happens that MySQL has chosen to use an index that you suspect is less efficient than another index on the same table. You can use one of two join hints to prod MySQL into action:

- The USE INDEX (*index_list*) hint tells MySQL to consider only the indexes contained in index_list during its evaluation of the table's access strategy. However, if MySQL determines that a sequential scan of the index or table data (index or ALL access types) will be faster using any of the indexes using a seek operation (eq_ref, ref, ref_or_null, and range access types), it will perform a table scan.

- The FORCE INDEX (*index_list*), on the other hand, tells MySQL not to perform a table scan,[3] and to always use one of the indexes in *index_list*. The FORCE_INDEX hint is available only in MySQL versions later than 4.0.9.

The IGNORE INDEX Hint

If you simply want to tell MySQL to *not* use one or more indexes in its evaluation of the access strategy, you can use the IGNORE INDEX (*index_list*) hint. MySQL will perform the optimization of joins as normal, but it will not include in the evaluation any indexes listed in *index_list*. Listing 7-38 shows the results of placing an IGNORE INDEX hint in a SELECT statement.

---

3. Technically, FORCE INDEX makes MySQL assign a table scan a very high optimization weight, making the use of a table scan very unlikely.

Listing 7-38. *Example of How the IGNORE INDEX Hint Forces a Different Access Strategy*

```
mysql> EXPLAIN
    -> SELECT p.name, p.unit_price, coi.price
    -> FROM CustomerOrderItem coi
    ->  INNER JOIN Product p
    ->   ON coi.product_id = p.product_id
    ->  INNER JOIN CustomerOrder co
    ->   ON coi.order_id = co.order_id
    -> WHERE co.ordered_on = '2004-12-07' \G
*************************** 1. row ***************************
           id: 1
  select_type: SIMPLE
        table: co
         type: ref
possible_keys: PRIMARY,ordered_on
          key: ordered_on
      key_len: 3
          ref: const
         rows: 1
        Extra: Using where; Using index
*************************** 2. row ***************************
           id: 1
  select_type: SIMPLE
        table: coi
         type: ref
possible_keys: PRIMARY
          key: PRIMARY
      key_len: 4
          ref: ToyStore.co.order_id
         rows: 1
        Extra:
*************************** 3. row ***************************
           id: 1
  select_type: SIMPLE
        table: p
         type: eq_ref
possible_keys: PRIMARY
          key: PRIMARY
      key_len: 4
          ref: ToyStore.coi.product_id
         rows: 1
        Extra:
3 rows in set (0.01 sec)

mysql> EXPLAIN
    -> SELECT p.name, p.unit_price, coi.price
    -> FROM CustomerOrderItem coi
```

```
    ->  INNER JOIN Product p
    ->   ON coi.product_id = p.product_id
    ->  INNER JOIN CustomerOrder co IGNORE INDEX (ordered_on)
    ->   ON coi.order_id = co.order_id
    -> WHERE co.ordered_on = '2004-12-07' \G
*************************** 1. row ***************************
            id: 1
   select_type: SIMPLE
         table: co
          type: ALL
 possible_keys: PRIMARY
           key: NULL
       key_len: NULL
           ref: NULL
          rows: 6
         Extra: Using where
*************************** 2. row ***************************
            id: 1
   select_type: SIMPLE
         table: coi
          type: ref
 possible_keys: PRIMARY
           key: PRIMARY
       key_len: 4
           ref: ToyStore.co.order_id
          rows: 1
         Extra:
*************************** 3. row ***************************
            id: 1
   select_type: SIMPLE
         table: p
          type: eq_ref
 possible_keys: PRIMARY
           key: PRIMARY
       key_len: 4
           ref: ToyStore.coi.product_id
          rows: 1
         Extra:
3 rows in set (0.03 sec)
```

As in the previous example, you see that the resulting query plan was less optimal than without the join hint. Without the IGNORE_INDEX hint, MySQL had a choice between using the PRIMARY key or the index on ordered_on. Of these, it chose to use the ref access strategy—a lookup based on a non-unique index—and used the constant in the WHERE expression to fulfill the reference condition.

In contrast, when the `IGNORE_INDEX` (ordered_on) hint is used, MySQL sees that it has the choice to use the `PRIMARY` key index (needed for the inner join from `CustomerOrderItem` to `CustomerOrder`). However, it decided that a table scan of the data, using a `WHERE` condition to filter out orders placed on December 7, 2004, would be more efficient in this case.

Subqueries and Derived Tables

Now we're going to dive into a newer development in the MySQL arena: the subquery and derived table abilities available in MySQL version 4.1 and later.

Subqueries are, simply stated, a `SELECT` statement within another statement. Subqueries are sometimes called sub-SELECTs, for obvious reasons. *Derived tables* are a specialized version of a subquery used in the `FROM` clause of your `SELECT` statements.

As you'll see, some subqueries can be rewritten as an outer join, but not all of them can be. In fact, there are certain SQL activities in MySQL that are impossible to achieve in a single SQL statement without the use of subqueries.

In versions prior to MySQL 4.1, programmers needed to use multiple `SELECT` statements, possibly storing results in a temporary table or program variable and using that result in their code with another SQL statement.

Subqueries

As we said, a subquery is simply a `SELECT` statement embedded inside another SQL statement. As such, like any other `SELECT` statement, a subquery can return any of the following results:

- A single value, called a *scalar* result

- A single-row result—one row, multiple columns of data

- A single-column result—one column of data, many rows

- A tabular result—many columns of data for many rows

The result returned by the subquery dictates the context in which the subquery may be used. Furthermore, the syntax used to represent the subquery varies depending on the returned result. We'll show numerous examples for each different type of query in the following sections.

Scalar Subqueries

When a subquery returns only a single value, it may be used just like any other constant value in your SQL statements. To demonstrate, take a look at the example shown in Listing 7-39.

Listing 7-39. *Example of a Simple Scalar Subquery*

```
mysql> SELECT *
    -> FROM Product p
    -> WHERE p.unit_price = (SELECT MAX(unit_price) FROM Product) \G
*************************** 1. row ***************************
```

```
       product_id: 6
              sku: SPT003
             name: Tennis Racket
      description: Fiberglass Tennis Racket
           weight: 2.15
       unit_price: 104.75
1 row in set (0.34 sec)
```

Here, we've used this scalar subquery:

```
(SELECT MAX(unit_price) FROM Product)
```

This can return only a single value: the maximum unit price for any product in our catalog.

Let's take a look at the EXPLAIN output, shown in Listing 7-40, to see what MySQL has done.

Listing 7-40. *EXPLAIN for the Scalar Subquery in Listing 7-39*

```
mysql> EXPLAIN
    -> SELECT *
    -> FROM Product p
    -> WHERE p.unit_price = (SELECT MAX(unit_price) FROM Product) \G
*************************** 1. row ***************************
           id: 1
  select_type: PRIMARY
        table: p
         type: ALL
possible_keys: NULL
          key: NULL
      key_len: NULL
          ref: NULL
         rows: 10
        Extra: Using where
*************************** 2. row ***************************
           id: 2
  select_type: SUBQUERY
        table: Product
         type: ALL
possible_keys: NULL
          key: NULL
      key_len: NULL
          ref: NULL
         rows: 10
        Extra:
2 rows in set (0.00 sec)
```

You see no real surprises here. Since we have no index on the unit_price column, no indexes are deployed. MySQL helpfully notifies us that a subquery was used.

The statement in Listing 7-39 may also be written using a simple LIMIT expression with an ORDER BY, as shown in Listing 7-41. We've included the EXPLAIN output for you to compare the two query execution plans used.

Listing 7-41. *Alternate Way of Expressing Listing 7-39*

```
mysql> SELECT *
    -> FROM Product p
    -> ORDER BY unit_price DESC
    -> LIMIT 1 \G
*************************** 1. row ***************************
 product_id: 6
        sku: SPT003
       name: Tennis Racket
description: Fiberglass Tennis Racket
     weight: 2.15
 unit_price: 104.75
1 row in set (0.00 sec)

mysql> EXPLAIN
    -> SELECT *
    -> FROM Product p
    -> ORDER BY unit_price DESC
    -> LIMIT 1 \G
*************************** 1. row ***************************
           id: 1
  select_type: SIMPLE
        table: p
         type: ALL
possible_keys: NULL
          key: NULL
      key_len: NULL
          ref: NULL
         rows: 10
        Extra: Using filesort
1 row in set (0.00 sec)
```

You may be wondering why even bother with the subquery if the LIMIT statement is more efficient. There are a number of reasons to consider using a subquery in this situation. First, the LIMIT clause is MySQL-specific, so it is not portable. If this is a concern for you, the subquery is the better choice. Additionally, many developers feel the subquery is a more natural, structured, and readable way to express the statement.

The subquery in Listing 7-39 is only a simple query. For more complex queries, involving two or more tables, a subquery would be required, as Listing 7-42 demonstrates.

Listing 7-42. *Example of a More Complex Scalar Subquery*

```
mysql> SELECT p.product_id, p.name, p.weight, p.unit_price
    -> FROM Product p
    -> WHERE p.weight = (
    ->   SELECT MIN(weight)
    ->   FROM CustomerOrderItem
    -> );
+------------+-------------------------+--------+------------+
| product_id | name                    | weight | unit_price |
+------------+-------------------------+--------+------------+
|          8 | Video Game - Car Racing | 0.25   | 48.99      |
|          9 | Video Game - Soccer     | 0.25   | 44.99      |
|         10 | Video Game - Football   | 0.25   | 46.99      |
+------------+-------------------------+--------+------------+
3 rows in set (0.00 sec)
```

Here, because the scalar subquery retrieves data from `CustomerOrderItem`, not `Product`, there is no way to rewrite the query using either a `LIMIT` or a join expression.

Let's take a look at a third example of a scalar subquery, shown in Listing 7-43.

Listing 7-43. *Another Example of a Scalar Subquery*

```
mysql> SELECT
    ->   p.name
    -> , p.unit_price
    -> , (
    ->     SELECT AVG(price)
    ->     FROM CustomerOrderItem
    ->     WHERE product_id = p.product_id
    ->   ) as "avg_sold_price"
    -> FROM Product p;
+--------------------------+------------+----------------+
| name                     | unit_price | avg_sold_price |
+--------------------------+------------+----------------+
| Action Figure - Tennis   | 12.95      | 12.950000      |
| Action Figure - Football | 11.95      | 11.950000      |
| Action Figure - Gladiator| 15.95      | 15.950000      |
| Soccer Ball              | 23.70      | 23.700000      |
| Tennis Balls             | 4.75       | 4.750000       |
| Tennis Racket            | 104.75     | 104.750000     |
| Doll                     | 59.99      | 59.990000      |
| Video Game - Car Racing  | 48.99      | NULL           |
| Video Game - Soccer      | 44.99      | NULL           |
| Video Game - Football    | 46.99      | 46.990000      |
+--------------------------+------------+----------------+
10 rows in set (0.00 sec)
```

The statement in Listing 7-43 uses a scalar subquery in the SELECT clause of the outer statement to return the average selling price of the product, stored in the CustomerOrderItem table. In the subquery, note that the WHERE expression essentially *joins* the CustomerOrderItem. product_id with the product_id of the Product table in the outer SELECT statement. For each product in the outer Product table, MySQL is averaging the price column for the product in the CustomerOrderItem table and returning that scalar value into the column aliased as "avg_sold_price".

Take special note of the NULL values returned for the "Video Game – Car Racing" and "Video Game – Soccer" products. What does this behavior remind you of? An outer join exhibits the same behavior. Indeed, we can rewrite the SQL in Listing 7-43 as an outer join with a GROUP BY expression, as shown in Listing 7-44.

Listing 7-44. *Listing 7-43 Rewritten As an Outer Join*

```
mysql> SELECT
    -> p.name
    -> , p.unit_price
    -> , AVG(coi.price) AS "avg_sold_price"
    -> FROM Product p
    -> LEFT JOIN CustomerOrderItem coi
    ->   ON p.product_id = coi.product_id
    -> GROUP BY p.name, p.unit_price;
```

name	unit_price	avg_sold_price
Action Figure - Football	11.95	11.950000
Action Figure - Gladiator	15.95	15.950000
Action Figure - Tennis	12.95	12.950000
Doll	59.99	59.990000
Soccer Ball	23.70	23.700000
Tennis Balls	4.75	4.750000
Tennis Racket	104.75	104.750000
Video Game - Car Racing	48.99	NULL
Video Game - Football	46.99	46.990000
Video Game - Soccer	44.99	NULL

10 rows in set (0.11 sec)

However, what if we wanted to fulfill this request: "Return a list of each product name, its unit price, and the average unit price of all products tied to the product's related categories."

As an exercise, see if you can write a single query that fulfills this request. Give up? You cannot use a single SQL statement, because in order to retrieve the average unit price of products within related categories, you must average across a set of the Product table. Since you must also GROUP BY all the rows in the Product table, you cannot provide this information in a single SELECT statement with a join. Without subqueries, you would be forced to make two separate SELECT statements: one for all the product IDs, product names, and unit prices, and another for the average unit prices for each product ID in Product2Category that fell in a related category. Then you would need to manually merge the two results programmatically.

You could do this in your application code, or you might use a temporary table to store the average unit price for all categories, and then perform an outer join of your Product resultset along with your temporary table.

With a scalar subquery, however, you can accomplish the same result with a single SELECT statement and subquery. Listing 7-45 shows how you would do this.

Listing 7-45. *Complex Scalar Subquery Showing Average Category Unit Prices*

```
mysql> SELECT
    -> p.name
    -> , p.unit_price
    -> , (
    ->    SELECT AVG(p2.unit_price)
    ->    FROM Product p2
    ->    INNER JOIN Product2Category p2c2
    ->    ON p2.product_id = p2c2.product_id
    ->    WHERE p2c2.category_id = p2c.category_id
    ->    ) AS avg_cat_price
    -> FROM Product p
    ->   INNER JOIN Product2Category p2c
    ->    ON p.product_id = p2c.product_id
    -> GROUP BY p.name, p.unit_price;
```

name	unit_price	avg_cat_price
Action Figure - Football	11.95	12.450000
Action Figure - Gladiator	15.95	15.950000
Action Figure - Tennis	12.95	12.450000
Doll	59.99	59.990000
Soccer Ball	23.70	23.700000
Tennis Balls	4.75	54.750000
Tennis Racket	104.75	54.750000
Video Game - Car Racing	48.99	48.990000
Video Game - Football	46.99	45.990000
Video Game - Soccer	44.99	45.990000

```
10 rows in set (0.72 sec)
```

Here, we're joining two copies of the Product and Product2Category tables in order to find the average unit prices for each product and the average unit prices for each product in any related category. This is possible through the scalar subquery, which returns a single averaged value.

The key to the SQL is in how the WHERE condition of the subquery is structured. Pay close attention here. We have a condition that states WHERE p2c2.category_id = p2c.category_id. This condition ensures that the average returned by the subquery is across rows in the inner Product table (p2) that have rows in the inner Product2Category (p2c2) table matching any category tied to the row in the outer Product table (p). If this sounds confusing, take some time to scan through the SQL code carefully, noting how the connection between the outer and inner queries is made.

Correlated Subqueries

Let's take a look at the EXPLAIN output from our subquery in Listing 7-43. Listing 7-46 shows the results.

Listing 7-46. *EXPLAIN Output from Listing 7-43*

```
mysql> EXPLAIN
    -> SELECT
    -> p.name
    -> , p.unit_price
    -> , (
    -> SELECT AVG(price)
    -> FROM CustomerOrderItem
    -> WHERE product_id = p.product_id
    -> ) as "avg_sold_price"
    -> FROM Product p \G
*************************** 1. row ***************************
           id: 1
  select_type: PRIMARY
        table: p
         type: ALL
possible_keys: NULL
          key: NULL
      key_len: NULL
          ref: NULL
         rows: 10
        Extra:
*************************** 2. row ***************************
           id: 2
  select_type: DEPENDENT SUBQUERY
        table: CustomerOrderItem
         type: ALL
possible_keys: NULL
          key: NULL
      key_len: NULL
          ref: NULL
         rows: 10
        Extra: Using where
2 rows in set (0.00 sec)
```

Here, instead of SUBQUERY, we see DEPENDENT SUBQUERY appear in the select_type column. The significance of this is that MySQL is informing us that the subquery that retrieves average sold prices is a *correlated subquery*. This means that the subquery (inner query) contains a reference in its WHERE clause to a table in the outer query, and it will be executed for each row in the PRIMARY resultset. In most cases, it would be more efficient to do a retrieval of the aggregated data in a single pass. Fortunately, MySQL can optimize some types of correlated subqueries, and it also offers another subquery option that remedies this performance problem: the derived table. We'll take a closer look at derived tables in a moment.

Correlated subqueries do not necessarily have to occur in the SELECT clause of the outer query, as in Listing 7-43. They may also appear in the WHERE clause of the outer query. If the WHERE clause of the subquery contains a reference to a table in the outer query, it is correlated.

Here's one more example of using a correlated scalar subquery to accomplish what is not possible to do with a simple outer join without a subquery. Imagine the following request: "Retrieve all products having a unit price that is less than the smallest sold price for the same product in any customer's order." Subqueries are required in order to fulfill this request. One possible solution is presented in Listing 7-47.

Listing 7-47. *Example of a Correlated Scalar Subquery*

```
SELECT p.name FROM Product p
WHERE p.unit_price < (
  SELECT MIN(price) FROM CustomerOrderItem
  WHERE product_id = p.product_id
);
```

Columnar Subqueries

We've already seen a couple examples of subqueries that return a single column of data for one or more rows in a table. Often, these types of queries can be more efficiently rewritten as a joined set, but columnar subqueries support a syntax that you may find more appealing than complex outer joins. For example, Listing 7-48 shows an example of a columnar subquery used in a WHERE condition. Listing 7-49 shows the same query converted to an inner join. Both queries show customers who have placed completed orders.

Listing 7-48. *Example of a Columnar Subquery*

```
mysql> SELECT c.first_name, c.last_name
    -> FROM Customer c
    -> WHERE c.customer_id IN (
    ->   SELECT customer_id
    ->   FROM CustomerOrder co
    ->   WHERE co.status = 'CM'
    -> );
+------------+-----------+
| first_name | last_name |
+------------+-----------+
| John       | Doe       |
+------------+-----------+
1 row in set (0.00 sec)
```

Listing 7-49. *Listing 7-48 Rewritten As an Inner Join*

```
mysql> SELECT DISTINCT c.first_name, c.last_name
    -> FROM Customer c
    -> INNER JOIN CustomerOrder co
    ->   ON c.customer_id = co.customer_id
```

```
      -> WHERE co.status = 'CM';
+------------+-----------+
| first_name | last_name |
+------------+-----------+
| John       | Doe       |
+------------+-----------+
1 row in set (0.00 sec)
```

Notice that in the inner join rewrite, we must use the DISTINCT keyword to keep customer names from repeating in the resultset.

ANY and ALL ANSI Expressions

As an alternative to using IN (*subquery*), MySQL allows you to use the ANSI standard = ANY ➥ (*subquery*) syntax, as Listing 7-50 shows. The query is identical in function to Listing 7-48.

Listing 7-50. *Example of Columnar Subquery with = ANY syntax*

```
mysql> SELECT c.first_name, c.last_name
    -> FROM Customer c
    -> WHERE c.customer_id = ANY (
    ->  SELECT customer_id
    ->  FROM CustomerOrder co
    ->  WHERE co.status = 'CM'
    -> );
+------------+-----------+
| first_name | last_name |
+------------+-----------+
| John       | Doe       |
+------------+-----------+
1 row in set (0.00 sec)
```

The ANSI subquery syntax provides for the following expressions for use in columnar result subqueries:

- *operand comparison_operator* ANY (*subquery*): Indicates to MySQL that the expression should return TRUE if any of the values returned by the *subquery* result would return TRUE on being compared to *operand* with *comparison_operator*. The SOME keyword is an alias for ANY.

- *operand comparison_operator* ALL (*subquery*): Indicates to MySQL that the expression should return TRUE if each and every one of the values returned by the *subquery* result would return TRUE on being compared to *operand* with *comparison_operator*.

EXISTS and NOT EXISTS Expressions

A special type of expression available for subqueries simply tests for the existence of a value within the data set of the subquery. Existence tests in MySQL subqueries follow this syntax:

```
WHERE [NOT] EXISTS ( subquery )
```

If the subquery returns one or more rows, the EXISTS test will return TRUE. Likewise, if the query returns no rows, NOT EXISTS will return TRUE. For instance, in Listing 7-51, we show an example of using EXISTS in a correlated subquery to return all customers who have placed orders. Again, the subquery is correlated because the subquery references a table available in the outer query.

Listing 7-51. *Example of Using EXISTS in a Correlated Subquery*

```
mysql> SELECT c.first_name, c.last_name
    -> FROM Customer c
    -> WHERE EXISTS (
    ->   SELECT * FROM CustomerOrder co
    ->   WHERE co.customer_id = c.customer_id
    -> );
+------------+-----------+
| first_name | last_name |
+------------+-----------+
| John       | Doe       |
| Jane       | Smith     |
| Mark       | Brown     |
+------------+-----------+
3 rows in set (0.00 sec)
```

There are some slight differences here between using = ANY and the shorter IN subquery, like the ones shown in Listing 7-50 and 7-48, respectively. ANY will transform the subquery to a list of values, and then compare those values using an operator to a column (or, more than one column, as you'll see in the results of tabular and row subqueries, covered in the next section). However, EXISTS does not return the values from a subquery; it simply tests to see whether any rows were found by the subquery. This is a subtle, but important distinction.

In an EXISTS subquery, MySQL completely ignores what columns are in the subquery's SELECT statement, thus all of the following are identical:

```
WHERE EXISTS (SELECT * FROM Table1)
WHERE EXISTS (SELECT NULL FROM Table1)
WHERE EXISTS (SELECT 1, column2, NULL FROM Table1)
```

The standard convention, however, is to use the SELECT * variation.

The EXISTS and NOT EXISTS expressions can be highly optimized by MySQL, especially when the subquery involves a unique, non-nullable key, because checking for existence in an index's keys is less involved than returning a list of those values and comparing another value against this list based on a comparison operator.

Likewise, the NOT EXISTS expression is another way to represent an outer join condition. Consider the code shown in Listings 7-52 and 7-53. Both return categories that have not been assigned to any products.

Listing 7-52. *Example of a NOT EXISTS Subquery*

```
mysql> SELECT c.name
    -> FROM Category c
```

```
    -> WHERE NOT EXISTS (
    -> SELECT *
    -> FROM Product2Category
    -> WHERE category_id = c.category_id
    -> );
+------------------------+
| name                   |
+------------------------+
| All                    |
| Action Figures         |
| Tennis Action Figures  |
| Football Action Figures|
| Video Games            |
| Shooting Video Games   |
| Sports Gear            |
+------------------------+
7 rows in set (0.00 sec)
```

Listing 7-53. *Listing 7-52 Rewritten Using LEFT JOIN and IS NULL*

```
mysql> SELECT c.name
    -> FROM Category c
    -> LEFT JOIN Product2Category p2c
    -> ON c.category_id = p2c.category_id
    -> WHERE p2c.category_id IS NULL;
+------------------------+
| name                   |
+------------------------+
| All                    |
| Action Figures         |
| Tennis Action Figures  |
| Football Action Figures|
| Video Games            |
| Shooting Video Games   |
| Sports Gear            |
+------------------------+
7 rows in set (0.00 sec)
```

As you can see, both queries return identical results. There is a special optimization that MySQL can do with the NOT EXISTS subquery, however, because NOT EXISTS will return FALSE as soon as the subquery finds a single row matching the condition in the subquery. MySQL, in many circumstances, will use a NOT EXISTS optimization over a LEFT JOIN … WHERE … IS NULL query. In fact, if you look at the EXPLAIN output from Listing 7-53, shown in Listing 7-54, you see that MySQL has done just that.

Listing 7-54. *EXPLAIN from Listing 7-53*

```
mysql> EXPLAIN
    -> SELECT c.name
    -> FROM Category c
    ->  LEFT JOIN Product2Category p2c
    ->   ON c.category_id = p2c.category_id
    -> WHERE p2c.category_id IS NULL \G
*************************** 1. row ***************************
          id: 1
 select_type: SIMPLE
       table: c
        type: ALL
possible_keys: NULL
         key: NULL
     key_len: NULL
         ref: NULL
        rows: 14
       Extra:
*************************** 2. row ***************************
          id: 1
 select_type: SIMPLE
       table: p2c
        type: index
possible_keys: NULL
         key: PRIMARY
     key_len: 8
         ref: NULL
        rows: 10
       Extra: Using where; Using index; Not exists
2 rows in set (0.01 sec)
```

Despite the ability to rewrite many NOT EXISTS subquery expressions using an outer join, there are some situations in which you cannot do an outer join. Most of these situations involve the aggregating of the joined table using a GROUP BY clause. Why? Because only one GROUP BY clause is possible for a single SELECT statement, and it groups only columns that have resulted from any joins in the statement. For instance, you cannot write the following request as a simple outer join without using a subquery: "Retrieve the average *unit* price of products that have *not* been purchased more than once."

Listing 7-55 shows the SELECT statement required to get the product IDs for products that *have* been purchased more than once, using the CustomerOrderItem table. Notice the GROUP BY and HAVING clause.

Listing 7-55. *Getting Product IDs Purchased More Than Once*

```
mysql> SELECT coi.product_id
    -> FROM CustomerOrderItem coi
    -> GROUP BY coi.product_id
    -> HAVING COUNT(*) > 1;
+------------+
| product_id |
+------------+
|          5 |
+------------+
1 row in set (0.00 sec)
```

Because we want to find the *average* unit price (stored in the Product table), we can use a correlated subquery in order to match against rows in the resultset from Listing 7-55. This is necessary because we cannot place two GROUP BY expressions against two different sets of data within the same SELECT statement.

We use a NOT EXISTS correlated subquery to retrieve products that do not appear in this result, as Listing 7-56 shows.

Listing 7-56. *Subquery of Aggregated Correlated Data Using NOT EXISTS*

```
mysql> SELECT AVG(unit_price) as "avg_unit_price"
    -> FROM Product p
    -> WHERE NOT EXISTS (
    ->   SELECT coi.product_id
    ->   FROM CustomerOrderItem coi
    ->   WHERE coi.product_id = p.product_id
    ->   GROUP BY product_id
    ->   HAVING COUNT(*) > 1
    -> );
+----------------+
| avg_unit_price |
+----------------+
| 41.140000      |
+----------------+
1 row in set (0.00 sec)

mysql> SELECT AVG(unit_price) as "avg_unit_price"
    -> FROM Product p
    -> WHERE product_id <> 5;
+----------------+
| avg_unit_price |
+----------------+
| 41.140000      |
+----------------+
1 row in set (0.00 sec)
```

We've highlighted where the correlating WHERE condition was added to the subquery. In addition, we've shown a second query that verifies the accuracy of our top result. Since we know from Listing 7-55 that only the product with a product_id of 5 has been sold more than once, we simply inserted that value in place of the correlated subquery to verify our accuracy.

We demonstrate an alternate way of approaching this type of problem—where aggregates are needed across two separate data sets—in our coverage of derived tables coming up soon.

Row and Tabular Subqueries

When subqueries use multiple columns of data, with one or more rows, a special syntax is required. The row and tabular subquery syntax is sort of a throwback to pre-ANSI 92 days, when joins were not supported and the only way to structure relationships in your SQL code was to use subqueries.

When a single row of data is returned, use the following syntax:

```
WHERE ROW(value1, value 2, … value N)
= (SELECT column1, column2, … columnN FROM table2)
```

Either a column value or constant value can be used inside the ROW() constructor.[4] Any number of columns or constants can be used in this constructor, but the number of values must equal the number of columns returned by the subquery. The expression will return TRUE if all values in the ROW() constructor to the left of the expression match the column values returned by the subquery, and FALSE otherwise. Most often nowadays, you will use a join to represent this same query.

Tabular result subqueries work in a similar fashion, but using the IN keyword:

```
WHERE (value1, value 2, … value N)
IN (SELECT column1, column2, … columnN FROM table2)
```

It's almost always better to rewrite this type of tabular subquery to use a join expression instead; in fact, this syntax is left over from an earlier period of SQL development before joins had entered the language.

Derived Tables

A *derived table* is simply a special type of subquery that appears in the FROM clause, as opposed to the SELECT or WHERE clauses. Derived tables are sometimes called *virtual tables* or *inline views*.

The syntax for specifying a derived table is as follows:

```
SELECT … FROM ( subquery ) as table_name
```

The parentheses and the as *table_name* are required.

---

4. Technically, the ROW keyword is optional. However, we feel it serves to specify that the subquery is expected to return a single row of data, versus a columnar or tabular result.

To demonstrate the power and flexibility of derived tables, let's revisit a correlated subquery from earlier (Listing 7-47):

```
mysql> SELECT p.name FROM Product p
    -> WHERE p.unit_price < (
    ->  SELECT MIN(price) FROM CustomerOrderItem
    ->  WHERE product_id = p.product_id
    -> );
```

While this is a cool example of how to use a correlated scalar subquery, it has one major drawback: the subquery will be executed once for each match in the outer result (Product table). It would be more efficient to do a single pass to find the minimum sale prices for each unique product, and then join that resultset to the outer query. A derived table fulfills this need, as shown in Listing 7-57.

Listing 7-57. *Example of a Derived Table Query*

```
mysql> SELECT p.name FROM Product p
    -> INNER JOIN (
    ->  SELECT coi.product_id, MIN(price) as "min_price"
    ->  FROM CustomerOrderItem coi
    ->  GROUP BY coi.product_id
    -> ) as mp
    ->  ON p.product_id = mp.product_id
    -> WHERE p.unit_price < mp.min_price;
```

So, instead of inner joining our Product table to an actual table, we've enclosed a subquery in parentheses and provided an alias (mp) for that result. This result, which represents the minimum sales price for products purchased, is then joined to the Product table. Finally, a WHERE clause filters out the rows in Product where the unit price is less than the minimum sale price of the product. This differs from the correlated subquery example, in which a separate lookup query is executed for each row in Product.

Listing 7-58 shows the EXPLAIN output from the derived table SQL in Listing 7-57.

Listing 7-58. *EXPLAIN Output of Listing 7-57*

```
mysql> EXPLAIN
    -> SELECT p.name FROM Product p
    -> INNER JOIN (
    ->  SELECT coi.product_id, MIN(price) as "min_price"
    ->  FROM CustomerOrderItem coi
    ->  GROUP BY coi.product_id
    -> ) as mp
    ->  ON p.product_id = mp.product_id
    -> WHERE p.unit_price < mp.min_price \G
```

```
*************************** 1. row ***************************
           id: 1
  select_type: PRIMARY
        table: <derived2>
         type: ALL
possible_keys: NULL
          key: NULL
      key_len: NULL
          ref: NULL
         rows: 8
        Extra:
*************************** 2. row ***************************
           id: 1
  select_type: PRIMARY
        table: p
         type: eq_ref
possible_keys: PRIMARY
          key: PRIMARY
      key_len: 4
          ref: mp.product_id
         rows: 1
        Extra: Using where
*************************** 3. row ***************************
           id: 2
  select_type: DERIVED
        table: coi
         type: ALL
possible_keys: NULL
          key: NULL
      key_len: NULL
          ref: NULL
         rows: 10
        Extra: Using temporary; Using filesort
3 rows in set (0.00 sec)
```

The EXPLAIN output clearly shows that the derived table is executed first, creating a temporary resultset to which the PRIMARY query will join. Notice that the alias we used in the statement (mp) is found in the PRIMARY table's ref column.

For our next example, assume the following request from our sales department: "We'd like to know the average order price for all orders placed." Unfortunately, this statement won't work:

```
mysql> SELECT AVG(SUM(price * quantity)) FROM CustomerOrderItem GROUP BY order_id;
ERROR 1111 (HY000): Invalid use of group function
```

We cannot aggregate over a single table's values twice in the same call. Instead, we can use a derived table to get our desired results, as shown in Listing 7-59.

Listing 7-59. *Using a Derived Table to Sum, Then Average Across Results*

```
mysql> SELECT AVG(order_sum)
    -> FROM (
    ->   SELECT order_id, SUM(price * quantity) as order_sum
    ->   FROM CustomerOrderItem
    ->   GROUP BY order_id
    -> ) as sums;
+----------------+
| AVG(order_sum) |
+----------------+
|     101.170000 |
+----------------+
1 row in set (0.00 sec)
```

Try executing the following SQL:

```
mysql> SELECT p.name FROM Product p
    -> WHERE p.product_id IN (
    ->   SELECT DISTINCT product_id
    ->   FROM CustomerOrderItem
    ->   ORDER BY price DESC
    ->   LIMIT 2
    -> );
```

The statement seems like it would return the product names for the two products with the highest sale price in the CustomerOrderItem table. Unfortunately, you will get the following unpleasant surprise:

```
ERROR 1235 (42000): This version of MySQL doesn't yet support \
'LIMIT & IN/ALL/ANY/SOME subquery'
```

At the time of this writing, MySQL does not support LIMIT expressions in certain subqueries, including the one in the preceding example. Instead, you can use a derived table to get around the problem, as demonstrated in Listing 7-60.

Listing 7-60. *Using LIMIT with a Derived Table*

```
mysql> SELECT p.name
    >  FROM Product p
    -> INNER JOIN (
    ->   SELECT DISTINCT product_id
    ->   FROM CustomerOrderItem
    ->   ORDER BY price DESC
    ->   LIMIT 2
    -> ) as top_price_product
    ->   ON p.product_id = top_price_product.product_id;
```

```
+---------------+
| name          |
+---------------+
| Tennis Racket |
| Doll          |
+---------------+
2 rows in set (0.05 sec)
```

Summary

We've certainly covered a lot of ground in this chapter, with plenty of code examples to demonstrate the techniques. After discussing some SQL code style issues, we presented a review of join types, highlighting some important areas, such as using outer joins effectively.

Next, you learned how to read the in-depth information provided by EXPLAIN about your SELECT statements. We went over how to interpret the EXPLAIN results and determine if MySQL is constructing a properly efficient query execution plan. We stressed that most of the time, it does. In case MySQL didn't pick the plan you prefer to use, we showed you some techniques using hints, which you can use to suggest that MySQL find a more effective join order or index access strategy.

Finally, we worked through the advanced subquery and derived table offerings available in MySQL 4.1.

In the next chapter, we build on this base knowledge, turning our attention to two more SQL topics. First, we'll look at how MySQL optimizes query execution and how you can increase query speed. Then we'll look at scenarios often encountered in application development and administration, and some advanced query techniques you can use to solve these common, but often complex, problems.

CHAPTER 8

■ ■ ■

SQL Scenarios

In the previous chapter, we covered the fundamental topics of joins and subqueries, including derived tables. In this chapter, we're going to put those essential skills to use, focusing on situation-specific examples. This chapter is meant to be a bridge between the basic skills you've picked up so far and the advanced features of MySQL coming up in the next chapters. The examples here will challenge you intellectually and attune you to the set-based thinking required to move your SQL skills to the next level. However, the scenarios presented are also commonly encountered situations, and each section illustrates solutions for these familiar problem domains.

We hope you will use this particular chapter as a reference when the following situations arise in your application development and maintenance work:

- OR conditions prior to MySQL 5.0

- Duplicate entries

- Orphan records

- Hierarchical data handling

- Random record retrieval

- Distance calculations with geographic coordinate data

- Running sum and average generation

Handling OR Conditions Prior to MySQL 5.0

We mentioned in the previous chapter that if you have a lot of queries in your application that use OR statements in the WHERE clause, you should get familiar with the UNION query. By using UNION, you can alleviate much of the performance degradation that OR statements can place on your SQL code.

As an example, suppose we have the table schema shown in Listing 8-1.

Listing 8-1. *Location Table Definition*

```
CREATE TABLE Location (
    Code MEDIUMINT UNSIGNED NOT NULL AUTO_INCREMENT
    , Address VARCHAR(100) NOT NULL
    , City VARCHAR(35) NOT NULL
    , State CHAR(2) NOT NULL
    , Zip VARCHAR(6) NOT NULL
    , PRIMARY KEY (Code)
    , KEY (City)
    , KEY (State)
    , KEY (Zip)
);
```

We've populated a table with around 32,000 records, and we want to issue the query in Listing 8-2, which gets the number of records that are in San Diego *or* are in the zip code 10001.

Listing 8-2. *A Simple OR Condition*

```
mysql> SELECT COUNT(*) FROM Location WHERE city = 'San Diego' OR Zip = '10001';
+----------+
| COUNT(*) |
+----------+
|       83 |
+----------+
1 row in set (0.49 sec)
```

If you are running a MySQL server version before 5.0, you will see entirely different behavior than if you run the same query on a 5.0 server. Listings 8-3 and 8-4 show the difference between the EXPLAIN outputs.

Listing 8-3. *EXPLAIN of Listing 8-2 on a 4.1.9 Server*

```
mysql> EXPLAIN SELECT COUNT(*) FROM Location
    -> WHERE City = 'San Diego' OR Zip = '10001' \G
*************************** 1. row ***************************
           id: 1
  select_type: SIMPLE
        table: Location
         type: ALL
possible_keys: City,Zip
```

```
        key: NULL
    key_len: NULL
        ref: NULL
       rows: 32365
      Extra: Using where
1 row in set (0.01 sec)
```

Listing 8-4. *EXPLAIN of Listing 8-2 on a 5.0.4 Server*

```
mysql> EXPLAIN SELECT COUNT(*) FROM Location
    -> WHERE City = 'San Diego' OR Zip = '10001' \G
*************************** 1. row ***************************
           id: 1
  select_type: SIMPLE
        table: Location
         type: index_merge
possible_keys: City,Zip
          key: City,Zip
      key_len: 37,6
          ref: NULL
         rows: 39
        Extra: Using union(City,Zip); Using where
1 row in set (0.00 sec)
```

In Listing 8-4, you see the new index_merge optimization technique available in MySQL 5.0. The UNION optimization essentially queries *both* the City and Zip indexes, returning matching records that meet the part of the WHERE expression using the index, and then *merges* the two resultsets into a single resultset.

■**Note** Prior to MySQL 5.0.4, you may see Using union (City, Zip) presented as Using sort_union (City, Zip).

Prior to MySQL 5.0, a rule in the optimization process mandated that no more than one index could be used in any single SELECT statement or subquery. With the new Index Merge optimization, this rule is thrown away, and some queries, particularly ones involving OR conditions in the WHERE clause, can employ more than one index to quickly retrieve the needed records.

However, with MySQL versions prior to 5.0, you will see EXPLAIN results similar to those in Listing 8-3, which shows a nonexistent optimization process: the optimizer has chosen to disregard both possible indexes referenced by the WHERE clause and perform a full-table scan to fulfill the query.

If you find yourself running these types of queries against a pre-5.0 MySQL installation, don't despair. You can play a trick on the MySQL server to get the same type of performance as that of the Index Merge optimization.

By using a UNION query with two separate SELECT statements on each part of the OR condition of Listing 8-2, you can essentially mimic the Index Merge behavior. Listing 8-5 shows how to do this.

Listing 8-5. *A UNION Query Resolves the Problem*

```
mysql> SELECT COUNT(*) FROM Location WHERE City = 'San Diego'
    -> UNION ALL
    -> SELECT COUNT(*) FROM Location WHERE Zip = '10001';
+----------+
| COUNT(*) |
+----------+
|       81 |
|        2 |
+----------+
2 rows in set (0.00 sec)
```

Listing 8-6 shows the EXPLAIN indicating the improved query execution plan generated by MySQL 4.1.9.

Listing 8-6. *EXPLAIN from Listing 8-5*

```
mysql> EXPLAIN
    -> SELECT COUNT(*) FROM Location WHERE City = 'San Diego'
    -> UNION ALL
    -> SELECT COUNT(*) FROM Location WHERE Zip = '10001' \G
*************************** 1. row ***************************
           id: 1
  select_type: PRIMARY
        table: Location
         type: ref
possible_keys: City
          key: City
      key_len: 37
          ref: const
         rows: 60
        Extra: Using where; Using index
*************************** 2. row ***************************
           id: 2
  select_type: UNION
        table: Location
         type: ref
possible_keys: Zip
          key: Zip
      key_len: 8
          ref: const
         rows: 2
        Extra: Using where; Using index
```

```
*************************** 3. row ***************************
            id: NULL
   select_type: UNION RESULT
         table: <union1,2>
          type: ALL
 possible_keys: NULL
           key: NULL
       key_len: NULL
           ref: NULL
          rows: NULL
         Extra:
3 rows in set (0.11 sec)
```

As you can tell from Listing 8-6, the optimizer has indeed used both indexes (with a const reference) in order to pull appropriate records from the table. The third row set in the EXPLAIN output is simply informing you that the two results from the first and second SELECT statements were combined.

However, we still have one problem. Listing 8-5 has produced two rows in our resultset. We really only want a single row with the count of the number of records meeting the WHERE condition. In order to get such a result, we must wrap the UNION query as a *derived table* (introduced in Chapter 7) from Listing 8-5 in a SELECT statement containing a SUM() of the results returned by the UNION. We use SUM() because COUNT(*) would return the number 2, as there are two rows in the resultset. Listing 8-7 shows the final query.

Listing 8-7. *Using a Derived Table for an OR Condition*

```
mysql> SELECT SUM(rowcount) FROM (
    -> SELECT COUNT(*) AS rowcount FROM Location WHERE City = 'San Diego'
    -> UNION ALL
    -> SELECT COUNT(*) AS rowcount FROM Location WHERE Zip = '10001'
    -> ) AS tmp;
+----------------+
| SUM(rowcount)  |
+----------------+
|            83  |
+----------------+
1 row in set (0.06 sec)
```

Dealing with Duplicate Entries and Orphaned Records

The next scenarios represent two problems that most developers will run into at some point or another: duplicate entries and orphaned records. Sometimes, you will inherit these problems from another database design team. Other times, you will design a schema that has flaws allowing for the corruption or duplication of data. Both dilemmas occur primarily because of poor database design or the lack of proper constraints on your tables. Here, we'll focus on how to correct the situation and prevent it from happening in the future.

Identifying and Removing Duplicate Entries

In the case of duplicate data, you need to be able to identify those records that contain redundant information and remove those entries from your tables.

As an example, imagine that we've been given a dump file of a table containing RSS feed entries related to job listings. A reader system has been reading RSS feeds from various sources and inserting records into the main RssEntry table. Figure 8-1 shows the E-R diagram for our sample tables, and Listing 8-8 shows the CREATE statements for the RssEntry and RssFeed tables.

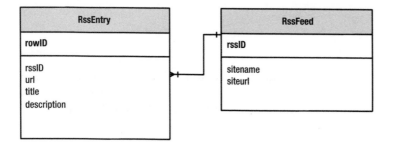

Figure 8-1. *Initial E-R diagram for the RSS tables*

Listing 8-8. *Initial Schema for the Duplicate Data Scenario*

```
CREATE TABLE RssFeed (
    rssID INT NOT NULL AUTO_INCREMENT
    , sitename VARCHAR(254) NOT NULL
    , siteurl VARCHAR(254) NOT NULL
    , PRIMARY KEY (rssID)
);

CREATE TABLE RssEntry (
    rowID INT NOT NULL AUTO_INCREMENT
    , rssID INT NOT NULL
    , url VARCHAR(254) NOT NULL
    , title TEXT
    , description TEXT
    , PRIMARY KEY (rowID)
    , INDEX (rssID)
);
```

After loading the dump file containing around 170,000 RSS entries, we decide that each RSS entry really should have a unique URL. So, we go about setting up a UNIQUE INDEX on the RssEntry.url field, like this:

```
mysql> CREATE UNIQUE INDEX Url ON RssEntry (Url);
ERROR 1062 (23000): Duplicate entry 'http://salesheads.4Jobs.com/JS/General/Job.asp\
?id=3931558&aff=FE' for key 2
```

MySQL runs for a while, and then spits out an error. It seems that the RssEntry table has some duplicate entries. The only constraint on the table—an AUTO_INCREMENT PRIMARY KEY— offers no protection against duplicate URLs being inserted into the table. The reader has apparently just been dumping records into the table, without checking to see if there is an identical record already in it. Before adding a UNIQUE constraint on the url field, we must eliminate these redundant records. However, first, we'll add a non-unique index on the rowID and url fields of RssEntry, as shown in Listing 8-9. As you'll see shortly, this index helps to speed up some of the queries we'll run.

Tip When doing work to remove duplicate entries from a table with a significant number of rows, adding a temporary, non-unique index on the columns in question can often speed up operations as you go about removing duplicate entries.

Listing 8-9. *Adding a Non-Unique Index to Speed Up Queries*

```
mysql> CREATE INDEX UrlRow ON RssEntry (Url, rowID);
Query OK, 166170 rows affected (5.19 sec)
Records: 166170  Duplicates: 0  Warnings: 0
```

The first thing we want to determine is exactly how many duplicate records we have in our table. To do so, we use the COUNT(*) and COUNT(DISTINCT *field*) expressions to determine how many URLs appear in more than one record, as shown in Listing 8-10.

Listing 8-10. *Determining How Many Duplicate URLs Exist in the Data Set*

```
mysql> SELECT COUNT(*), COUNT(*) - COUNT(DISTINCT url) FROM RssEntry;
+----------+-------------------------------+
| COUNT(*) | COUNT(*) - COUNT(DISTINCT url) |
+----------+-------------------------------+
|   166170 |                          8133 |
+----------+-------------------------------+
1 row in set (1.90 sec)
```

Subtracting COUNT(*) from COUNT(DISTINCT url) gives us the number of duplicate URLs in our RssEntry table. With more than 8,000 duplicate rows, we have our work cut out for us.

Now that we know the number of duplicate entries, we next need to get a resultset of the unique entries in the table. When retrieving a set of unique results from a table containing duplicate entries, you must first decide which of the records you want to keep. In this situation, let's assume that we're going to keep the rows having the highest rowID value, and we'll discard the rest of the rows containing an identical URL.

■Tip When removing duplicate entries from a table, first determine which rows having duplicate keys you wish to keep in the table. For instance, if you are removing a duplicate customer record, will you take the oldest or newest record? Or will you need to merge the two records? Be sure you have a game plan for what to do with the redundant data records.

To get a list of these unique entries, we use a GROUP BY expression to group the records in RssEntry along the URL, and find the highest rowID for records containing that URL. We'll insert these unique records into a new table containing a unique index on the url field, and then rename the original and new tables. Listing 8-11 shows the SELECT statement we'll use to get the unique URL records.

Listing 8-11. *Using GROUP BY to Get Unique URL Records*

```
mysql> SELECT MAX(rowID) AS rowID, url FROM RssEntry GROUP BY Url;
... omitted
| 114038 | http://www.zend.com/jobs/single_job.php?id=811    |
| 114039 | http://www.zend.com/jobs/single_job.php?id=812    |
| 114040 | http://www.zend.com/jobs/single_job.php?id=813    |
+--------+-----------------------------------------------------------+
158037 rows in set (3.13 sec)
```

As you can see, the query produces 158,037 rows, which makes sense. In Listing 8-10, we saw that the number of duplicates was 8,133, compared to a total record count of 166,170. Subtracting 8,133 from 166,170 yields 158,037.

Remember the index we added in Listing 8-9? We did so specifically to aid in the query shown in Listing 8-11. Without the index, on our machine the same query took around six minutes to complete. (Your mileage may vary, of course.)

So, now that we have a resultset of unique records, the last step is to create a new table containing the unique records from the original RssEntry table. Listing 8-12 completes the circle.

Listing 8-12. *Creating a New Table with the Unique Records*

```
mysql> CREATE TABLE RssEntry2 (
    ->   rowID INT NOT NULL AUTO_INCREMENT
    -> , rssID INT NOT NULL
    -> , title VARCHAR(255) NOT NULL
    -> , url VARCHAR(255) NOT NULL
    -> , description TEXT
    -> , PRIMARY KEY (rowID)
    -> , UNIQUE INDEX Url (url));
Query OK, 0 rows affected (0.37 sec)
```

```
mysql> INSERT INTO RssEntry2
    -> SELECT * FROM RssEntry
    -> INNER JOIN (
    ->  SELECT MAX(rowID) AS rowID, url
    ->  FROM RssEntry
    ->  GROUP BY url
    -> ) AS uniques
    ->  ON RssEntry.rowID = uniques.rowID;
Query OK, 158037 rows affected (11.42 sec)
Records: 158037  Duplicates: 0  Warnings: 0

mysql> ALTER TABLE RssEntry RENAME TO RssEntry_old;
Query OK, 0 rows affected (0.01 sec)

mysql> ALTER TABLE RssEntry2 RENAME TO RssEntry;
Query OK, 0 rows affected (0.00 sec)
```

If we wanted to drop the old table, we could have done so. Depending on your situation when you're dealing with duplicate records, you may or may not want to keep the original table. As a fail-safe, you may choose to preserve the old table, just in case your queries failed to produce the required results.

Note Some readers may have noticed that we could have also done a multitable DELETE statement, joining our unique resultset to the RssEntry table and removing nonmatching records. This is true, however, we wanted to demonstrate the table-switching method, because it often performs better for large table sets. We'll demonstrate the multitable DELETE method in the next section.

Identifying and Removing Orphaned Records

A more sinister data integrity problem than duplicate records is that of orphaned, or unattached, records. The symptoms of this situation often rear their ugly heads as inexplicable report data. For example, a manager comes to you asking about a strange item in a summary report that doesn't match up to a detail report's results. Other times, you might stumble across orphaned records while performing ad hoc queries. Your job is to identify those orphaned records and remove them.

To demonstrate how to handle orphaned records, we'll use the same schema that we used in the previous section (see Figure 8-1 and Listing 8-8). Listing 8-13 shows a series of SQL statements to select and count records. We begin with a simple summary SELECT that references the RssFeed table from the RssEntry table for a range of rssID values in the RssEntry table, and counts the number of entries in the RssEntry table, along with the sitename field from the RssFeed table. Then we show a simple count of the rows found for the same range in the RssEntry table, without referencing the RssFeed table. Notice that the counts are the same for each result.

Listing 8-13. *Two Simple Reports Showing Identical Counts*

```
mysql> SELECT sitename, COUNT(*)
    -> FROM RssEntry re
    ->  INNER JOIN RssFeed rf
    ->   ON re.rssID = rf.rssID
    -> WHERE re.rssID BETWEEN 420 AND 425
    -> GROUP BY sitename;
+--------------+----------+
| sitename     | COUNT(*) |
+--------------+----------+
| pickajob.com |      985 |
+--------------+----------+
1 row in set (0.40 sec)

mysql> SELECT COUNT(*) FROM RssEntry
    -> WHERE rssID BETWEEN 420 AND 425;
+----------+
| COUNT(*) |
+----------+
|      985 |
+----------+
1 row in set (0.01 sec)
```

Now, let's corrupt our tables by removing a parent record from the RssFeed table, leaving records in the RssEntry referencing a nonexistent parent rssID value. We'll delete the parent record in RssFeed for the rssID = 424:

```
mysql> DELETE FROM RssFeed WHERE rssID = 424;
Query OK, 1 row affected (0.43 sec)
```

What happens when we rerun the same statements from Listing 8-13? The results are shown in Listing 8-14.

Listing 8-14. *Mismatched Reports Due to a Missing Parent Record*

```
mysql> SELECT sitename, COUNT(*)
    -> FROM RssEntry re
    ->  INNER JOIN RssFeed rf
    ->   ON re.rssID = rf.rssID
    -> WHERE re.rssID BETWEEN 420 AND 425
    -> GROUP BY sitename;
+--------------+----------+
| sitename     | COUNT(*) |
+--------------+----------+
| pickajob.com |      850 |
+--------------+----------+
1 row in set (0.00 sec)
```

```
mysql> SELECT COUNT(*) FROM RssEntry WHERE rssID BETWEEN 420 AND 425;
+----------+
| COUNT(*) |
+----------+
|      985 |
+----------+
1 row in set (0.00 sec)
```

Notice how the count of records in the first statement has changed, because the reference to RssFeed on the rssID = 424 key has been deleted. Both reports should show the same numbers, but because a parent has been removed, the reports show mismatched data. The rows in RssEntry matching rssID = 424 are now orphaned records.

This is a particularly sticky problem because the report results *seem* to be accurate until someone points out the mismatch. If you have a summary report containing thousands of line items, and detail reports containing hundreds of thousands of items, this kind of data problem can be almost impossible to detect.

But, you say, if we had used the InnoDB storage engine, we wouldn't have had this problem, because we could have placed a FOREIGN KEY constraint on the rssID field of the RssEntry table! But we specifically chose to use the MyISAM storage engine here for a reason: it is the only storage engine capable of using FULLTEXT indexing.[1]

As you learned in Chapter 7, you can use an outer join to identify records in one table that have no matching records in another table. In this case, we want to identify those records from the RssEntry table that have no valid parent record in the RssFeed table. Listing 8-15 shows the SQL to return these records.

Listing 8-15. *Identifying the Orphaned Records with an Outer Join*

```
mysql> SELECT re.rowID, LEFT(re.title, 50) AS title
    -> FROM RssEntry re
    ->  LEFT JOIN RssFeed rf
    ->   ON re.rssID = rf.rssID
    -> WHERE rf.rssID IS NULL;
+--------+--------------------------------------------------+
| rowID  | title                                            |
+--------+--------------------------------------------------+
|  27008 | Search Consultant (Louisville, KY)               |
|  22377 | Enterprise Java Developer (Frankfort, KY)        |
... omitted
| 136167 | JavaJ2ee leadj2ee architects (Fort Knox, KY)     |
| 137709 | Documentum Architect (Louisville, KY)            |
+--------+--------------------------------------------------+
135 rows in set (1.44 sec)
```

As you can see, the query produces the 135 records that had been orphaned when we deleted the parent record from RssFeed.

---

1. In future versions of MySQL, FULLTEXT indexing may be supported by more storage engines. However, as we go to press, InnoDB does not currently support it.

Just as with duplicate records, it is important to have a policy in place for how to handle orphaned records. In some rare cases, it may be acceptable to leave orphaned records alone; however, in most circumstances, you'll want to remove them, as they endanger reporting accuracy and the integrity of your data store. Listing 8-16 shows how to use a multitable DELETE to remove the offending records.

Listing 8-16. *A Multitable DELETE Statement to Remove Orphaned Records*

```
mysql> DELETE RssEntry FROM RssEntry
    -> INNER JOIN (
    ->   SELECT re.rowID FROM RssEntry re
    ->   LEFT JOIN RssFeed rf
    ->   ON re.rssID = rf.rssID
    ->   WHERE rf.rssID IS NULL
    -> ) AS orphans
    ->   ON RssEntry.rowID = orphans.rowID;
Query OK, 135 rows affected (1.52 sec)
```

Multitable DELETE statements require you to explicitly state which table's records you intend to delete. In Listing 8-16, we explicitly tell MySQL we want to remove the records from the RssEntry table. We then perform an inner join on a derived table containing the outer join from Listing 8-15, referencing the rowID column (join and derived table techniques are detailed in Chapter 7). As expected, the query removes the 135 rows from RssEntry corresponding to our orphaned records. Listing 8-17 shows a quick repeat of our initial report queries from Listing 8-13, verifying that the referencing summary report contains counts matching a nonreferencing query.

Listing 8-17. *Verifying That the DELETE Statement Removed the Orphaned Records*

```
mysql> SELECT sitename, COUNT(*)
    -> FROM RssEntry re
    ->   INNER JOIN RssFeed rf
    -> ON re.rssID = rf.rssID
    -> WHERE re.rssID BETWEEN 420 AND 425
    -> GROUP BY sitename;
+---------------+----------+
| sitename      | COUNT(*) |
+---------------+----------+
| pickajob.com  |      850 |
+---------------+----------+
1 row in set (0.00 sec)

mysql> SELECT COUNT(*) FROM RssEntry
    -> WHERE rssID BETWEEN 420 AND 425;
+----------+
| COUNT(*) |
+----------+
|      850 |
+----------+
1 row in set (0.00 sec)
```

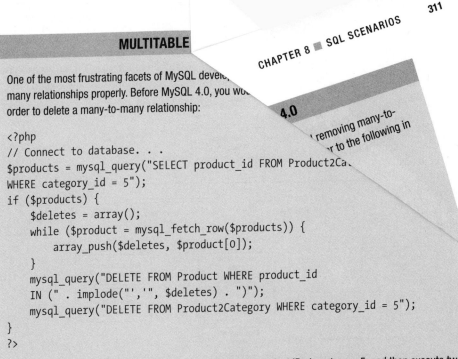

MULTITABLE

One of the most frustrating facets of MySQL devel~~op~~
many relationships properly. Before MySQL 4.0, you wo~~uld~~
order to delete a many-to-many relationship:

4.0

removing many-to-
~~r~~ to the following in

```php
<?php
// Connect to database. . .
$products = mysql_query("SELECT product_id FROM Product2Ca
WHERE category_id = 5");
if ($products) {
    $deletes = array();
    while ($product = mysql_fetch_row($products)) {
        array_push($deletes, $product[0]);
    }
    mysql_query("DELETE FROM Product WHERE product_id
    IN (" . implode("','", $deletes) . ")");
    mysql_query("DELETE FROM Product2Category WHERE category_id = 5");
}
?>
```

Notice that we needed to build a query to return the product IDs in category 5, and then execute two `DELETE` statements: one to remove the parent and another to remove the children in `Product2Category`. No temporary table solution is possible, because a join or subquery is not available in the `DELETE` statement before MySQL 4.0.

Dealing with Hierarchical Data

In this section, we'll look at some issues regarding dealing with hierarchical, or tree-like, data in SQL. For these examples, we'll use a part of our sample schema from Chapter 7, as shown in Figure 8-2. We'll use many of the techniques covered in that chapter, as well.

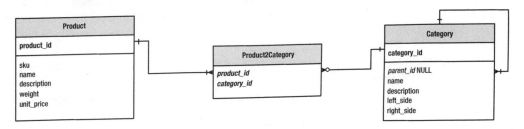

Figure 8-2. *Section of sample schema for hierachical data examples*

...minantly is the Category table. In order for you to get ...made a diagram of the relationship of the rows in this ...use this figure to graphically explain the SQL contained in ...category_id value for each row, or *node* in tree-based lan-

The data we ...
a visual feel fo... the category name.
table, as sho...
this section
guage, is ...

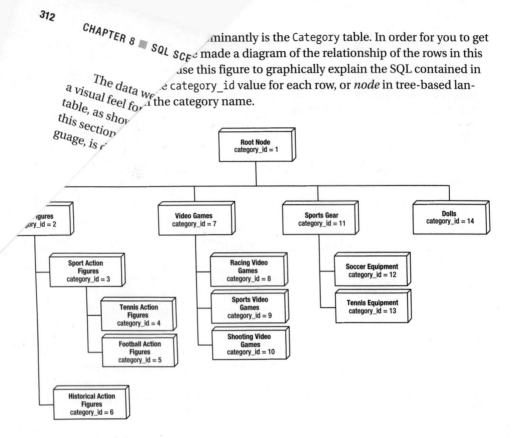

Figure 8-3. *Diagram of the category tree*

You can use a number of techniques to store and retrieve tree-like structures in a relational database management system. SQL itself is generally poorly suited for handling tree-based structures, as the language is designed to work on two-dimensional sets of data, not hierarchical ones. SQL's lack of certain structures and processes, like arrays and recursion, sometimes make these various techniques seem like "hacks." Although there is some truth to this observation, we'll present a technique that we feel demonstrates the most set-based way of handling the problems inherent with hierarchical data structures in SQL. This technique is commonly referred to as the *nested set model.*[2]

The nested set model technique emphasizes having the programmer update metadata about the tree at the time of insertion or deletion of nodes. This metadata alleviates the need for recursion in most aggregating queries across the tree, and thus can significantly speed up query performance in large data sets.

---

2. The nested set model was made popular by a leading SQL mind, Joe Celko, author of *SQL for Smarties*, among other titles.

THE ADJACENCY LIST AND PATH ENUMERATION MODELS

Perhaps the most common technique for dealing with trees in SQL is called the *adjacency list model*. In Chapter 7, you saw an example of this technique when we covered the self join. In the adjacency list model, you have two fields in a table corresponding to the ID of the row and the ID of its parent. You use the parent ID value to traverse the tree and find child nodes. Unfortunately, this technique has one major flaw: it requires recursion in order to "walk" through the hierarchy of nodes. To find all the children of a specific node in the tree, the programmer must make repeated SELECTs against the children of each child node in the tree. When the *depth* of the tree (number of levels of the hierarchy) is not known, the programmer must use a cursor (either a client-side or server-side cursor, as described in Chapter 11) and repeatedly issue SELECTs against the same table.

Another technique, commonly called the *path enumeration model*, stores a literal path to the node within a field in the table. While this method can save some time, it is not very flexible and can lead to fairly obscure and poorly performing SQL code.

We encourage you to read about these methods, as your specific data model might be best served by these techniques. Additionally, reading about them will no doubt make you a more rounded SQL developer. For those interested in hierarchies and trees in SQL, we recommend picking up a copy of Joe Celko's *Trees and Hierarchies in SQL for Smarties* (Morgan Kaufmann, 2004). The book is highly rooted in the mathematical foundations for SQL models of tree structures, and is not for the faint of heart.

Understanding the Nested Set Model

The nested set technique uses a method of storing metadata about the nodes contained in the tree in order to provide the SQL parser with information about how to "walk" the hierarchy of nodes. In our example, this metadata is stored in the two fields of Category labeled left_side and right_side. These fields store values that represent the left and right *bounds* of the part of the category tree that the row in Category represents.

The trick to the nested set model is that these two fields must be kept up-to-date as changes to the hierarchy occur. If these two fields are maintained, we can assume that for any given row in the table, we can find all children of that Category by looking at rows with left_side values *between* the parent node's left_side and right_side values. This is a critical aspect of the nested set model, as it alleviates the need for a recursive technique to find all children, regardless of the depth of the tree.

The nested set model gives the following rules regarding how the left and right numbers are calculated:

- For the root node in the hierarchy, the left_side value will always be 1, and the right_side value is calculated as 2*n where n is the number of nodes in the tree.

- For all other nodes, the right_side value will equal the left_side + (2*n) + 1, where n is the total number of child nodes. Thus, for the leaf nodes (nodes without children), the right_side value will always be equal to the left_side value + 1.

The second rule may sound a bit tricky, but, it really isn't. If you think of each node in the tree as having a left_side and right_side value, these values of each node are ordered counter-clockwise, as illustrated in Figure 8-4. The process of determining left_side and right_side values will become clear as we cover inserting and removing nodes from the tree in the upcoming examples. For right now, take a look at Figure 8-4 to get a feel for the pattern by which the left and right values are generated. Remember that for each node, the left and right value of all child nodes must fall *between* the left and right value of the parent node.

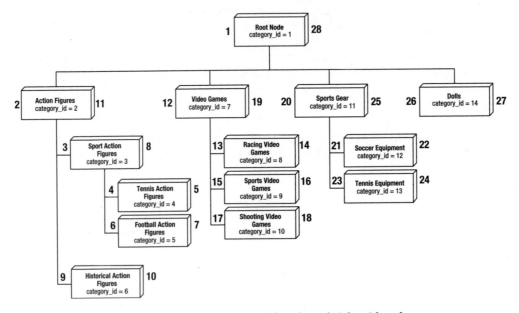

Figure 8-4. *Diagram of the category tree, showing left_side and right_side values*

Listing 8-18 shows all the data we'll be working with in the Category table. Use this listing, along with Figure 8-4, to follow along with the upcoming examples.

Listing 8-18. *The Category Table Data*

```
mysql> SELECT category_id, name, left_side, right_side FROM Category;
+-------------+--------------------------+-----------+------------+
| category_id | name                     | left_side | right_side |
+-------------+--------------------------+-----------+------------+
|           1 | All                      |         1 |         28 |
|           2 | Action Figures           |         2 |         11 |
|           3 | Sport Action Figures     |         3 |          8 |
|           4 | Tennis Action Figures    |         4 |          5 |
|           5 | Football Action Figures  |         6 |          7 |
|           6 | Historical Action Figures |        9 |         10 |
|           7 | Video Games              |        12 |         19 |
|           8 | Racing Video Games       |        13 |         14 |
|           9 | Sports Video Games       |        15 |         16 |
|          10 | Shooting Video Games     |        17 |         18 |
|          11 | Sports Gear              |        20 |         25 |
|          12 | Soccer Equipment         |        21 |         22 |
|          13 | Tennis Equipment         |        23 |         24 |
|          14 | Dolls                    |        26 |         27 |
+-------------+--------------------------+-----------+------------+
14 rows in set (0.00 sec)
```

Now, you're ready to look at how to accomplish the following common chores using the nested set technique:

- Find the depth of a node

- Find all nodes under a specific parent

- Find all nodes above a specific node

- Summarize across the tree

- Insert a node into the tree

- Remove a node from the tree

Finding the Depth of a Node

One of the first tasks you will run into with hierarchical data is how to find the depth of the tree as a whole, or the depth of a single node within the tree. In our Category example data, you might want to know how many levels there are in the category tree—how far down does the tree go? In Figure 8-3, you can see that currently, our category tree has four levels, with the root node being level 1.

Using the nested set method, you compare two *sets* of the same information against each other using the left and right side values. To get the depth of any node in the hierarchy, compare the base table, which we'll call set A, against a subset (or *nested* set) of the same data, which we'll refer to as set B. For each value in set A, you know that the level of each row is equal to the number of elements in set B in which the left side value of set A falls *between* the left and right side values of set B.

Let's take the first two rows in Category, and work through the equation:

- For the root node, we know the left_side = 1. We look for the number of rows in Category where the number 1 falls between the left_side and right_side values of the row. We find only one row: the root node itself. All other rows have a left_side value greater than 1, and so do not meet the BETWEEN expression's criteria. Therefore, the root node is at level 1.

- For the next node (category_id = 2), we know the left_side = 2. We look for the number of rows in Category where the number 2 falls between the left_side and right_side values of the row. We find two rows: the root node (1 => 2 <= 28) and the current node itself (2 => 2 <= 9). All other rows have a left_side value > 2, and so do not meet the BETWEEN expression's criteria.

Following through this logic, we can deduce the SQL shown in Listing 8-19, which outputs the level of the hierarchy at which each node happens to reside.

Listing 8-19. *Finding the Level of a Node in the Tree*

```
mysql> SELECT c1.name, COUNT(*) AS level
    -> FROM Category c1
    -> INNER JOIN Category c2
    -> ON c1.left_side BETWEEN c2.left_side AND c2.right_side
    -> GROUP BY c1.name;
```

```
+----------------------------+-------+
| name                       | level |
+----------------------------+-------+
| All                        |     1 |
| Action Figures             |     2 |
| Sport Action Figures       |     3 |
| Tennis Action Figures      |     4 |
| Football Action Figures    |     4 |
| Historical Action Figures  |     2 |
| Video Games                |     2 |
| Racing Video Games         |     3 |
| Sports Video Games         |     3 |
| Shooting Video Games       |     3 |
| Sports Gear                |     2 |
| Soccer Equipment           |     3 |
| Tennis Equipment           |     3 |
| Dolls                      |     2 |
+----------------------------+-------+
14 rows in set (0.03 sec)
```

Look carefully at Listing 8-19. The relationship between c1 and c2 is critical. We're comparing two copies of the Category table with each other using the BETWEEN clause. We'll be using this type of join in the rest of these examples, so make sure you understand what is going on here. The nesting of sets is occurring along the left_side and right_side values. As you'll see, we can derive almost any information about our hierarchy by making slight adjustments to the query style used in Listing 8-19.

How would we determine the depth of the tree as a whole? Well, the depth of the entire tree is equal to the maximum level returned by the query in Listing 8-19, as shown in Listing 8-20.

Listing 8-20. *Getting the Total Depth of the Tree*

```
mysql> SELECT MAX(level) FROM
    -> (
    -> SELECT c1.category_id, COUNT(*) AS level
    -> FROM Category c1
    -> INNER JOIN Category c2
    -> ON c1.left_side BETWEEN c2.left_side AND c2.right_side
    -> GROUP BY c1.category_id
    -> ) AS derived;
+------------+
| MAX(level) |
+------------+
|          4 |
+------------+
1 row in set (0.16 sec)
```

Finding All Nodes Under a Specific Parent

When dealing with hierarchical data, you may wish to find all the children under a specified node. For instance, what if we wanted to find all subcategories belonging to the Sport Action Figures category? If you look back to Figure 8-4, you'll see that both the Tennis Action Figures and Football Action Figures categories are contained in the Sport Action Figures category. Listing 8-21 shows how to retrieve all child nodes under a specified parent.

Listing 8-21. *Finding All Child Nodes Under a Parent Node*

```
mysql> SELECT c1.name, c1.description
    -> FROM Category c1
    -> INNER JOIN Category c2
    -> ON c1.left_side BETWEEN c2.left_side AND c2.right_side
    -> WHERE c2.category_id = 3
    -> AND c1.category_id <> 3;
+------------------------+------------------------+
| name                   | description            |
+------------------------+------------------------+
| Tennis Action Figures  | Tennis Action Figures  |
| Football Action Figures| Football Action Figures|
+------------------------+------------------------+
2 rows in set (0.08 sec)
```

If you want to retrieve a node itself and all its children, simply remove the WHERE expression for c1.category_id <> 3, as shown in Listing 8-22.

Listing 8-22. *Retrieving a Node and All Its Children*

```
mysql> SELECT c1.name, c1.description
    -> FROM Category c1
    -> INNER JOIN Category c2
    -> ON c1.left_side BETWEEN c2.left_side AND c2.right_side
    -> WHERE c2.category_id = 3;
+------------------------+--------------------------------------+
| name                   | description                          |
+------------------------+--------------------------------------+
| Sport Action Figures   | All Types of Action Figures in Sports|
| Tennis Action Figures  | Tennis Action Figures                |
| Football Action Figures| Football Action Figures              |
+------------------------+--------------------------------------+
3 rows in set (0.03 sec)
```

Finding All Nodes Above a Specific Node

Other times, you may be interested in finding nodes in the tree that correspond to parents of a specific node. Let's suppose that we want to get a list of all categories from which the Football Action Figures category derived. We use the *inverse* of our query in Listing 8-21 to return the results of set B (c2), instead of set A (c1), as Listing 8-23 demonstrates.

Listing 8-23. *Finding All Parent Nodes*

```
mysql> SELECT c2.name, c2.description
    -> FROM Category c1
    ->  INNER JOIN Category c2
    ->   ON c1.left_side BETWEEN c2.left_side AND c2.right_side
    -> WHERE c1.category_id = 5
    -> AND c2.category_id <> 5;
+----------------------+--------------------------------------+
| name                 | description                          |
+----------------------+--------------------------------------+
| All                  | All Categories                       |
| Action Figures       | All Types of Action Figures          |
| Sport Action Figures | All Types of Action Figures in Sports |
+----------------------+--------------------------------------+
3 rows in set (0.08 sec)
```

We've highlighted the areas of the query that changed from Listing 8-21. Notice we did *not* change the relationship between the two data sets—the ON condition. What changed was which *side* of the join we returned.

Summarizing Across the Tree

Let's go a step further and get some more meaningful information out of MySQL. Let's assume our operations manager presented this request: "Provide product names, total number of items sold, and total sales for all Sports Gear categories."

To break this request down, we first know that we will need to get the category IDs of all our Sports Gear categories, including the parent Sports Gear category. Listing 8-22 has already done most of this work for us; we simply need to return the category_id value, instead of the name and description values, and change the category_id to that of the Sports Gear category node, as shown in Listing 8-24.

Listing 8-24. *Retrieving All Sports Gear Categories and Subcategory IDs*

```
mysql> SELECT c1.category_id
    -> FROM Category c1
    ->  INNER JOIN Category c2
    ->  ON c1.left_side BETWEEN c2.left_side AND c2.right_side
    ->   WHERE c2.category_id = 11;
+-------------+
| category_id |
+-------------+
|          11|
|          12|
|          13|
+-------------+
3 rows in set (0.03 sec)
```

Next, we want to use the many-to-many relationship in the `Product2Category` table in order to join the `CustomerOrderItem` table, which houses our sales information. Listing 8-25 shows the join. Notice we use the query in Listing 8-24 as a derived table inner-joined to `Product2Category` in order to retrieve the appropriate products matching the needed categories.

Listing 8-25. *Getting Sales for Products Within a Node of a Tree*

```
mysql> SELECT
    ->    p.name AS Product
    ->    , SUM(coi.quantity) AS ItemsSold
    ->    , SUM(coi.quantity * coi.price) AS TotalSales
    -> FROM Product p
    ->  INNER JOIN CustomerOrderItem coi
    ->   ON p.product_id = coi.product_id
    ->  INNER JOIN Product2Category p2c
    ->   ON p.product_id = p2c.product_id
    ->  INNER JOIN (
    ->   SELECT c1.category_id
    ->   FROM Category c1
    ->    INNER JOIN Category c2
    ->    ON c1.left_side BETWEEN c2.left_side AND c2.right_side
    ->    WHERE c2.category_id = 11
    ->  ) AS c
    ->   ON p2c.category_id = c.category_id
    -> GROUP BY p.name;
+---------------+-----------+------------+
| Product       | ItemsSold | TotalSales |
+---------------+-----------+------------+
| Soccer Ball   |         1 |      23.70 |
| Tennis Balls  |        57 |     270.75 |
| Tennis Racket |         1 |     104.75 |
+---------------+-----------+------------+
3 rows in set (0.03 sec)
```

The query in Listing 8-25 is merely a combination of elements you've learned about so far. We're following the relationships from three tables back to a set of category IDs we've generated using our nested set model.

Now, let's see what happens to our SQL if we are asked to fulfill this request: "Provide the total number of products in our catalog for each category. For parent categories, provide aggregated numbers."

When you see a request for aggregated numbers, you know that you'll be summing information using the `SUM()` and `COUNT()` functions. However, in this request, we've been asked to provide a special type of aggregation, known as a *rollup* (because you're "rolling up" subcategories into their parent categories). To accomplish this, we're going to use the inverse technique described earlier in the "Finding All Nodes Above a Specific Node" section. Take a look at Listing 8-26.

Listing 8-26. *Finding Aggregated Totals*

```
mysql> SELECT c2.category_id, c2.name, COUNT(*) AS products
    -> FROM Category c1
    ->  INNER JOIN Category c2
    ->   ON c1.left_side BETWEEN c2.left_side AND c2.right_side
    ->  INNER JOIN Product2Category p2c
    ->   ON c1.category_id = p2c.category_id
    -> GROUP BY c2.category_id;
+-------------+--------------------------+----------+
| category_id | name                     | products |
+-------------+--------------------------+----------+
|           1 | All                      |       10 |
|           2 | Action Figures           |        3 |
|           3 | Sport Action Figures     |        2 |
|           6 | Historical Action Figures|        1 |
|           7 | Video Games              |        3 |
|           8 | Racing Video Games       |        1 |
|           9 | Sports Video Games       |        2 |
|          11 | Sports Gear              |        3 |
|          12 | Soccer Equipment         |        1 |
|          13 | Tennis Equipment         |        2 |
|          14 | Dolls                    |        1 |
+-------------+--------------------------+----------+
11 rows in set (0.00 sec)
```

Again, the trick is knowing which set (either c2 or c1) to return in the resultset. The set that is returned determines the aggregation of the resultset. In the case of rollups, you want to return the data set B (c2), which represents the part of the tree including and above the current node in the join. Note how we use a GROUP BY expression on the c2 set's category_id values, and use the COUNT(*) function to return the number of products in the Product2Category table that match c2's category_id value. If you don't understand the logic, work slowly through the SQL, writing down each set of data and how the join will match certain values. It's important that you understand the way the data sets relate through the BETWEEN operator. We'll be returning to this concept later in this chapter, in the "Generating Running Sums and Averages" section.

For our final query in this section, let's bring together our two requests: "Provide a list of all categories, with sales totals for each category. Include rollups for each parent category, and indent each subcategory appropriately from the root node by the number of levels deep."

Although it sounds complex, this request is really a simple adaptation of our last query, along with a trick you learned in the previous section about determining the node depth. Instead of finding counts of products with the Product2Category table, we're going to use it to join to CustomerOrderItem to get our sales totals. Listing 8-27 shows the SQL for this request.

Listing 8-27. *Sales Rollup Report by Category*

```
mysql> SELECT
    ->  CONCAT(REPEAT('--', levels.level - 1), c2.name) AS Category
    ->  , SUM(coi.quantity) AS TotalItems
```

```
->   , SUM(coi.quantity * coi.price) AS TotalSales
-> FROM Category c1
->   INNER JOIN Category c2
->    ON c1.left_side BETWEEN c2.left_side AND c2.right_side
->   INNER JOIN Product2Category p2c
->    ON c1.category_id = p2c.category_id
->   INNER JOIN CustomerOrderItem coi
->    ON p2c.product_id = coi.product_id
->   INNER JOIN
->   (
->    SELECT c3.category_id, COUNT(*) AS level
->    FROM Category c3
->     INNER JOIN Category c4
->      ON c3.left_side BETWEEN c4.left_side AND c4.right_side
->    GROUP BY c3.category_id
->   ) AS levels
->     ON c2.category_id = levels.category_id
-> GROUP BY c2.category_id;
+-------------------------------+------------+------------+
| Category                      | TotalItems | TotalSales |
+-------------------------------+------------+------------+
| All                           |         65 |     607.02 |
| --Action Figures              |          3 |      40.85 |
| ----Sport Action Figures      |          2 |      24.90 |
| ----Historical Action Figures |          1 |      15.95 |
| --Video Games                 |          1 |      46.99 |
| ----Sports Video Games        |          1 |      46.99 |
| --Sports Gear                 |         59 |     399.20 |
| ----Soccer Equipment          |          1 |      23.70 |
| ----Tennis Equipment          |         58 |     375.50 |
| --Dolls                       |          2 |     119.98 |
+-------------------------------+------------+------------+
10 rows in set (0.41 sec)
```

We realize Listing 8-27 has a lot going on. But this is a good example of how you can use all of the knowledge you've learned in the previous chapters to produce some pretty amazing reports. Using the building blocks of the derived tables you learned in Chapter 7, we took the query from Listing 8-19, which found the depth of each category node. We used the REPEAT function to insert two dashes for each level in the category from the root node. We made this section of the query bold in order for you to tell which piece of the overall query is involved in the depth calculation.

The italicized part of the query shows the rollup adaptation from our query in Listing 8-26. Instead of counting the products, we've simply used Product2Category to join to the sales information found in CustomerOrderItem and used the SUM function to provide some aggregated numbers.

■Note Notice that the query from Listing 8-27 shows only 10 results? But there are 14 categories. As an exercise, rewrite the query in Listing 8-27 to use an outer join to include the categories that have no product sales. Use the techniques you learned in Chapter 7.

Inserting a Node into the Tree

What happens to our nested set model when we need to insert a new category into our catalog? Clearly, our model depends on the left and right side metadata about each category. To keep our model from breaking, we need to update this metadata when our tree changes. Luckily, we have our rules from which we can derive a node-insertion strategy.

When you're inserting nodes into the tree, you must first decide what the *parent* of the new node will be—where will the node be inserted? Once you know which node is the parent, you can then update the metadata for all nodes according to the right side value of this parent.

Let's assume we want to add under the Video Games category a new category called Puzzle Video Games. Therefore, the *parent* is the Sports Video Games category node, and the rightmost child is the Shooting Video Games subcategory.

Figure 8-5 shows what we intend to happen to the category tree. The new node is shaded, and the updated metadata is circled. Notice the pattern of how the metadata changed from Figure 8-4. For those nodes with original left_side values greater than that of the parent's right_side value (19), their new left_side value was increased by two. Similarly, for those nodes whose original right_side value was greater than or equal to the rightmost sibling's right_side value (19), their new right_side value is also increased by two. The new node slides easily into the gap. If you're unsure, compare the two figures side by side until you see the pattern of changes.

Following from this insertion pattern, we use the SQL in Listing 8-28 to insert the new node to the right of the insertion point.

Listing 8-28. *Inserting a New Node and Updating the Metadata*

```
mysql> SELECT @insert_right := right_side FROM Category WHERE category_id = 7;
+----------------------------+
| @insert_right := right_side |
+----------------------------+
|                         19 |
+----------------------------+
1 row in set (0.11 sec)

mysql> UPDATE Category
    -> SET left_side = IF(left_side > @insert_right, left_side + 2, left_side)
    -> , right_side = IF(right_side >= @insert_right, right_side + 2, right_side)
    -> WHERE right_side >= @insert_right;
Query OK, 6 rows affected (0.16 sec)
Rows matched: 6  Changed: 6  Warnings: 0
```

```
mysql> INSERT INTO Category (parent_id, name, description, left_side, right_side)
    -> VALUES (7, 'Puzzle Video Games', 'Puzzle Video Games', @insert_right,
    -> (@insert_right + 1));
Query OK, 1 row affected (0.03 sec)
```

Notice the steps we take:

1. Assign the right_side value of the parent node to a user session variable called @insert_right.

2. Use the UPDATE expression to "bump up" the left_side and right_side values of the nodes above the insertion point, and update the right_side value of the parent node, according to the pattern shown in Figure 8-5.

3. Use a simple INSERT statement to push the new category into the tree at the insertion point.

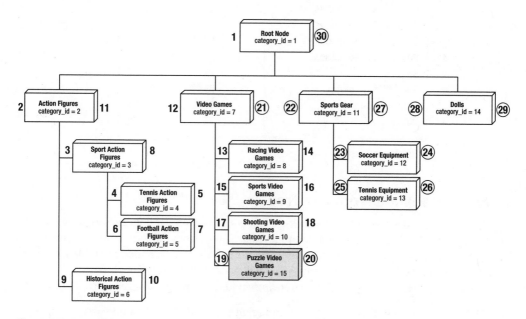

Figure 8-5. *Inserting a new node in the category tree*

Listing 8-29 shows a SELECT of the updated category tree to demonstrate the results of our node insertion.

Listing 8-29. *Verifying the New Node Insertion*

```
mysql> SELECT category_id, name, left_side, right_side
    -> FROM Category
    -> ORDER BY left_side, right_side;
+-------------+-------------------------+-----------+------------+
| category_id | name                    | left_side | right_side |
+-------------+-------------------------+-----------+------------+
|           1 | All                     |         1 |         30 |
|           2 | Action Figures          |         2 |         11 |
|           3 | Sport Action Figures    |         3 |          8 |
|           4 | Tennis Action Figures   |         4 |          5 |
|           5 | Football Action Figures |         6 |          7 |
|           6 | Historical Action Figures |       9 |         10 |
|           7 | Video Games             |        12 |         21 |
|           8 | Racing Video Games      |        13 |         14 |
|           9 | Sports Video Games      |        15 |         16 |
|          10 | Shooting Video Games    |        17 |         18 |
|          16 | Puzzle Video Games      |        19 |         20 |
|          11 | Sports Gear             |        22 |         27 |
|          12 | Soccer Equipment        |        23 |         24 |
|          13 | Tennis Equipment        |        25 |         26 |
|          14 | Dolls                   |        28 |         29 |
+-------------+-------------------------+-----------+------------+
15 rows in set (0.09 sec)
```

Removing a Node from the Tree

Finally, we also need a method for removing a category from our catalog. Let's assume that we want to remove the category named Shooting Video Games from the Video Games category. Figure 8-6 shows how we want the new category tree to look. We've shaded the node we wish to remove and circled the metadata values that will need to change.

As you would expect, the pattern for removing a node is basically the reverse of adding a node:

1. Start by determining the left_side and right_side values of the node we're going to delete, which are 17 and 18 in this case.

2. Subtract two from the left_side values of any node having a left_side value greater than the left_side value of the deleted node.

3. Subtract two from the right_side value of any node having a right_side value greater than the right_side value of the deleted node.

4. Finally, remove the category from both the Category table and the Product2Category table using a multitable DELETE statement. We use a LEFT JOIN to ensure that the category is deleted, even if it has not been assigned to any products.

Listing 8-30 shows the SQL to accomplish the node removal.

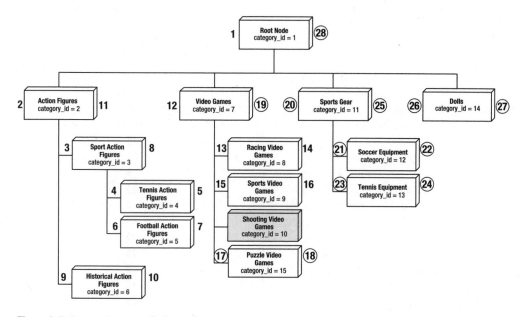

Figure 8-6. *Removing a node from the category tree*

Listing 8-30. *Removing a Node*

```
mysql> SELECT @delete_left := left_side, @delete_right := right_side
    -> FROM Category
    -> WHERE category_id = 10;
+---------------------------+----------------------------+
| @delete_left := left_side | @delete_right := right_side |
+---------------------------+----------------------------+
|                        17 |                         18 |
+---------------------------+----------------------------+
1 row in set (0.80 sec)

mysql> UPDATE Category
    -> SET left_side = IF(left_side > @delete_left, left_side - 2, left_side)
    -> , right_side = IF(right_side > @delete_right, right_side - 2, right_side)
    -> WHERE right_side > @delete_right;
Query OK, 7 rows affected (0.17 sec)
Rows matched: 7  Changed: 7  Warnings: 0

mysql> DELETE Product2Category, Category
    -> FROM Category
    ->  LEFT JOIN Product2Category
    ->   ON Category.category_id = Product2Category.category_id
    -> WHERE Category.category_id = 10;
Query OK, 1 row affected (0.09 sec)
```

Finally, we check the metadata status of our tree, as shown in Listing 8-31.

Listing 8-31. *Checking the Metadata Status*

```
mysql> SELECT category_id, name, left_side, right_side
    -> FROM Category
    -> ORDER BY left_side, right_side;
+-------------+-------------------------+-----------+------------+
| category_id | name                    | left_side | right_side |
+-------------+-------------------------+-----------+------------+
|           1 | All                     |         1 |         28 |
|           2 | Action Figures          |         2 |         11 |
|           3 | Sport Action Figures    |         3 |          8 |
|           4 | Tennis Action Figures   |         4 |          5 |
|           5 | Football Action Figures |         6 |          7 |
|           6 | Historical Action Figures |       9 |         10 |
|           7 | Video Games             |        12 |         19 |
|           8 | Racing Video Games      |        13 |         14 |
|           9 | Sports Video Games      |        15 |         16 |
|          16 | Puzzle Video Games      |        17 |         18 |
|          11 | Sports Gear             |        20 |         25 |
|          12 | Soccer Equipment        |        21 |         22 |
|          13 | Tennis Equipment        |        23 |         24 |
|          14 | Dolls                   |        26 |         27 |
+-------------+-------------------------+-----------+------------+
14 rows in set (0.03 sec)
```

Retrieving Random Records

In certain applications, you may need to return a random set of records from a given table. For instance, your web application might have a banner advertising system that displays a random image from a table of advertisements stored in MySQL. You can do this in a couple ways, using MySQL's extension functions. One method is to use the RAND() function along with the LIMIT clause. As an example, assume we have the simple table schema for storing advertisements shown in Listing 8-32.

Listing 8-32. *Sample Table Schema for Storing Advertisements*

```
CREATE TABLE Banner (
    banner_id INT NOT NULL AUTO_INCREMENT
    , image_url VARCHAR(255) NOT NULL
    , click_url VARCHAR(255) NOT NULL
    , expires_on DATE NOT NULL
    , PRIMARY KEY (banner_id)
);
```

If we wanted to return a single random record that is not expired, we could use the code in Listing 8-33 to do so. We've shown two runs of the same SQL to demonstrate the random return values from the Banner table.

Listing 8-33. *Returning a Single Random Banner Record*

```
mysql> SELECT * FROM Banner ORDER BY RAND() LIMIT 1;
+-----------+--------------------+----------------------+------------+
| banner_id | image_url          | click_url            | expires_on |
+-----------+--------------------+----------------------+------------+
|         2 | /images/banner2.jpg | http://www.google.com | 2005-06-01 |
+-----------+--------------------+----------------------+------------+
1 row in set (0.11 sec)

mysql> SELECT * FROM Banner ORDER BY RAND() LIMIT 1;
+-----------+--------------------+--------------------+------------+
| banner_id | image_url          | click_url          | expires_on |
+-----------+--------------------+--------------------+------------+
|         3 | /images/banner3.jpg | http://www.msn.com | 2005-06-01 |
+-----------+--------------------+--------------------+------------+
1 row in set (0.00 sec)
```

This method works just fine for tables that have small row counts. However, the performance of this query begins to degrade rapidly on larger tables. Let's select a random row from our larger RssEntry table and take a look at the results of an EXPLAIN statement, as shown in Listing 8-34.

Listing 8-34. *The Same Query on a Larger Table*

```
mysql> SELECT title FROM RssEntry ORDER BY RAND() LIMIT 1;
+-----------------------------------+
| title                             |
+-----------------------------------+
| HVAC Sheetmetal Worker (Aldie, VA) |
+-----------------------------------+
1 row in set (4.17 sec)

mysql> EXPLAIN SELECT title, url, rssID FROM RssEntry ORDER BY RAND() LIMIT 1 \G
*************************** 1. row ***************************
           id: 1
  select_type: SIMPLE
        table: RssEntry
         type: ALL
possible_keys: NULL
          key: NULL
      key_len: NULL
          ref: NULL
         rows: 157902
        Extra: Using temporary; Using filesort
1 row in set (0.00 sec)
```

As you can see, MySQL loads the data into a temporary table and sorts the data according to the randomizer. Even on a relatively small table (160,000 records), the performance of the query was abysmal.

To remedy the situation, we use a user variable to store the count of records in the table, and then randomize the returned record by retrieving a row ID, as Listing 8-35 shows.

Listing 8-35. *Returning a Single Random Record from a Larger Table*

```
mysql> SELECT @row_id := COUNT(*) FROM RssEntry;
+---------------------+
| @row_id := COUNT(*) |
+---------------------+
|              157902 |
+---------------------+
1 row in set (0.01 sec)

mysql> SELECT @row_id := FLOOR(RAND() * @row_id) + 1;
+----------------------------------------+
| @row_id := FLOOR(RAND() * @row_id) + 1 |
+----------------------------------------+
|                                  59569 |
+----------------------------------------+
1 row in set (0.00 sec)

mysql> SELECT title FROM RssEntry WHERE rowID = @row_id;
+---------------------------------+
| title                           |
+---------------------------------+
| Recruiter (TEKsystems Corporate) |
+---------------------------------+
1 row in set (0.00 sec)
```

This method performs *much* quicker than the previous method, and we suggest using this on any table that has more than a few thousand records.

Calculating Distances with Geographic Coordinate Data

In this section, we're going to have some fun with trigonometry! You'll see how, using some standard trigonometric formulas and your MySQL server, you can accomplish some pretty cool tricks with information freely available to you.

The Geographic Information System (GIS), in the simplest sense, is data that references a geographical location using coordinates. Though GIS data is often referred to as spatial data, we won't be using the spatial extensions of MySQL in our examples. Instead, we'll show you how to use standard MySQL functions and SQL to pull information from a data store of coordinates.

Although MySQL has made significant headway in implementing the OpenGIS standards in the spatial extensions, the MySQL implementation is still in its nascent stages. Currently, its spatial extensions support only Euclidean geometry, which deals with shapes and coordinates in flat measurements. Because the Earth is not a flat, planar surface, distance calculations must take into account the degree to which the lines of longitude converge as they move towards the poles. Therefore, doing calculations for *spherical* distances using Euclidean geometry produces less and less accurate results as you move away from the equator. Additionally, the lack of certain spatial SQL functions (for instance, for calculating the area within three points on a sphere) makes using the extension somewhat cumbersome.

In the examples in this section, we'll be using a data set of U.S. Census Bureau Zip Code Tabulation Areas (ZCTAs),[3] which is available for free from http://www.census.gov/geo/www/gazetteer/places2k.html. We have normalized this data set and removed the information we did not need for the examples.

Tip A wealth of GIS data is available from a number of sources. Check government web sites for this information, or go to http://en.wikipedia.org/wiki/GIS, which lists sites that offer free GIS information. Additionally, private companies offer standardized GIS data for a fee.

Understanding the Distance Calculation Formula

In our examples, we're going to be using a formula for calculating distances called the great circle distance formula. This formula calculates the distance between two coordinates on a spherical surface—in this case, the Earth.[4]

The great circle distance formula states that the distance (d) between two points (x_1, y_1) and (x_2, y_2), where the x values are latitude and the y values are longitude, on a sphere of radius r can be determined by this calculation:

$$d = \text{acos} \, (\, \sin(x_1) * \sin(x_2) + \cos(x_1) * \cos(x_2) * \cos(y_2 - y_1) \,) * r$$

The formula assumes that the latitude and longitude values are in *radians*. However, the latitude and longitude values available in the Census Bureau data were in degrees, not radians. You can see this in the initial design of our ZCTA table, shown in Listing 8-36.

Listing 8-36. *Initial Design for the ZCTA Table*

```
CREATE TABLE ZCTA (
  zcta CHAR(6) NOT NULL
, lat_degrees DECIMAL(9,6) NOT NULL
, long_degrees DECIMAL (9,6) NOT NULL
, PRIMARY KEY(zcta));
```

---

3.   ZCTAs are not *exactly* the same as U.S. Postal Service Zip Codes; however, in our testing, the ZCTAs match very closely to them and can be considered accurate for the purposes of these calculations.

4.   Technically, the Earth is not perfectly spherical, but given its size, the relatively minor imperfections in the Earth's surface will not skew the calculations significantly.

We populated the ZCTA table with 32,038 entries corresponding to the Census Bureau data latitude and longitude coordinates in degrees for each ZCTA. But since we know that we'll need to do at least some calculations using radians, we should save ourselves the repeated calculation of the degrees to radians conversion, and simply add two columns for the radian value of the latitude and longitude. In order to convert degrees to radians, we use the following formula:

radians = degrees * (π/180)

A quick SELECT statement of five random rows along with our formula yields the results shown in Listing 8-37.

Listing 8-37. *Determining the Converted Radian Values*

```
mysql> SELECT
    ->   zcta
    -> , lat_degrees
    -> , lat_degrees * (PI() / 180) AS lat_radians
    -> , long_degrees
    -> , long_degrees * (PI() / 180) AS long_radians
    -> FROM ZCTA
    -> ORDER BY RAND()
    -> LIMIT 5;
+-------+-------------+-------------+--------------+--------------+
| zcta  | lat_degrees | lat_radians | long_degrees | long_radians |
+-------+-------------+-------------+--------------+--------------+
| 61568 | 40.513657   | 0.70709671  | -89.474083   | -1.56161734  |
| 42728 | 37.123196   | 0.64792200  | -85.275620   | -1.48834034  |
| 75060 | 32.802681   | 0.57251479  | -96.954987   | -1.69218375  |
| 37316 | 34.995041   | 0.61077869  | -84.729515   | -1.47880901  |
| 71270 | 32.524761   | 0.56766417  | -92.646965   | -1.61699458  |
+-------+-------------+-------------+--------------+--------------+
5 rows in set (0.13 sec)
```

As you can see, the radian values will fit nicely in a column of DECIMAL(9,8). However, because our degrees columns are a DECIMAL(9,6), we'll experience some truncating of values down to the lowest common denominator when we INSERT the converted radian values. So, we add the columns as DECIMAL(9,6) and INSERT the converted degree values, as shown in Listing 8-38.

Listing 8-38. *Loading the New Radian Values*

```
mysql> ALTER TABLE ZCTA
    -> ADD COLUMN lat_radians DECIMAL(9,6) NOT NULL
    -> , ADD COLUMN long_radians DECIMAL(9,6) NOT NULL;
Query OK, 32038 rows affected (0.24 sec)
Records: 32038  Duplicates: 0  Warnings: 0
```

```
mysql> UPDATE ZCTA
    -> SET lat_radians = lat_degrees * (PI() / 180)
    -> , long_radians = long_degrees * (PI() / 180);
Query OK, 32038 rows affected, 64076 warnings (0.34 sec)
Rows matched: 32038  Changed: 32038  Warnings: 64076

mysql> SELECT * FROM ZCTA LIMIT 5;
+-------+-------------+--------------+-------------+--------------+
| zcta  | lat_degrees | long_degrees | lat_radians | long_radians |
+-------+-------------+--------------+-------------+--------------+
| 35004 | 33.606380   | -86.502495   | 0.586542    | -1.509753    |
| 35005 | 33.592587   | -86.959686   | 0.586301    | -1.517733    |
| 35006 | 33.451714   | -87.239578   | 0.583843    | -1.522618    |
| 35007 | 33.232422   | -86.808716   | 0.580015    | -1.515098    |
| 35010 | 32.903431   | -85.926697   | 0.574273    | -1.499704    |
+-------+-------------+--------------+-------------+--------------+
5 rows in set (0.00 sec)
```

Now that we have all the information stored in our ZCTA table, we'll look at how to do the following common distance-related calculations:

- Calculating the distance between two points

- Determining which zip codes fall within a given radius

Calculating the Distance Between Two Points

Let's say we have a list of store locations, and we want to find the distance between the two stores. Assume that store A is located in New York City, in zip code 10001, and store B is located in the Baltimore, Maryland, metropolitan area, in zip code 21236. We want to know how far the two stores are from each other.

In order to use the great circle distance formula, we first need the coordinates, in radians, of each store's zip code. Listing 8-39 demonstrates using user variables to store the needed radian coordinate values.

Listing 8-39. *Gathering Coordinate Information for Zip Codes*

```
mysql> SELECT
    -> @lat_A := lat_radians
    -> , @long_A := long_radians
    -> FROM ZCTA
    -> WHERE zcta = '10001';
+---------------------+----------------------+
| @lat_A := lat_radians | @long_A := long_radians |
+---------------------+----------------------+
| 0.711235            | -1.291483            |
+---------------------+----------------------+
1 row in set (0.00 sec)
```

```
mysql> SELECT
    -> @lat_B := lat_radians
    -> , @long_B := long_radians
    -> FROM ZCTA
    -> WHERE zcta = '21236';
+--------------------+------------------------+
| @lat_B := lat_radians | @long_B := long_radians |
+--------------------+------------------------+
| 0.687476           | -1.334952              |
+--------------------+------------------------+
1 row in set (0.00 sec)
```

The final piece of data we need to complete the equation is the radius of the Earth in miles. This constant is the number 3,956. To complete the distance request, we simply plug these user variables into the great circle distance formula to obtain the distance between the stores, as Listing 8-40 shows.

Listing 8-40. *Plugging the User Variables into the Distance Formula*

```
mysql> SELECT ACOS(SIN(@lat_A) * SIN(@lat_B)
    -> + COS(@lat_A) * COS(@lat_B)
    -> * COS(@long_B - @long_A)) * 3956 AS distance;
+-----------------+
| distance        |
+-----------------+
| 161.70380719616 |
+-----------------+
1 row in set (0.00 sec)
```

But did we need to use user variables to complete the request? Issuing three statements against the MySQL server seems like a lot of work, don't you agree? Instead, we could have done a cross join of the two entries with the coordinate information and done away with the user variables, as Listing 8-41 demonstrates.

Listing 8-41. *Using a Cross Join Rather Than User Variables*

```
mysql> SELECT ACOS(SIN(x1.lat_radians) * SIN(x2.lat_radians)
    -> + COS(x1.lat_radians) * COS(x2.lat_radians)
    -> * COS(x2.long_radians - x1.long_radians)) * 3956 AS distance
    -> FROM ZCTA x1, ZCTA x2
    -> WHERE x1.zcta = '10001'
    -> AND x2.zcta = '21236';
+-----------------+
| distance        |
+-----------------+
| 161.70380719616 |
+-----------------+
1 row in set (0.04 sec)
```

And voilà! We have an easy method of determining the distance in miles between two coordinates. Now, if you're wondering about the performance of this query, let's take a look at the EXPLAIN, in Listing 8-42.

Listing 8-42. *EXPLAIN of the Distance Query*

```
mysql> EXPLAIN
    -> SELECT ACOS(SIN(x1.lat_radians) * SIN(x2.lat_radians)
    -> + COS(x1.lat_radians) * COS(x2.lat_radians)
    -> * COS(x2.long_radians - x1.long_radians)) * 3956 AS distance
    -> FROM ZCTA x1, ZCTA x2
    -> WHERE x1.zcta = '10001'
    -> AND x2.zcta = '21236' \G
*************************** 1. row ***************************
           id: 1
  select_type: SIMPLE
        table: x1
         type: const
possible_keys: PRIMARY
          key: PRIMARY
      key_len: 6
          ref: const
         rows: 1
        Extra:
*************************** 2. row ***************************
           id: 1
  select_type: SIMPLE
        table: x2
         type: const
possible_keys: PRIMARY
          key: PRIMARY
      key_len: 6
          ref: const
         rows: 1
        Extra:
2 rows in set (0.40 sec)
```

You'll notice that this query will complete almost instantaneously, as the PRIMARY index of the ZCTA table is queried for a const (almost instant lookup), and the formula is then calculated with the values in the two lookups.

■**Tip** As you progress through the following chapters on stored procedures and functions, refer back to this and the next section. Once you learn how to write a stored procedure or function, you might want to consolidate the SQL code in the following code listings into compact procedures. It would be a good exercise for you.

What would happen if we removed the WHERE clauses in Listing 8-42? Without the WHERE clause, we would have a complete Cartesian product of all ZCTA rows crossed against each other. If we eliminated only part of the WHERE clause (say, for the second zip code), we would have the distances from the first zip code to all zip codes in our table, as Listing 8-43 shows.

Listing 8-43. *Distances from a Specific Zip Code to All Known Zip Codes*

```
mysql> SELECT x2.zcta AS Zip
    -> , ACOS(SIN(x1.lat_radians) * SIN(x2.lat_radians)
    -> + COS(x1.lat_radians) * COS(x2.lat_radians)
    -> * COS(x2.long_radians - x1.long_radians)) * 3956 AS "Distance from 10001"
    -> FROM ZCTA x1, ZCTA x2
    -> WHERE x1.zcta = '10001';
... omitted
| 00971 |      1617.0076621906 |
| 00976 |      1617.8210570274 |
| 00979 |      1612.0294495892 |
| 00982 |      1613.8683216421 |
| 00983 |      1613.8354440218 |
| 00985 |      1616.9707648494 |
| 00987 |      1616.8698513986 |
+-------+--------------------+
32038 rows in set (0.24 sec)
```

Removing the WHERE clause from Listing 8-43 entirely would lead to a table containing distances from every zip code to every other zip code. However, we don't recommend doing this, because you'll end up with a table of $32,038^2$, or 1,026,433,444 records!

Determining Zip Codes Within a Given Radius

Suppose that we are building a store locator for our e-commerce web site, and we want to give customers the ability to find a store within a certain number of miles from where they live. Following the logic from our example in Listing 8-43, we should be able to retrieve all zip codes falling within a certain distance from the first zip code by moving the distance calculation from the SELECT statement into the WHERE condition.

Let's assume that we have a customer in Maryland at the zip code 21236. We want to find all ZCTAs that fall within five miles of this zip code. Listing 8-44 shows the adaptation of Listing 8-43, moving the distance formula to the WHERE clause.

Listing 8-44. *Finding ZCTAs Within a Specific Radius*

```
mysql> SELECT
    ->   x2.zcta
    -> FROM ZCTA x1, ZCTA x2
    -> WHERE x1.zcta = '21236'
    -> AND ACOS(SIN(x1.lat_radians) * SIN(x2.lat_radians)
    ->   + COS(x1.lat_radians) * COS(x2.lat_radians)
    ->   * COS(x2.long_radians - x1.long_radians)) * 3956 <= 5;
```

```
+-------+
| zcta  |
+-------+
| 21057 |
| 21128 |
| 21162 |
| 21206 |
| 21214 |
| 21234 |
| 21236 |
| 21237 |
+-------+
8 rows in set (0.13 sec)
```

As you can see, this produced eight zip codes lying within five miles of the customer's home zip code of 21236. Now, what if we wanted to show these zip codes along with the distance from the home zip code, and order the results from nearest to farthest? Listing 8-45 shows an adaptation of our previous query to return this ordered result.

Listing 8-45. *Ordering Results from Nearest to Farthest*

```
mysql> SELECT
    ->    x2.zcta AS Zip
    -> , ACOS(SIN(x1.lat_radians) * SIN(x2.lat_radians)
    -> + COS(x1.lat_radians) * COS(x2.lat_radians)
    -> * COS(x2.long_radians - x1.long_radians)) * 3956 AS "Distance"
    -> FROM ZCTA x1, ZCTA x2
    -> WHERE x1.zcta = '21236'
    -> AND ACOS(SIN(x1.lat_radians) * SIN(x2.lat_radians)
    -> + COS(x1.lat_radians) * COS(x2.lat_radians)
    -> * COS(x2.long_radians - x1.long_radians)) * 3956 <= 5
    -> ORDER BY Distance;
+-------+-----------------+
| Zip   | Distance        |
+-------+-----------------+
| 21236 |               0 |
| 21128 | 2.2986385889254 |
| 21234 | 2.9331244776703 |
| 21162 | 3.9927939103667 |
| 21237 | 4.0496936110152 |
| 21206 | 4.4020674824977 |
| 21057 | 4.5535837161195 |
| 21214 | 4.8578974381478 |
+-------+-----------------+
8 rows in set (0.11 sec)
```

This looks about right. We know that the 21236 zip code distance should indeed be 0, since that is the home zip code. But, back to our original request, we wanted to find the stores located within five miles of the customer's home zip code. All we've done so far is return the zip codes within five miles of the customer's home zip code.

Assume we have a `StoreLocation` table containing around 10,000 stores, structured as shown in Listing 8-46.

Listing 8-46. *StoreLocation Table Definition*

```
CREATE TABLE StoreLocation (
  store_id INT NOT NULL AUTO_INCREMENT
, address VARCHAR(100) NOT NULL
, city VARCHAR(35) NOT NULL
, state CHAR(2) NOT NULL
, zip VARCHAR(6) NOT NULL
, PRIMARY KEY (store_id)
, KEY (zip));
```

We have a number of ways in which we can use the SQL from Listing 8-44 in order to retrieve records from our `StoreLocation` table that match the zip codes within our search radius. In our first attempt, we'll use a non-correlated subquery on the `StoreLocation.zip` field to match records returned in our resultset from Listing 8-44. In Listing 8-47, we've italicized the duplicated code from Listing 8-44, and bolded the new code using a non-correlated subquery to find `StoreLocation` records.

Listing 8-47. *Non-Correlated Subquery to Find StoreLocation Records Within Zip Radius*

```
mysql> SELECT
    -> LEFT(address, 30) as address
    -> , city
    -> , state
    -> , zip
    -> FROM StoreLocation
    -> WHERE zip IN (
    -> SELECT x2.zcta
    -> FROM ZCTA x1, ZCTA x2
    -> WHERE x1.zcta = '21236'
    -> AND ACOS(SIN(x1.lat_radians) * SIN(x2.lat_radians)
    -> + COS(x1.lat_radians) * COS(x2.lat_radians)
    -> * COS(x2.long_radians - x1.long_radians)) * 3956 <= 5
    -> );
+--------------------------------+-------------+-------+-------+
| address                        | city        | state | zip   |
+--------------------------------+-------------+-------+-------+
| WHITE MARSH MALL  8200 PERRY H | BALTIMORE   | MD    | 21236 |
| 8200 PERRY HALL BOULEVARD  WHI | WHITE MARSH | MD    | 21236 |
| 8641 PHILADELPIA ROAD          | BALTIMORE   | MD    | 21237 |
| 2401 CLEANLEIGH DRIVE          | PARKVILLE   | MD    | 21234 |
```

```
| 1971 EAST JOPPA ROAD          | TOWSON      | MD    | 21234 |
| 4921 CAMPBELL ROAD            | WHITE MARSH | MD    | 21162 |
| 7400 EAST BELAIR ROAD         | BALTIMORE   | MD    | 21236 |
| 5246 HARFORD ROAD             | HAMILTON    | MD    | 21214 |
| 9103 BELAIR ROAD              | PERRY HALL  | MD    | 21236 |
+-------------------------------+-------------+-------+-------+
9 rows in set (0.17 sec)
```

The SQL is not really all that complicated when you break the request into its requisite parts. We've added a very simple IN expression to fulfill the non-correlated subquery matching zip codes in the StoreLocation table to zip codes returned from the matched records in the ZCTA table x2. Let's take a look at the EXPLAIN to verify the optimizer is working as expected. Listing 8-48 shows the output.

Listing 8-48. *EXPLAIN Output from Listing 8-47*

```
mysql> EXPLAIN
    -> SELECT
    ->  LEFT(address, 30) as address
    -> , city
    -> , state
    -> , zip
    -> FROM StoreLocation
    -> WHERE zip IN (
    ->  SELECT x2.zcta
    ->  FROM ZCTA x1, ZCTA x2
    ->  WHERE x1.zcta = '21236'
    ->  AND ACOS(SIN(x1.lat_radians) * SIN(x2.lat_radians))
    ->  + COS(x1.lat_radians) * COS(x2.lat_radians)
    ->  * COS(x2.long_radians - x1.long_radians)) * 3956 <= 5
    -> ) \G
*************************** 1. row ***************************
           id: 1
  select_type: PRIMARY
        table: StoreLocation
         type: ALL
possible_keys: NULL
          key: NULL
      key_len: NULL
          ref: NULL
         rows: 9640
        Extra: Using where
*************************** 2. row ***************************
           id: 2
  select_type: DEPENDENT SUBQUERY
        table: x1
         type: const
possible_keys: PRIMARY
```

```
            key: PRIMARY
        key_len: 6
            ref: const
           rows: 1
          Extra:
*********************** 3. row **************************
             id: 2
    select_type: DEPENDENT SUBQUERY
          table: x2
           type: eq_ref
  possible_keys: PRIMARY
            key: PRIMARY
        key_len: 6
            ref: func
           rows: 1
          Extra: Using where
3 rows in set (0.00 sec)
```

From the EXPLAIN output, we see that our index on StoreLocation.zip is not being used. In fact, MySQL doesn't even consider it an option, as the zip key isn't listed in possible_keys. Instead, MySQL has chosen to do a full table scan (ALL). For each record in the StoreLocation result, MySQL is using a WHERE expression to look for any returned values in the subquery that match the zip field value in StoreLocation. Since the query apparently isn't using an index, perhaps there is a way in which we could rewrite the query so that an index is used.

Let's try rewriting the non-correlated subquery as a single derived table joined on the zip column of StoreLocation. Listing 8-49 shows our revised SQL. We've bolded the changes.

Listing 8-49. *Revised Query to Use a Single Derived Table*

```
mysql> SELECT
    ->   LEFT(address, 30) as address
    -> , city
    -> , state
    -> , zip
    -> FROM StoreLocation sl
    -> INNER JOIN (
    ->   SELECT x2.zcta
    ->   FROM ZCTA x1, ZCTA x2
    ->   WHERE x1.zcta = '21236'
    ->   AND ACOS(SIN(x1.lat_radians) * SIN(x2.lat_radians)
    ->   + COS(x1.lat_radians) * COS(x2.lat_radians)
    ->   * COS(x2.long_radians - x1.long_radians)) * 3956 <= 5
    -> ) AS zips
    -> ON sl.zip = zips.zcta;
+--------------------------------+--------------+-------+-------+
| address                        | city         | state | zip   |
+--------------------------------+--------------+-------+-------+
| 4921 CAMPBELL ROAD             | WHITE MARSH  | MD    | 21162 |
```

```
| 5246 HARFORD ROAD              | HAMILTON     | MD    | 21214 |
| 2401 CLEANLEIGH DRIVE          | PARKVILLE    | MD    | 21234 |
| 1971 EAST JOPPA ROAD           | TOWSON       | MD    | 21234 |
| WHITE MARSH MALL  8200 PERRY H | BALTIMORE    | MD    | 21236 |
| 8200 PERRY HALL BOULEVARD  WHI | WHITE MARSH  | MD    | 21236 |
| 7400 EAST BELAIR ROAD          | BALTIMORE    | MD    | 21236 |
| 9103 BELAIR ROAD               | PERRY HALL   | MD    | 21236 |
| 8641 PHILADELPIA ROAD          | BALTIMORE    | MD    | 21237 |
+-------------------------------+-------------+-------+-------+
9 rows in set (0.14 sec)
```

The results are almost identical to the first query, except that the order of the results has now been changed to use the zip field value instead of the store_id field. Why is this? It has to do with the order in which MySQL chooses to join the various resultsets together. In Listing 8-48, you saw that MySQL chose to first do a table scan on the StoreLocation data set. It then found matching rows in the ZCTA subquery. Since the natural order of the StoreLocation data is the store_id value, that is what the eventual order of the results became. In Listing 8-49, MySQL has chosen to perform a different join strategy, as evidenced by Listing 8-50.

Listing 8-50. *EXPLAIN Results from Listing 8-49*

```
mysql> EXPLAIN
    -> SELECT
    ->  LEFT(address, 30) as address
    -> , city
    -> , state
    -> , zip
    -> FROM StoreLocation sl
    -> INNER JOIN (
    ->  SELECT x2.zcta
    ->  FROM ZCTA x1, ZCTA x2
    ->  WHERE x1.zcta = '21236'
    ->  AND ACOS(SIN(x1.lat_radians) * SIN(x2.lat_radians)
    ->  + COS(x1.lat_radians) * COS(x2.lat_radians)
    ->  * COS(x2.long_radians - x1.long_radians)) * 3956 <= 5
    -> ) AS zips
    -> ON sl.zip = zips.zcta \G
*************************** 1. row ***************************
           id: 1
  select_type: PRIMARY
        table: <derived2>
         type: ALL
possible_keys: NULL
          key: NULL
      key_len: NULL
          ref: NULL
         rows: 8
        Extra:
```

```
*************************** 2. row ***************************
           id: 1
  select_type: PRIMARY
        table: sl
         type: ref
possible_keys: zip
          key: zip
      key_len: 8
          ref: zips.zcta
         rows: 2
        Extra:
*************************** 3. row ***************************
           id: 2
  select_type: DERIVED
        table: x1
         type: const
possible_keys: PRIMARY
          key: PRIMARY
      key_len: 6
          ref:
         rows: 1
        Extra:
*************************** 4. row ***************************
           id: 2
  select_type: DERIVED
        table: x2
         type: ALL
possible_keys: NULL
          key: NULL
      key_len: NULL
          ref: NULL
         rows: 32038
        Extra: Using where
4 rows in set (0.12 sec)
```

As you can see, MySQL first executes the derived table SELECT statement, and then uses the index on StoreLocation.zip to find the rows in StoreLocation that have a matching zip code. MySQL uses the natural order of the StoreLocation.zip index in the output of the query.

But there is still one nagging performance consideration that we might address in this query. Our derived table query execution plan has a table scan on the ZCTA x2 table. The previous subquery (Listing 8-47) had an eq_ref execution optimization performed from the main x1 ZCTA table (having 1 const row), as you saw in Listing 8-48. Is it possible to get the best of both worlds? Granted, 0.14 second isn't a long execution time for such an in-depth SQL statement, but this query might be run quite frequently. Using the knowledge you've gained so far, do you think there is a way to perform this query that will use the eq_ref optimization from the subquery, but have a chance to use the index on StoreLocation.zip?

Give yourself two points if you thought, "I can do this without a subquery *or* a derived table!" Indeed, you can. Listing 8-51 shows how we can simply join the x2 ZCTA subset to the StoreLocation table itself, along the StoreLocation.zip index.

Listing 8-51. *Removing the Derived Table in Favor of a Standard Inner Join*

```
mysql> SELECT
    -> LEFT(address, 30) as address
    -> , city
    -> , state
    -> , zip
    -> FROM ZCTA x1, ZCTA x2
    -> INNER JOIN StoreLocation sl
    ->  ON x2.zcta = sl.zip
    -> WHERE x1.zcta = '21236'
    -> AND ACOS(SIN(x1.lat_radians) * SIN(x2.lat_radians)
    -> + COS(x1.lat_radians) * COS(x2.lat_radians)
    -> * COS(x2.long_radians - x1.long_radians)) * 3956 <= 5;
+--------------------------------+--------------+-------+-------+
| address                        | city         | state | zip   |
+--------------------------------+--------------+-------+-------+
| WHITE MARSH MALL   8200 PERRY H | BALTIMORE    | MD    | 21236 |
| 8200 PERRY HALL BOULEVARD   WHI | WHITE MARSH  | MD    | 21236 |
| 8641 PHILADELPIA ROAD          | BALTIMORE    | MD    | 21237 |
| 2401 CLEANLEIGH DRIVE          | PARKVILLE    | MD    | 21234 |
| 1971 EAST JOPPA ROAD           | TOWSON       | MD    | 21234 |
| 4921 CAMPBELL ROAD             | WHITE MARSH  | MD    | 21162 |
| 7400 EAST BELAIR ROAD          | BALTIMORE    | MD    | 21236 |
| 5246 HARFORD ROAD              | HAMILTON     | MD    | 21214 |
| 9103 BELAIR ROAD               | PERRY HALL   | MD    | 21236 |
+--------------------------------+--------------+-------+-------+
9 rows in set (0.12 sec)
```

Well, this variation was marginally faster. Let's check out the EXPLAIN to see if what we expected to happen actually did. Listing 8-52 shows the results.

Listing 8-52. *EXPLAIN Output from Listing 8-51*

```
mysql> EXPLAIN
    -> SELECT
    -> LEFT(address, 30) as address
    -> , city
    -> , state
    -> , zip
    -> FROM ZCTA x1, ZCTA x2
    -> INNER JOIN StoreLocation sl
    ->  ON x2.zcta = sl.zip
    -> WHERE x1.zcta = '21236'
```

```
    -> AND ACOS(SIN(x1.lat_radians) * SIN(x2.lat_radians)
    -> + COS(x1.lat_radians) * COS(x2.lat_radians)
    -> * COS(x2.long_radians - x1.long_radians)) * 3956 <= 5 \G
*************************** 1. row ***************************
           id: 1
  select_type: SIMPLE
        table: x1
         type: const
possible_keys: PRIMARY
          key: PRIMARY
      key_len: 6
          ref: const
         rows: 1
        Extra:
*************************** 2. row ***************************
           id: 1
  select_type: SIMPLE
        table: sl
         type: ALL
possible_keys: zip
          key: NULL
      key_len: NULL
          ref: NULL
         rows: 9640
        Extra:
*************************** 3. row ***************************
           id: 1
  select_type: SIMPLE
        table: x2
         type: eq_ref
possible_keys: PRIMARY
          key: PRIMARY
      key_len: 6
          ref: jobs.sl.zip
         rows: 1
        Extra: Using where
3 rows in set (0.00 sec)
```

Did it work? Well, almost. This time, MySQL at least gave itself the *option* of using the index on StoreLocation.zip, but in the end, decided it was faster to simply use a table scan of the StoreLocation data.

■**Tip** Take the time to consider if there is a better or faster way of doing things. Rewrite your SQL queries to try other approaches, and do test iterations to see the results.

Finally, let's wrap up our examination of distance calculations by combining two queries from this section to output the stores located within five miles of the customer's home zip code, along with the distance to each store. Listing 8-53 shows this final report query.

Listing 8-53. *Combining Two Queries for a Distance to Store Report*

```
mysql> SELECT
    ->    LEFT(address, 30) AS address
    -> , city
    -> , state
    -> , zip
    -> , ROUND(ACOS(SIN(x1.lat_radians) * SIN(x2.lat_radians)
    -> + COS(x1.lat_radians) * COS(x2.lat_radians)
    -> * COS(x2.long_radians - x1.long_radians)) * 3956, 2) AS "Distance"
    -> FROM ZCTA x1, ZCTA x2
    ->   INNER JOIN StoreLocation sl
    ->    ON x2.zcta = sl.zip
    -> WHERE x1.zcta = '21236'
    -> AND ACOS(SIN(x1.lat_radians) * SIN(x2.lat_radians)
    -> + COS(x1.lat_radians) * COS(x2.lat_radians)
    -> * COS(x2.long_radians - x1.long_radians)) * 3956 <= 5
    -> ORDER BY Distance;
+--------------------------------+-------------+-------+-------+----------+
| address                        | city        | state | zip   | Distance |
+--------------------------------+-------------+-------+-------+----------+
| WHITE MARSH MALL   8200 PERRY H | BALTIMORE   | MD    | 21236 |     0.00 |
| 7400 EAST BELAIR ROAD          | BALTIMORE   | MD    | 21236 |     0.00 |
| 8200 PERRY HALL BOULEVARD   WHI | WHITE MARSH | MD    | 21236 |     0.00 |
| 9103 BELAIR ROAD               | PERRY HALL  | MD    | 21236 |     0.00 |
| 2401 CLEANLEIGH DRIVE          | PARKVILLE   | MD    | 21234 |     2.93 |
| 1971 EAST JOPPA ROAD           | TOWSON      | MD    | 21234 |     2.93 |
| 4921 CAMPBELL ROAD             | WHITE MARSH | MD    | 21162 |     3.99 |
| 8641 PHILADELPIA ROAD          | BALTIMORE   | MD    | 21237 |     4.05 |
| 5246 HARFORD ROAD              | HAMILTON    | MD    | 21214 |     4.86 |
+--------------------------------+-------------+-------+-------+----------+
9 rows in set (0.14 sec)
```

■Note Remember that the quality of the report is only as accurate as the data from which it is derived. The more accurate your GIS data, the more accurate your distance calculations will be. For instance, if you have GIS data specific not to a zip code, but to the latitude and longitude of your store locations, you could generate even more accurate calculations.

Generating Running Sums and Averages

Creating running sums and averages in reports is a common requirement. Running sums and averages simply display totals or averages for certain fields in the resultset on a line-by-line basis, with each line representing the "running," or up-to-this-point, accumulation or average of data.

To generate running sums in a report, you use a technique where a resultset is joined against itself—a self join—using the greater-than or equal-to operator (>=). When doing this type of join, the first instance of the resultset (call it set A) is referenced against itself to provide a sum of all rows in a second instance of the resultset (call it set B) that are greater than or equal to the row in the set A.

Recall from our earlier coverage of the nested set model for tree structures that we used the BETWEEN predicate to gather information about the nodes under or above a specific node in the tree. In the case of running sums and averages, you employ a similar concept, but using the >= instead of the BETWEEN operator.

Imagine we want to fulfill the following request from our sales manager regarding our online toy store sales: "Provide a report of all products along with total sales for each product. Provide a column with a running sum of total sales."

You already know how to complete the request without the running sum part, so let's start there. Listing 8-54 shows the piece of the request you already know how to fulfill.

Listing 8-54. *Retrieving Total Sales for Each Product*

```
mysql> SELECT p.name, SUM(coi.quantity * coi.price) AS total_sales
    -> FROM Product p
    ->  INNER JOIN CustomerOrderItem coi
    ->   ON p.product_id = coi.product_id
    -> GROUP BY p.name;
+--------------------------+-------------+
| name                     | total_sales |
+--------------------------+-------------+
| Action Figure - Football |       11.95 |
| Action Figure - Gladiator |      15.95 |
| Action Figure - Tennis   |       12.95 |
| Doll                     |      119.98 |
| Soccer Ball              |       23.70 |
| Tennis Balls             |      270.75 |
| Tennis Racket            |      104.75 |
| Video Game - Football    |       46.99 |
+--------------------------+-------------+
8 rows in set (1.13 sec)
```

In order to produce the running sums, we must join the resultset from Listing 8-54 to itself using a self join. But instead of using the standard equal-to operator, we use the greater-than or equal-to operator, so that the right side of the join contains all rows up to or equal to the comparison row on the left side of the join. Listing 8-55 shows how we accomplish this.

Listing 8-55. *Creating a Running (Cumulative) Sum Column*

```
mysql> SELECT
    ->   totals1.name AS Product
    ->  , totals1.total_sales AS "Product Sales"
    ->  , SUM(totals2.total_sales) AS "Cumulative Sales"
    -> FROM (
    ->   SELECT
    ->    p.name
    ->   , SUM(coi.quantity * coi.price) AS total_sales
    ->   FROM Product p
    ->     INNER JOIN CustomerOrderItem coi
    ->      ON p.product_id = coi.product_id
    ->   GROUP BY p.name
    ->  ) AS totals1
    -> INNER JOIN (
    ->   SELECT
    ->    p.name
    ->   , SUM(coi.quantity * coi.price) AS total_sales
    ->   FROM Product p
    ->     INNER JOIN CustomerOrderItem coi
    ->      ON p.product_id = coi.product_id
    ->   GROUP BY p.name
    ->  ) AS totals2
    ->    ON totals1.name >= totals2.name
    -> GROUP BY totals1.name;
+---------------------------+---------------+------------------+
| Product                   | Product Sales | Cumulative Sales |
+---------------------------+---------------+------------------+
| Action Figure - Football  |         11.95 |            11.95 |
| Action Figure - Gladiator |         15.95 |            27.90 |
| Action Figure - Tennis    |         12.95 |            40.85 |
| Doll                      |        119.98 |           160.83 |
| Soccer Ball               |         23.70 |           184.53 |
| Tennis Balls              |        270.75 |           455.28 |
| Tennis Racket             |        104.75 |           560.03 |
| Video Game - Football     |         46.99 |           607.02 |
+---------------------------+---------------+------------------+
8 rows in set (0.00 sec)
```

We've used two derived tables of the resultset produced by Listing 8-54, and then used the greater-than or equal-to predicate to join the two resultsets together. In the outermost SELECT statement, notice that the Product Sales column comes straight from the first derived table, while we used the matching rows from the joined table in order to produce the running sum column.

But, do we need to join on the Product Name column? Actually, no. We join on the result-set column we wish to order the results by. So, if we wanted to order the report by, for instance, Product Sales, we would order the derived tables accordingly and change the ON expression to use this field, as demonstrated in Listing 8-56. We've added a column for producing running average columns, to show you that the same technique applies for generating averages.

Listing 8-56. *Changing the Report Order and Generating Running Averages*

```
mysql> SELECT
    -> totals1.name AS Product
    -> , totals1.total_sales AS "Product Sales"
    -> , SUM(totals2.total_sales) AS "Cumulative Sales"
    -> , ROUND(AVG(totals2.total_sales), 2) AS "Running Avg"
    -> FROM (
    -> SELECT
    -> p.name
    -> , SUM(coi.quantity * coi.price) AS total_sales
    -> FROM Product p
    ->  INNER JOIN CustomerOrderItem coi
    ->   ON p.product_id = coi.product_id
    -> GROUP BY p.name
    -> ORDER BY total_sales
    -> ) AS totals1
    -> INNER JOIN (
    -> SELECT
    -> p.name
    -> , SUM(coi.quantity * coi.price) AS total_sales
    -> FROM Product p
    ->  INNER JOIN CustomerOrderItem coi
    ->   ON p.product_id = coi.product_id
    -> GROUP BY p.name
    -> ORDER BY total_sales
    -> ) AS totals2
    ->   ON totals1.total_sales >= totals2.total_sales
    -> GROUP BY totals1.name
    -> ORDER BY totals1.total_sales;
+----------------------------+---------------+------------------+-------------+
| Product                    | Product Sales | Cumulative Sales | Running Avg |
+----------------------------+---------------+------------------+-------------+
| Action Figure - Football   |         11.95 |            11.95 |       11.95 |
| Action Figure - Tennis     |         12.95 |            24.90 |       12.45 |
| Action Figure - Gladiator  |         15.95 |            40.85 |       13.62 |
| Soccer Ball                |         23.70 |            64.55 |       16.14 |
| Video Game - Football      |         46.99 |           111.54 |       22.31 |
| Tennis Racket              |        104.75 |           216.29 |       36.05 |
| Doll                       |        119.98 |           336.27 |       48.04 |
| Tennis Balls               |        270.75 |           607.02 |       75.88 |
+----------------------------+---------------+------------------+-------------+
8 rows in set (0.09 sec)
```

Summary

In this chapter, we've expounded on the basic principles you learned in Chapter 7, working through a number of common scenarios. You may not have realized it, but in the examples in this chapter, we used every join style covered in Chapter 7. Additionally, we practiced the art of using derived tables and subqueries to produce *exactly* the results you need from your schemata. You've sharpened your SQL skills considerably.

We started with a simple walk-through of how to rewrite OR expressions using UNION queries in MySQL servers prior to 5.0. From there, we headed into the maintenance aspect of removing duplicate entries and orphaned records from your databases.

Then the SQL started to fly as we examined the nested set model for tree structures in SQL. You learned some nifty techniques for managing the metadata necessary to keep the model accurate, and saw how the nested set model allows for aggregated reporting across the tree without the need for recursion.

After that, we looked at a couple methods for retrieving randomized rows from a resultset, and you saw the importance of always checking to see if one method of doing a task in SQL will perform on different table sizes.

Next, we put on our math hats and generated a system capable of returning distance calculations from GIS coordinates. You saw how using various derived table and subquery techniques can alter the execution plan of reports. Finally, we went over how to create running sums and averages to round out our coverage of SQL scenarios.

In the next chapters, you're going to learn about the brand-new features available to you in MySQL 5.0: stored procedures, stored functions, views, cursors, and triggers.

CHAPTER 9

■■■

Stored Procedures

The wait is finally over. MySQL has long been criticized for its lack of stored procedures by application developers, database administrators, business analysts, and rival databases. With the announcement of version 5.0 came the news that stored procedures are now an option for users of MySQL. This new functionality has generated some excitement in the MySQL community, as well as in the outlying database market. MySQL users who have wanted the ability to use stored procedures but are living with MySQL for other reasons are rejoicing. Likewise, folks who are using other databases because of a need for stored procedures are reevaluating MySQL as a possible alternative to their current database choice.

In this chapter, we'll cover the following topics related to stored procedures:

- The advantages and disadvantages of using stored procedures

- MySQL's implementation of stored procedures

- How to create stored procedures

- How to view, alter, remove, and edit stored procedures

- How to call stored procedures

- Stored procedure permissions

Stored Procedure Considerations

A *stored procedure* is a collection of SQL statements used together. Stored procedures allow you to go beyond the typical single-statement database query used to retrieve a set of records or update a row. Stored procedure syntax supports variables, conditions, flow controls, and cursors, so a stored procedure can perform complex processing within the database between the database call and the resulting return. Stored procedures can consist of as little as one statement, or they may contain hundreds or even thousands of lines.[1]

---

1. MySQL stores the procedure body in a BLOB column, which is limited to storing 64KB of data. If you average 60 characters per line, you can store around 1,000 lines in a single procedure.

■**Note** As of the writing of this chapter, MySQL has released version 5.0.6, which is labeled a beta release. While the stored procedure functionality in the database is stable enough to test and document, production users are encouraged to wait until a release of the 5.0.*x* branch that is labeled production. With MySQL, change is constant. Although the procedure syntax is fairly complete, we encourage you to refer to the MySQL documentation on stored procedures at `http://dev.mysql.com/doc/mysql/en/stored-procedures.html` for any updates.

With the ability to store complex processing inside the database, application developers and database administrators find that, in certain cases, they prefer to have some of the processing logic performed in the database before the data is returned to the client or application. Putting logic into the database is a heavily debated topic, and should not be done without first considering the advantages and disadvantages of doing so.

The Debate Over Using Stored Procedures

As with many technologies that allow multiple approaches to solving a business problem, there is passionate debate as to whether using stored procedures is a good thing, and if so, how they should be used. Here, we'll look at the arguments for and against using stored procedures, so you can decide if stored procedures make sense for your application. As with all technology, it's important to consider if that technology best fills your need before rushing into deployment.

Stored Procedure Advantages

Since this chapter is about how to use stored procedures, let's begin with a review of some of the arguments for using them:

- Stored procedures allow you to combine multiple queries into a single trip to the database. This means you can reduce traffic between the client and the database by not needing to make multiple requests for multiple actions. Depending on your application, saving network traffic can be significant enough to offset any counter argument.

- If you are grabbing many rows from the database and using business logic to limit the results, a stored procedure may be able to encapsulate that logic and reduce the amount of data returned to the client or application, as well as reduce the processing needed in the application before presenting the results.

- Stored procedures provide a clean interface to the data. Rather than needing to build a query in your code, you can reduce your SQL to a single, simple call statement.

- In some cases, having your SQL stored in the database makes managing queries much easier, especially in distributed or compiled systems, where deploying new code with embedded queries is very difficult.

- Keeping queries in the database allows the database administrator control over the creation and optimization of queries, tables, and indexes used in returning data to the calling client. The database administrator has a deeper understanding of the data model, relationships, and performance of the database. SQL statements coming from the database administrator will be optimized with the data model in mind, and perhaps will spur tweaks in the database configuration and indexes.

- Stored procedures abstract the structure of the data from the application, which can help when changes are needed in the data model by having a central location for all query changes. In programming, this is referred to as *class* or *package encapsulation*. The stored procedures represent a black box, where developers don't need to be familiar with the internals of the procedure. As long as developers know how to call the procedure and how the results will come back, they can be ignorant about the procedure details.

- Where security is important, stored procedures allow controlled access to viewing and changing data. Callers do not need to have permission on specific tables; if their query can be encapsulated in a stored procedure, they need only the ability to access that procedure. Chapter 15 has more details about creating and managing permissions, and database security is covered in Chapter 16.

- Using stored procedures means you are passing a single parameter or a small list of parameters to the database. Compared with building SQL statements in your application to pass to the database, the parameterized call is more secure. If you're building SQL on the fly in your code, you might be more open to attacks like SQL injection, where attackers attempt to spoof your program and alter your dynamically built query to expose, change, or destroy your data.

- Some databases optimize the statements of your stored procedure, parsing and organizing the pieces of the procedure when it is created.[2] This reduces the amount of work necessary when the procedure is called, meaning that queries and operations in the procedure are faster than if they were sent from the client to parse and process at run time.

Stored Procedure Disadvantages

Before you decide that you should start moving all your scripts into the database, consider some of the arguments against using stored procedures:

- Stored procedures put more load on the database server, for both processors and memory. Rather than being focused on the business of storing and retrieving data, you may be asking the database to perform any number of logical operations, which detract from the pure focus on representing data and data relationships.

- Working with stored procedures isn't as simple as editing a piece of code. You need to pull it out of the database, work on it, and then reinsert it into the database.

- Although using stored procedures can simplify the code, passing parameters can become unwieldy. While it's true that in any language, passing a lot of parameters gets ugly, in many languages, you can pass references to data objects that simplify the interface.

---

2. As it happens, MySQL does not do this. However, queries within the procedure can benefit from the query cache, which is discussed in Chapter 4.

- Needing to define an interface between the database and application adds an extra layer of complexity and coordination. Rather than writing queries to grab the data needed for a particular view, the developer must rely on the database administrator to provide a procedure to get that data. Coordinating updates in the application with this kind of reliance on an interface to the data, and on the database administrator, can add unnecessary complexity.

- In many cases, sticking logic in stored procedures eliminates potential cross-vendor database compatibility. Unless the syntax of your stored procedures is recognized by another vendor's database, the stored procedures will work only in your database.

- Using stored procedures in a database limits the processing to the databases on the physical server. Sometimes, data needed for decisions is pulled from multiple servers or locations—perhaps you need some pieces from databases on two different machines, or you want to use data from a database in conjunction with data from a web service. If you are pulling data from multiple machines or other services, you will be limited in how much of your logic can be moved into a stored procedure. Moving pieces of your system into procedures while leaving some in the application may add more confusion than it's worth.

- Debugging stored procedures can be a pain. Development and debugging tools typically work much better for programming languages than they do for database procedures.

- Specific to MySQL, functionality for stored procedures is new and not yet production-ready.

Having considered some of the major arguments against using stored procedures, we suggest that you consider a few other things as a part of your decision on if and how stored procedures fit into your application needs.

Other Considerations in Using Stored Procedures

Before we move into the implementation details for stored procedures in MySQL, you should be thinking about how stored procedures will fit into your application design. As you look at the possibilities for moving pieces of your application into the database, consider how you will draw lines between layers in your application. Perhaps you want just a few procedures to run some complex data manipulation, or maybe you are thinking about creating a complete data abstraction layer.

If you plan on creating more than one or two procedures, you should also be thinking about how you'll break the functionality of your procedures into small, reusable chunks. You may also consider creating a style guide and best-practices document to unify the interfaces and internals of your procedures.

Stored Procedures in MySQL

Database vendors use a variety of programming languages and syntax for building and managing stored procedures. Many of these databases share a set of core SQL commands, but most of them have added extensions to facilitate the level of complexity that can be attained within the stored procedure. Oracle procedures are written in PL/SQL. Microsoft SQL Server 2000 procedures are written in Transact-SQL (T-SQL). To write procedures for PostgreSQL, you use PL/psSQL. Each implementation includes some common commands, and then an extended syntax for accomplishing more advanced logic.

MySQL developers have taken the expected approach in their implementation of stored procedures. A database focused on simplicity and maximum performance would likely implement a simple set of features that supply the most amount of control to users wanting to move logic into the database. MySQL has done this by implementing the SQL:2003 standard for stored procedures and has added minimal MySQL-specific syntax. In the cases where MySQL provides an extended use of a statement, the MySQL documentation (and this book) notes the extension to the standard.

■**Note** The official standard for stored procedures is ISO/IEC 9075-*x*.2003, where *x* is a range of numbers between 1 and 14 that indicate many different parts of the standard. For short, the standard is often referred to as SQL:2003, SQL-2003, or SQL 2003. We refer to the standard a SQL:2003, since the official specification uses the : as a separator, and MySQL documentation uses this format. The standard can be found on the ISO web site (`http://www.iso.org`) by doing a search for 9075. The standard is available for a fee.

The SQL:2003 standard provides a basic set of commands for building multiple-statement interactions with the database. SQL:2003 was published in 2003 as the replacement for the previous SQL standard, SQL:1999. These standards include specifications for syntax and behavior for SQL commands that are used to build, create, and maintain stored procedures. MySQL's choice to stick to the SQL:2003 standard means that stored procedures created in MySQL can be seamlessly used in other databases that support this standard. Currently, IBM's DB2 and Oracle Database 10g are compliant with SQL:2003. The success of moving a stored procedure from Oracle or DB2 into MySQL will depend on whether any of the vendor extensions have been used. Even if the vendor supports SQL:2003, if a stored procedure uses vendor-specific syntax, MySQL will fail on an unrecognized command when attempting to create the procedure.

The MySQL implementation provides a wide array of controls for processing data and logic in the database. It doesn't have the extended syntax bells and whistles of other database systems, but it does provide a rich set of basic commands that can create some incredibly powerful procedures.

Stored procedures are processed by the MySQL server, and they are independent of the storage engine used to store your data. If you use a feature of a particular storage engine in your stored procedure statement, you will need to continue to use that table type to use the stored procedure. MySQL stores the data for stored procedures in the proc table in the mysql database. Even though procedures are all stored in one place, they are created and called by either using the current database or by prepending a database name onto the various procedure statements.

In the rest of this chapter, we'll cover how to create, manage, and call MySQL stored procedures.

Building Stored Procedures

SQL:2003 sets forth a set of commands to create procedures; declare variables, handlers, and conditions; and set up cursors and constructs for flow control.

In its simplest form, you can create a stored procedure with a CREATE statement, procedure name, and a single SQL statement. Listing 9-1 shows just how simple this can be.

Listing 9-1. *Creating a Single-Statement Procedure*

```
mysql> create procedure get_customers ()
SELECT customer_id,name FROM customer;
```

■**Caution** The stored procedure shown in Listing 9-1 has a SELECT statement as the last thing processed in the procedure, which returns a resultset to the caller. This is really convenient, but it is a MySQL extension to the SQL:2003 standard. The standard says you must put results into a variable or use a cursor to process a set of results.

However frivolous Listing 9-1 may appear, it contains the required parts: a CREATE statement with a procedure name and a SQL statement. Calling the stored procedure to get the results is simple, as demonstrated in Listing 9-2.

Listing 9-2. *Calling a Single-Statement Procedure*

```
mysql> call get_customers ();
+-------------+---------+
| customer_id | name    |
+-------------+---------+
|           1 | Mike    |
|           2 | Jay     |
|           3 | Johanna |
|           4 | Michael |
|           5 | Heidi   |
|           6 | Ezra    |
+-------------+---------+
6 rows in set (0.00 sec)
```

Other than abstracting the syntax of the query from the caller, this example doesn't really justify creating a procedure. The same result is just as easily available with a single query from your application.

As a more realistic example, let's consider the scenario of merging duplicate accounts in your online ordering system. Your online store allows a user to create an account, with a user-defined login and password, to use for placing orders. Suppose user Mike places an order or two, and then doesn't visit your site for a while. Then he returns and signs up again, inadvertently creating a second account. He places a few more orders. At some point, he realizes that he has two accounts and puts in a request to have the old account removed. He says that he would prefer to keep all the old orders on the newer account.

This means that in your database, you'll need to find all the information associated with the old account, move it into the new account, and delete the old account. The new account record probably has core pieces of information like name, address, and phone, which won't need to change. The data to be moved may include address book and payment information, as well as Mike's orders. Anywhere in your system where a table has a relationship with your customer, you'll need to make a change. Of course, you should check for the existence of the accounts, and the employee who makes that change may want to have a report of how many records were changed.

Creating the series of statements to process this data merge in your code is possible, but using a procedure to handle it would simplify your application. Listing 9-3 demonstrates how a stored procedure might solve the requirements of this merge account request.

Listing 9-3. *Creating a Multistatement Stored Procedure*

```
DELIMITER //
CREATE PROCEDURE merge_customers
(IN old_id INT, IN new_id INT, OUT error VARCHAR(100))
SQL SECURITY DEFINER
COMMENT 'merge customer accounts'
BEGIN
        DECLARE old_count INT DEFAULT 0;
        DECLARE new_count INT DEFAULT 0;
        DECLARE addresses_changed INT DEFAULT 0;
        DECLARE payments_changed INT DEFAULT 0;
        DECLARE orders_changed INT DEFAULT 0;

        ## check to make sure the old_id and new_id exists
        SELECT count(*) INTO old_count FROM customer WHERE customer_id = old_id;
        SELECT count(*) INTO new_count FROM customer WHERE customer_id = new_id;
        IF !old_count THEN
            SET error = 'old id does not exist';
        ELSEIF !new_count THEN
            SET error = 'new id does not exist';
        ELSE
            UPDATE address SET customer_id = new_id WHERE customer_id = old_id;
            SELECT row_count() INTO addresses_changed;
```

```
        UPDATE payment SET customer_id = new_id WHERE customer_id = old_id;
        SELECT row_count() INTO payments_changed;

        UPDATE cust_order SET customer_id = new_id WHERE customer_id = old_id;
        SELECT row_count() INTO orders_changed;

        DELETE FROM customer WHERE customer_id = old_id;

        SELECT addresses_changed,payments_changed,orders_changed;

     END IF;
END
//
DELIMITER ;
```

When entering multiple statement blocks into MySQL, you need to first change the default delimiter to something other than a semicolon (;), so MySQL will allow you to enter a ; without having the client process the input. Listing 9-3 begins by using the delimiter statement: DELIMITER //, which changes the delimiter to //. When you're ready to have your procedure created, type //, and the client will process your entire procedure. When you're finished working on your procedures, change the delimiter back to the standard semicolon with: DELIMITER ;, as you can see at the end of Listing 9-3. We'll explain the other parts of this listing in detail shortly.

Listing 9-4 shows how to call this procedure with the required parameters and get the results from the procedure. We'll look at the details of executing stored procedures in the "Using Stored Procedures" section later in this chapter.

Listing 9-4. *Calling the Stored Procedure*

```
mysql> call merge_customers (1,4,@error);
+-------------------+-------------------+----------------+
| addresses_changed | payments_changed | orders_changed |
+-------------------+-------------------+----------------+
|                 2 |                 2 |              2 |
+-------------------+-------------------+----------------+
1 row in set (0.23 sec)
```

Now, let's step through each part of the stored procedure to see how it's constructed and what options are available.

The CREATE Statement

You create a stored procedure using the CREATE statement, which takes a procedure name, followed by parameters in parentheses, followed by procedure characteristics, and ending with the series of statements to be run when the procedure is called. Here is the syntax:

```
mysql> CREATE PROCEDURE [database.]<name> ([<parameters>]) [<characteristics>]
<body statements>
```

The name may be prefixed with a database name, and it must be followed by parentheses. If the database is not provided, MySQL creates the procedure in the current database or gives a No database selected error if a database is not active. Procedure names can be up to 64 characters long.

■**Caution** Avoid conflicts with built-in functions by not using built-in function names for your procedure. If you must have a procedure with the same name as a MySQL function, putting a space between the name and the parentheses will help MySQL differentiate between the two. For example, a build in function for getting all uppercase text is upper(). We suggest you don't, but if you must create a stored procedure with the same name, use upper () (note the space between the name and the opening parenthesis) to distinguish it from the built-in function.

You can set parameters for a stored procedure using the following syntax:

```
[IN|OUT|INOUT] <name> <data type>
```

If you don't specify IN, OUT, or INOUT for the parameter, it will default to IN. These three types of parameters work as follows:

- An IN parameter is set and passed into the stored procedure to use internally in its processing.

- An OUT parameter is set within the procedure, but accessed by the caller.

- An INOUT parameter is passed into the procedure for internal use, but is also available to the caller after the procedure has completed.

The name and data type of the parameter are used in the stored procedure for referencing and setting values going in and out of the procedure. The data type can be any valid data type for MySQL, and it specifies what type of data will be stored in the parameter. You'll see a detailed example of passing arguments in and out of a procedure in the "Using Stored Procedures" section (Listings 9-13 and 9-16) later in this chapter.

The stored procedure characteristics include a number of options for how the stored procedure behaves. Table 9-1 lists the available options with a description of how they affect the stored procedure.

Table 9-1. *Characteristics Used to Create a Stored Procedure*

Characteristic	Value	Description
LANGUAGE	SQL	This is the language that was used to write the stored procedure. While MySQL intends to implement other languages with external procedures, currently SQL is the only valid option.
SQL SECURITY	DEFINER or INVOKER	The SQL SECURITY characteristic tells MySQL which user to use for permissions when running the procedure. If it's set to DEFINER, the stored procedure will be run using the privileges of the user who created the procedure. If INVOKER is specified, the user calling the procedure will be used for obtaining access to the tables. The default, if not specified, is DEFINER.
COMMENT		The COMMENT characteristic is a place to enter notes about a stored procedure. The comment is displayed in SHOW CREATE PROCEDURE commands.

■**Caution** The COMMENT characteristic is an extension to SQL:2003, which means that procedures with a comment in the definition may not easily move to another SQL:2003-compliant database.

The Procedure Body

The body of a stored procedure contains the collection of SQL statements that make up the actual procedure. In addition to the typical SQL statements you use to interact with data in your database, the SQL:2003 specification includes a number of additional commands to store variables, make decisions, and loop over sets of records.

■**Note** MySQL allows you to put Data Definition Language (DDL) statements (CREATE, ALTER, and so on) in the body of a stored procedure. This is part of the SQL:2003 standard, but it is labeled as an optional feature and may not be supported in other databases that comply with the standard.

BEGIN and END Statements

You use the BEGIN and END statements to group statements in procedures with more than one SQL statement. Declarations can be made only within a BEGIN . . . END block.

You can define a label for the block to clarify your code, as shown here:

```
customer: BEGIN
<SQL statement>;
<SQL statement>;
END customer
```

The labels must match exactly.

The DECLARE Statement

The DECLARE statement is used to create local variables, conditions, handlers, and cursors within the procedure. You can use DECLARE only as the first statements immediately within a BEGIN block. The declarations must occur with variables first, cursors second, and handlers last.

A common declaration is the local variable, which is done with a variable name and type:

```
DECLARE <name> <data type> [DEFAULT];
```

Variable declarations can use any valid data type for MySQL, and may include an optional default value. In Listing 9-3, several declarations are made, including a number of variables for counting items as the statements in the procedure are processed:

```
DECLARE new_count INT DEFAULT 0;
```

Here, we'll look at how to declare variables, conditions, and handlers. Cursors are covered in more detail in Chapter 11.

Variables

Stored procedures can access and set local, session, and global variables. Local variables are either passed in as parameters or created using the DECLARE statement, and they are used in the stored procedure by referencing the name of the parameter or declared variable.

You can set variables in several ways. Using the DECLARE statement with a DEFAULT will set the value of a local variable:

```
DECLARE customer_count INT DEFAULT 0;
```

You can assign values to local, session, and global variables using the SET statement:

```
SET customer_count = 5;
```

MySQL's SET statement includes an extension to the SQL:2003 standard that permits setting multiple variables in one statement:

```
SET customer_count = 5, order_count = 50;
```

Using SELECT . . . INTO is another method for setting variables within your stored procedure. This allows you to query a table and push the results into a variable as a part of the query. SELECT . . . INTO works only if you are selecting a single row of data:

```
SELECT COUNT(*) INTO customer_count FROM customer;
```

You can also select multiple values into multiple variables:

```
SELECT customer_id,name INTO new_id,new_name FROM customer LIMIT 1;
```

Conditions and Handlers

When making declarations in your stored procedure, your list of declarations can include statements to indicate special handling when certain conditions arise. When you have a collection of statements being processed, being able to detect the outcome of those statements and proactively do something to help the procedure be successful can be important to your caller.

Suppose one of the stored procedures created for your online store included a statement to update the customer's name. The column for the customer's name is CHAR(10), which is smaller than you would like, but is the most your legacy order-entry system can handle. The normal behavior for MySQL when updating a record is to truncate the inserted value to a length that fits the column. For numerous reasons, this is unacceptable to you. Fortunately, when MySQL does a truncation, it issues a warning and returns an error, and also sets the SQLSTATE to indicate that during the query, the data was truncated.

Handlers are designed to detect when certain errors or warnings have been triggered by statements and allow you to take action. A handler is declared with a handler type, condition, and statement:

```
DECLARE <handler type> HANDLER FOR <condition> <statement>;
```

Handler Types

The handler type is either CONTINUE or EXIT.[3] CONTINUE means that when a certain error or warning is issued, MySQL will run the provided statement and continue running the statements in the procedure. The EXIT handler type tells MySQL that when the condition is met, it should run the statement and exit the current BEGIN . . . END block.

Here's a handler statement with an EXIT handler type:

```
DECLARE EXIT HANDLER FOR truncated_name
        UPDATE customer SET name = old_name WHERE customer_id = cust_id;
```

In this statement, the EXIT handler type tells the procedure to execute the statement, and then exit when a truncation occurs.

Conditions

The handler condition is what triggers the handler to act. You can define your own conditions and reference them by name, or choose from a set of conditions that are provided by default in MySQL. Table 9-2 shows the MySQL handler conditions.

Table 9-2. *MySQL Handler Conditions*

Condition	Description
SQLSTATE '<number>'	A specific warning or error number, which is described in the MySQL documentation. The number must be enclosed in quotes (typically single).
<self-defined condition name>	The name of the self-defined condition you created using the DECLARE . . . CONDITION statement.
SQLWARNING	Matches any SQLSTATE that begins with 01. Using this condition will allow you to catch a wide range of states.
NOT FOUND	Matches any SQLSTATE beginning with 02. Using this state lets you catch any instance where the query references a missing table, database, and so on.
SQLEXCEPTION	Matches every SQLSTATE except those beginning with 01 or 02.
<MySQL error>	Using a specific error will cause the handler to execute for the specific MySQL error.

■Tip Creating self-defined conditions improves readability of your code. Rather than using the MySQL error or SQLSTATE number, you are assigning a name to that state, which will be more understandable than just having the number.

---

3. The UNDO handler type, which is part of the SQL:2003 specification, is not currently supported in MySQL.

To create a self-defined condition, use a condition declaration with a name and a value:

```
DECLARE <condition name> CONDITION FOR <condition value>;
```

The condition name will be used in a DECLARE . . . HANDLER definition. The condition value can be either a MySQL error number or a SQLSTATE code. For example, to catch when some data has been truncated, the condition declaration with the MySQL error number looks like this:

```
DECLARE truncated_name CONDITION FOR 1265;
```

Or if you wanted to use the SQLSTATE number, you would write the same statement like this:

```
DECLARE truncated_name CONDITION FOR SQLSTATE '01000';
```

■**Caution** A single SQLSTATE value can be assigned to multiple MySQL error numbers, meaning that if you use the SQLSTATE numbers, you may have different errors that generate the same SQLSTATE. This can help or hinder the effectiveness of your handler. In some cases, you want to match all occurrences of a certain type of error, which are grouped under a certain SQLSTATE. In the example, we want to find a very specific error, so it makes more sense to use the MySQL error code.

Statements

The last piece of the handler declaration is a statement, which will be run before the stored procedure either continues or exits, depending on the handler type you chose. For example, to catch a case where the name had been truncated, your stored procedure might look like the one shown in Listing 9-5.

Listing 9-5. *Declaring a Condition and Handler*

```
DELIMITER //
CREATE PROCEDURE update_name (IN cust_id INT, IN new_name VARCHAR(20))
BEGIN
        DECLARE old_name VARCHAR(10);
        DECLARE truncated_name CONDITION for 1265;
        DECLARE EXIT HANDLER FOR truncated_name
            UPDATE customer SET name = old_name WHERE customer_id = cust_id;

        SELECT name INTO old_name FROM customer WHERE customer_id = cust_id;
        UPDATE customer SET name = new_name WHERE customer_id = cust_id;

        SELECT customer_id,name FROM customer WHERE customer_id = cust_id;
END
//
DELIMITER ;
```

The update_name procedure accepts a customer ID (cust_id) and a new name (new_name). The first two statements declare a variable to store the old name and a condition named truncated_name, which specifies MySQL error 1265 as the condition. MySQL error 1265 indicates that a field in the statement was truncated when the statement was processed. The third declaration is a handler statement that tells the procedure that if the truncated_name state is reached, to update the customer record to the old name and exit.

The stored procedure runs the declarations first, and then selects the current name for that customer into the old_name variable. On the following UPDATE statement, depending on the length of the name to be inserted, the query result may be a MySQL error 1265. If so, the handler for truncated_name runs the statement associated with the handler:

```
UPDATE customer SET name = old_name WHERE customer_id = cust_id;
```

This query sets the name back to the original value. The procedure then exits, and no record is returned to the client.

■**Note** The handler example demonstration here is really just an elaborate rollback mechanism. The SQL:2003 standard contains specifications for an UNDO handler type, which would roll back the transaction block if a particular condition is met. MySQL doesn't currently support the UNDO handler type, but promises it is coming.

Flow Controls

SQL:2003 flow constructs give you a number of statements to control and organize your statement processing. MySQL supports IF, CASE, LOOP, LEAVE, ITERATE, REPEAT, and WHILE, but does not currently support the FOR statement.

IF

The IF statement behaves as you would expect if you've written code in another language. It checks a condition, running the statements in the block if the condition is true. You can add ELSEIF statements to continue attempting to match conditions and also, if desired, include a final ELSE statement.

Listing 9-6 shows a piece of a procedure where the shipping cost is being calculated based on the number of days the customer is willing to wait for delivery. delivery_day is an integer parameter passed into the procedure.

Listing 9-6. *IF Statement*

```
IF delivery_day = 1 THEN
        SET shipping = 20;
ELSEIF delivery_day = 2 THEN
        SET shipping = 15;
ELSEIF delivery_day = 3 THEN
        SET shipping = 10;
ELSE
        SET shipping = 5;
END IF;
```

CASE

If you're checking a uniform condition, such a continual check for number of shipping days, you might be better off using the CASE construct. Listing 9-7 shows how this same logic demonstrated in Listing 9-6 could be processed using the CASE statement. Not only does it seem to improve the readability of the code, but the code in Listing 9-7 runs at least twice as fast as the code in Listing 9-6. delivery_day is an integer parameter passed into the procedure.

Listing 9-7. *CASE Statement*

```
CASE delivery_day
WHEN 1 THEN
        SET shipping = 20;
WHEN 2 THEN
        SET shipping = 15;
WHEN 3 THEN
 SET shipping = 10;
ELSE
        SET shipping = 5;
END case;
```

The CASE control can also operate without an initial case value, evaluating a condition on each WHEN block. Listing 9-8 shows the shipping calculator using this syntax. As with Listing 9-7, Listing 9-8 runs significantly faster than the IF-based logic in Listing 9-6.

Listing 9-8. *CASE Statement with Condition Checks*

```
CASE
WHEN delivery_day = 1 THEN
        SET shipping = 20;
WHEN delivery_day = 2 THEN
        SET shipping = 15;
WHEN delivery_day = 3  THEN
        SET shipping = 10;
ELSE
        SET shipping = 5;
END CASE;
```

Now that you are up to speed with checking values, we'll turn our attention to the constructs for repeating. The LOOP, LEAVE, ITERATE, REPEAT, and WHILE statements provide methods to work through a given number of conditions.

LOOP and LEAVE

The LOOP statement creates an ongoing loop that will run until the LEAVE statement is invoked. Optional to the LOOP is a label, which is a name and a colon prefixed to the LOOP statement, with the identical name appended to the END LOOP statement. Listing 9-9 demonstrates a LOOP and LEAVE construct.

Listing 9-9. *LOOP Statement with LEAVE*

```
increment: LOOP
SET count = count + 1;
IF count > in_count THEN LEAVE increment;
END IF;
END LOOP increment;
```

The LEAVE statement is designed to exit from any flow control. The LEAVE statement must be accompanied by a label.

ITERATE

You can use ITERATE in a LOOP, WHILE, or REPEAT control to indicate that the control should iterate through the statements in the loop again. Listing 9-10 shows ITERATE added to the increment example in Listing 9-9. Adding the IF condition to check if the count is less than 20, and if so iterating, means that the value of count, when the loop is complete, will never be less than 20, because the ITERATE statement ensures that the addition statement is run repeatedly until the count reaches 20.

Listing 9-10. *Loop with ITERATE Statement*

```
DELIMITER //
CREATE PROCEDURE increment (IN in_count INT)
BEGIN
DECLARE count INT default 0;

increment: LOOP
SET count = count + 1;
IF count < 20 THEN ITERATE increment; END IF;
IF count > in_count THEN LEAVE increment;
END IF;
END LOOP increment;

SELECT count;
END
//
DELIMITER ;
```

WHILE

The WHILE statement is another mechanism to loop over a set of statements until a condition is true. Unlike LOOP, where the condition is met within the loop, the WHILE statement requires specification of the condition when defining the statement. As with loops, you can add a name to give a name to the WHILE construct. Listing 9-11 shows a simple use of this statement.

Listing 9-11. *WHILE Statement*

```
WHILE count < 10 DO
SET count = count + 1;
END WHILE;
```

REPEAT

To loop over a set of statements until a post-statement condition is met, use the REPEAT state-ment. Listing 9-12 shows a simple use. The check_count label is optional, as is the label with other constructs.

Listing 9-12. *REPEAT Statement*

```
check_count: REPEAT
SET count = count + 1;
UNTIL count > 10
END REPEAT check_count;
```

Using Stored Procedures

If you've gone to all the trouble of creating a procedure, you probably want to put it to use. You may be calling the procedures directly from the MySQL command-line client or from a program written in PHP, Java, Perl, Python, or another language. Here, we'll look at how to call procedures from the command line and from PHP, just to demonstrate calling procedures from a program. Check the documentation for the specific language you're using to see which driv-ers are needed and how the interface for procedures and parameters work in that language.

Calling Procedures from the MySQL Client

From the MySQL client, you use the CALL statement to execute a procedure, providing the procedure name and correct number of arguments.

```
CALL [database.]<procedure name> ([<parameter>, <parameter>, …]);
```

Calling a simple procedure without any parameters is fairly straightforward, as you saw earlier in the chapter, when we demonstrated calling the get_customer procedure (Listing 9-2).

Listing 9-13 shows an example of calling a stored procedure that requires three arguments: an old customer ID as the first IN argument, a new customer ID as the second IN argument, and an OUT argument used in the procedure for setting an error message. Once the stored procedure has been executed, the @error variable contains a string set inside the stored procedure.

Listing 9-13. *Calling a Stored Procedure with IN and OUT Parameters*

```
mysql> CALL merge_customers (8,9,@error);
Query OK, 0 rows affected (0.01 sec)

mysql> SELECT @error;
+----------------------+
| @error               |
+----------------------+
| old id does not exist |
+----------------------+
1 row in set (0.30 sec)
```

If you call a procedure with the wrong number of arguments, MySQL gives an error:

```
mysql> CALL shop.merge_customers (1,2);
ERROR 1318 (42000): Incorrect number of arguments for PROCEDURE merge_customers; \
expected 3, got 2
```

Calling Procedures from PHP

In PHP, stored procedures must be called using PHP's `mysqli` extensions. This requires your PHP code to be compiled with the `--with-mysqli` option. Listing 9-14 shows how you would call the get_customers procedure from PHP and report the results.

Listing 9-14. *Calling a Stored Procedure from PHP*

```php
<?
$mysqli = mysqli_connect("localhost","mkruck","ProMySQL","shop");

if (mysqli_connect_errno()) {
        printf("Failed to connect: %s\n", mysqli_connect_error());
        exit();
}

if ($result = $mysqli->query("CALL get_customers ()")) {
        printf("%d records found\n",$result->num_rows);
        while ($row = $result->fetch_row()) {
            printf("%d - %s\n",$row[0],$row[1]);
        }
}
else {
        echo $mysqli->error,"\n";
}
$mysqli->close();
?>
```

This script makes a connection to the database (checking for failure), calls the stored procedure, and then prints the number of rows that were returned along with a line for each piece of the data. If the CALL statement fails, the error is printed.

Running the PHP script in Listing 9-14 generates the output shown in Listing 9-15.

Listing 9-15. *Output from a Stored Procedure Called in PHP*

```
6 records found
1 - Mike
2 - Jay
3 - Johanna
4 - Michael
5 - Heidi
6 - Ezra
```

The output from Listing 9-15 shows that six records were returned from the get_customers procedure.

To merge two of these customers by calling the `merge_customers` procedure (created in Listing 9-3) adds a little more complexity because you must pass IN and OUT parameters to the procedure. A simple way to do this is shown in Listing 9-16.

Listing 9-16. *Calling a Stored Procedure with Parameters from PHP*

```php
<?
$mysqli = mysqli_connect("localhost","mkruck","ProMySQL","shop");

if (mysqli_connect_errno()) {
    printf("Failed to connect: %s\n", mysqli_connect_error());
    exit();
}
$old_customer = 1;
$new_customer = 4;

$mysqli->query("CALL merge_customers ($old_customer,$new_customer,@error)");

$result = $mysqli->query("SELECT @error");
if ($result->num_rows) {
        while ($row = $result->fetch_row()) {
                printf("%s\n",$row[0]);
        }
}
else {
        print "Customer merge successful";
}

$mysqli->close();
?>
```

This PHP script will print a success message if the call to the procedure didn't set the `@error`:

```
Customer merge successful
```

But if the procedure encountered a problem, such as that one of the records couldn't be found, and sets the `@error` variable with an error message, the PHP script will print that error. Running the PHP script again, after customer records 1 and 4 have already been merged, results in the PHP script printing the error message from the procedure:

```
old id does not exist
```

■Tip The `mysqli` extension allows significantly more complex database interaction, such as creating prepared statements, binding parameters, and so on. For more information, see the PHP documentation at `http://www.php.net/mysqli`.

Managing Stored Procedures

Most of the work in an environment where stored procedures are used is in creating the stored procedure. However, at some point, you will need to manage the procedures in your database. MySQL provides a set of commands for this purpose.

Viewing Stored Procedures

You have several options when viewing information about stored procedures. To get a summary of the procedures across all databases in your system, use SHOW PROCEDURE STATUS, which will give you a summary of information about all the stored procedures in your system. Listing 9-17 shows the output for three procedures used for listings in this chapter. Using the \G option outputs in rows instead of columns.

Listing 9-17. *Output of SHOW PROCEDURE STATUS*

```
mysql> SHOW PROCEDURE STATUS\G
*************************** 1. row ***************************
           Db: shop
         Name: get_customers
         Type: PROCEDURE
      Definer: mkruck01@localhost
     Modified: 2005-01-10 23:23:20
      Created: 2005-01-10 23:23:20
Security_type: DEFINER
      Comment:
*************************** 2. row ***************************
           Db: shop
         Name: get_shipping_cost
         Type: PROCEDURE
      Definer: mkruck01@localhost
     Modified: 2005-01-10 22:45:57
      Created: 2005-01-10 22:45:57
Security_type: DEFINER
      Comment:
*************************** 3. row ***************************
           Db: shop
         Name: merge_customers
         Type: PROCEDURE
      Definer: mkruck01@localhost
     Modified: 2005-01-10 23:23:20
      Created: 2005-01-10 23:23:20
Security_type: DEFINER
      Comment: get rid of unnecessary data
```

This command can be limited by appending a LIKE clause, in this case limiting the output to just returning the merge_customer procedure.

```
mysql> SHOW PROCEDURE STATUS LIKE 'merge%'\G
```

The SHOW PROCEDURE STATUS statement gives you a nice summary view of all the procedures in the databases on your machine. To get more details on a stored procedure, use the SHOW CREATE PROCEDURE statement:

```
SHOW CREATE PROCEDURE [<database>.]<procedure name>;
```

This statement shows you the name and the CREATE statement. Listing 9-18 shows an example of the output for the get_shipping_cost procedure.

Listing 9-18. *Output of SHOW CREATE PROCEDURE*

```
mysql> SHOW CREATE PROCEDURE shop.get_shipping_cost\G
*************************** 1. row ***************************
       Procedure: get_shipping_cost
        sql_mode:
Create Procedure: CREATE PROCEDURE `shop`.`get_shipping_cost`(IN delivery_day INT)
    COMMENT 'determine shipping cost based on day of delivery'
BEGIN
        declare shipping INT;
        case delivery_day
        when 1 then set shipping = 20;
        when 2 then set shipping = 15;
        when 3 then set shipping = 10;
        else set shipping = 5;
        end case;
        select shipping;
END
1 row in set (0.12 sec)
```

Neither of the views we've discussed thus far shows you everything there is to know about a procedure. The summary provides only a few pieces of summary information, and SHOW ➥ CREATE PROCEDURE shows the name, along with the body as a large, unreadable CREATE statement. If you have SELECT access on the proc table in the mysql database, a SELECT statement will show you everything there is to know about all procedures or a particular procedure. Listing 9-19 shows the output from a SELECT of the get_shipping_cost procedure, which shows the procedure's database, name, language, security type, parameter list, body, definer, comment, and other information.

Listing 9-19. *Output of SELECT from the mysql.proc Table*

```
mysql> SELECT * FROM mysql.proc WHERE name = 'get_shipping_cost'\G
*************************** 1. row ***************************
                db: shop
              name: get_shipping_cost
              type: PROCEDURE
     specific_name: get_shipping_cost
          language: SQL
  sql_data_access: CONTAINS_SQL
  is_deterministic: NO
```

```
    security_type: DEFINER
       param_list: IN delivery_day INT
           returns:
              body: BEGIN
          declare shipping INT;
          case delivery_day
          when 1 then set shipping = 20;
          when 2 then set shipping = 15;
          when 3 then set shipping = 10;
          else set shipping = 5;
          end case;
          select shipping;
END
          definer: mkruck01@localhost
          created: 2005-01-11 00:01:47
         modified: 2005-01-11 00:01:47
         sql_mode:
          comment: determine shipping cost based on day of delivery
1 row in set (0.12 sec)
```

As you can see, if you want to view everything there is to know about a procedure, the direct SELECT on the mysql.proc table will provide the most information.

Altering and Removing Stored Procedures

The ALTER statement lets you change the characteristics of a stored procedure. It has the following syntax:

```
ALTER PROCEDURE [<database>.]<procedure name> <characteristics>
```

The ALTER statement can change any of the characteristics used to create the procedure, as shown earlier in Table 9-1. For example, to change the SQL SECURITY and COMMENT on the get_customers procedure, you would use the following ALTER statement:

```
mysql> ALTER PROCEDURE get_customers SQL SECURITY INVOKER
COMMENT 'show all customers';
```

To remove a stored procedures, use the DROP statement, which has the following syntax:

```
DROP PROCEDURE [database.]<procedure name>
```

Editing Stored Procedures

Editing stored procedures doesn't happen interactively with the database, as with the SHOW, ALTER, or DROP statements. The process of editing a stored procedure means opening it in an editor, making the necessary changes, and replacing the existing procedure in the database with the new one using a DROP and then a CREATE statement.

Choosing an environment for editing stored procedures is similar to finding one for any kind of programming. If you prefer to work in a text editor like Emacs, vi, or Notepad, you'll probably be most comfortable doing the same when working on your procedures. A GUI tool will make more sense if that's where you find most of your other development happens.

Regardless of your tool for editing stored procedures, you should use a versioning system like Subversion or CVS to store and keep track of changes in your stored procedures. Stored procedures should be treated like any other piece of code in this respect—you've spent time developing it and should take measures to protect your time and effort.

■**Tip** If you prefer working in a GUI, you might try MySQL Query Browser, a GUI tool for Windows and Linux that has en excellent interface for editing procedures. The tool will allow you to update the existing procedure with a DROP and CREATE from a button on the interface. More information on the freely available MySQL Query Browser is available at `http://dev.mysql.com/doc/query-browser/en/index.html`.

Stored Procedure Permissions

For permissions to create and call stored procedures, MySQL relies on the existing permissions scheme, which is covered in Chapter 15. Specific to procedures, the MySQL permissions scheme has the CREATE ROUTINE, ALTER ROUTINE, and EXECUTE privilege.

The permissions required for working with stored procedures are as follows:

Viewing permissions: To view stored procedures with SHOW PROCEDURE STATUS, you must have SELECT access to the mysql.proc table. To be able to use the SHOW CREATE PROCEDURE, you must have either SELECT access to the mysql.proc table or the ALTER ROUTINE privilege for that particular procedure. Both SHOW PROCEDURE STATUS and SHOW CREATE PROCEDURE were covered earlier in this chapter.

Calling permissions: To call a stored procedure, you need the ability to connect to the server and have the EXECUTE permission for the procedure. EXECUTE permissions can be granted globally (in the mysql.user table), at the database level (in the mysql.db table), or for a specific routine (in the mysql.procs_priv table).

Creating and altering permissions: To govern creating and altering a stored procedure, MySQL uses the CREATE ROUTINE and ALTER ROUTINE privilege. As with the EXECUTE privilege, permissions for creating or changing procedures can be granted globally (in the mysql.user table), at the database level (in the mysql.db table), or for a specific routine (in the mysql.procs_priv table).

Dropping permissions: To drop a procedure, you must have the ALTER ROUTINE privilege. Permissions for dropping procedures can be granted globally (in the mysql.user table), at the database level (in the mysql.db table), or for a specific routine (in the mysql. procs_priv table).

The success of a stored procedure call is also affected by the procedure's SQL SECURITY characteristic. If set to DEFINER, the procedure will be run with the permissions of the user who created the procedure. Procedures will be run as the calling user if SQL SECURITY is set to INVOKER. In either case, the INVOKER or DEFINER must have appropriate access to the tables used in the stored procedure or calling the procedure will result in a permission error.

Having the option to run procedures with the permissions of the creator means that you can create a set of procedures by a user with access to all of the tables, and allow a user who has no permissions in the tables but does have the ability to connect to the server and execute the procedure, to run it. This can be a simple, but excellent, way to simplify and enforce security in your database.

WHAT'S MISSING IN MYSQL STORED PROCEDURES?

The MySQL AB developers continue to develop stored procedure features in MySQL. As of version 5.0.6, a few documented statements are still missing from the syntax:

- `SIGNAL`: Used in a handler to return a `SQLSTATE` and message text.

- `RESIGNAL`: Allows you to indicate that a handler should send a `SQLSTATE` other than the one originally caught.

- UNDO: Used in defining a handler. This handler type specifies that if a certain condition is reached, the database should undo the statements previously run within the `BEGIN . . . END` block.

- `FOR`: Used to loop over a set of instructions a given number of times.

Summary

Stored procedures in MySQL are a welcome and exciting addition to the 5.0 release. While there's a lot of power, and perhaps some efficiency, in moving logic into your database, it's important to consider if and how procedures fit into your existing application. Hasty decisions based on excitement to use cool technology usually lead to problems down the road.

As mentioned in the chapter, users should exercise caution in adopting the stored procedure functionality until the stability of the 5.0 server matches their environment requirements. For most users, waiting for the stable release is probably the best choice.

MySQL's choice of SQL:2003 provides a good set of statements for developing procedures and a standard for potential inter-database procedure exchange. MySQL provides a good set of tools for creating, altering, dropping, and viewing procedures.

As MySQL developers continue to develop and flush out their implementation of stored procedures, we look forward to further developments of the stored procedure functionality and anxiously await the stable release of the 5.0 branch of MySQL.

In the next chapter, we'll look at stored functions, another technology available in MySQL versions 5.0 and later.

CHAPTER 10

■■■

Functions

More than likely, you're already familiar with database functions. If you haven't defined them yourself in a database that allowed user-defined functions, you've probably used one or more of the functions built into your database. If you've ever stuck a LENGTH() function in a query to find the number of bytes in a string, or used an UPPER() function to make the data you select return in all uppercase letters, you're familiar with at least the use of functions.

You may have encountered situations where, within a query, you've wanted to use one of the built-in database functions to perform some simple calculation or manipulation on a piece of data, but found that the database didn't offer a function suitable to your needs. Or maybe the database had a function that looked like it would work, but when you tried it, that function didn't give you the kind of results you wanted.

Stored functions, available in MySQL versions 5.0 and later, are the solution many need for encapsulating pieces of logic. In this chapter, we'll cover the following topics related to stored functions:

- Uses of database functions

- Database functions compared with other database tools

- MySQL's implementation of stored functions

- How to create stored functions

- An example of using functions

- How to view, change, and remove stored functions

- Stored function permissions

- Benchmarks to determine the overhead in using functions

Database Function Uses

To illustrate the usefulness of stored functions, let's look at how they might offer a solution for a problem in the online store application we've used in previous chapters. Part of your system is a table full of customer records. The customer records are used on your web site to customize the users' pages by displaying their name when they are at the site. In addition, the data is used for mailing periodic promotional flyers and for invoicing wholesale customers. Users create their own accounts on the site, and they can update their contact information if it changes. The self-service account management leads to variations in the format of the records. Many users use mixed uppercase and lowercase characters, but some users enter data in all uppercase or all lowercase.

For your web site and mailings, you're particularly interested in having the customer's first and last name look professional, with the first letter uppercase and the remainder lowercase. To ensure the name is formatted correctly, you want to handle this as part of the queries that pull data from the database, as opposed to in the code for the site or mailing list. MySQL has built-in UPPER() and LOWER() functions, but a thorough review of the string functions reveals nothing that will achieve the formatting you need. What you need is a function that will take a string and return the string with the first character converted to uppercase and the remainder in lowercase.

Stored functions to the rescue. MySQL versions 5.0 and later offer a means for defining functions to be used in standard SQL statements for performing an endless number of tasks, including calculations, data validation, data formatting, and data manipulation.

■**Note** As we write this chapter, MySQL has released version 5.0.6, which is labeled a beta release. While the database is stable enough to test and document the functionality of stored functions, production users are encouraged to wait until a release of the 5.0.*x* branch that is labeled production.

Database functions are a method for encapsulating logic that can be performed with any number of input arguments, and require that one, and only one, value be returned. Database functions are called within SELECT, INSERT, or UPDATE statements, generating values on the fly to be used within the query to change data being saved into a table or returned in a set of results. A function always returns a single, predefined type set in the definition of the function.

Examining MySQL's built-in functions, you might conclude that a function is intended to perform some calculation or manipulation of one or more values to return a value for output from a SELECT statement or storage in the database (think of the LENGTH() function). When building your own functions, you can also use other pieces of data (like a session variable) as a part of the SQL statements that make up the function body. For example, if you created a ucasefirst() function to solve the problem of customer name formatting, you would use it in a SQL statement like this:

```
SELECT user_id, ucasefirst(firstname), ucasefirst(lastname),
email_address FROM user;
```

We'll return to this sample ucasefirst() function at the very end of this chapter, after we've covered the details of creating functions.

Functions Compared with Other Database Tools

Database functions can be used in many ways, so you need to consider how to best use them for your applications. Throughout this book, we continue to emphasize careful consideration of the various database technologies as you design and implement your database. As you consider the possible uses for functions in your application and database, you should be thinking about how functions fit into the bigger picture and if a stored function in the database is the best choice for the required logic. To help you figure this out, let's take a look at how functions compare with some other database tools for manipulating data: stored procedures, views, and triggers.

While we can't provide definitive answers as to where each tool fits best, we do suggest that you think carefully about your overall database and application architecture, and keep your use of the various database tools consistent and well documented.

Stored Functions vs. Stored Procedures

The syntax for defining the body of stored functions includes the same set of statements defined for stored procedures, covered in Chapter 9. As we've discussed, MySQL's stored procedures provide a rich set of syntax to perform logic operations in the database. Like the body of a procedure, the function body can include things like variables and flow constructs to encapsulate both small and large pieces of functionality.

So why not just use stored procedures then? While you can do a lot with stored procedures, they aren't always the best fit for encapsulating pieces of logic. Furthermore, creating a stored procedure for each piece of logic can be overkill, and needing to call and then process the results from a procedure is sometimes more work that it's worth if you need only a small piece of data to use in another query.

A function can be used directly from within a SELECT, INSERT, or UPDATE statement, and the result of that function is either saved in the table or returned with the output (depending on whether you're getting or saving data). Stored procedures may not return any results, or they might return a large set of records for further processing and presentation. In contrast, a stored function always returns a single value.[1] The required single-value return makes a function perfect for logic needed within an existing query.

In summary, the main difference between stored procedures and database functions is the way they are called and what they return. A stored procedure is executed with an explicit statement: the CALL command. Stored procedures don't necessarily return any value, but can set OUT values and can return one or more data records. A stored procedure can also execute without returning any data to the client.

Note that the debate surrounding the use of stored procedures, discussed in Chapter 9, also applies to using stored functions (as well as views and triggers) in the database. Many of the arguments for and against stored procedures also pertain to using functions in your database, and you should be aware of these arguments when assessing the merits of incorporating such features into your application.

---

1.   The returned value can be NULL, if there is nothing for the function to return.

Functions vs. Views

A *view* provides a way to create a virtual representation of data in one or more tables, which might include calculating a value on the fly, as a part of the view definition. We will discuss views in detail in Chapter 12. Here, we would like to point out some overlap they share with functions.

Like a view, a function can be used to create a column of data on the fly. A difference is that a function can include many rows of statements and conditional logic, whereas a view can present only data that can be calculated or formatted within a single SQL SELECT statement.

Before jumping into defining a function, it might be wise to determine whether a view is better suited to the task. Consider the data set in Listing 10-1, which contains a simple list of entries from cust_order, a table responsible for representing customer orders.

Listing 10-1. *Sample Listing from a Customer Order Table*

```
+---------------+----------+----------+
| cust_order_id | item_sum | shipping |
+---------------+----------+----------+
|             1 |    30.95 |    20.00 |
|             2 |    40.56 |    20.00 |
|             3 |   214.34 |    30.01 |
|             4 |   143.65 |    24.99 |
|             5 |   345.99 |    30.01 |
|             6 |   789.24 |    30.01 |
|             7 |     3.45 |    10.00 |
+---------------+----------+----------+
```

Suppose you want to create a fourth column that is a calculation of the item_sum multiplied by your current sales tax rate and added to the shipping to produce a total_cost column.[2] Based on a tax rate of 5%, this desired output might look something like Listing 10-2.

Listing 10-2. *Sample Listing of Orders with Calculated Total*

```
+---------------+----------+----------+--------+
| cust_order_id | item_sum | shipping | total  |
+---------------+----------+----------+--------+
|             1 |    30.95 |    20.00 |  52.50 |
|             2 |    40.56 |    20.00 |  62.59 |
|             3 |   214.34 |    30.01 | 255.07 |
|             4 |   143.65 |    24.99 | 175.82 |
|             5 |   345.99 |    30.01 | 393.30 |
|             6 |   789.24 |    30.01 | 858.71 |
|             7 |     3.45 |    10.00 |  13.62 |
+---------------+----------+----------+--------+
```

---

2. We're assuming you want to have the database make this calculation, but it could be easily made in the calling program as well as a part of the code's business logic or presentation of the data.

■**Note** Storing calculated columns is sometimes considered taboo in database design and administration circles. But before you blindly agree, consider how not having a calculated column will affect your data. In the example in Listing 10-2, the total is calculated on the fly and not stored in the database. What happens when the tax rate increases? If you haven't stored the total for your customer orders, you end up having old orders in the system that start looking like they weren't paid in full because the calculation of the total column now results in a slightly higher total than it did before the tax increase. It could be argued that the tax rate could be stored in the table, or a tax table be kept with dates for when particular tax rates were active. Gives you something to think about, right?

The output from Listing 10-2 has a fourth column, which contains the total cost of the order, with shipping and tax included. This is fairly easily accomplished with a standard SQL statement, as shown in Listing 10-3.

Listing 10-3. *SELECT Statement with Total Calculated in SQL*

```
mysql> SELECT cust_order_id, item_sum, shipping,
item_sum * .05 + item_sum + shipping AS total
FROM cust_order;
```

But you're trying to get away from having your application build SQL statements that contain calculations, so you're looking at how a function might be able to encapsulate the calculation made in the second line of Listing 10-3. You could generate the same output as in Listing 10-2 by creating a `calculate_total()` function and using it in the `SELECT`, as shown in Listing 10-4.

Listing 10-4. *SELECT Statement with Total Calculated in Function*

```
mysql> SELECT cust_order_id, item_sum, shipping,
calculate_total(item_sum,shipping)
AS total FROM cust_order;
```

Details on how to create the `calculate_total()` function are coming later in the chapter, in the "Creating Functions" section (for now, just rest assured that it works). The SQL in Listing 10-4 abstracts the actual calculation of the total. However, it still requires a specific piece of syntax, `calculate_total(item_sum,shipping)`, to be written into the query. We'll revisit Listings 10-3 and 10-4 when we talk about benchmarking the overhead in processing a function, in the "Performance of Functions" section.

By using a view, the `SELECT` statement to output the same results from Listing 10-2 doesn't require any special syntax into the query. You can just run the `SELECT` against the view, which represents `total` in a virtual column as part of the view definition. With a view, the calling SQL doesn't need to know anything about the calculation:

```
mysql> SELECT cust_order_id, item_sum, shipping, total FROM cust_order_view;
```

Again, you'll have to wait until Chapter 12 to get details on how to build a view to support this query. This simple example demonstrates one instance where functions and views overlap in their ability to solve a requirement. You can probably think of other scenarios where the two overlap.

Which should you choose? We can't answer that question because the decision ultimately rests on the particular situation. If you are well versed in stored functions, and your database administrator applauds the use of functions and heckles anyone who asks to have a view created, you might be better off with the function. On the other hand, if you've designed your database to include use of views to meet similar requirements elsewhere in your system, you might find that a view fits better.

As a general rule, use a view when the calculation or manipulation is needed every time a record is pulled from the table. If the virtual data is not required every time the data is retrieved, it's better to use a function that is put in the query only when the manipulated data is needed as a part of the results.

Functions vs. Triggers

A *trigger* is a statement, or set of statements that are stored and associated with a particular event, like an UPDATE or DELETE, that happens on a particular column or table. When the event happens, the statements in the trigger are executed. We will cover triggers in detail in Chapter 13. Again, our purpose here is to point out where a trigger might be an alternative to a function.

The same example we used in the previous section to compare functions with views can also be solved by using a trigger. You'll recall that Listing 10-2 calculated the cost of various items based on their price, shipping fee, and tax. Triggers provide a set of functionality that would allow you to calculate the total whenever data is inserted or updated in the table, storing the total in the table without needing to specify the calculation in the SQL. While you can get the output from Listing 10-2 to look identical, the solution isn't exactly the same, because a trigger requires you to actually store the calculated total in a real column.[3] When using a function or a view, the total can be calculated on the fly and represented in a virtual data column.

You've now seen three different tools—functions, views, and triggers—as potential ways to calculate the order total within the database. Isn't it nice to have these choices?

Functions in MySQL

MySQL's function implementation reflects the overall goal of MySQL AB: to provide a simple but speedy database that doesn't go overboard on providing unnecessary, or unnecessarily complex, functionality. The syntax for creating stored functions in MySQL follows closely with the SQL:2003 syntax used for creating stored procedures. Our experience with MySQL and other databases shows that if you have ever dabbled in user-defined functions in Microsoft SQL Server, DB2, Oracle, Informix, or PostgreSQL, creating functions in MySQL will be quite familiar.

---

3. Interestingly enough, you can actually use the function from within the trigger to perform the calculation of the value to be stored in the table when a trigger statement executes.

Note The official standard for syntax used to build stored functions is ISO/IEC 9075-*x*:2003, where *x* is a range of numbers between 1 and 14 that indicate many different parts of the standard. For short, the standard is often referred to as SQL:2003, SQL-2003, or SQL 2003. We refer to the standard as SQL:2003, since the official specification uses the colon (:) as a separator, and MySQL documentation uses this format. The standard can be found on the ISO web site (`http://www.iso.org`) by doing a search for 9075. The standard is available for a fee.

Like stored procedures, MySQL functions are stored in the `proc` table in the `mysql` database. Also, as with stored procedures, MySQL loads functions into memory when the database starts up or when the function is created or modified. The server does not dynamically load the function from where it is stored in the `mysql.proc` table when you issue a statement that requires the function. Given the overlap between stored procedures and stored functions, it shouldn't surprise you that in the documentation, MySQL lumps both stored procedures and functions into one term: *routines*.

USER-DEFINED AND NATIVE FUNCTIONS

In versions prior to 5.0, the options for adding functions to MySQL were to either create a user-defined function (UDF) or add a native function. UDFs and native functions are still a part of MySQL in versions later than 5.0.

The UDF requires writing a piece of code in C or C++ that is compiled and then referenced from within MySQL with the `CREATE FUNCTION` statement. The `CREATE FUNCTION` statement includes a `SONAME` keyword that tells MySQL where to find the shared object that will execute the logic of the function. When MySQL starts, or when the `CREATE FUNCTION` statement is issued with the `SONAME` keyword, MySQL loads in the active UDFs and makes them available for use in queries to the database (unless you started the database with `--skip-grant-tables`; in which case, no functions are loaded).

To create a native function in MySQL, you are required to make modifications to the MySQL source code, defining your function as a part of the source to be built in the MySQL binary.

In MySQL 5.0, the stored function shares the `CREATE FUNCTION` syntax with UDFs. The `CREATE` ➥ `FUNCTION` and other statements for building and managing functions also apply to the stored function, which is a set of SQL statements stored in the database and loaded from the `mysql.proc` table when MySQL starts up. There is no compiled C or C++ code involved in writing a stored function. The difference between a stored function and a UDF is that in the `CREATE` statement, the stored function will have a set of SQL statements, where the UDF will have the `SONAME` keyword that points to the compiled C or C++ code.

Because UDFs run on the system, not in the database, they have access to system information. Stored functions, on the other hand, have access to data and settings in the MySQL server, but not to the system or server. Depending on what logic you need from the function, one or the other may better suit your needs.

For documentation on creating native functions in MySQL, see `http://dev.mysql.com/doc/mysql/en/functions.html`.

Creating Functions

In our discussion about how stored functions fit in with other database tools, we hinted at using a function to calculate some values on the fly. In this first example, we aim to show you just how simple creating a function can be. Let's review the customer order scenario we presented earlier in our discussion of functions versus other database tools. Listing 10-5 shows some sample data from a table that contains customer orders.

Listing 10-5. *Sample Listing from a Customer Order Table*

```
+---------------+----------+----------+
| cust_order_id | item_sum | shipping |
+---------------+----------+----------+
|             1 |    30.95 |    20.00 |
|             2 |    40.56 |    20.00 |
|             3 |   214.34 |    30.01 |
|             4 |   143.65 |    24.99 |
|             5 |   345.99 |    30.01 |
|             6 |   789.24 |    30.01 |
|             7 |     3.45 |    10.00 |
+---------------+----------+----------+
```

You are trying to generate a fourth column representing the total cost, which is the item_sum with 5% sales tax and the shipping charges added. Listing 10-6 shows the CREATE statement for the calculate_total() function.

Listing 10-6. *CREATE Statement for calculate_total()*

```
CREATE FUNCTION calculate_total
(cost DECIMAL(10,2), shipping DECIMAL(10,2))
RETURNS DECIMAL(10,2)
RETURN cost * 1.05 + shipping;
```

Listing 10-6 presents a CREATE statement with a function name, two incoming parameters, a declaration of the type that will be returned, and a body. The body consists of a single statement that returns the calculation of the cost, multiplied by the tax and added to the shipping cost.

Any SELECT statement using the function simply needs to pass the correct parameters to the function, as shown in Listing 10-7.

Listing 10-7. *Using the calculate_total() Function*

```
mysql> SELECT cust_order_id, item_sum, shipping,
calculate_total(item_sum,shipping) AS total
FROM cust_order;
```

When the query is executed, the function will be called for each row, performing the calculation and returning the result to be included in the output of the resultset. The resulting output is shown in Listing 10-8.

Listing 10-8. *Output from SELECT Using the calculate_total() Function*

```
+--------------+----------+----------+--------+
| cust_order_id | item_sum | shipping | total  |
+--------------+----------+----------+--------+
|            1 |    30.95 |    20.00 |  52.50 |
|            2 |    40.56 |    20.00 |  62.59 |
|            3 |   214.34 |    30.01 | 255.07 |
|            4 |   143.65 |    24.99 | 175.82 |
|            5 |   345.99 |    30.01 | 393.30 |
|            6 |   789.24 |    30.01 | 858.71 |
|            7 |     3.45 |    10.00 |  13.62 |
+--------------+----------+----------+--------+
7 rows in set (0.00 sec)
```

CREATE Statement

As you've seen, a function is brought into existence in the database with a CREATE statement. This statement requires a function name, some input parameters, a return type, and one or more SQL statements in the function body with at least one return statement. The complete CREATE statement syntax looks like this:

```
CREATE FUNCTION [database.]<name> (<input parameters>)
  RETURNS <data type> [characteristics] <body>;
```

The syntax for building functions allows for endless possibilities for putting pieces of logic under a simple interface for calling from within your SQL statements. Let's examine the pieces of the statement and discuss how each affects the behavior of the function.

■**Tip** Before you embark on defining functionality to encapsulate a bit of processing, check the MySQL documentation on the existing built-in functions. MySQL provides a rich set of functions for manipulating strings, numbers, dates, full-text search, variable casts, and groupings.

Function Name

The name of the stored function must not be the same as another stored function in the database. It can be the same as a built-in function (although we strongly discourage it), in which case you refer to the stored function by using a space between the name and the opening parenthesis for input parameters. The name of any database in the system can be prepended to the function name to create a stored function outside the currently active database.

■**Tip** For clarity and consistency, you may want to have your style guide require that SQL statements always include a space after the function name when using stored functions. This will prevent the accidental use of a built-in function. Calling a nonexistent stored function resulting in an error is better than using the wrong function and moving on with erroneous data.

For example, if you want to create a procedure to determine the amount of tax that should be added to the order, your function name might be `calculate_tax`:

```
CREATE FUNCTION calculate_tax . . .
```

Input Parameters

Enclosed in parentheses after the function name is a list of input parameters that are required to run the function, along with the data type that is expected for the parameter. Each parameter must have a name and a data type. The data type can be any valid MySQL data type. Parameters are separated by a comma. For example, if you were going to accept a dollar amount in your `calculate_tax()` function, the input parameters would be added immediately after the function name:

```
CREATE FUNCTION calculate_tax (cost DECIMAL(10,2)) . . .
```

When calling a stored function, if you do not specify the correct number of parameters, MySQL will return an error indicating an incorrect number of arguments.

■**Note** In Chapter 9, we explained how procedure parameters can be specified as IN, OUT, or INOUT. Stored functions do not allow for this syntax. All parameters after the function name are passed into the function, and the only value that comes out of the function is the return. A CREATE FUNCTION statement will fail if the IN, OUT, or INOUT syntax is used in defining the parameters, because these keywords are not part of the CREATE FUNCTION statement.

Return Value

The stored function is required to have the RETURNS keyword with a valid MySQL data type. The RETURNS keyword comes directly after the input parameters, and is followed by the data type:

```
CREATE FUNCTION calculate_tax (cost DECIMAL(10,2))
RETURNS DECIMAL(10,2)
. . .
```

When the function is called, the result of the function will be placed in the query as the value to be returned with the record (for SELECT) or saved into the table (for INSERT and UPDATE).

■**Caution** With both input and return values in a function, the data type is required to define the function. However, when calling the function, MySQL doesn't verify that you are passing in the correct data type. Passing in an unmatching data type can lead to some interesting and unpredictable results. MySQL will cast the values into the appropriate type for the function, which leads to return values that might be different than expected. For your own sanity, make sure that when you call a function, you pass in arguments with the correct data type and use the returned data type appropriately.

Characteristics

Characteristics in the definition of a stored function give the parser hints as to how the function is written and should be processed. Table 10-1 describes the available characteristics.

Table 10-1. *Characteristics Used to Create a Stored Function*

Characteristic	Value	Description
[NOT] DETERMINISTIC		MySQL currently accepts this keyword but does nothing with it. In the future, setting a function to be deterministic will tell the query parser that for a given set of parameters, the results will always be the same. Knowing a function is deterministic will allow the MySQL server to optimize the use of the function. The default is NOT DETERMINISTIC. The DETERMINISTIC characteristic isn't allowed in function ALTER statements.
LANGUAGE	SQL	The language that was used to write the body of the function. Currently, SQL is the only valid option (and the default). MySQL has suggested that in the future, other languages will be supported.
SQL SECURITY	DEFINER or INVOKER	Tells MySQL which user to use for permissions when running a function. If it's set to DEFINER, the stored function will be run using the privileges of the user who created the function. If INVOKER is specified, the user calling the function will be used for obtaining access to the tables. DEFINER is the default if this characteristic is not specified.
COMMENT		A place to enter notes about a stored function. The comment is displayed in SHOW CREATE ➡ FUNCTION commands.

■**Caution** The COMMENT characteristic is an extension to SQL:2003, which means that functions with a comment in the definition may not easily move to another SQL:2003-compliant database.

In the CREATE statement, characteristics are entered immediately following the return data type. For a function where you want to be sure the caller's permissions are used in running the function, add that syntax, as follows:

```
CREATE FUNCTION calculate_tax (cost DECIMAL(10,2))
RETURNS DECIMAL(10,2)
SQL SECURITY DEFINER
 . . .
```

The Function Body

The body of the stored function is a collection of SQL statements that contain the logic to take place in the function. As you saw in the example in Listing 10-6, the body can consist of one simple statement. While the single-statement function is useful, you can do considerably more in a function by using multiple statements. The length of the body is limited to 64KB of data, because the body is stored in a BLOB field.[4]

If you've dabbled in stored procedures (and/or read Chapter 9), the syntax used for functions will be familiar, because it's the same. Here, we'll review blocks, declarations, variables, and flow constructs as they are used in functions.

BEGIN . . . END Statements

The BEGIN and END statements are used to group statements, and they are required for functions with more than one SQL statement. Any declarations must be made within this block and appear before any other statements in a BEGIN . . . END block.

The block can be modified with labels for clarifying code, as shown in Listing 10-9. The label on the BEGIN and END must match exactly.

Listing 10-9. *BEGIN . . . END Block with Labels*

```
DELIMITER //
CREATE FUNCTION calculate_tax (cost DECIMAL(10,2))
RETURNS DECIMAL(10,2)
SQL SECURITY DEFINER
tax: BEGIN
DECLARE order_tax DECIMAL(10,2);
SET order_tax = cost * .05;;
RETURN order_tax;
END tax
//
DELIMITER ;
```

As when you're creating a stored procedure with multiple statements, when entering multiple statement blocks into MySQL, change the default delimiter to something other than a semicolon (;), so MySQL will allow you to enter a semicolon without having the client process the input. Change the delimiter by using the delimiter statement: DELIMITER //. When you're ready to have your function created, type //, and the client will process the entire set of statements that make up your stored function. When you're finished working on your functions, change the delimiter back to the standard semicolon with DELIMITER ;.

---

4. A storage amount of 64KB for the function body allows you to store around 1,000 lines of code, provided you average 60 characters on each line.

DECLARE Statements

As demonstrated in Listing 10-9, the DECLARE statement is used to create local variables, conditions, handlers, and cursors within the procedure. DECLARE can be used only in the first statements immediately within a BEGIN block. The declarations must occur variables first, cursors second, and handlers last. A common declaration is the local variable, which is done with a variable name and type:

```
DECLARE <name> <data type> [default];
```

The default value is optional when declaring a variable.

The following is an example of declaring an integer named order_tax with an initial value of 0:

```
DECLARE order_tax DECIMAL(10,2) DEFAULT 0;
```

Here, we'll take a closer look at declaring variables, conditions, and handlers. Cursors, which are also created with the DECLARE statement, are covered in more detail in Chapter 11.

Variables

Functions can access and set local, session, and global variables. Local variables are either passed in as parameters or created using the DECLARE statement, and are used in the stored function by referencing the name of the parameter or declared variable.

LOCAL, SESSION, AND GLOBAL VARIABLES IN MYSQL

MySQL has three different kinds of variables:

- *Local variables*: These variables are set in the scope of a statement or block of statements. Once that statement or block of statements has completed, the variable goes out of scope. An example of a local variable is order_tax: DECLARE order_tax DECIMAL(10,2);.

- *Session variables*: These variables are set in the scope of your session with the MySQL server. A session starts with a connection to the server and ends when the connection is closed. Variables can be created and referenced throughout the time you maintain your connection to the MySQL server, and go out of scope once the connection is terminated. Variables created during your connection cannot be referenced from other sessions. To declare or reference a session variable, prefix the variable name with an @ symbol: SET @total_count = 100;.

- *Global variables*: These variables exist across connections. They are set using the GLOBAL keyword: SET GLOBAL max_connections = 300;. Global variables are not self-defined, but are tied to the configuration of the running server. As shown, the global variable max_connections is used by MySQL to determine how many concurrent sessions, or connections, it will allow.

You can set variables in several ways. Using the DECLARE statement with a DEFAULT will set the value of a local variable, as shown in the previous example.

Values can be assigned to local, session, and global variables using the SET statement:

```
SET @total_shipping_cost = @total_shipping_cost + 5.00;
```

MySQL's SET statement includes an extension that permits setting multiple variables in one statement:

```
SET shipping_cost = 5, @total_shipping_cost = @total_shipping_cost + 5.00;
```

Note that this extension is not SQL:2003-compliant.

Conditions and Handlers

By declaring conditions and handlers, MySQL allows you to catch certain MySQL errors or SQLSTATE conditions. Errors are raised for many different reasons (MySQL includes more than 2,000 error conditions), but are predominantly centered on permissions, changes in the database structure, and changes in the data. Declaring conditions and handlers in functions works just as it does in stored procedures, which was covered in detail in Chapter 9.

Listing 10-10 shows an example of declaring a condition and handling the rise of that condition.

Listing 10-10. *Declaring a Condition and Handler*

```
DELIMITER //

CREATE FUNCTION perform_logic (some_input INT(10)) returns INT(10)
BEGIN
        DECLARE problem CONDITION FOR 1265;
        DECLARE EXIT HANDLER FOR problem
                RETURN NULL;

        # do some logic, if the problem condition is met
        # the function will exit, returning a NULL

        RETURN 1;
END
//
DELIMITER ;
```

In this example, the MySQL error number 1265 means that data was truncated when saving to a table. Any truncated field would raise the condition and cause the function to exit with a return of NULL. The complete list of SQLSTATE values and MySQL error codes is available at http://dev.mysql.com/doc/mysql/en/error-handling.html.

Flow Constructs

SQL:2003 flow constructs give you a number of statements to control and organize your statement processing. MySQL supports IF, CASE, LOOP, LEAVE, ITERATE, REPEAT, and WHILE, but does not currently support the FOR statement.

Flow controls for functions are identical to flow controls for stored procedures, which were discussed in Chapter 9. Here, we'll review the constructs and look at some examples using functions. We'll begin with the IF and CASE constructs for checking values, and then turn our attention to the looping constructs: LOOP, LEAVE, ITERATE, REPEAT, and WHILE statements.

IF

The IF statement checks a condition and runs the statements in the block if the condition is true. If needed, you can add ELSEIF statements to continue attempting to match conditions, and you can include a final ELSE statement. Listing 10-11 shows a piece of a function where the shipping cost is being calculated based on the number of days the customer is willing to wait for delivery. delivery_day is an integer parameter passed into the function when it's called.

Listing 10-11. *IF Statement*

```
DELIMITER //
CREATE FUNCTION delivery_day_shipping (delivery_day INT(1)) RETURNS INT(2)
BEGIN

DECLARE shipping_cost INT(2) DEFAULT 0;

IF delivery_day = 1 THEN
        SET shipping_cost = 20;
ELSEIF delivery_day = 2 THEN
        SET shipping_cost = 15;
ELSEIF delivery_day = 3 THEN
        SET shipping_cost = 10;
ELSE
        SET shipping_cost = 5;
END IF;

RETURN shipping_cost;

END
//
DELIMITER ;
```

CASE

For checking a uniform condition, you can use a CASE construct rather than an IF construct. Listing 10-12 shows how to use a CASE statement to accomplish the same conditions as the previous IF ... ELSEIF ... ELSE statement in Listing 10-11. Not only do they improve the readability of your code, but CASE statements generally run faster than the corresponding IF constructs. In this example, the integer parameter delivery_day is passed into the function from the caller.

Listing 10-12. *CASE Statement in a Function*

```
DELIMITER //
CREATE FUNCTION delivery_day_shipping (delivery_day INT(1)) RETURNS INT(2)
BEGIN

DECLARE shipping_cost INT(2) DEFAULT 0;

CASE delivery_day
WHEN 1 THEN
        SET shipping_cost = 20;
WHEN 2 THEN
        SET shipping_cost = 15;
WHEN 3 THEN
        SET shipping_cost = 10;
ELSE
        SET shipping_cost = 5;
END CASE;
RETURN shipping_cost;

END
//
DELIMITER ;
```

■**Caution** Unlike IF statements, CASE statements must find a match; otherwise, MySQL will return an error. However, you can get around this by using an ELSE statement, which makes sure that a catchall executes when no other condition is met.

The CASE control can also operate without an initial case value, evaluating a different condition on each WHEN statement. This is useful if you want to check different conditions in the same CASE statement. Listing 10-13 shows the shipping calculator using this syntax. The function is similar to the one in Listing 10-12, but adds the ability to pass in a preferred status. If preferred is 1, the shipping is always returned as 2, a special shipping price for preferred customers. By using the CASE statements with the condition checked on each line, you can first check the case where preferred is set, and then move on to the other cases. As with Listing 10-12, Listing 10-13 runs significantly faster than the IF-based logic in Listing 10-11.

Listing 10-13. *CASE Statement with Condition Checks*

```
DELIMITER //
CREATE FUNCTION delivery_day_shipping (delivery_day INT(1),preferred INT(1))
RETURNS INT(2)
BEGIN

DECLARE shipping_cost INT(2) DEFAULT 0;

CASE
WHEN preferred = 1 THEN
        SET shipping_cost = 2;
WHEN delivery_day = 1 THEN
        SET shipping_cost = 20;
WHEN delivery_day = 2 THEN
        SET shipping_cost = 15;
WHEN delivery_day = 3  THEN
        SET shipping_cost = 10;
ELSE
        SET shipping_cost = 5;
END CASE;
RETURN shipping_cost;

END
//
DELIMITER ;
```

LOOP and LEAVE

The LOOP statement creates a repeating loop that will run until the LEAVE statement is invoked. Optional to the LOOP is a label, which is a name and a colon prepended to the LOOP statement, with the identical name appended to the END LOOP statement. To exit the loop, a LEAVE statement can be invoked. The LEAVE keyword requires a loop label. The LEAVE statement must be accompanied by a label, which means that to use a LEAVE, you must have a name assigned to the loop.

Listing 10-14 demonstrates use of both LOOP and LEAVE in the round_down_tenth() function. This function takes an integer and returns the next lowest integer that is a multiple of ten. Where is this useful? Suppose you are dynamically creating a graph of number of orders each day for the past month, but for clarity, you want to center numbers around multiples of ten, but not round up and risk presenting data that's not based in reality. round_down_tenth() will give you the closest multiple of ten lower than the number passed to the function.

Listing 10-14. *LOOP Statement with LEAVE*

```
DELIMITER //
CREATE FUNCTION round_down_tenth (quantity INT(10)) RETURNS INT(10)
BEGIN
```

```
increment: LOOP

IF quantity MOD 10 < 1 THEN
LEAVE increment;
END IF;

SET quantity = quantity - 1;

END LOOP increment;

RETURN quantity;

END
//
DELIMITER ;
```

ITERATE

The ITERATE statement is used in the LOOP, WHILE, and REPEAT controls to indicate that control should iterate through the statements in the loop again. You can use this to prevent the loop from reaching a secondary piece of logic until the looping has satisfied the first condition.

For example, suppose you needed to order a supply of baseball caps, based on the volume of orders from last month. The supplier provides them by the dozen, so you are required to order them in quantities of 12. However, you sell them in batches of 8, so you want to make sure that the quantity you order will match the requirements of both the supplier and your sales. Listing 10-15 shows a function that can accomplish this by finding the next highest multiple of two numbers.

Listing 10-15. *LOOP Statement with ITERATE*

```
DELIMITER //
CREATE FUNCTION find_common_multiple (quantity INT(10)) RETURNS INT(10)
BEGIN

increment: LOOP

IF quantity MOD 12 > 0 THEN
SET quantity = quantity + 1;
ITERATE increment;
END IF;

IF quantity MOD 8 < 1 THEN
LEAVE increment;
END IF;

SET quantity = quantity + 1;

END LOOP increment;
```

```
RETURN quantity;

END
//
DELIMITER ;
```

Using the `find_common_multiple()` function first finds a multiple of 12, iterating in a smaller loop because of the `ITERATE increment` statement early in the logic. Once a dozen is found, the loop then considers if the number is also a multiple of 8; if not, it increments the quantity and goes back to the first condition.

WHILE...DO

Another mechanism to loop over a set of statements until a condition is true is the `WHILE` statement. Unlike `LOOP`, where the condition is met within the loop, the `WHILE` statement requires specification of the condition when defining the statement. As with `LOOP` constructs, a label can be placed before and after the `WHILE` constructs.

Listing 10-16 shows a simple use of this statement in a function that takes an integer and returns the next value that is a multiple of 12. This kind of function is helpful if you have something like an order fulfillment system that automatically submits an order for restocking of the warehouse based on last month's order volume, but is required to order by the dozen.

Listing 10-16. *WHILE Statement*

```
DELIMITER //
CREATE FUNCTION round_up_dozen (quantity INT(10)) RETURNS INT(10)
BEGIN

WHILE quantity MOD 12 > 0 DO
SET quantity = quantity + 1;
END WHILE;

RETURN quantity;

END
//
DELIMITER ;
```

REPEAT

To loop over a set of statements until a post-statement condition is met, use the `REPEAT` statement. The `REPEAT` statement ensures that your instructions will be run at least once.

Building on a previous example, let's say that each month you take the quantity of a product sold and place an order for that many, plus whatever it takes to make the ordered quantity come out in dozens. But you need to have at least one of the products available every month for a charity donation, so you really need the amount sold last month, plus one for this month rounded up to the nearest dozen. The function in Listing 10-17 does just that.

Listing 10-17. *REPEAT Statement*

```
DELIMITER //
CREATE FUNCTION order_quantity (quantity INT(10)) RETURNS INT(10)
BEGIN

REPEAT
SET quantity = quantity + 1;
UNTIL quantity MOD 12 = 0
END REPEAT;

RETURN quantity;

END
//
```

The function in Listing 10-17 first adds one to the incoming quantity before it starts the process of determining when it will reach the next quantity divisible by 12.

■**Caution** When a stored function is created, the syntax of the body isn't fully checked to determine if the function will fail at runtime. You should verify the validity of each function by testing it with a sample data set before releasing it into production.

Using Functions

As you've seen, functions are executed by using the function name from within SELECT, INSERT, and UPDATE statements. When using functions, you can prepend the database name to the function name. If the function you are referencing doesn't exist in the currently active database, a function does not exist error will occur.

In this section, we'll take a look at a stored function that uses several of the available statements.

■**Note** Although the examples in this chapter focus on numeric calculations and text manipulation, stored functions can also access data in your tables with SQL statements like SELECT . . . INTO or UPDATE to retrieve and manipulate data in your tables.

For the client, order data includes a date the order was placed, a sum of all the items on the order, and a column that contains the number of days until the customer wants the order delivered to a home or work address (contained in the rush_ship column). Listing 10-18 shows the table output.

Listing 10-18. *Sample Listing from the order Table*

```
+---------------+------------+----------+------------------+
| cust_order_id | order_date | item_sum |     rush_ship    |
+---------------+------------+----------+------------------+
|             1 | 2005-08-31 |    30.95 |                1 |
|             2 | 2005-08-27 |    40.56 |                3 |
|             3 | 2005-09-27 |   214.34 |             NULL |
|             4 | 2005-09-01 |   143.65 |             NULL |
|             5 | 2005-09-10 |   345.99 |                5 |
|             6 | 2005-08-28 |   789.24 |                1 |
|             7 | 2005-09-01 |     3.45 |                1 |
+---------------+------------+----------+------------------+
7 rows in set (0.00 sec)
```

Your client has provided you with a few rules on how to calculate the shipping, rush shipping, and tax charges. Your client wants to be able to see this data, along with the total for the customer's order. Based on the client-provided information, you will create a number of functions to generate this data. Let's start with a calc_tax() function, as shown in Listing 10-19, which takes the item cost and returns the amount of tax required.

Listing 10-19. *Function to Calculate Tax*

```
DELIMITER //
CREATE FUNCTION calc_tax (cost DECIMAL(10,2)) RETURNS DECIMAL(10,2)
RETURN cost * .05
//
DELIMITER ;
```

The next function will calculate the shipping charges, based on the sum of the items. Listing 10-20 shows the calc_shipping() function, which calculates the shipping charges based on the sum of the items and the client's shipping ranges.

Listing 10-20. *Function to Calculate Shipping*

```
DELIMITER //
CREATE FUNCTION calc_shipping (cost DECIMAL(10,2)) RETURNS DECIMAL(10,2)
BEGIN

DECLARE shipping_cost DECIMAL(10,2);

SET shipping_cost = 0;
IF cost < 25.00 THEN
        SET shipping_cost = 10.00;
ELSEIF cost < 100.00 THEN
        SET shipping_cost = 20.00;
ELSEIF cost < 200.00 THEN
        SET shipping_cost = 30.00;
```

```
ELSE
        SET shipping_cost = 40.00;
END IF;

RETURN shipping_cost;
END
//
DELIMITER ;
```

Listing 10-20 takes the cost of the items in the order and returns a flat-rate shipping charge. Now that you have the shipping charge, you need to add in any additional rush-shipping charges, depending on how many days the customer is willing to wait for the package to arrive. Listing 10-21 shows the calc_rush_shipping() function, which has the breakdown of days and costs.

Listing 10-21. *Function to Calculate Rush Shipping Charges*

```
DELIMITER //
CREATE FUNCTION calc_rush_shipping (rush_ship INT(10)) RETURNS DECIMAL(10,2)
BEGIN

DECLARE rush_shipping_cost DECIMAL(10,2);

CASE rush_ship
WHEN 1 THEN
        SET rush_shipping_cost = 20.00;
WHEN 2 THEN
        SET rush_shipping_cost = 15.00;
WHEN 3 THEN
        SET rush_shipping_cost = 10.00;
ELSE
        SET rush_shipping_cost = 0.00;
END CASE;

RETURN rush_shipping_cost;

END
//
DELIMITER ;
```

Lastly, you need a calc_total() function, which will calculate the total of all these items. Listing 10-22 shows the CREATE statement for a function that takes two arguments, and calls the calc_tax(), calc_shipping(), and calc_rush_shipping() functions to create a total cost for this customer's order.

Listing 10-22. *Function to Calculate Total Cost*

```
DELIMITER //
CREATE FUNCTION calc_total (item_sum DECIMAL(10,2), rush_ship INT(10))
RETURNS DECIMAL(10,2)
BEGIN

DECLARE order_total DECIMAL(10,2);

SET order_total = item_sum + calc_tax(item_sum) +
calc_shipping(item_sum) + calc_rush_shipping(rush_ship);
RETURN ROUND(order_total,2);

END
//
DELIMITER ;
```

The calc_total() function takes the item_sum and rush_ship values and encapsulates the three previously created functions to create a total order cost.

Notice how functions can be called from within functions. In Listing 10-22, the calc_total() function calls the calc_tax(), calc_shipping(), and calc_rush_shipping() functions to create a calculation of the return values from all three.

■**Note** Theoretically, there is no limit to the number of layers in defining functions. However, you might start to find that after just a few layers, keeping track of them becomes unwieldy. Again, it's always good to plan the implementation details before doing something like embarking on a multilevel function scheme.

Also, notice that the function definition in Listing 10-22 uses the built-in ROUND() function. For all of these function and variable declarations, the data type is DECIMAL(10,2), which should give a dollar and cent decimal, but when all the functions were compiled together in the calc_total() function, digits four and five places to the right of the decimal started to appear. To ensure that the results make sense for the application or client, the ROUND() function forces the data to output with just two decimal places.

The query to get the information the client has requested is shown in Listing 10-23.

Listing 10-23. *SELECT Statement Using Created Functions*

```
SELECT cust_order_id AS id, order_date, item_sum, rush_ship,
calc_tax(item_sum) AS tax,
calc_shipping(item_sum) AS shipping,
calc_rush_shipping(rush_ship) AS rush,
calc_total(item_sum,rush_ship) AS total
FROM cust_order;
```

The output from this query produces a nice table filled with the appropriate results, as shown in Listing 10-24.

Listing 10-24. *Output from SELECT Using Created Functions*

```
+----+------------+----------+-----------+-------+----------+-------+--------+
| id | order_date | item_sum | rush_ship | tax   | shipping | rush  | total  |
+----+------------+----------+-----------+-------+----------+-------+--------+
|  1 | 2005-08-31 |    30.95 |         1 |  1.55 |    20.00 | 20.00 |  72.50 |
|  2 | 2005-08-27 |    40.56 |         3 |  2.03 |    20.00 | 10.00 |  72.59 |
|  3 | 2005-09-27 |   214.34 |      NULL | 10.72 |    40.00 |  0.00 | 265.06 |
|  4 | 2005-09-01 |   143.65 |      NULL |  7.18 |    30.00 |  0.00 | 180.83 |
|  5 | 2005-09-10 |   345.99 |         5 | 17.30 |    40.00 |  0.00 | 403.29 |
|  6 | 2005-08-28 |   789.24 |         1 | 39.46 |    40.00 | 20.00 | 888.70 |
|  7 | 2005-09-01 |     3.45 |         1 |  0.17 |    10.00 | 20.00 |  33.62 |
+----+------------+----------+-----------+-------+----------+-------+--------+
7 rows in set (0.00 sec)
```

Managing Functions

After you've created a collection of functions in the database, you'll likely need to manage them. As with stored procedures, you can view, change, and remove stored functions.

Viewing Functions

MySQL offers several ways to view the existing functions in your database. To see all of the functions across all databases, use the SHOW FUNCTION STATUS command, as shown in Listing 10-25.

■**Note** In the examples here, we use the \G switch from the mysql client utility to display the results in rows, rather than in columns.

Listing 10-25. *Output of SHOW FUNCTION STATUS*

```
mysql> SHOW FUNCTION STATUS\G
*************************** 1. row ***************************
             Db: shop
           Name: calc_rush_shipping
           Type: FUNCTION
        Definer: mkruck@localhost
       Modified: 2005-02-09 20:13:06
        Created: 2005-02-09 20:13:06
  Security_type: DEFINER
        Comment:
```

```
*************************** 2. row ***************************
           Db: shop
         Name: calc_shipping
         Type: FUNCTION
      Definer: mkruck@localhost
     Modified: 2005-02-09 20:13:06
      Created: 2005-02-09 20:13:06
Security_type: DEFINER
      Comment:
*************************** 3. row ***************************
           Db: shop
         Name: calc_tax
         Type: FUNCTION
      Definer: mkruck@localhost
     Modified: 2005-02-09 20:13:06
      Created: 2005-02-09 20:13:06
Security_type: DEFINER
      Comment:
*************************** 4. row ***************************
           Db: shop
         Name: calc_total
         Type: FUNCTION
      Definer: mkruck@localhost
     Modified: 2005-02-09 20:13:06
      Created: 2005-02-09 20:13:06
Security_type: DEFINER
      Comment:
4 rows in set (0.00 sec)
```

This command displays a few pieces of information about each function in all databases. The Db indicates the database where the function is defined, and the Name indicates the name used to create and call the function. For SHOW FUNCTION STATUS, the Type will always have a value of FUNCTION. The Definer is the person who created the function.

■**Note** The definer of a function is not changed when an ALTER statement is processed for a function. To change who defined a function, the function must be dropped and then re-created by the desired user.

The Modified and Created fields tell you when the function was last changed and when it was first created in the database, respectively. The Security_type indicates whether the function is being executed using the permissions of the user who defined the function or the user who is calling the function.

The SHOW FUNCTION STATUS command presents a nice summary, but to see what's in a function, you'll want to use the SHOW CREATE FUNCTION command. Listing 10-26 shows the output of this statement for the calc_total() function.

Listing 10-26. *Output of SHOW CREATE FUNCTION*

```
mysql> SHOW CREATE FUNCTION shop.calc_total\G
*************************** 1. row ***************************
       Function: calc_total
       sql_mode:
Create Function: CREATE FUNCTION `shop`.`calc_total`(item_sum decimal(10,2),
rush_ship int) RETURNS decimal(10,2)
begin
declare order_total decimal(10,2);
set order_total = item_sum + calc_tax(item_sum) +
calc_shipping(item_sum) + calc_rush_shipping(rush_ship);
return round(order_total,2);
end
```

This command lets you view the CREATE statement for any function in any database. It provides the name, SQL mode, and the CREATE statement.

In Listings 10-25 and 10-26, you don't see the deterministic and language settings. If you want to get at the raw data for a function, and you have access to the mysql database, you can select information from the mysql.proc table and get all the underlying data. A raw view of the data gives you slightly more information than what you can get from the SHOW commands. For example, Listing 10-27 shows the SELECT statement for the calc_total() function and its output.

Listing 10-27. *Output of Function Data from mysql.proc Table*

```
SELECT * FROM mysql.proc WHERE name = 'calc_total'\G
*************************** 1. row ***************************
               db: shop
             name: calc_total
             type: FUNCTION
    specific_name: calc_total
         language: SQL
 sql_data_access: CONTAINS_SQL
 is_deterministic: NO
    security_type: DEFINER
       param_list: item_sum decimal(10,2), rush_ship int
          returns: decimal(10,2)
             body: begin
declare order_total decimal(10,2);
set order_total = item_sum + calc_tax(item_sum) +
calc_shipping(item_sum) + calc_rush_shipping(rush_ship);
return round(order_total,2);
end
          definer: mkruck@localhost
          created: 2005-02-09 20:45:53
         modified: 2005-02-09 20:45:53
         sql_mode:
          comment:
```

Here, you see the various pieces of the function, including `language` and `is_deterministic`, broken into separate fields. This view of the defined functions is cleaner if you are looking for a quick list of parameters or return types.

Changing and Removing Functions

MySQL provides an `ALTER` statement for stored functions, but as with stored procedures, the `ALTER` statement can change only the characteristics of a function, not the SQL statements that make up the body. The `ALTER` statement has the following syntax:

```
ALTER FUNCTION [database.]<name> <characteristics>;
```

Here is an example:

```
mysql> ALTER FUNCTION shop.calc_total
COMMENT 'encapsulate all functions for one big total';
```

You can change multiple characteristics within a single `ALTER` statement. If a characteristic isn't specified in the statement, the value is left as it was when the function was created. You can change all the characteristics listed in Table 10-1, shown earlier in the chapter, with one exception: the `DETERMINISTIC` characteristic isn't allowed in the `ALTER` statement.

To remove a stored function, use the `DROP` command:

```
DROP FUNCTION [database.]<name>
```

Here is an example:

```
mysql> DROP FUNCTION shop.calc_shipping;
```

As expected, the `DROP` statement removes the function from the `mysql.proc` table.

Function Permissions

When speaking of permissions in regard to stored functions, two main sets are involved: permissions to create and manage stored functions, and permissions to use functions.

To create a function in a database, the user must have the `CREATE ROUTINE` privilege. To change an existing function, the user must have the `ALTER ROUTINE` privilege. Permissions for creating or changing procedures can be granted globally (in the `mysql.user` table), at the database level (in the `mysql.db` table), or for a specific routine (in the `mysql.procs_priv` table).

To use a function, the caller must have the `EXECUTE` privilege for the particular database. When the function is called, the actions in the function are performed either by the user who is executing the function or the user who defined the function, depending on if the `SQL SECURITY` is set to `DEFINER` or `INVOKER`. As with the `CREATE` and `ALTER` statements, permissions for executing a function can be granted globally (in the `mysql.user` table), at the database level (in the `mysql.db` table), or for a specific routine (in the `mysql.procs_priv` table).

When a stored function is created, the creator is automatically granted the `ALTER ROUTINE` and `EXECUTE` privilege for that routine.

Chapter 15 addresses account administration and permissions, and provides more details on granting users appropriate permissions for managing and using stored functions.

Performance of Functions

We discussed benchmarking in detail in Chapter 6. As you might expect, you can perform various benchmarks to look at how functions affect the performance of a query. Here, we were primarily interested in creating a simple example that demonstrated the overhead required to send parameters to a function and get the result back, rather than focusing on the actual processing within the function itself.

To benchmark the overhead in using a function, we took the statement from Listing 10-3 and compared performance of that SELECT statement with the statement in Listing 10-4. Because this is a fairly simple function, the differences in performance should be primarily due to the time it takes to pass the item_sum and shipping values into the function and get the result.

The metrics were performed on MySQL 5.0.2, running on a single AMD64 2800+, with 1GB of RAM and a 10KB RPM SCSI data disk (separate from the boot disk). The database is using the prebuilt binary for AMD64 downloaded from the MySQL web site and is using all default options on startup (no .my.cnf file used on startup).

What we found is that repeated tests running the calculation ten million times directly in the SQL statement took an average of 6.8 seconds, or 1.47 million operations per second. Listing 10-28 shows the statement.

Listing 10-28. *Simple Calculation Directly in Query*

```
mysql> SELECT cust_order_id, item_sum, shipping,
item_sum * .05 + item_sum + shipping AS total
FROM cust_order;
```

We then created a function, calculate_total() shown in Listing 10-29, to abstract the calculation shown in the second line of Listing 10-28.

Listing 10-29. *CREATE Statement for calculate_total()*

```
CREATE FUNCTION calculate_total
(cost DECIMAL(10,2), shipping DECIMAL(10,2))
RETURNS DECIMAL(10,2)
RETURN cost * 1.05 + shipping;
```

With this function defined in the database, we ran the query in Listing 10-30 repeatedly on the same ten million rows that we ran the query from Listing 10-28. In this instance, instead of the calculation happening directly in the query, we used the calculate_total() function.

Listing 10-30. *Simple Calculation Using Function*

```
mysql> SELECT cust_order_id, item_sum, shipping,
calculate_total(item_sum,shipping) AS total
FROM cust_order;
```

We found on average it took 9.4 seconds to process the rows, or about 1.06 million operations per second.

Are those numbers significant? A lot depends on how much data you need to process. If you have billions of rows of data that you're considering filtering through a function, you may want to perform some benchmarks of your own to determine the impact the functions will have on your performance. For anyone processing smaller amounts of data (tens of thousands), the difference of having a function in the statement will be insignificant.

■Caution Throughout this chapter, we've discussed using functions in SELECT, INSERT, and UPDATE statements. To be sure we're clear, we do not suggest putting a function in the WHERE clause of a query, unless there is deliberate reason to have it there. Using functions in the WHERE clause invalidates any benefit of using an index. Using functions prevents the database from performing lookups on those index keys, meaning that your query will require a full-table scan. Use caution when building the WHERE clause of your SQL statements, and use a function only if you are sure you do not need the indexes.

Summary

We've been through a lot of details on using stored functions in MySQL. We started the chapter looking at functions in general, and how functions compare with other database-level tools. In addition to finding the right use for functions to meet the requirements set for your database, you should be familiar with the specifics of MySQL's implementation of functions before diving into moving pieces of your business logic into functions.

After reviewing the general concepts of stored functions, we dug into examples and details of the commands used to build functions. We looked at how to create functions to encapsulate calculations, and how to create functions that use other functions. We also went through details on managing existing functions with the SHOW, ALTER, and DROP commands.

We concluded the chapter by discussing the permission scheme for functions and looked into the significance of functions on query performance.

At the beginning of the chapter, we talked about needing a function to convert a statement to make the first character uppercase and the rest in lowercase. To bring the chapter full circle, here's the ucasefirst() function:

```
CREATE FUNCTION ucasefirst (phrase VARCHAR(255)) RETURNS VARCHAR(255)
RETURN CONCAT(UCASE(SUBSTR(phrase,1,1)),SUBSTR(LCASE(phrase),2));
```

And here's how it works:

```
mysql> SELECT ucasefirst("tEST THe caSE-CHANGING funCtion!");
+------------------------------------------------+
| ucasefirst("tEST THe caSE-CHANGING funCtion!") |
+------------------------------------------------+
| Test the case-changing function!               |
+------------------------------------------------+
```

The ability to create your own functions in MySQL—whether to perform a calculation, manipulate data, or format data using native SQL statements—gives you a simple, yet powerful set of commands and syntax. Using stored functions, you can now encapsulate and organize logic, extending your database to better meet the needs of your application and users.

CHAPTER 11

■■■

Cursors

In the previous chapters, we looked at both stored procedures and stored functions, and the new possibilities they bring to MySQL 5.0. As we explored these new routines, we left out a very useful piece of syntax that opens up even more possibilities in the use of stored routines: the syntax for cursors.

Cursors, like stored procedures and functions, are new to MySQL in version 5.0. Cursors are a welcome addition for people who are coming from cursor-capable databases or have been using MySQL but grumbling about not being able to use cursors. Most major databases provide cursor functionality, including DB2, Oracle, SQL Server, Sybase, and PostgreSQL. With 5.0, MySQL joins the ranks of other cursor-capable database systems.

Even if you haven't used cursors in a database before, this chapter will provide the information you need to try them out. In this chapter, we will cover the following topics related to cursors:

- Database cursor basics

- MySQL's implementation of cursors

- How to create cursors

- An example of using cursors

Database Cursors

Back in Chapter 9, all of the stored procedure examples looked at data in singular form, selecting one or two columns from a single record in a table into a variable or two to use in making a decision. You might have places where using single pieces of data meets your needs, but you're probably left thinking that unless a routine can work with sets of data, stored procedures or functions aren't of much use to you. For example, you might have a stored procedure that needs to be capable of processing a large set of records, inserting data into a set of tables based on the values in each record. Doing all of this within a stored procedure makes a lot of sense, but you need to be able to issue a SELECT statement, retrieve the rows, and loop through them one at a time to determine how each record should be handled.

With the addition of support for cursors in MySQL 5.0, processing sets of data within a stored routine is possible. The database cursor allows you to issue a SELECT statement in a procedure, either on a single table or joining multiple tables, and use a pointer to the data in the results to iterate over each record. With each record, you can use all of the available routine logic discussed in Chapter 9 and 10 to make decisions about what needs done with each record.

■Note As of writing this chapter, MySQL has released version 5.0.6, which is labeled a beta release. While the cursor functionality in the database is stable enough to test and document, production users are encouraged to wait until a release of the 5.0.x branch that is labeled production.

In database terms, a *cursor* is a pointer to a record in a set of results in the database. Using a database cursor allows you to issue a query, but rather than getting back the set of query records, you get back a pointer to the data that allows you to interact with the set of records. The cursor provides a mechanism to use the data, allowing you to issue commands to read information, move to another record, make a change to the data, and so on. Once the cursor has been created, it remains actively pointed at the data until it is closed or the connection to the database is closed.

A popular use of cursors is to issue a query that requests a cursor in return, and then have code control the cursor to iterate through the set of records, performing logic based on the information in each row.

As with stored procedures, stored functions, and other technologies, there is a debate as to where cursors are appropriate. Some suggest that cursors should be a last resort. They say that, in most cases, it's better to return the entire resultset to the client to work with than to tie up the database keeping track of a cursor over a period of time. Others suggest that cursors are a preferred method for interacting with large sets of data. They say that using cursors allows for more immediate access to the data and reduces the load on the database, because cursors can return the data to the client incrementally, and only as needed by the client. Whether cursors are appropriate for your application is a question you must answer when looking at the needs of your users and the stewards of the data. Before you decide to invest time and energy into using cursors, you should carefully weigh the implications of moving data processing for multiple-row data sets out of your application and into the database.

Before looking at the details of using cursors with MySQL, let's review some basic cursor concepts, to give you some context for MySQL's cursor implementation.

Server and Client Cursors

The two major types of cursors are server-side cursors and client-side cursors. *Server-side cursors* let you open a cursor in code that is run inside the database. You are not able to send the cursor, or a pointer to control the cursor, to an external client for interaction with the database. Server-side cursors are opened, used, and closed from within a routine inside the database. The cursor is opened and closed without any interaction with an external client, other than calling the procedure that may use a cursor internally.

A database system that allows *client-side cursors* provides the ability to open a cursor from a client outside the database (for example, in your application) and have the database return the cursor to the external client for control. Where client-side cursors are in use, you will see the client or application make a query to the database that asks for a cursor, instead of the record set, in the return. The client gets the cursor from the database, and then uses logic built into the application to control the cursor's movement, retrieval, and modification of data. Once the application has finished, it is expected to close the cursor.

MySQL offers only server-side cursors.

Cursor Movement

Depending on the database, control over the movement of the cursor varies. In its simplest form, a cursor moves forward one record at a time and gives you no control over the direction or spacing of the movement.

More sophisticated implementations will allow you to move the cursor both forward and backward. Beyond the ability to move backward is the capability to skip to certain records, based on either a record number or a position relative to where the cursor is currently positioned. It's also common to see a command to move the cursor back to the first or forward to the last record.

MySQL cursors are of the forward-only type.

Data Behind the Cursor

You might wonder exactly where the cursor resides and what data it's using when you're scrolling around. The SQL standard specifies that cursors can be either insensitive or asensitive.

An *insensitive* cursor is one that points at a temporary copy of the data. Any changes in the data while the cursor is open are hidden from the cursor, because the cursor is looking at a snapshot of the data taken at the time the cursor was requested. The snapshot of the data sticks around until the cursor is closed.

An *asensitive* cursor points at the real data, not a cached or temporary copy. A cursor that points at the actual data becomes available faster than an insensitive cursor, because the data doesn't need to be copied to a temporary place. However, when using a cursor that points at the actual data, changes in the underlying data from another connection may affect the data being used by the cursor.

MySQL cursors are asensitive.

Read and Write Cursors

The most common type of cursor returned from a database is a cursor used for reading data. However, some cursors can make changes to the record where the cursor is currently positioned.

The ability to write via a database cursor opens up a lot of additional options for your cursor use. With a write cursor, you could run a query, perform some logic on the fields in the query, and make updates to the fields in the record based on the logic. To do this same kind of thing from the client would take getting the entire resultset and then performing numerous updates on each row.

MySQL cursors are read-only.

Cursors in MySQL

MySQL comes with cursor functionality in version 5.0 and later. As you would expect, MySQL has implemented a small core of cursor functionality that can accomplish a lot.

MySQL's cursor implementation can be summarized in one statement: MySQL cursors are read-only, server-side, forward-moving, and asensitive. As our earlier discussion indicated, because they are server-side cursors, they can be used only within stored routines in the database. You cannot request a cursor from a client, and the database is not capable of returning a cursor for external control.

Being ready-only, MySQL cursors are limited to the use of the cursor to retrieve information from the database, not to make changes. If you want to make changes to the data retrieved through a cursor, you'll need to issue a separate UPDATE statement.

MySQL cursors can move only forward, one record at a time. The FETCH statement is used to move the cursor forward one record. If you need to move forward more than one record—for example, because you want to process every fifth record—you could use IF statements with a variable to perform your logic every so many FETCH statements.

MySQL supports asensitive, but not insensitive, cursors. This means that when you open a cursor to read information from a table, the actual table data is used when grabbing information, as opposed to a cached copy or temporary table to isolate the cursor's interaction with the data from other client interaction. With cursors in MySQL being asensitive, you aren't required to wait until the data is loaded from the main table storage to a temporary location to start fetching the data. This also means that you might find that data changes through other connections to the database at the time you are using your cursor. These changes may show up as you move through the records retrieved by your cursor declaration.

■**Note** In the case of using a recursive procedure or function with a cursor, you are allowed to keep the cursor open while the stored procedure or function hands control to another instance of itself. There is no limit to the number of cursors that can be open, but too many open cursors can consume enough resources to crash your database. Look for a configuration option in the near future that will let you limit the number of open cursors.

Creating Cursors

Let's start with a simple example so you can get some idea of what a function with a cursor looks like. For this example, suppose we have been asked to build an easy way for employees to get a list of the cities where we have order-processing facilities. Since we took great care to normalize our data, all cities are stored in a central table. The employees could just SELECT from the city table, but the vertical list of city names output from the SELECT isn't acceptable.

The employees use this information to dynamically generate documents that must put the city names in a sentence.

■**Note** In the examples in this chapter, we focus on using cursors in stored procedures and stored functions, but cursors can also be used in triggers. However, we recommend that you keep trigger processing to a minimum, using triggers only for simple tasks that verify or manipulate the data. Use extended processing, like cursors, in a trigger only if absolutely necessary. Triggers are covered in Chapter 13.

We could write a tool that goes to the database, gets the list, and formats the results in a string to be used in a paragraph, or we could put this into a function and let the employees call the function. Listing 11-1 shows how we might build the city_list() function.

Listing 11-1. *city_list() Function*

```
DELIMITER //
CREATE FUNCTION city_list() RETURNS VARCHAR(255)
BEGIN

        DECLARE finished INTEGER DEFAULT 0;
        DECLARE city_name VARCHAR(50) DEFAULT "";
        DECLARE list VARCHAR(255) DEFAULT "";
        DECLARE city_cur CURSOR FOR SELECT name FROM city ORDER BY name;
        DECLARE CONTINUE HANDLER FOR NOT FOUND SET finished = 1;

        OPEN city_cur;

        get_city: LOOP
                FETCH city_cur INTO city_name;
                IF finished THEN
                        LEAVE get_city;
                END IF;
                SET list = CONCAT(list,", ",city_name);
        END LOOP get_city;

        CLOSE city_cur;

        RETURN SUBSTR(list,3);

END
//
DELIMITER ;
```

When entering multiple statement blocks into MySQL, you need to first change the default delimiter to something other than a semicolon (;), so MySQL will allow you to enter a ; without having the client process the input. Listing 11-1 begins by using the delimiter statement: DELIMITER //, which changes the delimiter to //. When you're ready to have your procedure created, type //, and the client will process your entire procedure. When you're finished working on your procedures, change the delimiter back to the standard semicolon with DELIMITER ;, as you can see at the end of Listing 11-1.

The differences in this function definition from the ones you saw in Chapter 10 are the DECLARE...CURSOR, OPEN, FETCH, and CLOSE statements, as well as the HANDLER declaration. These are the statements for using cursors.

Before we look at the syntax for the statements related to cursors, let's step through what's happening in the city_list() function. It starts with a number of variable declarations, a cursor declaration to get city names from the city table, and a handler declaration to help you determine when you've reached the end of the results. It then opens the cursor and iterates through the results, fetching each record, checking if the fetch failed, and adding the name of the current city to our string. Finally, it returns the string to the caller. Using this function is simple, as shown in Listing 11-2.

Listing 11-2. *Using the city_list() Function*

```
mysql> SELECT city_list() AS cities;
+---------------------------------+
| cities                          |
+---------------------------------+
| Berlin, Boston, Columbus, London |
+---------------------------------+
1 row in set (0.05 sec)
```

The employees who need to have a string list of all the cities in the system can now use this function where required. It will always get the list of current city names in the city table.

The statements for using cursors are intertwined with statements to build the overall routine, but appear in the order DECLARE, OPEN, FETCH, and CLOSE as you build a procedure or function that uses a cursor.

DECLARE Statements

When building a stored procedure or function that requires a cursor, a few DECLARE statements are needed. You may recall from our coverage of stored procedures in Chapter 9 that declarations must be ordered variables first, cursors second, and handlers last.

Variables

When using a cursor, you need to declare at least two variables. One is the variable that will be used to indicate that the cursor has reached the end of the record set. In Listing 11-1, we used the finished variable for this purpose:

```
DECLARE finished INTEGER DEFAULT 0;
```

The finished variable was initialized to 0. During the loop over the record, this variable is checked with an IF statement to determine if the last record has been reached. We'll look at the loop shortly, when we discuss the HANDLER statement.

Beyond the variable for exiting the loop, you also need to declare a variable for each field that you will FETCH from the cursor. In this example, we're getting only one field from each row, so we declare only one variable to store the field value being pulled from the row of data:

```
DECLARE city_name VARCHAR(50) DEFAULT "";
```

When you're iterating over the records, the FETCH statement gets the field value from the cursor and assigns the value to the variable. We'll cover fetching data from the records in the upcoming section about the FETCH statement.

Each time the loop iterates, city_name will be set to the value of name for the current row and be available for use in whatever logic you're performing in the loop. In this case, we're building a string.

We also have declared a list variable that is created to store the joined city names. This variable will eventually be used for the return to the client.

Cursor

Once we've declared the variables for the procedure, we can declare the cursor itself. The statement to create the cursor is shown here:

```
DECLARE <cursor name> CURSOR FOR <SELECT statement>;
```

This statement simply defines the cursor, but does not actually process the statement or create the pointer to the data. The DECLARE statement from Listing 11-1 shows how this looks in practice:

```
DECLARE city_cur CURSOR FOR SELECT name FROM city ORDER BY name;
```

Here, we create a cursor named city_cur, which is defined as a pointer to the data from a SELECT statement that will retrieve all the names from the city table.

Handler

A HANDLER statement is required to detect and handle when the cursor cannot find any more records. Each time the FETCH statement is processed, it attempts to get the next row of data. When it has reached the end of the set of results, it will not be able to find another set of data. At that time, a condition will be raised, the handler will be activated, and the handler will set up for the iteration over the records to exit. (Refer to Chapter 9 for more information about handlers.)

In the example in Listing 11-1, we declared a finished variable, initially set to 0. We then created a handler that says, "When FETCH has raised the condition that it couldn't find a record to read, set the finished variable to 1," as follows:

```
DECLARE CONTINUE HANDLER FOR NOT FOUND SET finished = 1;
```

Each time the loop iterates, it attempts to FETCH, and then immediately checks the finished variable to see if it was changed by the condition being raised. If the finished variable wasn't changed by an activation of the HANDLER statement, the loop continues. This logic is repeated for each iteration through the loop:

```
get_city: LOOP
                FETCH city_cur INTO city_name;
                IF finished THEN
                        LEAVE get_city;
                END IF;
                SET list = CONCAT(list,", ",city_name);
END LOOP get_city;
```

If the FETCH can't get a row, a NOT FOUND condition is raised. This condition is handled by the handler, which sets finished to 1. The IF finished THEN statement will then be satisfied, and the loop will exit on the LEAVE statement. A loop label, get_city in this example, is required to use the LEAVE statement. (See Chapter 9 for details on flow constructs, including the LOOP, IF... THEN, and LEAVE statements.)

■Caution You may be tempted to use the REPEAT statement for your iterations, but be careful. The REPEAT mechanism is problematic because it doesn't allow you to check to see if the FETCH caused the reset of the finished variable until the bottom of the loop. If you don't check if the loop should exit immediately after the FETCH, you will execute statements, even though the end of the resultset has been reached.

OPEN Statement

After you have declared the necessary variables and the cursor itself, you can activate the cursor by using the OPEN statement:

```
OPEN <cursor name>;
```

For our example, where the cursor was declared as city_cur, the OPEN statement looks like:

```
OPEN city_cur;
```

When you issue this statement, the SELECT statement in the cursor declaration is processed, and the cursor is pointed at the first record in the statement, ready for a FETCH to happen.

■Tip A cursor declaration can be opened multiple times within a stored procedure. If the cursor has been closed, the OPEN statement can be used to run the SQL statement again and give you a pointer to the data. This might be helpful if you have a set of records that needs to be used several times in a procedure or function.

FETCH Statement

The FETCH statement gets the data from the record, assigns it to a variable, and tells the cursor to move to the next record. The FETCH statement requires a cursor name and a variable:

```
FETCH <cursor name> INTO <variable name>[, <variable name>, …];
```

The example in Listing 11-1 fetches the record from the city_cur cursor and puts that single value into the city_name variable:

```
FETCH city_cur INTO city_name;
```

If your SELECT statement in DECLARE…CURSOR contains more than one column, you'll be required to provide a comma-delimited list of variables to use when assigning the value of each field to a variable. For example, if the SELECT statement in Listing 11-1 had also specified the city_id, we would have needed to declare a variable to hold the city_id when it was fetched.

CLOSE Statement

When you are finished with the cursor, you should close it. The CLOSE statement to accomplish this is simple:

```
CLOSE <cursor name>;
```

In Listing 11-1, we close the city_cur cursor as follows:

```
CLOSE city_cur;
```

Closing the cursor removes the pointer from the data. If you don't issue the CLOSE statement, the cursor will remain open until your connection to the database is closed.

■**Tip** You can have multiple cursors within a single stored procedure, each with its own DECLARE statement. You can have them opened at the same time and FETCH from them within the same loop, or in separate iterations at different points in your procedure or function. Be aware that the NOT FOUND condition will be met when any of the FETCH statements finds that it is at the end of the record set. There is no way to assign a condition to a specific cursor.

Using Cursors

We started the chapter with a scenario where you needed to process multiple records and move them to a set of other tables in your system, with the appropriate table for a row being decided by the data in the row. Now, let's see how you might solve this type of problem with a stored procedure and cursor.

Sticking with the online store example we've been using in previous chapters, suppose we have a login table that keeps track of when a customer logs in to our system. We use this information to keep a customer login history for statistics, as well as to record login information in case a security issue arises. We also use this table to show users their login history for the past week. Because we have user counts in the hundreds of thousands at any given point, and users log in to the system many times throughout each day, the table that tracks their access grows quickly, as expected. Within just a few months, the login process, which checks the last login and inserts a new record, and the page that displays the recent login information both show signs of problems with scalability.

Since we really want only the logins from the past week, we don't need all the information to stay in the login table. To reduce the size of our login table, we decide to create a login_archive table and push the older information in the login table into this archive.

From our customer support group and reps, we learn that the data would be even more useful if it were separated using the region of the user and placed in tables replicated out to the regional offices during the archive process. To do this, we create an archive table for each of three main regions: login_archive_south, login_archive_northeast, and login_archive_northwest. However, we still need a way to go through all of the data and move it to the right place.

This scenario is perfect for a stored procedure that uses a cursor to go through each line of the data and move it into different tables. Since we don't actually need to see any of the data in the client during this process, using a stored procedure will give us better performance, because data does not need to flow back and forth between the client and the database. The interaction with the data and the data itself stays inside the database until the process is complete. Listing 11-3 shows the login_archive() procedure built to accomplish this task.

Listing 11-3. *login_archive() Procedure*

```
DELIMITER //

CREATE PROCEDURE login_archive()
BEGIN
        DECLARE finished INTEGER DEFAULT 0;
        DECLARE cust_id INTEGER;
        DECLARE log_id INTEGER;
        DECLARE time DATETIME;
        DECLARE moved_count INTEGER DEFAULT 0;
        DECLARE customer_region INTEGER;

        DECLARE login_curs CURSOR FOR SELECT l.customer_id, l.login_time,
                c.region, l.login_id
                FROM login l, customer c
                WHERE l.customer_id = c.customer_id
                AND to_days(l.login_time) < to_days(now())-7;

        DECLARE CONTINUE HANDLER FOR NOT FOUND SET finished = 1;

        OPEN login_curs;

        move_login: LOOP
```

```
      FETCH login_curs INTO cust_id, time, customer_region, log_id;

      IF finished THEN
             LEAVE move_login;
      END IF;

      IF customer_region = 1 THEN
             INSERT INTO login_northeast SET customer_id = cust_id,
             login_time = time;
      ELSEIF customer_region = 2 THEN
             INSERT INTO login_northwest SET customer_id = cust_id,
             login_time = time;
      ELSE
             INSERT INTO login_south SET customer_id = cust_id,
             login_time = time;
      END IF;

      DELETE from login where login_id = log_id;

      SET moved_count = moved_count + 1;

      END LOOP move_login;

      CLOSE login_curs;

      SELECT moved_count as 'records archived';

END
//
DELIMITER ;
```

This stored procedure starts with the expected declaration of the finished variable and other variables for storing fetched data, as well as the cursor and handler declaration. We also create the moved_count variable for keeping track of how many records are moved. The SQL statement that defines the cursor is a bit more complex than our first example, but nothing out of the ordinary. It joins two tables and includes a WHERE clause to limit the results to records that are older than seven days.

We then open the cursor and use the LOOP statement to go through each record. Notice that the FETCH statement assigns values to multiple variables, correlated with the number of columns in the SELECT statement that defined city_cur. After the FETCH, we first check to see if we've reached the end of the records, exiting if we have. If we're not ready to exit, we use the values in the record to determine which region the customer belongs in, and INSERT the record into the appropriate table. Finally, in the loop, we DELETE the record that was just moved so it isn't in the login table (one of the main purposes for the archive process) and increment the moved_count variable.

Let's try this to make sure that the procedure is moving the data appropriately. A look at the record counts shows that there's a lot of information in the login table, and none in the region-specific tables. Listing 11-4 shows the output from four queries to get record counts.

Listing 11-4. *Record Counts Before Calling archive_login()*

```
mysql> SELECT COUNT(*) AS login FROM login;
+-------+
| login |
+-------+
| 10000 |
+-------+
1 row in set (0.17 sec)

mysql> SELECT COUNT(*) AS login_northwest FROM login_northwest;
+-----------------+
| login_northwest |
+-----------------+
|               0 |
+-----------------+
1 row in set (0.01 sec)

mysql> SELECT COUNT(*) AS login_northeast FROM login_northeast;
+-----------------+
| login_northeast |
+-----------------+
|               0 |
+-----------------+
1 row in set (0.01 sec)

mysql> SELECT COUNT(*) AS login_south FROM login_south;
+-------------+
| login_south |
+-------------+
|           0 |
+-------------+
1 row in set (0.00 sec)
```

Now, let's see what happens when we execute the stored procedure, with its internal cursor mechanism, using the CALL statement, as shown in Listing 11-5.

Listing 11-5. *Running login_archive()*

```
mysql> CALL login_archive();
+------------------+
| records archived |
+------------------+
|             3757 |
+------------------+
1 row in set (9.58 sec)
```

The return from `login_archive()` tells us that 3,757 of our 10,000 records were archived.

To verify that records were moved into the appropriate place, we can run the queries to check the counts of each table, as shown in Listing 11-6.

Listing 11-6. *Record Counts After Calling archive_login()*

```
mysql> SELECT COUNT(*) AS login FROM login;
+-------+
| login |
+-------+
|  6243 |
+-------+
1 row in set (0.24 sec)

mysql> SELECT COUNT(*) AS login_northwest FROM login_northwest;
+-----------------+
| login_northwest |
+-----------------+
|            1344 |
+-----------------+
1 row in set (0.01 sec)

mysql> SELECT COUNT(*) AS login_northeast FROM login_northeast;
+-----------------+
| login_northeast |
+-----------------+
|            1256 |
+-----------------+
1 row in set (0.01 sec)

mysql> SELECT COUNT(*) AS login_south FROM login_south;
+-------------+
| login_south |
+-------------+
|        1157 |
+-------------+
1 row in set (0.00 sec)
```

The output from the counts on the tables indicates that some of the `login` table's records were moved to the three regional archive tables, and that there are still 6,243 records left. A look at the `login` table reveals that the remaining records are from logins from the past seven days, as we anticipated.

Summary

With the ability to add cursors into stored procedures and functions, you gain a powerful set of commands to process data, specifically in sets of results in your tables.

Cursors are used in stored procedures, functions, and triggers to iterate through sets of data, assigning local variables to the field values in the data and using those values to perform logic or additional SQL statements. As with all database tools, you must carefully consider how cursors meet the needs of your users and application and determine whether using them within a procedure or function will provide the best solution to the problem you are attempting to solve.

The cursor syntax is simple and easy to add into the syntax for stored routines in the database. With just four additional statements, MySQL keeps focused on doing the most with the least.

The chapter worked through two examples: a simple function and a stored procedure. Both examples provide a starting point for thinking about how your database could benefit from the use of cursors.

All said, cursors are the icing on the cake of stored routines. The ability to process large sets of data within your database opens up countless new options in planning and implementing the functionality and tools that are required of any database administrator or application programmer.

## CHAPTER 12

Views

MySQL is all about storing and retrieving relational data. A lot of data stored in a database is dynamic, in the sense that data is being added, updated, or removed. Data is also dynamic in the sense that as you collect it, you find new questions to ask about the data and new ways to arrange the relationships between various pieces of data. A part of this forward motion includes looking at the data in different ways—including new columns, joining tables not previously associated with one another, summarizing data in new ways, and so on.

Views offer one solution to the ever-changing need for rearranging and changing how data is presented. Views are new to MySQL as of version 5.0. Perhaps you've started using them already, or have used them in another database system. Maybe you've heard other developers or database administrators describe using views. Even if you have no idea what views are, this chapter is the right place to be to learn why and how views can make things easier for everyone.

This chapter delves into views in MySQL, and covers the following areas:

- Uses for database views

- MySQL's implementation of views

- How to create views

- Updatable views

- Views of views

- How to display, change, and remove views

- View permissions

- Performance of views

Database View Uses

Have you ever wanted to let a user build queries that would look at only certain rows of data in a particular table? Have you ever wanted to have data from several tables merged together into a single, dynamically updated table? Have you ever wanted to create an "alias" for a table, having it appear under two names but contain the same data? One way to accomplish these goals, which involve virtual representations of tables, is to use views.

A view provides a mechanism for interacting with rows and columns of data contained in one or more tables. From the client, a view behaves like a table, in that it has a specific number of columns and contains any number of rows of data. The view can be used in a SELECT statement, just like any other table. The view can also be used to update data in certain circumstances.

In the database, a view is defined primarily by a query that performs a SELECT on one or more tables. A view definition also includes some keywords to help the database know how to process interactions with the data through the view. A view can even contain columns that are results of database functions or column aggregation. In essence, a view is a way for you to take a SELECT statement, put it inside the server, and make the results into a table that can be queried and is always current with the tables in the FROM clause in the defining query.

Another way to think of a view is that it's like telling the server that, before it runs an incoming SQL statement, it needs to first issue a predefined SELECT statement. Once the predefined statement has been executed, the server should run the incoming SQL statement on the data retrieved in the predefined SELECT statement.

For example, suppose you have a customer table with id, name, age, and household_income fields. A SELECT on this table can get any of those four fields. If you wanted to hide the house_hold_income field from certain employees, or hide it from your application, you could define a view with a SELECT statement like this:

```
SELECT id, name, age FROM customer;
```

If you named the view customer_info, any SELECT statements against the view would be able to retrieve only columns and records that show up in the predefined statement—id, name, and age—from the table. Since the customer_info table is based on a SELECT from the customer table, results from the customer_info table will always be exactly what you would find in the customer table, less the household_income column.

The following are some reasons why database designers, database administrators, developers, and other database folks might want to implement views in their database or application:

Query abstraction: You want a way to abstract queries from the user, resulting in a simplified data interface, reduced network traffic, and data representations different from the actual tables. Complex queries can be cumbersome in the code, as well as a burden on network bandwidth.

Limited access: For efficiency or security, you want to limit access to a subset of data in a particular table or set of tables. For example, a table must consist of product orders from around the world, but have fulfillment centers in certain regions that should see only orders for their region. You might create a view for each region to provide that region the ability to view and update its data but not data from another region.

Backward-compatibility: For backward-compatibility, you want to provide access to a particular table under a separate name, which acts as an interface to the referenced table. For instance, if you are refactoring a particular table, you might use a view to continue to return results based on the original table structure to mask changes in the table.

Security: Some database systems support only read-only views, or give you the ability to specify that a view is read-only. In systems where views can be created as read-only, they can be used to enforce security, giving people access to a view of the table that cannot be updated.

Development: Views can allow multiple developers to point their development code to a single database, yet make changes in specific tables. This can be useful in multiuser development environments, where each developer possesses his or her own database for development. To begin, the developer's database contains views of the tables in the central database. In the instance where a developer needs to alter a table for development, that developer can change the view, or drop the view and create a local copy of the table. After completing the code changes, the ALTER statements made to the local tables are made in the central database, and the developer replaces his or her local copies of the tables with views of the newly altered tables in the central database.

Virtual fields: In a database design where storing calculated fields is not permitted, or in situations where new calculated fields need to be added, views can provide a virtual representation of those columns that are calculated as the query is executed. A view will solve a problem like having a basket table with a quantity and unit_cost field where you want to display the total_price (product of quantity and price_each) but don't want to store it in a table. A view can join the columns of a physical table with dynamically calculated columns to provide calculations without needing to store those calculations in the database.

Views in MySQL

MySQL's implementation of views conforms to the SQL:2003 standard, except in a few cases, which are noted as appropriate throughout the chapter.

Views are associated with a specific database and are stored in a MySQL data dictionary file, located in /<datadir>/<database_name>/<view_name>.frm. Data dictionary files for views are stored in plain-text format, which means you can view the SQL that defines the view, as well as the other attributes of the view, with a text viewer or editor.

■**Note** As we write this chapter, MySQL has released version 5.0.6, which is labeled a beta release. While the database is stable enough to test and document the functionality of views, production users are encouraged to wait until a release of the 5.0.x branch that is labeled for production.

The MySQL server processes queries of views in two different ways:

- MySQL creates a temporary table of the data results from the view's defining SELECT statement, and then executes the incoming SQL against the temporary table.

- MySQL combines the incoming SQL statement with the view's defining SELECT statement, creating a new, single SQL statement. This SQL statement is executed against the tables.

Both methods, and how to control MySQL's choice of which method to use, are covered in more detail in the next section.

Queries against a view will be stored in the query cache if the cache is enabled and the query can be stored in the cache.[1] If available, data is always pulled from the buffering subsystem to avoid making a call to the disk. (See Chapter 4 for more information about MySQL buffering subsystems.)

MySQL supports views of views. The SELECT statement that defines a view can contain references to other views in the database.

MySQL views contain a built-in versioning system. When a view is altered or replaced, a copy of the data dictionary file (.frm file) for the existing view is copied into the arc (archive) directory within the directory of that particular database. The three most recent data dictionary files are stored for each replaced or altered view. The archive copies of the data dictionary files are kept even after the view is dropped. The archive files are deleted when the database is dropped.

Now that we've described how MySQL implements views, we can move on to the details of building and maintaining views.

■**Note** If you're familiar with MySQL's MERGE storage engine, you might be wondering how its tables differ from views. As explained in Chapter 5, the MERGE storage engine allows you to join multiple identical tables into one virtual table. The tables must be identical, and when creating a MERGE table, you aren't allowed to limit the columns or rows by a SELECT statement. In contrast, views afford you a great deal of flexibility on what columns and rows to choose, from any number of varied tables.

Creating Views

At a minimum, creating a view requires a view name and a SQL statement:

```
CREATE VIEW <name> AS <SELECT statement>;
```

Suppose you have a customer table that has a customer_id, region, and name column. A sample output of a few rows from this table is shown in Listing 12-1.

Listing 12-1. *Records in customer Table*

```
+-------------+--------+---------+
| customer_id | region | name    |
+-------------+--------+---------+
|           1 |      1 | Mike    |
|           2 |      1 | Jay     |
|           3 |      2 | Johanna |
|           4 |      2 | Michael |
|           5 |      3 | Heidi   |
|           6 |      3 | Ezra    |
+-------------+--------+---------+
```

---

1. Details on what makes a query qualify for the query cache are available at http://dev.mysql.com/doc/mysql/en/query-cache-how.html.

A view might come in handy if you want certain employees to see the data in this table, but limit them to seeing only the customers in region 1. Listing 12-2 shows how to create a simple view to serve as an alias for the customer table, limiting the records to just those in region 1.

Listing 12-2. *Creating a Simple View*

```
mysql> CREATE VIEW customer_region1 AS
SELECT customer_id, name FROM customer WHERE region = 1;
```

Once the view is created, you can query it in the same way as any other table. Listing 12-3 shows a query against the customer_region1 view with the returned results.

Listing 12-3. *Selecting from a View*

```
mysql> SELECT * FROM customer_region1;
+-------------+------+
| customer_id | name |
+-------------+------+
|           1 | Mike |
|           2 | Jay  |
+-------------+------+
```

The statement in Listing 12-3 is just like any other SELECT, but instead of getting data directly from some tables, it goes through the view. This view has been defined as the customer_id and name columns of all records in the customer table where the region is 1. When you use SELECT *, you get the two columns defined in the view instead of the three columns in the underlying table.

The CREATE Statement

Much of the power of a view is contained in the SQL statement that defines the view. However, a number of syntax options in addition to the SELECT statement are important in building a view. The CREATE statement, with a complete list of user-defined fields looks like this:

```
CREATE [OR REPLACE] [<algorithm attributes>] VIEW [database.]< name> [(<columns>)]
AS <SELECT statement> [<check options>]
```

When creating a view, you can use the OR REPLACE syntax to prevent a MySQL error in the instance that the view is already defined. In some cases, such as when you would rather be notified that you are overwriting an existing view, not using the OR REPLACE is preferred.

■Note Permissions for creating, using, and managing views are covered later in the "View Permissions" section. If you are experiencing permission problems, refer to that section to clarify what privileges are necessary when working with views.

Let's break this statement down into each of the user-defined components to further explore how a view is created.

Algorithm Attributes

As mentioned earlier in the chapter, views are processed one of two ways. The algorithm attributes for a view allow you to have some control over which of these mechanisms MySQL uses when executing the query. These attributes are MERGE, TEMPTABLE, and UNDEFINED. Let's see what each one of these attributes means.

■**Caution** The ALGORITHM syntax is not included in the SQL:2003 specification. While this syntax is helpful in controlling the behavior of your view, it may mean your view definition statements aren't compatible with other database systems that support the SQL:2003 syntax standard.

MERGE

Specifying a MERGE algorithm tells the query parser to attempt to combine the incoming SQL statement with the SELECT statement that defines the view and create one SQL statement to process. If MySQL can do this, it can run just one query, which is more efficient than creating a temporary table. For this reason, MERGE is the preferred algorithm.

To demonstrate how this works, let's look at the view we used in Listing 12-2 and see how a SELECT statement could be combined with the view definition. Here is the statement to create the customer_region1 view using the MERGE algorithm:

```
CREATE ALGORITHM = MERGE VIEW customer_region1 AS
SELECT customer_id, name FROM customer WHERE region = 1;
```

Let's say we wanted to get the name of the customer with customer_id of 1 from this view. The SELECT statement would look like this:

```
SELECT name FROM customer_region1 WHERE customer_id = 1;
```

With a MERGE algorithm, MySQL combines the query with the SELECT statement in the view definition to come up with a single query to execute:

```
SELECT name FROM customer WHERE customer_id = 1 AND region = 1;
```

In this case, MySQL used the column name from the incoming SELECT and combined the WHERE clauses from both the incoming query and the SELECT statement that defines the customer_region1 view.

When the view doesn't represent a one-to-one relationship with records in the underlying tables, MERGE isn't allowed. A relationship between the view and its underlying tables that is not one-to-one is created by using aggregation functions (SUM(), MIN(), MAX(), and so on) or by using the DISTINCT, GROUP BY, HAVING, and UNION keywords. In instances where the MERGE algorithm isn't allowed, the database switches the ALGORITHM value to UNDEFINED.

TEMPTABLE

The TEMPTABLE algorithm forces a view to load the data from the underlying tables into a temporary table, using the SELECT statement that defines the view. Once the data is loaded to the temporary table, the incoming statement is executed against the temporary table.

Using a temporary table for a view adds overhead because all the data must be moved into the temporary table before the incoming statement can be processed. However, moving the data to a temporary table means the underlying tables can be released from any locks while the temporary table is used to finish the execution of the query. In some systems, minimal lock time is important. The TEMPTABLE option for views will mean the least amount of lock time for the view's underlying tables.

Views that reference only literal values are required to use a temporary table. Views that use temporary tables are never updatable. Updatable views are covered in the "Creating Updatable Views" section later in the chapter.

UNDEFINED

Setting the view algorithm to UNDEFINED tells the query parser to make the choice between the MERGE and TEMPTABLE algorithms. The parser prefers the MERGE method, so it will use that method unless a condition forces it to use a temporary table. As noted earlier, the MERGE method can't be used when the view doesn't represent a one-to-one relationship with records in the underlying tables.

UNDEFINED is the default, and it will be used if you omit the ALGORITHM keyword (or you can explicitly specify ALGORITHM = UNDEFINED). UNDEFINED is also used if the view specifies MERGE but can be processed only by using a temporary table.

View Name

The view name is the name used in SQL statements to query the view. Names of views share the same namespace as tables in the database, which means you can't have a view with the same name as a table within the same database.

The NAME parameter can be prefixed with a database name, which allows you to explicitly specify the database where the view should be created. If the database name isn't prepended, the view will be created in the currently active database. If there is no currently active database, the CREATE statement will return an error.

■**Tip** If you want to create views as aliases for security or abstraction, consider creating a separate database where your views are defined. Doing this means that the client uses a completely different database to view data, and you can use the same names as your tables for your views, because they aren't in the same namespace as the database where your tables are stored.

Column Names

Setting optional column names in a view allows you to change how the results are labeled when returned to the client. The number of columns specified in the column list must match the number of columns returned from the SELECT statement that defines the view. Listing 12-4 demonstrates creating the customer_region1 view, using the optional column names to specify the column labels returned with the query results.

Listing 12-4. *Creating a View with Specified Column Names*

```
mysql> CREATE VIEW customer_region1 (id, firstname) AS
SELECT customer_id, name FROM customer WHERE region = 1;
```

The results returned from the customer_region1 view will now label the columns as specified in the CREATE statement, as demonstrated in Listing 12-5.

Listing 12-5. *Selecting from the View with Specified Column Names*

```
mysql> SELECT * FROM customer_region1;
+----+-----------+
| id | firstname |
+----+-----------+
|  1 | Mike      |
|  2 | Jay       |
+----+-----------+
```

■**Note** You may discover that column names can also be changed in the output from a view by using the AS keyword for renaming columns with the SQL statement that defines the view. While this works, we recommend avoiding it and using the method demonstrated in Listing 12-4. Using AS in your defining SELECT statement complicates combining SQL statements when using the MERGE algorithm. In addition, the SQL:2003 standard specifies using the column list when changing the names of your columns.

The SELECT Statement

The SELECT statement can query a single table, multiple tables, or a union of multiple SELECT statements. Any table or column referenced in the SQL statement of the view must exist. The query parser checks these tables when the view is created.

A few things aren't allowed in a query that defines a view:

- A view definition cannot contain a subquery in the FROM clause of the SQL statement.

- User, system, or local variables are not allowed in the SQL SELECT statement.

- Views can't point at temporary tables (temporary views cannot be created).

- Triggers cannot be associated with a view.

- Views created within stored procedures can't reference parameters in the stored procedure.

■**Caution** When creating a view, the underlying tables and columns are checked. If the structure of those underlying tables is changed after the view has been created, the view will need to be updated; otherwise, queries to the view may return errors.

We've already reviewed a few examples of a view representing data from a single table in Listings 12-2 and 12-4. In the following sections, we'll go through using multiple tables with a join and combining multiple SELECT statements with UNION. These techniques allow you to create complex views of the data.

Joining Tables

Continuing with the order fulfillment theme, let's suppose that the general fulfillment manager wants to be able to view all orders going out from all fulfillment centers. In addition to the order_id and the ship_date, she also wants to see customer and address information for the order. To satisfy this request, we create a view called all_orders, which combines the order, customer, and address tables. The SELECT statement is fairly complex, so giving the manager a view that is easy to select from makes finding the data much easier. Listing 12-6 shows the CREATE statement.

Listing 12-6. *Creating a View with Joined Tables*

```
mysql> CREATE ALGORITHM = TEMPTABLE VIEW all_orders
(order_id, ship_date, region, customer_id, name, address) AS
SELECT o.cust_order_id, o.ship_date, c.region, c.customer_id, c.name, a.address
FROM customer c, address a, cust_order o
WHERE o.customer_id = c.customer_id
AND c.customer_id = a.customer_id
AND o.customer_id = a.customer_id
AND o.address_id = a.address_id;
```

When creating the all_orders view, we use the TEMPTABLE algorithm to ensure the view, and its underlying tables, won't be updated through the view. A simple SELECT statement retrieves all of the important information, as shown in Listing 12-7.

Listing 12-7. *Output of the View with Joined Tables*

```
mysql> SELECT * FROM all_orders;
+----------+------------+--------+-------------+---------+------------------------+
| order_id | ship_date  | region | customer_id | name    | address                |
+----------+------------+--------+-------------+---------+------------------------+
|        1 | 2005-08-31 |      1 |           1 | Mike    | 123 My Street          |
|        2 | 2005-08-27 |      1 |           1 | Mike    | 456 My Business Street |
|        3 | 2005-09-27 |      1 |           2 | Jay     | 123 That Street        |
|        4 | 2005-09-01 |      1 |           2 | Jay     | 123 That Street        |
|        6 | 2005-08-28 |      2 |           3 | Johanna | 123 Home Street        |
|        5 | 2005-09-10 |      2 |           3 | Johanna | 456 Work Street        |
|        7 | 2005-09-01 |      2 |           4 | Michael | 123 My Street          |
+----------+------------+--------+-------------+---------+------------------------+
7 rows in set (0.00 sec)
```

The results returned from a query to the all_orders view is a nice summary of information from three different tables, yet the manager can get at the data without needing to issue a sophisticated query each time. Also, if the manager wants to sort results by different fields, or limit the results, she can easily add the ORDER BY or LIMIT syntax, without needing to deal with such a large statement, as shown in Listing 12-8.

Listing 12-8. *Adding ORDER BY to the Joined Table View*

```
mysql> SELECT * FROM all_orders ORDER BY ship_date;
+----------+------------+--------+-------------+---------+------------------------+
| order_id | ship_date  | region | customer_id | name    | address                |
+----------+------------+--------+-------------+---------+------------------------+
|        2 | 2005-08-27 |      1 |           1 | Mike    | 456 My Business Street |
|        6 | 2005-08-28 |      2 |           3 | Johanna | 123 Home Street        |
|        1 | 2005-08-31 |      1 |           1 | Mike    | 123 My Street          |
|        7 | 2005-09-01 |      2 |           4 | Michael | 123 My Street          |
|        4 | 2005-09-01 |      1 |           2 | Jay     | 123 That Street        |
|        5 | 2005-09-10 |      2 |           3 | Johanna | 456 Work Street        |
|        3 | 2005-09-27 |      1 |           2 | Jay     | 123 That Street        |
+----------+------------+--------+-------------+---------+------------------------+
7 rows in set (0.00 sec)
```

If the manager prefers the order to be sorted a certain way all the time, we could specify the sort as an ORDER BY clause in the SQL statement that defines the view.

■**Note** In the case that a view has an ORDER BY clause, the results will be sorted before being returned to the client. If the client has also specified a sort, the results returned from the view will be resorted so the final output matches the query sent by the client. This is true for LIMIT statements as well. If the view limits the results to a given number, the limit defined in the view will be applied before a limit in the calling query. The query to get data from a view will never override the query used to define the view.

The manager is indeed quite content with this new feature; however, she also wants to be able to see the number of orders shipped on each date. We can supply this information by creating a view of the orders table with a GROUP BY clause, as shown in Listing 12-9.

Listing 12-9. *Using a GROUP BY Clause to Create a View*

```
mysql> CREATE ALGORITHM = TEMPTABLE VIEW ship_summary
(date, number_of_orders) AS
SELECT ship_date, count(ship_date)
FROM cust_order
GROUP BY ship_date;
```

Listing 12-10 shows the output of selecting all of the fields in the ship_summary view.

Listing 12-10. *Output of a View with a GROUP BY Clause*

```
mysql> SELECT * FROM ship_summary;
+------------+------------------+
| ship_date  | number_of_orders |
+------------+------------------+
| 2005-08-27 |                1 |
| 2005-08-28 |                1 |
| 2005-08-31 |                1 |
| 2005-09-01 |                2 |
| 2005-09-10 |                1 |
| 2005-09-27 |                1 |
+------------+------------------+
6 rows in set (0.00 sec)
```

The ship_summary view could easily be tweaked to further break down statistics by adding a HAVING clause to the GROUP BY statement. Just as you can when using SQL statements to get data from tables, you can add all kinds of limits to the grouped results when creating a view. For example, Listing 12-11 shows how to limit the output of the ship_summary to include only dates where one order was shipped.

Listing 12-11. *Using HAVING with GROUP BY to Create a View*

```
mysql> CREATE ALGORITHM = TEMPTABLE VIEW small_ship_dates
(ship_date, number_of_orders) AS
SELECT ship_date, count(ship_date)
FROM cust_order
GROUP BY ship_date
HAVING count(ship_date) < 2
ORDER BY ship_date;
```

A query of the data using the small_ship_dates view gives us a list of dates where only one order was shipped, as shown in Listing 12-12.

Listing 12-12. *Output of a View with a HAVING Clause*

```
mysql> SELECT * FROM small_ship_dates;
+------------+------------------+
| ship_date  | number_of_orders |
+------------+------------------+
| 2005-08-27 |                1 |
| 2005-08-28 |                1 |
| 2005-08-31 |                1 |
| 2005-09-10 |                1 |
| 2005-09-27 |                1 |
+------------+------------------+
5 rows in set (0.00 sec)
```

Unioned Tables

Views can also be created by two or more SELECT statements joined together with a UNION statement. As explained in Chapter 7, the UNION statement allows you to join multiple queries that have the same fields.

To illustrate how multiple SQL statements might be joined with a UNION, suppose our online ordering system forwards the order to a certain fulfillment center based on the geographic location of the person placing the order. Each center keeps a separate record of the customers. We want to provide a way to query customers across all centers, so we pull their databases onto a single server and create a view that centralizes their databases onto a single table using a UNION statement. Listing 12-13 shows a sample of the customer table from the region 1 database.

Listing 12-13. *Sample Customer Database from Region 1*

```
mysql> SELECT * FROM region1.customer;
+-------------+---------+
| customer_id | name    |
+-------------+---------+
|           1 | Mike    |
|           2 | Jay     |
+-------------+---------+
2 rows in set (0.00 sec)
```

We can easily create a view that pulls data from all three regions with the CREATE statement shown in Listing 12-14.

Listing 12-14. *Creating a View with UNION*

```
mysql> CREATE VIEW all_customers AS
SELECT * FROM region1.customer
UNION SELECT * FROM region2.customer
UNION SELECT * FROM region3.customer;
```

A simple SELECT statement will now present results from all three tables, as shown in Listing 12-15.

Listing 12-15. *Output of Selecting from the View Created with UNION*

```
mysql> SELECT * FROM all_customers;
+-------------+---------+
| customer_id | name    |
+-------------+---------+
|           1 | Mike    |
|           2 | Jay     |
|           3 | Johanna |
|           4 | Michael |
|           5 | Heidi   |
|           6 | Ezra    |
+-------------+---------+
6 rows in set (0.00 sec)
```

Listing 12-15 offers a convenient snapshot of the customer data pulled from the three different regions. The view might be more useful if, along with the combined data, we also included the data source for each customer record. Listing 12-16 presents a statement for creating a view that will include a column indicating from which region the customer record originates.

Listing 12-16. *Creating a UNION View with a Data Source*

```
mysql> CREATE OR REPLACE VIEW all_customers (region, customer_id, name) AS
SELECT 1, customer_id, name FROM region1.customer
UNION SELECT 2, customer_id, name FROM region2.customer
UNION SELECT 3, customer_id, name FROM region3.customer;
```

The output from a simple SELECT statement applied to the all_customers table now includes the number of the region where the data resides, as shown in Listing 12-17.

Listing 12-17. *Output of a UNION View with a Data Source*

```
mysql> SELECT * FROM all_customers;
+--------+-------------+---------+
| region | customer_id | name    |
+--------+-------------+---------+
|      1 |           1 | Mike    |
|      1 |           2 | Jay     |
|      2 |           3 | Johanna |
|      2 |           4 | Michael |
|      3 |           5 | Heidi   |
|      3 |           6 | Ezra    |
+--------+-------------+---------+
6 rows in set (0.00 sec)
```

Check Options

When creating an updatable view (a view that is part of an UPDATE, INSERT, or DELETE statement, as described in the next section), MySQL allows you to specify how much the parser will do when processing an update. This is done with the WITH CHECK OPTION syntax tacked onto the end of your SQL statement when creating a view. Enabling check options tells the parser to review the WHERE clause that defines the view when processing a statement to update a record or set of records in the view. With check options enabled, you aren't allowed to insert, update, or delete any records from the view (and subsequently the underlying table) unless the INSERT, UPDATE, or DELETE statement affects rows available within the view.

Two keywords can be added to the WITH CHECK OPTION statement: LOCAL and CASCADING. The default, LOCAL, tells the query parser that when a user is attempting to update a view, a check should be made of the SELECT statement that defines the view to ensure that the data being updated is part of the view. Consider a previous example from Listing 12-2, which created a view to display customer records from region 1. The view is updatable, but its CREATE statement doesn't include the CHECK OPTION syntax. In this case, a user can create an entry in the table for region 2, even though the view doesn't permit the user to see customers from region 2. Listing 12-18 shows the CREATE statement with the WITH LOCAL CHECK OPTION set to limit updates.

Listing 12-18. *Creating a View with Check Options*

```
mysql> CREATE OR REPLACE VIEW customer_region1 AS
SELECT customer_id, name, region FROM customer
WHERE region = 1 WITH LOCAL CHECK OPTION;
```

An attempted update to the customer_region1 view to set the region to a value not included in the view results in a MySQL error is shown in Listing 12-19.

Listing 12-19. *Illegal Update of a View with Check Options*

```
mysql> UPDATE customer_region1 SET region = 2 WHERE customer_id = 1;
ERROR 1369 (HY000): CHECK OPTION failed 'shop.customer_region1'
```

■**Note** WITH CHECK OPTION is used with only an updatable view. If the algorithm is set to TEMPTABLE, or the SQL statement uses syntax or a keyword that makes the view not updatable, specifying WITH CHECK OPTION will result in a MySQL error: ERROR 1368 (HY000) at line 5: CHECK OPTION on ➥ non-updatable view.

The CASCADING option checks both the current view, and if the current view is based on another view, the check looks at that view as well to verify that the change conforms to the view definition. With the CASCADING keyword, the query parser continues down through all views until the parser reaches a table to verify that all column and row changes that are in the issued statement are defined in the hierarchy of views. Creating views based on other views is covered in the "Defining Views of Views" section later in this chapter.

■**Caution** The CASCADE modifier to WITH CHECK OPTION is not part of the SQL:2003 specification. Use of this option, while helpful for views of views, may result in incompatible CREATE statements in other database systems.

Creating Updatable Views

Depending on the complexity of your views, you may be able to create views that can do more than provide output of data. Views in MySQL are meant to be updatable, as long as the SQL statement that creates the view doesn't represent the underlying tables in such a way that an update to the underlying data would be impossible to map through the view. We use the term *updatable* to mean that a view can be a part of an UPDATE, an INSERT, or a DELETE statement.

To be updatable, the records in the view must have a one-to-one relationship with the records in the underlying tables. Beyond that general restriction, a few other rules determine if a view can be updated. The easiest way to describe what kinds of views are updatable is to define the conditions under which a view becomes disqualified from being updatable. Views are *not* updatable in the following cases:

- The view is created with the algorithm specified as TEMPTABLE.

- A table in the FROM clause is reference by a subquery in the WHERE statement.

- There is a subquery in the SELECT clause.

- The SQL statement defining the view joins tables.

- One of the tables in the FROM clause is a non-updatable view.

- The SELECT statement of the view contains an aggregate function such as SUM( ), COUNT( ), MAX( ), MIN( ), and so on.

- The keywords DISTINCT, GROUP BY, HAVING, UNION, or UNION ALL appear in the defining SQL statement.

As MySQL parses the query, it will consider the rules and mark the view as non-updatable if any of the conditions are met. If none of these conditions is met, you will have an updatable view.

To illustrate, let's go back to our example where we created a view to control which customers could be viewed for employees in different regions. The data in the customer table is shown in Listing 12-20.

Listing 12-20. *Records in the customer Table*

```
+-------------+--------+---------+
| customer_id | region | name    |
+-------------+--------+---------+
|           1 |      1 | Mike    |
|           2 |      1 | Jay     |
|           3 |      2 | Johanna |
|           4 |      2 | Michael |
|           5 |      3 | Heidi   |
|           6 |      3 | Ezra    |
+-------------+--------+---------+
```

Creating a view that shows just the records from region 3 will give us a one-to-one relationship between the records in the view and those in the customer table. Listing 12-21 shows the creation of the customer_region3 view.

Listing 12-21. *Creating an Updatable View*

```
CREATE OR REPLACE VIEW customer_region3 AS
SELECT customer_id, name, region FROM customer
WHERE region = 3 WITH LOCAL CHECK OPTION;
```

A SELECT statement of all the records in this view shows that we're getting only the appropriate records, as shown in Listing 12-22.

Listing 12-22. *Records in the customer_region3 View*

```
mysql> SELECT * FROM customer_region3;
+-------------+-------+--------+
| customer_id | name  | region |
+-------------+-------+--------+
|           5 | Heidi |      3 |
|           6 | Ezra  |      3 |
+-------------+-------+--------+
2 rows in set (0.00 sec)
```

Because this view doesn't violate any of the criteria for creating an updatable view, we are allowed to update one of the records:

```
mysql> UPDATE customer_region3 SET name = 'David' WHERE customer_id = 6;
Query OK, 1 row affected (0.01 sec)
```

If we had specified TEMPTABLE as the algorithm, or had used some other syntax that would cause the parser to mark the view as non-updatable, we would have a different response to our attempt to update:

```
mysql> UPDATE customer_region3 SET name = 'David' WHERE customer_id = 6;
ERROR 1288 (HY000): The target table customer_region3 of the UPDATE is not updatable
```

Becoming familiar with the different rules for making a view updatable takes some time and practice. For more reading on MySQL's view implementation and the rules regarding updatable views, see http://dev.mysql.com/doc/mysql/en/create-view.html.

Defining Views of Views

Not only does MySQL allow you to create virtual representations of data in tables, you can also create a virtual representation of a view, or a view of a view. This can go as many levels deep as you can maintain.

Creating a view of a view is identical to creating a view of a table. You use the same CREATE ➥ VIEW statement, but instead of naming a table in the SQL statement, you use the name of a view.

A view of a view can be a handy way to create cascading levels of access to data. One scenario might involve a table filled with customer order and payment information. At the global level, you might have a view that excludes payment information, for the global support staff. At the regional level, you might provide two views: one with all information for a particular region and a second view of everything except for the payment information. This scenario is outlined in Table 12-1.

Table 12-1. *Cascading Levels of Information for an Online Ordering System*

View Name	Staff Position	Available Information
manage_all_orders	Global manager	Customer number, address, ordered items, payment information for all regions
support_all_orders	Global customer support	Customer number, address, ordered items for all regions
manage_region_orders	Regional manager	Customer number, address, ordered items, payment information for single region
support_region_orders	Regional customer support	Customer number, address, ordered items for single region

As discussed earlier in the section on creating views, the CASCADING parameter of WITH ➥ CHECK OPTION is designed to ensure that when you are using views of views, the statement checks to determine if permissions on making updates to a table will cascade down through all the view levels. As the check moves down through the levels of views, it checks to make sure the INSERT, UPDATE, or DELETE operation is being made on data that is available in your view.

As you add more layers with views, it's important to consider performance issues with views. View performance is discussed near the end of this chapter. Also, consider if using views of views adds an extra layer of unnecessary complexity.

Managing Views

Once you have a set of views in place, you'll likely need to manage those views. MySQL provides commands to display, change, and remove views.

Displaying Views

You can use the `SHOW CREATE VIEW` command to view the entire `CREATE` syntax used when creating a view:

```
SHOW CREATE VIEW [<database name>.]name
```

Listing 12-23 displays the output from the `SHOW CREATE VIEW` for the `all_customers` view (using the `\G` option for output in rows).

Listing 12-23. *Output of SHOW CREATE VIEW*

```
mysql> SHOW CREATE VIEW all_customers\G
*************************** 1. row ***************************
       View: all_customers
Create View: CREATE ALGORITHM=UNDEFINED VIEW `shop`.`all_customers`
AS select 1 AS `region`,`region1`.`customer`.`customer_id`
AS `customer_id`,`region1`.`customer`.`name`
AS `name` from `region1`.`customer`
union select 2 AS `2`,`region2`.`customer`.`customer_id`
AS `customer_id`,`region2`.`customer`.`name`
AS `name` from `region2`.`customer`
union select 3 AS `3`,`region3`.`customer`.`customer_id`
AS `customer_id`,`region3`.`customer`.`name`
AS `name` from `region3`.`customer`
1 row in set (0.00 sec)
```

`SHOW CREATE VIEW` doesn't produce the most readable output (we've inserted some line breaks for formatting), but it will provide you with a statement that can be used to re-create the view. If you require something more readable, and are more interested in seeing the column names and data types, the `DESCRIBE` statement works on a view just as it does on a table. Listing 12-24 shows the output from a `DESCRIBE` on the `all_customers` table.

Listing 12-24. *Output of DESCRIBE all_customers*

```
mysql> DESCRIBE all_customers;
+-------------+-------------+------+-----+---------+-------+
| Field       | Type        | Null | Key | Default | Extra |
+-------------+-------------+------+-----+---------+-------+
| region      | bigint(20)  | NO   |     | 0       |       |
| customer_id | int(11)     | NO   |     | 0       |       |
| name        | varchar(10) | YES  |     | NULL    |       |
+-------------+-------------+------+-----+---------+-------+
3 rows in set (0.00 sec)
```

One other place to find information about your views is in the data dictionary file. The data dictionary file is stored in the directory with the data files for the database. The view name is used to name the .frm file. If your data directory is /data/mysql, the ship_summary view dictionary file can be found at /data/mysql/shop/ship_summary.frm. A look inside this file reveals numerous expected fields and values, plus some additional ones, as shown in Listing 12-25.

Listing 12-25. *The ship_summary.frm Data Dictionary File*

```
shell> cat /data/mysql/shop/ship_summary.frm
TYPE=VIEW
query=select `shop`.`cust_order`.`ship_date` AS `date`,
count(`shop`.`cust_order`.`ship_date`) AS `number_of_orders`
from `shop`.`cust_order`
group by `shop`.`cust_order`.`ship_date`
md5=492eb8a32a6bd3b57b5f9f73be4db621
updatable=0
algorithm=1
with_check_option=0
revision=1
timestamp=2005-04-27 19:44:43
create-version=1
source=CREATE ALGORITHM = TEMPTABLE VIEW ship_summary\n
(date,number_of_orders) AS\n
SELECT ship_date, count(ship_date)\n
FROM cust_order\n
GROUP BY ship_date
```

The TYPE, updatable, algorithm, with_check_option, and source fields contain values we set and would expect to be in the definition. The following fields are used internally by MySQL, but they can provide valuable information:

- query: This information is the internal representation of the view's SELECT statement.

- md5: This field stores a hash of the view for verification that the data dictionary hasn't changed.

- revision: This keeps track of the version number of the view.

- timestamp: This maintains the date and time of the CREATE or last ALTER statement.

- create-version: This is always set to 1 and doesn't appear to be currently in use, but perhaps will serve a purpose in the future.

■**Note** You may notice that in the ship_summary.frm data dictionary file, the query field looks different from the source. When MySQL gets the CREATE statement, it takes the field labels specified after the view name and maps them to the <column name> AS <label> syntax for internal use. While we continue to recommend using the label definitions instead of the AS statement, it is interesting to see how MySQL transforms the CREATE statement for internal use. In this case, we're seeing the syntax of the SQL:2003 standard being mapped to the syntax understood by the existing MySQL query parser.

Changing Views

The ALTER VIEW statement is the same as the CREATE statement, except for the omission of the OR REPLACE option. In fact, the ALTER VIEW statement does the same thing as CREATE OR ➡ REPLACE, except that in the case of ALTER, a view of the same name must already exist. Lack of a view with the same name will result in a MySQL error. In altering a view, you are required to specify the attributes, columns, and SQL statement. None of these items is required to stay the same as the currently defined view, except for the name. The full ALTER statement looks like this:

```
ALTER [<algorithm attributes>] VIEW [<database>.]< name> [(<columns>)] AS
<SELECT statement> [<check options>]
```

The algorithm attributes, database, name, columns, SELECT statement, and check options are covered in detail in the previous section detailing the syntax of the CREATE statement.

To demonstrate using the ALTER VIEW command, suppose the customer support staff has been using the view created in Listing 12-16, which uses a UNION of multiple customer tables, but now they have started complaining about it. They would like to see the following changes:

- The query results return a region number, but the regions had been recently assigned names, and nobody remembers the region numbers anymore. Rather than seeing region numbers in their SELECT statements, they want to have the appropriate region name instead.

- Case-sensitivity issues involving the customer table's name have prompted requests to capitalize the output of the name column (the names are being used to programmatically compare customer data with names from a purchased mailing list).

- The shipping labels have problems if the names are too long, prompting a request to provide a column highlighting the name length, so they can scan down and ensure none of the labels will be misprinted.

All of these requests are easy to accommodate with a few changes to the previous view definition: change the region to the appropriate names, add a function that changes the name to uppercase, and add a new column that is a count of the characters in the name column. The ALTER VIEW statement to make these changes is shown in Listing 12-26.

Listing 12-26. *ALTER VIEW Statement*

```
mysql> ALTER VIEW all_customers (region,customer_id,name,name_length)
AS SELECT 'northeast', customer_id, upper(name), length(name) FROM region1.customer
UNION SELECT 'northwest', customer_id, UPPER(name), LENGTH(name)
FROM region2.customer
UNION SELECT 'south', customer_id, upper(name), length(name) FROM region3.customer;
```

Now the customer support folks will be happier with the query results, and perhaps be less prone to making mistakes with the zones and package labels. Listing 12-27 shows the output of the altered view.

Listing 12-27. *Output from the Altered View*

```
mysql> SELECT * FROM all_customers;
+-----------+-------------+---------+-------------+
| region    | customer_id | name    | name_length |
+-----------+-------------+---------+-------------+
| northeast |           1 | MIKE    |           4 |
| northeast |           2 | JAY     |           3 |
| northwest |           3 | JOHANNA |           7 |
| northwest |           4 | MICHAEL |           7 |
| south     |           5 | HEIDI   |           5 |
| south     |           6 | EZRA    |           4 |
+-----------+-------------+---------+-------------+
6 rows in set (0.00 sec)
```

■**Note** Listings 12-26 and 12-27 demonstrate a simple example of using functions in the view definition to create new data, which isn't part of the underlying tables. In the `all_customers` view, the `name_length` column doesn't exist in the underlying tables, but is the value returned from a function. Views are an excellent way to present new results derived from performing functions on or calculations with existing data.

Removing Views

To delete a view, use the DROP VIEW command. As with all DROP commands (index, table, procedure, database, and so on), DROP VIEW takes one argument: the name of the view to be dropped.

```
DROP VIEW [IF EXISTS] [<database>.]<name>
```

For example, to drop the `all_customers` view, issue this statement:

```
mysql> DROP VIEW all_customers;
```

A database name can be prepended to the view name if you want to be explicit or are dropping a view in a database other than the current, active database. You can add the IF EXISTS syntax if you would like to prevent an error from occurring if the view does not exist. A warning is generated when removing a nonexistent view with the IF EXISTS syntax.

■**Tip** When a view is altered or replaced, MySQL makes a backup copy of the data dictionary file in `<datadir>/<database name>/arc`. A copy is not made when the view is dropped. If you accidentally drop a view, check the `arc` directory for an old copy that was saved on an ALTER or REPLACE operation. You may be able to use that copy for re-creating the view.

View Permissions

Permissions on views are fairly straightforward. To create views, you must have the CREATE VIEW privilege in the database where you are creating a new view. In addition, the creator must have some privilege on each of the columns specified to be used in the view output, and SELECT privilege for columns used in the WHERE clause of the SQL statement that is a part of the view creation.

To use the ALTER VIEW statement, you must have CREATE VIEW and DROP privileges for the view you're attempting to change. As when you're creating a view, you must have permissions on the underlying table.

When removing a view, you are required to have the DROP privilege for the view. The DROP privilege can be granted globally in the mysql.user table or for a specific view in the tables_priv table.

To use a view, users can be granted SELECT privileges for a specific view, and they can then select from that view without having any additional privileges on the underlying tables:

```
GRANT SELECT ON shop.all_customers TO mkruck@localhost;
```

To update the data in a view, the updating user needs to INSERT, UPDATE, or DELETE permissions on the underlying table or tables to be changed. Managing table permissions is covered in Chapter 15.

Performance of Views

Perhaps you're wondering what kind of impact going through a view to the data will have on the performance of your SQL statements.

First, it's important to remember that the performance of a view is not going to be any better than the performance of the underlying tables. If your tables aren't optimized, or are organized poorly, a view to clean things up might help the interface, but it won't help performance of your queries.

Second, views rely on the indexes of the underlying tables. If your view is created on a table with ten million records, using a WHERE clause referencing columns without indexes, the view will perform just as poorly as the query. For the best performance, indexes on underlying tables should be designed to match the SELECT statement used in defining views.

■**Note** Views do not have indexes of their own. They rely on the indexes of the underlying tables to provide optimized lookups.

If your data is well organized and your indexes are in good condition, your views will perform well. In essence, when using the MERGE algorithm, MySQL creates a new, single query, which pulls the appropriate data from the table or tables. There is minimal processing between the view and the data, meaning your query can execute quickly without a lot of layers or logic to go through to get to the data. In addition, queries against views are stored in the buffer subsystem and query cache, if enabled. This means that, in some instances, your query of a view doesn't even look at the view or underlying table, but goes directly to the query cache. (See Chapter 4 for more information about MySQL's buffer subsystem and query cache.)

You will see more of a performance hit if your view uses the TEMPTABLE algorithm. As explained earlier in the chapter, using this method, the database first retrieves the records from the underlying tables and puts them in a temporary table, where it then runs the incoming SELECT statement. Depending on the size of your underlying tables, creating and populating a temporary table can be a significant performance hit.

Running Performance Tests

We ran a number of tests to try to get a sense of the performance implications of using views. For SELECT, INSERT, UPDATE, and DELETE, we ran a million statements into the database and averaged the amount of queries processed every second, both when running directly against the customer table and when running against a view of the customer table, customer_view. The SELECT statement grabbed all rows in the customer table or customer_view view, sending the output of eight records into a log file a million times. The INSERT created a million new customer records in the customer table or customer_view view, and the UPDATE performed a million updates on existing records in the customer table or customer_view view. The DELETE statement removed all million customer records, one at a time. The customer table uses the MyISAM storage engine.

The metrics were performed on MySQL 5.0.2, running on a single AMD64 2800+, with 1GB of RAM and a 10,000 RPM SCSI data disk. The database is the prebuilt binary for AMD64 and was configured with all default options (no .my.cnf file used on startup), except for when using the query cache, where the only configuration item was query_cache_size=1000000. (See Chapter 14 for details on configuring MySQL.) Table 12-2 shows the results in queries per second.

Table 12-2. *Performance Tests for MySQL Views*

SQL Statement	Queries/Second on Table	Queries/Second on View
Select all rows in customer table, query cache disabled	11,494	7,936
Select all rows in customer table, query cache enabled	21,052	21,052
Insert customer record	16,694	10,111
Update customer record	17,241	9,803
Delete customer record	13,698	8,984

Both the insert and update metrics are against views with simple definitions, not including WHERE clauses and check options. We ran some additional tests, using a view with a definition that included a WHERE clause and check options. The difference between a simple view and a complex view was negligible, adding only a total of five or six seconds when processing a million records.

We also tested the performance of views of views and found that adding in another view layer was comparable to the difference between the table and the first view, meaning that every view you add will decrease your performance by that much again.

We did not perform tests with views that used temporary tables. Why? We really wanted to get at how much overhead it takes for MySQL to process a SQL statement, merge it with the view definition, and return results from the new statement. When you use views with temporary tables, performance is largely affected by how much data is in your tables. The bottom line is that test results on temporary tables will be more useful if the tests are performed in your environment.

Using EXPLAIN

As with queries against tables, you can use the EXPLAIN syntax on a query of a view:

```
EXPLAIN SELECT * FROM all_orders WHERE customer_id = 1;
```

The output of the EXPLAIN will reflect the indexes of the underlying tables, not the view itself, as views do not have indexes. See Chapters 6 and 7 for details on interpreting the output of EXPLAIN.

Summary

In this chapter, we've introduced you to the general concept of views, and some ideas for general application of view technology. We discussed the views as implemented by MySQL and dug into the details of creating and maintaining views. We also went through the updatable nature of views, using views of views, and performance issues in implementing a view of a real table. The examples throughout this chapter demonstrated the power of using views in your application.

As we've emphasized throughout the book, it is always important to make technology a part of your larger application, or even organizational, plans. Using views can be extremely helpful, but can also cause problems if they aren't the right fit for the particular need. Always make an assessment of the organizational, application, and data needs before jumping to a conclusion about which technology to implement to meet that need.

That being said, views can be a lifesaver to a database administrator, application developer, end user, or anyone who comes in contact with your database or data. The ability to rearrange, compile, combine, limit, relabel, hide, and sort data in virtual tables opens up endless possibilities in meeting the demands of your data destinations.

■ ■ ■

## CHAPTER 13

Triggers

With the introduction of triggers in versions 5.0.2 and greater, MySQL provides more built-in support for helping you manage changes to your data. Triggers are a powerful tool for associating a set of SQL statements with a particular event in your database. As with the other new features we covered in the previous chapters—stored procedures, stored functions, and cursors—triggers are available in other database systems, such as DB2, Oracle, SQL Server, and PostgreSQL.

We have a lot of ground to cover in using MySQL's trigger functionality. This chapter will discuss the following topics:

- Database trigger basics

- The advantages and disadvantages of using triggers

- MySQL's implementation of triggers

- How to create triggers

- An example of using triggers

- Trigger permissions

- Performance of triggers

Database Triggers

A database may process changes to its data on the order of thousands of requests per second. Each request may INSERT, ALTER, or DELETE data from any number of tables. While this possibility of robust data management is what brought a database into the picture in the first place, it stands to reason that with each change in the data, you may want to associate particular pieces of logic. Perhaps you want to avoid inconsistencies by doing some extra data validation before saving a row. Maybe you would also like to keep track of changes in your tables by saving the current values into an audit table, before the data changes are made to the table.

Prior to version 5.0.2, you could rely on MySQL to ensure columns matched, and even use foreign key restraints to ensure integrity, but any further validation would be left to the application. Maintaining an audit table would require the application to load the rows that would be affected by the change prior to making the INSERT, UPDATE, or DELETE; save those rows to the audit table; and then perform the changes in the data. With MySQL version 5.0.2 and later, you can now accomplish these tasks with triggers.

A *trigger* is a statement, or set of statements, that is stored and associated with a particular event happening on a particular column or table. The current SQL standard, SQL:2003, specifies that the events allowed to activate a trigger are INSERT, UPDATE, or DELETE. The intention is to provide a mechanism to run any number of SQL statements whenever data changes in a given table as a result of one of the activating events. When the specified event occurs, the trigger is activated, and the statements defined in the trigger are run—either before or after the event, based on the definition of the trigger. Additionally, triggers are similar to stored procedures in that you can tap into the power of variables and control structures when creating the body of the trigger.

Before we look at more details of how MySQL implements triggers, let's consider the pros and cons of using triggers in your database applications.

■**Note** As we write this chapter, MySQL has released version 5.0.6, which is labeled a beta release. While the database is stable enough to test and document the functionality of triggers, production users are encouraged to wait until a release of the 5.0.*x* branch that is labeled for production.

The Debate Over Using Triggers

As you might expect, some application developers and database administrators believe that using triggers is good practice, and others are passionately against it. A review of some of the arguments both for and against triggers will give you a sense of the strengths and weaknesses of development that relies on having triggers in the database. As with all technologies, you need to determine how your unique application might benefit or suffer from using triggers.

The statements for and against triggers are not MySQL-specific, and include points pertaining to triggers in general, across all varieties of database systems. Thus, some of the arguments might apply specifically to functionality available in other database systems but not currently available in MySQL.

■**Note** The debate over whether to use a specific technology is often based on favorable or unfavorable experience with that technology, which may include forced use of technology where it was actually inappropriate. This can lead to some vehement and emotional opinions about how useful and appropriate a particular technology is for an application. When making decisions on how to use technology, you should attempt to be objective and see both sides of the argument, focusing on how the technology might meet the requirements for your database or application needs.

Trigger Advantages

Since this chapter is about using triggers, let's start with a review of the reasons you may find triggers appropriate for your database:

- Triggers provide a complementary, and more robust, integrity checking mechanism to foreign keys. Triggers can check more than just the presence of a certain foreign key; they can verify that the foreign key record has certain other characteristics. Using the advanced capabilities for integrity checking available with triggers, you can avoid needing to put some or all data integrity checks in your application.

- You can catch business process errors using triggers. This goes beyond simple data validation and into the enforcement of more complex rules. For example, if you want to limit the number of unprocessed orders for an individual customer to five, a trigger on INSERT could check to make sure there weren't already five unprocessed orders.

- When enforcing complex rules with triggers, you ensure that in every case where a change is made, the trigger code is run. If the data rules were contained only in the code that makes up your web-based application, any changes made in the database from the MySQL client tools or from other programs outside your web pages wouldn't get the same functionality.

- If scheduled tasks or scripts run periodically to perform checks or cleanup of data, triggers can provide a method to put those checks directly in the database. This means you don't need to wait for the cron task to run to have the data changed. One example of this is a cache table that removes expired entries when a new entry is inserted.

- If you need to make changes in one table based on changes in another table, a trigger handles moving the existing values into a new table more efficiently than the application can. An example might be a customer_history table that keeps track of all changes in the customer table. Before you change a customer record, you write a record to the customer_history table with the current field values. If you were to put this kind of functionality in the application, you would need to first select the row of the customer table and insert the values into the customer_history table before updating the customer record. That involves execution of three queries from your application. With a trigger, this functionality is handled in the database, and the application only needs to send the UPDATE statement.

- Triggers are useful if you need to perform a calculation before inserting or updating a row. For example, you might want to calculate the total cost based on the item cost and the shipping, and insert that value in another column. A trigger can take care of automatically calculating and setting the value for the total cost column.

Before you run off to your database and start moving your validation and business logic into database triggers, let's consider the reasons why you might not want to use triggers.

Trigger Disadvantages

Although there aren't as many arguments against using triggers as there are in favor, you should nonetheless weigh them carefully:

- While triggers might provide extended validation, they aren't a replacement for all validation. For instance, using a client-side scripting language to validate a web form is a simple, user-friendly way to alert the user of an issue, without needing to submit the form. In most cases, going all the way from the user's browser through the network and application to the database just to validate a form field doesn't make a lot of sense.

- The proliferation of triggers across many tables could result in a situation where a change in one table sets off a chain of trigger activations that are ultimately difficult to track and therefore hard to debug. An example might be an update in the customer table that triggers a change in the address table that activates a trigger in the order table. If one of the triggers is dropped, or has a bug in how it processes data, tracking down a problem spread across many triggers on a number of tables can quickly turn into a nightmare.

- Development tools for triggers aren't as slick and sophisticated as application development tools. If you need a proven development environment for developing your business logic, the tools for writing database triggers won't be as readily available as tools for writing business logic in languages such as PHP, Perl, and Java.

- Editing a PHP script on the file system is more straightforward than getting the trigger statement out of the database, making changes, and going through the steps to drop and re-create the trigger.

■**Note** Chapter 9 includes a discussion regarding the practicality of using stored procedures. That discussion contains a number of points similar to the arguments presented in this chapter for using triggers, and might provoke some additional thoughts on how to decide to use database technology.

Triggers in MySQL

MySQL aims at using the SQL standards when implementing new or updating existing functionality. MySQL triggers adhere to this rule. With one exception—the use of the NEW and OLD keywords—the syntax used in MySQL matches the syntax defined for the SQL:2003 standard. However, there is syntax in the standard that MySQL doesn't support, such as the ATOMIC and REFERENCING keywords, the ability to specify column names for an UPDATE trigger, and a WHERE clause for conditional checks.

If you're coming from another database environment where you've used triggers, you may find that MySQL's implementation is similar. In most cases, the MySQL syntax is a smaller subset of the functionality that is used elsewhere.[1] Most database systems have trigger support with helpful syntax extensions, which are not available in MySQL.

---

1. While the concepts for creating triggers are similar, SQL Server has a unique syntax for creating triggers that differs from the syntax in the current documentation for Oracle, DB2, and PostgreSQL.

MySQL triggers are independent of the storage engines used to store the data. They can be used with any of the available storage engines. (See Chapter 5 for details on MySQL storage engines.)

In MySQL, triggers are stored in *<data directory/<database name>/<table name>*.TRG, a text file that contains the definitions of all triggers created for events on that table. This file can contain multiple trigger definitions, which are added to and removed from the file as they are created and dropped from the MySQL client. Since the file is plain text, it is possible to view the file in a text viewer or editor. Within the file, you'll find triggers=, followed by numerous trigger statements, each surrounded in single quotation marks. Be warned, with longer trigger definitions, the file becomes seriously unreadable.

■**Caution** We advise against editing the .TRG file manually with a text editor. It can be done, but direct editing of the .TRG file could lead to problems in future versions of MySQL if the internal storage mechanism or format changes.

MySQL triggers are loaded into the database memory when they are created or when the database is started. Each time an update is made that activates the trigger, the SQL statements of the trigger are already in memory and don't need to be read from the trigger file.

When you're using triggers in MySQL, you should be aware of the following restrictions:

- Triggers cannot call stored procedures.[2]

- Triggers cannot be created for views or temporary tables.

- Transactions cannot be started or ended within a trigger. This means you can't do something like start a transaction in your application, and then close the transaction with a COMMIT or ROLLBACK statement from within the trigger. (See Chapter 3 for details on MySQL transactions.)

- Creating a trigger for a table invalidates the query cache. If you rely heavily on the query cache, be warned that queries being pulled from the cache will need to be regenerated from the data tables after a trigger is created. (See Chapter 4 for details on the query cache.)

- Triggers share table-level namespaces. This means that currently you can't have two triggers with the same name on a particular table. MySQL encourages using unique trigger names across an entire database, should the namespace be moved to the database level.[3]

---

2. We found that you can actually put the CALL statement in a trigger, but when the trigger fires, it fails on a procedure does not exist error, even if the procedure exists and can be called from outside the trigger.

3. The SQL:2003 specification calls for the trigger namespace to be at the database level. MySQL hints at a future release moving the trigger namespace to the database level, requiring unique trigger names across an entire database, not just for a specific table.

> ■**Note** MySQL is constantly under active development. While we feel it's important to document the exist-
> ing implementation details of triggers in MySQL, we also want to note that the functionality is improving and
> will likely mean some of the noted implementation details and limitations will be changed. You can find more
> details and current information about MySQL's trigger implementation at `http://dev.mysql.com/doc/`
> `mysql/en/triggers.html`.

Now that we've gone through the significant pieces that characterize MySQL's implementation of triggers, let's move on to the details of writing SQL to create database triggers.

Creating MySQL Triggers

To get started, let's go through a simple example. Going back to the scenario introduced earlier
in the chapter, suppose that we need to track changes to our `customer` table. Rather than needing to program our application to keep a history of the changes, we want to use the database
to take care of the audit trail, creating a record of the current data before it is changed. This
seems like a perfect place to put trigger functionality.

To demonstrate how triggers work, we'll begin with the same `customer` table we've used in
previous chapters, as shown in Listing 13-1.

Listing 13-1. *Records in the customer Table*

```
mysql> SELECT * FROM customer;
+-------------+---------+
| customer_id | name    |
+-------------+---------+
|           1 | Mike    |
|           2 | Jay     |
|           3 | Johanna |
|           4 | Michael |
|           5 | Heidi   |
|           6 | Ezra    |
+-------------+---------+
6 rows in set (0.00 sec)
```

In order to keep track of changes in the `customer` table, we want to add a `customer_audit`
table. The `customer_audit` table structure is shown in Listing 13-2.

Listing 13-2. *Description of the customer_audit Table*

```
mysql> DESC customer_audit
+-------------+-------------+------+-----+---------+----------------+
| Field       | Type        | Null | Key | Default | Extra          |
+-------------+-------------+------+-----+---------+----------------+
| id          | int(11)     | NO   | PRI | NULL    | auto_increment |
| action      | char(50)    | YES  |     | NULL    |                |
| customer_id | int(11)     | YES  |     | NULL    |                |
| name        | varchar(50) | YES  |     | NULL    |                |
| changed     | datetime    | YES  |     | NULL    |                |
+-------------+-------------+------+-----+---------+----------------+
```

Every time either an UPDATE or DELETE is made to the customer table, we want to record the action, current customer_id, name, and the time of the change. While doing this in the application is possible, it requires getting all matching records before the UPDATE or DELETE statement and using the application to insert the records into the audit table. With a trigger, the database can be programmed to take care of creating the log of changes.

To be sure updates are saved as a part of the audit, we create a trigger on the customer table that will be activated on any UPDATE to the table. Listing 13-3 shows a trigger that is built to handle updates, named before_customer_update.

Listing 13-3. *Creating the before_customer_update Trigger*

```
DELIMITER //

CREATE TRIGGER before_customer_update BEFORE UPDATE ON customer
FOR EACH ROW
BEGIN
INSERT INTO customer_audit
SET action='update',
customer_id = OLD.customer_id,
name = OLD.name,
changed = NOW();
END

//
DELIMITER ;
```

We will look more closely at the CREATE TRIGGER statement shortly. This trigger, as indicated in the CREATE TRIGGER statement, is set to activate prior to an update to records in the table. The before_customer_update trigger inserts a row into the customer_audit table each time a record is updated. We can see this in action by issuing an UPDATE statement, as shown in Listing 13-4.

Listing 13-4. *Updating customer Records*

```
mysql> UPDATE customer SET name=UCASE(name);
Query OK, 6 rows affected (0.01 sec)
```

■**Note** As of MySQL version 5.0.6, there is a bug with locking the correct tables when a trigger is activated. If your trigger contains data-changing statements, you will need to lock the tables used in your trigger. For this example, the customer and customer_audit tables need to be locked, changing the UPDATE statement in Listing 13-4 to LOCK TABLES customer WRITE, customer_audit WRITE; UPDATE customer SET ➥ name = ucase(name); UNLOCK TABLES;. As of this writing, this bug is marked as critical and should be resolved in an upcoming release.

The UPDATE statement in Listing 13-4 will change all the values in the name column of the customer table to uppercase, as shown in Listing 13-5.

Listing 13-5. *Records in the customer Table After Updating*

```
mysql> SELECT * FROM customer;
+-------------+---------+
| customer_id | name    |
+-------------+---------+
|           1 | MIKE    |
|           2 | JAY     |
|           3 | JOHANNA |
|           4 | MICHAEL |
|           5 | HEIDI   |
|           6 | EZRA    |
+-------------+---------+
```

Listing 13-5 demonstrates that the record change to uppercase took effect. Now, let's see if the trigger activated and logged the previous record. Listing 13-6 shows the records in the customer_audit table.

Listing 13-6. *Records in the customer_audit Table After Updating*

```
mysql> SELECT * FROM customer_audit;
+----+--------+-------------+---------+---------------------+
| id | action | customer_id | name    | changed             |
+----+--------+-------------+---------+---------------------+
|  1 | update |           1 | Mike    | 2005-05-10 22:20:44 |
|  2 | update |           2 | Jay     | 2005-05-10 22:20:44 |
|  3 | update |           3 | Johanna | 2005-05-10 22:20:44 |
|  4 | update |           4 | Michael | 2005-05-10 22:20:44 |
|  5 | update |           5 | Heidi   | 2005-05-10 22:20:44 |
|  6 | update |           6 | Ezra    | 2005-05-10 22:20:44 |
+----+--------+-------------+---------+---------------------+
6 rows in set (0.00 sec)
```

As you can see in Listing 13-6, the customer_audit table contains the previous value for name and the time it was changed.

As part of our audit trail, we also want to keep track of any records that are removed from the customer table. The before_customer_delete trigger defined in Listing 13-7 does this for deletions to the customer table.

Listing 13-7. *Creating the before_customer_delete Trigger*

```
DELIMITER //

CREATE TRIGGER before_customer_delete BEFORE DELETE ON customer
FOR EACH ROW
BEGIN
INSERT INTO customer_audit
SET action='delete',
customer_id = OLD.customer_id,
name = OLD.name,
changed = NOW();
END

//
DELIMITER ;
```

Listing 13-7 looks a lot like the before_customer_update trigger, but the trigger is modified to respond to DELETE statements against the customer table. Before any row is deleted from the customer table, a record is inserted into the customer_audit table with the values of that row.

To test the trigger, we issue a command to delete all the records in the customer table:

```
mysql> DELETE FROM customer;
Query OK, 6 rows affected (0.01 sec)
```

This statement removes all the records from the `customer` table and activates the `customer` table's trigger for record deletions. If we look at the `customer_audit` table, we'll see a row inserted for each of the deletions from the `customer` table, as shown in Listing 13-8.

Listing 13-8. *Records in the customer_audit Table After Deletions*

```
mysql> SELECT * FROM customer_audit;
+----+--------+-------------+---------+---------------------+
| id | action | customer_id | name    | changed             |
+----+--------+-------------+---------+---------------------+
|  1 | update |           1 | Mike    | 2005-05-10 22:20:44 |
|  2 | update |           2 | Jay     | 2005-05-10 22:20:44 |
|  3 | update |           3 | Johanna | 2005-05-10 22:20:44 |
|  4 | update |           4 | Michael | 2005-05-10 22:20:44 |
|  5 | update |           5 | Heidi   | 2005-05-10 22:20:44 |
|  6 | update |           6 | Ezra    | 2005-05-10 22:20:44 |
|  7 | delete |           1 | MIKE    | 2005-05-10 23:00:20 |
|  8 | delete |           2 | JAY     | 2005-05-10 23:00:20 |
|  9 | delete |           3 | JOHANNA | 2005-05-10 23:00:20 |
| 10 | delete |           4 | MICHAEL | 2005-05-10 23:00:20 |
| 11 | delete |           5 | HEIDI   | 2005-05-10 23:00:20 |
| 12 | delete |           6 | EZRA    | 2005-05-10 23:00:20 |
+----+--------+-------------+---------+---------------------+
12 rows in set (0.00 sec)
```

As you can see, the table has entries for both the UPDATE and the DELETE statements we ran, giving us a history of the changes to the `customer` table.

Now that you've seen some of the syntax and a working example, let's take a look at the details of each piece of the CREATE TRIGGER statement.

■**Tip** When you're building triggers, we recommend you use a versioning system like CVS or subversion for the source of the trigger creation statements. Trigger development, like other pieces of your database and application, results in a piece of code that is valuable to your organization.

The CREATE Statement

The CREATE TRIGGER statement is used to define a trigger and associate it with changes occurring in a table. It has the following syntax:

```
CREATE TRIGGER <name> <time> <event>
ON <table>
FOR EACH ROW
<body statements>
```

As you can see here, and in Listings 13-3 and 13-7, the CREATE TRIGGER statement takes five required pieces: the name, time, event, table name, and one or more body statements. With the time and event, you must choose from an enumerated set of options:

```
CREATE TRIGGER <name> [BEFORE | AFTER] [INSERT | UPDATE | DELETE]
```

As with stored procedures, functions, and cursors, when entering multiple-statement blocks into MySQL, change the default delimiter to something other than the semicolon (;), so MySQL will allow you to enter a semicolon without having the client process the input. Change the delimiter by using the delimiter statement: DELIMITER //. This will change the delimiter to //, meaning that you can use ; as many times as necessary. When you're ready to have your trigger created, type //, and the client will process your entire trigger statement. When you're finished working on the trigger, change the delimiter back to the standard semicolon with DELIMITER ;.

ALSO IN SQL:2003

MySQL contains a subset of the SQL:2003 syntax for database triggers. More of the syntax will be added in the future, but currently, the following key items of the SQL:2003 database trigger specification are not included in MySQL's trigger syntax:

- When a trigger is declared using the UPDATE event, SQL:2003 allows you to specify a list of specific columns, restricting the firing of the trigger to updates happening to the defined columns, not just the entire row.

- Trigger definitions can contain a WHERE clause as a part of FOR EACH ROW. This clause lets you perform conditional checks on data in the record and limit running the trigger statements to specific rows of data.

- The SQL:2003 standard indicates that the BEGIN statement can be followed by an optional ATOMIC keyword, to make the block execute as one unit.

- The SQL:2003 standard specifies the use of a REFERENCING keyword that can follow the table name. This part of the statement allows you to assign a name to the current record as well as to the incoming record. Rather than needing to use OLD and NEW in your body statements, you can assign the old and new records names like existing_customer and updated_customer, which make the trigger statements more readable.

An update to the trigger functionality is coming with MySQL 5.1, which promises to have a more full-featured implementation of the SQL:2003 syntax.

Trigger Name

When you name a trigger, it must conform to database rules for naming objects. The rules for legal names can be found at http://dev.mysql.com/doc/mysql/en/legal-names.html. Also, the trigger name must be unique for the table.

Since tables can have multiple triggers defined for different time and event types, we recommend using a combination of the event type, time, and table name when naming your triggers. This allows for creating multiple triggers on a single table without having conflicting names. The SQL:2003 standard calls for unique trigger names across the entire database, so we also recommend that you use the name of the table when naming your triggers, to avoid conflicts with other triggers in the database.

Before adding triggers to your database, you should choose a naming convention that can be used for triggers throughout your database and help clarify the purpose of the trigger. For example, the names we used in the `customer_audit` example gave an indication of the scope of the trigger:

```
CREATE TRIGGER before_customer_update . . .
CREATE TRIGGER before_customer_delete . . .
```

Activation Time

You must specify an activation time when you define a trigger. The time can be BEFORE or AFTER, to run the statements in the trigger either before or after the event occurs. For example, if you define the trigger to run AFTER an update, when the UPDATE statement is received by the database, it will perform the update on the table, and then run the statements in the trigger body. If you need to check the integrity of the fields in an INSERT statement, you will want the statements in the body of the trigger to run BEFORE the record is inserted into the table.

How do you know what trigger timing is right?

- Use BEFORE when you want to perform an action prior to the change being made in the table. This might include calculating a value or getting the current record's values for use elsewhere.

- Use AFTER if the action you want needs to happen after the changes are made in the table. For example, if you need to create an empty placeholder entry in a `customer_address` table after a new `customer` record is created, you probably don't want to create the `customer_address` record until after the `customer` record insertion is completed.

Choosing the trigger time affects what can be done in the body of SQL statements. When you choose AFTER, the trigger is activated after the event completes, which means you cannot change the values of the incoming query because the record has already been written to the table.

In our earlier `customer_audit` example, both triggers had BEFORE timing:

```
CREATE TRIGGER before_customer_update BEFORE . . .
CREATE TRIGGER before_customer_delete BEFORE . . .
```

Event for Activation

When defining a trigger, you are required to specify the event during which the trigger will activate: INSERT, UPDATE, or DELETE. To make a trigger fire on more than one event, you must create multiple triggers, one for each event.

As with the activation time for a trigger, the event you specify in the trigger declaration changes the kinds of SQL statements and logic that can be used in the body of the trigger. For an INSERT event, there is no OLD record, because this is the initial creation of the record, not the replacement of an existing one. If the trigger event is DELETE, there will not be a NEW record, because no new data is being created; it involves only removal of the existing, or OLD, record.

In our customer_audit example, we had one trigger for an UPDATE event and one trigger for a DELETE event:

```
CREATE TRIGGER before_customer_update BEFORE UPDATE . . .
CREATE TRIGGER before_customer_delete BEFORE DELETE . . .
```

Table to Activate the Trigger

When defining a trigger, you are required to specify the table that will activate the trigger on the given event. As noted in the previous section about MySQL's implementation of triggers, the table cannot be a view or a temporary table.

The table name follows the timing and event parts of the trigger definition:

```
CREATE TRIGGER before_customer_update BEFORE UPDATE ON customer . . .
CREATE TRIGGER before_customer_delete BEFORE DELETE ON customer . . .
```

Trigger Body Statements

The SQL statements that compose the body of a trigger are where the real action happens. Prior to the body definition, MySQL requires the keywords FOR EACH ROW, which means that as an INSERT, UPDATE, or DELETE happens, the defined SQL statement or statements will be executed one time for each of the records that are affected.

The trigger body can be a single SQL statement, or if wrapped within a BEGIN and END clause, the body can contain multiple statements. This allows you to run a limitless number of statements within a single trigger.[4]

OLD and NEW Keywords

Two keywords are unique to SQL statements used in defining triggers: OLD and NEW. These keywords allow you to refer to the data before and after the activating event takes place. For example, if you have defined a trigger that is activated before an update, you will be able to reference fields in the current database record with OLD.*<fieldname>*. You can also reference fields in the incoming record with NEW.*<fieldname>*. Listings 13-3 and 13-7 showed examples of using the OLD syntax:

```
customer_id = OLD.customer_id,
name = OLD.name,
```

You'll see examples of the NEW syntax in getting and setting record values in upcoming examples.

---

4. We attempted to find a limit for the number of lines in a trigger. However, after successfully running a script-generated, one million-line trigger (which required a change to the max_allowed_packet setting to process the CREATE statement), we figured we would call it limitless.

■**Note** The OLD and NEW keywords are extensions to SQL:2003. However, the OLD and NEW keywords are more like predefined names that the SQL:2003 standard allows for when using the REFERENCING syntax. MySQL doesn't currently support the REFERENCING keyword, so rather than letting you specify the name of the old and new record, MySQL predefines them as OLD and NEW. In some ways, this makes the coding less clear, because you can't specify the names for the records, but it also means you'll have uniform syntax throughout all your triggers.

Variables and Flow Control Statements

Just like stored procedures and functions, triggers support the use of variables and flow controls. Refer to Chapters 9 and 10 when you need to build triggers using flow controls. (Also see http://dev.mysql.com/doc/mysql/en/flow-control-constructs.html.)

Using Triggers

Now that we've gone through the details on the syntax used to build a trigger, let's look at a second, more involved example to demonstrate the usefulness of triggers.

For this example, let's suppose we're working on the table that keeps track of customer orders. The cust_order table, as shown in Listing 13-9, contains the order ID, date the order was shipped, the sum of all the items, a discount percentage to be applied, the shipping cost, and a total.

Listing 13-9. *Description of the cust_order Table*

```
mysql> DESC cust_order;
+-----------------+------------------+------+-----+---------+----------------+
| Field           | Type             | Null | Key | Default | Extra          |
+-----------------+------------------+------+-----+---------+----------------+
| cust_order_id   | int(10) unsigned | NO   | PRI | NULL    | auto_increment |
| ship_date       | date             | YES  |     | NULL    |                |
| item_sum        | decimal(10,2)    | YES  |     | NULL    |                |
| discount_percent| int(2) unsigned  | YES  |     | NULL    |                |
| shipping        | decimal(10,2)    | YES  |     | 0.00    |                |
| total           | decimal(10,2)    | YES  |     | NULL    |                |
+-----------------+------------------+------+-----+---------+----------------+
```

As records are inserted into this table, we want to automatically calculate the total, which is derived from multiplying the sum of the items with the discount and adding in the shipping charges. A single-statement procedure would accomplish this, as shown in Listing 13-10.

Listing 13-10. *Trigger to Calculate the Total*

```
CREATE TRIGGER before_cust_order_insert BEFORE INSERT ON cust_order
FOR EACH ROW
SET NEW.total = NEW.item_sum -
(NEW.discount_percent/100 * NEW.item_sum) + NEW.shipping;
```

Listing 13-10 shows the use of the NEW keyword, which sets the value of the incoming record's total field by performing a calculation on a few of the other fields. You'll notice that if you insert a record into the cust_order table with a NULL or zero value for the discount_percent, you get some unpredictable results in the total.

This is corrected by adding a check, using an IF statement, to the trigger. The check determines whether the discount_percent needs to be a part of the calculation, as shown in Listing 13-11.

Listing 13-11. *Trigger to Calculate the Total with a Discount Check*

```
DELIMITER //

CREATE TRIGGER before_cust_order_insert BEFORE INSERT ON cust_order
FOR EACH ROW
BEGIN

IF NEW.discount_percent IS NULL OR NEW.discount_percent = 0 THEN
        SET NEW.total = NEW.item_sum + NEW.shipping;
ELSE
        SET NEW.total = NEW.item_sum -
        (NEW.discount_percent/100 * NEW.item_sum) + NEW.shipping;
END IF;

END

//
DELIMITER ;
```

Now, the trigger will only use the discount as a part of the calculation if the value is not NULL and greater than zero.

■**Note** The trigger definition in Listing 13-11 shows the use of the IF . . . THEN . . . ELSE flow control syntax that can be used in the trigger body. For more information about flow controls, see Chapters 9 and 10.

Let's take this example one step further and add a limit to the discount_percent. Perhaps there's been some abuse of this field, and the manager of the store places a maximum 15% discount on any order. He asks if you can do some magic in the database to make sure the rule is enforced. You already have the trigger in place to calculate the total, so adding a statement to limit the value inserted into the discount_percent field is as simple as the three lines shown in Listing 13-12.

Listing 13-12. *Limiting the Discount Field to 15%*

```
IF NEW.discount_percent > 15 THEN
        SET NEW.discount_percent = 15;
END IF;
```

The IF statement in Listing 13-12 catches any instance where the incoming record has a discount greater than 15%, and resets the value for the discount_percent to 15. The complete trigger definition is shown in Listing 13-13.

Listing 13-13. *Complete cust_order Insert Trigger*

```
DELIMITER //
CREATE TRIGGER before_cust_order_insert BEFORE INSERT ON cust_order
FOR EACH ROW
BEGIN

IF NEW.discount_percent > 15 THEN
        SET NEW.discount_percent = 15;
END IF;

IF NEW.discount_percent IS NULL OR NEW.discount_percent = 0 THEN
        SET NEW.total = NEW.item_sum + NEW.shipping;
ELSE
        SET NEW.total = NEW.item_sum -
        (NEW.discount_percent/100 * NEW.item_sum) + NEW.shipping;
END IF;

END

//
DELIMITER ;
```

Now, let's see what happens when we try to insert a record into the cust_order table and ask for a discount of 24%, as shown in Listing 13-14.

Listing 13-14. *Inserting into the cust_order Table with an Invalid Discount*

```
mysql> INSERT INTO cust_order SET ship_date='2005-08-12',
item_sum = 123.43,
discount_percent = 24,
shipping = 12.45;
```

Listing 13-15 shows that not only was the total calculated on the insertion, but also the discount was limited to 15%, reduced from the value of 24% specified in the INSERT statement.

Listing 13-15. *Output of cust_order Table After Insert*

```
+---------------+------------+----------+------------------+----------+--------+
| cust_order_id | ship_date  | item_sum | discount_percent | shipping | total  |
+---------------+------------+----------+------------------+----------+--------+
|             1 | 2005-08-12 |   123.43 |               15 |    12.45 | 117.37 |
+---------------+------------+----------+------------------+----------+--------+
1 row in set (0.00 sec)
```

The trigger created in Listing 13-13 does a good job of performing the simple check and calculation we want, but the user can invalidate the total field and exceed the discount by updating the table. In order to ensure the same table behavior when the records are updated, we need to create a similar trigger that activates on the UPDATE event, as shown in Listing 13-16.

Listing 13-16. *Complete cust_order Update Trigger*

```
DELIMITER //

CREATE TRIGGER before_cust_order_update BEFORE UPDATE ON cust_order
FOR EACH ROW
BEGIN

IF NEW.discount_percent > 15 THEN
        SET NEW.discount_percent = 15;
END IF;

IF NEW.discount_percent IS NULL OR NEW.discount_percent = 0 THEN
        SET NEW.total = NEW.item_sum + NEW.shipping;
ELSE
        SET NEW.total = NEW.item_sum -
        (NEW.discount_percent/100 * NEW.item_sum) + NEW.shipping;
END IF;

END

//
DELIMITER  ;
```

Before leaving this example, let's add one more restriction on the update, to demonstrate the interaction between OLD and NEW rows of data. Suppose the manager now says that on any update, the discount_percent should never increase by more than 2%. Adding this restriction requires a check of the existing value and making sure that the new value isn't any more than two greater than the previous value. Comparing the OLD and NEW values, as shown in Listing 13-17, makes it easy to create this restriction.

Listing 13-17. *Limiting the Increase in discount_percent*

```
IF OLD.discount_percent + 2 <= NEW.discount_percent THEN
        SET NEW.discount_percent = OLD.discount_percent + 2;
END IF;
```

The entire update trigger, with the discount increase restrictions, discount limit restrictions, and the calculated columns, is shown in Listing 13-18. You'll notice that before we can create a new trigger, we need to remove the existing trigger.

Listing 13-18. *Complete cust_order Update Trigger*

```
DELIMITER //

DROP PROCEDURE cust_order.before_cust_order_update //

CREATE TRIGGER before_cust_order_update BEFORE UPDATE ON cust_order
FOR EACH ROW
BEGIN

IF OLD.discount_percent + 2 <= NEW.discount_percent THEN
        SET NEW.discount_percent = OLD.discount_percent + 2;
END IF;

IF NEW.discount_percent > 15 THEN
        SET NEW.discount_percent = 15;
END IF;

IF NEW.discount_percent IS NULL OR NEW.discount_percent = 0 THEN
        SET NEW.total = NEW.item_sum + NEW.shipping;
ELSE
        SET NEW.total = NEW.item_sum -
        (NEW.discount_percent/100 * NEW.item_sum) + NEW.shipping;
END IF;

END

//
DELIMITER ;
```

Let's test this on another record in our cust_order table, as shown in Listing 13-19.

Listing 13-19. *Current cust_order Record*

```
+--------------+------------+----------+------------------+----------+-------+
| cust_order_id | ship_date | item_sum | discount_percent | shipping | total |
+--------------+------------+----------+------------------+----------+-------+
|             2 | 2005-08-27 | 40.56    |               10 | 10.34    | 46.84 |
+--------------+------------+----------+------------------+----------+-------+
```

This record has a discount of 10%. Let's try to bump that up to 14%, using the statement in Listing 13-20.

Listing 13-20. *Update with discount_percent Increase Limit*

```
mysql> UPDATE cust_order SET discount_percent = 14 WHERE cust_order_id = 2;
```

Without having a trigger to limit the increase of the discount to 2%, the discount should increase to 14% with this update. With the trigger in place to limit the increase, the new discount_percent for this cust_order record is 12, 2 greater than the previous value of 10. The output from the table is shown in Listing 13-21.

Listing 13-21. *Output from cust_order Table with a Limited Increase*

```
+--------------+------------+----------+-----------------+----------+-------+
| cust_order_id | ship_date  | item_sum | discount_percent | shipping | total |
+--------------+------------+----------+-----------------+----------+-------+
|            2 | 2005-08-27 | 40.56    |              12 | 10.34    | 46.03 |
+--------------+------------+----------+-----------------+----------+-------+
```

The example could continue, adding additional checks into the trigger until it accomplished every last bit of data integrity checking needed for the business logic, but we think you probably get the general idea. Let's move on to how to manage your database triggers.

Managing Triggers

After you've created a collection of triggers in the database, you'll likely need to manage them. As with stored procedures and functions, you can view, change, and remove stored functions.

Viewing Triggers

As we write this chapter, a recent commit to the MySQL source code indicates that there will soon be a TRIGGERS view in the INFORMATION_SCHEMA. In order to view information about triggers in your database, use the following statement:

```
SELECT * FROM INFORMATION_SCHEMA.TRIGGERS;
```

This statement will give you a set of records for the triggers in your database, including the following columns:

- TRIGGER_CATALOG

- TRIGGER_SCHEMA

- TRIGGER_NAME

- EVENT_MANIPULATION

- EVENT_OBJECT_CATALOG

- EVENT_OBJECT_SCHEMA

- EVENT_OBJECT_TABLE

- ACTION_ORDER

- ACTION_CONDITION

- ACTION_STATEMENT

- ACTION_ORIENTATION

- ACTION_TIMING

- ACTION_REFERENCE_OLD_TABLE

- ACTION_REFERENCE_NEW_TABLE

- ACTION_REFERENCE_OLD_ROW

- ACTION_REFERENCE_NEW_ROW

- CREATED

For more information about the INFORMATION_SCHEMA, see Chapter 21. Another option is to look at the CREATE statement in the data directory:

`<data directory>/<database name>/<table name>.TRG`

As noted earlier, this is a somewhat unreadable representation of your CREATE statement, but it will show you what is currently defined in the database.

■Note In MySQL, to get access to data dictionary information, you typically use the SHOW command. There is currently no SHOW CREATE or SHOW STATUS for triggers, as there is for tables, views, stored procedures, and so forth.

Modifying and Removing Triggers

If you need to modify one of your triggers, you must first issue a DROP statement, and then a CREATE statement to redefine the trigger. The SQL:2003 standard does not provide for something like an ALTER TRIGGER or CREATE OR REPLACE TRIGGER statement to drop and create a trigger in one statement.

The DROP TRIGGER statement is similar to the statement for dropping a table, database, or view. In a DROP TRIGGER statement, the table name must be prepended to the name of the trigger:

`DROP TRIGGER <table name>.<trigger name>`

For example, to drop the after_customer_update trigger we created for the customer table in the shop database, first make the shop database active:

`mysql> USE shop;`

Once you are in the shop database, you can drop the trigger using the table and trigger name:

```
mysql> DROP TRIGGER customer.after_customer_update;
```

You may have noticed that we didn't just prepend the database name in front of the table name. Unlike other DROP commands, where you can prefix the database name to the table or other item, you cannot drop a trigger unless the currently active database contains the table associated with the trigger.

Trigger Permissions

Trigger permissions control access to creating and dropping triggers, as well as trigger activation.

To manage triggers, you'll need the ability to create and drop triggers. Both of these commands require the SUPER privilege for the database. See Chapter 15 for more information about granting permissions to users.

To have a trigger activate, you need to have permission to run a SQL statement that matches the event on the trigger. If you don't have permission to INSERT into a table, you won't be able to make an INSERT trigger on that table activate. This is true for all of the trigger event types, including INSERT, UPDATE, and DELETE.

When the trigger activates, if a statement in the body sets a variable equal to a field in the NEW record, the calling user must have the ability to perform SELECT operations of the table. This is because the user is attempting to pull a value from the record into a variable.

When attempting to set a field in the NEW record equal to a variable, the results of a calculation or function, or another field, the caller needs to have UPDATE permissions on the table. If the user is setting a field, this changes the value of the field that will go into the table, which requires the ability to update the table.

If you don't have the appropriate permissions on the table when attempting to interact with the trigger's table, you will get an access denied error.

■**Note** The MySQL source code hints at future use of a trigger privilege. Look for a change in a future release where you can differentiate between users with SUPER privileges and those who have permissions to create and drop triggers.

Trigger Performance

For databases that need the functionality available through triggers, even significantly degraded performance will be worth the trade-off for having event-triggered database-level logic. Perhaps you are on the fine line, trying to decide if introducing triggers to your environment is worth the performance trade-off. In either case, it's probably worth looking at what kind of overhead is added to interacting with a table when a trigger is set to activate on a certain event.

For these tests, we took a series of SQL statements with randomly generated values and ran sets of 10,000 and 50,000 statements into the database. We calculated the queries per second for both the set of statements with no trigger defined and against the same table with each statement passed through one of three triggers. Two of these triggers were used in examples shown earlier in this chapter, in Listings 13-13 and 13-18. The third was a simple DELETE trigger, shown in Listing 13-22.

Listing 13-22. *Delete Trigger for Performance Testing*

```
DELIMITER //
CREATE TRIGGER after_cust_order_delete AFTER DELETE on cust_order
FOR EACH ROW
BEGIN

IF @insert_count IS NULL THEN
        SET @insert_count = 0;
END IF;
SET @insert_count = @insert_count + 1;

END
//

DELIMITER ;
```

Our intention in testing was to determine how much overhead is involved in the inclusion of the trigger in the statement processing. For this reason, we did not use triggers that interacted with other tables, as that additional interaction would add overhead to the execution time that is beyond the execution of the trigger.

The metrics were performed on MySQL 5.0.2 alpha, running on a single AMD64 2800+, with 1GB of RAM and a 10,000 RPM SCSI data disk (separate from the boot disk). The database is using the prebuilt binary for AMD64 downloaded from the MySQL web site, with all the default options on startup (no my.cnf file used on startup). Table 13-1 shows the results.

Table 13-1. *Performance Test for MySQL Triggers*

SQL Statement	Queries/Sec Without Trigger	Trigger	Queries/Sec with Trigger
INSERT INTO cust_order	166.2	From Listing 13-13	165.8
UPDATE cust_order	174.2	From Listing 13-18	184.8
DELETE FROM cust_order	165.7	From Listing 13-22	165.8

As we ran the benchmark queries, and as you can see in the results, we found very little difference between having a trigger handling the data and putting the data directly into the table (and with the UPDATE and DELETE, having the trigger improves performance). There are a few explanations for this:

- The triggers execute extremely quickly. In the case of one-statement triggers, this is likely. In the instance where a trigger contains a significant amount of logic that must be run for every record, it's more likely that performance will drop.

- Because INSERT, UPDATE, and DELETE statements interact with data on the disk, we may be seeing the I/O of the disks as the most significant piece of the performance here, making the trigger processing time insignificant.

- The examples used in our performance tests were too simplistic to truly test the impact that triggers have on the data going into a table. While this is possible, the second trigger example is typical of the kind of processing that would be likely in a real-world scenario.

We can't suggest how significant these numbers are. You'll need to decide if the additional overhead is worth having trigger functionality in your database. As with all database functionality, you should spend time benchmarking your database. Before you roll out your trigger-based implementation, take time to benchmark each trigger under real-world loads, and be sure that you can accept whatever performance degradation your application will experience as a result.

Summary

Triggers can provide a valuable set of functionality to complement referential integrity checks in your data, and can provide additional functionality in adjusting and creating data as data in the tables is changed. Before jumping into using triggers, it's important to consider their advantages and disadvantages, and make sensible decisions based on the needs of your database and application.

MySQL has a great start on implementing the SQL:2003 standard for database triggers, with a few key pieces missing. Triggers in MySQL are far enough along to allow database users to start to experiment and develop with the functionality, and plan for the arrival of a stable MySQL release with triggers.

A trigger definition requires a single CREATE statement with a few parameters and one or more SQL statements to make up the body. The body can include declaration and flow control statements to build decision-making mechanisms into the trigger.

Tools for managing triggers are limited. The CREATE and DROP statements are the only tools provided for managing triggers in the database. Triggers are viewed using the INFORMATION_ SCHEMA in MySQL. Check MySQL's trigger documentation for up-to-the-minute information about the release of more administrative tools.

Triggers offer an exciting and powerful mechanism to interact with data at the database level. With the ability to run a series of SQL statements whenever data is changed in the database, you gain much more control over what is happening as data changes stream into your database.

PART 2

■■■

Administration

MySQL Installation and Configuration

Installing and configuring MySQL can take anywhere from five minutes to five hours, or even span multiple days, depending on your requirements. One of the long-time goals of MySQL AB has been to keep the installation of MySQL quick and simple. By providing an easy installation process with preconfigured options, MySQL makes it possible to have a database running with almost no effort. However, while the easy installation and default configuration work for many, when deploying MySQL in an esoteric or somewhat more complicated environment, you might want to take advantage of the numerous options it offers for building, installing, configuring, and tuning MySQL to fit your needs. Depending on your specific architecture and database requirements, you may spend a significant amount of time setting up the database before it is ready for use.

The MySQL web site provides a wide range of precompiled binaries for numerous platforms. You are encouraged to use these precompiled binaries, and benefit from the MySQL AB team's years of experience and wealth of knowledge about various platforms. The precompiled binaries are well documented in the notes on the download page, and they often are faster than a self-compiled binary. In some cases, MySQL AB uses commercial compilers for speed improvements. However, in some situations, the existing binaries won't meet your needs, and you'll want to build from the source package or even directly from the top of the source tree.

After you've installed MySQL, you may need to perform some other setup tasks, such as having MySQL start up when you start your operating system. You might also need to set some of MySQL's myriad configuration options. And since MySQL is under constant development, it is likely that, at some time, you will want to upgrade to the latest version.

This chapter covers MySQL installation, configuration, upgrading, and related issues. Specifically, we'll discuss the following topics:

- Existing MySQL installations

- Prebuilt binary installation

- Source and development source tree builds

- MySQL startup and shutdown

- Post-installation steps

- MySQL configuration options

- Upgrading techniques

- MySQL uninstallation

- Multiple database servers on a single machine

Using an Existing Installation

The simplest way to get up and running with MySQL is to use a version of the database included in your operating system installation. Many Linux distributions include a package for MySQL that is installed with the operating system. If the preinstalled version meets your needs, it may be ready to use.

However, often, a preinstalled version of MySQL lags behind the current release, because new MySQL versions are released on a frequent basis. If, for reasons of functionality or performance, you need a more recent version of MySQL, you'll want to upgrade—if not now, then at some point. In most cases, this will require uninstalling the package and upgrading to a package or tarball from the MySQL web site.

Additionally, you may find that support is more readily available for the standard, MySQL-defined installation. In some operating systems, the preinstalled MySQL's organization is different from the standard MySQL installation's organization. MySQL AB and the community may not provide assistance if your installation varies from the standard organization.

If you choose to use an existing installation, take the time to review the "Performing Post-Installation Setup," "Configuring MySQL," and "Upgrading MySQL" sections in this chapter.

Installing Prebuilt Binaries

With the exception of having MySQL preinstalled with the operating system, using prebuilt binaries from the MySQL web site is the quickest, and recommended, method for installation. These binaries are carefully compiled, and they are based on years of experience in creating the most stable and highest performing build. For certain architectures, MySQL uses commercial compilers, which net as much as 20% performance boost over the open-source alternative.

Beyond choosing the right build for your architecture and operating system, you must choose from a few build types. In some cases, you'll also have a choice of installation mechanisms: the command-line installed tarball or a package with an installer.

Here, we'll describe how to use the MySQL binaries to install MySQL on Unix, Windows, and Mac OS X systems.

MYSQL DIRECTORY STRUCTURE

MySQL installs more than a thousand files and directories on your system. The location of these files differs depending on the installation mechanism you choose. The tarball root directory structure contains the following:

- `bin`: This directory contains the `mysqld` server program and all client programs and tools you will run to use and administer MySQL.

- `data`: The data files, where MySQL reads and writes its data, are stored here, along with log files for the server.

- `docs`: The documentation directory contains an HTML and text file with version-specific documentation.

- `include`: The binary tarball includes a set of header files, which may be used when writing or compiling other programs.

- `lib`: The `lib` directory contains MySQL library files.

- `scripts`: This directory contains the `mysql_install_db` script, which is used to install initial data files and accounts.

- `share`: The `share` directory contains SQL scripts for fixing privileges, as well as a set of language files for using MySQL in a variety of languages.

- `sql-bench`: MySQL includes a set of benchmarking tools (discussed in Chapter 6).

- `support-files`: The MySQL installation includes a directory with several confiiguration file examples and other support scripts.

If you aren't using the Unix tarball, see the MySQL document at `http://dev.mysql.com/doc/mysql/en/Installation_layouts.html` for information about file layouts for different operating systems.

Supported Operating Systems

MySQL AB provides prebuilt binaries for a wide range of operating systems, along with documentation on the build process for each binary. (See `http://dev.mysql.com/doc/mysql/en/MySQL_binaries.html` for more details on the MySQL binaries.) You'll find downloadable binaries for Linux (for x86, S/390, IA64, Alpha, Sparc, PowerPC, AMD64, and EMT64 processors), Solaris, FreeBSD, Windows, Mac OS X, HP-UX, IBM-AIX, QNX, Novell NetWare, SCI Irix, and Dec OSF. Binaries are available for two or more recent operating system versions, except for QNX, Novell NetWare, and OSF, which have a single download available.

All platforms are not considered equal for running a MySQL server. MySQL AB is clear that it doesn't want to suggest, in general, that a specific operating system is better than another, but certain platforms better meet an outlined set of requirements for running the database server. When evaluating a platform, MySQL AB works through a list of criteria to determine how well suited the platform is for running MySQL:

- How good are the threading libraries on the operating system? MySQL is threaded and relies on the operating system for its threading libraries. The database server will be reliable only if the threading on a platform is stable.

- Will the operating system use multiple CPUs? The database gets a great deal of performance if threads, which are handling connections and queries, can run on more than one processor.

- How stable and robust is the file system? MySQL relies heavily on reading and writing data to the file system. The stability and performance of the file system will have a big effect on the performance of the database. Also important to consider is how well the file system handles large files.

- How much is the operating system used and how well is it understood? When considering recommendations for an operating system, MySQL AB assesses how many users have had success running MySQL on a platform, how much MySQL-related expertise is available for that operating system, and the amount of MySQL history and testing that has been done.

The answers to all of these questions culminate in a few recommendations from MySQL AB. Currently, MySQL recommends Linux on x86, Solaris on SPARC, and FreeBSD as the platforms that best meet the criteria for a MySQL database server.

MySQL Build Types

For most platforms, MySQL is available in three different build types, each with a different set of features:

- *Standard*: Includes MySQL server with MyISAM and InnoDB storage engines, client tools, benchmarking suite, and MySQL libraries.

- *Max*: Includes the features in the standard build, plus the NDB Cluster and Berkeley DB (BDB) storage engines (where supported), user-defined functions, and other features not in the standard binaries. More details on the max binaries are available from `http://dev.mysql.com/doc/mysql/en/mysqld-max.html`.

- *Debug*: Binaries compiled with debugging support, with reduced performance (not recommended for production use).

On Windows, you can choose between a zip file for manual installation or two types of installers. Unlike with the Unix tarballs, where you choose a build type, Windows downloads contain all of the binary types. When you install manually or with a GUI installer, the standard, max, and debug binaries are all installed along with two additional binaries, standard-nt and max-nt, which are optimized for Windows NT, 2000, and XP and have support for Named Pipes.

Manual Installation

For Unix, the manually installed tarball format is the most widely used and recommended method for installing your database. A manual installation process is also available for Windows, but it is not as easy or thorough as the Windows installer option.

Manually Installing Tarball on Unix

Tarred binaries unpack into a single directory, named by its build type (standard, max, or debug), version, and platform (for example, `mysql-max-5.0.6-pc-linux-i686`). All binaries, configuration files, data, libraries, and documentation are in this directory.

MySQL documentation recommends putting the untarred directory into `/usr/local` and symbolically linking it to `/usr/local/mysql`. The tarred binaries include a range of configuration files to match a range of database needs, as well as an `init.d`-style startup script for starting, stopping, restarting, and checking the status of a running MySQL server. Tarballs are available for all listed platforms.

Installing the tarball for a prebuilt binary takes relatively few steps, which include creating a `mysql` group and user, untarring the file, installing the data files, changing the permissions for the files and directories, and starting the database. Here is the procedure (all commands run using the root user):

1. Create the `mysql` group, which is used with the `mysql` user for controlling permissions of the files installed with MySQL, as well as the data files and logs.

   ```
   # groupadd mysql
   ```

2. Create the `mysql` user, whose primary group is the `mysql` group. The `mysql` user is used for both file permissions and running the `mysql` server as a non-root user.

   ```
   # useradd -g mysql mysql
   ```

3. Move to the recommended location for installing the MySQL files.

   ```
   # cd /usr/local
   ```

4. Untar the MySQL tarball.

   ```
   # tar -xzvf /path/to/mysql-VERSION-OS.tar.gz
   ```

5. Create a symbolic link, for ease in accessing the database.

   ```
   # ln -s /full/path/to/mysql-VERSION-OS mysql
   ```

6. Move into the install directory.

   ```
   # cd mysql
   ```

7. Run the script to install the initial database files used for MySQL accounts and testing. Specify to install the files as the `mysql` user.

   ```
   # scripts/mysql_install_db --user=mysql
   ```

8. Change user ownership of all installed files and directories to root.

   ```
   # chown -R root .
   ```

9. Change user ownership of the data directory to `mysql`.

   ```
   # chown -R mysql data
   ```

10. Change group ownership of all installed files and directories to `mysql`.

    ```
    # chgrp -R mysql .
    ```

11. Start the database using `mysqld_safe`, specifying that the database should be run by the `mysql` user.

    ```
    # bin/mysqld_safe --user=mysql &
    ```

At this point, you should have a running instance of MySQL.

Note On Unix, the recommended method for starting a MySQL server is `bin/mysqld_safe`, not `bin/mysqld`. `mysqld_safe` provides security to the database server if an error occurs, by restarting the server and logging runtime information to your error log.

Manually Installing the Windows Binary

Using the Windows installer option, as described in the next section, is the recommended way to install MySQL on Windows platforms. However, if you need to manually install MySQL on Windows for some reason, you can do so. Download the `noinstall.zip` file, and then follow these steps:

1. Unzip the Windows zip file.

   ```
   C:\> C:\path\to\unzip.exe mysql-VERSION-win-noinstall.zip
   ```

2. Rename the Windows zip file to `mysql`.

   ```
   C:\> rename mysql-VERSION-win mysql
   ```

3. Create a configuration file and start a `mysqld` group. (MySQL groups are covered in the "Configuration Groups" section later in this chapter.)

   ```
   C:\> echo [mysqld] > my.ini
   ```

4. Add the `basedir` option to your configuration file. (Configuration file options are covered in the "Configuring MySQL" section later in this chapter.)

   ```
   C:\> echo basedir=C:\mysql >> my.ini
   ```

5. Add the data directory option to your configuration file.

   ```
   C:\> echo datadir=C:\mysql\data >> my.ini
   ```

6. Start the MySQL server.

   ```
   C:\> C:\mysql\bin\mysqld
   ```

You will now have a running instance of MySQL on your Windows system.

Windows Installer

The easiest and most thorough option for installing MySQL on Windows is to use the Windows Essentials download. The Essentials download comes with a Microsoft Windows installer file that installs server binaries, command-line utilities, and libraries.

After downloading Windows Essentials, run the installer to install the necessary files using the MySQL Installation Wizard. If you leave the Configure option checked, after you click Finish, the MySQL Configuration Wizard starts automatically. The wizard prompts you with a series of screens to determine how the database server will be used. At the end of the wizard, it creates a configuration file based on your preferences. The MySQL Configuration Wizard can also be run separately to modify an existing installation.

The MySQL Configuration Wizard steps you through the following screens:

- *Machine Type*: Choose developer, server, or dedicated server. This choice dynamically sets temporary table and buffer pool sizes based on your machine's memory.

- *Storage Type*: Choose whether your database will be multifunctional, transactional, or nontransactional. Your storage type choice sets the default storage engine and determines which engines to enable. If you need a combination of transactional and nontransactional tables, choose multifunctional. If you choose nontransactional, the default storage engine will be set to MyISAM, which is faster but does not include support for transactions. (See Chapter 5 for details on the MySQL storage engines.)

- *Tablespace Settings*: Specify the path to the folder that will contain the data files for the database.

- *Connection Load*: Choose how many connections MySQL will allow. Your choice sets the `max_connections` parameter in the configuration file.

- *TCP Networking*: Choose to enable MySQL network availability and specify a port, or disable networking altogether.

- *Default Character Set*: Choose a default character set. This sets the `default-character-set` option in the configuration file, which tells MySQL what set of characters to use.

- *Windows Options*: Indicate whether you would like a Windows service installed, including choosing the name of the service. Also specify if you would like MySQL programs added to your Windows `PATH` variable.

- *Security*: Secure the database by setting the root password and removing the anonymous account, which does not have a password.

When the wizard completes, the configuration file is created. The database will start if you selected to run it.

RPMs

RPM package files for standard, max, and debug builds are available in generic form for x86 Linux, as well as in specific builds for the Red Hat and SUSE Linux distributions. What makes a complete tarball is broken into several RPMs, allowing you to install the server, client, libraries, and so on separately. As it should, the RPM spreads the installed files across various directories (`/usr/bin`, `/usr/libexec/`, `/usr/share/man`, `/var/lib`, `/etc`, and others). The server package creates the required `mysql` group and user, installs the application, creates the data files, and starts the database. Table 14-1 provides a brief description of the RPM packages.

Table 14-1. *RPM Packages*

Name	Description
server	Installs the server binaries, configuration, and data files
bench	Installs all the benchmarking tools and test suites (see Chapter 6)
client	Installs the client RPM, for client and tool programs (`mysqladmin`, `mysqldump`, and so on)
devel	Includes header files and libraries needed if you are compiling other programs to use MySQL
shared	Includes dynamic client libraries that can be used by other applications that want to interact with a MySQL server
embedded	Installs a server that can be included in other applications
shared-compat	Includes dynamic client libraries available in the shared package, as well as the older, 3.23.x libraries for compatibility

Mac OS X Packages

Tarballs are available for Macintosh systems running OS X 10.2 and above, and they can be installed using the manual install instructions for Unix. If you don't want to go through the manual installation, download the Mac installer for a GUI-based installation.

The Mac installer is downloaded as a disk image, which, when mounted, contains a database install package and a startup install package. The database installer expects an existing `mysql` user, which is already set up by default in OS X version 10.2 and greater, even if MySQL has never been installed on your OS X machine. The database installer uses the same directory structure as the tarball, but it is smart about not deleting existing installations, moving any existing `mysql` directory to `mysql.old`. Use the `MySQLStartupItem.pkg` to create an entry in the OS X operating system startup programs.

Once you've completed the OS X installer process, either using the manual Unix instructions or the OS X GUI installer, you can start the database using the following commands:

```
# cd /usr/local/mysql
# ./bin/mysqld_safe &
```

If you've installed the `MySQLStartupItem` package, you can use the following startup script command:

```
# /Library/StartupItems/MySQLCOM/MySQLCOM start
```

Building from Source or the Development Source Tree

We start this section with a reminder that MySQL strongly encourages you to use the prebuilt binaries. MySQL AB developers expend significant effort into their build process, and in many cases, this provides the fastest and most stable build. In instances where you need support for a problem, using the prebuilt binaries will reduce the resistance to assistance. With that said, we realize that, in some cases, the binaries may not fit your needs. You may be considering building from source for the following reasons:

- MySQL isn't available for your architecture or operating system.

- You prefer to install MySQL in a different location than the one provided by the binary.

- You want extra features that are not included in a binary for your system.

- You don't need certain features built into the binary for your system.

- You want to use different compiler options, or a different compiler altogether.

- Before MySQL is built, you need to change some of the source code. Perhaps you need to apply a patch from MySQL AB or have customized functions to compile with the source.

- You want the additional tests and examples, which are in the source, but left out of the prebuilt binaries.

- You rest better when you know the exact details of how your MySQL binary was built.

If any of those reasons ring true for you, then download the tarball from mysql.com and get started.

■Note If you need to build from source on Windows (a rare requirement), see the MySQL documentation's instructions for using VC++ to build the source, available from http://dev.mysql.com/doc/mysql/en/Windows_source_build.html.

Manually Installing the Source Tarball on Unix

Building MySQL from source is fairly straightforward on Unix-like platforms, especially if you've compiled other software. Installation of the source tarball on a Unix system is similar to installing the binary tarball, with a few extra steps to configure and compile the MySQL binaries. Here are the steps:

1. Create the mysql group, which is used with the mysql user for controlling permissions of the files installed with MySQL, as well as the data files and logs.

   ```
   # groupadd mysql
   ```

2. Create the mysql user, whose primary group is the mysql group. The mysql user is used for both file permissions and running the MySQL server as a non-root user.

```
# useradd -g mysql mysql
```

3. Untar the source tarball.

```
# tar -xzvf mysql-VERSION.tar.gz
```

4. Move into the directory created when untarring.

```
# cd mysql-VERSION
```

5. Run the configure script, specifying options for building MySQL (see Table 14-2).

```
#./configure --prefix=/usr/local/mysql-VERSION (other options)
```

■**Note** When running `configure` to build MySQL, unless you are building as part of a packaging tool, we highly recommend installing everything into /usr/local/mysql. Using /usr or /usr/local as a prefix will spread files throughout several directories. Unless you have a packaging tool to help keep track of the files, having everything installed into one directory will simplify future upgrades.

---

6. Compile the software.

```
# make
```

7. Test the compiled software.

```
# make test
```

8. Install the software.

```
# make install
```

If things go well, you'll watch the build process take its time dumping status messages onto the screen, and then end up back at your shell prompt, with an OK or success message. At that point, you can continue with the following steps.

■**Note** As you run `configure`, `make`, and `make test`, you may run into complications—perhaps `configure` will complain about missing files or `make` will dump a dozen screens of errors. In many cases, the problem is misused `configure` options, missing libraries, incomplete paths, or incompatible options. Look at the first lines that indicate trouble and see if you can find keywords that indicate what the `compile` or `make` is working on at the point of failure. Verify that your options for that functionality are correct. For help, you can use a search engine to find the error string, or scan the configure script and makefile to see if you can gather clues on the point where the compile is failing and what's causing problems.

---

9. Move to the recommended location where you installed the MySQL files.

   ```
   # cd /usr/local
   ```

10. Create a symbolic link, for ease in accessing the MySQL server directory.

    ```
    # ln -s mysql-VERSION mysql
    ```

11. Move into the install directory.

    ```
    # cd mysql
    ```

12. Run the script to install the initial database files used for MySQL accounts and testing.

    ```
    # scripts/mysql_install_db
    ```

13. Change user ownership of all installed files and directories to root.

    ```
    # chown -R root .
    ```

14. Change user ownership of the data directory to mysql.

    ```
    # chown -R mysql data
    ```

15. Change group ownership of all installed files and directories to mysql.

    ```
    # chgrp -R mysql .
    ```

16. Start the database using mysqld_safe, specifying that the database should be run by the mysql user.

    ```
    # bin/mysqld_safe --user=mysql &
    ```

Your main reason for tackling the source build may be to set specific configuration options. Table 14-2 lists commonly used configuration options. For a full list, check the MySQL documentation or run ./configure --help in your source directory.

Table 14-2. *Common MySQL Configuration Options*

Option	Description
--disable-largefile	Do not include large file support.
--enable-local-infile	Enable LOAD DATA LOCAL INFILE. This is disabled by default.
--enable-thread-safe-client	When compiling the client, enable threads.
--prefix=<dir>	Install files at this location. The default is /usr/local.
--with-archive-storage-engine	Enable the ARCHIVE storage engine.
--with-berkeley-db=<dir>	Use this directory for the BDB storage engine.
--with-berkeley-db-includes=<dir>	Use this directory for the BDB headers.
--with-berkeley-db-libs=<dir>	Use this directory for BDB libraries.
--with-charset=<name>	Specify the default character set. The choices are binary, armscii8, ascii, big5, cp1250, cp1251, cp1256, cp1257, cp850, cp852, cp866, dec8, euckr, gb2312, gbk, geostd8, greek, hebrew, hp8, keybcs2, koi8r, koi8u, latin1, latin2, latin5, latin7, macce, macroman, sjis, swe7, tis620, ucs2, ujis, and utf8.

Continued

Table 14-2. *Continued*

Option	Description
`--with-client-ldflags`	Additional arguments for linking clients.
`--with-comment`	Add a comment about the compilation process.
`--with-csv-storage-engine`	Enable the CSV storage engine.
`--with-example-storage-engine`	Enable the example storage engine.
`--with-lib-ccflags`	Additional CC library options.
`--with-libwrap=<dir>`	Compile in support for TCP wrappers.
`--with-low-memory`	Try to use less memory to compile to get around memory limitations.
`--with-mysqld-ldflags`	Additional `ld` linking arguments for `mysqld`.
`--with-mysqld-user=<username>`	Use this username to run the `mysqld` daemon.
`--with-mysqlfs`	Include the MySQL file system (CORBA-based).
`--with-ndb-docs`	Include documentation for the NDB Cluster.
`--with-ndb-port-base`	Use this port for the NDB Cluster.
`--with-ndb-sci=<dir>`	Give MySQL a location for the `sci` library. The libraries should be in `<dir>/lib` and header files in `<dir>/include`.
`--with-ndb-shm`	Include the shared memory transporter for the NDB Cluster.
`--with-ndb-test`	Include test programs for the NDB Cluster.
`--with-ndbcluster`	Enable the NDB Cluster storage engine.
`--with-openssl=<dir>`	Include support for OpenSSL.
`--with-openssl-includes=<dir>`	Look in `<dir>` for OpenSSL.
`--with-openssl-libs=<dir>`	Look for OpenSSL libraries in `<dir>`.
`--with-pstack`	Enable the `pstack` backtrace library.
`--with-pthread`	Use the `pthread` library.
`--with-raid`	Enable support for RAID.
`--with-tcp-port=<number>`	Specify the port to use for MySQL services. The default is 3306.
`--with-unix-socket-path=<file>`	Specify the file for MySQL to use for creating and using the Unix socket.
`--with-vio`	Include support for virtual I/O.
`--with-zlib-dir=<dir>`	Give MySQL a location for the compression library. The libraries should be in `<dir>/lib` and header files in `<dir>/include`.
`--without-bench`	Skip building the MySQL benchmark suite.
`--without-debug`	Build a production version without debugging code.
`--without-docs`	Do not include MySQL documentation.
`--without-innodb`	Exclude the InnoDB storage engine.
`--without-libedit`	Use system's `libedit`, instead of the copy bundled with MySQL.
`--without-man`	Do not include man pages when building.
`--without-query-cache`	Skip building the query cache.
`--without-readline`	Use the system's `readline`, instead of the copy bundled with MySQL.
`--without-server`	Do not build the server. Build only the client.

FINDING LIBRARIES WITH LDPATH

While building MySQL, you may link to libraries that are dynamically loaded. Perhaps you want to include the ability for SSL encryption on database connections, which will require links to the OpenSSL libraries on your server. To ensure these libraries can be found at build and runtime, you may need to give the compiler some help. Many folks set `LD_LIBRARY_PATH` to contain a list of paths, which the compiler and binaries use when looking for needed libraries. This can cause problems if binaries are started outside your environment where the paths aren't included.

To better assist the compiler in finding libraries to link against at compile time, and help the binary find these libraries at runtime, use `LDFLAGS`. `LDFLAGS` are passed to the linker, and can tell the linker to use certain paths when looking for libraries at compile time as well as runtime. Setting `LDFLAGS` to `-L/some/path` tells the linker to look in that path during compile time. Adding `-R/some/path` will append that path to a list of directories considered at runtime.

Installing from the Development Source Tree on Unix

You may consider setting up a build that uses the latest source from the MySQL AB development source tree because building from a specific version of the source doesn't provide what you need. Or perhaps you want to play with some of the latest functionality in MySQL, but a release with that functionality isn't available. Or you may have submitted a bug that has been committed for release in the next version, but you need that fix sooner than the next release. These are all valid reasons for working with the very latest builds. Thankfully, the process is well documented and not much more work than building from a source tarball.

MySQL AB uses BitKeeper, a configuration management system, for its code repository. BitKeeper allows multiple users to keep their own repository with revision history and provides tools for moving changes between repositories. You may not be interested in modifying the source code, but you will need to get a copy of the source via the BitKeeper tools in order to build from the development source tree. BitKeeper is a free download from `http://www.bitkeeper.com` (you will need to register first). Once you have the client, grabbing a clone of the source code requires one simple command.

To build from the development tree, you'll need up-to-date versions of GNU `make`, `autoconf`, `automake`, `libtool`, and `m4`. On some Unix machines, these tools are installed by default, or the operating system has a developer tools package that includes them. If you can't find a package, you can always get these tools from `http://www.gnu.org`.

Installation from the source tree on a Unix system is similar to installing from the source tarball, with a few extra steps to get and set up the source code. Here are the steps:

1. Create the `mysql` group, which is used with the `mysql` user for controlling permissions of the files installed with MySQL, as well as the data files and logs.

   ```
   # groupadd mysql
   ```

2. Create the `mysql` user whose primary group is the `mysql` group. The `mysql` user is used for both file permissions and running the MySQL server as a non-root user.

   ```
   # useradd -g mysql mysql
   ```

3. Get the source tree from the MySQL BitKeeper site. *BRANCH* is one of 4.1, 5.0, 5.1, and so on.

   ```
   # bk clone bk://mysql.bkbits.net/mysql-BRANCH mysql-BRANCH
   ```

4. Move into the source directory.

   ```
   # cd mysql-BRANCH
   ```

5. Tell BitKeeper you are going to work with the files.

   ```
   # bk -r edit
   ```

6. Run commands to generate the `configure` script and makefiles.

   ```
   # aclocal; autoheader; autoconf; automake
   ```

7. Run commands to generate the configure script and makefile for the InnoDB storage engine, if you want to use this storage engine.

   ```
   # (cd innobase; aclocal; autoheader; autoconf; automake)
   ```

8. Run the configure script, specifying options for building MySQL (configuration options are summarized in Table 14-2).

   ```
   #./configure --prefix=/usr/local/mysql (other options)
   ```

9. Compile the software.

   ```
   # make
   ```

10. Test the compiled software.

    ```
    # make test
    ```

11. Install the software.

    ```
    # make install
    ```

12. Move to the recommended location where you installed the MySQL files.

    ```
    # cd /usr/local/mysql
    ```

13. Run the script to install the initial database files used for MySQL accounts and testing.

    ```
    # bin/mysql_install_db
    ```

14. Change user ownership of all installed files and directories to root.

    ```
    # chown -R root .
    ```

15. Change user ownership of the data directory to `mysql`.

    ```
    # chown -R mysql var
    ```

16. Change group ownership of all installed files and directories to `mysql`.

    ```
    # chgrp -R mysql .
    ```

17. Move a configuration file to /etc for use in starting the database.

    ```
    # mv support-files/my-medium.cnf /etc/my.cnf
    ```

18. Start the database using mysqld_safe, specifying that the database should be run by the mysql user.

    ```
    # bin/mysqld_safe --user=mysql &
    ```

Starting and Stopping MySQL

Although each of the sections on installing MySQL included a step to start the database, we want to call particular attention to the recommended method for starting your database server. Also, inevitably there will be a point where you need to stop the database server.

■Tip If you don't find an example that matches your server, you can use the mysqladmin tool to stop the database: mysqladmin -u root -p shutdown.

Unix Startup and Shutdown

On Unix, the server program is contained in mysqld, but the recommended script for running the database is mysqld_safe, which runs a process to monitor the database and keep it running. Using mysqld_safe also logs extra pre-startup steps, which may help in troubleshooting problems with the mysqld binary.

On many Unix flavors, an rc script named mysql or mysql.server will be installed in /etc/init.d, /etc/init.d/rc.d, or /usr/local/etc/rc.d, which can be given the start argument to start the database. These scripts wrap around the mysqld_safe script. If it's available, using an rc script is recommended over running mysqld_safe manually. This script can also be given the stop argument to shut down the database:

```
/etc/init.d/mysql stop
```

Windows Startup and Shutdown

If you are running MySQL on Windows, you should probably set up a service, as described in the "Performing Post-Installation Setup" section of this chapter. The service allows you to use the Services tool in the Control Panel to start the database, or run NET START MySQL at the C:\> prompt. If you don't have a service installed for MySQL, use C:\mysql\bin\mysqld.

If you have a service running, you can stop it through the Services tool in the Control Panel, or use NET STOP MySQL at the C:\> prompt. If you don't have the service installed, use the following command to shut down the database:

```
C:\mysql\bin\mysqladmin -u root shutdown
```

Mac OS X Startup and Shutdown

If you've installed the `MySQLStartupItem` package, you can use the shell script for automatic startup:

```
# /Library/StartupItems/MySQLCOM/MySQLCOM start
```

Otherwise, you can use the Unix command for starting with `mysqld_safe`.

If you've installed the `MySQLStartupItem` package, you can use the shell script for shutting down MySQL:

```
# /Library/StartupItems/MySQLCOM/MySQLCOM stop
```

Performing Post-Installation Setup

Depending on your installation mechanism, the following are some additional steps you may need to perform after you've installed MySQL:

Add MySQL to operating system startup: If your installation mechanism didn't create a service or an entry in the appropriate place to have the MySQL server start automatically when the server boots up, you may want to add it now, so the server will always be running, even if the machine is rebooted. Table 14-3 summarizes instructions for several operating systems.

Secure the database: Secure the database using various techniques, as outlined in Chapter 16. Securing your database includes important steps like removing networking if it's not needed, setting the root password, and removing the no-password anonymous account.

Create accounts: You'll need to create accounts for yourself and others to use the database. Set up your account first, with all permissions necessary to create other accounts so you can avoid using the root user, which is considered bad security practice. Then, for each user who needs access to the database, create a login and a set of appropriate permissions to control that account's access to the data. Chapter 15 covers setting up user accounts.

Review prebuilt configuration files: Based on your intended use of MySQL, if you aren't planning on spending time digging into configuration details, you may want to take a few minutes to consider using one of the prebuilt configuration files provided with the installation. In the `support-files` folder of your installation are four configuration files: `my-small.cnf`, `my-medium.cnf`, `my-large.cnf`, and `my-huge.cnf`. Depending on the size of memory on the machine, and what other processes you plan on running on the server, you may be able to realize some benefits by trying different prebuilt configuration files.

Move data directory: To ease in upgrading, you might consider putting your data in a directory other than the installed MySQL directory. If you put your data files into another directory, perhaps even on a separate disk, you ease the upgrade process because you won't need to move data files into the `mysql` install folder after a new version is installed. You also get performance improvements by putting your data files on a disk separate from the operating system. Use the `--datadir` option in your configuration file to specify the location of your data files.

Put tools in your path: To ease use of the MySQL tools, you may want to make sure the binaries are in your path, and perhaps in all server users' paths. This isn't important if you've installed using an RPM where the binaries are installed in /usr/bin, which is in the PATH environment variable by default. However, if you've installed into /usr/local/mysql, adding /usr/local/mysql/bin to the PATH environment variable of users allows them to use the tools without needing to type the full path /usr/local/mysql/bin/mysql to start their client.

Table 14-3. *Adding MySQL to Operating System Startup*

Operating System	Instructions
Linux	Depending on the distribution, adding MySQL to the startup can differ. The Red Hat or Fedora distributions use chkconfig, which allows you to move support-files/mysql.server to /etc/init.d/mysql and run chkconfig ➥ --add mysql. Gentoo Linux uses rc-update; with support-files/mysql.server moved to /etc/init.d/mysql, you run rc-update add mysql default. See the documentation for your Linux distribution for specific details.
FreeBSD	Add mysql_enable="YES" to /etc/rc.conf.
Solaris	Copy support-files/mysql.server to /etc/init.d/mysql and create symbolic links from /etc/rc1.d/K99mysql and /etc/rc2.d/S99mysql.
Windows	Create a Windows service with C:\mysql\bin\mysqld --install.
Macintosh	Install the MySQLStartupItem package.

Configuring MySQL

In many cases, the default configuration provided by the installer or included in the support-files folder will meet your needs. Even so, you'll want to know how MySQL uses the configuration files, along with the options on the command line, and be aware of the available settings. Then, if the defaults for MySQL do not perform as you expected, you'll be able to change the configuration.

■**Note** This section gives an overview of how configuration works and what options are available. Chapter 6 digs deeper into profiling your database. Use the techniques outlined in Chapter 6 when tweaking these configuration options to determine how configuration changes affect performance.

Location of Configuration Files

MySQL uses text-based configuration files (commonly referred to as *option files*). By allowing you to use multiple levels of configuration files, cascading to create a complete set of options, MySQL offers a powerful mechanism to customize the interaction with the server and tools.

Unix Configuration Files

On Unix systems, MySQL first looks in /etc/my.cnf and loads global options, applied to all servers and users. MySQL then loads options from a my.cnf file in MYSQL_HOME, an environment variable that points to a directory. If MYSQL_HOME isn't set, the database first looks in the data directory and then in the base directory for a configuration file. For a binary installation, the data directory is typically /usr/local/mysql/data. For a source installation, the data directory is /usr/local/var. Some packages, like RPM, are configured to store the data in /var/lib/mysql.

After looking in the data directory, MySQL will check for the command-line --defaults-extra-file=/*some/path*/my.cnf, and load those options. The last configuration MySQL loads is your user-specific, ~/.my.cnf file, which resides in your home directory. After processing all configuration files, MySQL processes the options given on the command line.

Windows Configuration Files

On Windows, MySQL first looks for my.ini in your WINDIR, and then for C:\my.cnf. To determine the value of WINDIR, use the following command:

```
C:\> echo %WINDIR%
```

Configuration Groups

As if having multiple configuration file levels didn't provide enough flexibility, the configuration files for MySQL can be further delineated by using groups, which let you set configuration options for specific tools, and even specific versions of the mysqld server. This means you can have one buffer size for mysqldump and another one for your mysql client, or one username/password for the program mysqladmin and another for mysqlshow.

The configuration file should start with options for all commands, before a group is specified. After options are set for all servers and tools, a group declaration starts the move into more specific options. A group section is specified by using brackets ([*group*]). All options after the group declaration will apply to servers or tools that fall into that group. A group section ends when a new group starts or the end of the file is reached. Table 14-4 lists the common configuration groups.

Table 14-4. *Common Configuration Groups*

Group	Applies to
server	The mysqld server program and mysqld_safe and mysql.server startup scripts
mysqld	The mysqld server program, regardless of startup mechanism
mysqld_safe	Database process started with the mysqld_safe script
safe_mysqld	Database process started using the mysqld_safe script
mysql.server	mysql.server startup script only
mysqld-4.0	mysqld for version 4.0; use mysqld-MAJOR.MINOR for other server versions
client	Any client program, not mysqld
mysql	MySQL client only
myisamchk	myisamchk tool, which checks and repairs MyISAM tables
myisampack	myisampack tool, which packs MyISAM tables into smaller, read-only format
mysqladmin	mysqladmin tool, which is used for database administration commands

Group	Applies to
mysqlbinlog	mysqlbinlog tool, which converts binary logs to text
mysqlcheck	mysqlcheck tool, which checks the health of tables
mysqldump	mysqldump tool, which creates SQL statements for rebuilding databases or tables
mysqlhotcopy	mysqlhotcopy tool, which copies data files
mysqlimport	mysqlimport, a command-line interface to LOAD DATA INFILE
mysqlshow	mysqlshow tool, which is used for showing information about databases, tables, columns, and so on
mysql_multi	mysql_multi tool, which is used for managing multiple running databases on one machine
mysqld1	mysql_multi with server 1 group number specified; use mysqld<*group number*> to create mysql_multi groups with options for each server

With the wide array of configuration groups and unending list of configuration options (covered in the next section), a configuration file can become quite complex. Listing 14-1 provides a simple configuration file with common groups and options.

Listing 14-1. *Sample my.cnf File with Groups*

```
[client]
username=michael
password=my_secret
port=3306
socket=/tmp/mysql.sock

[mysql]
prompt=mysql-prod>

[mysqld]
socket=/tmp/mysql.sock
key_buffer_size=8M
max_allowed_packet=4M
port=3306
```

Configuration Options

The meat of configuring MySQL is in the options—several hundred of them. The values are typically Boolean (no value needed; if the option is present, it will be used), strings, or integers. Options can be specified on the command line when starting the server or running a tool. However, in most instances, putting the options in a file will work better, since using a number of options can get unwieldy on the command line. In addition, if you're trying to ensure that the server or tools are consistently started with the same options, it is best to have them saved in an option file that can be loaded by the server or tool, without the risk of an option being left out.

Here, we will briefly outline commonly used options, grouped in the following functional areas:

- Client configuration
- Server configuration
- Logging configuration
- Engine-specific configuration
- Replication configuration
- Buffer and cache allocation configuration
- Server SSL configuration

For details on why or when you might use particular configuration options, see the chapters in this book that correspond with that functional area. Also, refer to the MySQL documentation at `http://dev.mysql.com/doc/mysql/en/Option_files.html`. You'll notice we use both underscore and dash when writing out configuration options in the following tables. You can use either underscore (_) or dash (-) when writing configuration options.

Client Configuration Options

Table 14-5 lists the common options used by client programs, including the `mysql` command-line interface and the administrative tools.

Table 14-5. *Common Client Configuration Options*

Option	Description
password=<password>	Password used to connect to server
port=<number>	Port number for clients to connect to server
socket=<file>	Socket file for client connections
ssl	Use SSL for your database connection
user=<name>	Username used for connecting to server

Server Configuration Options

The options outlined in Table 14-6 are directed at running the `mysql` server and the core functionality provided by the server.

Table 14-6. *Server Configuration Options*

Option	Description
ansi	Use ANSI SQL syntax, not MySQL syntax
basedir=<dir>	Path to installation directory; most paths are relative to this
bind-address=<ip address>	IP to use when binding server to address
character_set_server=<name>	Set the default character set
console	Use screen for error output; keep Windows console window open
chroot=<name>	During startup, chroot mysqld daemon

Option	Description
datadir=<dir>	Path to the data files
default-storage-engine=<name>	Use this as the default storage engine for tables
default-time-zone=<name>	Set the default time zone
init-file=<name>	At startup, read SQL commands from this file
join_buffer_size=<number>	Size of buffers used for full joins
key_buffer_size=<number>	Size of buffer allocated for index blocks for MyISAM tables
long_query_time=<number>	Query execute time which, when exceeded, triggers entry in slow query log
low-priority-updates	Make SELECT statements take priority over INSERT, UPDATE, or DELETE
lower_case_table_names[=<number>]	Set to 1 when tables are created in lowercase on disk and table names are case-insensitive; set to 2 for a case-insensitive file system
max_allowed_packet=<number>	Maximum packet length to send/receive from/to server
max_binlog_size=<number>	Binary log will be rotated automatically when the size exceeds this value (minimum value is 4096)
max_connections=<number>	Number of simultaneous clients allowed
max_connect_errors=<number>	Connections from a host will be blocked if number of interrupted connections from the host exceeds this number
max_join_size=<number>	Error returned if join statement will return more than this number of records
max_length_for_sort_data=<number>	Maximum number of bytes in a set of sorted records
max_sort_length=<number>	Maximum number of bytes for sorting BLOB or TEXT values
max_tmp_tables=<number>	Maximum number of temporary tables a client can keep open at a time
max_user_connections=<number>	Maximum number of active connections for a single user; set to 0 for no limit
memlock	Lock mysqld in memory, don't use swap disk; must run server as root
old-passwords	Use old password encryption (useful for versions 4.0 and earlier)
pid-file=<file>	PID file used by safe_mysqld
port=<number>	Use this port number for connections
safe-user-create	Don't allow new user creation by the user who has no write privileges to the mysql.user table
read-only	Except for replication and users with SUPER privilege, make tables read-only
skip-grant-tables	Don't load grant tables on startup; open all tables to all users
skip-networking	Don't allow TCP/IP connections

Continued

Table 14-6. *Continued*

Option	Description
skip-show-database	Prevent SHOW DATABASE commands
skip-stack-trace	If database fails, don't print stack
skip-symbolic-links	Prevent symbolic linking of tables
skip-thread-priority	Give all threads identical priorities
socket=<file>	Socket file to use for database connections
sort_buffer_size=<number>	When a thread needs to sort, this size is used for allocating the buffer for that sort
symbolic-links	Support symbolic links
sync-binlog=<number>	Every *n*th event, the binary log is synchronized to disk; set to 0 for no synchronization
tmp_table_size=<number>	If an in-memory temporary table exceeds this size, MySQL will automatically convert it to an on-disk MyISAM table
tmpdir=<dir>	Location for temporary files; specify multiple paths separated by a colon, which will be used in round-robin order
user=<name>	Run mysqld server daemon as user

Logging Configuration Options

The options listed in Table 14-7 are geared toward the logging functions of MySQL, allowing you to specify types of information to log, location of logs, detail level, and log sizes. These options are discussed in more detail in Chapters 18 and 20.

Table 14-7. *Common Logging Configuration Options*

Option	Description
binlog-do-db=<name>	Log updates for the specified database, and exclude all others not explicitly mentioned
binlog-ignore-db=<name>	Do not log updates in the binary log for this database
log[=<file>]	File to log connections and queries
log-bin[=<file>]	Log updates using binary format
log-bin-index=<file>	File that keeps track of binary log filenames
log-error[=<file>]	Log error file
log-isam[=<file>]	File to log all MyISAM changes
log-queries-not-using-indexes	Log queries that are executed without using an index
log-short-format	Log minimal information for updates and slow queries
log-slave-updates	Slave will log updates made to the slave database; turn on for daisy-chain slaves
log-slow-queries[=<file>]	Log slow queries to this log file; default name is *hostname*-slow.log
log-warnings[=<number>]	Send noncritical warnings to the log file

Engine-Specific Configuration Options

Engine-specific configuration options are outlined in Table 14-8. Storage engines are discussed in more detail in Chapters 5 and 19.

Table 14-8. *Common Engine-Specific Configuration Options*

Option	Description
bdb	Enable BDB (if this version of MySQL supports it); disable with skip-bdb (to save memory)
bdb-home=<path>	Location for BDB data files; should be same as datadir
bdb-logdir=<path>	Location for BDB log files
bdb_max_lock=<number>	Maximum locks on a BDB table
bdb-tempdir=<path>	Location for BDB temporary files
innodb	If MySQL binary allows, enable InnoDB
innodb_buffer_pool_size=<number>	Size of memory used by InnoDB to cache data and indexes
innodb_data_file_path=<path>	Path to individual files and their sizes (combines with innodb_data_home_dir)
innodb_data_home_dir=<path>	The common part for path to InnoDB tablespaces
innodb_fast_shutdown	Faster server shutdown
innodb_file_per_table	Breaks InnoDB tables into separate .ibd file in data directory
innodb_flush_log_at_trx_commit[=<number>]	Value of 0 will write and flush every second; value of 1 (recommended and the default) will write and flush at each commit; value of 2 writes at commit, flushes every second
innodb_log_arch_dir=<path>	Location for log archives
innodb_log_archive[=<number>]	If you want archived logs, set to 1
innodb_log_buffer_size=<number>	Buffer size for InnoDB when writing logs to disk
innodb_log_file_size=<number>	Size of each InnoDB log file in group, specified in megabytes; once size is reached, MySQL creates new log file
innodb_log_group_home_dir=<path>	Path to InnoDB log files
innodb_max_dirty_pages_pct=<number>	Percentage of dirty pages allowed in buffer pool
innodb_open_files=<number>	Maximum number of files InnoDB keeps open simultaneously
innodb_safe_binlog	InnoDB truncates the binary log after the last not-rolled-back transaction after a recovery from a crash
isam	Enable ISAM (if this version of MySQL supports it)
max_heap_table_size=<number>	Don't allow creation of heap tables bigger than this
myisam-recover[=<name>]	Syntax is myisam-recover[=option[,option...]], where option can be DEFAULT, BACKUP, FORCE, or QUICK
myisam_sort_buffer_size=<number>	Size of buffer for sorting when recovering tables or creating indexes
ndbcluster	Enable NDB Cluster (if this version of MySQL supports it).
skip-bdb	Disable BDB table type

Replication Configuration Options

MySQL replication enables you to create near-real-time duplication of your data onto another database server. Table 14-9 lists the configuration options for controlling replication. Replication is covered in Chapter 18.

Table 14-9. *Common Replication Configuration Options*

Option	Description
`master-connect-retry=<number>`	Number of seconds the slave thread will sleep before retrying to connect to the master in case the master goes down or the connection is lost
`master-host=<name>`	Master hostname or IP address for replication (required for slave to run); can also exist in `master.info` file
`master-password=<password>`	Slave thread will use this password when connecting to the master
`master-port=<number>`	Port on master for slave connections
`master-retry-count=<number>`	Number of tries the slave will make to connect to the master before giving up
`master-ssl`	Enable the slave to connect to the master using SSL
`master-user=<name>`	Slave thread will use this name when connecting to the master
`max_relay_log_size=<number>`	Size at which relay log is rotated (minimum is 4096); set to 0 to have relay log rotated with `max_binlog_size`
`relay-log=<file>`	File location and name where relay logs are stored
`replicate-do-db=<name>`	Tells slave to replicate a specific database; use directive multiple times to specify multiple databases
`replicate-do-table=<name>`	Tells slave to replicate only the named table; use directive multiple times to specify more than one table
`replicate-ignore-db=<name>`	Tells slave to ignore this database; use directive multiple times to specify multiple databases
`replicate-ignore-table=<name>`	Tells slave to ignore this table; use directive multiple times to specify multiple tables
`relay-log-info-file=<file>`	File that maintains the position of the replication thread in the relay logs; default is in data directory
`replicate-wild-do-table=<name>`	Slave replicates tables matching the wildcard pattern; use directive multiple times to specify multiple databases
`replicate-wild-ignore-table=<name>`	Slave ignores tables matching the wildcard pattern; use directive multiple times to specify multiple wildcard patterns
`server-id=<number>`	Unique identifier for server when a part of replication system
`slave-load-tmpdir=<dir>`	Location for slave to store temporary files when replicating a `LOAD DATA INFILE` command
`slave-skip-errors`	Slave continues replication when an error is returned from processing a query
`skip-slave-start`	Don't automatically start slave

Buffer and Cache Allocation Configuration Options

Table 14-10 lists the buffer and cache allocation options. These are tightly aligned with server performance. Details on the buffer and cache subsystems are covered in more depth in Chapter 4.

Table 14-10. *Common Buffer and Cache Allocation Configuration Options*

Option	Description
binlog_cache_size=<number>	Cache size for holding SQL statements headed to the binary log
flush_time=<number>	Flush all tables at the given interval (in seconds); handled by at dedicated thread
query_cache_limit=<number>	Queries with results larger than this are not cached
query_cache_size=<number>	Memory allocated for storing results from queries

Server SSL Configuration Options

Table 14-11 shows the configuration options for using SSL with MySQL. These are an integral part of securing remote connections to the database, as discussed in Chapter 16.

Table 14-11. *Server SSL Configuration Options*

Option	Description
skip-ssl	Do not allow SSL connections
ssl	Allow secure connections (ssl-ca, ssl-cert, and ssl-key must be present)
ssl-ca=<file>	File that contains a list of trusted Certificate Authorities
ssl-capath=<dir>	Directory with trusted Certificate Authority .pem files
ssl-cert=<file>	SSL certificate used in creating secure connections
ssl-key=<file>	SSL key used in creating secure connections

Upgrading MySQL

Upgrading MySQL is fairly straightforward. For the most part, you can remove the existing installation and put a new one in its place. In cases where the MySQL-provided instructions indicate, you'll need to upgrade the permissions tables using the mysql_fix_privilege_tables script, depending on the version of your existing installation and the upgrade version. See the MySQL documentation at http://dev.mysql.com/doc/mysql/en/Upgrade.html for version-specific upgrade requirements.

Before you start an upgrade, you want be sure to preserve two pieces of the existing installation: your configuration files and your data files. It is wise to make copies of both before an upgrade.

Upgrade your version of MySQL as follows:

Manually installed tarball on Unix: After copying the configuration files and data files, shut down your database. Unpack the new tarball to /usr/local and move the mysql symbolic link to the new version. If you keep your data and configuration files in /usr/local, copy your data and configuration file into the data directory within the new mysql install directory. Start the server and run mysql_fix_privilege_tables if necessary.

Manually installed on Windows: After copying the configuration files and data files, shut down your database. Unpack the zip file at C:\ and rename the directory to mysql. If necessary, copy the backup configuration files and data files into the new installation directory. Start the database and run the mysql_fix_privilege_tables script if necessary.

Installed with the Windows installer: The Windows installer is designed to handle upgrades. After downloading the new installer, stop your server. If you're upgrading from a version prior to 4.1.5, remove the MySQL service with C:\mysql\bin\mysqld --remove. After the database is stopped and service removed, double-click the installer and go through the installation.

Installed with an RPM: Upgrading an RPM is fairly simple. The RPM upgrade process respects added data files and changed configuration files, but it's always a good idea to back up your files before beginning the installation. Get the latest set of RPM files and use the rpm tool to upgrade your packages.

Installed with the Mac installer: Upgrading on a server where the Mac installer has been used for install is similar to upgrading a tarball. Make a copy of your configuration and data files, shut down the server, and then run the installer program for the new version. This will install the new version in /usr/local and create a symbolic link for the new install to /usr/local/mysql. Copy the configuration files and data into the new install folder, if necessary, and start the database. Run the mysql_fix_privilege_tables script if required.

Uninstalling MySQL

While we hope you aren't uninstalling MySQL because you don't want to use it anymore, it is important to know just how to get a MySQL installation off a machine. For example, you may want to cleanly install a new instance of the database or move your database server to a new machine.

■**Caution** Before starting the process of uninstalling MySQL, make sure you have a copy of your data and configuration files if you plan to use them again. Also, be sure to shut down the database before starting to remove the database.

The ease of uninstalling MySQL depends on which mechanism you used to install it. If you installed with an RPM or the Windows Installer, you can run an uninstall program that will remove the previously installed files. If you installed from a binary tarball or source into the recommended /usr/local/mysql location, you can delete that directory. If you've installed from source into /usr/local, you are faced with manually determining all the files installed with your MySQL and removing them individually.

Once you've removed the binaries and main mysql directory, you might want to check in the data directory and in common locations for configuration files to verify that all files have been removed.

Last, if the machine shouldn't be running a MySQL server, you should verify that the server isn't in the startup or Windows service. Table 14-3 indicates how to add MySQL to the startup of a machine. Reverse those instructions to disable automatic startup, using a command or editing a particular file to change the start option.

Running Multiple Database Servers on a Single Machine

Running multiple instances of a MySQL database is fairly simple. The recommended method is to use the mysql_multi script, which will let you set options for the different server numbers in one configuration file, organized by groups. The mysql_multi script can start and stop any number of servers based on mysqld group numbers defined in the configuration file and passed to mysql_multi on the command line. If using mysql_multi doesn't work for you, you can also run a separate, simultaneous instance of mysqld by starting up with the command-line option --defaults-file pointed at files with different settings to allow for multiple server instances.

The key parameters that can't overlap on multiple instances of the server are the port, Unix socket (Unix only), process ID file (Unix only), and shared memory base name (Windows only). By changing these options, you can run any number of servers. If you have logging options turned on, you must specify different locations for each server. These include log, log-bin, log-update, log-error, log-isam, and bdb-logdir.

You most likely want to change the data directory for each server instance. Running multiple servers against one set of data files is not recommended, as it can cause problems if the system locking isn't perfect.

Except for the port and socket, all of the options can be more automatically set for each server instance by changing the basedir option. Using basedir tells the MySQL server to put the data, process ID file, and log files in a location relative to the basedir. Listing 14-2 shows a sample configuration file using the basedir option.

Listing 14-2. *Sample my.cnf File for mysql_multi*

```
# my.cnf
[mysqld1]
basedir=/usr/local/mysql/server1
port=3306
socket=/tmp/mysql.sock1

[mysqld2]
basedir=/usr/local/mysql/server2
port=3307
socket=/tmp/mysql.sock2
```

When using client tools on a multiple-instance server, it's important to be clear about which server you intend to use. You can use your local `~/.my.cnf` file to specify the port or socket to use when connecting, or specify the port or socket file on the command line when running the client or tool. Another option is to create `~/.my.cnf1` and `~/.my.cnf2`, and use the `--defaults-extra-file=~/.my.cnf2` command to load the options for connecting to the correct instance.

Summary

In this chapter, we've covered the wide spectrum of installation options for MySQL. These vary from simple, no-configure binary package installations to the complexity of building from source and digging into varying levels of configuration files and option details. MySQL AB places a great deal of emphasis on creating what the users of the database need, and attempts to provide an installation process for the novice or small-scale user, all the way to the expert, large-scale-deployment user.

Once you've installed MySQL, there are a number of post-installation steps to consider in making sure the database is set up to run smoothly. Part of this may include switching to another prebuilt configuration file, and possibly editing your configuration to make the database behave and perform to your needs. Becoming familiar with all the configuration options for MySQL is a daunting task, but as you learn how to tweak the settings, you can create a set of options that make your server and tools hum along in perfect harmony with the needs of your organization.

As you watch development move forward and new releases become available, you'll want to review the steps for upgrading your MySQL installation.

CHAPTER 15

■ ■ ■

User Administration

In this chapter, we will look at the methods you, as a database administrator, have to control the access and permissions of users within the database server. To effectively and securely manage multiple user accounts on one or more database servers, it's helpful to understand how MySQL determines if a user has the rights to perform a specific action, or whether the user account even has access to the system at all.

Because seemingly small user administration mistakes can lead to users gaining access to information that should not be available to them, it is important for you to understand the subtle differences between MySQL's many privileges. Additionally, you may be surprised to learn the order in which MySQL determines if privileges are granted. We'll step you through these topics in this chapter, as well as demonstrate how to accomplish user administration tasks in both a console and a graphical environment.

Specifically, we will cover the following topics:

- The MySQL privileges

- How MySQL authenticates users and verifies user privileges

- User account management from the command line

- User account management with the MySQL Administrator GUI tool

- Role-based management considerations

- Guidelines for administering users

MySQL Privileges

MySQL uses a set of tables in the mysql database called the *grant tables* to check incoming connections and requests. These grant tables are loaded into memory when the database server starts. Depending on the commands used to grant access or change permissions, this in-memory table data is reloaded immediately or after a FLUSH PRIVILEGES command is executed. When the grant tables are manually changed (using an INSERT, UPDATE, or DELETE command on the actual grant table), changes are not reflected in the in-memory table data (which is the data on which the server operates) until a FLUSH PRIVILEGES command is executed. On the other hand, changes made to the grant tables through the GRANT, REVOKE, and CREATE USER (which, in MySQL 5.0.2 and later, adds users with no privileges) commands are reflected in the in-memory data immediately. It is for this reason that we recommend using the GRANT and REVOKE commands over direct manipulation of the grant tables.

Granting and Revoking Privileges

The list of actions that the current user can perform is called the user's set of *privileges*. MySQL's privileges (or permissions) are either granted or not granted—the user has the ability to execute the needed request or the user does not have this ability.

■**Note** In other database servers, permissions are often kept in a three-state format: granted, not granted (revoked), or default. The default permission works with the server's role-based security, where a user can belong to multiple *groups* of users, with each group having a set of permissions. If the user's permission for an action is set to default, the user *inherits* the permissions of the groups to which they belong. Since MySQL does not implement group-, or role-, based security, it does not use a third logic state to handle security inheritance. We will discuss role-based user organization in the "Thinking in Terms of User Roles" section later in this chapter.

To grant a user account privileges on the system, use the GRANT command, which follows this basic syntax:

GRANT *priv_type* ON {*.* | * | *db_name*.* | *table_name*} TO *username*;

To remove a privilege for a user account, use the REVOKE command:

REVOKE *priv_type* ON {*.* | * | *db_name*.* | *table_name*} FROM *username*;

Both the GRANT and REVOKE commands can alter privileges for multiple users in a single command. To do so, simply provide a delimited list of usernames after the TO or FROM clauses. You'll see many examples of GRANT and REVOKE commands in this chapter.

Understanding Privilege Scope Levels

The MySQL privileges are organized into various scope levels. The *scope* of the privilege is the level at which the permission to do something is applied. While some privileges pertain to actions that are performed at the server level—such as the PROCESS or SHUTDOWN privilege— other permissions may apply to actions performed inside a specific database, table, or even a specific column of a table. MySQL arranges privileges in this way so that database administrators can allow users to execute various requests against one database object but not another. MySQL 5.0.3 and later versions include five scope levels for privileges, with a corresponding table in the mysql database for each:

- Global scope, corresponding with the user grant table

- Database scope, corresponding with the db grant table

- Table scope, corresponding with the tables_priv grant table

- Column scope, corresponding with the columns_priv grant table

- Routine scope, corresponding with the procs_priv grant table

To determine if a user may perform a given request, MySQL looks for privileges at the highest scope level (global) first. If the needed privilege is *not* granted at that level, MySQL looks for the permission at the next scope level down. If the privilege is found at *any* level, the request is granted. Some privileges exist only at certain levels; others exist at more than one level. As we cover each of the privilege scope levels, you will see the logical overlap of certain privileges, such as the SELECT privilege, which may be granted for various levels of database objects, from an entire database to a single column.

In the following sections, we'll review the privileges available at each scope level. The exact list of privileges that are used to evaluate the incoming request depends on the version of MySQL you are using, as new features added in later versions have required additional privilege sets. In this chapter, we present the privileges in the MySQL 5.0.4-beta.

Note When upgrading MySQL versions, always check to make sure that you have upgraded the grant tables appropriately. In your upgrade installation, under the /scripts directory, you will find a file named mysql_fix_privilege_tables.sql. Executing this script (using the MySQL client SOURCE command) will add new privilege fields and tables to the mysql system database. Ensure changes to the grant tables are reflected by issuing a FLUSH PRIVILEGES command after running this script.

Global Privilege Scope

All privileges contained in the mysql.user table pertain to privileges available to the user on a global level. These privileges apply to all databases on the server. If a privilege is granted at the global level, it will override all other scope levels. Therefore, it is imperative to verify that users receiving global privileges should indeed be allowed such access.

To grant a user globally scoped privileges, follow the ON keyword of the GRANT statement by *.*. Here is an example of granting the PROCESS privilege (which allows the user to use the SHOW PROCESSLIST command) to a user:

```
mysql> GRANT PROCESS ON *.* TO 'root'@'localhost';
Query OK, 0 rows affected (0.00 sec)
```

Note The results output of GRANT statements will always show Query OK, 0 rows affected. This does not mean the query had no effect. If anything was wrong with the GRANT statement, an error will be returned.

Table 15-1 lists all the privileges available under the global scope, along with which version of MySQL the privilege became active and a brief explanation regarding what function the privilege enables the user account to perform. In addition to the privileges listed in Table 15-1, the GRANT OPTION and ALL privileges are available.[1] We'll cover these special cases later in the chapter.

---

1. Additionally, there is a REFERENCES privilege available at the global, database, table, and column scope levels; however, this privilege is not currently used by MySQL.

Table 15-1. *Global Scope Privileges*

Privilege Name	Versions	Access Allowed
ALTER	All	Change table structures for any database.
ALTER ROUTINE	5.0.3+	Change or drop any stored procedures, triggers, and functions (routines) in any database.
CREATE	All	Create databases, and create tables and indexes in all databases.
CREATE ROUTINE	5.0.3+	Create stored procedures, triggers, and functions in any database.
CREATE TEMPORARY TABLES	4.0.2+	Use the TEMPORARY keyword when creating tables in the connection.
CREATE USER	5.0.3+	Create other users in the system.
CREATE VIEW	5.0.1+	Create views in any database.
DELETE	All	Remove rows from any table in any database. The REPLACE command requires both this and the INSERT permission.
DROP	All	Remove any database object, including the database itself using the DROP DATABASE statement.
EXECUTE	5.0.3+	Run stored procedures, triggers, and functions in any database.
FILE	All	Issue LOAD DATA INFILE and SELECT . . . INTO FILE commands. Note that the only files that can be read using this command are files that are globally readable (world-readable) or readable by the MySQL server daemon. Generally, anything in the data_dir will be readable. The user can also write files in those same directories (using the SELECT . . . INTO FILE command), but cannot overwrite existing files. Also note that the FILE privilege is not needed if the user uses the LOCAL keyword in the LOAD DATA INFILE command.
INDEX	All	Create and remove (DROP) indexes on existing tables in all databases. Note that the CREATE privilege allows for creation of indexes in the CREATE TABLE statement as well.
INSERT	All	Insert rows into a table in any database. The REPLACE command requires both this and DELETE permission.
LOCK TABLES	4.0.2+	Used in conjunction with the SELECT privilege to determine if the current user can explicitly execute a LOCK TABLES command.
PROCESS	All	Execute the SHOW PROCESSLIST commands, enabling the user to view the contents of currently executing queries.
RELOAD	All	Various refresh tasks, including the ability to flush (refresh) various database objects like privileges and tables.
REPLICATION CLIENT	4.0.2+	Issue the SHOW MASTER STATUS and SHOW SLAVE STATUS commands.

Privilege Name	Versions	Access Allowed
REPLICATION SLAVE	4.0.2+	Must be given to the connecting slave's client user to enable subscription to the master server.
SELECT	All	Retrieve the information in a table in any database.
SHOW DATABASES	4.0.2+	Execute the SHOW DATABASES command and obtain a list of the server's databases.
SHOW VIEW	5.0.1+	Execute the SHOW CREATE VIEW command.
SHUTDOWN	All	Shut down the database server via mysqladmin. There is no ability to shut down the server from any mysql client, for obvious reasons.
SUPER	4.0.2+	Kill a process. Of course, this privilege would be fairly useless unless the user was also granted the PROCESS permission. Additionally, this privilege enables the CHANGE MASTER, PURGE MASTER LOGS, and SET GLOBAL commands.
UPDATE	All	Update rows in a table in any database.
USAGE	All	Used to create a user with no privileges.

In order to specify more than one privilege at a time, simply separate privilege names using a comma in the GRANT statement, as in this example:

```
mysql> GRANT SELECT, INSERT, DELETE, UPDATE ON *.*
    -> TO 'jpipes'@'localhost';
Query OK, 0 rows affected (0.01 sec)
```

■**Note** To change a table with an ALTER TABLE statement, the user must actually have the CREATE, ALTER, and INSERT permissions. Additionally, the ALTER permission allows a user to rename a table, and so is a security risk, since the current user might rename system tables (grant tables) used by MySQL in its access control.

Database Privilege Scope

Privileges applied at the database scope level pertain to the specified database and all objects contained within it, including tables and routines. To specify database-level privileges, you can use either one of two conventions:

- If you follow the ON keyword of the GRANT statement with a single asterisk (*), the privileges will be applied to the currently selected database. However, be aware that if no database is currently selected, and you follow the ON keyword with a single asterisk, the privileges will be applied on a global scope!

- You may follow the ON keyword with *db_name*.*, where *db_name* is the name of the database for which you are granting privileges. This is the recommended way to grant database-level privileges, as it provides more specificity and avoids the risk of accidentally granting global privileges.

Here is an example of granting multiple user accounts SELECT rights on the ToyStore schema by chaining usernames together after the TO clause:

```
mysql> GRANT SELECT ON ToyStore.*
    -> TO 'mkruck'@'localhost', 'jpipes'@'localhost';
Query OK, 0 rows affected (0.01 sec)
```

Table 15-2 lists all of the privileges available at a database level.

Table 15-2. *Database Scope Privileges*

Privilege Name	Versions	Access Allowed
ALTER	All	Change table structures for the specified database.
ALTER ROUTINE	5.0.3+	Change or drop any stored procedures, triggers, and functions in the specified database.
CREATE	All	Create databases, and create tables and indexes in the specified databases.
CREATE ROUTINE	5.0.3+	Create stored procedures, triggers, and functions in the specified database.
CREATE TEMPORARY TABLES	4.0.2+	Use the TEMPORARY keyword when creating tables in the specified database within the user session.
CREATE VIEW	5.0.1+	Create views in the specified database.
DELETE	All	Remove rows from any table in the specified database.
DROP	All	Remove all objects within the specified database, including the database itself using the DROP DATABASE statement.
EXECUTE	5.0.3+	Run stored procedures, triggers, and functions in the specified database.
INDEX	All	Create and remove (DROP) indexes on existing tables in the specified database.
INSERT	All	Insert rows into a table in the specified database.
LOCK TABLES	4.0.2+	Used in conjunction with the SELECT privilege to determine if the current user can explicitly execute a LOCK TABLES command for tables within the specified database.
SELECT	All	Retrieve the information in a table in the specified database.
SHOW VIEW	5.0.1+	Execute the SHOW CREATE VIEW command.
UPDATE	All	Update rows in a table in the specified database.

PERMISSIONS FOR TEMPORARY TABLES

You can't give users separate sets of permissions to regular tables and to temporary tables. If you're in a situation where you need to allow users to create and work with temporary tables, but not regular database tables, consider implementing a solution described by Dietrich Feist on the MySQL web site. He recommends creating a separate database strictly for working with temporary tables, which would allow you to grant different permissions to temporary tables than you grant to regular tables. You can grant users all the needed permissions in this database, but restrict certain permissions (like CREATE, ALTER, and so on) on your regular databases. To create temporary tables, users would need to explicitly reference the temporary database name before all table names.

The following are the steps to set up a separate database for temporary tables (using the company database and an imaginary user some_restricted_user):

1. Set up a database for temporary table usage:

```
mysql> CREATE DATABASE tmp;
```

2. Grant the restricted user the ability to do needed work in the new tmp database:

```
mysql> GRANT SELECT, INSERT, UPDATE, DELETE,
    ->DROP, ALTER, CREATE TEMPORARY TABLES
    -> ON tmp.*
    -> TO 'some_restricted_user'@'localhost';
```

3. Grant restricted permissions on the regular company database:

```
mysql> GRANT SELECT, INSERT, UPDATE, DELETE
    -> ON company.*
    -> TO 'some_restricted_user'@'localhost';
```

Keep in mind that some_restricted_user would need to prefix CREATE TEMPORARY TABLE statements with the tmp. database prefix if the table were created using data from another database and some_restricted_user had already selected another database:

```
mysql> USE company;
mysql> CREATE TEMPORARY TABLE tmp.Employee SELECT * FROM Employee;
```

This approach is similar to how other database servers allow you to manage different permission sets for temporary and regular tables. See http://dev.mysql.com/doc/mysql/en/Privileges_provided.html for more details on the strategy.

Table Privilege Scope

Privileges applied at the table scope level pertain to a specific table only. To specify table-level privileges, you follow the ON keyword with the full name of the database table for which you are granting privileges, in the form *db_name.table_name*.

Suppose you have a user account responsible for some automated mailers running from cron job on a remote server. The script needs to access and change only the information in the ToyStore.Customer table. Here's how you might grant this limited access to such a user:

```
mysql> GRANT SELECT, INSERT, UPDATE, DELETE
    -> ON ToyStore.Customer TO 'responder'@'mail.example.com';
Query OK, 0 rows affected (0.33 sec)
```

The GRANT command will *create a new user* if no existing user account is found for the one used in the statement. Therefore, executing the preceding statement will create the user account for responder@mail.example.com, if such a user did not already exist on the server. Table 15-3 lists all privileges available at the table scope level.

Table 15-3. *Table Scope Privileges*

Privilege Name	Versions	Access Allowed
ALTER	All	Change the structure of the specified table.
CREATE	All	Create the specified table. The CREATE privilege is needed for the ALTER TABLE command to succeed.
DELETE	All	Remove rows from the specified table.
DROP	All	Remove the specified table and any indexes attached to it.
INDEX	All	Create and remove (DROP) indexes on the specified table.
INSERT	All	Insert rows into the specified table.
SELECT	All	Retrieve the information in the specified table.
UPDATE	All	Update rows in a table in the specified database.

Column Privilege Scope

Privileges applied at the column scope level pertain to one or more columns within a specific table. To specify column-level privileges, you must follow the ON keyword with the full name of the database table for which you are granting privileges, in the form *db_name.table_name*, just as you do with table-level privileges. In addition, you must specify the columns you are changing privileges for in parentheses after the privilege list.

To continue our example in the previous section, suppose that after some consideration, you decide that the responder@mail.example.com user account should not be able to retrieve the contents of the password column of ToyStore.Customer. You may be tempted to simply use the REVOKE command to remove the SELECT privilege from the user account for this column. Doing so, however, will result in an error:

```
mysql> REVOKE SELECT (password) ON ToyStore.Customer
    -> FROM 'responder'@'mail.example.com';
ERROR 1147 (42000): There is no such grant defined for user 'responder' \
on host 'mail.example.com' on table 'Customer'
```

MySQL is helpfully informing you that you have not specifically granted any column privileges. Remember that you have already granted responder@mail.example.com table-level rights to the Customer table. To remove rights to a specific column of the table, you must first revoke the table-level rights you have granted, and then grant column-specific privileges to those fields you wish the user to see. Listing 15-1 illustrates this process.

Listing 15-1. *Revoking Table-Level Privileges and Granting Column-Level Privileges*

```
mysql> REVOKE SELECT, INSERT, UPDATE, DELETE ON ToyStore.Customer
    -> FROM 'responder'@'mail.example.com';
Query OK, 0 rows affected (0.00 sec)

mysql> GRANT SELECT (customer_id, login, created_on, first_name
    -> , last_name, shipping_address, shipping_city, shipping_province
    -> , shipping_postcode, shipping_country)
    -> ON ToyStore.Customer TO 'responder'@'mail.example.com';
Query OK, 0 rows affected (0.32 sec)
```

Notice that each column you wish to assign rights to must be included in the column list after the SELECT privilege keyword in the GRANT statement.

Table 15-4 lists the privileges available at the column scope level.

Table 15-4. *Column Scope Privileges*

Privilege Name	Versions	Access Allowed
INSERT	All	Insert data into the specified column(s) of the table.
SELECT	All	Retrieve the data from the specified column(s) of the table.
UPDATE	All	Update data in the specified column(s) of the table.

■**Note** If a user who does not have rights to insert data into a column attempts to do so, the default value for the column is inserted and the INSERT request proceeds as normal. This is a deviation from the SQL standard, which dictates that the user must have the INSERT privilege on all columns in the table in order to insert a row of data.

Routine Privilege Scope

The routine privilege scope level applies to individual stored procedures and functions. You must specify the database name and the routine name when granting rights at the routine level, as in this example:

```
mysql> GRANT EXECUTE ON test.ShowIndexSelectivity TO 'jpipes'@'localhost';
Query OK, 0 rows affected (0.32 sec)
```

Table 15-5 lists the two privileges available at the routine scope level.

Table 15-5. *Routine Scope Privileges*

Privilege Name	Versions	Access Allowed
ALTER ROUTINE	5.0.3+	Modify the definition of the stored procedure or function.
EXECUTE	5.0.3+	Run the stored procedure or function.

■**Note** For the routine, column, and table-level privileges, the referenced object must be present in the database before privileges can be granted to a user for the object. This is not the case for database-level privileges. You may assign database-level privileges to a user account for a database that has not yet been created.

The GRANT OPTION Privilege

A special privilege provides users with the ability to grant privileges to other users. This is an extremely critical privilege to understand, as not knowing its impact can seriously undermine the security of your database server.

Essentially, when the GRANT statement is issued with the WITH GRANT OPTION clause, it means that the user being granted privileges has the ability to grant other users the same privileges they have. While this may seem like a fairly harmless ability, there are some serious drawbacks to using WITH GRANT OPTION frivolously.

Imagine you have set up one user with only the SELECT, LOCK TABLES, and RELOAD privileges (for doing backups), and you have another user set up with SELECT, CREATE, ALTER, DROP, INSERT, DELETE, and INDEX privileges (for database design work). You have wisely created separate users for doing separate tasks, and as the database administrator, you would like to keep it that way. However, a sticky situation could develop if you created the accounts with the WITH GRANT OPTION clause: the two users could grant each other their own privileges, thereby negating all your hard work to try to prevent the database designer from having the LOCK ➥ TABLES privilege. Even more problematic, you now have two more users who can create new user accounts. As we mentioned earlier, issuing a GRANT statement for a user that does not yet exist prompts MySQL to create a new user account for that user. So, as always with the GRANT statement, be careful what privileges you are bestowing.

■**Caution** Unless you are working on a large database system with a number of database administrators, there are very few reasons to use the WITH GRANT OPTION clause. It is a security headache and produces, in our opinion, very little benefit. User privileges should be granted by very few individuals, preferably only one. This ensures consistency and conformity to company security policies.

Granting All Privileges

When you want to grant or revoke all available privileges for a user (except for the GRANT ➡ OPTION privilege) at a specific privilege scope level, you can substitute the keyword ALL for the (much longer and cumbersome) list of privileges. For instance, if you wanted to provide mkruck@localhost all privileges on the ToyStore.Customer table, you could issue the following:

```
GRANT ALL ON ToyStore.Customer TO 'mkruck'@'localhost';
```

This would affect all table-level privileges: SELECT, INSERT, UPDATE, DELETE, CREATE, DROP, INDEX, and ALTER.

Issuing GRANT ALL requests at other scope levels yields similar results. Consider this example:

```
GRANT ALL ON ToyStore.* TO 'mkruck'@'admin.example.com';
```

This would grant the user account mkruck@admin.example.com the database-level privileges of ALTER, ALTER ROUTINE, CREATE, CREATE ROUTINE, CREATE TEMPORARY TABLES, CREATE VIEW, DELETE, DROP, EXECUTE, INSERT, UPDATE, INDEX, SELECT, SHOW VIEW, and LOCK TABLES. By using the *.* modifier, you grant the user every privilege except the GRANT OPTION privilege, so take care when using the ALL keyword to use the correct scope modifier after the ON keyword!

To revoke all privileges issued to a user account, use the REVOKE ALL command:

```
REVOKE ALL ON *.* FROM 'mkruck'@'localhost';
```

This would remove all global privileges from mkruck@localhost except for the GRANT OPTION privilege.

To include the GRANT OPTION privilege in the REVOKE command, issue the following version:

```
REVOKE ALL, GRANT OPTION ON *.* FROM 'mkruck'@'localhost';
```

This syntax is available from MySQL 4.1.2. Prior to this version, two statements are necessary to remove all privileges for a user:

```
REVOKE ALL ON *.* FROM 'mkruck'@'localhost';
REVOKE GRANT OPTION ON *.* FROM 'mkruck'@'localhost';
```

Viewing User Privileges

You can use a number of methods to obtain information regarding a user's granted or revoked privileges. Which method you choose is a really just a matter of formatting preference. Here, we'll cover using the SHOW GRANTS command and querying the grant tables directly. Another method of viewing user privileges is to use the new support for the INFORMATION_SCHEMA virtual database, which we'll cover in Chapter 21.

Using SHOW GRANTS

One way to check a user's grants is to use the SHOW GRANTS statement:

```
SHOW GRANTS FOR username;
```

This will show, in reproducible GRANT statements, the privileges available to the user (helpful in reminding you of the syntax for the GRANT statement). Listing 15-2 shows the output of SHOW GRANTS.

Listing 15-2. *SHOWS GRANTS Output*

```
mysql> SHOW GRANTS FOR 'jpipes'@'localhost';
+---------------------------------------------------------------------+
| Grants for jpipes@localhost                                         |
+---------------------------------------------------------------------+
| GRANT SELECT, INSERT, UPDATE, DELETE ON *.* TO 'jpipes'@'localhost'  |
| GRANT SELECT ON `ToyStore`.* TO 'jpipes'@'localhost'                 |
| GRANT EXECUTE ON `test`.`ShowIndexSelectivity` TO 'jpipes'@'localhost' |
+---------------------------------------------------------------------+
3 rows in set (0.00 sec)
```

You may notice a peculiarity in the results in Listing 15-2. The privileges for jpipes@localhost on a global level completely negate the need for the SELECT privilege on the ToyStore database. So, why do both lines appear? This is because MySQL does not remove grant table entries just because a more encompassing privilege level has been granted to the user. Keep this in mind when changing user privileges. If at some point, you loosen a user's restrictions by granting global privileges, and later revoke the global privileges, the database-specific privileges will still exist.

Querying the Grant Tables

Another option for determining a user's privileges involves querying the actual grant tables (which are described in the next section). To see global permissions for jpipes@localhost, query the user grant table, as Listing 15-3 demonstrates.

Listing 15-3. *Querying the user Grant Table Directly*

```
mysql> SELECT * FROM mysql.user
    -> WHERE User = 'jpipes' AND Host = 'localhost' \G
*************************** 1. row ***************************
            Host: localhost
            User: jpipes
        Password:
     Select_priv: Y
     Insert_priv: Y
     Update_priv: Y
     Delete_priv: Y
     Create_priv: N
       Drop_priv: N
     Reload_priv: N
   Shutdown_priv: N
    Process_priv: N
       File_priv: N
```

```
              Grant_priv: N
         References_priv: N
              Index_priv: N
              Alter_priv: N
            Show_db_priv: N
              Super_priv: N
   Create_tmp_table_priv: N
        Lock_tables_priv: N
            Execute_priv: N
         Repl_slave_priv: N
        Repl_client_priv: N
        Create_view_priv: N
          Show_view_priv: N
     Create_routine_priv: N
      Alter_routine_priv: N
        Create_user_priv: N
                ssl_type:
              ssl_cipher:
             x509_issuer:
            x509_subject:
           max_questions: 0
             max_updates: 0
         max_connections: 0
    max_user_connections: 0
1 row in set (0.31 sec)
```

Here, you can see all privileges except the SELECT, INSERT, UPDATE, and DELETE privileges are set to N, which makes sense; the first line from the previous output of Listing 15-2 shows the global GRANT statement having these privileges enabled.

Querying each of the grant tables as in Listing 15-3 will produce similar output for each of the privilege scope levels. The user and db tables store privilege information in separate fields of type ENUM('Y','N'). The tables_priv, columns_priv, and procs_priv grant tables store privilege information in a single SET() field containing a list of the available privileges. Listing 15-4 shows the output of a SELECT on the tables_priv table to illustrate this difference.

Listing 15-4. *Querying the columns_priv Grant Table Directly*

```
mysql> SELECT Db, Table_name, Table_priv FROM mysql.tables_priv
    -> WHERE User = 'mkruck' AND Host = 'localhost';
+----------+------------+---------------+
| Db       | Table_name | Table_priv    |
+----------+------------+---------------+
| ToyStore | Customer   | Select,Insert |
+----------+------------+---------------+
1 row in set (0.00 sec)
```

Now that you've seen how to grant and revoke privileges, it's important to understand how MySQL actually applies and verifies those privileges.

How MySQL Controls Access and Verifies Privileges

MySQL controls access to the database server through a two-step process. In the first step of the process, MySQL identifies and authenticates the user connecting through a MySQL client. The second part of the process entails determining what the authenticated user can do once inside the system, based on that user's privileges.

Figure 15-1 illustrates the flow of events in the MySQL access control and privilege verification system. You can see how the different steps of the process are designed to ensure that the requests issued by the client, including the actual connection request, are allowed. When requests or connections do not meet all access criteria, MySQL returns an error code corresponding to the reason for request refusal.

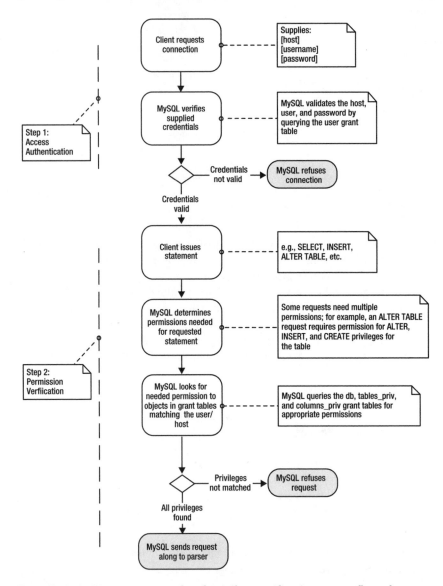

Figure 15-1. *MySQL access control and privilege verification system flow of events*

> **Note** See http://dev.mysql.com/doc/mysql/en/Access_denied.html for an explanation of common reasons for access denied messages.

How MySQL Authenticates Users

MySQL uses a two-part label to identify the user issuing a connection request. This label is composed of the *username* and the *host* values. The host value represents the machine from which the connection originates. The username part of the label is the specific user connecting from the host.

The user grant table stores information needed to authenticate incoming connections, along with a set of global privileges tied to each entry in the table (discussed earlier in the chapter). The three columns of the user grant table that are used in the connection authentication decision are Host, User, and Password. The User column value can be either an actual username (for example, joe_smith) or a blank string (' '). Wildcard matches can be used in the Host column. An underscore (_) character represents a single character, and a percent (%) represents any number of characters. The Host column value can be in any of the following formats:

- Host (or domain) name: www.mycompany.com, %.mycompany.com

- Host IP address: 123.124.125.255, 123.124.125.%

- Local machine client: localhost, and on some Linux systems, localhost.localdomain

MySQL compares the username and host values of the connection with entries in the user grant table in a special way. When the mysql.user table data is loaded into memory, it is first sorted based on how *specific* the User and Host column values are. Because the Host column values can contain wildcard characters, and the User column can be blank (meaning any user at the specified Host), some table entries will be more specific than others.

For example, Listing 15-5 shows some sample rows from the user grant table on a test database server we've set up for the examples in this chapter.

Listing 15-5. *The user Grant Table*

```
mysql> SELECT User, Host FROM mysql.user;
+-----------+------------------+
| User      | Host             |
+-----------+------------------+
|           | %                |
| mkruck    | %                |
| jpipes    | %.example.com    |
| mkruck    | admin.example.com |
|           | localhost        |
| jpipes    | localhost        |
| mkruck    | localhost        |
| root      | localhost        |
| responder | mail.example.com |
+-----------+------------------+
9 rows in set (0.00 sec)
```

When MySQL sorts this list according to specificity, it will be ordered by the most specific Host value to the least specific. Since IP addresses or domain names are more specific than a host specification that contains a wildcard, the actual order in which MySQL would see the entries in Listing 15-5 would be as listed in Table 15-6.

Table 15-6. *The user Table Results Ordered by Specificity of Username and Host Label*

User	Host
jpipes	localhost
jpipes	%.example.com
mkruck	localhost
mkruck	admin.example.com
mkruck	%
responder	mail.example.com
root	localhost
	localhost
	%

If the label jpipes@groups.example.com were passed to the identification system, MySQL would first search for all entries matching the supplied username *or* having a blank entry in the User column. Then it would go down the returned list of entries, looking first for a Host column value that matches the incoming tag. Four entries in the sample user grant table match this username part of the identification label, as shown in Table 15-7.

Table 15-7. *Possible Entries That Could Match Label jpipes@groups.example.com*

User	Host
jpipes	localhost
jpipes	%.example.com
	localhost
	%

Of these four, the top row contains the most specific username and host combination. However, the groups.example.com domain clearly does not match the Host column value localhost. The next row, with the Host value of %.example.com matches our supplied domain, and so this row is used in order to determine access and privileges to the system. If the Host value did *not* match, the next row would be checked, and so on down the line.

We cover this sorting logic here because of the confusion some MySQL users experience regarding why certain privileges have not been granted to them when executing queries. This confusion can be tracked to a misunderstanding of which entry in the user grant table has been loaded for their current connection. Often, if a number of entries have been made to the user grant table with similar Host and User column values, it may not be clear which entry has been loaded. If you are unsure about which entry has been loaded for a connection, use the CURRENT_USER() function, as shown in Listing 15-6.

Listing 15-6. *Using the CURRENT_USER() Function to Determine Active Entry*

```
mysql> SELECT CURRENT_USER();
+----------------+
| CURRENT_USER() |
+----------------+
| root@localhost |
+----------------+
1 row in set (0.00 sec)
```

DEFAULT CONNECTION PARAMETERS

Clients can connect to a MySQL server in numerous ways. Regardless of the client or API used to connect, MySQL executes the same authentication procedures to authorize the incoming requests. Even so, it is possible through the use of option files, to configure clients to send a default host, username, and password along with each connection. This is done by altering the MySQL configuration file (described in Chapter 14) and inserting one or more of the following entries under the [client] configuration section:

- host=*hostname*

- user=*username*

- password=*your_pass*

Setting a default password for the MySQL client is not a secure practice, and should not be done on anything but test or development servers that do not have any sensitive data.

Also be aware that, by default, MySQL accepts connections from anonymous users; that is, MySQL allows connections that do not supply a username. Though the default access of this anonymous user is limited, and only the test database can be accessed, it is still a security threat, as discussed in Chapter 16.

How MySQL Verifies User Privileges

After MySQL has verified that the user connecting has access to the database server, the next step in the access control process is to determine what, if anything, that user may do while connected to the server. In order to determine if a user can issue a command, the privileges at the different scope levels are checked from the broadest scope (global) to the finest scope (column level). An additional grant table, mysql.host, is consulted in special circumstances.

Logically, MySQL follows this equation to determine if a user has appropriate privileges to a database-specific object:

- Global privileges

- *Or* (database privileges *and* host privileges)

- *Or* table privileges

- *Or* column privileges

Take a look at Figure 15-2 to get a feel for how this logic is processed by the privilege verification system for a simple request. In Figure 15-2, let's assume that the connection was authenticated as jpipes@localhost, and sent the following request:

```
SELECT login, password FROM ToyStore.Customer WHERE ID=1;
```

MySQL would first look to see if an entry existed in the user grant table matching the supplied user and host and having the SELECT privilege enabled (found in the select_priv column). If the value of the SELECT privilege were 'Y', MySQL would stop the privilege verification process and continue with the request's execution. If the value of the SELECT privilege were 'N', MySQL would continue down the grant table chain to the db table.

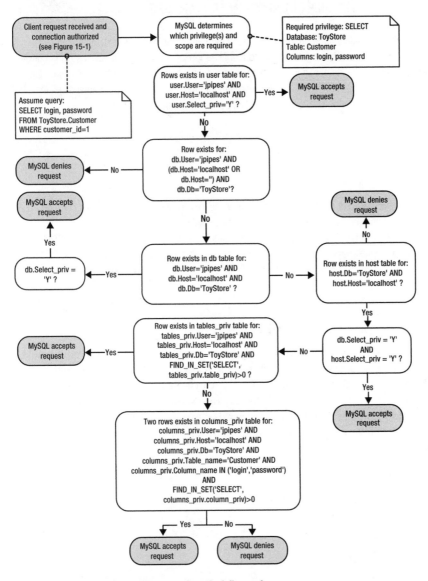

Figure 15-2. *Privilege verification detailed flow of events*

MySQL looks for an entry in the db table matching db.User='jpipes' AND ➥ db.Host='localhost' AND db.Database_name='ToyStore'. If a row exists in mysql.db for this combination, the db.Select_priv column is checked. If it found a 'Y' value for the db.Select_priv column, MySQL would accept the request. If a row did not exist in mysql.db matching db.User='jpipes' AND db.Host='localhost' AND db.Database_name='ToyStore' but a row that matched db.User='jpipes' AND db.Host='' AND db.Database_name='ToyStore' *did exist*, then the mysql.host grant table is queried.

If no rows in mysql.host match host.Host='localhost' AND host.Db='ToyStore', MySQL denies the request. If a row in mysql.host *does* match host.Host='localhost' AND ➥ host.Db='ToyStore', then the Select_priv column in both rows in mysql.db and mysql.host are checked for a 'Y' value. If this is the case, MySQL accepts the request. (We'll discuss the relationship between the db and host grant tables in just a moment.) If not, MySQL continues to the tables_priv grant table.

If MySQL has reached the tables_priv grant table, it determines if there is a row in the table that matches the condition WHERE User='jpipes' AND Host='localhost' AND Db='ToyStore' AND Table_name='Customer' AND FIND_IN_SET('SELECT', Table_priv)>0.[2] If such a row exists, MySQL accepts the request. If not, it repeats a similar process in the columns_priv grant table. If MySQL does not find rows in the columns_priv table for the requested columns of the SELECT statement, MySQL denies the request.

The Purpose of the host Grant Table

The host grant table stores entries that are used when the db grant table does not have adequate information to process the privilege verification request (see Figure 15-2). Neither the GRANT nor REVOKE statements affect entries in mysql.host. Entries must be added and removed manually.

The host grant table has an almost identical schema to the db grant table, except it does not have a User column. When a statement request is evaluated by the access control system, and it comes to the database grant level (meaning the user's global privileges were insufficient to grant the request and the object requiring privileges is of a database scope level or below), the access control system checks to see if there is an entry in mysql.db for the supplied user. If one is found, and the Host column value is *blank* (not '%', which means any database) then mysql.host is consulted for further information. If an entry is found in mysql.host for the supplied Host value in the identification label, then the privileges contained in both mysql.db *and* mysql.host are combined (with a logical AND expression) to determine if the request should be granted.

So, why would you even bother using the host table? That's a good question. Most database administrators never even touch it. Many don't even know it exists, and if they do, they don't know why it's there. The primary reason that mysql.host was added to the grant table mix was to provide database administrators the ability to grant or deny access requests coming from certain hosts or domains, regardless of the username. Remember that the MySQL access control system is not denial-based. It uses an OR-based system to search for any granted level of needed privilege, instead of searching first for the explicit denial of that privilege.

---

2. MySQL doesn't actually use the FIND_IN_SET() function, but rather does a bitwise & operation on the privileges loaded into memory for the queried user. We use the FIND_IN_SET() function here to demonstrate the concept.

However, there are times when it is necessary to create what are known as *stop lists*, or lists of items to which access specifically is denied. `mysql.host` can be used to create just such lists for domains, *regardless of the user part of the identification label*. Let's say we have three server hosts in our network: `sales.example.com`, `intranet.example.com`, and `public.example.com`. Of these, the only server that we don't want to have access to any databases is `public.example.com`, as it poses a security risk. So, we run the following code:

```
mysql> INSERT INTO mysql.host SET Host='public.example.com', Db='%';
mysql> INSERT INTO mysql.host SET Host='%.example.com', Db='%'
    -> , Select_priv='Y', Insert_priv='Y', Update_priv='Y', Delete_priv='Y'
    -> , Create_priv='Y', Drop_priv='Y',  Index_priv='Y',Alter_priv='Y'
    -> , Create_tmp_table_priv='Y';
```

This allows us to put a stop list together (currently containing only one entry for the `public.example.com` host) and deny access to connections originating from that server. Using the % wildcard this way in the `Db` column and in the `Host` column means that the access control system will always find a match in the host table for any internal `example.com` server, regardless of the request. Since any privilege columns we leave out in the `INSERT` statement will default to `'N'`, we can rest assured that no unintended privileges have been granted.

Remember, however, that the MySQL access control system will use privileges in the global `mysql.user` entry first in the privilege verification process. Therefore, if the account `some_user@public.example.com` had privileges set to `'Y'` at the global level, that entry would override the host table entries.

Managing User Accounts from the Command Line

You can use SQL commands to add and remove user accounts, including several GRANT clauses to place restrictions on accounts. Here, we'll look at those commands. In the next section, we'll cover using the MySQL Administrator GUI tool to manage user accounts.

Adding User Accounts

As mentioned earlier, you can use the GRANT command to create new user accounts. Any time you issue a GRANT statement for a username and host combination that does not currently exist in the `mysql.user` table, a new user account is created. A row is inserted in the `mysql.user` table for the username and host specified in your GRANT statement. If the scope of the privileges granted in the statement is global, the user account's global permissions will be set in this new row and no other tables will receive an entry. If the scope of privileges was below the global scope, a new entry will be inserted in the grant table corresponding to the privilege level.

The IDENTIFIED BY clause of the GRANT statement allows you to specify a password for the user account, like so:

```
GRANT SELECT ON ToyStore.*
TO 'some_user'@'localhost' IDENTIFIED BY 'my_password';
```

Another way to add new user accounts is to insert rows directly into the mysql.user table. This is a convenient way to add multiple users at once, however we don't recommend this method for just the odd user or two. To add only a few users, stick to the GRANT command. If you do insert directly into mysql.user, note the password supplied in the IDENTIFIED BY clause is actually encrypted in the mysql.user grant table. If you add the row to the user table directly, you must use the PASSWORD() function to encrypt the password:

```
INSERT INTO mysql.user  SET Host='localhost', User='some_user',
 Password=PASSWORD('my_password'), Select_priv='Y';
```

Otherwise, the connecting user would not be able to access the server, as the supplied password would be encrypted and compared to the (plain-text) Password column value in the user table.

Starting in MySQL 5.0.2, you can also add users with no privileges by using the CREATE ➥ USER command. The following two statements are identical in function:

```
CREATE USER 'some_user'@'localhost' IDENTIFIED BY 'my_password';
GRANT USAGE ON *.* TO 'some_user'@'localhost' IDENTIFIED BY 'my_password';
```

Restricting User Accounts

In addition to the user account's global privileges, the mysql.user grant table also houses a number of additional fields that can aid you as a database administrator in restricting the account's use of the database server. Starting with version 4.0.2, MySQL provides three fields—max_questions, max_updates, and max_connections—which allow you to limit the interaction a particular account has with the server. Before 4.0.2, all you could do was set the max_connections configuration variable to limit the number of connections made by a single user account, meaning you couldn't vary the setting per user. Now, you have much more flexibility in how you handle resource usage.

You can use the following to restrict user accounts:

- WITH MAX_QUERIES_PER_HOUR *n*, where *n* is the number of queries the user may issue, limits the number of queries a user may issue against the server in one hour.

- WITH MAX_UPDATES_PER_HOUR *n* changes the number of update requests the user may issue.

- WITH MAX_CONNECTIONS_PER_HOUR *n* changes the number of times a user may log in to the database server in a single hour.

- MAX_USER_CONNECTIONS, available in MySQL 5.0.3 and later, differs from the MAX_CONNECTIONS_PER_HOUR setting in that it is not time limited and refers to the total amount of connections simultaneously made by the user account. Use this option if you have a user that consistently opens too many user connections to the server, leaving many of them idle or sleeping.

One good use of the USAGE privilege is in changing these variables without affecting any other privileges. Listing 15-7 demonstrates changing all three of these variables, as well as a direct query on mysql.user to show the change.

Listing 15-7. *Using the USAGE Privilege to Change Global User Restriction Variables*

```
mysql> GRANT USAGE ON *.* TO 'jpipes'@'localhost'
    -> WITH MAX_QUERIES_PER_HOUR 1000
    -> MAX_UPDATES_PER_HOUR 1000
    -> MAX_CONNECTIONS_PER_HOUR 50;
Query OK, 0 rows affected (0.00 sec)

mysql> SELECT max_questions, max_updates, max_connections
    -> FROM mysql.user
    -> WHERE User='jpipes' AND Host='localhost';
+---------------+-------------+-----------------+
| max_questions | max_updates | max_connections |
+---------------+-------------+-----------------+
|          1000 |        1000 |              50 |
+---------------+-------------+-----------------+
1 row in set (0.01 sec)
```

Using a combination of these resource limiters, you can achieve a fine level of control over the resource usage of user accounts. They are useful when you have a high-traffic, multi-user database server, as is typical in shared hosting environments, and you want to ensure that the database server shares its available resources fairly.

Removing Accounts

If you are using a MySQL version 4.1.1 or later, you can remove a user account with the DROP USER command:

```
DROP USER 'some_user'@'%';
```

In versions prior to MySQL 4.1.1, you need to issue the following two statements to remove an account:

```
DELETE FROM mysql.user WHERE user='some_user' AND Host='%';
FLUSH PRIVILEGES;
```

Here, we're manually deleting the entry, and issuing FLUSH PRIVILEGES to ensure that changes are reflected in the in-memory copy of the grant tables, as discussed in the next section.

Effecting Account Changes

As stated earlier, MySQL keeps privilege information in-memory from when the server is started. When making changes to privileges, you should be aware of when the in-memory copy of the grant tables contains the most up-to-date privilege information and when it does not.

When In-Memory Tables Are Updated

In all of the following situations, the in-memory grant tables contain the most up-to-date privilege and access information:

- After issuing a GRANT, REVOKE, CREATE USER, or DROP USER statement

- After issuing the FLUSH PRIVILEGES statement

- Immediately after the server starts and before any requests are made to the mysql database

If, however, you alter the mysql grant tables directly, as is necessary when altering mysql.host or deleting a user account before version 4.1.1 of MySQL, the in-memory copies of the privilege tables *will not* contain the most current information, and you should immediately issue a FLUSH PRIVILEGES statement to make the changes current.

When Current Connection Requests Use the New Privileges

If you make high-priority changes to the privilege system—for instance, because a security violation was detected and you want to take immediate action—you will want to know exactly when MySQL will use the privileges you have changed.

When you change a user's database-level access and privileges (those stored in mysql.db), the new privileges will take effect *after* the next issue of a USE *db_name* statement. While this is okay for most web-based systems, where a new USE statement is issued on each HTTP request, this can be more problematic if the offending user is logged in to a persistent session (a console or client/server application session). If the security risk is high, you may be forced to KILL the offending user's process (identified using the SHOW FULL PROCESSLIST command) in order to ensure a new USE *db_name* request is generated.

When you make changes to the user's global privileges, as well as passwords, the next time the correct privileges will be read is when a new connection request is received with the same identification tag. Again, it may be necessary in some situations to identify the offending process IDs and KILL the processes to effectively "log out" the offending user.

When you change a user's table or column-level privileges, the new privileges will take effect on the very next request to the server, so, in general, you do not need to worry about enforcing privilege changes at that level.

Using the MySQL Administrator GUI Tool

MySQL AB released the GUI tools MySQL Administrator and MySQL Query Browser in different stages over 2004. New database administrators will find the GUI tools more intuitive than their command-line counterparts. In some cases, particularly for user management tasks, the GUI can reduce a number of fairly repetitive SQL statements down to a few clicks of the mouse.

Here, we'll discuss how to use the MySQL Administrator tool to manage user accounts. Your first step is to set up your connection to the server. Then you can navigate to the User Administration section and use those tools to add and remove accounts, as well as specify user privileges.

> **■Note** To administer the user accounts, you must first connect to the server as a user with GRANT OPTION privileges (database administrator). Otherwise, all the options detailed here are unavailable (grayed-out) to you.

Connecting to the Server

When you start up the MySQL Administrator program, you are greeted with the dialog box shown in Figure 15-3.

> **■Note** The figures in this section come from a computer running Fedora Core 3 Linux using the KDE desktop environment. Although you may notice slight variations in the MySQL Administrator functionality, depending on the operating system you use, the interface runs in a very similar fashion on Windows and Macintosh operating systems. See http://dev.mysql.com/downloads/ for the version for your system.

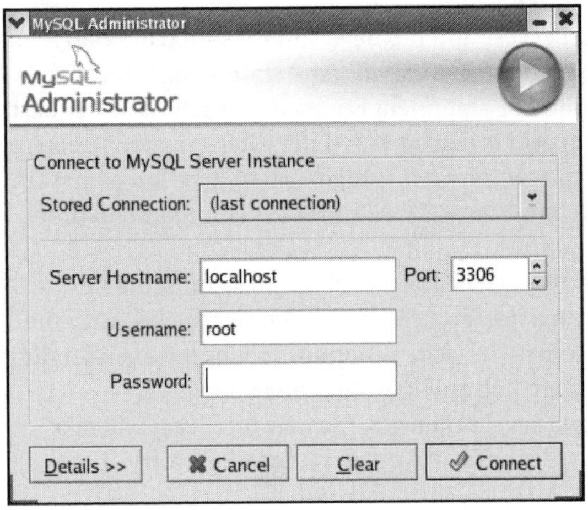

Figure 15-3. *The MySQL Administrator common connection dialog box*

You can enter your information in to the text boxes provided for server hostname, username, and password. However, since you'll presumably be using this tool more than once, you can set up a stored connection so you don't need to repeatedly enter this information. To do so, select Open Connection Editor in the Stored Connection drop-down box. This will bring up the Preferences dialog box, shown in Figure 15-4.

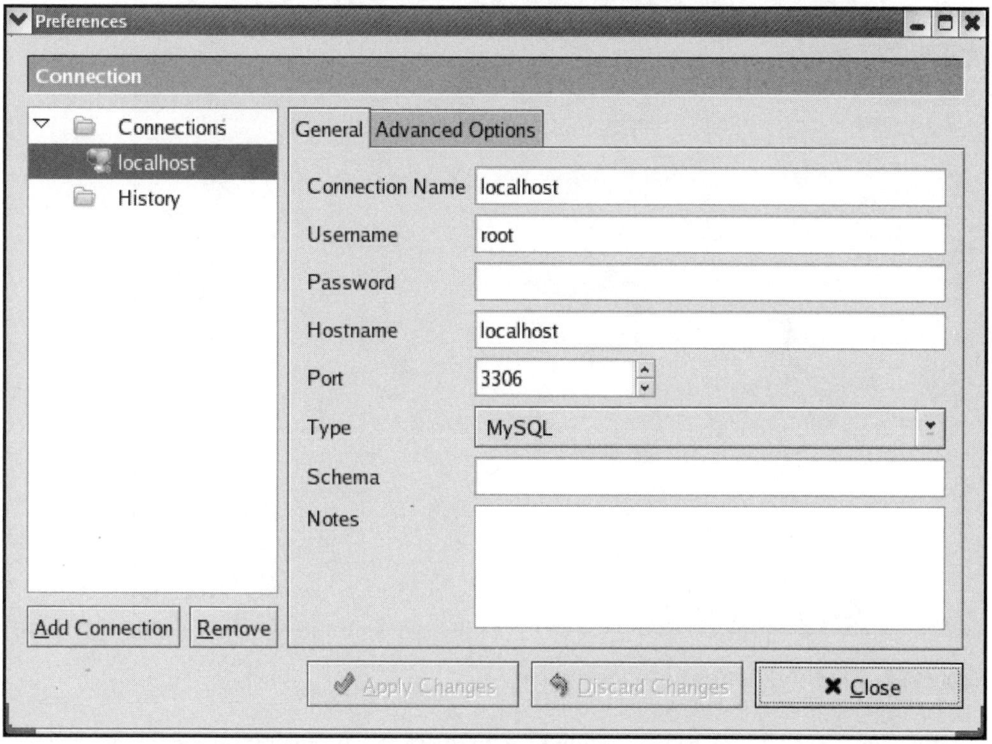

Figure 15-4. *The MySQL Administrator Connection Preferences dialog box*

Click the Add Connection button in the lower-left corner, and then fill in the appropriate information to the space in the right of the dialog box. When you're finished, click Apply Changes, then Close. You will be taken back to the Connection dialog box, where you can now select the new stored connection you just saved. Enter your password and click Connect.

Navigating User Administration

After you connect to the server, you will find yourself in the MySQL Administrator interface, with a number of options in the left pane, as shown in Figure 15-5.

Tip If you're a Linux user, you can avoid needing to retype your passwords every time you enter MySQL Administrator or MySQL Query Browser. In either application, select File ➤ Preferences, and then click General Options tab and select Store Connection Passwords. Optionally, you can obscure the password storage by selecting Obscured in the Storage Method drop-down list.

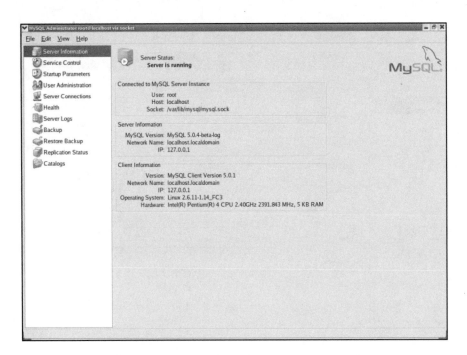

Figure 15-5. *The MySQL Administrator console*

Click the User Administration option to go to the User Administration section of MySQL Administrator, as shown in Figure 15-6.

As you can see, in the bottom-left pane of the window is a tree-view-like User Accounts list. The server's user accounts are listed by username. Clicking the username will display zero, one, or more hostnames preceded by an @ sign, depending on how many entries in mysql.user have a User column value matching the username. If no hosts are listed, it means that the only entry in mysql.user with that username is one where the Host column value is '%'.

In Figure 15-6, notice that while we have selected jpipes@% (the top-level of the node for jpipes), the Schema Privileges and Resource Limits tabs in the main window area are grayed-out. This is because there actually is no record in mysql.user for jpipes@%. There is, however, a record in mysql.user for jpipes@localhost, which is why, as demonstrated in Figure 15-7, the Schema Privileges and Resource Limits tabs are active and available when we select that part of the tree.

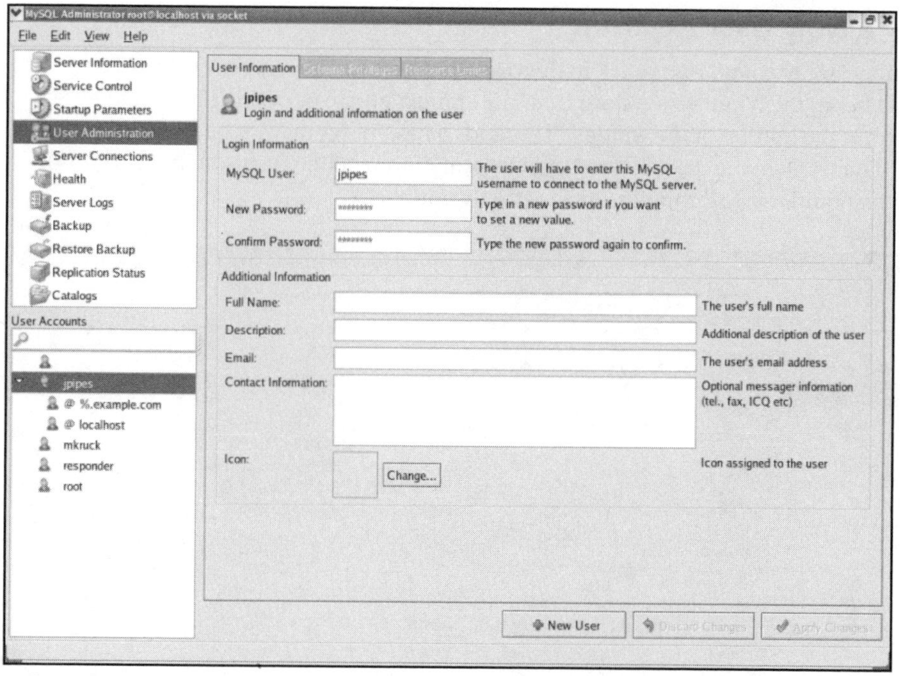

Figure 15-6. *The User Administration section of MySQL Administrator*

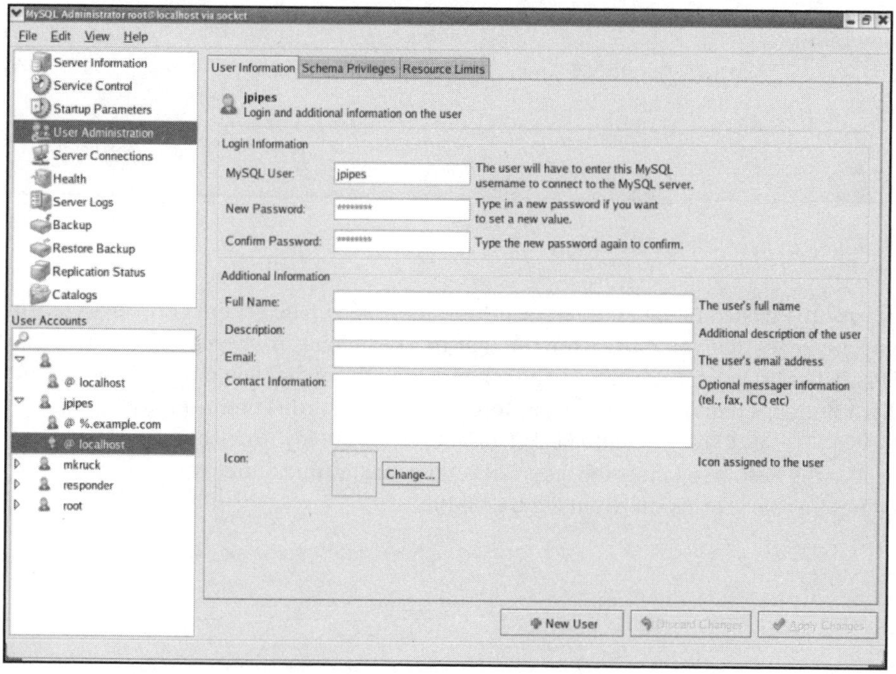

Figure 15-7. *Selecting a user account with a matching entry in mysql.user*

Adding a New User Account

To add a new user account, right-click in the User Accounts section and select New User (Add New User in the Windows version) from the context menu, or optionally, click the New User button at the bottom of the window. This adds a new_user entry in the User Accounts list. In the right pane, fill in the fields in the Login Information section, as shown in Figure 15-8. Filling in the Additional Information area is strictly optional.[3]

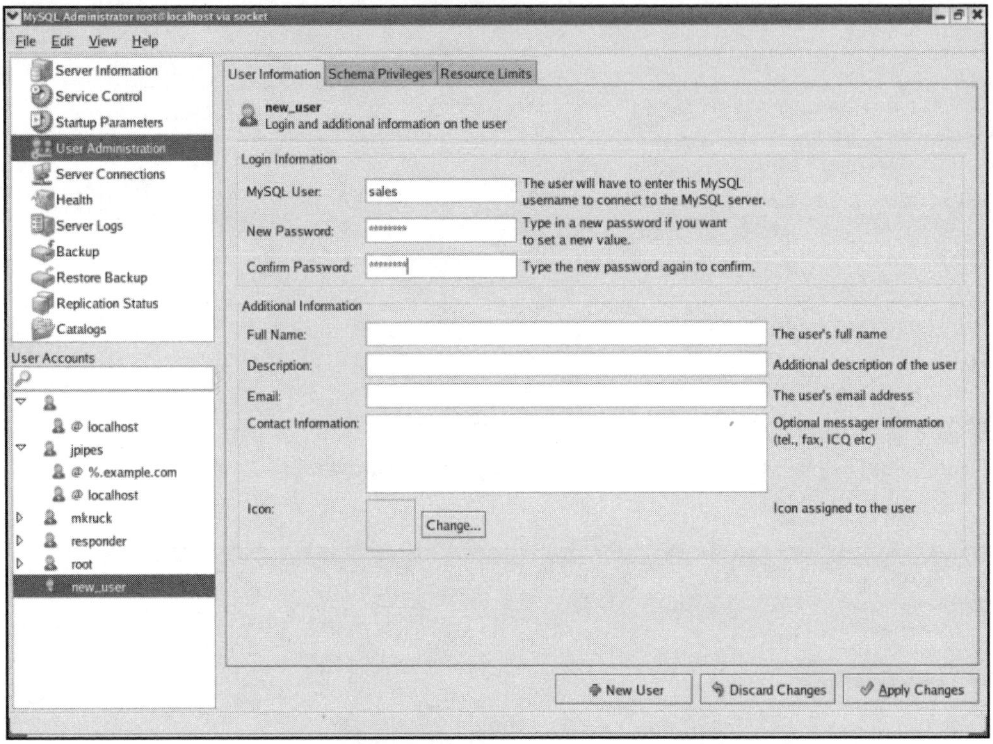

Figure 15-8. *Filling in new user information*

When you are finished filling in the basic information, select the Schema Privileges tab. In this tab, any privileges that you move from the rightmost Available Privileges list to the middle Assigned Privileges list will be granted for the schema (database) that you have selected in the leftmost list, entitled Schema. In Figure 15-9, you can see that for this new user, we have granted the SELECT, INSERT, UPDATE, and DELETE privileges for the ToyStore schema.

If you click the Resource Limits tab, you can set the maximum connections, queries, and updates values for this user, as shown in Figure 15-10.

---

3. Information you enter in the Additional Information is stored in the mysql.user_info system table.

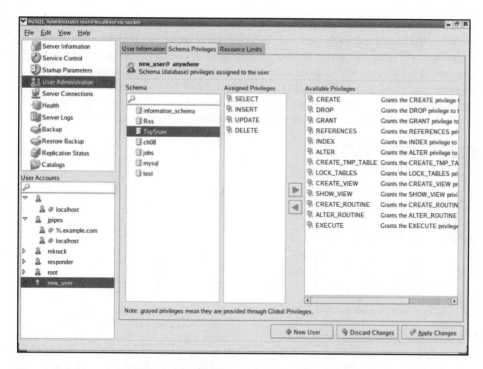

Figure 15-9. *Granting the new user privileges on the ToyStore schema*

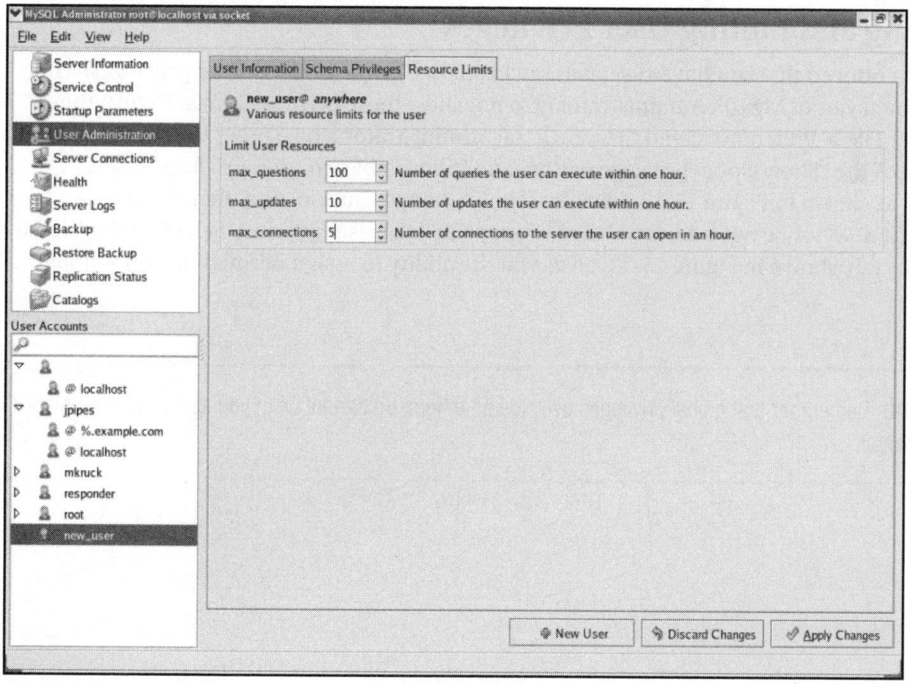

Figure 15-10. *Setting the new user's resource limitations*

When you have finished making your changes, click the Apply Changes button. Your user will be added to the user grant table with the Host column value of '%'. Usually, this is not what you really want, since it is better to have a more specific entry for the Host column. To create an entry in mysql.user with a more specific Host value, right-click the username in the User Accounts area and select Add Host. In the Add Host dialog box, shown in Figure 15-11, select the Hostname or IP option and type in your desired domain or host address. Click OK, and you will see an additional node under the new username in the User Accounts area.

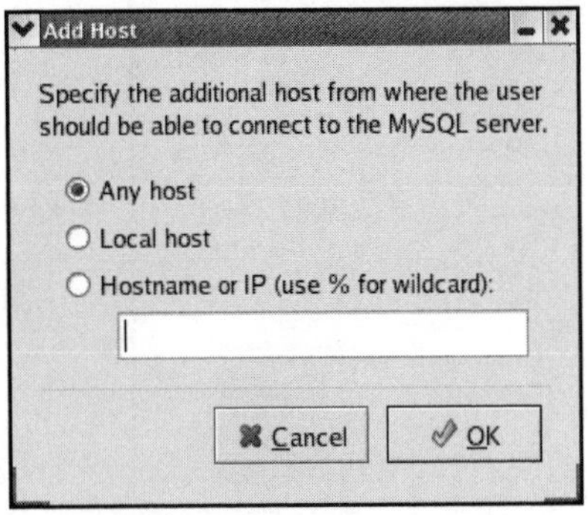

Figure 15-11. *The Add Host dialog box*

Selecting the new node will change the right content area to display the entry for the node.

Viewing and Editing User Privileges

Have you noticed that you haven't seen a way to change global or table-level privileges? The default behavior of MySQL Administrator is to not show these privilege levels. To turn them on, select File ➤ Preferences, and then click the Administrator icon. Under User Administration, check the "Show global privilege editor" and "Show table/column privilege editor" options, as shown in Figure 15-12. Click the Apply Changes button, and then click Close.

You'll now notice two additional tabs when you click a user account. Selecting the Global Privileges tab, shown in Figure 15-13, gives you the ability to assign permissions on a global level.

Caution Remember that global privileges override all others. Be careful what you assign through MySQL Administrator.

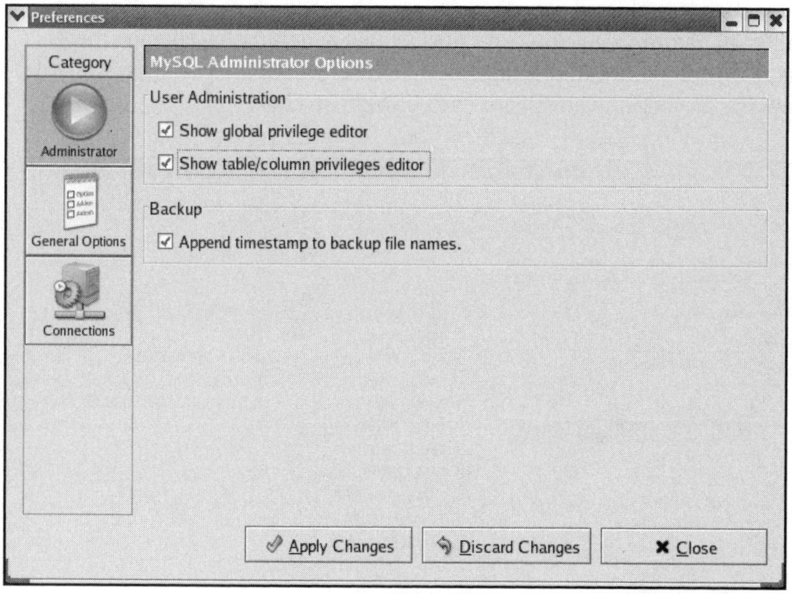

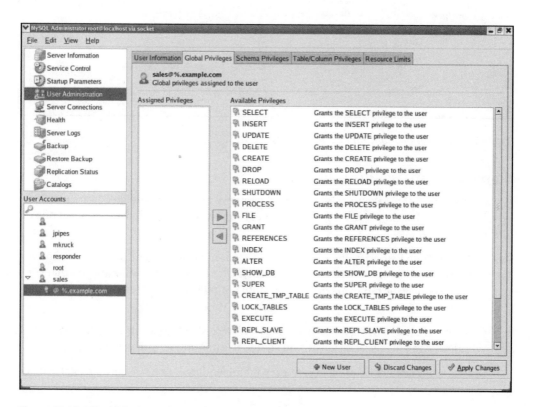

Figure 15-12. *Turning on the global privilege editor*

Figure 15-13. *The Global Privileges editor in MySQL Administrator*

Similarly, you can change table and column privileges by selecting the Table/Column Privileges tab, as shown in Figure 15-14. You can select a table or column by clicking the appropriate schema in the left pane and drilling down to the object of interest. The Available Privileges list displays the privileges available for each object you click.

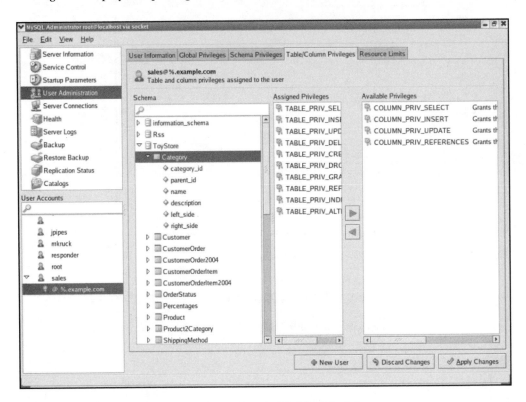

Figure 15-14. *The Table/Column Privileges editor in MySQL Administrator*

Removing an Account

MySQL Administrator makes it (a bit too) easy to remove users (and all related user/host `mysql.user` records). Simply right-click the user account you wish to remove and select one of the following options:

- *Remove Host*: Removing the host removes that user/host entry and all associated privileges. If there is only one user/host entry, MySQL Administrator will warn you that you will essentially be removing the user account entirely, since no remaining `mysql.user` entries will be available.

- *Remove User*: Removing the user will delete all record of the user and any host combinations it might have. Obviously, you should use this option with caution.

MySQL Administrator asks you to confirm your impending action, as shown in Figure 15-15.

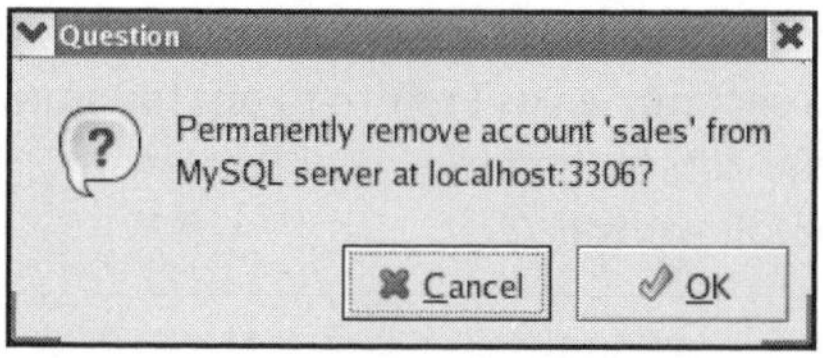

Figure 15-15. *The Remove Account confirmation dialog box*

For more information about using MySQL Administrator, see `http://dev.mysql.com/doc/administrator/en/mysql-administrator-introduction.html`.

Thinking in Terms of User Roles

Up until now, we've been speaking about the access control and privilege verification systems strictly in terms of user accounts. However, many other database vendors have implemented an alternate, more complex, account management subsystem. The primary difference between MySQL and other popular vendors is that MySQL does not have a role-based implementation.[4]

Sticking to their original goals for ease of use and simplicity, the MySQL developers have chosen not to overcomplicate the access control process by adding new layers of complexity to the grant system. It is unlikely that you will see a role-based implementation in the near future. However, that does not mean you should disregard the notion of account management by roles. The concept is just as important, whether MySQL implements the roles systematically or leaves the implementation to your own devices.

Many of you who are systems administrators are already intimate with group-based account management. All major server operating systems provide a mechanism to place user accounts into one or more usually function-oriented groups. By function-oriented, we mean that the group's members generally share similar work goals: server administrators, power users, regular users, server daemons, and so on. It is often helpful to think of the user accounts you manage for a MySQL database server in similar terms. Users of the database server almost always can be categorized into groups based on the *roles* they play in the overall scheme of the database server's daily activity.

More than likely, if you already manage a MySQL database server, you, perhaps unknowingly, think in terms of role-based management. When you add a new user account, you find out what the user will need to accomplish on a daily basis and which databases the account will need to access. In doing so, you are effectively determining the role that the user will play in the system.

The primary advantage to role-based account management is that user accounts and privileges are controlled in a consistent manner. If you administer database servers with more than just a few users, it is important to have a written policy detailing the roles having access to the system. This written policy provides a reference for administrators to use when adding, removing, or changing user accounts.

---

4. MySQL's MaxDB product already has a role-based account management system. If you feel MySQL's normal user access and privilege verification system will not meet the needs of your organization, head over to `http://dev.mysql.com/doc/maxdb/en/default.htm` to check out how MaxDB implements its role-based system through an extended SQL variant.

As you start down the road to role-based management, begin with a list of the roles that can be played by database users in your system. For this section, we will return to our toy store sample schema. After a few minutes of thinking about the different types of users that will have access to the database server, we come up with the following list:

- Database Administrators

- Database Users

The Database Administrators group (role) is fairly self-explanatory. For our Database Users role, we can further break down the list to the following:

- *Super Users*: Users who have access to all databases and can do all simple table-related tasks, as well as have full rights on a database named tmp.

- *Regular Users*: Users who have access to specified databases and may do simple table-related tasks.

- *Designers*: Users who have all database-related access and privileges on some databases (schema).

We want to ensure that users belonging to each role (and sub-role) have only the privileges that they need to do their activities, and no more. Also, we're assuming here that Super Users have some general database knowledge and know how to use MySQL, so we've given them a database (tmp) to use for their own measures. Thus, we put together a matrix to show which *global* and *database* level privileges member users should be granted as *defaults*, as shown in Table 15-8. This kind of table serves as an important written policy to guide database administrators for large projects. This document should be maintained as changes to the account management system are implemented.

Table 15-8. *Role-Privilege Matrix for the Toy Store Database Server*

Role	Global Privileges	Database-Level Privileges
DB Admins	ALL	N/A[5]
DB Users	NONE	NONE
DB Users: Super Users	NONE	SELECT, INSERT, UPDATE, DELETE on all schema; ALL on schema called tmp
DB Users: Regular Users	NONE	SELECT, INSERT, UPDATE, DELETE on select schema
DB Users: Designers	NONE	ALL on select schema

Now, we have a working strategy for setting defaults for our system's users based on their roles. You would use a list like the one in Table 15-8 as a reference when making account management changes. Instead of remembering the exact privileges a specific user account should be granted, you need to know only which role a new user will play.

Finally, you might streamline the process of account management further, by encapsulating the account management into stored procedures or shell scripts that add appropriate permissions based on these well-defined roles.

---

5. Remember that global privileges override database-level privileges.

Practical Guidelines for User Administration

In this chapter, we've covered a number of topics related to user account management. Here, is a simple list of strategies we consider to be best practices:

- Grant as few privileges as is absolutely necessary for users to accomplish their daily activities.

- Avoid using `WITH GRANT OPTION`.

- Avoid issuing any global privileges to anyone but the topmost database administrator.[6]

- Keep privileges as simple as possible. If you don't need table or column-level privileges, don't use them. This only slows down the access control system and overcomplicates your setup.

- Think in terms of role-based management. This will allow you to more effectively manage large groups of users by grouping them by like activities.

- Use scripts to consolidate role-based management into a secure, well-organized environment.

Summary

In this chapter, we've covered some essentials of MySQL user administration, as well as some advanced aspects. To review, we started by explaining MySQL privileges and their scopes. Then we took an in-depth look at how the two-step access control and privilege verification system works. You learned how the decision to allow or deny a certain request is made, and stepped through some common misunderstandings regarding that decision-making process.

Next, we reviewed how to add users into the system, modify permissions for those users, and eventually remove them. Along the way, we pointed out some occasional "gotchas," and walked you through the more unique, but nonetheless important, scenarios of limiting a user's resources and setting up a host stop list using the `mysql.host` grant table.

We then looked at how to manage users using the MySQL Administrator GUI, walking through setting up a connection, and working in the User Administrator section.

Finally, we switched gears a bit and talked about the major difference between MySQL's user administration implementation and other database vendors: MySQL's lack of role-based account management. We demonstrated some techniques for thinking in terms of role-based management and finished up with some guidelines to follow as you administer users in your databases.

---

6. An exception to this would be specific roles such as a backup job user account that requires global `RELOAD`, `LOCK TABLES`, and `SELECT` privileges.

Security

You recently released a new piece of functionality to your users and are starting to see the data moving in and out of the database with speed and efficiency. You're happily watching the quick response of your system and thinking that your work is done. Yet, while you enjoy the compliments of management and co-workers, you have this nagging feeling about the data. It's nothing major, just a twinge of uneasiness about the new functionality and the sensitive nature of some of the data. Then you're reminded of a conversation you had a month back with a customer who needed to get some summary information from many tables in the database. Because you didn't have time to grant SELECT at the table levels for all 18 tables he needed to access, you granted him the privilege to SELECT at the database level. This gave him the ability to select from any table in the database. Now, you've added another 5 tables with more sensitive data that shouldn't be available to this customer. You rush back to your desk and quickly revoke his SELECT privileges and grant SELECT on the original 18 tables, hoping that the sensitive data hasn't been exposed.

End users—whether employees, customers, students, clients, or any other number of users—rely on their data being available when they need it, accurate in that it has been stored correctly and hasn't been tampered with, and protected in the sense that only the right people will be able to see their data. A compromise of data in any of these ways leads to lack of trust from those who store and use data in your system. In addition, a flaw in the protection of data can lead to long interruptions in business processes, and wasted employee time and company funds while data integrity issues are resolved.

In writing a chapter on database security, we don't want to just provide a seemingly endless list of random thoughts on how to secure your system. We don't want to shake our finger at you, delivering yet another security lecture. Unfortunately, the list of things to consider when securing your database is hard to avoid, and we'll end up there eventually. But we want to spend some time focusing on the reasons behind the emphasis on using secure practices. Therefore, we'll begin by addressing some broad questions about security. Then we'll look at some critical items related to MySQL security, followed by a scenario with specifics on how you might implement a security plan. Finally, we'll address the different parts of a system that affect the database and offer suggestions for securing those parts.

In this chapter, we'll cover the following topics:

- Common reasons for security problems
- Biggest security threats
- Security policy and plan implementation
- A MySQL security quick list
- An example of implementing a security plan
- Security for each part of a system

Understanding Security Requirements

Why are we so interested in security practices? To answer that question, we need to address three other questions.

Why Aren't We Secure?

These days, we are constantly warned about computer exploits and ways to protect against them. Despite this barrage of information, we still learn of, or experience firsthand, security breaches of various types. Why does this continue to happen?

In relation to databases and database applications, we think the following are some of the common reasons for security problems:

Time constraints: Time is a major factor in the attention given to security. Many managers will be pushing for the next piece of functionality before the current one is complete, leaving developers and administrators no time to give attention to making sure things are locked down.

Lack of security knowledge: Developers and administrators might not know enough about security in general or lack awareness of the specifics of database access controls. Perhaps in giving someone access based on an IP address range, the wildcard matching wasn't quite right, and access was granted to a much wider range of machines.

Lack of information about data: It might not be a lack of understanding of security practices that leaves data exposed, but lack of knowledge about the data itself. Suppose your database server is managed by a third party in an off-site data center. If the system administrator of the server isn't aware of the sensitive nature of your data, he may make a decision about security that puts your data at risk. This may be as simple as copying a database backup to a remote machine over a publicly available network.

Communication issues: Lack of communication between application developers, database administrators, and data owners can lead to poor security practices. The database may be heavily guarded, but in most cases, a privileged account will be used by the application to view and change data. If the application programmer doesn't understand the sensitive nature of the data, it may be exposed to unauthorized access, regardless of good security at the database level.

Habits are hard to break: If you've done something a certain way for years, it can be hard to change that behavior. If your team has always granted SELECT privileges at the database level because it's simpler than figuring out which specific tables are required, it may be difficult to change the process. Even if you get team members together and explain a new policy and its significance, you may find that people subconsciously revert to the mechanism they know best. This also applies to a habit of not giving security proper attention.

Acceptance of risk: Willingness to take risks can also be another reason for lack of good security. If a database administrator thinks there is little chance someone will find and gain access to the database, or be interested in toying with the data, she may not bother expending any effort on security. After all, what are the chances that someone will find the machine on the network?

■**Caution** Don't be fooled by a statement like, "Our site is completely public, so there's no need to protect the database." Securing a database isn't just about hiding data. It's about preventing unauthorized changes in the data, as well as keeping the data available. It's also about protecting the server from compromise through the database. In the end, there aren't many operators of databases-driven systems that don't care if their system is down.

It is important not only to acknowledge the fact that you might not be practicing good security, but also to determine how to resolve the deficiency. If lack of knowledge or understanding about security is one reason you have holes in your database, then do some more reading (starting with the rest of this chapter), join appropriate mailing lists, and/or attend a security conference (or a database conference with a security track). If the major barrier is time, tell your manager that there may be some security issues with the database that could lead to disaster and you would like a few days to research and resolve them.

Security incidents are never pleasant and can lead to drastic things like termination of employment. Whatever the issue, find a way to get through it so you can move forward with a clear conscience about your system, and keep your job, too.

Where's the Security Threat?

In planning your security, you want to have an idea of where the threat is coming from. In most cases, the biggest security threat to your organization is not the hacker outside your organization mounting a brute-force attack on your database. More often, the threat is the person sitting two offices down, or someone who already has an account in your database. Consider the opening example of this chapter, where an existing customer had permissions that were inadvertently granted.

Of course, you want to protect your system against outside intruders, but employees, clients, consultants, and others who already have access to your data pose the biggest threat. This is because the chance of them having misconfigured permissions and getting access to unauthorized data is more likely than a stranger getting all the way through the human and technological barriers around your system. In addition, people who understand the organization and technology are more likely to be able to circumvent barriers to get access to the data.

Consider the case of a consultant who has been working with the database administrator on a number of projects. The database administrator probably wouldn't question a request from that consultant to get access to a particular table. Database administrators are likely to be less rigorous about verifying a request for access if it comes from someone who is in the office and working with other parts of the system. If each request for access must go up against a formal security policy and plan, there is less chance that inappropriate access will be granted, even if it's an internal request.

What Does It Mean to Be Secure?

With all that's being written and said about security, you might think that securing your database is just a matter of going through a list of predefined steps to lock down your database. Yes, you can find a lot of information about securing database systems, but all systems are not the same. Your system presents a unique set of variables. What does it mean to be secure?

That's not an easy question to answer, and one that has created an industry of security professionals who are passionately working to determine what and how to secure systems and the data that lives within them.

To be clear, when we say that we want to secure a database, we're generally referring to controlling access to data. This applies to the ability to see, change, and remove the system's data. We might also lump into that the requirement that the database be available; that is, we would like to prevent the intentional or accidental shutdown of the database or the server where it runs.

Building a Security Plan

As we've hinted, protecting your system isn't about just following a set of prescribed steps from a security how-to guide. You need to develop *security policies* to define why different pieces of data need to be protected and what parts of the system should be available to users. This can be a time-consuming and challenging process. Sometimes, just making sure you have all the right people involved in the conversation to define the security requirements can be a challenge.

Defining security policies warrants a thorough process of identifying all the stakeholders of the data and bringing them together to define the rules of viewing, changing, and removing data from the system. Ideally, this process is well documented and results in readily available documentation, a mapping between user roles and database permissions, and a set of tools for managing the defined roles and permissions. You should also include access beyond the database access rules, such as who can have a shell account on the machine and access the data and log files.

The policy definition will likely require several iterations, allowing stakeholders to review the policy and provide feedback over a period of time. It's important to at least have the decision makers provide input into how you implement access control to the data in your database.

Don't plan on creating a timeless masterpiece; the policy document should be revisited regularly, particularly when a security breach has occurred, changes have been made in the data structure, or a new piece of functionality has been added.

Not only can it be difficult to get everyone together to define all your data and the meaning of its relationships, you may have the responsibility of educating policy makers, developers, and users of the data about the importance of knowing the data and the rules of how it should be protected. That can be difficult, because new issues involving data access and restriction arise every day, and the rules are changing as data and data aggregation continue to move our society in new directions.

The implementation of a security policy is your *security plan*. The security plan contains the action to support the policy. The complexity of your security plan will have a lot to do with the complexity of your security policy, database, data, application, and system. While there are security issues to consider with all databases, you will find that the requirements of one system are more demanding and require more planning and attention than you devote to another. Some of this is tied to the sensitive nature of the data. The security implementation for a database that stores credit card information or student grades requires more scrutiny than a database filled with a list of recommended novels.

Implementing and enforcing a security policy can be a daunting task. Going through the work to define who should have access to what and how data should be protected significantly eases the task. With a policy, the implementation is about understanding how your database access control lists work and creating the appropriate access rules.

■**Note** A big part of securing the data is being able to properly manage the access control lists for users who are looking at the data. Refer to Chapter 15 for details on managing user permissions to control user access.

To help you develop a security plan for your particular requirement, Table 16-1 provides a list of potential sections in a security document, with explanations of what might go into the section.

Table 16-1. *Potential Security Policy Sections*

Section	Description
Index	Overview of sections in your document. Provides readers with a summary of the sections addressed in the policy and easy access for referencing sections.
Organizational Policy	Summary of your organization's security policy, specifically how it relates to the database.
Physical Security	Information about where database machines are stored, how access is controlled, and what groups have access to the servers. Also describes who is responsible for granting access for specific parts of the database.
Operating System	Overview of operating system procedures as they relate to the database. Includes information about who has access to the server.
MySQL Installation	Details about how MySQL is installed and configured. Defines where data files are stored, what configuration options are specified, and whether networking is enabled.
Applications	Information about how applications interact with the database. Details who authorizes accounts and what permissions are associated with different applications. Also provides information about communication protocols.
Account Management	Definition of permission groups (based on roles, departments, or other groupings). Includes information about what permission groups exist, who grants access to accounts and assigns user IDs, what types of permissions are granted for different groups, who determines the access level, and how and when permissions are revoked.
Security Audit	Details about how often a security audit is suggested for security, including physical, operating system, database configuration, and accounts.

■**Tip** The SANS Institute has a Security Policy Project geared toward helping organizations and individuals quickly develop security policies. Sample policies can be downloaded from http://www.sans.org/ resources/policies/. Additionally, numerous organizations offer prebuilt security policies, and even a selection of books to help you work through the process.

Using Security Incidents

While we don't wish security problems on anyone, an event that usually triggers a careful look and improved commitment to security is a security incident. This can be anything from suspicious activity on the server to unexplained data changes. Even if the problem is resolved with a logical explanation that doesn't end up being related to a security issue, security awareness is heightened.

Use the security breach as a time to create or update your security policy and plan, and to reinforce with employees the importance of following the plan. Make it clear that if the plan is followed, the recently experienced security incident will not happen again.

As a part of your security plan, create a set of steps to go through when a security breach is suspected or detected. Determine how the issue should be escalated and who should be involved in clearing up the issue. Here is an example of a set of steps to take when a security breach is suspected or detected:

1. Alert team members.

2. Conduct technical research to explain or support suspicions.

3. Alert management. Provide technical support to claims.

4. Get management input on action.

5. Take action(s):

   • Security tightened

   • Permissions revoked

   • Compromised database restored from backup

   • Appropriate action taken against violating person

   • Alert data stakeholders and users

Obviously, the reaction and response should be adjusted accordingly, depending on the sensitivity of the data.

Keeping Good Documentation

Maintaining good documentation on your security policy and plan is key to keeping users' access in check. This documentation should be actively updated as changes are made in your database or application.

If you're just getting started, a core piece of your security plan should be the development of a table with mapping between user roles and permissions in the database. Table 16-2 includes a few sample records from a permissions mapping document from an online store.

Table 16-2. *Sample Permissions Mapping Document*

User/Group	Database	Table	Permission
Customer Reps	shop	customer	SELECT, UPDATE, INSERT, DELETE

Notes: Customer representatives use and maintain the customer table.

web_user	shop	product	SELECT

Notes: The web_user is an anonymous account used in the web application to display product information.

web_administrator	shop	customer, product	SELECT
web_administrator	shop	customer_order	SELECT, INSERT, UPDATE

Notes: The web_administrator is a user in the web application that is used specifically for creating and displaying customer orders.

DB Admins	All	All	All

Notes: Database administrators have full access to the database.

Maintaining a table such as the one shown in Table 16-2 is helpful to technical and management folks, because it centralizes details about who can do what in the database.

IMPROVING SECURITY EFFORTS

Don't try to completely overhaul your security practices in one shot. Such an attempt will most likely end in frustration and lead to no security policy or plan at all. Start by selecting one or two of the most important things and commit to always following good practice in those one or two things. Once those few critical things are taken care of, identify the next few items and work toward them.

Identify existing pieces of your system that could be more secure and take time to go back and give them the attention they need. If you've created a number of accounts with too widespread permissions, go back and clean up the accounts.

When you start a new project, spend some time on implementing security rules for the new functionality, completing the database administration work before any code is written.

A key to improving your security practices is to be knowledgeable about security. Increase your awareness and understanding of security topics by reading one of the hundreds of books on security, or by subscribing to a magazine or mailing list focused on the topic.

If you don't have the time, but can justify the expense, hire an outside security professional to perform a security audit. This can provide a significant boost to your security policy and plan. Having someone from the outside assess the situation provides an added measure of authority if you are given the task of convincing management that security is worth the time and energy.

Getting Started: A MySQL Security Quick List

We hope that your security policy development and implementation is a slow, careful, and deliberate process. But we also understand that, in many cases, security is something that must be wrapped into numerous other responsibilities and doesn't always get the attention it deserves. Here, we've provided a list of things that are imperative when running a MySQL database. These are the most serious of all the recommendations:

Set the root user password: By default, MySQL includes a database account for a root user that has no password. This means that until the root user password is changed, anyone can connect with full database privileges, without needing to enter a password. If you haven't changed the MySQL root account password, do so immediately:

```
SET PASSWORD FOR 'root'@'localhost' = PASSWORD('newpwd');
SET PASSWORD FOR 'root' = PASSWORD('newpwd');
```

Remove the anonymous account: By default, MySQL includes an anonymous account that, like the default root user account, has no password. The anonymous account makes it easy to immediately be able to use the database, because you can connect without needing to set up credentials. Unless the password is set, or the account is removed, anyone can connect to the MySQL database. The anonymous user has limited permissions, but still should be removed, unless it is used as a part of your security plan.[1] Remove the anonymous user account by revoking any accounts that do not have a name (specified with empty single quotation marks, '').

Run MySQL as a non-root user: Do not use the root Unix account to run the database. For database users who have the FILE privilege (described in Chapter 15), running as root means that interactions with files are doing so with root privilege, which could allow access like reading otherwise-protected files from the operating system into a database table for viewing. Typically, you will create a mysql user account and use it for running the database. Then, if the MySQL server has a security vulnerability, the potential for damage to the rest of the operating system is limited to what the mysql user is allowed to do.

Use the mysql group: Create a mysql group, and use that group to control access to the log files. Depending on how much logging you do, having exposed log files in MySQL can be just as bad as having exposed data files.

Check data file permissions: Make sure your data files are available only to the mysql user (and maybe mysql group, if circumstances require). Even if users don't have an account to connect to the database, if they have the ability to read the data and log files on the server's filesystem, they can copy them elsewhere to use.

Disable networking: If you use MySQL only on the local machine (you are physically at the machine, are using a secure connection to run a shell, or are using an application running on the same machine), turn off networking. You can do this by setting --skip-networking in your server startup configuration (see Chapter 14 for details on configuring MySQL).

---

1. You may use the anonymous account to make certain pieces of information available. Perhaps you have tables that many people need to see, so you keep the anonymous account for access to that data. That way, people can connect and view the data without needing to remember a username or password.

Secure network traffic: If MySQL must be used across a network, use a private network or SSL encryption for the traffic that flows between the database and client. If you're just looking at data, this prevents snooping, but if you're resetting passwords, granting permissions, or looking at the process lists (where you can see executing queries), having privacy for your data means you are not exposing the sensitive data as it comes across the wire.

This list gives you a starting point by stressing the most critical items, but it does not provide a complete picture. Once you've implemented the items on this list, we encourage you to continue reading to get a more thorough idea of the steps for securing your database.

Setting Up Database Security: An Example

To highlight some of the ways a database can be secured, let's consider a real-world scenario. Suppose you have an office for an online shopping store (to stick with a familiar example). For your ordering system, you have a web site for the public to shop, place orders, and check order status, backed by a database. You also have a web-based application used for order processing and order fulfillment, pointed at the same database. You have a team of ten order processing and eight order fulfillment employees. Besides yourself, three other members of the IT staff work on the applications and maintain the database. Figure 16-1 shows the different players in this scenario, depicting the customers and employees, and a server that handles the requests from your public web site and your employee interface to the data.

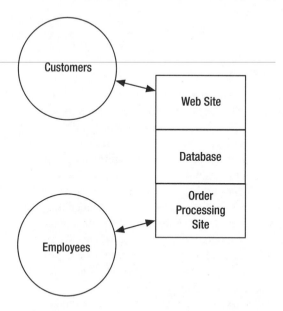

Figure 16-1. *Users and servers in a single-server online shopping configuration*

Locking Up the Server

Regardless of how many servers are required to run the site, the first thing to consider is the physical location and accessibility between the pieces of the system in Figure 16-1. You should have the machines in a secure location, with no access allowed by the public (not in a closet in the office lobby), and limited physical access by all employees, even your IT staff. To physically get access to the machines should require obtaining a key to unlock the server rack.

Locking Down Network Access

Next, consider how your server is available via the network. You need to make sure the operating system is updated. You also must deny access to services on the machine via a firewall or by disabling unnecessary programs and processes.

The public web site will obviously need to be accessed by anyone coming in from the Internet. The order-processing and order-fulfillment pieces of the system are needed only by users within your office. You might control access by using an internal network and binding an internal domain name or IP address to the those pieces of the site or service.[2]

Because MySQL is running on the same machine as the sites, and the interaction with the database happens through tools built into the site, you should be able to disable the networking capabilities of MySQL. This involves adding the `skip-networking` option to your startup. Adding this option means that MySQL will not listen for data requests via the network, which can be a security risk.

■**Note** If you are using SSH to connect to a machine, and then using the MySQL client to interact with the database, you are not using MySQL's networking capabilities. The network connection is handled by SSH, and the database connection is made using the Unix socket.

Controlling Access to Data

With the networking locked down, you should next consider how to control access to data in the system. Presumably, you have a database with a set of tables used to store information about categories, products, users, and user orders. These tables drive the site. In addition, you may have data for internal use in processing, packaging, and shipping the orders. If you don't already, it's not a bad idea to separate those functional areas into two separate databases, which will give you more options for controlling access down the road.

Of course, you've removed the anonymous account from the database and have set the root user's password, as noted in the quick list earlier in this chapter. Now, you need to figure out how to give access to the applications. For the public web site, you will create one user specifically designed to interact with the database on behalf of the user of the site. This database account should have the bare minimum access to allow the web user to browse products, put them in a shopping basket (and remove them), and process the order. This account will be programmed into the web application to get a database handle.

The employees' interaction can be managed in a variety of ways. You might maintain MySQL accounts for each employee and require employees to type their username and password into the application and use their credentials to get a database handle from the database.

---

2. We're thinking of Apache's VirtualHost directive, which allows you to bind different domain names or IP addresses to a particular directory with a set of pages or scripts letting you create multiple sites on a single machine. For more information about configuring virtual hosts, see `http://httpd.apache.org/docs/mod/core.html#virtualhost`.

This provides a great deal of granularity in controlling access to the data, but can be difficult to maintain if you have a lot of employees. Another approach is to create a special user to obtain a database handle and interact with the database on behalf of the user.

Besides having an account for the database administrator, you should need only two accounts for access to MySQL (or one plus the number of employees if you're granting accounts to employees).

Making sure the rules for each user are correct is a matter of reviewing the security plan access documentation and running GRANT statements for each permission needed. In addition, for both the public and internal site, MySQL connections can be limited to those coming from localhost, because the only connections made to the database are coming from processes on the same machine. When granting permissions, everything should be done with @localhost appended to the user. When looking at the mysql.user table, you should not see any entries with host set to something other than localhost.

This simple scenario provides a very rudimentary review of the process of securing a system and database. By no means does this cover the details necessary to call your security work complete, but it does give you a sense of the process. Before we leave our example, let's consider a few more elements that add some complexity to the plan.

Adding Remote Access

Suppose that one of the order-processing employees has arranged to work some hours from home and needs access to the database from a remote location. You have several options, which may vary in acceptability, depending on what kind of work the employee will be doing from home:

Shell account over SSH: You could grant remote access to the command-line tools by creating a shell account on the server, with access to the mysql client program. This model would require creating and maintaining shell accounts for users requiring remote access, but you would not need to open the database to network requests you previously disabled with the skip-networking option.

MySQL Administrator over SSH: If the user needs a GUI to interact with the database, but SSH is still your preferred connection method, you could install the MySQL Administrator tool on the server and have it run remotely in an X window on the user's remote desktop. You wouldn't need to open up mysql to network connections, but you would still need to maintain shell accounts. You also would need a decent pipe between the server and the user's home to get acceptable response from MySQL Administrator running via the X Windowing System. (MySQL Administrator is introduced in Chapter 15; also visit http://www.mysql.com/products/administrator/ for more information.)

SSL client connection: If creating, maintaining, or allowing a user to have a shell account on the server is out of the question, another option is to run MySQL in a mode that will listen (on port 3306) for requests to the database. The risk here is that you open the database to network-based attacks. Also, unless the network connections are on a private network, you would want to require use of SSL encryption in the account privileges. This is accomplished by adding REQUIRE SSL or REQUIRE X509 in the GRANT statement for the user's MySQL account. You would also limit the host to the employee's remote IP address (or at least an IP range) by specifying <user>@<ip> in the GRANT statement. Then, if an attempt were made to connect from another IP address, or without SSL enabled, the connection attempt would be refused.

Note that MySQL doesn't have SSL enabled by default. This means that it's unlikely that a version provided with your operating system will have SSL support. In addition, the MySQL binaries available from the MySQL web site do not have SSL enabled. To use SSL connections, you need to build MySQL yourself. The OpenSSL libraries must be installed on your system to rebuild MySQL and enable SSL support. See Chapter 14 for more information about compiling MySQL and using configuration options during the process.

MySQL Administrator via SSL: If network connections are allowed (and, in this case, SSL encryption should be required), the user could also connect to the database using tools like MySQL Administrator instead of a command-line client on their remote machine.

As you can see, each piece of the security puzzle brings more options to consider, and these also require reconsideration of the original assumptions made when developing the security policy for your data and database.

Adding Servers

Having a single server responsible for handling the online customers as well as the employees and database is not always the case. Another likely scenario is to have one or more classes or groupings of servers, responsible for functional areas of the site. Figure 16-2 shows our original scenario with servers broken into three classes: public web site, order processing site, and database.

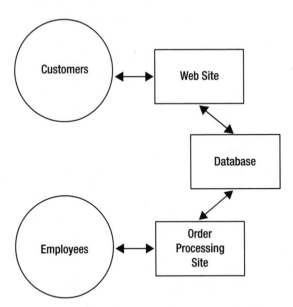

Figure 16-2. *Users and servers in a multiple-server online shopping configuration*

The primary difference between this and the system shown in Figure 16-1 is that with multiple servers, you can further segregate the functions and get better control over access to the servers. In this scenario, you can put just the server needed for the customer web site on the public network, and protect the order-processing site on a private network available only to employees in the office. The database server doesn't need to reside in either of these networks;

it could be connected to the web servers via a separate network. Figure 16-3 shows a revamped diagram of the servers, illustrating where each piece of the site fits into this model for securing the systems.

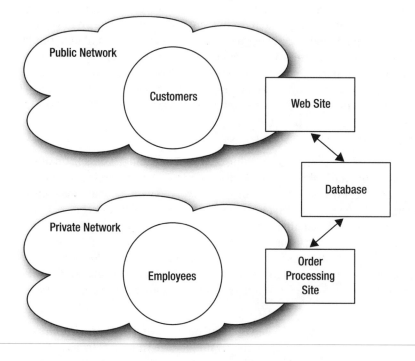

Figure 16-3. *Users and servers segregated from network segments*

Having the machines separated like this means you'll be required to turn on networking on the MySQL server and change the access rules to allow traffic from the IP addresses or domain names of your web site and the order-processing site.

Implementing this configuration will also put you at odds with the employees who are using the database remotely. Before you implement this plan, you'll want to think about how you're going to get them from the public Internet to the database server living on a private network. Perhaps you'll put an old desktop up on the public Internet to serve as a gateway into the private network. Or maybe you'll create a secure tunnel through the public web server. In either case, you have some homework to do before proposing this security improvement.

Now that we've looked at an example of setting up security, we'll move on to a collection of suggestions for ensuring your system is secure.

Securing Your Whole System: Seven Major Areas

Because your system is built with various parts, deciding how to secure a database involves a lot more than just protecting the database itself. When deciding how to protect your data, you should be thinking about methods to secure physical access to the server, operating system, files and processes, network, database configuration, users and application access, and the data itself.

Physical Access to the Server

Even if your account permissions are locked down to the most granular details, if people have physical access to a server, they could power down the machine, pull network cables, or take drives out of the database machine. If users can power cycle the server and boot from a CD in the drive, they can easily mount up drives and have full root access to the data on those drives.

While tales of social engineering to convince a data center operator to grant unauthorized physical access to a server seem far-fetched, consider how long it takes your organization to communicate word that an employee has lost access rights. Will security personnel at your data center know in time that an employee has lost rights to the server room if that employee immediately drives (or takes the elevator) to where your servers are housed and attempts to gain access?

Here are a few suggestions to secure physical access:

Lock the server: Do you have a database running on a machine under a desk in an office that gets cleaned during the night? Do the employees on the cleaning crew know not to unplug cords or dust near the power switch of your servers? If your database machines are in a location that is traveled by other people (strangers or employees), consider getting a locking rack, or at least machines with keyed power or a lockable front bezel. In larger organizations, considering using an access card and physical log for the name, time, and purpose for physical access. Even if you trust your employees, logging the entry to the server area sends a message about the importance of caution during physical interaction with the machines. In some cases, it may deter an employee from being at the machine when not necessary.

Protect the cords: Are your machines locked up tight, but receiving power or network connectivity via a publicly accessible area? You may want to move your machines or rack to a place where intentional or accidental removing of cables is not a risk to your server.

Protect remote hardware: The physical security of your machines might extend to physical protection of external hardware. Do you have a laptop or desktop somewhere that has passwords stored or public-key authentication to the database servers? Even if you don't store passwords in a file on your system, if your SSH or database tools have the Remember Password box checked, you should treat your desktop or laptop computer as if it were part of the set of machines necessary to physically protect.

Consider off-site hosting: If you have your servers in-house (or in-office), but use them over a network, you might look into co-location or dedicated server services to provide a secure environment for your machines. In most cases, a data center will provide better physical protection on your machine than you can at an office.

Protect backups: If you have a backup of your system written to tape or onto another server, that physical storage should be protected as rigorously as the servers themselves are guarded.

These are just a few ideas about how you might protect your servers. Since there are so many variables in controlling physical access to your servers, we recommend that you look closely at your particular situation and implement any measures that would improve the physical security of your machines.

Operating System

Taking the time to properly configure and secure your database accounts will be pointless if your operating system remains open to intruders. A user could get access to the root account on your server via a security hole in the operating system (or an application or library on the server) and be able to do a lot of damage—copy, remove, or change database files; reset the root MySQL password (or any other password on the system); and more. Even without root access, if a user can execute commands with the privileges of an existing user on the system, he may be able to copy the data files onto another system.

To ensure a machine is secure, be diligent about keeping the applications and libraries on your machines up-to-date, especially when a known exploit is announced for a piece of code on your server. Be sure, in cases like SSL libraries, that any dependent applications are rebuilt with the newest libraries.

■**Tip** Many books are dedicated to operating system security. For example, *Hardening Windows*, by Jonathan Hassell (Apress, 2004), and *Hardening Linux*, by James Turnbull (Apress, 2005) provide thorough coverage of securing your operating system.

Files, Directories, and Processes

An extension of the operating system, the files, directories, and processes on your server also need to be protected to secure your database. If a user has read access to the directory and files of your database, she can easily copy them to another server and have MySQL load them. With access to the MySQL binary logs, a user can view any insert, update, or delete statements in the database. Having this information exposed is almost as bad as having the data files themselves open.

Here are a few suggestions to secure access to files, directories, and processes:

Run MySQL as a non-root user: This is one of the critical items on the MySQL security quick list presented earlier in the chapter. We want to stress that it's important to make sure your database is running as a non-root user, to protect the resources on your server.

Protect the socket file: Make sure your `mysql.sock` file, used for database interactions on the local machine, is protected. This file is typically stored in the `/tmp` directory (`/tmp/mysql.sock`). On some operating systems, any user can remove files from the `/tmp` directory. Removing `mysql.sock` will prevent any interaction with the database. To protect against this, you can either set permissions on `/tmp` files or move `mysql.sock` to another location using the `socket=/path/to/socket` option in your database and client configuration. Refer to `http://dev.mysql.com/doc/mysql/en/problems-with-mysql-sock.html` for more information about protecting the `mysql.sock` file.

Secure log files: If you are logging database activity, include your log files in the list of files to secure. Give log files read and write permissions to only the `mysql` user (and perhaps the `mysql` group).

Consider an encrypted file system: If protecting your data files is critical, you might consider using an encrypted file system, which will store data on the disks in an encrypted format. An encrypted file system means that even if your disk is removed from the machine and mounted elsewhere, your data is still protected (provided the key hasn't been discovered). Using an encrypted file system adds overhead in retrieving and saving data. Also, you'll need to account for encrypted files when backing up and restoring data.

Prevent symbolic links: If you don't need to use symbolic links, disable this feature by specifying the `skip-symbolic-links` option in the database configuration (see Chapter 14). This will prevent users from creating symbolic links within MySQL to files they don't have permission to view but can get to through the server (running MySQL as root makes this problem even more serious). However, in some cases, using a symbolic link for tables is necessary to spread the data across several different disks for space and performance.

Just as when you're protecting access to data and database management functions from within MySQL, it is important to look at all the user accounts on your server and determine how to make sure the data and log files are available to only those who have authorization to access the files. Some pieces of this will be implemented with the security plan; others are just a part of being diligent about locking down your system.

Network

The network is another point of entry to your database, and it should be a part of your security audit on your database servers. As we've suggested earlier in this chapter, if you don't need network access on your MySQL server, turn it off. There's no reason to leave it up and listening if it's not being used. It poses an unnecessary security threat.

Here are a few other ideas for securing your network:

Restrict host connections: Use the `HOST` field restrictively in your `GRANT` statements, making sure that you are granting access only to connection requests from a set of specific DNS or IP addresses.

Secure traffic: If network connectivity is required for your database server, use a private network or SSL encryption for the data. If funds allow, obtain an extra network interface for each server and a switch to run the traffic through. For instances where the private network isn't an option, use MySQL's SSL encryption, or set up a secure tunnel using SSH or an SSL tunnel. If the only reason you need networking is for users to query the data from their desktop, you might consider creating a shell account that provides the ability to log in to the database or run administrative tools.

Use a firewall: Adding a firewall to your machine not only blocks unwanted MySQL traffic, but it is also good practice for keeping your operating system secure.

Use IP addresses if your DNS is unreliable: If you don't have a trusted DNS source, use IP addresses for connection control. An untrusted DNS means that you can't be sure that someone won't change the entry for `trustedhost.promysql.com` to `untrusted.badhacker.net`. In this case, your database, thinking connections are allowed from `trustedhost.promysql.com`, would let the connection through, even though the request was really coming from an untrusted machine.

These are a few things to think about when looking at access to your data over a network. Your server configuration might call for additional considerations, which should be carefully weighed when choosing the right protection for your database networking.

User Access

User access is where most of the action happens when securing the data in your database. This involves creating accounts, granting access to databases and tables, restricting users to connections from certain hosts, and so on. Refer to Chapter 15 for specifics on how to set up and modify user accounts.

As we noted in the MySQL security quick list earlier in the chapter, when you first get MySQL up and running, be sure to set the root password. By default, this password is blank, which allows anyone on the server to connect as root. Then don't use the root account to manage your database. Set up another account for that purpose. We also said that you should remove the anonymous user account, which is part of the default table setup in MySQL. For more information on securing initial MySQL accounts, see `http://dev.mysql.com/doc/mysql/en/default-privileges.html`.

Other areas related to user access include passwords, account privileges, and connections, as discussed in the following sections.

Requiring Passwords

You should require passwords, and make sure that they are good ones. MySQL doesn't enforce periodic password changes; in fact, it doesn't enforce having passwords at all. When you create a user account, make sure the user is assigned a password or creates a good password. You may choose to manually force a password change periodically, but it's a social, not technical process. Users can reset their passwords by using this command:

```
SET PASSWORD FOR '<user>'@'localhost' = PASSWORD('newpwd');
```

Controlling Account Privileges

The following are a few ideas for controlling account privileges:

- Grant the minimal amount of access necessary for users to do their work. Do not fall into the trap of thinking that you don't have time now, so you will just grant everything and then come back and fix the permissions later. This is dangerous, because you're probably not thinking of the entire set of data (if you're in a rush), and the chances you'll come back later and make changes are slim (based on personal experience).

- Don't grant access at all, if it can be avoided. The user who runs a report once a year probably doesn't need access if you can have another user or administrator store the query and run it for him. The best security for an account is to not have the account at all.

- Never grant access, or permission to directly change, the MySQL privilege tables. If a user has INSERT, UPDATE, or DELETE privileges on the `mysql.user` table, she can make all kinds of trouble. We recommend using the GRANT syntax for controlling all accounts and permissions.

- Grant the PROCESS and SUPER privileges only to database administrators, and with caution. With these permissions, a user can issue a SHOW PROCESSLIST command, which allows the user to see all queries issued against the database, including password resets.

- Grant the FILE privilege only to administrative users. This privilege allows a user to create files on the file system as the user running MySQL (underscoring why you shouldn't be running mysqld as the root user).

- Rather than giving a user direct access to a table or set of tables, create a stored procedure that contains the statements he needs to run and give him only the ability to connect to the database and execute that procedure.

- If the user only needs to view certain pieces of data, create a view that is not updatable that contains only the data she requires.

Controlling Connections

A major part of securing your database is controlling the connections to the database. Denying connections is your first defense in keeping unauthorized people and actions out of your database. Here are some ways that you can control connections:

- Revoke the ability for the root to connect from anywhere except from the localhost. This assumes you have a shell account on the database server. If you do not, you may want to change the host of the root to a specific domain name or IP address to ensure that there is only one place to connect as root.

- Restrict the number of connections that can be made by a user.

- Restrict the number of bad connection attempts that can come from a host before connections are blocked, using the max_connect_errors setting (see Chapter 14). By default, this is limited to 10, which usually works well.

- Force SSL connections from remote hosts, unless you know the hostname is coming from a private network. This is done by adding REQUIRE SSL or REQUIRE X509 in the GRANT statement.

■**Note** As mentioned earlier in the chapter, MySQL doesn't have SSL enabled by default. In order to use SSL connections, you must install the OpenSSL libraries on your system and build MySQL yourself to enable SSL support. See Chapter 14 for details on compiling and configuring MySQL.

Securing user accounts is an ongoing process. You should periodically look through your user (and other permission tables) and verify that the policies you have defined are still intact. As time passes, different users touch the system, new functionality in the database and application are added, and your security policy changes. Doing an audit of the user accounts in MySQL is a good way to pinpoint potential security holes and get them closed before an incident.

Application Access

Building a secure application is important to protecting your database. The security of the data is closely tied to how well the application protects the data from attacks.

When the data is extremely sensitive, you may choose to not create a general-use application account. You may do this if you want to be sure you have authentication credentials presented via the application for any change in the data. This can be a headache to maintain, especially if you don't create scripts or procedures to manage the accounts. However, having accounts specifically assigned to users means you control the ability to change data from the MySQL permissions structure and don't need to rely on the application to manage permissions. Also, when a change is made with the binary log enabled, you have a trail of changes that can be tied to specific user connections.

In most instances with a web application, a general-use account for connections from the application will be easier to deal with and more appropriate. Be careful when creating accounts used by the application to read and manipulate records in your database. If your system is heavy on reads, you may want to create an account with SELECT-only permissions to be used in most places in the application. Create a more privileged user to perform data-manipulation tasks.

Data Storage and Encryption

Up to this point, we've looked at only how to protect access to or prevent unauthorized changes of data, not the data itself. As we've said before, because the contents of databases vary wildly—from grocery lists to banking transactions—you should assess how secure your data must be. For most applications, protection against getting into the database is enough. However, in some cases, the data in the database requires an extra layer of protection.

For instances where data is extremely sensitive and damaging to individuals if tampered with, you might want to consider using one-way encryption, two-way encryption, or no encryption at all (by not storing the data in your system). We'll take a brief look at each of these approaches here. For details on encryption functions in MySQL, refer to http://dev.mysql.com/doc/mysql/en/encryption-functions.html.

One-Way Encryption

Use one-way encryption for information that doesn't need to be reversed. This technique is used for passwords. The password is encrypted once with a nonreversible algorithm, and then on future attempts to verify the password, the data is run through the algorithm again and compared to the previously computed result.

Functions in MySQL for one-way encryption are password(), old_password(), md5(), encrypt(), and sha1(). These functions are easy to use, and like all functions, are embedded directly into your SQL statements, as in this example:

```
mysql> SELECT sha1("a horrible secret") AS sha1;
```

The following is the result from this SELECT statement:

```
+------------------------------------------+
| sha1                                     |
+------------------------------------------+
| 06bc43a7c4c03fb37553c3f42bad928c9a8d1aa1 |
+------------------------------------------+
1 row in set (0.00 sec)
```

■**Caution** Do not invent your own encryption algorithm. Many well-tested and widely used algorithms are available in MySQL to produce cryptographically secure results.

Two-Way Encryption

Two-way encryption functions allow you to encrypt data using a value and a key. With the encrypted value and the key, you can get back to the original value.

MySQL functions that support two-way encryption are aes_encrypt(), aes_decrypt(), encode(), decode(), des_encrypt(), and des_decrypt(). The Advanced Encryption Standard (AES) is currently regarded as the most sound encryption routines currently available in MySQL. The encoding is performed with a 128-bit key, which is significantly secure and still speedy.

■**Note** The Data Encryption Standard (DES) functions work only if MySQL has been compiled with SSL support, and uses DES key files from the file system.

As with other MySQL functions, you use the two-way encryption functions directly in your SQL statements, as in this example:

```
mysql> SELECT aes_decrypt(aes_encrypt("a horrible secret","SecRet"),
"SecRet") AS AES;
```

Because the AES functions generate binary information, an attempt to show the output from the function in text is futile. In this example, we are encrypting a string with the key "SecRet", and then immediately decrypting the result of that encryption using the same key. This use wouldn't be that useful in your application, but it demonstrates using two-way encryption. Here is the output of the statement:

```
+-------------------+
| AES               |
+-------------------+
| a horrible secret |
+-------------------+
1 row in set (0.00 sec)
```

Attempting to use the incorrect key for decryption will result in a NULL response from the decryption function:

```
mysql> SELECT aes_decrypt(aes_encrypt("a horrible secret","SecRet"),
"PubLic") AS AES;
+-----+
| AES |
+-----+
| NULL|
+-----+
1 row in set (0.00 sec)
```

Two-way encryption functions in MySQL provide a powerful tool for encrypting data so its value in the database is meaningless unless coupled with the key for decryption.

No Encryption

The most reassuring way of keeping data secured in your system is to not have the data stored anywhere in your system. Yes, that sounds obvious, but it is an important option to think about.

When you accept a credit card in your application, is it really necessary to keep the credit card information in your database? If part of your application fires off a request to a third party to charge the card and credit your account, you may not need to keep the credit card information around after that point. If your payment-processing vendor creates an entry in its system and passes back a token that can be used for future reference, storing that key in your database and using it, instead of the credit card number, makes more sense. As the processing of the order moves through your system, you don't need to worry about the sensitive nature of that credit card number, because it is not housed anywhere in your system as the processing of the order moves along.

Summary

We've been through a lot of information regarding security. We started by discussing the importance of understanding security requirements and making a security policy and implementation plan before undertaking the actual work of making changes in your database. You saw that security involves much more than just looking at what tables a user can access. It starts early on when decisions are made about what and how data will be stored and who will have access to that data. Once decisions have been made (please document those, it will save you a lot of time), you can put together a road map for implementing the plan, including building tools to manage the security policy.

Next, we considered a real-world scenario and the steps a database administrator might take to make sure the database was properly secured from unauthorized access. Then we dove into seven major areas to consider when reviewing and attempting to improve the security of your database: physical access, operating system, files and directories, network, user access, application access, and data storage. Each of these sections offered suggestions for improving the security of your system.

Remember that, in many cases, the biggest security threat is internal to your organization. Yes, you do want to protect against the bad hacker who is running a port scan across your system. However, you also need to have measures in place to secure against intentional and accidental attacks from within. You don't want the experience of having an innocent developer accidentally delete everything in a table in the production database, where he had no reason being, just because he got mixed up and issued the command intended for the development database.

The important goal is to get your system to a state where you are relatively comfortable with the security you have in place. It's not easy to get to this state, because it seems you can always find room for improvement. Just moving in this direction will help your system and make you feel better about your security. Oh, and it will also help you sleep better at night.

Backup and Restoration

Data continues to become more important to the functioning of organizations and the services they provide to customers. Along with this trend, the value of the organization becomes more centered on the availability of the data. This reinforces the importance of having backups of data readily available to reduce interruptions in service should the data become unavailable or compromised. Even though the consequences of not having a backup can be detrimental to the organization (and employee), commitment to backing up data varies.

Backups are often left until the last minute, which means they are done in a hurry and without proper consideration to the requirements of the backup. The method to restore data gets even less attention.

This chapter begins by reviewing the reasons, requirements, and principles of backing up and restoring data. Then it covers the specific backup and restore methods available in MySQL. We will cover the following topics related to backing up and restoring data in MySQL:

- Reasons for creating backups

- Backup and restoration planning

- Methods for backing up and restoring MySQL data, including `mysqldump`, `mysqlhotcopy`, InnoDB backups, and MySQL Administrator

- Binary logs for up-to-date tables

Why Do We Create Backups?

Perhaps this seems the question of a novice, but have you ever asked yourself why you are (or should be) backing up your data? If you asked that question of several people in your organization, you might be surprised that you get a variety of answers. There are many reasons for having backups of data, and those reasons affect how you should implement both your backup strategy and your recovery strategy.

Here are some of the reasons why you might create a backup of your database:

- Computer hardware is not 100% reliable. You back up your data so that if your database server or disks have a hardware failure, you have a snapshot that can be used to bring back the data.

- Human interactions with the database aren't reliable. Whether accidental or intentional, people working in the database can cause unwanted changes in the data, requiring a restore from a backup.

- Programs have bugs, or unexpected interactions with the database, and you may find that your application is making unwanted changes in your data. With a backup, you can return to a previous version of the data.

- A backup of a database can sometimes be used to preserve a snapshot of the data for historical reasons. These backups might be kept around for years.

- Servers can be compromised and need to be rebuilt. If you have a snapshot of your data from before the breach, you'll be able to go back to that point once the server is rebuilt.

- Viruses, SQL-injection, and other web-based scripting attacks can bring down your database server or play tricks with the data in your database, requiring a restoration.

- Having a backup allows you to run tests against data, and then quickly restore the data to a previous state. Most testing of a system backed with data relies on data being in a certain state. Having a backup of that state allows you to easily return to that state to rerun the tests.

- In some instances, you might want a periodic backup with just the database structure, without any data. This can be useful if you need to share your schema with other people or systems, or for version control of the structure.

- You may need to export data to other systems. Perhaps you have a local copy of the database running on a desktop for running statistics queries, or you have a testing server for releasing new code that requires a production database refresh. The database snapshot from a backup is also helpful in setting up a replicated database.

■**Tip** Jeremy Zawodny created a tool, called `mysqlsnapshot`, for creating snapshots of your database, intended for use when creating a point-in-time view of the data to transfer to another machine to be the base data for starting a replicated server. You can download `mysqlsnapshot` from the project page he maintains (`http://jeremy.zawodny.com/mysql/mysqlsnapshot/`).

You may back up your data for one or many of these reasons, or other reasons. Your backup needs are the basis for your backup and restore plan, as described next.

Creating a Backup and Restore Plan

If you've held any responsibility for data backups and restorations, you've probably had the experience of a user requesting something from the backup that wasn't available. You then needed to clarify exactly what could and couldn't be done with a backup. Maybe the user was looking for a few hundred records that were deleted from a table three weeks ago, and you explained that backups are kept for only one week.

If you've had a conversation like this, you may have been asked to clarify precisely what is and isn't available through the backups of the system. This kind of interaction with users of your data points to the need for a backup plan, which includes both how the data is backed up and how it is restored.

If you need motivation to take the time to properly develop a backup plan, imagine that tomorrow when you get to work (or you were woken up by the phone), every one of your databases, on all of your live database servers, had been dropped. Where does that leave you? Do you have the data somewhere, and how easy is it to get to for a restoration?

If you're wondering why you need a restore plan, imagine you have a backup of every table in your database, allowing you to restore a single table. After you restore a single table (that had 100 rows accidentally deleted), you realize that there are problems with dependencies from other tables. You now have orphaned records after the restoration, all because you didn't have time to think through all the relationships and restore the referencing tables. Without a practiced plan and set of methods in place to restore the data, you may find that restoring the files from the backup does not bring the data back to the correct state.

Developing Your Backup Plan

The backup plan should be a document that outlines the requirements for your backup strategy and implementation. Owners and users of the data should be a significant part of creating this document. Stakeholders are ultimately the people who must deal with the loss of data, and they should be at the table helping define what the backup plan should look like. The data owners and users will be able to provide a lot of detail on when and how the data is used, and what types of situations might arise that would require data restoration. Getting a sense for what the users prioritize as reasons to keep a backup of the data will help in determining the implementation details for your backup. Having the stakeholders and technical folks at the same table allows technical folks to give input on what is technically possible (outside of uncommitted transactions, there is no "undo" button in MySQL).

Once you have been refreshed on how the other stakeholders use the data, and have a sense of why and how stakeholders would use a backup, you should discuss the implementation details. The following are some questions to pose:

- How often should the backups run? Depending on the application, this might be weekly, nightly, or even every hour.

- Does all the data require the same backup interval? Some data might never change, and some data may change constantly. Should you back up everything once a week and certain other databases or tables every night?

- How long should backups be preserved? Is two days' worth of history enough, or do you need to provide a month's worth of backup?

- Where should the backup be stored? Is it necessary to have it on the database server for faster restoration, or should it be moved to a remote server for protection against theft or disaster? Should it be on disks or on a tape? Should a copy be kept off-site?

- Is it acceptable to lose any data? It's possible that your backup plan will leave gaps in the data. For example, suppose you have a nightly backup, and you plan to use the binary logs to bring any of your tables up-to-date. If the database server goes down, and the data is not available, you've lost access to the binary logs. A restore from the backup brings you up-to-date with last night's backup, but without the binary logs, you have no way to bring the database up to what was last available on your now-unavailable database. Replication, discussed in Chapter 18, can help solve this problem.

All of these questions will lead to the technical details for implementing the backup plan. The answers to these questions will also be directly tied to how the data is restored.

■**Note** In some cases, the requirements for a backup are better met by database replication. With a replicated database, a current, live copy of the data is maintained on a separate server and can be brought into service without the trouble of restoring data from another disk or tape. A replicated server doesn't solve data integrity or deletion issues, as it mirrors the primary database, but it can be available when the primary database or database server becomes unavailable. See Chapter 18 for more information about replication.

Developing Your Restore Plan

The conversation and document outlining the backup plan is incomplete if it does not address the process of restoring data. While you have the stakeholders and technical people in the room, be sure to get their input on how the data is restored to the database server.

The following are some questions to address to help define the restore policy:

- Who, of the data owners, is authorized to request that a table be restored to a previous state? Maybe you can agree on a list of people or positions that are authorized to make the request.

- What is the process of identifying a needed restoration, communicating the restoration request, and having the data restored? In most cases, data restorations are critical, and the natural process is for the data owner to make a frantic call or visit to the database administrator, who drops everything and processes the request for restored data. Documenting that process, with office locations, phone numbers, and e-mail addresses, will help during those frantic moments.

- Who, of the technical staff, is authorized to have access to the backup files and the necessary permission to restore data? If you have a large staff of database folks, only some of them might have access to the server and data. Does that need to be expanded so someone is always available to help in a data emergency?

- How does the data owner or user specify what to restore? Depending on what happened with the data to require a restoration from backup, it might be difficult to specify what needs to be restored. If there is a single table that was dropped, the administrator will most likely need to restore the data from the most recent backup, and then bring the table current with statements from the binary log. If the problem was with an update that went awry, the administrator will need to restore the table, and then run the binary logs up until the statement immediately before the UPDATE statement. This requires some detailed communication, and might prompt you to write a clause in the backup plan requiring the database administrator and data owner to sit together and restore the data.

- What are the restrictions on how data can be restored, based on the database constraints? You might have rules that say if one table gets restored to a previous state, the five tables that rely on it will also be restored. It's easy to create a mess in your database if you restore tables that leave orphaned records in other tables.

- What kind of downtime is acceptable while the restoration is happening? When restoring data to the database, the data will not be available for a period of time. Depending on the type of restoration, you might need to take the database server offline completely while the files are copied back. The downtime is exacerbated by larger tables, which require more time to restore.

- If there's a chance some data will be lost during a restore from backup, is that acceptable? Suppose you had a backup of the data from last night, but your database server went down today and lost all the data from this morning.

The process of deciding and defining how the backup and restoration will work will likely go through many iterations as the needs for your database are discovered and ironed out. This policy will be refined by application in real-world situations within your organization. The finalized plan should be available to all stakeholders for reference and reviewed regularly. Each time a situation arises where a restore from a backup is needed, the plan should be consulted to ensure that the backup and restoration met the outlined plan.

Backing Up a Database: A Quick Example

If you aren't interested in wading through the details of the various types of backup, this section is for you. Ideally, you should be aware of all your options and thoughtfully consider the different methods for backing up your data. However, we're aware that you don't always have time to consider all the options. In this case, mysqldump is a quick way to create a backup of an entire database or tables in a database.

The mysqldump program generates a set of SQL statements that you can send into MySQL to re-create the table and data using DROP TABLE, CREATE TABLE, and INSERT statements.

For this simple example, we'll use mysqldump in a way that accepts a database and table name, in this form:

```
shell> mysqldump <database> <table> > backup_file.sql
```

For example, to create a backup of the customer table in the shop database, use this statement:

```
shell> mysqldump -u backup_user -p shop customer > customer_backup.sql
```

The -u (username) and -p (password) options are used for the database connection. Details on using command-line arguments with mysqldump are covered in the next section of this chapter. The output, which was put into the customer_backup.sql file, is shown in Listing 17-1 (some comments and optional SET statements have been removed for clarity).

Listing 17-1. *Output of mysqldump for the customer Table*

```
-- Host: localhost     Database: shop
-- -------------------------------------------------------

-- Table structure for table `customer`
DROP TABLE IF EXISTS `customer`;
CREATE TABLE `customer` (
  `customer_id` int(11) NOT NULL auto_increment,
  `name` varchar(10) default NULL,
  PRIMARY KEY  (`customer_id`)
) ENGINE=InnoDB DEFAULT CHARSET=latin1;

-- Dumping data for table `customer`
LOCK TABLES `customer` WRITE;
INSERT INTO `customer` VALUES (1,'Mike'),(2,'Jay'),(3,'Johanna'),
(4,'Michael'),(5,'Heidi'),(6,'Ezra');
UNLOCK TABLES;
```

To restore the customer table to the same state that it was in when you created the backup, you simply send that file to the mysql client with the database where MySQL should re-create the table:

```
shell> mysql -u restore_user -p shop < customer_backup.sql
```

This is a very simplistic view of backing up and restoring MySQL data, but it does work. Read on for more details on mysqldump and other backup utilities available for MySQL.

Using MySQL Tools to Make and Restore Backups

After you've discovered your backup requirements and created a policy for your backup and restore practices, you are ready to dig into the technical details of creating a backup and restoring from it. We've whetted your appetite in the previous section with a quick overview of one of the tools, and will now go through a complete set of options, including mysqldump, mysqlhotcopy, InnoDB Hot Backup, innobackup, and the MySQL Administrator tools.

■**Note** This discussion does not cover the methods for backing up a MySQL cluster or data in tables using the NDB Cluster storage engine. You can use mysqldump, which works with all storage engines, or the cluster tools built specifically for backing up the data across the cluster nodes. The cluster management console provides a command to initiate a backup of the data and another command to restore data. These commands are covered in Chapter 19.

FILE SYSTEM BACKUPS

You may already have a backup process for your file system. Many hosting services, data centers, and server rooms have a network-based backup system in place that you can subscribe to. In that case, using a file system backup might make it more convenient to create backups. It's also a way to ensure that everything about your database gets backed up, including configuration and log files.

However, unless you are stopping your database or read-locking all tables when the backup happens, the actual data files aren't well suited for the typical file system backup. Your database files may be actively changing during the backup, and you can't be sure how consistent your data will be if you've simply had those files copied to another location. In addition, if you are using in-memory (heap) tables, a file system backup of those tables will not capture that data, because the data stored in heap tables does not get written to disk (for efficiency and speed purposes).

A possible solution is to use one of the other MySQL backup tools in conjunction with the file system backups. You might do a `mysqldump` of your database into a specific directory, and then have the backup of the files taken care of by the file system backup. The dump gives you a consistent snapshot, and the file system backup provides the remote storage and history of the dump.

If you do need to restore some data, and a file system backup of the native data files is all you have to work with, have the files or directory restored to your server, and then shut down the database to move the previous files into the correct location on the server. Even though it is not the recommended method for backing up and restoring a database, we have seen it work in a pinch.

Using mysqldump

A utility called `mysqldump` is installed along with MySQL client programs. `mysqldump` takes the current structure and data in your database and converts them into sets of SQL statements that can be used to re-create the table structures and data. `mysqldump` is an excellent option for smaller databases, if you're running backups remotely, or if you aren't using the MyISAM table type. This tool works with all storage engines, and it can output SQL formatted to match a number of different standards and database systems.

■**Caution** Currently (as of MySQL version 5.0.6), the `mysqlbackup` program does not capture all meta information about a database or table. Triggers are not a part of any dump, and stored procedures and functions are dumped with only a `mysqldump` of the `mysql.proc` table. View creation statements are included in the output of the database.

Backing Up with mysqldump

`mysqldump` gives you numerous options to control the output of the SQL statements. Depending on what you're attempting to back up, you can run the utility in three ways:

- To back up a single table, or a few tables from a single database, use a statement like this:

```
mysqldump [<options>] <database> [<table> <table>. . .]
```

- To back up multiple databases, but not all of them, use the command arrangement shown here:

```
mysqldump [<options>] --databases [<options>] <database
[database database. . .]>
```

- To back up all the databases in the MySQL server, use this form:

```
mysqldump [<options>] --all-databases [<options>]
```

For any of the three ways, using options will let you control the specifics of what and how the output is created. Table 17-1 describes common mysqldump options. Understanding these options will be helpful when you are working on the policy for backing up and restoring data, and will enable you to guide the policy based on technical feasibility. Additionally, knowing which options are available will help you implement the backup and restore policy.

■Tip The options for mysqldump can be included in your configuration files, as well as specified on the command line. mysqldump reads options from the [client] and [mysqldump] configuration groups. For more information about using configuration files, refer to Chapter 14.

Table 17-1. *Common mysqldump Options*

Option	Description
-A, --all-databases	Include all databases in output.
--add-drop-table	Put a DROP TABLE statement before each CREATE ➥ TABLE. This is useful if you are importing the dump file into a database to replace existing tables.
--add-locks	Surround each INSERT statement with a LOCK statement.
--allow-keywords	Allow column names to be created using keywords.
--character-sets-dir=<dir>	Location of directory with character sets.
-i, --comments	Add comments to the dump file. This is useful for making notes about the dump.
--compatible=<name>	Specify a mode for the dump. The default is a dump optimized for MySQL. Modes can be ansi, mysql323, mysql40, postgresql, oracle, mssql, db2, maxdb, no_key_options, no_table_options, or no_field_options. You can use several modes, using a comma to separate them.
--compact	mysqldump output is less verbose. Removes header, footer, and structure comments. Using this option also enables --skip-add-drop-table, --no-set-names, --skip-disable-keys, and --skip-lock-tables.

Option	Description
-c, --complete-insert	When building INSERT statements, include field names in INSERT statements. This is helpful if you're dumping data to put into another table that has additional columns.
--create-options	Use MySQL-specific options in CREATE statements.
-B, --databases	Use to dump one or more databases, specified as arguments after this option. A USE <database> statement is added to the output.
--default-character-set=<value>	Specify the default character set to be used.
--delayed-insert	All INSERT statements generated will be INSERT ➡ DELAYED.
--delete-master-logs	After the backup is complete, delete the master logs. --master-data is also enabled with this option.
-K, --disable-keys	Two statements will be wrapped around the sets of INSERT statements for a table, /*!40000 ALTER TABLE tb_name DISABLE KEYS */; and /*!40000 ALTER TABLE tb_name ENABLE KEYS ➡ */;. Having keys disabled improves performance of the restore operation.
-e, --extended-insert	Use the multirecord INSERT syntax, where a single INSERT statement contains multiple value sets and is significantly faster. Starting with MySQL version 5.0, this option is on by default.
--fields-terminated-by=<value>	Used with the --tab option, allows you to specify a character or set of characters to insert after each field when the records are saved into the tab-delimited file.
--fields-enclosed-by=<value>	Used with the --tab option, allows you to specify a character or set of characters to enclose each field with when the records are saved into the tab-delimited file.
--fields-optionally-enclosed-by=<value>	Used with the --tab option, allows you to specify a character or set of characters to optionally enclose each field with when the records are saved into the tab-delimited file. Optionally means that the field won't be enclosed if it's not necessary according to the SQL rules. String fields (CHAR, VARCHAR, and so on) are enclosed, and numeric fields (INTEGER, FLOAT, and so on) are not.
--fields-escaped-by=<value>	Used with the --tab option, allows you to specify a character to place in front of any tab, newline, or \ character that appear within fields.

Continued

Table 17-1. *Continued*

Option	Description
-F, --flush-logs	Before the dump is started, flush the server log files. Each database mysqldump encounters will cause mysqldump to flush the log files. If you are dumping multiple databases with --databases or --all-databases, and don't want the logs flushed every time, use the --lock-all-tables or --master-data option. If either of those options is specified, mysqldump will flush the logs once, at the time the lock is obtained on all the tables.
-f, --force	Report errors as they occur but keep processing statements.
-?, --help	Show the help information.
--hex-blob	Fields that are binary strings (BLOB, BINARY, and VARBINARY) are put into the output file in hexadecimal format.
-h, --host=<*name*>	The server to connect to when running the dump. This can be an IP address or DNS name.
--lines-terminated-by=<*value*>	In conjunction with the --tab option, allows you to specify a character or set of characters to end the lines in the tab-delimited file.
-x, --lock-all-tables	Get a read lock for all tables, across all databases while the dump occurs. With this option, --lock-tables and --single-transaction are disabled.
-l, --lock-tables	Before the dump starts, lock all the tables that are going to be dumped.
--master-data[=<*number*>]	Put the filename and binary log position in the dump file. Specifying a value of 1 adds a CHANGE ➥ MASTER statement with the master log position and filename, which causes the slave to start from that file and position. A value of 2 (the default) writes the same CHANGE MASTER statement, but puts it in a comment for reader reference. Specifying this option requires the RELOAD privilege.
--max_allowed_packet=<*number*>	Set the maximum allowed buffer size, which is used for communication between the client and server. This can be set as high as 1GB.
--net_buffer_length=<*number*>	Set the initial buffer size for communication between client and server. Be sure the --net_buffer_length of the server is at least as large as what you're setting for mysqldump.
--no-autocommit	Before each set of INSERT statements that create a table's worth of data, add an autocommit=0; statement. After each table, commit the INSERTs. This is applicable only if you are restoring data into tables that use a storage engine that supports transactions.

Option	Description
`-n, --no-create-db`	Don't put any database `CREATE` statements in the dump. This option applies only to instances where you are dumping entire databases with `--database` or `--all-databases`. This is useful if you are backing up and restoring tables within a database or the entire database, but aren't dropping the database as a part of your restoration.
`-t, --no-create-info`	Don't put table creation statements into the dump. As with `--no-create-db`, this option is useful if you are planning on restoring a single table by doing a `TRUNCATE <table>;` or `DELETE ➥ FROM <table>;` and then importing the records. In either case, you leave the table intact and want only the `INSERT` statements for the restoration, not the `CREATE TABLE` statement.
`-d, --no-data`	Do not put any `INSERT` statements used to re-create the records in the table or database. For example, use this if you need a snapshot of the database structure, but not any of the data.
`--opt`	A shortcut option to turning on several common options. Using `--opt` has the same effect as using `--quick`, `--disable-keys`, `--lock-tables`, `--add-drop-table`, `--add-locks`, `--create-options`, `--extended-insert`, and `--set-charset`. This option is enabled by default. It can be turned off by using `--skip-opt`.
`-p, --password[=password]`	Use the password provided on the command line to connect to the database, or prompt for one on the terminal if the password isn't specified.
`-P, --port=<number>`	Use this port to connect to the database server.
`--protocol=<name>`	Specify the protocol used to connect to the MySQL server. Valid values are `tcp`, `socket`, `pipe`, and `memory`.
`-q, --quick`	Send the dump directly to standard output, without buffering the query.
`-Q, --quote-names`	Use backticks to quote column and table names. This reduces problems with spacing and reserved words.
`-r, --result-file=<name>`	Put the output from the dump into the specified file, rather than to standard output. On Windows, this option prevents newlines (\n) from becoming a carriage return and line feed (\r\n), which is typically not desired on Windows.
`--set-charset`	Insert a `SET NAMES default_character_set` statement into the dump file. This option is enabled by default, but can be turned off with `--skip-set-charset`.

Continued

Table 17-1. *Continued*

Option	Description
--single-transaction	Create a snapshot of tables that is multiversion-capable (as of version 5.0.6, this applies to only InnoDB). If this option is enabled, a BEGIN statement is issued before the dump starts, which gives mysqldump access to the tables as they appeared at the time the BEGIN statement was issued, regardless of how long the dump takes. With this option specified, --lock-tables is disabled.
--skip-opt	Turn off the options that are enabled with the --opt command alias. This disables --quick, --disable-keys, --lock-tables, --add-drop-table, --add-locks, --create-options, --extended-insert, and --set-charset.
-S, --socket=<*file*>	Connect to the MySQL server using this socket file.
-T, --tab=<*dir*>	Create two files for each table being dumped: a file with SQL statements and a tab-separated text file with data. For each table, a <*table name*>.sql file and <*table name*>.txt file are generated in the specified directory. The .sql file contains the table DROP and CREATE statements, and the .txt file contains all the data in tab-delimited format. The --tab option is complemented by the --fields-terminated-by, --fields-enclosed-by, --fields-optionally-enclosed-by, --fields-escaped-by, and --lines-terminated-by options.
--tables	All values after this option are names of tables. This allows you to override the --databases option.
-u, --user=*name*	Connect to the database using this username. By default, MySQL uses the account name of the current user.
-v, --verbose	Generate a helpful printout of statements indicating the steps mysqldump is going through.
-V, --version	Print the version information for mysqldump.
-w, --where=<*WHERE clause*>	Use the specified WHERE clause when selecting data from the database. If you want to dump only certain records from a table, this is the way to do it. A properly formatted where option looks like --where="customer_id > 1 AND ➥ customer_id < 4". The fields specified in the WHERE clause must match fields in the table. The quotation marks around the clause are required.
-X, --xml	Output the table in well-formed XML. XML support in MySQL is limited. For more information about XML and MySQL, see http://solutions.mysql.com/software/?item=292 and http://www.kitebird.com/articles/mysql-xml.html.

As you can see, there is no lack of options when running mysqldump. By putting the right combination of options together, you can adjust the output to what you need. See http://dev.mysql.com/doc/mysql/en/mysqldump.html for more information about mysqldump.

Restoring with mysqldump

Restoring from files created with mysqldump should be fairly straightforward. The restore process doesn't require you to shut down the database, but the default dump locks the tables while they are restored. This can be disabled, but you probably don't want someone making an INSERT into that table during the restoration anyway.

Since the file contains a set of SQL statements, you can usually just send the contents of the file into the MySQL client, like this:

```
shell> mysql <database> < database_backup.sql
```

And the table magically gets restored to its former state.

When you are creating the dump, if you do not specify any options, the file will contain a DROP, CREATE, and set of INSERT statements for each table. If you send that file into the client, it will re-create every table in the dump file with its state at the time of the dump.

However, maybe you don't want to restore the entire database, but just need one table restored. In this instance, you either need to create an individual dump file for that table or parse through the *database_backup*.sql backup file and pull out the DROP, CREATE, and INSERT statements for the table you need to restore. If you have a large database and your dump files are many gigabytes, this process can take a lot of time. If you have some extremely large tables, you may consider creating a few dump files as a part of your backup to ease the work needed to restore the data. Typically, when a restoration is needed, you are under pressure and time is constrained. It's worth the extra work to create restore-ready files when the backup runs. As we noted earlier, an important consideration when deciding what is right for your backup implementation is looking at how the backup will be restored.

mysqldump Backup and Restore Example

Before we move on to the next option for backing up your MySQL database, let's look quickly at an example. Suppose that your backup and restore plan, in its simplest form, was to create a dump of the tables every morning at 6 a.m., and that you would create a dump of just your orders table every hour, on the hour. It is important to have a recent copy of the cust_order table, as your customer support folks are busy entering orders and hate having to reenter orders. On your Unix box, you would create two entries in your crontab,[1] as shown in Listing 17-2.

Listing 17-2. *crontab Entries to Automate Backup*

```
0 6 * * * mysqldump -A > /backup/full_backup-`date +%F`.sql
0 * * * * mysqldump shop cust_order > /backup/cust_order_backup-`date +%F_%R`.sql
```

---

1. A more secure solution is to create a Unix account for backups, with a matching, limited-privileges (just enough to make a backup) MySQL account.

Tip If space is an issue, and your data dump files are large, you may want to add compression to your backup process. To add `bzip2` compression to the first `crontab` entry in Listing 17-2, use this statement: `mysqldump -A | bzip2 -c > /backup/full_backup-`date +%F`.sql.bz2`.

If you put those `crontab` entries from Listing 17-2 in just before 6 a.m. and wait for a few hours, an `ls -1 /backup` will show something like Listing 17-3.

Listing 17-3. *Output of Backup Directory*

```
full_backup-2005-08-05.sql
cust_order_backup-2005-08-05_06:00.sql
cust_order_backup-2005-08-05_07:00.sql
cust_order_backup-2005-08-05_08:00.sql
```

Now, your restore plan indicates that in the case where just the orders table has a problem, you will restore it to the data from the most recent top of the hour. You don't want to take the entire database offline, but just want to replace all the data in that table.

The data in the `cust_order` backup file will look something like Listing 17-4 (we cleaned out some statements for clarity). Note that because we haven't specified to not include them, the DROP TABLE and CREATE TABLE statements are in the file.

Listing 17-4. *Output of mysqldump for the cust_order Table*

```
-- MySQL dump 10.9
-- Host: localhost     Database: shop
-- -------------------------------------------------------

-- Table structure for table `cust_order`
DROP TABLE IF EXISTS `cust_order`;
CREATE TABLE `cust_order` (
  `cust_order_id` int(10) unsigned NOT NULL auto_increment,
  `ship_date` date default NULL,
  `item_sum` decimal(10,2) default NULL,
  `discount_percent` int(2) unsigned default NULL,
  `shipping` decimal(10,2) default '0.00',
  `total` decimal(10,2) default NULL,
  PRIMARY KEY  (`cust_order_id`)
) ENGINE=InnoDB DEFAULT CHARSET=latin1;

-- Dumping data for table `cust_order
LOCK TABLES `cust_order` WRITE;
INSERT INTO `cust_order` VALUES (1,'2005-08-31','30.95',14,'3.25','29.87'),…
UNLOCK TABLES;
```

The command in Listing 17-5 shows that to restore the `cust_order` table to the way it was at 8 a.m. is pretty simple.

Listing 17-5. *Restoring a Single Table*

```
shell> mysql shop < orders_backup-2005-08-05_08:00.sql
```

This runs all of the statements in the backup file into the MySQL database. The table is dropped, created, locked, filled with data from the INSERT statement, and then unlocked.

■**Note** For those of you who are thinking that a backup and recovery plan that allows restored data to be anywhere up to an hour old is a joke, hang on. We understand, and will get to ways to make sure your data is brought up to the last second or statement before the destructive change. Information about restoring using the binary logs is covered in the "Using Binary Logs for Up-to-Date Tables" section later in this chapter.

Using mysqlhotcopy

If you are using the MyISAM storage engine, mysqlhotcopy may be the right choice for your backup implementation. mysqlhotcopy takes advantage of the fact that MyISAM tables are stored in separate files in the data directory on the file system, organized into a directory for each database. mysqlhotcopy is a Perl script that locks tables through a Perl client connection to the database and makes file system copies of the data while the tables are locked, which prevents the tables from changing. After the files are copied, the locks are released.

The primary reason to use mysqlhotcopy over mysqldump is for performance. Using the operating system to copy the data files to a backup location is significantly faster than creating a set of INSERT statements for a table or database of tables. mysqlhotcopy is also pretty easy to use.

However, mysqlhotcopy runs only on Unix and NetWare machines, and requires that the database be stopped to restore a file from the backup. You must run the program on the machine where the MySQL data files are located, which rules out being able to call it from a remote server and place the files on that remote backup machine.

■**Note** mysqlhotcopy is a Perl script. It requires the Perl DBI module and DBD::mysql drivers to be installed on your system.

Backing Up with mysqlhotcopy

To back up with mysqlhotcopy, you issue a command in the following form:

```
mysqlhotcopy <options> <db_name>[<./table regular expression/>] [<new database> |
<directory>]
```

The directory for saving the data files must exist before you run the program, or you will get an error. Listing 17-6 shows the command in its simplest form, using two arguments to create a copy of the shop tables in /backup/shop.

Listing 17-6. *Simple Backup with mysqlhotcopy*

```
shell> mysqlhotcopy shop /backup
```

The regular expression for table matching allows you to be more specific about which tables to copy; for example, you could back up all of your tables having to do with your customers. Listing 17-7 demonstrates the use of regular expressions in the command arguments.

Listing 17-7. *Using a Regular Expression with mysqlhotcopy*

```
shell> mysqlhotcopy shop./cust/ /backup
```

The output from `mysqlhotcopy` steps through what it's doing, as shown in Listing 17-8.

Listing 17-8. *Output from mysqlhotcopy*

```
Locked 2 tables in 0 seconds.
Flushed tables (`shop`.`cust_order`, `shop`.`customer`) in 0 seconds.
Copying 6 files...
Copying indices for 0 files...
Unlocked tables.
mysqlhotcopy copied 2 tables (6 files) in 0 seconds (0 seconds overall).
```

Here, you see that the tables were locked, flushed, copied, and then unlocked. Looking at the backup directory, you will find copies of the two tables, with the data, index, and data dictionary files. Listing 17-9 shows the contents of the /backup/shop directory.

Listing 17-9. *Listing of the /backup/shop Directory*

```
cust_order.MYD
cust_order.MYI
cust_order.frm
customer.MYD
customer.MYI
customer.frm
```

■**Note** If you've ever used the SQL command BACKUP TABLE <table_name> TO '/directory', you'll notice that `mysqlhotcopy` performs a very similar action, although the `mysqlhotcopy` utility is run in the Unix shell instead of MySQL client shell. BACKUP TABLE is deprecated, but it is still available in the current builds of MySQL. RESTORE TABLE is the complementary command to BACKUP TABLE. It pulls the table from the backup directory into the live database. Plans for MySQL version 5.1 include replacements for these commands.

One other way that you can use `mysqlhotcopy` is to create a new database in the active MySQL server, by specifying a database name instead of a directory when running the program. An example of a command for making a new database is shown in Listing 17-10.

Listing 17-10. *Creating a New Database with mysqlhotcopy*

```
shell> mysqlhotcopy shop shop_old
```

This command creates a new database, shop_old, by creating the directory in the active data directory and making a copy of the table files from the shop database into the new directory. Having the backup available as a live database may be helpful to the users of the data. Also, at a minimum, it means you can access and look at the data as it stood when the data was copied, without needing to perform a restore from the copied data files.

■**Caution** If you run mysqlhotcopy as any user other than the user used to run your MySQL server, the file permissions on the newly created database won't be right. The directory and table files created when running the command in Listing 17-10 resulted in a shop_old directory and table files owned by the user we were using to run the command. Before you attempt to use the table, you'll need to change the permissions on the directory and files.

The options for mysqlhotcopy allow you to change how you interact with the utility and its behavior. The common options are shown in Table 17-2.

Table 17-2. *Common Options in mysqlhotcopy*

Option	Description
--addtodest	Rather than renaming the destination directory if it exists, add new copies of files to the existing directory.
--allowold	Instead of exiting with an error because the database directory for backup of the tables already exists, rename the directory with _old appended and continue.
--checkpoint=<db.table>	Make periodic entries into this table to indicate progress. The table needs to have the following columns: time_stamp ➡ TIMESTAMP NOT NULL, src VARCHAR(32), dest VARCHAR(60), and msg VARCHAR(255).
--chroot=<dir>	Location of the base chroot jail directory where mysqld runs.
--debug	Provide a lot of extra information while copying the files, including a dump of an object structure containing all the tables found to be copied.
-n, --dryrun	Go through the checks and processing, but don't actually perform any of the copying of data.
--flushlog	Once all the tables are locked, flush the logs.
-h, --host=<name>	The name of the server to connect to when running the copy program via a TCP/IP connection. This can be an IP address or DNS name, but must be the local server.
--keepold	When --allowold is specified, the renamed _old directory is removed at the end of the process. This option tells mysqlhotcopy to skip the deletion of that directory.
--noindices	Do not include full index files in copy of tables.

Continued

Table 17-2. *Continued*

Option	Description
--method=*<name>*	Copy the tables using the specified method. cp is currently the only supported value.
-p, --password=*<password>*	Use the password provided on the command line to connect to the database, or prompt for one on the terminal if the password isn't specified.
-P, --port=*<number>*	Use this port to connect to the database server on the local machine.
-q, --quiet	Except for errors, don't create any output.
--record_log_pos=*<db.table>*	Make an entry in the specified table with slave and master status. The table must have these columns: host VARCHAR(60), time_stamp TIMESTAMP(14), log_file VARCHAR(32), log_pos INT(11), master_host VARCHAR(60), master_log_file VARCHAR(32), and master_log_pos INT.
--regexp=*<string>*	Copy databases that match the regular expression.
--resetmaster	Once all the tables are locked, reset the binary log.
--resetslave	Once all the tables are locked, re-create the master.info file.
-S, --socket=*<file>*	Connect to the MySQL server using this socket file on the local machine.
--suffix=*<name>*	Append this string onto the names of databases copied with mysqlhotcopy.
--tmpdir=*<dir>*	Instead of using /tmp for temporary files, use this directory.
-u, --user=*<name>*	Connect to the database using this username. By default, MySQL uses the account name of the current user.

See http://dev.mysql.com/doc/mysql/en/mysqlhotcopy.html for more information about mysqlhotcopy options.

Restoring with mysqlhotcopy

The restore process for MyISAM files copied with mysqlhotcopy is pretty straightforward. You want to make sure the database is not being used, by shutting down the database server, or the tables are locked (with a READ lock). Then simply copy the files for the database or tables from your backup directory into the MySQL data directory. You need to copy every file, including the .MYD, .MYI, .frm, and .TRG files for the table. The easiest way to make sure you have everything is to use a wildcard, as shown in Listing 17-11.

Listing 17-11. *Restoring MyISAM Data Files with a Wildcard Character*

```
cp /backup/shop/cust_order* /data/mysql/shop/.
```

After you've copied the files, make sure the permissions on the directories and files are set correctly. The recommended setting is to have the directories and files owned by the user running your server (we hope that's mysql, not root), and to make the directories and files accessible only to that user (chmod 700). Release the lock on the table, and you are up and running with the previous version of the table.

> ■**Caution** Remember that, if you copy individual tables into your database from a previous time, you may leave records in other tables orphaned. For example, if your `customer` table has a number of recent records that point to entries in your `cust_order` table, and then you restore the `customer` table to a previous state, you will have `cust_order` records that do not have a corresponding `customer` record. This can lead to numerous problems in the database and may affect the application as well (for example, you're trying to look at an order but the query returns nothing because it's joined to the `customer` table and no record exists).

Creating Backups of InnoDB Files

For folks who have been using MyISAM for years, the introduction of InnoDB and its mysterious `ibdata1` file may have caused some uncertainty and reluctance to embrace the new storage engine. Because InnoDB is a transactional, multiversioning, and self-restoring table type, moving data to InnoDB may have felt like letting go of some of your control.

Using the `innodb_file_per_table` option brings some familiarity back, in that, rather than storing everything in one large database file, the storage engine creates an individual `.ibd` file for each table in the corresponding database-named directory within your data directory. This also means you can interact with the tables independently, instead of needing to work with the entire set of databases and tables in one large `ibdata` file.

The truth is, while InnoDB is a more full-featured storage engine, InnoDB tables are nothing to be nervous about. The primary thing to remember is that, at any given point, there may be uncommitted transactions that aren't yet saved to the data files. Any interaction with the files themselves requires all transactions to be complete and all tables to be locked.

InnoDB tables can be easily backed up with `mysqldump`, just like the other table types. Any version of MySQL greater than 4.0.2 supports the `--single-transaction` option, which should be used if you have InnoDB tables, because it will give you a consistent snapshot of your database without needing to maintain a lock on the tables.

As with MyISAM tables, you can use other methods and tools specific to InnoDB tables for creating backups.

Manually Backing Up and Restoring InnoDB Files

Before we look at some of the InnoDB-specific programs, we want to mention that you can manually copy InnoDB data files. To do this properly, you need to shut down your MySQL server. Once the database server is shut down, you can take a backup manually by copying files (or letting your file system backup do the work). Once the database server is down, copy the `ibdata*`, `*.ibd`, `*.frm`, `ib_logfile*`, and `my.cnf` files to an alternate location.

To restore to the state when the backup was taken, shut down the database, copy the files that were backed up to their original location, make sure the permissions on the files are correct, and start up the database.

It is also possible to manually back up and restore individual tables if you are using the `innodb_file_per_table` option, which creates individual data files for each table. To copy a table file, you need to stop all activity on the table and make sure all transactions are committed. One way to do this is to obtain a READ lock on the table with `LOCK TABLES <table_name>` ➥ `READ`. However, be aware that issuing this LOCK statement is dangerous, because if there are uncommitted transactions, it forces those transactions to be committed to obtain the lock. It might be better to use other means to stop interaction with the table. Use SHOW INNODB STATUS to verify that the database has no active transactions, and then copy the .ibd data file.

To restore a single InnoDB table, use the following set of steps:

1. Stop writes coming to the table.

   LOCK TABLES <*table_name*> WRITE;

2. Remove the table.

   ALTER TABLE <*table_name*> DISCARD TABLESPACE;

3. Copy the individual .ibd file into the appropriate database directory.

4. Re-create the tablespace.

   ALTER TABLE <*table_name*> IMPORT TABLESPACE;

5. Release the lock.

   UNLOCK TABLES;

Understanding how to manually copy the entire database or individual files means you can perform the backup and restore tasks manually, or write a script to put together your own mechanism for backing up and restoring InnoDB databases and tables.

Using InnoDB Hot Backup (ibbackup)

Although it is a commercial product, for a long time, the recommended tool for working with InnoDB data files was InnoDB Hot Backup, or ibbackup. This utility allows you to create a backup of a running MySQL InnoDB database, without any noticeable effect on the database performance. You can purchase the license for InnoDB Hot Backup online from the InnoDB web site (http://www.innodb.com/).

Note that innobackup, which is covered in the next section, may better meet your needs. However, innobackup relies on ibbackup to back up the InnoDB data files, so having an understanding of ibbackup is helpful, even if you plan to use the other tool.

The process of creating a backup with ibbackup is simple: you create a second configuration file that matches some of the configuration options from your live database, and use that second configuration file to give ibbackup information about how and where to perform the backup. Listing 17-12 shows a snippet of the InnoDB options from a my.cnf file.

Listing 17-12. *Sample Options from a Live my.cnf for ibbackup*

```
[mysqld]
datadir = /data/mysql
innodb_data_home_dir = /data/mysql
innodb_data_file_path = ibdata1:10M:autoextend
innodb_log_group_home_dir = /data/mysql
set-variable = innodb_log_files_in_group=2
set-variable = innodb_log_file_size=20M
```

Listing 17-13 shows an example of a second configuration file, called mybackup.cnf, with a few of the options changed.

Listing 17-13. *Sample Options from mybackup.cnf for ibbackup*

```
[mysqld]
datadir = /backup
innodb_data_home_dir = /backup
innodb_data_file_path = ibdata1:10M:autoextend
innodb_log_group_home_dir = /backup
set-variable = innodb_log_files_in_group=2
set-variable = innodb_log_file_size=20M
```

After you have the two configuration files in place, run the ibbackup command. Listing 17-14 shows how the command is formatted, using the live and the backup configuration files.

Listing 17-14. *ibbackup Command and Arguments*

```
shell> ibbackup /etc/my.cnf /etc/mybackup.cnf
```

This command will generate some output to show its progress. It will finish with a statement that the backup has completed. If you then do an ls -1 /backup (from where the mybackup.cnf file indicated to put the backup), you'll see a log of the backup and all of your data files. Listing 17-15 shows the contents of /backup. Note that ibbackup will not overwrite files, so before you run the utility, you'll need to make sure the contents of the backup directory are copied elsewhere or removed.

Listing 17-15. *Contents of the backup Directory*

```
ibbackup_logfile
ibdata1
ibdata2
```

The process of restoring from an ibbackup backup involves two steps, and it takes an unusual approach to restoring data. Instead of moving files into the data directory, you use the backup configuration file as the main configuration file and run MySQL off the data files in the backup directory. So, rather than having a backup directory, you have several data directories that you can switch between, or use a symbolic link for your primary data directory. This also means that you are required to take a snapshot of your other, non-InnoDB tables and put them in the data directory. Unless you do this, you won't have all your data in the new directory when making it your live MySQL data directory.

First, apply the ibbackup_logfile to the backed-up data files. This rolls the data files forward to make them consistent with the log files. Applying the log file is a simple command, as shown in Listing 17-16.

Listing 17-16. *Applying the Log File to Data Files*

```
shell> ibbackup --apply-log /etc/mybackup.cnf
```

After you have the data files ready, stop MySQL and start it using the configuration file that was used to create the backup, as shown in Listing 17-17.

Listing 17-17. *Moving MySQL to Backed-Up Data Files*

```
shell> /use/local/mysql/bin/safe_mysqld --defaults-file=/etc/mybackup.cnf
```

We've provided an extremely limited overview of the ibbackup utility. Many command arguments and options are available to customize the backup. For example, you can specify compression, regular expression matches on table names, and to suspend the backup at the end for additional processing. Refer to http://www.innodb.com/manual.php for more information.

Using innobackup

Although ibbackup has been around for a while, in most cases, it's no longer the best choice for backup when you consider that you need to do some scripting to have your non-InnoDB tables added to the backup. The innobackup program was written to allow you to back up both your MyISAM and InnoDB table types. The reason we say "in most cases" is because innobackup issues a FLUSH TABLES WITH READ LOCK statement to get a snapshot of the non-InnoDB tables. If you have large MyISAM tables or long queries against the MyISAM tables, this command could cause a significant interruption in database availability.

The way that innobackup backs up and restores files is very similar to how ibbackup works, except it includes all of the database, including database directories and all .frm, .MYI, and .MYD files. Although innobackup is open source, it works by first running ibbackup. You are required to have a licensed copy of ibbackup to run the database backup.

To create a backup, first create a second configuration file, just like the one shown earlier in Listing 17-13, to be used by ibbackup. Then use the innobackup script, passing it a user, a password, the configuration file location, and a backup directory, as shown in Listing 17-18.

Listing 17-18. *Backup Using innobackup*

```
innobackup --user=<username> --password=<password> /etc/mybackup.cnf /backup
```

The innobackup script will create a new directory in /backup, using the current date and time, and place all of the database directories and files within that directory. Listing 17-19 shows that, unlike the /backup directory contents for ibbackup, an ls -1 /backup/2005-08-15_13-27-09 (the backup directory) shows all of your database directories and files.

Listing 17-19. *Contents of the innobackup Backup Directory*

```
backup-my.cnf
ibbackup_logfile
ibdata1
ibdata2
ib_logfile0
ib_logfile1
mysql
mysql-stderr
mysql-stdout
test
```

As a part of the backup, innobackup creates the backup-my.cnf file with the current database options. Also, the mysql-stderr and mysql-stdout files are created and contain messages generated during the backup.

The restore process is similar to the process for ibbackup. It first requires running the logs forward, as shown in Listing 17-20. Note that you need to specify the directory with the date and time for the desired backup.

Listing 17-20. *Applying Log Files to InnoDB Data Files*

```
shell> innobackup --apply-log /etc/mybackup.cnf /backup/2005-08-15_13-27-09
```

After you've applied the log files, you must create a new configuration file, with the options in your backup configuration (/etc/mybackup.cnf) and those saved by innobackup into backup-my.cnf. A simple cat command, as shown in Listing 17-21, will do the trick and create a valid configuration file for running the MySQL server.

Listing 17-21. *Creating the Complete Configuration File for ibbackup*

```
shell> cat /etc/mybackup.cnf /backup/2005-08-15_13-27-09/backup-my.cnf >\
/backup/2005-08-15_13-27-09/my.cnf
```

Now that you have a complete configuration file, you can start the database using the backed-up structure, index, and data files. Listing 17-22 shows the appropriate command.

Listing 17-22. *Moving MySQL to Backed-Up Data Files*

```
shell> /use/local/mysql/bin/safe_mysqld \
--defaults-file=/backup/2005-08-15_13-27-09/my.cnf
```

We've provided the basics of using innobackup, but we have not covered all of the options available. Refer to http://www.innodb.com/manual.php for more information about innobackup options.

Using MySQL Administrator

Our last stop on the backup options tour is MySQL Administrator. This is a GUI tool that is available for Windows, Linux, and Macintosh systems. We introduced MySQL Administrator's User Administration section in Chapter 15. MySQL Administrator also includes a set of interfaces to back up and restore data in your MySQL database. MySQL Administrator can connect to a local database or run remotely and connect using TCP/IP.

■**Note** In Chapter 15, we used the Linux version of MySQL Administrator for interacting with the database. In this chapter, we use the Mac OS X version to give you a sense of the differences. The most notable difference is that the major functional areas are in a bar across the top of the GUI in OS X, rather than on the left side, as they are in the Linux program.

The output generated by the MySQL Administrator Backup utility is like that of mysqldump. Your backup file contains a collection of DROP, CREATE, and INSERT statements that are used to re-create the table as it was at the time of backup.

Although the MySQL Administrator makes backing up your data simple while you're at the GUI, we don't recommend that you use this method as a replacement for a scheduled backup. Either use the scheduling functionality of MySQL Administrator to schedule a regular backup of your data or set up a cron entry to do a regular backup.

Making Backups with MySQL Administrator

As shown in Figure 17-1, the MySQL Administrator Backup tool has a Project tab that allows you to define projects. After you start up the MySQL Administrator and go through the steps of connecting to your database (as described in Chapter 15), click on the Backup option in the navigation bar. In this example, we've already connected to the MySQL server that pulled the list of databases and tables into the tool. With the click of a mouse, you can create new projects and associate any number of databases or tables to be a part of the backup.

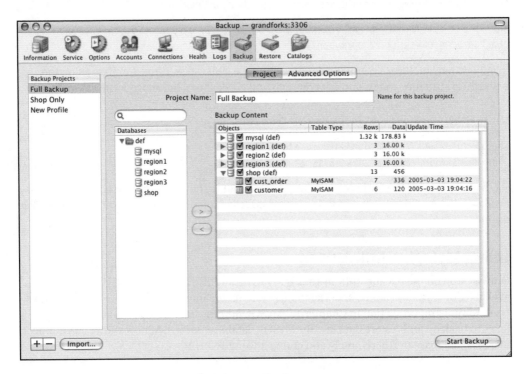

Figure 17-1. *Project tab of MySQL Administrator Backup*

To customize the output in the dump file created by the Backup utility, click the Advanced Options tab. As you can see in Figure 17-2, you have some control over how the backup runs and what is put into the backup file. These options are a subset of those available for the `mysqldump` utility. Refer to Table 17-1 for more information about the `mysqldump` options.

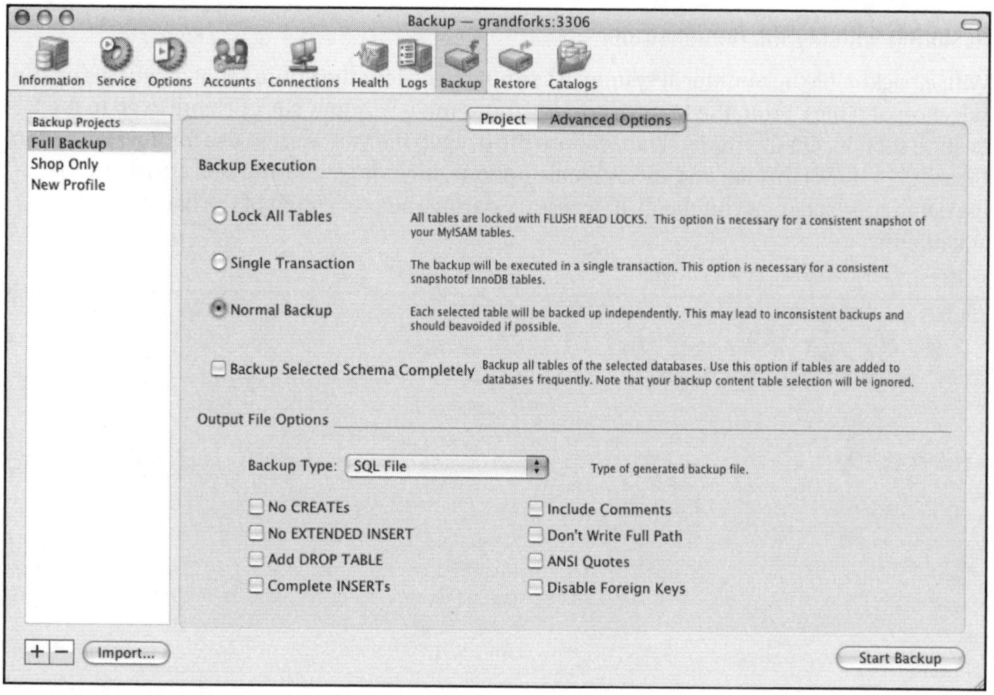

Figure 17-2. *Advanced Options tab of MySQL Administrator Backup*

After you've chosen your backup project and tweaked the output accordingly, click the Start Backup button to create a backup file. You will be prompted to specify a backup location and filename on your local machine, as shown in Figure 17-3.

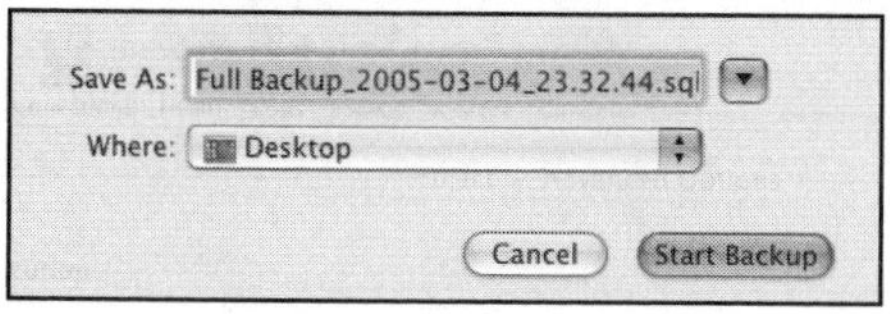

Figure 17-3. *Prompt for backup directory and filename*

After you've specified where to save the backup, click Start Backup. That's all you need to do to make your backup with MySQL Administrator.

The Windows and Linux versions of MySQL Administrator have an area for scheduling daily, weekly, or monthly backups. (We hope this feature will soon be available in the Mac OS X version.) For more information about backup scheduling with MySQL Administrator, refer to `http://dev.mysql.com/doc/administrator/en/mysql-administrator-backup-schedule.html`.

Restoring with MySQL Administrator

With a backup file on your local system, it's simple to restore the entire set of databases or any selection of tables. From the MySQL Administrator main window, click Restore to go to the Restore section. On the General tab, choose the backup file you want to use for the restoration. Figure 17-4 shows this tab and the available options, including ignoring SQL errors and creating databases (schemas) on the fly if necessary during the processing of the backup statements.

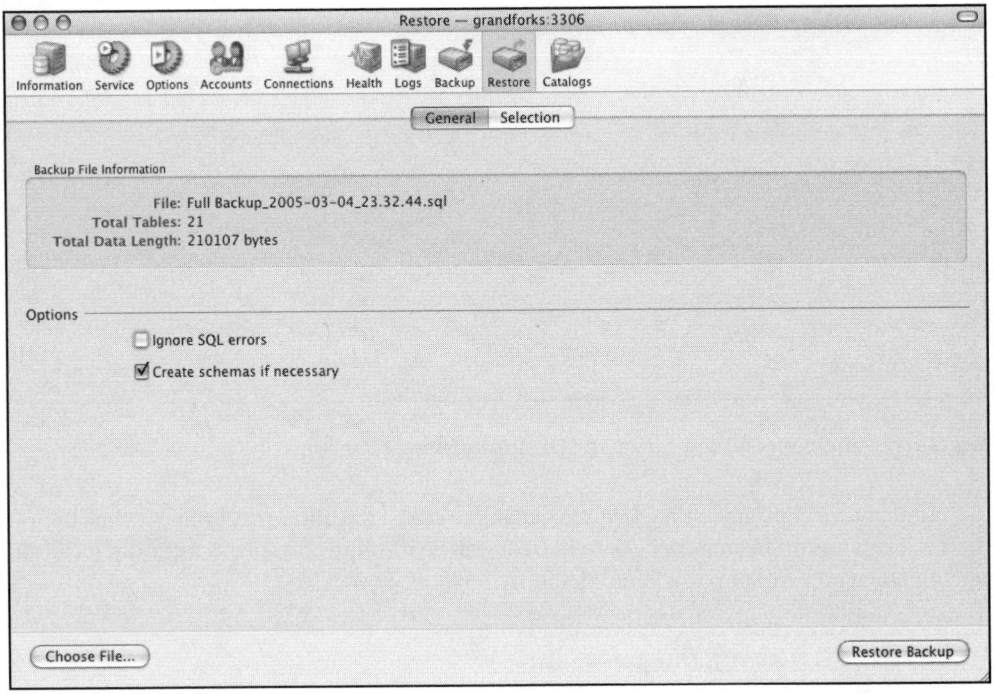

Figure 17-4. *General tab of MySQL Administrator Restore*

Once you've chosen the backup file and specified the options, you should move to the Selection tab, where you can choose the databases and tables to restore when running Restore. Figure 17-5 shows this tab.

When you've chosen the databases and tables you would like to restore, click the Restore Backup button, and the statements will be run against the MySQL database.

For more information about MySQL Administrator, see http://dev.mysql.com/doc/ administrator/en/mysql-administrator-introduction.html.

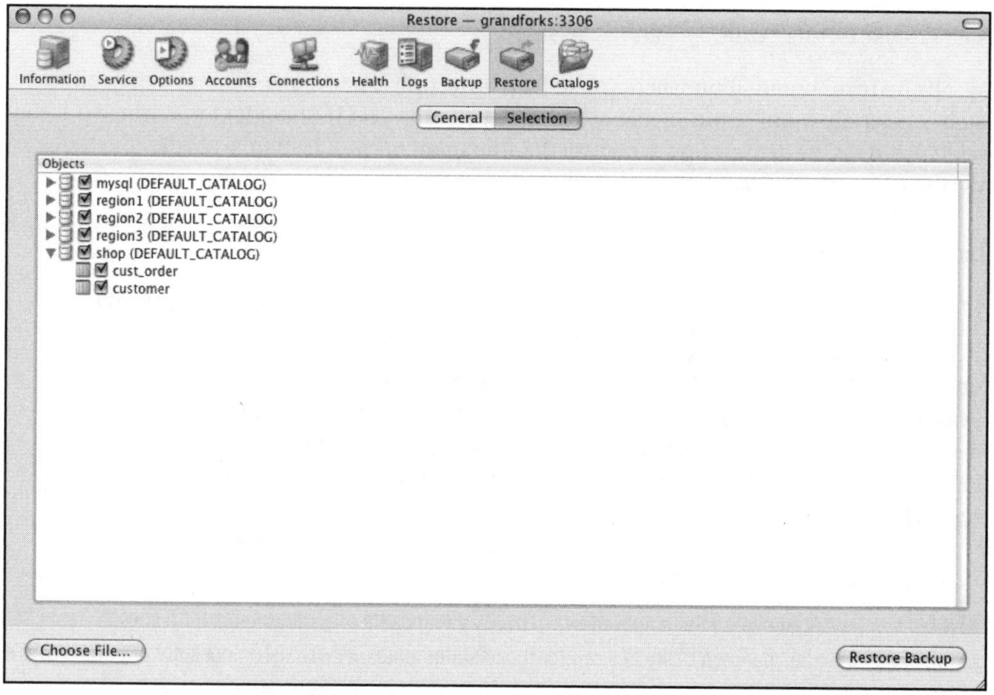

Figure 17-5. *Selection tab of MySQL Administrator Restore*

Using Binary Logs for Up-to-Date Tables

Throughout this chapter, we've stopped the process of restoring data at the point where the most recent backup file was restored. In some cases, this is okay; in other cases, it is not acceptable. In the projects we've worked on, restoring data that is hours or days old is not acceptable.

In the instances where you need your data to be more up-to-date than the last backup, MySQL's binary log files are your key to bridging that gap. Binary logs are enabled with the log-bin option in your server configuration file, which causes any statement that changes the data to be written to the binary file. (See Chapter 14 for details on configuring MySQL.)

To make using the binary log easier, we recommend that each time you take a backup of the database, you flush the binary logs, which you can do with the FLUSH LOGS SQL statement or the RESET MASTER command. Flushing the logs creates a new log file in the series, each numbered incrementally. Resetting the master removes existing binary log files and starts a new one. The option to restart with a new binary log file is available with many of the backup tools, which makes them easier to use (see the options listed in Tables 17-1 and 17-2). If you start a new binary log file as a part of your backup (or immediately after), it will make bringing the data forward in time much easier.

To bring all of the databases in your server up to the last statement before you restored the data, use the mysqlbinlog tool to create text SQL statements from the binary log and pipe them to your database, like this:

```
shell> mysqlbinlog <binlog file> | mysql
```

If you're in the situation where you are restoring only a particular database, or need to stop at a certain point in the log file before you get to the DELETE statement that wiped out the table, mysqlbinlog has options to control the statement output. Listing 17-23 demonstrates the use of these options.

Listing 17-23. *Limiting the mysqlbinlog Output*

```
shell> mysqlbinlog --database=shop --stop-position=4193 <binlog file> | mysql
```

The options given to mysqlbinlog in Listing 17-23 will ensure that only statements destined for tables in the shop database are sent to MySQL, and that the statements will stop when the log position reaches 4193, the position of the binary logs immediately before a destructive statement was issued. You can find the log position by running the mysqlbinlog tool on the binary log file and piping the output to grep or sending it into a file for text-based searching.

■**Note** If you want to control the output of mysqlbinlog to include only statements for a specific table, you will need to write your own utility to grep for those statements. mysqlbinlog does not offer a --table option.

Review the statements in the binary log that come after the unwanted statement. You may want to process those as well if they affect other tables. Do this by finding the binary log position after the problem statement and run the same statement from Listing 17-23, but use the --start-position option, setting it to the binary log position of the next statement.

Refer to http://dev.mysql.com/doc/mysql/en/mysqlbinlog.html for more information about mysqlbinlog options.

Summary

In this chapter, you've seen the great deal of flexibility you have in implementing a backup and restore strategy for your MySQL databases. However, before you think about the technical details, consider how your backups and restorations will be a part of your organization, and get the right people around the table to discuss the requirements. Be sure to document the conversation and review the document periodically to make adjustments.

Regardless of the table type, you have several options for how to get the data out of the database to store in an alternate location. For each of the methods to back up data, there is a process to use the backup files for a restoration. Backup tools and restore tools both give you a lot of options for customizing the way data is formatted and processed. Being aware of these options helps in planning and implementing the backup and restore procedure. If you find that your backup plan requires some hybrid combination of several tools, or repeated use of a single tool for each database, you might consider writing your own backup script that calls on any of the existing tools.

General discussions of data backup and restore topics often refer to these tasks as uninteresting, boring, tedious, and worse than a needle under your fingernail. Yes, there are probably more exciting things to be involved with, but there's no reason why procedures for protecting your data can't be interesting as well. We hope that, as you've read this chapter, you've gotten a sense of how this process can be more than a mundane, last-minute, and dreaded responsibility.

■ ■ ■

Replication

Imagine, for a moment, that there was a single, physical phone book for the entire country where you lived. This phone book was housed in a building in one city, and had specific hours in which you were permitted to visit. Imagine that phone numbers weren't available from any other source. To look up a friend's phone number, or find the number to call to make a reservation for dinner, you'd be required to travel to the phone book building, get in line, and wait for your turn to flip through the pages. You might imagine that over time, special services would arise in which you could call in a request to the phone book office or a third-party service that would retrieve the number for you. You might argue that this arrangement makes having the phone book pointless, and the data stored in the book of little value to anyone who needs immediate access to the data, or who doesn't live within close proximity to the phone book office.

Much like our phone book example, organizations or applications often require multiple instances of their database, either within the same physical space for scalability or redundancy, or spread halfway around the world for geographic diversity. In either case, the data needs to be available in multiple instances to provide value to the organization. Although issues with geographic diversity can sometimes be solved with good network connections, there are plenty of cases in which having a separate instance of the data better serves the needs of the organization.

Fortunately, we don't live in a world where data has to be confined to a single physical location. With replication, a MySQL database can exist partially, or in its entirety, in many different locations, with each replicated instance following close behind the primary database.

In the context of databases, replication means creating a copy of the data in an alternate location. In most instances, this means the data is available via a second or third server, either in the same location or a geographically separate location. However, there's nothing to prevent you from using replication between two databases on a single server. Replication is as much about having an alternate copy as it is about active synchronization of the data, either real-time or at some interval. The goal of replication is to make data from one database available in more than that one place.

Replication in MySQL can be fairly simple to set up, depending on the complexity of your replication requirements. For a single replicated database with a small amount of data, you're just a few commands away from having a replicated database—but more on that later.

By the time you've completed this chapter, you'll have learned about the following topics:

- What replication is

- Why you should replicate data

- What replication doesn't solve

- How to plan for replication

- How MySQL implements replication

- Setting up replication initially

- Understanding your configuration options

- Monitoring and managing MySQL replication

- Replication performance

- Examples of replication

Without further delay, let's start our look into replication with a discussion of what we mean by replication.

What Is Replication?

Depending on your previous experience with replication, you may have some ideas about what it means to replicate your data between servers or systems. Data replication tools are available in most widely used database systems (Oracle, SQL Server, Sybase, PostgreSQL, and so on), but the feature sets and management tools of each system vary.

Terminology

The terminology for replication varies between database systems. However, all seem to split the replicated databases into two groups: databases that provide data and databases that consume data.[1] You might think of these groups as some databases exporting their data and other databases importing data. To further complicate replication, you can set up a database to provide data to another database while at the same time being a consumer of data. We'll get into a few configuration examples later in the chapter to illustrate why and how you might use a database as both data provider and consumer. Terminology to describe the process of replicating data varies between different vendors. In MySQL, databases that are replicated from, or that export their data, are called masters. Databases that replicate the data, or import it from another server, are called slaves.

---

1. SQL Server separates databases into publishers and subscribers, but also has a third player called the distributor. The distributor isn't a database, but a process that can run independently on a separate machine to move data between publishers and subscribers.

REPLICATION TERMINOLOGY

If you're new to replication, or are coming from another database system, you might not be familiar with the replication terminology in MySQL. Following is a list of terms with corresponding definitions:

- *Master*: A database that serves as the primary source of data for other databases. A master exports data to another database.

- *Slave*: The slave replicates, or imports data changes, from another database.

- *Snapshot*: A snapshot refers to making a point-in-time copy of the data on the primary database to be moved to a slave database. Creating a snapshot gives a starting point for replication to move forward.

- *Merge or multimaster*: Merge or multimaster replication is a concept in which a system has multiple databases that feed each other updates. MySQL doesn't support this.

Synchronous vs. Asynchronous Replication

Before we talk about the feature sets of replication systems, note that, regardless of a system's features, the databases are kept in sync either synchronously or asynchronously. MySQL's replication implementation is asynchronous, meaning that the data in the replicated systems lags behind that on the master, anywhere from fractions of a second to several seconds. Let's look more closely at the differences between the two synchronization types.

Synchronous Replication

In synchronous replication, the data is committed to the primary database as well as the replicated database as a part of the same transaction. This is also known as dual commit or dual phase commit. The transaction is written and committed on both the master and the slave as a part of the transaction. In synchronous replication, the primary database and all replicated databases are always in sync. Figure 18-1 visually represents the process of synchronous replication.

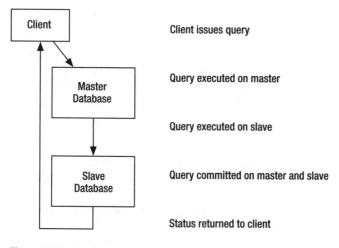

Figure 18-1. *Synchronous replication*

As you can see in the diagram in Figure 18-1, the query is executed on both the master and the slave, and then committed on both before the client receives the return status. With the query changing data in both places before returning a response, all databases in the environment are kept in sync.

Asynchronous Replication

Asynchronous replication means that a query isn't picked up on the replicated servers until after the transaction is complete on the primary database. Typically, a process pulls or pushes data changes from the primary database at a scheduled interval and makes those changes in the replicated system. In MySQL, data is pulled from the master by a process on the slave after the master has completed the query and made an entry in the binary log.

With asynchronous replication, the replicated databases are always some amount of time behind the primary database. The amount of time depends on numerous factors: how frequently the replication process grabs updates, how much data must be transferred to the replicated systems, and how fast the network will allow the data to move between those systems. Figure 18-2 shows the flow of data in asynchronous replication.

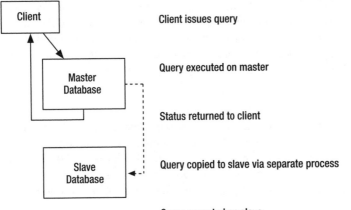

Figure 18-2. *Asynchronous replication*

Figure 18-2 illustrates how an asynchronous replication system processes the query on the master server and returns status to the client before the query is replicated on the slave. At some future point the query is pulled to the slave and executed. Again, we want to point out that MySQL replication is asynchronous, the flow of data matching that in Figure 18-2.

One-Way vs. Merge

Replication technology lives on a continuum that goes from simple to complex. Each database vendor has its own set of tools to accomplish replicating data from one system to another. Some of the tools are sophisticated, and include endless configuration options for controlling and optimizing the data moving between your systems. Others are fairly simple, giving just enough control to set up the system and let it take over.

At the simpler end of the continuum are replication mechanisms that provide read-only copies of the data, or one-way replication. In a one-way replication arrangement, all updates to the database are directed to the master server, and then those changes are pulled down to the replicated databases. The communication is one-way in that any change on a slave is never communicated back to the master.

It is possible to set up a replication system in which a segment of your databases or tables is replicated from a master and some tables are maintained locally. In that case, local data changes to the nonreplicated tables on the slave won't cause problems. Otherwise, if you've got a set of replicated tables, you shouldn't make updates on the slave, as the updates may cause problems with future updates from the master, and the data will most likely be lost the next time you do a complete refresh of the data.

In more advanced database replication systems, replication allows for both reading and writing in the replicated database, and provides a mechanism to merge changes from multiple databases into every other replicated database. Having multiple primary databases, with reads and writes happening in each, presents some interesting problems. The replication software has to make decisions about which records take precedence when there are conflicts.

MySQL's replication falls on the simpler end of the spectrum, and doesn't provide data merging in its replication feature. Data is replicated to read-only servers. If changes are made in the replicated data, they aren't replicated back to the master. More information about enabling merge replication in MySQL is available at `http://dev.mysql.com/books/ hpmysql-excerpts/ch07.html#hpmysql-CHP-7-SECT-7.3`.

Why Replicate Data?

Before running out and setting up a server to replicate your data, it's good to consider what role replication will play in the requirements of your database or database-backed application. In many instances, replication is just the thing you've been looking for, and will make a huge, positive impact on your system. However, in some cases it can be more hindrance than help, as discussed in the section "What Isn't Solved with Replication." Let's look at a few areas where MySQL's replication may help.

Performance

Having replicated databases can improve performance of your application. Perhaps you want to be able to spread the load of database queries across several database servers. If you're at a point where the CPU or memory on your database server has peaked, or the network traffic for database transactions is reaching capacity, you may find that replicating your data onto several machines and balancing queries across multiple machines improves your database response.

Even if you don't have ongoing demand for performance improvements provided by replication, sometimes providing a separate database for certain users or specific queries can offer a great deal of relief for your primary database. Reporting or summary queries can be extremely intensive, and can slow or stop other queries to those tables. Replicating the data, and moving user accounts or pointing reporting tools to the replicated data, can be of great benefit to the primary database.

Geographic Diversity

Replication is a good way to solve situations in which data is needed in multiple locations. Perhaps you have offices located across the country or around the world and need to provide a local copy of the data for each office. Using a replication mechanism could allow each office local access to its data, but also make its data available to other offices, and vice-versa.

Limited Connectivity

If you have inconsistent network availability, replication may be a way to provide more uptime. Perhaps you have customers in a certain part of the country with an intermittent pipe to the public Internet, but a very good network within their region. Setting up a database within the region that replicates off a master when the connection is up gives your customers a constantly available database. The data is only as current as the latest successful connection to the master, but the database is always available for use within the region.

Redundancy and Backup

A replicated database is an excellent way to provide redundancy and high availability. Having one or more slave databases running all the time means that you can roll onto one of the slave servers in the instance of a machine failure or disaster. You can do the switch manually, or you can program the application to make the switch if the primary machine isn't available.

In addition to providing redundancy, a replicated database is an excellent stand-by backup for instances where you need to restore from a backup. Unlike a nightly dump of the data, the replicated data is as current as the last statement read from the binary log on the master database, which is likely to be more current than your most recent backup. Using a replicated server as a backup means your backup is constantly updated, and if your primary database server goes down you've got an almost-current copy of the database ready to start the restore process.

■**Caution** Be careful when relying on a replicated database for restoring data. If you're attempting to restore data from an accidental query, the data change will likely happen in the slaves before you can get to them to restore the data. Using replication as a backup is more appropriate for instances in which a restore is required after a disk or server failure.

Storage Engine and Index Optimization

Replication can allow you to take advantage of multiple storage engines for a single table or database. What does that mean? With replication it's possible to use one table type on the master and another table type on the slave. Perhaps you want to have foreign keys, which are only allowed using the InnoDB and BDB table types, but you also want to be able to use the full-text indexing feature of the MyISAM table type. Because replication simply executes queries from one server on another server, it's possible to have the master database use InnoDB tables, which provides referential integrity. You can alter the tables replicated to the slave to be MyISAM, including the definition of full-text indexes. If you wanted to run queries against the full-text index, you would send those queries to the slave with the MyISAM tables and full-text index. Presumably, you'd use the InnoDB features on the master to enforce data integrity, but get the advantages of the MyISAM performance, and so on.

We've hinted at it with the full-text indexes in our multiple-storage-engines example, but it's worthy to note that a slave database can have a different set of indexes than the master. This can be helpful if you have fundamentally different methods for accessing the data that require multiple indexes on a single table. Spreading those indexes across two different databases and sending the queries to the appropriate machine can mean reduced index sizes and improved performance.

What Isn't Solved with Replication

Replication can be helpful, and necessary in many situations, but it doesn't solve every problem. Just to give a few examples:

- Replication doesn't solve data validation or integrity problems. Whatever changes are made to the master database are also made in the slave.

- As cautioned earlier, using replication as a backup system to restore data from accidental updates or deletes doesn't work. Because a replicated server has most likely executed the same query within seconds of the master, going to a slave to retrieve records that were accidentally updated or deleted on the master proves unsuccessful.

- Because MySQL replication is asynchronous, it isn't useful in a system where data is needed in real time by the slaves.

- By default, replication in MySQL doesn't allow you to merge data from two different servers into one. If you have updates happening in two databases and you need to represent them in one, you might be better served by replicating the separate databases and then creating a view that brings the tables together. See Chapter 12 for more information on views in MySQL.

- Replication in MySQL doesn't natively give you the ability to run updates in two different databases and have them reflect each other's changes by replicating each other. This is also known as multimaster replication.

You now should have a sense of what replication can and can't do, and why you might embark on creating replicated data in your environment.

Planning for Replication

Before we leave the replication why and get into the how, we encourage you to stop and think about how replication fits into your organization. When looking at how to build replication into your system, or expand a system to include replicated data, you should think about how you can go about fully understanding the requirements. We encourage you to identify the owners of the data and gather their expectations for the data in the system.

Armed with that knowledge, consider the things replication can and can't do, and work with the stakeholders to develop a technically viable policy on replicating data. Go through things such as the requirements for synchronization and privacy. Help the stakeholders understand the possibilities available through replication and the process of establishing and maintaining a system with replicated data. Together, document a policy for replicating data that is technically possible and meets the requirements of your organization.

Armed with the policy, put together an implementation plan that includes information on the details of where and how the data is replicated. Good documentation of this plan will serve as a fallback when you've been focused on other things and don't recall the details, as well as an aid for anyone who has to step in to help with implementation or problems in the system.

We understand it's rare to be a database administrator or application developer who loves to write documentation, especially on something as nontechnical as policies. Hopefully, the potential gains from having the process documented will be motivation enough to forge through well-written policy and implementation documents. This will ensure that as you move forward, you remain on the right track and don't cause a lot of extra work for yourself or others by not having documentation available for clarification.

How MySQL Implements Replication

In its simplest form, MySQL's replication moves data from one database to another by copying all the queries that change the data in one database and running those exact statements in the replicated database. In effect, the slave databases are shadowing the master database by copying the master's queries.

■**Note** Replication has been available since version 3.23.15, but underwent some significant changes in 4.0.2. If you're attempting to set up replication that involves versions prior to 4.0.2, see MySQL's documentation on replication for more information on replication with earlier versions of MySQL.

Binary Log

How does replication actually work? That's what we're here to look into. You're probably familiar with the binary log, a logging mechanism that keeps track of all changes in your MySQL tables. Because replication relies on the binary log, you must enable it with the log-bin option in your database startup to successfully replicate data. Chapters 4, 17, and 20 talk about the binary log a bit, but in different contexts, so we'll do a quick review here, keeping replication in mind.

Every time a query makes a change in your database, or has the potential to make a change, that query is executed and then appended to the binary log.[2] Test this by issuing the statement in Listing 18-1 in your MySQL client.

Listing 18-1. *DELETE Statement to Test Binary Log*

```
DELETE FROM customer;
```

After you've issued the statement, check the last entry in the binary log. If you aren't familiar with the binary log file, it's in your data directory. By default, if you haven't specified it in the options, it's named <server name>-bin.00000x (the currently active binary log is the highest numbered). It's necessary to use the myslqbinlog tool included with MySQL to convert the binary to ASCII to make it readable. You can see that the last entry in the binary log looks like that of Listing 18-2, except your time will be different.

Listing 18-2. *Last Statement in Binary Log*

```
# at 716
#050319 12:07:21 server id 1  end_log_pos 793   Query   thread_id=120   exec_time=0
    error_code=0
USE shop;
SET TIMESTAMP=1111252041;
DELETE FROM customer;
```

As you can see in Listing 18-2, the last item in the binary log is the DELETE statement. There are a few other pieces of information. First, the log entry tells us the position of the binary log when starting: #at 716. The next line gives us, among other things, the time, the server number, the binary log position at the end of the statement, the time it took to execute the query, and if there was an error. The binary log then includes a USE shop; statement to ensure you're in the right database, a SET TIMESTAMP statement to adjust the time to the time this statement was entered, and the actual SQL statement that was processed. As you might sense, this information all comes in handy when attempting to keep another database in sync with this one. It's as if you could copy these five lines to another identical database and see the same changes in the data on the other database. Series of statements that are part of a transaction are written to the binary log once the transaction has successfully completed. Transactions that fail and roll back, or are rolled back manually, don't change the data and thus aren't written to the binary log.

Because we're here to talk about replication, we won't explain the binary log further, but you can find more information in the MySQL documentation at http://dev.mysql.com/doc/mysql/en/binary-log.html.

---

2. As of MySQL version 4.1.3, any statement that could potentially change data, like a DELETE where no rows were matched, is still written to the binary log.

Replication Process

Now that you're familiar with the binary log, and we've hinted at how the binary log might be used in replication, let's look at the steps that happen when data is replicated to another server:

1. INSERT, UPDATE, DELETE or some other data-changing query is issued to the master database.

2. The query is parsed, executed, and written to the binary log on the master.

3. The I/O thread on the slave asks for new queries from the I/O thread on the master, and pulls anything new from the binary log on the master into a log on the slave called the relay log.

4. A processing thread on the slave reads the relay log and executes the query.

The simple explanation is that for any data change on the master, an entry is made into the binary log. That statement is copied to the slave and executed there as well, making the exact change to the slave as was made on the master and thus keeping the data in sync.

We hinted at different threads in these four steps. Running a replication slave requires three threads, in addition to those already used to keep your database's non-replication-related features running. Two threads run on the slave, the first to communicate with the master for entries in the master's binary log and to pull the statements onto the slave machine. The second slave thread reads the queries in the relay log (which were pulled from the master) and processes them. The third thread runs on the master and is responsible for communicating changes in the master's binary log. If you have multiple slaves pointing at a single master, the master will run a separate thread to communicate with each of the slaves.

Relay Log

The binary log is the master's representation of changes in the data. As you've seen in the replication steps, the entries in the master's binary log get copied to the slave. Where do those statements go?

The queries pulled from the master are stored in what's called a *relay log*, named something like <machine>-relay-bin.00001. The relay log files typically reside in your data directory, but you can specify to have them stored elsewhere. The relay log is a delayed copy of the master's binary log, and you only see it in your data directory if the database is set up to run as a slave of another database. If you're running replication, the relay log will grow at the same rate as the binary log on the master. In fact, the format of the binary log and relay log are the same; you can view the text version of the relay log by using mysqlbinlog on the relay log file. Watching the entries in the relay log can give you a rudimentary sense of what data is being replicated to your database, and how quickly.

As of MySQL 5.0, a new relay log is created each time the I/O thread starts (prior to 5.0, a new log was created only on the first startup). You can control the size of relay logs by the max_relay_log_size, a new file being generated when the size of the currently active log file reaches the specified limit.

Unlike the binary log, MySQL automatically purges the relay logs when the slave no longer needs them (because every statement has been processed in the database).

info Files

When running replication, two new files appear in your data directory: `master.info` and `relay-log.info`. MySQL uses these files to save information about your replication state, and they're used when MySQL starts up, if they're available.

■**Caution** MySQL considers the information contained in the `master.info` and `relay-log.info` file before looking for settings in the configuration files. This means that changes in your `my.cnf` file may be ignored, if the information is stored in the `info` files.

Both of these files provide information about the configuration and status of your replication, but shouldn't be used as configuration files to make changes. The primary purpose for these files is to keep state information between database restarts, and for database backups. The slave threads control both of these files, and you should only use them for information. You can make changes to these files with the `CHANGE MASTER` command, which is discussed in more detail in the section "CHANGE MASTER."

master.info File

The `master.info` file contains a number of lines detailing the configuration and status of the master database. The information in this file, and much more, is also available with the `SHOW SLAVE STATUS` command, which is covered in the section "SHOW SLAVE STATUS." Listing 18-3 shows a sample `master.info` file.

Listing 18-3. *Sample master.info File*

```
14
master-database-bin.000002
5813
master-database.example.com
replicate
r3p1!c8
3306
60
0
(6 blank lines removed)
```

In Listing 18-3, we've removed six blank lines that are place holders for SSL information. The complete listing of entries in the `master.info` file is shown in Table 18-1. Lines 9 through 14 contain information about the use of SSL connections for the replication threads.[3] These lines may be blank if values aren't specified on startup.

---

3. The SSL connection options are new to the `master.info` file as of MySQL version 4.1. Previous versions of MySQL included only seven lines, represented by lines 2–8 in Table 18-1.

Table 18-1. *Line Descriptions for master.info File*

Line Number	Example	Description
1	14	Indicates to the I/O thread how many lines of data are in the file.
2	master-database-bin.000002	The name of the current binary log file on the master.
3	5813	The read position of the I/O thread in the binary log file on the master database.
4	master-database.example.com	The DNS name or IP address of the master database.
5	replicate	The name of the user for connections to the master for replication.
6	r3p1!c8	The password used when connecting to the master database. This is not shown in the SHOW SLAVE STATUS command.
7	3306	Port number for connections to the master.
8	60	Number of seconds to wait until the connection to the master is retried.
9	0 or 1	Boolean value that indicates if SSL is allowed on the master.
10	/data/mysq/ssl/master-ca-list	Path to a file containing a trusted CA.
11	/data/mysql/ssl	Path to the directory where CA certificates exist.
12	master.cert	Name of the master SSL certificate file.
13	ALL:-AES	List of ciphers allowed in SSL encryption, separated by a colon.
14	master.key	Name of the master SSL key file.

relay-log.info File

The relay-log.info file contains information about the state of the thread that is responsible for reading and processing the statements in the relay log. Listing 18-4 shows a sample file.

Listing 18-4. *Sample relay-log.info File*

```
./slave-database-relay-bin.000054
32
master-database-bin.000002
5813
```

As you can see, the relay log information file contains four lines. A sample and description of these lines are shown in Table 18-2.

Table 18-2. *Line Descriptions for relay-log.info File*

Line Number	Example	Description
1	./slave-database-relay.bin.000034	Name of the file to read for pulling in queries.
2	32	Position in the relay log file where the thread is currently reading.
3	master-database-bin.000002	Name of the master log that is being read.
4	5813	Position in the master binary log where the thread is currently reading.

■**Note** The `master.info` and `relay-log.info` files aren't the only flat files that appear in your data directory. Under normal operation, MySQL keeps a `<machine>-bin.index` to help it keep track of the binary log files. The same is true for replication. If you're replicating data from a master machine, the slave will keep a `<machine>-relay-bin.index` file in your data directory to help MySQL keep track of the existing relay log files.

Initial Replication Setup

We've been through a lot of discussion about creating policies and implementation plans for replication, and have looked at the details of how MySQL accomplishes replication. Now let's turn to the hands-on details of setting up a replicated environment. We'll start with the simplest replication setup to illustrate the required steps to configure a master and slave, and get the slave replicating data from the master. These steps are minimal, but show how easy it can be to get basic replication up and running. After you've gotten a simple replicated environment established, you'll most likely want to look deeper into the configuration options and example configurations for more in-depth information on customizing your replication.

Adjust Configuration

For the master database, assign a unique server ID (usually 1, 2, 3, and so on) and enable binary logging with two entries in the `mysqld` section of the server startup configuration file. These options come preset in the default configuration files, so you might already have something configured as such in your master:

```
[mysqld]
server-id=1
log-bin
```

For the slave, assign a unique server ID with one entry in the `mysqld` section of the configuration file used on startup:

```
[mysqld]
server-id=2
```

■**Tip** For replication to work properly, the master and slave need to be able to communicate via TCP/IP on a designated port. For MySQL, the default port is 3306. Ensure that the `--skip-networking` option isn't in your configuration file, and that the firewall allows this traffic through on port 3306, or the port you've designated for MySQL.

You can also set the `server_id` from within the MySQL client by issuing this command:

```
mysql> SET global server_id=2;
```

This allows you to set server IDs without restarting your database. Be sure to make corresponding changes in the configuration files so the server IDs will stick on a restart.

Create Replication Account

For the slave to get data from the master, you need to establish an account for the slave to connect through to grab updates from the binary log. We recommend setting up a specific user for replication, with permissions limited to replication.

On the master, create an account for replication with this statement:

```
mysql> GRANT REPLICATION SLAVE ON *.* TO 'replicate'@'%' IDENTIFIED BY 'r3p1!c8';
```

The `REPLICATION SLAVE` piece of this statement indicates that the only permission this user has is to pull statements from the master's binary log. The tables (`*.*`) and host (`'%'`) pieces of this statement should follow after your privilege rules. If you're only replicating from one machine, you should probably limit the @ to that specific machine. See Chapter 15 for more information on specifying privileges based on the host, and for specific databases or tables.

■**Note** Versions of MySQL prior to 4.0.2 did not have the `REPLICATION SLAVE` privilege. Creating permissions for replication on older versions requires granting the `FILE` privilege.

Schema and Data Snapshot

Before you can start replicating your data, your slave server needs to have a copy of the database structure and any existing data on the master. You need a snapshot of your data that represents your database at a single point in time. When you start replicating the data, you'll start replicating from the time you made a snapshot of your master database. When the slave database starts, it begins pulling data from the master starting at a particular point in time. To avoid any overlap or gap in data, you'll want to be sure that the point at which the replicated machine starts reading your data is the exact point where you made your data snapshot. For the purposes of this simple setup, we'll assume you'll replicate all databases, including your permissions tables in the `mysql` database.

The most universal tool for making a snapshot is `mysqldump`. This tool works with all storage engines and gives you a file that's easy to work with to create a duplicate set of data on a second server. Listing 18-5 goes through the list of steps to create a dump.

Tip Although it's the easiest way to copy data for the purposes of showing how to get a simple replication up and running, mysqldump might not be the right tool for you. There are several other ways to create a snapshot. Two other shell tools, mysqlhotcopy and mysqlsnapshot, may fit your needs better if you have large tables that use the MyISAM storage engine. If you're using MyISAM, you should also look at the possibility of using the LOAD DATA FROM MASTER command, which you can run from within the MySQL client to pull data from the master and set your relay log position. You can find more information about LOAD DATA FROM MASTER at http://dev.mysql.com/doc/mysql/en/load-data-from-master.html. mysqlhotcopy documentation can be found at http://dev.mysql.com/doc/mysql/en/mysqlhotcopy. html, and information on mysqlsnapshot is at http://jeremy.zawodny.com/mysql/mysqlsnapshot/. Chapter 17 also contains details about ways to create data snapshots.

Listing 18-5. *Lock Tables and Find Binary Log Position*

```
mysql> FLUSH TABLES WITH READ LOCK;
mysql> SHOW MASTER STATUS\G
*************************** 1. row ***************************
            File: master-bin.000002
        Position: 6016
    Binlog_Do_DB:
Binlog_Ignore_DB:
```

Make a note of the File and Position settings on the master—you'll use these later in configuring the slave. Leave the MySQL client connection open (closing it removes the lock). While you still have the client connection open, issue the mysqldump command from another shell, as shown in Listing 18-6.

Listing 18-6. *Create a Snapshot of the Data*

```
shell> mysqldump -A > all_database.sql
```

Once your entire database is dumped to the file, you can go back into your client and unlock the table. You can either simply exit the client tool, which releases the lock; go back and release the lock from the tables by exiting the client; or issue the lock release statement shown in Listing 18-7.

Listing 18-7. *Release the Tables Lock*

```
mysql> UNLOCK TABLES;
```

Move the all_database.sql file to your slave server. Start your slave server database, if it's not running already. Other than having a server ID, you don't need any additional options in the configuration file because the replication options will be specified as a part of starting the replication.

With your slave database running, send the dump of your master database to the client, using the statement in Listing 18-8.

Listing 18-8. *Create Slave Tables from Master Snapshot*

```
shell> mysql < all_database.sql
```

Running the command in Listing 18-8 brings your slave database to the exact point in time that your master was when the snapshot was taken. With the data in place, we're ready to start the replication processes and start pulling updates from the master.

Start Replication

We're finally there. With the slave machine's database set to a particular point in time, we're ready to start replication, which will pull statements from the master's binary log and keep the slave synced closely with the master database.

How do you ensure you won't miss any statements that have changed data on the master since you took the snapshot? If you recall, we made note of the position of the binary log when the snapshot was taken. If we tell the slave to start pulling statements at that point, it will pull everything that has happened since the snapshot. Setting the master log position is a part of the configuration of the slave. Listing 18-9 shows the command to configure the replication on your slave server.

Listing 18-9. *Set up Slave for Replication with CHANGE MASTER*

```
mysql> CHANGE MASTER TO
MASTER_HOST='master.example.com',
MASTER_USER='replicate',
MASTER_PASSWORD='r3p1!c8',
MASTER_LOG_FILE='master-bin.000002',
MASTER_LOG_POS=6016;
```

With these options set, you're ready to start replication, which is done with a simple statement:

```
mysql> START SLAVE;
```

Your slave server is now running, right? How do you know it's working? There are a number of ways to check the status of the slave. You can verify that the statements from the master are being copied into your relay log files by performing a `mysqlbinlog` on the latest relay log. You can also check records in the database on the master and compare the counts or highest ID for different tables. These methods are nice ways to watch replication in action, but don't always provide the summary information about your replication process. In addition, if the replication isn't running, you won't find the reason by looking through the replicated data. To really see what's going on in your server, you should be familiar with the monitoring and management commands. But before you do that, we have to look at all the remaining configuration options available for your replication setup. Let's take a few minutes and go over all the options that will enable you to take our simple example and build it up to meet your needs.

Configuration Options

We've gone through the entire process of setting up replication in a MySQL database, but in a somewhat simplistic way. We didn't show most of the available configuration options during the process. Although simple replication works pretty well, we suspect that most folks will require more granular control over their replication. MySQL's replication configuration options give you a lot of flexibility to control what's happening in your replication environment.

We've grouped the options into three main categories: core options used on the first startup of the slave and stored in the master.info file, options that can be controlled from within a running MySQL instance, and options that must reside in the configuration file.

■**Note** We refer to your configuration files a lot in this section, and want to point out that replication options are just like any other MySQL options. They can be a part of the configuration file hierarchy described in Chapter 14.

Core Options

We'll call the configuration options in Table 18-3 core options. They're options that are stored in the master.info file and are considered essential options to running replication. You can also specify these options in the CHANGE MASTER command.

If you want replication to start immediately upon startup of the slave, place these configuration options and their values in your configuration file. When the slave server starts, it pulls these options from your configuration file, stores them in master.info, and attempts to start replication.

If you want to start replication by hand after your slave server is already running, you *shouldn't* have these options in your configuration file. After the slave database is up and running, issue the CHANGE MASTER command, specifying values for each of the options as a part of the command, and then issue the START SLAVE command. A sample of the CHANGE MASTER command is shown in Listing 18-9, and this command is covered later in the chapter.

Whether you have replication start automatically by getting values from your configuration file or start using CHANGE MASTER, be aware that from that point forward the core options are always pulled from the master.info file. The only way to reset these options is to issue another CHANGE MASTER command, or remove the master.info file prior to a startup. Table 18-3 shows the core replication options.

Table 18-3. *Core Replication Options*

Option	Description
`--master-host=<hostname>`	This is the hostname or IP address of the master database, where the slave should connect to retrieve statements from the binary log.
`--master-user=<user>`	The thread that retrieves queries from the master uses this name for its connection to the master database.
`--master-password=<password>`	This is the password used along with the `--master-user` to connect to the master server.
`--master-port=<port number>`	This is the port number to connect to the master server. The default port for MySQL is 3306.
`--master-connect-retry=<number of seconds>`	This option tells the slave how often to check for the presence of a master if a connection cannot be made. If the slave attempts to connect, and can't get through to the master, it waits this number of seconds until it makes another attempt.
`--master-ssl=<0|1>`	Tells the slave whether it should be using SSL to connect with the master. If SSL is turned on, you need to set the other `master-ssl-*` options.
`--master-ssl-ca=<file>`	Path to a file containing trusted CA certificates.
`--master-ssl-capath=<dir>`	Path to the directory where CA certificates exist.
`--master-ssl-cert=<name>`	Name of the master SSL certificate file.
`--master-ssl-cipher=<cipher:cipher>`	List of ciphers allowed in SSL encryption, separated by a colon.
`--master-ssl-key=<name>`	Name of the master SSL key file.

Other Options

Beyond the core set of configuration options stored in the `master.info` file, there's quite a list of available options for your configuration file. You can also specify any of these options on the command line when starting MySQL. Table 18-4 shows these options with a description of the behavior changes based on the specified value.

Table 18-4. *Startup Replication Options*

Option	Description
`--log-slave-updates`	Turn on logging for updates made in the slave database. Normally, statements that are pulled from the master to run on the slave aren't logged to the binary log. With this option specified, the statements from the master will be logged into the binary log after they're run.
`--log-warnings`	Add additional information to the error log, such as network connection success after failure and how slaves are started. This is enabled by default after version 4.0.19 and 4.1.2. Use `--skip-log-warnings` to disable.

Option	Description
`--master-info-file=<file>`	Use this file to store and read information about the master. See Table 18-1 for information on the contents of this file.
`--max-relay-log-size=`➥ `<number of bytes>`	The maximum size of the relay log before a new one is created. The default setting is 0, which causes MySQL to use the `--max_binlog_size` setting.
`--read-only`	Prevents writes to the slave database except for those users with SUPER privilege. This is useful if you want to protect replicated databases from accidental data changes.
`--relay-log=<file>`	Name of the file where the slave writes and reads queries coming from the master. You can use this option to put your log files onto a disk separate from the disks with your data for improved performance.
`--relay-log-index=<file>`	Name of the file with information about the current relay log and position.
`--relay-log-info-file=<file>`	Name of the file used to store the list of available relay log files.
`--relay-log-purge=<0|1>`	Specifies if the replication process should remove relay log files once they are processed. The default is 1.
`--relay-log-space-limit=`➥ `<number of bytes>`	Forces MySQL to keep the combined relay log size under a certain size. If this size is reached, MySQL will suspend replication until the slave has caught up and the relay log files can be purged. MySQL may ignore this setting temporarily to prevent a deadlock when it conflicts with `--max-relay-log-size`.
`--replicate-do-db=<database name>`	Specifies the name of a database to replicate. Use this option multiple times to specify multiple databases. The slave replicates statements in which this database was the currently active database, not queries with a qualified database, such as UPDATE `db.table`. Unless the query is issued while `<database name>` is the active database, the statements won't be replicated. To get around this, use `--replicate-wild-do-table=<database name>.%`.
`--replicate-do-table=`➥ `<database name>.<table name>`	Specifies the name of a table, within a database, to be replicated. Use this option multiple times to specify multiple tables. Works with queries qualified with a database, such as INSERT INTO `db.table`.
`--replicate-ignore-db=`➥ `<database name>`	Ignores statements that update data in this table. Use this option multiple times to specify multiple databases. The slave ignores statements where this database was the currently active database, not queries with this as the qualified database, such as UPDATE `db.table`. Unless the query is issued while `<database name>` is the active database, the statements won't be ignored. To get around this, use `--replicate-wild-ignore-table=`➥ `<database name>.%`.

Continued

Table 18-4. *Continued*

Option	Description
`--replicate-ignore-table=`➡ `<database name>.<table name>`	Ignores statements issued to this table, within the specified database. Works to ignore queries qualified with a database, such as `INSERT INTO db.table`.
`--replicate-wild-do-table=`➡ `<database name>.<table name>`	Similar to `--replicate-do-table`, but allows you to specify wild-card characters. "_" matches a single character and "%" matches any number of characters. You can use wild-card characters multiple times in both the database and table names. For example, to replicate the `customer`, `customer_order`, `customer_address`, and `customer_payment` tables in the `shop` database, use `shop.customer%`.
`--replicate-wild-ignore-table=`➡ `<database name>.<table name>`	Like `--replicate-ignore-table`, but allows you to use wild-card characters. "_" matches a single character and "%" matches any number of characters. You can use wild-card characters multiple times in both the database and table names. For example, to ignore the `customer`, `customer_order`, `customer_address`, and `customer_payment` tables in the `shop` database, use `shop.customer%`.
`--replicate-rewrite-db=`➡ `<master name>-><new name>`	Translates the name of the database on the master to a new name on the slave. This only works for updates made to the database when it's the default database, not for statements to tables qualified with the database name, such as `DELETE FROM shop.customer`. Be aware that the rewrite happens before any of the matching to determine whether the statement should be replicated, so your matching rules need to use the `<new name>`.
`--replicate-same-server-id`	The default behavior is to ignore statements in the relay log that have a server ID that indicates the statement originated from itself. This prevents infinite loops in replication ring configurations. Use this option if you need to disable this so you can run statements marked as being from this server.
`--report-host=<hostname>`	The hostname to register with the master. In most cases this should be the hostname of the slave, but it can be any string. Each registered slave shows in the `SHOW SLAVE HOSTS` statement on the master.
`--report-port=<port>`	The port number the slave should use for registering with the master. Leave unset to use the default port.
`--skip-slave-start`	When starting up the database, don't start up the slave. Use this option if you want to have some of the slave options in your configuration file, but don't want the slave to start replicating automatically.
`--slave_compressed_protocol=<0|1>`	If the master and slave support it, a value of 1 will cause them to use compression for data exchange during replication.

Option	Description
`--slave-load-tmpdir=<file>`	Specifies an alternate location for temporary file storage. Used in replication of `LOAD DATA INFILE` statements where files need to be stored somewhere temporarily while being imported into the database.
`--slave-net-timeout=`➥ `<number seconds>`	Waits for this number of seconds for the master to send more data, and then considers the connection broken and retries.
`--slave-skip-errors=`➥ `<err_code, err_code,...	all>`	In replication, the default is that on any error, replication stops. This option allows you to tell the replication process to ignore certain error numbers, or all errors. This option can be dangerous, as problems in replication can get hidden. Use it cautiously. For more information on MySQL error numbers, see `http://dev.mysql.com/doc/mysql/en/error-handling.html`.

How Does MySQL Decide What to Replicate?

We've just looked at all the configuration options for replication in MySQL. A number of them are designed to allow you to control which tables are replicated. These include `replicate-do-`➥ `*`, `replicate-ignore-*`, and `replicate-wild-*`. You may wonder how MySQL parses these statements and prioritizes what statements to respect when there are multiple matches for a table.

MySQL uses a specific set of logical steps in determining whether each statement will get replicated. The logic used to decide where to stop in the tree is more fully documented in the MySQL documentation, but in general the rules are considered in the following order:

1. `replicate-do-db`

2. `replicate-ignore-db`

3. `replicate-do-table`

4. `replicate-ignore-table`

5. `replicate-wild-do-table`

6. `replicate-wild-ignore-table`

You can find more information on the details of the decision-making process at `http://dev.mysql.com/doc/mysql/en/replication-options.html`.

■**Tip** You can also control what gets replicated to slave servers by limiting what gets written to the binary log with the `binlog-do-db` and `binlog-ignore-db` options in your MySQL configuration. If a statement isn't written to the binary log, it won't be replicated to the slave machines. Use care with this option. If you're using the binary log to roll forward to a point in time after a restore from backup, you may run into trouble if you aren't writing all changes to the binary log.

Monitoring and Managing

Whether you're just embarking on setting up replication, or have been at it for years, being familiar with the tools to monitor and manage MySQL replication is the key to having well-performing, successfully replicating copies of your data. In this section, we'll go through seven key commands to keep your eyes on and to tweak your data replication.

■**Note** The tools provided with MySQL to monitor replication are designed to be run manually. For most production situations, you'll want to have an automated status update and alert system in place. Several scripts are available for building an alert system. See this URL for some of these scripts: http://dev.mysql.com/books/hpmysql-excerpts/ch07.html#hpmysql-CHP-7-SECT-5.4.2.

SHOW MASTER STATUS

The SHOW MASTER STATUS statement gives you information on the status of the master server as it relates to replication. Example output from this statement is shown in Listing 18-10.

Listing 18-10. *Output from SHOW MASTER STATUS*

```
mysql> SHOW MASTER STATUS;
+--------------------+----------+--------------+------------------+
| File               | Position | Binlog_Do_DB | Binlog_Ignore_DB |
+--------------------+----------+--------------+------------------+
| master-bin.000002  |     6016 |              |                  |
+--------------------+----------+--------------+------------------+
```

The output of this command includes the currently active binary log, the current position that MySQL is writing to the log, and the value of Binlog_Do_DB and Binlog_Ignore_DB. These last two columns show the value of the corresponding configuration options to limit the statements that are written to the binary log.

As you can see, this particular host is using binary log master-bin.000002 at position 6016. If you're running this statement as a part of creating a snapshot of your data, take note of the log name and position for use in your CHANGE MASTER command on the slave.

SHOW SLAVE HOSTS

This statement is run on the master server and returns a list of all the slaves that have registered and are replicating data from this machine. A replication slave registers with the master if the --report-host option is specified in the slave configuration options. Slaves that don't have --report-host won't appear in the SHOW SLAVE HOSTS command. Listing 18-11 shows an example of the output of this statement.

Listing 18-11. *Output from SHOW SLAVE HOSTS*

```
mysql> SHOW SLAVE HOSTS;
+-----------+-------------------+------+-------------------+-----------+
| Server_id | Host              | Port | Rpl_recovery_rank | Master_id |
+-----------+-------------------+------+-------------------+-----------+
|         2 | slave.example.edu | 3306 |                 0 |         1 |
+-----------+-------------------+------+-------------------+-----------+
```

The output includes the ID of the server, the host string that was reported, the port that replication is running on, the ranking of the machine for priority in getting updates from the master, and the ID of the master server.

SHOW SLAVE STATUS

The SHOW SLAVE STATUS command gives you a dump of information about the status of replication from the slave's point of view. Listing 18-12 shows a sample output. Using the \G option outputs in rows instead of columns.

Listing 18-12. *Output from SHOW SLAVE STATUS*

```
mysql> SHOW SLAVE STATUS\G
*************************** 1. row ***************************
               Slave_IO_State: Waiting for master to send event
                  Master_Host: master.example.edu
                  Master_User: replicate
                  Master_Port: 3306
                Connect_Retry: 60
              Master_Log_File: master-bin.000002
          Read_Master_Log_Pos: 6016
               Relay_Log_File: slave-relay-bin.000005
                Relay_Log_Pos: 232
        Relay_Master_Log_File: master-bin.000002
             Slave_IO_Running: Yes
            Slave_SQL_Running: Yes
              Replicate_Do_DB:
          Replicate_Ignore_DB:
           Replicate_Do_Table:
       Replicate_Ignore_Table:
      Replicate_Wild_Do_Table:
  Replicate_Wild_Ignore_Table:
                   Last_Errno: 0
                   Last_Error:
                 Skip_Counter: 0
          Exec_Master_Log_Pos: 6016
              Relay_Log_Space: 232
               Until_Condition: None
               Until_Log_File:
```

```
            Until_Log_Pos: 0
        Master_SSL_Allowed: No
        Master_SSL_CA_File:
        Master_SSL_CA_Path:
          Master_SSL_Cert:
        Master_SSL_Cipher:
           Master_SSL_Key:
     Seconds_Behind_Master: 0
```

This is a way to see all the settings that were specified in the options file or in the CHANGE MASTER statement, and to see the active log files and corresponding positions. The Slave_IO_Running and Slave_SQL_Running columns indicate that both slave threads are running, or more generally that the replication processes designated for the slave are operating. Three items deserve closer attention: slave state, last error, and seconds behind master.

Slave State

The slave's I/O thread is always in a state, which is displayed in the SHOW SLAVE STATUS command. Understanding the different states can be helpful in troubleshooting problems with replication. State messages point you to the specific step in the replication process that is having problems. Table 18-5 shows a list of the different states and a description of what's happening during that state.

Table 18-5. *Slave State Descriptions for Slave I/O Thread*

State	Description
Connecting to master	The thread is trying to create a connection to the master.
Checking master version	After the connection to the master is made, the slave checks the version of the master. This state happens immediately after the slave makes the connection, and is very brief.
Registering slave on master	The slave, after connecting, is now registering with the master. The slave is only in this state briefly.
Requesting binlog dump	The I/O thread on the slave is making a request to get the statements from the binary log.
Waiting to reconnect after a failed binlog dump request	The thread is sleeping while it waits for the next time to try to connect. The slave goes into this state on a failed attempt to get statements from the binary log.
Reconnecting after a failed binlog dump request	The thread is attempting to connect to the master after a failed attempt.
Waiting for master to send event	The thread has requested binary log entries from the master, and is waiting for the master I/O thread to respond with some data. This state is common, and in most cases means that the master doesn't have any statements to send just now.
Queuing master event to the relay log	The thread is putting entries returned from the master's binary log into the relay log on the slave.
Waiting to reconnect after a failed master event read	When reading the statements sent from the I/O on the master, an error occurred. Waiting to reconnect and try again.

State	Description
Reconnecting after a failed master event read	The last connection failed during a read of the statements sent from the master's binary log. Attempting to connect again.
Waiting for the slave SQL thread to free enough relay log space	The I/O thread is waiting for more space to be made for relay logs. This state occurs when the `relay_log_space_limit` option is specified and the slave needs to rotate those logs to free up more space.
Waiting for slave mutex on exit	The thread is in the process of stopping. The slave is only in this state briefly.

Last Error

The *last error* is the error number and message from the most recently executed SQL statement from the relay log. If the statement had no error, the value will be 0 for `Last_Errno`, and there will be no value in `Last_Error`. The errors are helpful in troubleshooting a failing replication.

Seconds Behind Master

The `Seconds_Behind_Master` column compares the time a statement was brought in from the I/O thread to the time that statement was processed. If your network is fast, and statements are getting to the slave quickly, the value of `Seconds_Behind_Master` will give you a pretty good sense of how long it takes for a statement to be processed. The slower the network connection, the less accurate this value.

To find the real value of how long it was between issuing a statement on the master and its execution on the slave, you need to create some monitoring or health-check scripts to test. Replication performance is addressed in the upcoming section "Replication Performance."

CHANGE MASTER

We looked at the `CHANGE MASTER` command back when we did the initial setup of our replication server. All the name/value pairs are optional, and you can use the `CHANGE MASTER` command to change any or all of the options. Table 18-1 and Table 18-3 laid out details about the values. Listing 18-13 recaps the command and shows all the available options.

Listing 18-13. *CHANGE MASTER Statement*

```
mysql> CHANGE MASTER TO MASTER_HOST = '<host name>',
MASTER_USER = '<user name>',
MASTER_PASSWORD = '<password>',
MASTER_PORT = <port number>,
MASTER_CONNECT_RETRY = <number seconds>,
MASTER_LOG_FILE = '<master log name>',
MASTER_LOG_POS = <master log position>,
RELAY_LOG_FILE = '<relay log name>',
RELAY_LOG_POS = <relay log position>,
MASTER_SSL = <0|1>,
MASTER_SSL_CA = '<ca file name>',
```

```
MASTER_SSL_CAPATH = '<ca directory path>',
MASTER_SSL_CERT = '<certificate file name>',
MASTER_SSL_KEY = '<key file name>',
MASTER_SSL_CIPHER = '<cipher list>';
```

■**Caution** When making changes to the configuration, be sure that either replication is stopped or that relay logs aren't being processed. You may want to check SHOW SLAVE STATUS for the state before executing a CHANGE MASTER statement.

START SLAVE

To start a slave running, issue the START SLAVE command. This will start replication using the options set with CHANGE MASTER, or in the master.info file from a previous start. By default this command starts both the I/O and the SQL threads, which start retrieving and processing statements from the master.

If you want to start only the I/O thread to read statements from the master, or only the SQL thread to process statements in the relay log, you can specify which thread to start. To start just the I/O thread, use the statement in Listing 18-14.

Listing 18-14. *Starting the I/O Thread*

```
START SLAVE IO_THREAD;
```

To start just the SQL thread, use the statement in Listing 18-15.

Listing 18-15. *Starting the SQL Thread*

```
START SLAVE SQL_THREAD;
```

You can also add conditions to the SQL thread startup with the UNTIL keyword. Adding this keyword tells the SQL thread to process statements up to a certain point in the binary or relay log. Listing 18-16 shows the syntax for a statement using the UNTIL clause.

Listing 18-16. *Starting the SQL Thread with the UNTIL Clause*

```
START SLAVE [sql_thread]
[UNTIL relay_log_file = '<log name>', relay_log_pos = <log position>] |
[UNTIL master_log_file = '<log name>', master_log_pos = <log position>];
```

With the UNTIL clause, you aren't allowed to mix the relay log options with the master log options. If you leave the sql_thread syntax out, both the I/O and SQL threads will start.

STOP SLAVE

You use the STOP SLAVE statement to tell the threads that have been running the replication processes to quit. You can execute it without any arguments to stop both the I/O and SQL threads, or specify which slave thread to stop, as shown in Listing 18-17.

Listing 18-17. *Stopping Replication*

```
STOP SLAVE [io_thread, sql_thread];
```

RESET SLAVE

The RESET SLAVE statement deletes the master.info and relay-log.info files, removes all relay logs, and starts fresh with a new relay log. This statement initiates a clean start. Along with the STOP SLAVE and CHANGE MASTER commands, the RESET SLAVE statement gives you the control to remove any connection with previous replication settings or positions.

■**Caution** When using RESET SLAVE, be aware that all relay logs are removed, even if statements in the relay log haven't been processed.

Replication Performance

Everyone wants to know how fast MySQL replicates data from a master to its slaves. That's a difficult question to answer. One thing is for sure: the data isn't available in the slave until after the statement is completed in the master. The fact is, the statement isn't written to the master's binary log until after the statement execution is complete on the master. This means that, at best, the statement is picked up the instant it's in the master's binary log, quickly copied to the slave server, and then run the instant it's appended to the relay log on the slave. How long does that process take?

Unfortunately, there's no concrete answer. Cursory tests in a single-slave environment with smaller records, on a server under little load, indicate a nearly undetectable delay.[4] However, a lot depends on your environment, including the servers, network, database load, and record size.

To answer how quickly the data will replicate in your environment, our recommendation is that you set up a test server for replication. This could be a full-blown testing environment, or if you don't have a large budget, an older server or unused desktop. Set up replication, with data changes in the master representative of the changes you see in your production database. Watch the Seconds_Behind_Master value from the SHOW SLAVE STATUS command, or create a script to test time differences between queries on the master and slave.[5] Perhaps you want to automate a regular check of the slave and record its health during different periods of activity on the master server. After you get a sense of how fast replication is working for your data, start to put some test loads on the slave server to see how offloading queries from the master, or accepting queries from elsewhere, would affect the delay between the master and slave.

Our sense is that replication works as fast as the environment allows it, which is nearly instantaneous in situations where the database load isn't overbearing and the hardware and

---

4. Information about this test can be found at http://dev.mysql.com/books/hpmysql-excerpts/ch07.html#hpmysql-CHP-7-SECT-1.3.

5. If you have the time on the machines synced, one idea is to insert a record into a table using the time() function, or have a timestamp column. Because the time() function is in the replicated statement, the insert into the table on the slave is a certain number of seconds later than the insert into the master.

network are sufficient. We encourage you to consider the following five factors as you try to assess (or improve) the performance of your replication environment.

Hardware

First, replication is only going to be as fast as your disks and CPU can save, retrieve, and process statements from the binary and relay log files. This applies to more than just replication, but is a factor in how fast the server can communicate an addition to the binary log out to a slave server.

Network

Your network is a key link in replication speed. Every statement logged on the master server needs to be sent across the network to your slave servers. A slow or congested network has a significant effect on the delay on your slave servers.

MySQL replication doesn't do any network magic that enables it to push traffic across a network at lightning speed. It uses TCP/IP for communicating changes, and is subject to the same bandwidth limits, bottlenecks, and packet failures that normal network traffic encounters. If you have a slow connection between your servers, and someone decides to copy a 5GB log file from one machine to the other, your replication speeds will suffer accordingly.

Database Load

The load on your master database affects the speed of your replication. Not only does it take more work to keep feeding the ever-increasing binary log statements to the slave, the thread has to compete with the other MySQL threads for access to the disk and CPU time.

Record Size

Records executed on the master have to be read from the binary log file, transferred across the network, saved into the relay log file, read from the relay log file, and executed in the slave database. The size of your record plays a role in how fast MySQL can move through all these steps. If you have a record with three char(10) columns, the transfer will be much faster than a record with a 15MB BLOB.

Amount of Data and Types of Queries

The amount of data and types of queries you run against that data will have an effect on how quickly changes are seen in the slave. Suppose you have several million rows of data in a table. You perform an update with a WHERE clause that requires a full-table scan and updates half the records in the table. If the statement takes 20 seconds to run on the master, it will be at least 20 seconds until those changes are seen in the slave. Even if it only takes 1 millisecond to get the statement from the master to the slave, it will take the same amount of time to process on the slave.[6]

---

6. This is assuming you haven't done some trickery with the indexes on the slave, which could make the statement run faster (or slower) on the slave.

Replication Examples

To get a better sense of what kind of configurations are possible, we provide a few configuration options in this section, complete with diagrams.

Simple Replication

The simplest type of replication is to have one master and a single slave that replicates the master's data. This is the easiest environment to set up and maintain. This setup provides a hot-backup copy of your data, or a separate database to use to take backups without interrupting the production database. Figure 18-3 shows the simplest of replication setups.

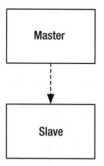

Figure 18-3. *Single-server replication*

The single-server replication is the easiest to restore when there are replication problems. If replication has stopped, getting it back up and running involves working with just one master and one slave machine. The worst-case scenario to get back up and running is that you have to go through the setup process, starting with taking another snapshot of the master, and so on.

Multiple Slaves

A slightly more involved replication environment is where you have multiple slaves getting data from the same master. Figure 18-4 shows four slaves pointing at a single master.

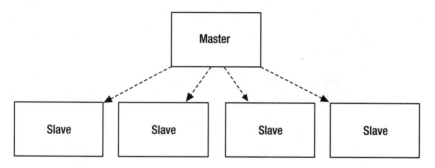

Figure 18-4. *Multislave replication*

This type of setup is good for environments with heavy loads of read queries, with fewer writes. All write statements are directed to the master, and reads are spread across many slave servers. This reduces the load on any single server and can also provide redundancy. If one of the slaves fails, traffic can easily be pushed off to one of the other slaves.

Note A master can have multiple slaves, but a slave can only have one master. As we discussed in the section "How MySQL Implements Replication," there are no tools to merge updates from multiple servers. Even if you were tempted to try, MySQL's configuration file only allows you to specify one `master_host` parameter.

Daisy Chain

Although having multiple slaves pointed to a single master works well in certain situations, there may be other cases where creating a chain of replicated machines meets your needs better. Perhaps having many machines replicating from a single master requires too much work for your master, or your replication environment is spread across such a large geographic area that chaining the closest ones together gives you better replication speed.

Whatever the reason, it's entirely possible to set up a slave server to one machine as a master to another. As long as you have a unique server ID in the configuration of a server, and have binary logging enabled, any server can be a master, even if its statements are coming from another master. Figure 18-5 shows a sample configuration where servers are daisy-chained together.

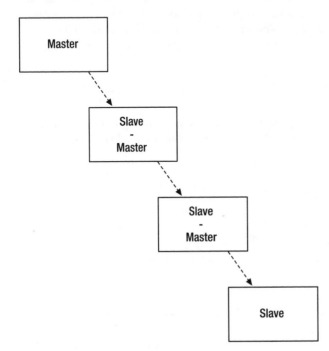

Figure 18-5. *Daisy chain of replicated servers*

To make this possible, be sure that each slave is recording updates from the master in its binary log with the `--log-slave-updates` option.

Repairing a daisy-chain replication environment can be tricky, especially if a catastrophic failure on one of the middle machines sets off a failure in all the slaves below. In an ideal situation, you would repair the faulty machine and start replication back up to find that the slaves downstream have continued to wait for the next update and picked right back up where they left off. A more difficult scenario would be a failure that required a new snapshot from the master, going down through each replicated machine restoring from the snapshot, and manually restarting replication.

Other

You're probably getting the sense that there's little restriction on the kinds of replication environments you can build. Indeed, with the configuration options and ability for a slave to be a master, there is a ton of flexibility with MySQL replication configurations. You might have a large tree of replicated databases that contains three, four, or five levels of replication, each level with different fine-grained controls over the list of databases and/or tables that get replicated down to the next level. Or you might have a daisy chain of servers with multiple slaves running off each master in the chain. There are no limits, except your sanity.

Remember, with each layer you add to your environment, the environment becomes that much more difficult to maintain. Resolving an issue with a server that feeds to a tree of ten other database servers can lead to a lot of work. Be careful of how creative and deep your investment into replication goes.

■**Note** There's a chance that reading about replication in MySQL has made you uneasy, or you wish that replication was more full-featured, or implemented in another way. If that's the case, you might want to look at the available third-party solutions. Many commercial products offer replication as well as clustering for redundancy and high availability, including multimaster replication. A few open-source projects also offer wrappers for MySQL. Rather than getting into specific vendors, check out this link for a list of MySQL partners, in which you can find MySQL-endorsed products that offer third-party replication tools: http://solutions.mysql.com/.

Summary

Replication in MySQL opens up possibilities for significant expansion of your database system. Hopefully we've conveyed the importance of careful planning to determine why and how replication fits into your system.

We spent a good deal of time throughout the chapter focusing on setting up, configuring, monitoring, and maintaining your replication servers. Armed with this information, you're equipped to embark on a venture into replication, or improve your existing replication setup.

Replication is an exciting technology, and although MySQL's implementation doesn't have all the bells and whistles of other database systems, it gives you a lot of room to build a customized system.

We hope your environment has replication requirements, or areas where replication could meet an unmet need. We see implementing a replication system as one of those fun, exciting technical challenges. We hope you look at replication in the same way.

CHAPTER 19

■ ■ ■

Cluster

Most database administrators spend time worrying about the availability of their database, and how to provide uninterrupted access to the data. In the past two chapters, we've gone over backups and replication and talked about how they might fit into building a system in which you can minimize downtime if a server or database fails. With a backup on hand, you can minimize the downtime for a database to as little as the time it takes to restore the data from your backup. Replicating your data to a second machine to serve as a hot copy of your data should mean even less downtime than waiting for a backup to restore. In both these instances you still have some downtime. You can reduce the downtime even further by building your application, or a database access layer under your application, to move automatically to the replicated database if the primary database becomes unavailable. To do this requires a significant design and development effort.

Part of determining the effectiveness of your backup or replication plan is to assess just how much downtime is acceptable. Most managers will respond with, "We cannot have any downtime," but when presented with information about the cost associated with trying to provide an uptime guarantee, the response usually softens. Many organizations can live with the one or two hours it takes to restore a backup of the data to a machine, or the few minutes it takes to point the application at a new database server that has been replicating the data.

But what if you can't afford that kind of downtime? What if you're running an application that contains critical data for a hospital information system, or are running a high-volume e-commerce site that loses money each second the database is down? Even if you don't have this kind of critical situation, you may have a client or manager who requires that his or her database be capable of having a server die and to have no interruption in the flow of data to the application.

To meet the needs of those who require a highly available database, MySQL provides the NDBCLUSTER storage engine, which spreads data redundantly across many servers and provides access to the data as if the servers were all one. The cluster spreads data across the servers in a way that allows any one of the servers to go offline and not interrupt the availability of the database or data either to users or your application. If you're running a system with a set of load-balanced web servers spread across several data centers, and are looking for a database to back your application that requires the same level of scalability, redundancy, and availability, MySQL Cluster is worth a close look.

■**Note** You don't have to have a huge data center filled with servers to be interested in, or even benefit from, MySQL Cluster. It can be set up on as few as three servers and still provide complete redundancy.

If you've come to MySQL with clustering technology experience from another database, this chapter should give you an idea of how MySQL implements clustering.

Through the remainder of the chapter we'll discuss the following topics:

- What clustering is

- How MySQL implements clusters

- How to install MySQL Cluster

- Configuring and setting up a cluster implementation

- Using `ndb_mgmd`, `ndbd`, and `ndb_mgm`

- Options for configuring your cluster

- Managing the cluster

- What the log files contain

- Protecting your cluster

Once you've finished reading this chapter, you should have a good idea of what's going on under the hood of MySQL's cluster engine, and how to set up and maintain a clustered database successfully.

■**Caution** While we've been writing this book, a large percentage of the development activity for MySQL has been on the cluster code. With a lot of development activity, things change quickly. Although most of the concepts will remain the same, the details of MySQL's cluster engine may change. As of this writing, MySQL is using version 4.1.12 for production, and makes reference to how things used to be done in 4.1.9. If you're using an older or newer version than these, please review MySQL's online documentation to get up-to-date information at `http://dev.mysql.com/doc/mysql/en/ndbcluster.html`. Information about new cluster features is available at `http://dev.mysql.com/doc/mysql/en/mysql-5-1-cluster-roadmap.html`.

What Is Clustering?

The concept of clustering has been around for a long time—almost as long as computers themselves. In general, the cluster concept is about grouping multiple computers together to behave as one, either to provide parallel computing power or for redundancy if one of the machines goes down. A cluster is an abstract representation of the individual computers, which allows the individual computers to come and go without any visible interruption to the user interacting with the computer cluster.

Database clustering flows right along those lines. A database cluster spreads data across a set of servers to provide scalability and redundancy. Just like a computer cluster, a database cluster can withstand a machine going down and still continue to provide access to the data. A properly configured cluster has duplicate copies of the data in multiple machines in the cluster. A cluster also provides scalability, in that you can easily add servers to the cluster for more processing power, memory, or storage space. If you need more storage space, or want improved performance, you add more servers to the cluster to assume some of the database burden.

In the database world, we tend to look at clusters primarily as a way to provide guaranteed uptime. With a set of clustered databases, any one of the machines can go offline and not interrupt the database availability. The cluster also provides more processing power as the cluster size increases.

As hinted at in the introduction, MySQL's clustered database technology started in 2003 with the purchase of an Ericsson division called Alzato. Alzato was developing a database product for use in telecommunications. This database uses cluster concepts to provide highly available databases.

■**Note** Throughout this book, we've pushed for good policy and implementation plans for your database. Using MySQL Cluster shouldn't be any different. Before you embark on getting servers allocated, set up, and configured, be sure you've taken time to sit down with your data owners and explain the advantages and disadvantages of MySQL Cluster. Make a formal document outlining your implementation plan, including how the cluster will be configured and managed.

MySQL's Cluster Implementation

MySQL makes cluster technology available through its NDBCLUSTER storage engine. From the client perspective, using the cluster engine is just like interacting with any other storage engine. Because MySQL provides clients with a unified mechanism to access data in the various storage engines, using the cluster involves using the same familiar command-line interface or programmatic access method you've been using to get to tables in other storage engines.

To be fair, although client access is similar to using the other storage engines, this storage engine isn't exactly the same. The MyISAM and InnoDB storage engines come prebuilt and are ready to use upon installation and startup of the database. Any initialization required of these storage engines is performed when the database is started up. Using the cluster engine is more involved. Because a cluster involves several servers, there are a number of steps to go through before the cluster engine is available to the client. These steps are covered in more detail in the section "Initial Configuration and Startup," but before we get into that, let's first go through an overview of how MySQL clustering works. The cluster engine is similar to HEAP tables in that it stores all the data in memory. Like InnoDB, the cluster storage engine supports transactions. Any transaction that isn't complete when a node dies is rolled back. Failed transactions should be handled in the application.

Nodes

MySQL uses the term *node* to describe a specific process within the cluster system. Often, a process is associated with an individual server, but it's also possible to run multiple processes, or nodes, on one machine.

There are three kinds of nodes: SQL, storage, and management. Each node serves a specific purpose in a functioning cluster.

SQL Node

A SQL node provides client access to the data in the storage nodes. The SQL node runs inside a MySQL server process. On startup, the SQL node consults the cluster configuration information on the management node to obtain information on the available storage nodes. Once up and running, the MySQL server accepts queries, and after appropriate parsing and permission checking, passes the required information to the cluster storage engine to retrieve the data.

■**Note** The MySQL Cluster SQL and storage nodes operate independently enough that you can run both on the same server. Although this might have some financial gain and mean fewer machines to administrate, it means your system won't be as scalable or highly available. If you run a cluster with the SQL node on the same server as your storage node and the machine crashes, you risk losing both the data and access to the data.

Storage Node

A storage node is typically associated with a single server, but multiple storage nodes can exist on one machine. The storage node runs an ndbd process to coordinate storage and retrieval activity with the other nodes and communicate with the management server. Along with the ndbd process, storage nodes store data in memory.

It's natural to be curious about how the storage nodes interoperate to coordinate multimachine storage and retrieval of data. Each storage node has three main components: a transaction coordinator, index storage, and data storage. When the SQL node receives a request and is ready to retrieve the data, it makes a request of the transaction coordinator on one of the storage nodes. Storage nodes are chosen in round-robin fashion. If a particular storage node is unavailable, the transaction coordinator from the next storage node is used.

The transaction coordinator is capable of retrieving data from the index and data storage that's a part of its own node, as well as indexes and data from any of the other nodes. If the data needed is spread across four nodes, the transaction coordinator will retrieve the information from the data storage on all four nodes and return it to the SQL node. Each storage node keeps a pool of I/O threads for processing requests for data.

Management Node

The management node is responsible for providing information about the cluster to each SQL and storage node as it starts up. When a SQL or storage node starts up, it looks to the management node to get information about the cluster configuration and storage nodes in the cluster. Thus, the management node must be configured and running before any of the storage nodes can be started. The management node is also responsible for collecting log entries from the nodes and writing them to central log files.

Once the SQL and storage nodes are running, they can operate independently from the management node. If the management node becomes unavailable, the other nodes will continue normal operation, minus the central logging provided by the management node. Having said that, it's a good idea to keep your management node up and running because it provides a set of tools to manage your cluster, even if it's busy checking the status of your cluster, stopping or starting nodes, or running backups. We'll cover commands in the management client later in the chapter.

■**Note** To be clear, the management node has two different processes that run: the management server and the management client. The management server is a daemon that interacts with all the nodes in the cluster. The management client is a command-line tool you use to issue commands that control and check the status of the cluster.

Node Arrangement

Like replication in MySQL, clustering offers a lot of flexibility. We're including a few example arrangements to give you some ideas about how your set of nodes might be arranged.

Your node arrangement is based on both the data availability policy you've defined with your stakeholders, and what hardware is necessary to meet the demands of your system. Once you've decided that a MySQL cluster can meet your policy, you need to determine how many machines are needed to meet your query demands and provide the appropriate amount of redundancy. Here are a few sample arrangements to get you thinking.

Simple Arrangement

To have redundant storage you need at least two storage nodes. Figure 19-1 shows a simple node arrangement. In this configuration the storage nodes each have a complete set of the data, and are independent of the SQL node.

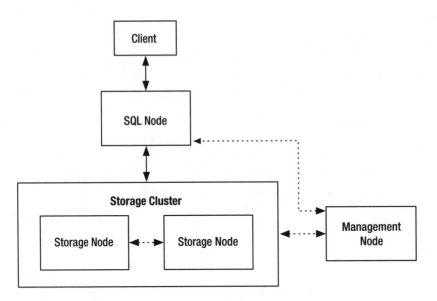

Figure 19-1. *Simple node arrangement*

As Figure 19-1 shows, the client connects to a SQL node, which has obtained information about the storage cluster from the management node at startup. The storage cluster contains redundant storage nodes with duplicate copies of the data. In this configuration, either of the storage nodes could go down and the cluster would remain up, serving data from the remaining storage node.

Robust Arrangement

You might be curious about what will happen if the SQL node in Figure 19-1 goes down. To make your system completely redundant, you should have multiple SQL nodes. Figure 19-2 shows a more robust configuration.

In this configuration, we've specified redundant SQL nodes and have doubled the storage nodes. We've assigned each client to a node, which provides two different independent interfaces to the data. This arrangement might fit well into a web environment where the web servers are behind a load balancer. If either of the SQL nodes goes down and pages aren't available on the associated web server, the load balancer pushes traffic to the other machine until you have a chance to repair the failing SQL node.

Minimalist Arrangement

Before leaving the conversation about node arrangements, we want to show how you can build a redundant cluster with just three servers. We've mentioned this previously in the chapter, and the three-server setup is the example featured in an article on MySQL's site at `http://dev.mysql.com/tech-resources/articles/mysql-cluster-for-two-servers.html`.[1] To get redundancy in both SQL and storage nodes with three servers, you combine the SQL and storage nodes onto the same machines. Figure 19-3 shows this arrangement.

---

1. The article claims to be geared toward a two-server setup, but immediately discloses that three machines are needed for true redundancy.

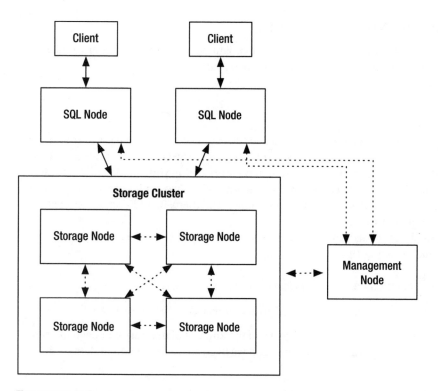

Figure 19-2. *Robust node arrangement*

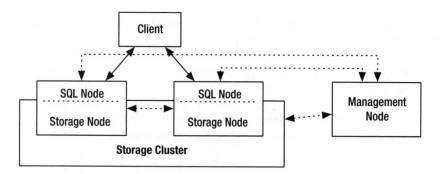

Figure 19-3. *Minimalist node arrangement*

As shown in Figure 19-3, the SQL nodes can run on the same machines as the storage nodes. Because the SQL node (mysqld) and storage node (ndbd) are separate processes, they can run on the same machine without conflict. If one of the machines in this arrangement goes down, you still have an available database on the other machine.

Again, we reiterate that finding the right node arrangement is a matter of your data availability policy, combined with the anticipated load that will be put on the cluster.

Calculating the Number of Nodes

Having looked at a few sample configurations, you might be wondering how many nodes you should have in your cluster. You need to consider two primary factors, besides cost: memory and performance.

Memory

The first and most concrete factor when choosing how many nodes to have is the amount of memory you need to store your data. As we've mentioned, a MySQL cluster stores all data in memory, which means you need to have enough memory within your storage nodes to store all your data twice. Why twice? Because the cluster always has two copies of your data, so when one of the storage nodes goes down, your data is still there. In addition, the storage nodes need memory to run the ndbd process.

You can calculate the recommended amount of memory needed in each of your nodes by using the formula in Listing 19-1.

Listing 19-1. *Formula for Calculating Required Memory*

```
(MB of data * number of replicas * 1.1)/number of nodes = MB in each node
```

Listing 19-1 shows the calculation to give you the amount of memory you need in each machine. Listing 19-2 shows an example in which we need space for 500MB of data on a cluster with two replicas and four nodes.

Listing 19-2. *Example Calculation of Required Memory*

```
(500 * 2 * 1.1)/4 = 275
```

Based on this calculation, the layout shown in Figure 19-2 would require each of the storage nodes to have 275MB of memory available to be successful in the cluster. Obviously, as your data needs grow the amount of memory on each server becomes significantly larger. A system with 50GB of data will take either a few very expensive machines with a lot of memory or a slew of less expensive machines with less memory.[2]

You should be generous when calculating the amount of space you need in the cluster machines. Expanding memory can be significantly more difficult than adding disk space, especially if you have machines that already have their memory slots filled.

Performance

The second thing to consider when deciding how many nodes to put in your cluster is performance and scalability. A busy storage node can easily consume the CPU of a server. As you explore using the NDBCLUSTER engine, run some tests with data from your production database to get a sense of how scalable the engine is. You can set up a single SQL/storage node to run these tests to begin with, just to experiment. As you get more serious about moving your storage to a cluster, you'll want to perform more significant tests on dedicated hardware to get results that can be used for projections on hardware needs and expected performance.

---

2. At some point in the near future, 50GB of memory in a system will be standard, and we'll chuckle about this paragraph.

Using the Cluster

Like any other storage engine, you must use a `mysqld` server that's compiled with the cluster engine into the database when it's built. We recommend using a prebuilt max binary, which has the cluster engine and tools built in.

Because a cluster involves several servers and has a set of its own configuration variables, the configuration of the cluster involves some setup that isn't required with the MyISAM or InnoDB engines. Once the cluster is configured and started, you can create tables in the cluster just like in any other storage engine by using the `engine=NDBCLUSTER` statement at the end of the `CREATE TABLE` or `ALTER TABLE` statement.

Note As of the writing of this chapter, MySQL only provides binaries with built-in support for MySQL Cluster for Linux, Solaris, and Mac OS X. A Windows version is promised to be coming.

Limitations of MySQL Cluster

Cluster technology is fairly new to MySQL. Even though the cluster engine now available in MySQL is a solid storage engine, it was developed for requirements that may differ from what you might think should be standard for a database. Since adding the `NDBCLUSTER` storage engine, MySQL's developers have been actively working on the cluster code to integrate it more fully into MySQL and provide a clustered storage engine that looks and behaves more like the other storage engines (MyISAM, InnoDB, and so on).

We'd like to point out a few of MySQL Cluster's current limitations, not as a comprehensive list, but to show you some of the primary limitations and give you an idea of how using the NDB storage engine might be different from MyISAM or InnoDB:

Note It's clear, from looking at the activity in the source code, that the MySQL developers are busily working on removing these limitations. Although it's important to document them, we encourage you to look to the online documentation to verify that a limitation is still valid if it's a concern. You can find the change history of MySQL Cluster at `http://dev.mysql.com/doc/mysql/en/mysql-cluster-change-history.htm`.

- Except for `BLOB` fields, each record can only contain up to 8K of data.

- MySQL Cluster currently uses memory for all data storage. Although this makes the database operations extremely fast, it can be an issue when there are large amounts of data. The MySQL documents suggest that developing disk-based storage as an option is high on the priority list.

- The combined database and table name for a particular table must be less than 122 characters. If you have a database name that is 22 characters (for example, `east_fullfilment_centr`), the tables within that database only have 100 of the total 122 characters to use for their name.

- Column names can be no longer than 31 characters. If a table is created with column names longer than 31 characters, the column names are truncated. Truncation may result in an error if the truncated columns aren't unique.

- In MySQL Cluster, all fields are fixed length. This means that even if you use a VARCHAR data type, the entire space for that record will be allocated when storing the data, even if the data doesn't require all the space.

- In total, the number of database, table, index, and BLOB objects cannot exceed 1,600.

- Each table is limited to having 128 attributes (columns).

- Foreign keys aren't supported. Foreign key statements are ignored in CREATE or ALTER commands.

- Although you can stop and start defined nodes without causing any cluster unavailability, adding a new node to the cluster requires a change to the management's configuration file. Changes in the configuration require a complete stop and start of all the nodes in the cluster to become aware of the new node. This means some downtime for your cluster.

- Not all character sets are supported. As of writing this chapter, the following character sets are supported: big5, binary, euckr, gb2312, gbk, latin1, sjis, tis620, ucs2, ujis, and utf8.

- Prefix indexes (indexing of first few characters of a field) aren't supported. Indexes always cover the entire field.

- WKT and WKB geometric data types are not supported.

- There's no support for partial rollback in transactions. NDB tables always roll back the entire transaction on a failure.

- Query cache support is disabled because there is no way for invalidation of the cache on nodes other than the local node.

- Because each server in the cluster maintains its own binary log, replication from the cluster requires making all data changes on one machine in the cluster.

- You cannot mix big-endian and little-endian systems in your cluster. The management and storage nodes must be the same architecture. Clients' connections can come from any architecture.

MySQL maintains a list of current limitations, which is longer than the list we've presented here and gets into more detail. As MySQL continues its integration and enhancement of the cluster engine, the limitation list will get smaller. You can watch the progress on the cluster software by looking at the change history, which provides a general overview of the improvements being made to the software. Here's a pointer to MySQL's cluster limitations and change history documents: http://dev.mysql.com/doc/mysql/en/mysql-cluster-limitations-in-4-1.html.

Installing MySQL Cluster

To use or try MySQL's cluster technology, you need the clustering tools installed on your server. If you're running version 4.1.3 or later, and have installed using the max binaries, the necessary tools are already installed on your machines. If you're using an older version of MySQL, or have installed from the standard binary package, you need to update to a more current version of MySQL.

The max binary package includes binaries that have cluster support compiled inside them. The installation also sticks a collection of binaries in your bin directory, including the storage node daemon (ndbd), the management node daemon (ndb_mgmd), and the management client, ndb_mgm.

■Note MySQL's instructions for installing the management node include making a copy of only the necessary binary files ndb_mgmd and ndb_mgm into a directory and discarding the rest of the installation. This reduces the number of files on your system, but isn't necessary for running the cluster management node. If you've installed the max binary, it's not necessary to remove the extra files.

Initial Configuration and Startup

With all your machines equipped with the latest max binary, you're ready to get in, do some configuring, and start up your cluster. You'll first configure and start the management server, then configure and start the storage nodes, and finally start up with SQL nodes. For the purpose of our example, we'll use the setup shown in Figure 19-3, which has a management node, two storage nodes, and two SQL nodes.

Management Node

The management server is the first place to start. You must configure and start it before the storage and SQL nodes are started, or they'll fail on startup.

Configure

The management node requires the most significant configuration, but it's still fairly straightforward to put together. You should put the configuration file in a location that will be used for the cluster log files. For our example, we put it at /var/lib/mysql, but you may have another preference. With your favorite editor, create a file /var/lib/mysql/config.ini that looks like Listing 19-3.

Listing 19-3. *Sample Management Node Configuration*

```
[NDBD DEFAULT]
NoOfReplicas=2
DataMemory=80M
IndexMemory=52M

[TCP DEFAULT]

[NDB_MGMD]
hostname=<ip of your management node>
datadir=/var/lib/mysql

[NDBD]
hostname=<ip of first storage node>
datadir=/var/lib/mysql

[NDBD]
hostname=<ip of second storage node>
datadir=/var/lib/mysql

[MYSQLD]
hostname=<ip of SQL node>

[MYSQLD]
hostname=<ip of SQL node>
```

We'll go into more detail on what's happening in this configuration file later in the chapter. For now, you get an idea that we have several different sections, similar to the my.cnf file, the first two applying to all nodes and the remaining four applying to individual nodes in the cluster. The configuration file has one [NDBD] section for each storage node and one [MYSQLD] section for every SQL node in the cluster.

Start

With the configuration file created for the management server, it's time to start the management server. Listing 19-4 shows the command to run as root (change the path if your MySQL binaries are located elsewhere).

Listing 19-4. *Command to Start the Cluster Management Daemon*

```
shell> /usr/local/mysql/bin/ndb_mgmd -f /var/lib/mysql/config.ini
```

You shouldn't see any output when starting up the management daemon. In fact, if you do see some output, it's likely to be about an error in the configuration file. Listing 19-5 displays what might show up if you had an error on line 3 of your configuration file.

Listing 19-5. *Sample Error from the Management Daemon*

```
Error line 3: Parse error
Error line 3: Could not parse name-value pair in config file.
Unable to read config file
```

If you see output like Listing 19-5, look at the line number in your configuration file and check it against the documentation.

Storage Nodes

With the management node up and running, you're ready to configure and start up the storage nodes. You'll need to follow these steps for each storage node in your cluster.

Configure

The configuration for storage nodes goes right into your standard my.cnf file. Add the lines shown in Listing 19-6.

Listing 19-6. *Sample Storage Node Configuration*

```
[MYSQL_CLUSTER]
ndb-connectstring=<ip of management node>
```

The storage node daemon uses the MYSQL_CLUSTER section options when starting up. You only need one option for the storage node to operate: the location of the management server. For our initial setup, everything else is contained in the management node's configuration file.

Before you move on to starting up the node, be sure the data directory you specified in the management node exists.

Start

To start the storage node for the first time, use the command in Listing 19-7. You should only pass the --initial option the first time the daemon is started, or any time you want to reload the configuration. Using this option removes all node recovery files.

Listing 19-7. *Command to Start the Cluster Storage Node Daemon*

```
shell> /user/local/mysql/bin/ndbd --initial
```

If the management server isn't available, you'll get an error during startup indicating that it couldn't find the management server.

SQL Node

With the management node and storage nodes up, we're ready to configure and start the final piece: the SQL node that allows us to interact with the storage engine.

Configure

The configuration options for the SQL node go into your my.cnf file, right in the [mysqld] section of your configuration, as shown in Listing 19-8.

Listing 19-8. *Sample Configuration for the SQL Node*

```
[MYSQLD]
ndbcluster
ndb-connectstring=<ip of management node>[:<port>]
```

The ndbcluster option tells this MySQL server that it will have the cluster as an engine and that it should pull information about the cluster from the management server. The default port is 1186. The port isn't required, but if your SQL nodes aren't connecting when you start them, add the port to the ndb-connectstring.

Start

To start up a SQL node, you simply start the MySQL server as you would normally. Listing 19-9 shows the startup command we're so familiar with, to be run as root.

Listing 19-9. *Start the SQL Node of the Cluster*

```
shell> /usr/local/mysql/bin/mysqld_safe &
```

If the management server isn't available, you'll get an error during startup indicating that it couldn't find the management server.

Check Processes

We'll cover the management client in greater detail later in the chapter, but before we call our initial startup good, let's take a quick peek at the cluster from the view of the management client. On the management server, start the management client and issue the SHOW command as shown by the two statements in Listing 19-10.

Listing 19-10. *Start the Cluster Management Client*

```
shell> /usr/local/mysql/bin/ndb_mgm
ndb_mgm> show
```

The result of this command should be something like the output in Listing 19-11.

Listing 19-11. *Output from the Cluster SHOW Command*

```
Cluster Configuration
---------------------
[ndbd(NDB)]     2 node(s)
id=2    @10.0.0.103  (Version: 4.1.12, Nodegroup: 0, Master)
id=3    @10.0.0.104  (Version: 4.1.12, Nodegroup: 0)
```

```
[ndb_mgmd(MGM)] 1 node(s)
id=1    @10.0.0.102  (Version: 4.1.12)

[mysqld(API)]   2 node(s)
id=4    @10.0.0.103  (Version: 4.1.12)
id=5    @10.0.0.104  (Version: 4.1.12)
```

You can see from the output in Listing 19-11 that we have two storage nodes, one management node, and two SQL nodes running. You can also see that the storage node with ID 2 is specified to serve as the master record for the data. If you get output indicating the node isn't connected, you may need to go back to the machine and verify that the process started and that the configuration file is correct on the node. If complications continue, you may want to look in the logs, which will be discussed shortly.

Once the cluster is set up, you probably want to see it in action. To do so, let's get on one of our SQL nodes and interact with the cluster.

To start, we'll get on the SQL node with the ID of 4 and create a table, customer, and insert some data, as shown in Listing 19-12.

Listing 19-12. *Create a Table in the Cluster*

```
mysql-node4> CREATE TABLE customer (
    -> customer_id INTEGER NOT NULL AUTO_INCREMENT PRIMARY KEY,
    -> name VARCHAR(10)
    -> ) ENGINE=NDBCLUSTER;
Query OK, 0 rows affected (0.69 sec)
mysql-node4> INSERT INTO customer VALUES (1,'Mike'),
    -> (2,'Jay'),
    -> (3,'Johanna'),
    -> (4,'Michael'),
    -> (5,'Heidi'),
    -> (6,'Ezra');
Query OK, 6 rows affected (0.01 sec)
Records: 6  Duplicates: 0  Warnings: 0
```

■**Note** When creating databases to be used in MySQL Cluster, you must issue the CREATE DATABASE statement on each SQL node in the cluster, as the statement isn't propagated to each node in the cluster.

The CREATE TABLE statement in Listing 19-12 is like any other statement to create a table, except it specifies that the cluster should be used for storing the table and data with the ENGINE = NDBCLUSTER syntax.

With the table created and data inserted in the cluster, you should be able to see those changes from the other SQL node. Listing 19-13 shows a SELECT statement issued on SQL node 5.

Listing 19-13. *SELECT Data from the Other SQL Node*

```
mysql-node5> SELECT * FROM customer;
+-------------+---------+
| customer_id | name    |
+-------------+---------+
|           1 | Mike    |
|           3 | Johanna |
|           5 | Heidi   |
|           6 | Ezra    |
|           2 | Jay     |
|           4 | Michael |
+-------------+---------+
6 rows in set (0.11 sec)
```

The SELECT statement on the other SQL node demonstrates that you can get at the data from either of the SQL nodes.

To further prove that the cluster is operating correctly, let's simulate a situation where one of the nodes becomes unavailable and make sure that you can still use the database and bring the node back from the crash.

First, remove the customer table from the cluster:

```
mysql-node4> DROP TABLE customer;
Query OK, 0 rows affected (0.50 sec)

mysql-node4> SHOW tables;
Empty set (0.01 sec)
```

Now, to see what happens when a storage node is removed from the cluster, pull the node identified with ID 2 for storage and ID 4 for SQL. When we remove this node (whether it be by pulling the power or network cord), the SHOW statement on the management node indicates that nodes in the configuration aren't connected. Listing 19-14 shows the status after this node is removed.

Listing 19-14. *Output from the Cluster SHOW Command with Disconnected Nodes*

```
Cluster Configuration
---------------------
[ndbd(NDB)]     2 node(s)
id=2 (not connected, accepting connect from 10.0.0.103)
id=3    @10.0.0.104  (Version: 4.1.12, Nodegroup: 0)

[ndb_mgmd(MGM)] 1 node(s)
id=1    @10.0.0.102  (Version: 4.1.12)

[mysqld(API)]   2 node(s)
id=4 (not connected, accepting connect from 10.0.0.103)
id=5    @10.0.0.104  (Version: 4.1.12)
```

With the server at IP 10.0.0.103 missing, the SHOW command indicates that an expected storage and SQL node aren't connected.

However, even while those two nodes are missing, you can still connect to SQL node 5 and interact with the data. With a node down, you can continue to create tables and data as if the database were completely available. Listing 19-15 shows how you'd look at the existing tables and create the customer table again. This time you're creating it on node 5 while nodes 4 and 2 are offline.

Listing 19-15. *Creating a Table with Unavailable Database Nodes*

```
mysql-node5> show tables;
Empty set (0.01 sec)

mysql-node5> CREATE TABLE customer (
    -> customer_id INTEGER NOT NULL AUTO_INCREMENT PRIMARY KEY,
    -> name VARCHAR(10)
    -> ) ENGINE=NDBCLUSTER;
Query OK, 0 rows affected (0.55 sec)

mysql-node5> INSERT INTO customer VALUES (1,'Mike'),
    -> (2,'Jay'),
    -> (3,'Johanna'),
    -> (4,'Michael'),
    -> (5,'Heidi'),
    -> (6,'Ezra');
Query OK, 6 rows affected (0.01 sec)
Records: 6  Duplicates: 0  Warnings: 0
```

You've just created a new table and inserted a number of rows of data while node 4 was completely unavailable. If you bring node 4 back up, as shown in Listing 19-16, the SHOW command on the management node indicates that the storage and SQL nodes are back up and functioning on that server.

Listing 19-16. *Output from the Cluster SHOW Command with Reconnected Nodes*

```
Cluster Configuration
---------------------
[ndbd(NDB)]     2 node(s)
id=2    @10.0.0.103  (Version: 4.1.12, Nodegroup: 0)
id=3    @10.0.0.104  (Version: 4.1.12, Nodegroup: 0, Master)

[ndb_mgmd(MGM)] 1 node(s)
id=1    @10.0.0.102  (Version: 4.1.12)

[mysqld(API)]   2 node(s)
id=4    @10.0.0.103  (Version: 4.1.12)
id=5    @10.0.0.104  (Version: 4.1.12)
```

You might ask, "Will the node that was unavailable be brought up to speed with data in the other node?" The answer is yes. When the unconnected node is brought back online, the data from the good node is replicated back onto the server. A SELECT on node 4, which was unavailable as you created the table and inserted data on node 5, shows that the data is also available on node 4 after it comes back online. Listing 19-17 shows the records in the customer table.

Listing 19-17. *Records in the Formerly Failing Node*

```
mysql-node4> SELECT * FROM customer;
+-------------+---------+
| customer_id | name    |
+-------------+---------+
|           4 | Michael |
|           1 | Mike    |
|           3 | Johanna |
|           5 | Heidi   |
|           6 | Ezra    |
|           2 | Jay     |
+-------------+---------+
6 rows in set (0.02 sec)
```

This simple example demonstrates that data is duplicated across storage nodes, and that the nodes communicate changes in data as nodes come and go from the cluster. This means that you can get data from any connected SQL node. It also means you can trust that if a node goes down, your data will be available through the other nodes, and when you bring the failing node back up it will automatically get up to speed on data from the other storage nodes.

Cluster Processes

As we ran through the quick configuration and startup details, you used a few cluster tools that deserve more attention. These tools are ndb_mgmd, the management server daemon; ndbd, the storage node daemon; and ndb_mgm, the management client.

Management Server

The management node runs a server that provides management commands to control the cluster. This daemon, ndb_mgmd, also holds the configuration information for all nodes in the cluster and provides central logging for each of the nodes. Table 19-1 shows a complete list of startup options.

Table 19-1. *ndb_mgmd Startup Options*

Option	Description
-?, --usage, --help	Show help information and exit.
-V, --version	Display information about the version and exit.

Option	Description
`--ndb-connectstring=<connect string>`	Set the connection string for making contact with the management node. Format is `[nodeid=<id>;]`➥`<hostname>[:<port>]`. In most cases, this will be just an IP address or hostname.
`--ndb-shm`	Enable shared memory connections if available.
`--ndb-optimized-node-selection`	Use an optimization mechanism to choose nodes for transactions. Default is round robin.
`-f, --config-file=<file>`	Use the specified configuration file on startup.
`-d, --daemon`	Run in daemon mode. This is on by default.
`--interactive`	Run in interactive mode (a shell). Used for testing, there isn't much you can do from the shell.
`--no-nodeid-checks`	Do not check node IDs.
`--nodaemon`	Do not run as a daemon. It is keeping the process running in the terminal.

Storage Node

Each storage node runs a daemon that's responsible for responding to requests for retrieving and storing data. This process is started up after the management server is running, and pulls information about the cluster from the management node's configuration file. Table 19-2 shows the available startup options that can be passed to `ndbd` on the command line.

Table 19-2. *ndbd Startup Options*

Option	Description
`-?, --usage, --help`	Show help information and exit.
`-V, --version`	Display information about the version and exit.
`-c, --ndb-connectstring=<connect string>`	Set the connection string for making contact with the management node. Format is `[nodeid=<id>;]`➥`<hostname>[:<port>]`. In most cases, this will be just an IP address or hostname.
`--ndb-shm`	Enable shared memory connections if available.
`--ndb-optimized-node-selection`	Use an optimization mechanism to choose nodes for transactions. Default is round robin.
`--initial`	Perform file cleanup and read configuration options from the management server. Use caution with this option; using it at the wrong time can remove important files. This option is intended for use on first start of `ndbd` and only for subsequent starts where the logs need to be removed and configuration reread.
`-n, --nostart`	Run the daemon, but don't start full operation until the management node issues the `start` command.
`-d, --daemon`	Run in daemon mode. This is the default.
`--nodaemon`	Do not run as a daemon. It is keeping the process running in the terminal.

Management Client

The management client is a command-line tool that allows you to monitor and manage the cluster. Most of this tool's usefulness comes from the commands you can issue in interactive mode, but there are also a number of startup options. The startup options are shown in Table 19-3.

Table 19-3. *nbd_mgm Startup Options*

Option	Description
-?, --usage, --help	Show help information and exit.
-V, --version	Display information about the version and exit.
-c, --ndb-connectstring=<connect string>	Set the connection string for making contact with the management node. Format is [nodeid=<id>;]➡ <hostname>[:<port>]. In most cases, this will be just an IP address or hostname.
--ndb-shm	Enable shared memory connections if available.
--ndb-optimized-node-selection	Use an optimization mechanism to choose nodes for transactions. Default is round robin.
-e, --execute=<command>	Instead of launching the interactive shell, execute the command, print the.output, and exit. See Table 19-8 for a complete list of commands.
-t, --try-reconnect=<number>	Try to connect to the management server every 5 seconds for this number of times. Default is 3.

For more information on the commands when the management client is running, or that can be used with the -e flag, see the section "Managing the Cluster."

Configuration File Options

You got a taste for some of the configuration file options in your initial cluster setup, and now you are familiar with all the startup options for the various cluster programs. Now let's take a close look at the configuration file options for each of the nodes—meaning the management, storage, and SQL nodes. Options are stored in either the config.ini or my.cnf configuration files. Even if you won't use all these options, having an awareness of the different sections in the configuration files and what options are available in each is helpful to understanding how the cluster runs, and all the option possibilities.

Management Server Configuration File

The management server configuration file is typically config.ini, and goes in the data directory on the machine where the management node will run. Six different configuration groups are in your config.ini: COMPUTER, MYSQLD, NDB_MGM, NDBD, TCP, and SHM. Each of these sections has different options and values. Let's look at the significant ones, which exclude TCP and SHM. More information on all the options can be found at this URL: http://dev.mysql.com/doc/mysql/en/mysql-cluster-config-example.html.

Tip The use of DEFAULT within the section declaration (for example, [MYSQLD DEFAULT]) tells the management server that the options and values apply to any node of that section type. If you want to have some options apply to all nodes, and then some that apply to a node individually, you can use both a [MYSQLD DEFAULT] that applies to all SQL nodes and several [MYSQLD] sections that apply to specific SQL nodes.

COMPUTER

Table 19-4 shows all the options available in the COMPUTER section of config.ini. This section is a place to define the machines in the cluster. If the COMPUTER section is used, the id and hostname options are required.

Table 19-4. *COMPUTER Options in Management Server Configuration*

Option	Description
id=<number>	ID of the server.
hostname=<name>	IP address or hostname of the computer.

MYSQLD

The MYSQLD section is used one time for every SQL node in the cluster. Table 19-5 has all the options available for this section.

Table 19-5. *MYSQLD Options in Management Server Configuration*

Option	Description
arbitrationdelay=<number>	Number of milliseconds the SQL node will delay before responding to an arbitration.
arbitrationrank=<number>	A SQL node's arbitration power can be set to 0, 1, or 2 to indicate no arbitration, high priority, or low priority in arbitration. Only SQL and management nodes can arbitrate.
batchbytesize=<number>	Set the number of byte increments to use when fetching records from the data node.
batchsize=<number>	Set the number of record increments used when fetching records from the data node.
executeoncomputer=<name>	A pointer to a machine named in the COMPUTER section. Takes the computer ID as the value.
id	ID of the server.
maxscanbatchsize=<number>	Limits the amount of data coming to the SQL node from all data nodes. The default is 256KB, maximum is 16MB.

NDB_MGMD

Table 19-6 has all the options available in the NDB_MGMD section of the management configuration file. You can also identify this section using [MGM].

Table 19-6. *NDB_MGMD Options in Management Server Configuration*

Option	Description
arbitrationdelay=<number>	Number of milliseconds the management server will delay before responding to an arbitration.
arbitrationrank=<number>	Management node's arbitration power can be set to 0, 1, or 2 to indicate no arbitration, high priority, or low priority in arbitration. Only management and SQL nodes can arbitrate.
datadir=<dir>	Directory where log files should be stored.
executeoncomputer=<name>	A pointer to a machine named in the COMPUTER section. Use the defined ID.
id=<number>	ID of the server.
logdestination=<name>	The place where the management server should send the logs; can be any combination of console, syslog, or file. Multiple logging options are separated by a semicolon. See the MySQL documentation for information on customizing the management logging at http://dev.mysql.com/doc/mysql/en/mysql-➥ cluster-event-reports.html.
portnumber=<number>	The port number that the management node uses to communicate with the other nodes.

■**Note** In the configuration file for the management and SQL node, you see some settings for arbitration. Arbitration is required when nodes in the cluster become unavailable and a process needs to decide if enough nodes are left to represent the data fully, and which of those nodes will constitute the new cluster while some of the nodes are unavailable.

NDBD

The NDBD section is used for defining storage nodes in the cluster, and should appear once for each storage node. In addition, the configuration must have an [NDBD DEFAULT] section with noofreplicas and either hostname or executeoncomputer. Table 19-7 shows the most significant options for this section; see this web site for the complete list of options and explanations: http://dev.mysql.com/doc/mysql/en/mysql-cluster-config-example.html.

Table 19-7. *NDBD Options in Management Server Configuration*

Option	Description
backupdatadir=<dir>	Directory for backup files. By default, backupdatadir is stored in a BACKUP folder in the filesystempath directory (which defaults to datadir).
datadir=<dir>	Directory where trace, log, and error files should be stored.
datamemory=<number>	Specifies the amount of memory that can be used for storing data.
executeoncomputer=<name>	A pointer to a machine named in the COMPUTER section. Takes the computer ID as the value.
filesystempath=<path>	Location where metadata, UNDO, and REDO logs are stored. Default is datadir. Directory must exist before ndbd starts.
hostname=<name>	IP address or hostname of the computer.
id=<number>	ID of the server.
indexmemory=<number>	Specifies the amount of memory that can be used for storing indexes.
noofreplicas=<number>	Number of duplicates of the data to be stored on the storage nodes. In most cases, 2 provides enough redundancy. Maximum value is 4.
serverport=<number>	Port number other storage nodes should use when attempting to connect to this node.

Storage Node Configuration

The options for configuring the storage node are put into the standard my.cnf file, in the [MYSQL_CLUSTER] section. There is only one option and value, the ndb-connectstring, which should be pointed at the management node of your cluster.

SQL Node Configuration

Configuration options for the SQL node go into the standard my.cnf file. There's no special section for the SQL node, configuration options going under the standard [MYSQLD] section.[3] There are only two options that are related to the SQL node in this section: ndbcluster and ndb-connectstring.

Putting the ndbcluster option in the configuration file tells the MySQL server to bring up the NDBCLUSTER storage engine when it starts up. The ndb-connectstring is the IP address or hostname for the management server. The connect string can also contain the node ID and port to get to the management server.

---

3. For more information on the [MYSQLD] configuration group and the MySQL configuration files in general, see Chapter 14.

Managing the Cluster

Managing a cluster, especially when there's a large pool of storage and SQL nodes, can be a daunting task. When your cluster is up and running, you'll need to think about things such as how to stop and start nodes to perform server upgrades, when and how to back up your data, and what to do if you've had a disaster and your data is corrupt or gone.

Management Client

The management client is a good place to start when learning about cluster management and putting together a plan for how you'll carry out backup, recovery, or scheduled maintenance. The set of commands available in the management client give you a good deal of control over the nodes in your cluster. Table 19-8 shows a complete list of commands available in the ndb_mgm tool. In many commands, a <severity> option is specified. These values can be any combination of alert, critical, error, warning, info, or debug.

Table 19-8. *ndb_mgm Client Commands*

Command	Description
HELP	Print all the commands, with their descriptions.
SHOW	Output a complete status for the cluster. This includes information on and status of the management node and all storage and SQL nodes.
START BACKUP [NOWAIT | WAIT ➥ STARTED | WAIT COMPLETED]	Start the backup process. When running the backup, either don't wait for the process to start before returning, wait until the backup has started to return, or wait until the backup has completed before returning to the shell.
ABORT BACKUP <id>	Stop the backup with the specified ID. The ID is returned from the START BACKUP command.
SHUTDOWN	Stop all processes in the cluster. This command stops all storage and SQL nodes, then stops the management server.
CLUSTERLOG ON [<severity>]	Turn on cluster logging, with an optional severity label.
CLUSTERLOG OFF [<severity>]	Turn off cluster logging for the specific severity level if included.
CLUSTERLOG FILTER [<severity>]	For the specified severity, toggle logging on or off.
CLUSTERLOG INFO	Print information about cluster logging. The output is a list of severities that are enabled.
<id> START	Start a particular database node (or all of them with ALL).
<id> RESTART	Restart a particular database node (or all of them with ALL).
<id> STOP	Stop a particular database node (or all of them with ALL).
ENTER SINGLE USER MODE <id>	Go into single user mode with the specified node as the only one to accept updates from. The specified node must be a SQL node.
EXIT SINGLE USER MODE	Go out of single user mode, allowing all SQL nodes to resume sending statements to the storage nodes.
<id> STATUS	Show status information for the specified node (or all of them with ALL).

Command	Description
PURGE STALE SESSIONS	Have the management server reset reserved node IDs.
CONNECT [<connectstring>]	Connect, or reconnect if already connected, to the specified management server.
QUIT	Exit the management client.

■**Note** To be clear, a proper shutdown and startup of a node won't result in the loss of data, even though the data is cleared from where it's stored in memory when ndbd stops. When the shutdown statement is issued from the management node, each storage node writes its data to disk before exiting. When the node starts back up, the data is loaded from the disk back into memory.

Single User Mode

The single user mode command is in the list of commands in Table 19-8, but we thought it important to talk about in more detail. If you're trying to pinpoint a problem with your application or database and want to restrict access temporarily to the cluster, the single user mode is a helpful command in the features of MySQL Cluster.

Single user mode allows you to specify that updates to the storage nodes should be limited to a specific node. The command, shown in Listing 19-18, demonstrates how to stop all commands except for those from SQL node 2.

Listing 19-18. *Command to Enter Single User Mode*

```
ndb_mgm> ENTER SINGLE USER MODE 2
```

■**Note** Entering a node ID of a node that isn't a SQL node causes the command to fail.

After entering single user mode, only that node is allowed to send statements to the storage nodes. Once you're finished with your debugging, you can exit single user mode with the statement in Listing 19-19, which reinstates all SQL nodes in the cluster.

Listing 19-19. *Command to Exit Single User Mode*

```
ndb_mgm>EXIT SINGLE USER MODE
```

Backing Up and Restoring

Even if you have completely redundant systems, backing up and being capable of restoring your cluster's data is important. Remember, until the MySQL development team implements a disk-based storage mechanism, all your data is in the memory of your storage nodes. If you ever have a power outage, or a problem with enough of your storage nodes that you lose your data, you'll need a way to restore the data back into memory once the machines come back up. Chapter 17 covered creating backup policies and implementation plans in detail.

mysqldump

Because mysqldump is storage-engine independent, you can always use it to create a scheduled (or unscheduled) dump of your data. This is wise if you want to have backups for the purpose of restoring single databases or tables. For complete details on using the mysqldump utility to back up and restore data, see Chapter 17.

Cluster Backup and Restore

The other backup option is to use the built-in cluster backup tools that come with MySQL. These tools allow you to create a complete backup of your cluster data. You issue the backup command in the management client, as shown in Listing 19-20.

Listing 19-20. *Starting a Cluster Backup*

```
ndb_mgm> START BACKUP
```

When the backup is started, the management client prints a few statements that show the ID that has been assigned to the backup. Listing 19-21 shows the statement that's printed when the backup has started, showing that the backup ID assigned is 3.

Listing 19-21. *Finding the Backup ID*

```
Backup 3 started
```

Make note of this backup ID—you'll need it if you want to restore, and it's necessary if you decide to cancel the backup. When the backup has completed, each node will have a set of backup files: one for the data dictionary information, a second with the actual data, and a third with the transaction log with information about when and how data was stored in the nodes.

To restore from this backup, the cluster database must first be empty. You can do this by shutting down the storage nodes and starting them back up with the --initial option, which cleans out the log and data files. You must issue the restore command on each storage node, but you also need to restore the metadata (table structures) on the first node to be restored. Listing 19-22 shows the command that should be issued on the first node that's restored. You need to be in the directory where the backup files were created on the node.

Listing 19-22. *Cluster Restore with Schema Create*

```
/usr/local/mysql/bin/ndb_restore --restore_meta --nodeid=<node id>
--backup_id=<backup id>
```

Once the first node has been restored, you can issue the same statement on the remaining nodes, but without the --restore_meta option to finish the restore.

Log Files

We've seen some of the configuration options and commands to set up and change output to the log files. We haven't seen the different log files, and what they might contain.

Your cluster contains two kinds of logs: a cluster log and a node log. Both these types of log files contain information about node connections, checkpoints, startup, restarts, statistics, and errors.

Cluster Log

The cluster log is located in the data directory of the management server, and contains information about the entire cluster, including the management, storage, and SQL nodes. The cluster log file is named ndb_<id>_cluster.log, the ID being the ID of the management node. Listing 19-23 shows a few lines from a cluster log file.

Listing 19-23. *Sample Output from a Cluster Log File*

```
shell> more ndb_1_cluster.log
2005-07-08 15:54:29 [MgmSrvr] INFO      -- NDB Cluster Management Server.
Version 4.1.12
2005-07-08 15:54:29 [MgmSrvr] INFO      -- Id: 1, Command port: 1186
2005-07-08 15:54:29 [MgmSrvr] INFO      -- Node 1: Node 2 Connected
2005-07-08 15:54:29 [MgmSrvr] INFO      -- Node 1: Node 3 Connected
```

In this cluster log, we see that the management node has started and two nodes have connected to the cluster.

Node Log

The node log lives in the data directory of each node, and only contains information specific to that node. This log file is named ndb_<id>_out.log, the ID being the ID of the node. Listing 19-24 shows a sample of a few lines from a storage node log file.

Listing 19-24. *Sample Output from a Node Log File*

```
shell> more ndb_2_out.log
2005-07-08 16:19:23 [NDB] INFO      -- Angel pid: 738 ndb pid: 739
2005-07-08 16:19:23 [NDB] INFO      -- NDB Cluster -- DB node 2
2005-07-08 16:19:23 [NDB] INFO      -- Version 4.1.12 --
2005-07-08 16:19:23 [NDB] INFO      -- Configuration fetched at 10.0.0.2 port 1186
```

Listing 19-24 shows that the storage node started up and was able to pull configuration information from the configuration file on the management node.

The MySQL documentation contains detailed information about what kinds of messages you'll see in the logs.

Security

By default, MySQL Cluster isn't secure. There are no permission checks when connections are made to the management server, which can leave you open to all kinds of unwanted behavior. Data transfer between nodes in the cluster and interaction between the management server and nodes aren't encrypted, and are left open for anyone to sniff. If you run your cluster on a public network, you expose all the data in your database and leave yourself open for anyone to connect to the management server to play with the cluster configuration and possibly shut down the cluster.

For these reasons, we recommend implementing a network-layer mechanism for protection. Your best bet is to use a private network for cluster communication, and limit connections to the management server to within the private network. If this isn't possible, you might want to implement a set of firewall rules that restrict database communication between the management server and nodes to those on your network.

The MySQL permissions tables still control access to the actual data in the cluster databases and tables. Any connection to the SQL node with a database statement goes through the rigors of MySQL's authentication and authorization mechanism. Chapter 15 fully explains authentication and authorization.

Summary

Cluster technology in MySQL is exciting, and holds a lot of promise for the future of highly available databases. Although there are some limitations in MySQL's cluster implementation, the storage engine is stable and being developed actively enough to make concerns about the limitations short-term.

Using the cluster engine is no different from any other storage engine, but setting up the cluster requires some extra work, and extra servers. The configuration and startup of the cluster nodes is fairly straightforward, and should be familiar to those who have worked with the MySQL configuration files and server before. You can use many configuration options to customize the cluster to meet your implementation needs.

If you need a database that has high availability, MySQL Cluster is worth a close look. Although MySQL continues to provide simplicity in its MyISAM and InnoDB engines, this storage engine demonstrates that MySQL is serious about meeting the rigorous demands of mission-critical, highly available databases.

CHAPTER 20

■■■

Troubleshooting

If you've been using MySQL as the database back-end for your application for any amount of time, you've probably experienced problems of some sort. For example, a user may have been attempting to run her query in the database, and after several attempts to get to the mysql> prompt, gave up in frustration and sent you an e-mail containing the message she saw on her terminal:

```
ERROR 2002 (HY000): Can't connect to local MySQL server through socket
'/tmp/mysql.sock'
```

Or maybe, as you executed the final steps of the release of a new piece of functionality on your web-based software, you went to the site to start browsing around. After a few proud clicks, you came across the following message on your web browser:

```
Warning: mysqli_connect(): Access denied for user 'webuser'@'localhost'
(using password: YES) in /home/promysql/web/customer_basket.php on line 32
Failed to connect: Access denied for user 'webuser'@'localhost'
(using password: YES)
```

No matter how much time you spend working to anticipate and prevent problems in your database-backed system, you should be prepared to resolve issues that arise. Even if you've designed the perfect application and database, pieces within the systems change over time, require upgrades, rely on external resources, and are used in unexpected ways. At some point, you will need to figure out what might be the cause of poor performance, or you may even need to deal with a system that is totally unavailable.

Troubleshooting is a very general term, covering a wide expanse of technical ground. In this chapter, we'll begin by covering what types of tools are useful for MySQL troubleshooting. Then we'll discuss a spectrum of issues that will help you in determining the cause of performance bottlenecks or a completely unavailable database. This chapter will cover the following topics:

- Troubleshooting tools

- Common problems: indicators and suggested solutions

- MySQL bug reporting

- MySQL support options

Troubleshooting Toolkit

A number of tools can be helpful when you're troubleshooting a problem with your database. These include MySQL logs, the MySQL thread list, your operating system process list, and monitoring programs.

Error Logs

The first time MySQL starts, it creates a file where it logs information about startup, shutdown, and critical errors. By default, this file is put in your data directory and is named *<server_name>*.err. You can change the name and location of the error log by using the --log-error=*<file>* startup option.

Error log entries start with the date and time, in *YYMMDD HH:MM:SS* format, and then contain a message indicating what is happening in the database at that particular time.

The error log is a valuable resource when troubleshooting issues with your server. It not only contains a record of details about problems the server has encountered, but it also has a history of when your server was stopped, started, and restarted (manually, as well as automatically with mysqld_safe). When you're troubleshooting, knowing what errors are occurring and when the database was last restarted can be critical pieces of information.

■**Tip** MySQL maintains a document about using the log files to find errors. The document can be found at http://dev.mysql.com/doc/mysql/en/using-log-files.html.

Startup Entries

For a server startup using mysql.server to start the database, without configuration options, the log file will contain something like the output shown in Listing 20-1.

Listing 20-1. *Entries in Log for Startup*

```
050430 13:45:48  mysqld started
050430 13:45:48  InnoDB: Started; log sequence number 0 43655
050430 13:45:48  InnoDB: Starting recovery for XA transactions...
050430 13:45:48  InnoDB: 0 transactions in prepared state after recovery
050430 13:45:48 [Note] /usr/local/mysql/bin/mysqld: ready for connections.
Version: '5.0.6-beta-max-log'  socket: '/tmp/mysql.sock'  port: 3306
MySQL Community Edition - Experimental (GPL)
```

As you can see, this example shows messages from the MySQL daemon as well as the InnoDB storage engine as they start. In the end, you see a ready for connections message, with a log of information about the version, socket, and port used by the server. This indicates that the server has successfully started.

The startup entries in the error log can be more extensive. If you're starting MySQL for the first time after going through the installation process, you'll see a lot more information about InnoDB getting the environment set up. Listing 20-2 shows the log entries during initial startup of a MySQL server.

Listing 20-2. *Entries in Log for Initial Startup*

```
050430 13:22:49  mysqld started
InnoDB: The first specified data file ./ibdata1 did not exist:
InnoDB: a new database to be created!
050430 13:22:49  InnoDB: Setting file ./ibdata1 size to 10 MB
InnoDB: Database physically writes the file full: wait...
050430 13:22:50  InnoDB: Log file ./ib_logfile0 did not exist: new to be created
InnoDB: Setting log file ./ib_logfile0 size to 5 MB
InnoDB: Database physically writes the file full: wait...
050430 13:22:50  InnoDB: Log file ./ib_logfile1 did not exist: new to be created
InnoDB: Setting log file ./ib_logfile1 size to 5 MB
InnoDB: Database physically writes the file full: wait...
InnoDB: Doublewrite buffer not found: creating new
InnoDB: Doublewrite buffer created
InnoDB: Creating foreign key constraint system tables
InnoDB: Foreign key constraint system tables created
050430 13:22:50  InnoDB: Started; log sequence number 0 0
050430 13:22:50  InnoDB: Starting recovery for XA transactions...
050430 13:22:50  InnoDB: 0 transactions in prepared state after recovery
050430 13:22:50 [Note] /usr/local/mysql/bin/mysqld: ready for connections.
Version: '5.0.6-beta-max-log'  socket: '/tmp/mysql.sock'  port: 3306
MySQL Community Edition - Experimental (GPL)
```

Shutdown Entries

When MySQL shuts down normally, you see lines like those shown in Listing 20-3 in your error log.

Listing 20-3. *Entries in Log for Shutdown*

```
050430 16:05:23 [Note] /usr/local/mysql/bin/mysqld: Normal shutdown
050430 16:05:23  InnoDB: Starting shutdown...
050430 16:05:25 [Note] /usr/local/mysql/bin/mysqld: Shutdown complete
050430 16:05:25  mysqld ended
```

If the InnoDB storage engine isn't a part of your server, your log won't contain the notice about the storage engine shutting down.

Critical Error Entries

Beyond showing a record of the database starting and stopping, the error log provides a place to look for information about critical problems in the database. For example, suppose you attempt to start MySQL using the `mysql.server` script but get a failure:

```
Starting MySQL................................. ERROR!
```

You can look in the error log to see if it has any information that would help identify the problem:

```
050430 15:39:02  mysqld started
050430 15:39:02 [ERROR] /usr/local/mysql/bin/mysqld: unknown variable 'default-
sorage=InnoDB'
050430 15:39:02  mysqld ended
```

This example shows that somewhere in your configuration files, there is an unknown variable. Armed with this information, you should be able to resolve the issue.

We could go on for pages talking about everything you might see in your MySQL error log. The point is to be familiar with the kind of information that is written to the log. Then, when you're attempting to resolve an issue with your server, you'll be able to identify any abnormalities.

General Query Log

Another helpful place to look for information while troubleshooting a MySQL server is the general query log. In this log file, MySQL logs every connection made and every statement sent to the server. The general query log is enabled with the `--log` option in your configuration file. The default location for this log is in your data directory, with the filename `<hostname>.log`. You can change the path and location of the log file by specifying a value in your `--log` configuration option, such as `--log=/var/log/mysql/query.log`. Queries are entered into this log file as the server receives them, not after they are executed, as they are entered in the binary log.

The general query log stores data in plain text, readable by any text viewer or editor. The log contains the time of the command, the connection `identifier` (each connection has a unique ID), the command type, and the command itself. Listing 20-4 shows a section from the general query log of the server used for running examples for this book.

Listing 20-4. *General Query Log Entries*

```
Time                 Id Command    Argument
050501 13:16:25       1 Connect     root@localhost on
                      1 Query       drop database if exists shop
                      1 Query       create database shop
                      1 Query       SELECT DATABASE()
                      1 Init DB     shop
                      1 Query       create table city
  (city_id integer not null auto_increment primary key,
```

```
name varchar(50))
                        1 Query        insert into city (name)
values ('Boston'),('Columbus'),('London'),('Berlin')
                        1 Query        create table customer
(customer_id integer not null auto_increment primary key,
name varchar (10),
region integer)
                        1 Query        insert into customer values (1,'Mike',1)
                        1 Query        insert into customer values (2,'Jay',2)
                        1 Query        insert into customer values (3,'Johanna',2)
                        1 Query        insert into customer values (4,'Michael',1)
                        1 Query        insert into customer values (5,'Heidi',3)
                        1 Query        insert into customer values (6,'Ezra',3)
                        1 Query        load data infile
'/home/mkruck/ProMySQL/examples/Chapter11/customer_data.csv'
into table customer fields terminated by ',' (name,region)
                        1 Query        create table login
(login_id integer not null auto_increment primary key,
customer_id integer,
login_time datetime,
login_unixtime integer)
                        1 Query        load data infile
'/home/mkruck/ProMySQL/examples/Chapter11/login_data.csv'
into table login fields terminated by ',' (customer_id,login_unixtime)
                        1 Query        update login set login_time = from_unixtime
(login_unixtime)
                        1 Query        create index name on customer (name)
                        1 Query        create index region on customer (region)
                        1 Query        create index customer_id on login (customer_id)
050501 15:23:11         2 Query        show tables
050501 15:23:14         2 Query        select * from customer
050501 15:23:19         2 Quit
```

The query log shows the statements used to create the shop database and set up the city, customer, and login tables. All of these statements were issued through one connection, with an ID of 1. The last three statements were through a second connection.

For troubleshooting, the value of the general query log is that you can look at the syntax of the queries being sent to the database. If you're experiencing performance problems or client connection issues, reviewing the general query log can help you determine if a particular query is causing issues in your system.

■**Note** Chapter 6 covers how to use the general query log and slow query log for profiling your system. See that chapter for more details about these logs.

Slow Query Log

The slow query log is a lot like the general query log, except that it logs only queries that reach a specified time threshold during execution. The slow query log is enabled with the --log-slow-query option in your configuration file. The default location for this log is in your data directory, with the filename <*hostname*>-slow.log. You can change the path and location of the log file by specifying a value in your --log-slow-query configuration option, such as --log-slow-query=/var/log/mysql/slow-query.log. To set the threshold for how many seconds must pass before the query is logged, use --long-query-time=<*number_of_seconds*>.

For every slow query, MySQL logs the current date and time, user, execution time, lock time, the number of rows sent to the client, the number of rows examined by the query, and the SQL statement itself. Listing 20-5 shows a few entries from a slow query log on a server where --long-query-time is set to 1.

Listing 20-5. *Slow Query Log Entries*

```
# Time: 050501 15:54:49
# User@Host: root[root] @ localhost []
# Query_time: 4  Lock_time: 0  Rows_sent: 0  Rows_examined: 0
use shop;
SET insert_id=1;
load data infile '/home/mkruck/ProMySQL/examples/Chapter11/login_data.csv'
into table login fields terminated by ',' (customer_id,login_unixtime);
# Time: 050501 15:54:53
# User@Host: root[root] @ localhost []
# Query_time: 4  Lock_time: 0  Rows_sent: 0  Rows_examined: 0
update login set login_time = from_unixtime(login_unixtime);
# Time: 050501 16:01:52
# User@Host: root[root] @ localhost []
# Query_time: 2  Lock_time: 0  Rows_sent: 0  Rows_examined: 0
SET timestamp=1114981312;
update login set login_time = now() where customer_id > 1000;
```

In this example, the slow query log shows that three queries exceeded the one-second limit: one to load data into the database and two UPDATE statements.

Familiarity with the slow query log will come in handy when you have a situation where one query is tying up many tables for long periods of time and interrupting other queries.

MySQL Server Thread List

If it hasn't happened yet, at some point in your use of MySQL, you'll want to see a real-time list of all the connections to the server and what each one is doing. If you have the SUPER privilege, the SHOW PROCESSLIST command will show you all connections to the database and what each connection is doing.[1]

---

1. If you do not have the SUPER privilege, SHOW PROCESSLIST will show you the connections for your account only.

■Note An alternative to running SHOW PROCESSLIST at the MySQL client prompt is to use the `mysqladmin` ➡ `processlist` script, which can be run from the Unix shell. You might prefer this approach if you're attempting to set up some automated monitoring of the MySQL connections with a shell script.

The SHOW PROCESSLIST command gives you the connection identifier, user, host, database, current command, time, and state for each open connection. A sample output of the SHOW PROCESSLIST command is shown in Listing 20-6.

Listing 20-6. *Output from SHOW PROCESSLIST*

```
mysql> SHOW PROCESSLIST\G
*************************** 1. row ***************************
     Id: 4
   User: root
   Host: localhost
     db: NULL
Command: Query
   Time: 0
  State: NULL
   Info: SHOW PROCESSLIST
*************************** 2. row ***************************
     Id: 6
   User: root
   Host: localhost
     db: shop
Command: Query
   Time: 7
  State: Repair by sorting
   Info: CREATE INDEX customer_id ON login (customer_id)
2 rows in set (0.00 sec)
```

Here, you see two active connections to the database. One is running the SHOW PROCESSLIST command, and the other is building an index. Note the Time row, which indicates that the query has been running for seven seconds.

Using the SHOW PROCESSLIST command is a helpful tool in identifying what's currently running in MySQL. If you have a slow or unresponsive database and you can get on the machine to run this command, you may be able to find the troublesome query.

If you do find a problematic query in your list of connections, you may want to stop it. The KILL command can either terminate the connection altogether (KILL <*connection_id*>) or terminate the currently running query but leave the connection intact (KILL QUERY ➡ <*connection_id*>). To stop the CREATE INDEX query in Listing 20-6, where the connection ID is 6, the command is KILL QUERY 6. You must have the SUPER privilege to stop queries.

Operating System Process List

Most operating systems provide a mechanism to get information about running processes, CPU usage, memory availability, disk I/O, and so on. While we tend to focus on MySQL, it doesn't run in a vacuum. Being able to figure out what is going on at the operating system and hardware level can often help in resolving an issue.

Whether you use `ps`, `top`, or `prstat` on Unix or the Windows Task Manager, the key is being able to get a sense of what processes are running on the machine. At a minimum, the process list will tell you if a MySQL server is running. You may also find the output valuable to identify issues like an overworked CPU or unavailable memory hindering MySQL's ability to respond to queries.

Monitoring Programs

System monitoring and alert tools can be homegrown scripts that regularly parse log files and alert you when certain events are detected. They also can be full-blown services that receive or request periodic status indicators from your server, and plot the history of the health of your database and machine over days, months, and years.[2] Whether homegrown or out of the box, these monitoring tools are designed to make sure you are immediately notified when a problem arises, give you a view of the load on your database and server over time, and provide other functions to help you watch your system.

When you are responsible for a production database, you'll want to know as soon as possible that a problem occurred, and get as much information as you can from a monitoring program. This will allow you to more quickly assess the situation and start using the tools necessary to determine the cause of the problem and move toward resolving it.

Commonly Encountered Issues

Now that we've considered the basic troubleshooting tools, we're going to spend some time outlining common issues you may encounter in your day-to-day administration of a MySQL server or server cluster. For each issue, we'll explain how to diagnose the problem, and then suggest one or more solutions.

Obviously, we can't cover every single issue that might occur when you're using MySQL. However, reviewing the specific steps to solve some of the problems will help familiarize you with using the MySQL tools for resolving other issues as well.

■**Note** Our commonly encountered issues summary isn't far off from a list that MySQL maintains at `http://dev.mysql.com/doc/mysql/en/common-errors.html`. You may find it helpful to review suggestions from both this section and the MySQL documentation. You'll see other pointers to sources for more information throughout this chapter.

---

2. A popular open-source monitoring tool is Nagios (`http://www.nagios.org/`), which includes clients on each machine and a central server that collects reports on various processes on servers. Also, a number of web-based monitoring services can do anything from ping your server to test specific services and functionality on a machine.

We've divided the common scenarios by general category, though to be sure, some scenarios cross categorical lines, as you'll see. We'll cover the following broad range of possible trouble areas:

- User, connection, and client issues
- Server installation, restart, and shutdown problems
- Data corruption

Troubleshooting User, Connection, and Client Issues

A fairly common category of troubleshooting is the group of errors and issues associated with client connections to the server. In this section, we'll cover how to handle these extremely pesky occurrences:

- `Can't connect through socket` errors
- `Can't connect to host` errors
- `Access denied for user` messages
- Permissions issues (user denied `SELECT`, `INSERT`, `UPDATE`, or `DELETE`)
- `Too many connections` errors
- `MySQL server not responding` errors
- `Packet length too big` messages
- `MySQL server has gone away` messages

Can't Connect Through Socket Errors

When connecting to a MySQL server on the same machine as the client, MySQL uses the Unix socket instead of the network.[3] If you do not specify a hostname, or use `localhost` as the host to connect with, your client will attempt to connect via the Unix socket. If your client can't find the socket file, it will fail when attempting to connect to the MySQL server.

The `mysql.sock` file is created by the MySQL server when it starts up, and it is removed when the server shuts down. When the client can't find the socket file, it can't connect to the local database server.

Evidence of the Problem

When a client cannot connect to MySQL through the socket file, it returns an error. This message might appear on the command line, as a page in your web browser, or in any window that displays error messages from the MySQL client. The message will look something like this:

```
ERROR 2002 (HY000): Can't connect to local MySQL server through socket
'/tmp/mysql.sock'
```

---

3. A Unix socket file connection is faster than a network connection using TCP/IP, but it is limited to a connection on the same machine.

This error is an indication that either the server is not running or the socket file can't be found when attempting a connection to the server.

If this error is happening in your production environment, and you have an alert system in place, that alert system should tell you that MySQL is unavailable. In the case of the mysql.sock socket file, you might have your alert system monitor for that file as a part of its checks of the MySQL process. If you are just getting MySQL up and running, and are tweaking your configuration or needing to periodically restart the database, you (or another user) may actually see this error message.

■**Note** Windows servers do not use socket files, so you will not see the Can't connect through socket error on Windows. The comparable technology on Windows is Named Pipes, which serves a similar purpose, allowing you to connect to MySQL without using the network.

Solutions

When confronted with a socket error, the following set of suggestions will likely reveal the source of your problem:

- Using your process monitor, check to be sure your MySQL server is running. Starting the server is a good start to removing the problem. If the server should have been running, you may want to spend some time figuring out what happened to make it stop.

- If the server is running, make sure the socket file is where the server and client expect to find it. By default, the socket is created at /tmp/mysql.sock, but this can be changed when compiling the database and in the MySQL configuration. The configuration options that go in your my.cnf file for the server and client files are socket=/path/to/mysql.sock, in both the [mysqld] and [client] sections. As you can imagine, if the client and server options don't match, you won't be able to connect and will have trouble getting the client to connect to the server.

- If MySQL is running, and mysql.sock is where it should be, check the permissions on the socket file. When the server creates it, the ownership is as follows:

  srwxrwxrwx 1 mysql   mysql   0 May 2 16:05 mysql.sock

  If the ownership or permissions of the socket file have changed, your error may be caused by inability to access the socket file.

- If your socket file is missing altogether, a restart of the server will re-create it in the default location (or the location where you've configured it to go).

- If circumstances prevent you from having or using a socket file, you can force a TCP/IP connection to the server by specifying the hostname of your computer or the loopback address with -h 127.0.0.1.

For more information about server connection failures, see http://dev.mysql.com/doc/mysql/en/can-not-connect-to-server.html. You can find more details on protecting mysql.sock at http://dev.mysql.com/doc/mysql/en/problems-with-mysql-sock.html.

Can't Connect to Host Errors

When you are in an environment where your MySQL connections are network-based, you may run into a problem connecting to the server. The network may be down, or the server might not be responding.

Evidence of the Problem

When a client cannot connect to MySQL via the network, it returns an error. As with any MySQL errors, this message might appear on the command line, as a page in your web browser, or in any window that displays error messages from the MySQL client. The message will look something like this:

```
ERROR 2003 (HY000): Can't connect to MySQL server on '10.0.0.200' (111)
```

This error is an indication that the server is not running on the given host machine.

If there are network problems, or the network address does not exist, you will either experience a long wait or see a message indicating that the host is unknown:

```
ERROR 2005 (HY000): Unknown MySQL server host '10.0.0.300'
```

If this error is happening in your production environment, and you have an alert system in place, that system should let you know that MySQL is unavailable. Some alert systems simply check to see if the MySQL process is running; others actually attempt to make a connection to the database and run a query. If you are just getting MySQL up and running, and are tweaking your configuration, you (or another user) may actually see this error.

Solutions

Following are some suggestions for dealing with a host connection problem:

- Check the processes on the host machine where you are attempting to connect. Check your process list to verify that MySQL is running. If not, starting it should resolve your problem.

- Verify that the MySQL server is allowing TCP/IP connections. This is set with the --skip-networking configuration option. If SHOW VARIABLES LIKE 'skip_networking'; indicates that the option is set to ON, your server won't allow network connections until you change that value to OFF.

- Verify that the port used by the MySQL server matches the one being used in your client. By default, MySQL uses port 3306, but this is easily changed with the --port option in the server or client configuration files, or with the -P option when starting the MySQL command-line client.

For more information, see http://dev.mysql.com/doc/mysql/en/can-not-connect-to-server.html.

Access Denied for User Messages

We started the chapter with an example of a user getting a message from a PHP page about denied access. You may find that as much as you try to keep on top of your privilege assignments, this error gets its fair share of exposure to users.

When a user attempts to connect to MySQL and issue a SQL statement, the database first checks if the user is allowed to connect, and then checks to see if the user has permission to execute the submitted statement. In either of these phases of authentication, MySQL may find that the user is not permitted access, and the client will receive an error. The access denied message is specifically about not having permission to connect to the database from a host with the supplied username and password.

Evidence of the Problem

The access denied error occurs when a user's credentials don't align correctly with permissions in MySQL. In the instance that you are using a general account for your web site interactions with the database, but MySQL is not allowing the connection, you or your users will see a message like this on your site page:

```
Warning: mysqli_connect(): Access denied for user 'webaccount'@'localhost'
(using password: YES) in /home/promysql/web/customer_basket.php on line 32
Failed to connect: Access denied for user 'webaccount'@'localhost'
(using password: YES)
```

If you have a system that implements user-level connection rules and permissions, where users make individual connections, the message will be more specific to the particular user account. You may also see the same message, but with an indication that no password is being used, like this:

```
Warning: mysqli_connect(): Access denied for user 'webaccount'@'localhost'
(using password: NO) in /home/promysql/web/customer_basket.php on line 32
Failed to connect: Access denied for user 'webaccount'@'localhost'
(using password: NO)
```

Solutions

To resolve an issue where access is denied, use the following suggestions to delve into the problem:

- Verify that the username is a valid MySQL account.

- Check that you are actually sending a password.

- Determine if the user's username and password in the connection match those in the MySQL database.

- Review the connection permissions for the user and verify that the user has the ability to connect from the given host.

- If permission is lacking, GRANT appropriate connection permission.

MySQL's privilege system is fairly complex. To fully understand how a user gains access to the MySQL server, read Chapter 15, which covers the privilege system in detail. You can also refer to `http://dev.mysql.com/doc/mysql/en/privilege-system.html`.

Permission Issues

Beyond the ability to connect to a MySQL server is the permission to execute a particular statement. As we noted, MySQL has a complex permission structure, which allows for a great deal of granularity in controlling user access to the server and data.

Evidence of the Problem

User denied errors come up frequently when new users or new functionality that requires changes in the user permissions are added to your system. Even with the most carefully planned rollout, as the changes settle, you are likely to see a few users have problems with queries they attempt to run.

The problem shows up in the form of an error message indicating that the given user is denied permission to run a given SQL command, as in this example:

```
mysql> SELECT * FROM customer;
ERROR 1142 (42000): SELECT command denied to user 'mkruck'@'localhost'
for table 'customer'
```

The user denied messages do not appear in the MySQL log files, so you'll often learn about the problem from specific users, in the form of an e-mail message or phone call. If you are using a client, either desktop or web-based, you may be able to find information about a user's problem by reviewing the log files from the web server or from your desktop application logs.

Solutions

Resolving issues with permissions can be tricky, especially if you haven't mastered the MySQL permission scheme. In the instances we've seen, these two suggestions have solved most permission problems:

- Use the `SHOW GRANTS FOR <username>` command and verify that the output shows that permission has been granted for the appropriate action on that table.

- If the rule seems to be there, check for instances where a more specific rule may be blocking a more general rule. An `UPDATE` permission for a specific IP address will block a `SELECT` rule for % (any host). If this is the case, you'll need to `GRANT` a more specific `SELECT` permission for the IP address or revoke the `UPDATE`.

As we recommended for access denied issues, see Chapter 15 of this book and `http://dev.mysql.com/doc/mysql/en/privilege-system.html` for more information about the MySQL access privilege system.

Too Many Connections Error

Each client that runs a query in MySQL requires a connection to the database. MySQL wisely allows you to set how many connections are allowed to the database with the `--max_connections` configuration option, which defaults to 100.

Evidence of the Problem

The problem arises when a connection is attempted after MySQL has reached the limit allowed with `--max_connections`. When this happens, the user will get a `Too many connections` error, in the command-line client, web interface, or other location that is displaying the response from a MySQL connection failure.

Solutions

You can deal with the problem of too many connections in these ways:

- Increase the value of your `--max_connections` configuration option to be large enough to handle the number of clients you anticipate at your highest volume. Depending on your operating system, you can set the value to accommodate anywhere from 400 to 4,000 connections.

- Use persistent database connections or implement a connection pooling mechanism to lower the number of connections to MySQL. Many languages provide persistent database connections, where instead of making a new connection for each query, connections are kept in memory for a period of time and reused. If your language does not have this capability, it is not difficult to implement your own connection pooling mechanism.

- Do a code review and look for places where you can consolidate or eliminate connections to the database.

For more information, refer to `http://dev.mysql.com/doc/mysql/en/too-many-connections.html`.

MySQL Server Not Responding

In your experience as an administrator or developer using MySQL, you've probably been in a situation where you can connect to the server, but when you attempt to issue a query, the server doesn't seem to respond. Based on our experience, the unresponsive server isn't actually the entire database server; instead, one or more tables have been locked and are preventing another user from querying those tables. This could be caused by another user running an intensive report, your system taking a point-in-time backup, or an update on a large table that is central to your system.

Evidence of the Problem

For web-based applications, the first sign of an unresponsive server is a hung web page that won't load, waiting for data from the web server. This behavior can also be duplicated in the command-line client: you type in a query, and you just sit there, waiting for minutes without anything happening.

Your users will certainly let you know about an unresponsive server, if the problem lasts for any amount of time. To be more proactive, a homegrown script or a good monitoring system can provide alerts based on predefined queries to your database.

Solutions

If you find yourself in the position of having a database-backed page or a client query that is not responding, here are some immediate steps you can take to get to the bottom of the problem:

- If you can connect to the database, issue SHOW PROCESSLIST and look at the query execution times to see if you can pinpoint a specific query that might be blocking the other ones. If you find such a query, the fastest way to get your database moving again is to kill the query (KILL QUERY <connection_id>). This might not be wise if the query is important, but, in most cases, we've found that the query is a noncritical, poorly written SQL statement being run by an unaware user.

- If you have a query that seems to overwhelm the database, rebuild it, making sure your syntax accounts for references between all tables. Use the EXPLAIN syntax to analyze the indexes and create or change indexes as appropriate. See Chapter 6 for details on using EXPLAIN and other profiling techniques.

- If you can't obtain a connection to the database at all, and your connection attempt seems to stall and not return, you may have a network-related issue like a firewall blocking your connection. If your firewall is configured to drop unwanted packets, you won't see the Unknown MySQL server host message. Instead, MySQL will just wait for a response (which isn't coming).

Packet Length Too Big Messages

If you are sending large queries to your database, or retrieving large BLOB fields of data from your database, you may experience a Packet too large error. This is caused by having the --max_allowed_packet configuration option set too small. A packet is considered one incoming SQL statement or an outgoing row of data.

Evidence of the Problem

Having packets that are larger than allowed can be quite a puzzler. When MySQL determines that the incoming query or outgoing record exceeds the maximum allowed size, it logs a Packet too large error and closes the connection. In the clients we've used, this results in the client reporting a Lost connection to MySQL server during query error. To determine what really happened, you need to look in the server's error log, where you'll see the Packet too large error.

This error occurs in client-to-server communication as well in server-to-server communication for replication. In either case, it's only when you look at the error messages in the logs or the replication status report that you see what the issue is.

Solutions

The following are two ways to deal with the large packet problem:

- Increase your `--max_packet_length` setting to be large enough to accommodate any SQL statement being sent to the database and any single row of data that is returned to the client. There's no blanket rule of thumb for calculating this value; just make sure it's larger than any piece of data you need to store in your database. For a database that stores large documents or images, you will need to set the `--max_packet_length` value much higher than if you're keeping track of customer addresses.

- If you have huge rows or large `BLOB` fields that are so big you cannot make the `--max_packet_length` setting large enough (either because of memory limitations or because the maximum limit is 1GB), or you want to break up the data for performance reasons, you might consider this suggestion: before you insert the large data object, break it into smaller chunks and insert a row for each piece of data, using a common identifier to group the pieces of data together. When you need the data, a single `SELECT` statement gets all of the records that contain the data, and the application assembles the data into one large chunk for use.

For more information, see `http://dev.mysql.com/doc/mysql/en/packet-too-large.html`.

The Server Has Gone Away Messages

On rare occasions, when you are using the MySQL client, you get the pleasure of seeing this message: `MySQL server has gone away`. The first time it happens, you panic and frantically get to the database server and start the process of figuring out why the database has shut down. After a little looking around, you find that the database is still running. A review of the error log reveals the database has not stopped, started, or restarted in the past few days or weeks. You probably spend some time puzzling over what happened, even trying to figure out why MySQL didn't log the server crash.

Evidence of the Problem

The `MySQL server has gone away` message is sent to a client for several reasons, each one resulting in the client's connection to MySQL being lost:

- The database administrator has used the `KILL` command to terminate your connection.

- You attempt to run a query after the connection is closed.

- The client or server has timed out for the connection.

- The size of your SQL statement is too large, or the results have a record that is too large for the `--max_allowed_packet` setting.

- You send an incorrect query to the server.

- You have found a MySQL bug and the database died during the query execution.

Solutions

The following are a few ways of discovering the cause of a broken MySQL connection:

- To verify that it was a connection problem, reconnect and issue the statement again. If the statement runs successfully, you probably encountered a timeout.

- If the connection is broken when you run the query a second time, check the value of your `--max-allowed-packet` setting. You can also look in the error log to see if a `Packet too large` message is logged. If so, increase the `--max-allowed-packet` value.

- Check with your database administrator to see if he killed your connection.

■**Note** The database administrator should immediately contact users with a notification that their connection was causing a problem and was killed, and help them work through the problem.

- If you don't have a problem with the packet size, carefully examine the syntax of your query. MySQL will sometimes close the connection if the query syntax is incorrect. Make sure all of your join fields are specified. You may want to reduce the complexity of the query, and gradually build it piece by piece to get back to the original complex query.

- If, in building a query, you find that some combination of valid SQL syntax generates this error, you may have stumbled into a MySQL bug (rare, but possible). See the "How to Report MySQL Bugs" section later in this chapter for information about finding and reporting bugs to MySQL AB.

For more information, refer to `http://dev.mysql.com/doc/mysql/en/gone-away.html` and `http://dev.mysql.com/doc/mysql/en/communication-errors.html`.

Troubleshooting Start, Restart, and Shutdown Issues

In this section, we'll discuss common problems related to starting and shutting down the server properly, including the following:

- Determining whether the server crashed

- Problems starting the MySQL server

- Problems stopping the MySQL server

- Unexpected restarts

■**Note** While MySQL aims to make every server installation a bump-free and quick process, you may run into trouble when installing or upgrading your server. See Chapter 14 for information that will help if you have problems installing or upgrading a MySQL database.

Did the Server Crash?

Depending on the message you get from the client, you may not be sure if the database server restarted or if you just had an issue with a client or a query. It is sometimes confusing trying to determine how significant the event was. Although a client connection getting closed is important to resolve, most administrators would consider a server restart far more serious. Being aware of where the problem occurred is important.

You have several ways to determine when the server last restarted. One way is to use the `mysqladmin version` command and check the uptime to determine if the server has recently restarted. Output from this command is shown in Listing 20-7. As you can see on the `Uptime` line, the server has been up for ten days, meaning that, in this example, the message you just got from the client was not because the server restarted.

Listing 20-7. *Output from mysqladmin version*

```
# mysqladmin version
mysqladmin  Ver 8.41 Distrib 5.0.6-beta, for unknown-linux-gnu on x86_64

Server version          5.0.6-beta-max-log
Protocol version        10
Connection              Localhost via UNIX socket
UNIX socket             /tmp/mysql.sock
Uptime:                 10 days 21 hours 58 min 21 sec

Threads: 1  Questions: 858  Slow queries: 0  Opens: 0  Flush tables: 1
Open tables: 3  Queries per second avg: 0.001
```

You can also get the uptime in seconds from within the MySQL shell, by using the `SHOW VARIABLES LIKE 'uptime'` command. The output of this command is shown in Listing 20-8.

Listing 20-8. *Uptime from MySQL Client*

```
mysql> SHOW VARIABLES like 'uptime';
+---------------+-------+
| Variable_name | Value |
+---------------+-------+
| Uptime        | 84472 |
+---------------+-------+
1 row in set (0.00 sec)
```

Another method for seeing if the database has recently restarted, and to get the history of activity over time, is to check the error log. Listing 20-9 shows the output of the log with an egrep for messages that indicate the server has stopped, started, or restarted. If you find unexplained entries in this output, you should look more closely at the error log and general query log to compare database activity with the unexplained server restarts to determine what might be the cause of the problem.

Listing 20-9. *egrep of Error Log*

```
shell> egrep "(ended|started|restarted)" promysql.err
050501 13:16:10  mysqld started
050501 15:51:32  mysqld ended
050501 15:51:33  mysqld started
050502 15:41:29  mysqld ended
050502 15:41:31  mysqld started
050502 15:41:43  mysqld ended
050502 16:02:04  mysqld started
050502 16:04:50  mysqld ended
050502 16:05:03  mysqld started
050505 17:48:40  mysqld ended
050505 17:54:07  mysqld started
```

For more information about the `mysqld_safe` startup script, see `http://dev.mysql.com/doc/mysql/en/mysqld-safe.html`. For what to do if MySQL keeps crashing, refer to `http://dev.mysql.com/doc/mysql/en/crashing.html`.

Problems Starting MySQL Server

Have you ever started the MySQL server only to find that, before you can connect, the MySQL server daemon ended? In MySQL version 5.0.4, the `mysql.server` script changed a bit to prevent the server from indicating it started up only to shut right back down. As of MySQL 5.0.4, when you issue the start command, you wait until the database has started, and then get a success message:

```
/etc/init.d/mysql start
Starting MySQL SUCCESS!
```

Evidence of the Problem

The most common way to find that your server won't start is to wait in suspense as the server startup process runs, and then see it finally indicates an error occurred:

```
/etc/init.d/mysql start
Starting MySQL................................. ERROR!
```

If you aren't using the startup script, the common indicator is the `mysql ended` message in the logs or on the console where the server was started. Also, starting the server using the MySQL binary itself will keep the process and messages in the forefront, as shown in Listing 20-10.

Listing 20-10. *Running MySQL Without a Startup Script*

```
./bin/mysqld
050430 14:56:32 [Warning] Can't create test file /data/mysql/promysql.lower-test
./bin/mysqld: Can't change dir to '/data/mysql/' (Errcode: 2)
050430 14:56:32 [ERROR] Aborting
```

Seeing the error about /data/mysql shown in Listing 20-10, you would check what's going on in the /data/mysql directory where your data files are stored. You might learn that the data directory is not properly mounted.

Solutions

Following are some steps to take when you have problems starting up MySQL:

- Check to see if MySQL is already running, or if the network port you are using for MySQL is being used by another process.

- Check the error logs to determine if any abnormal event was logged.

- Be sure your directories and data file permissions are set for the MySQL user and group.

- If the startup fails with an unknown option, fix the offending option.

- Check to see if there are missing data or log directories specified in the configuration file.

- If all of your existing options seem correct and your directories are fine, but you still are not seeing any log information, start MySQL using just the daemon itself with ./bin/mysqld, and see what kind of output is generated.

For more information about the MySQL startup script, see http://dev.mysql.com/doc/mysql/en/mysql-server.html.

Problems Stopping MySQL Server

In rare cases, you may find that you cannot seem to stop the MySQL server. Most often, this is related to a thread being busy in the database.

Evidence of the Problem

You'll see this problem when you attempt to stop the MySQL server:

```
sudo /etc/init.d/mysql stop
```

And instead of the typical, few seconds to stop the database, the wait continues until your database indicates it can't be stopped:

```
Killing mysqld with pid 32441
Wait for mysqld to exit............................... gave up waiting!
```

Or, with the MySQL 5.0.4 and later mysql.server script, you'll see that the stop process ends in an error:

```
/etc/init.d/mysql stop
Shutting down MySQL.................................. ERROR!
```

Solutions

Here are a few things to check and do if you are having a problem shutting down MySQL:

- You may have a thread that is busy and is preventing the server from stopping. Use the SHOW PROCESSLIST command to identify queries that are in progress. Killing the connection may be what's required to stop MySQL.

- Before stopping the database, stop resources (like Apache) that maintain connections to MySQL that could prevent the database from stopping.

- Is the MySQL server actually running? Look at processes and verify that MySQL is running. If the PID file exists, the error will come back even if the process isn't running. If your server stopped abnormally and didn't have a chance to remove the PID file, it will attempt to shut down as if it were running.

■**Caution** When you're having issues with shutting down a server, you may be tempted to use the operating system to force MySQL to exit. If MySQL won't shut down because it's busy writing data and you force it to, you may end up with corrupt or missing data. Use the operating system-level process termination command or tool only as a last resort.

For more information, see http://dev.mysql.com/doc/mysql/en/mysql-server.html.

Problems with Unexpected Restarts

A server unexpectedly restarting can lead to a lot of stress. If you are in an environment where every second counts, not knowing when the next server restart is going to happen may be unacceptable. For other database uses, unexpected restarts are less damaging, but still unnerving. If you have experienced unexpected restarts, you'll want to know what caused them and how to prevent them in the future.

Evidence of the Problem

Although a restart by mysqld_safe happens quickly, it is easily noticed by an application under heavy usage when connections can't be made for the small amount of time the server is down during the restart. If a restart goes unnoticed, or to figure out the exact timing, you can see the entry (or entries) by doing a grep "restarted" host.err.

Solutions

If you have problems with unexpected server restarts, the following items may help you resolve the problem:

- Not having enough memory can cause unexpected restarts. This can happen if MySQL needs more memory than is physically available on the server or another process is consuming a lot of memory. If you have a system that monitors your server's resources, check to see whether the low amount of memory available correlates to the times when the MySQL server restarted.

- Server restarts are a sign of corruption in the database tables. You should go through the steps to check the status of your tables and repair them if necessary. The next section provides more information about data corruption.

- Perform troubleshooting tasks on the operating system and hardware. A defective disk, damaged RAID controller, or faulty RAM can affect MySQL's ability to function and may cause the database to restart during certain failures.

- Check the following MySQL documentation:

    - What to do if MySQL keeps crashing: `http://dev.mysql.com/doc/mysql/en/reproduceable-test-case.html`

    - Table maintenance: `http://dev.mysql.com/doc/mysql/en/table-maintenance.html`

    - Check MyISAM tables: `http://dev.mysql.com/doc/mysql/en/myisamchk-syntax.html`

    - Repair MyISAM tables: `http://dev.mysql.com/doc/mysql/en/repair.html`

Resolving Data Corruption

As hard as MySQL developers work to perfect the database software, and database administrators work to keep their systems protected, data corruption does occur. The MySQL development team takes data corruption very seriously and provides a set of instructions to follow to create a reproducible bug that will allow them to identify where the corruption is happening.

Evidence of the Problem

The corrupted data files often show up in the form of a server crash or unexpected restart. They cause queries to fail or to return unexpected results (or no results). A more proactive approach for databases using the MyISAM storage engine is to regularly run the `mysqlcheck` script to determine if any tables are corrupted.

The following are some reasons that you might experience data file corruption:

- The server was killed in the middle of an update.

- A bug caused MySQL to stop while writing to disk.

- An external program is manipulating the data files.

- Multiple servers are pointed to the same data files.

- A corrupted data file caused the server to act improperly and corrupt other data.

- A storage engine bug caused bad data to be written.

- The operating system, hardware, or disks may be faulty.

Solutions

If you encounter a corrupt data file, here are some areas to look into:

- Be sure you have backups of your data. Yes, once you've discovered there is corruption it may be too late, but we hope you've had enough foresight to create regular backups (see Chapter 17 for details about backing up MySQL).

- If you are using MyISAM tables, run the `mysqlcheck` or `myisamchk` script to repair the table.

- If you can still get your database to run and use the table, do a `mysqldump` of the table, `DROP` the table, and then import the data from the dump. (Chapter 17 describes how to use `mysqldump`.)

- Follow MySQL's steps to create a repeatable situation and contact MySQL with the necessary information. You can find these steps at `http://dev.mysql.com/doc/mysql/en/reproduceable-test-case.html`.

You can refer to the MySQL documentation for checking and recovering MyISAM tables, at `http://dev.mysql.com/doc/mysql/en/myisamchk-syntax.html` and `http://dev.mysql.com/doc/mysql/en/crash-recovery.html`, respectively.

How to Report MySQL Bugs

It is possible that, in your use of MySQL, you encounter a bug. MySQL doesn't release software marked as production-ready until all known fatal bugs are resolved. MySQL defines a *fatal bug* as one that causes the server to crash under normal use, gives the wrong answer for a normal query, or contains a security problem. That being said, there is an active bug-tracking system that allows database users to submit bugs and track their status as they go through the system.

If you think you've found a bug, follow the steps outlined in the MySQL documentation for submitting a bug report (`http://dev.mysql.com/doc/mysql/en/bug-reports.html`). This involves the following steps:

- Make sure it's a repeatable bug (`http://dev.mysql.com/doc/mysql/en/reproduceable-test-case.html`).

- Search the existing documentation and mailing lists to see if there is a resolution.

- Search through the bug reports to see if it has been reported (`http://dev.mysql.com/doc/mysql/en/open-bugs.html`).

- Finally, submit the bug report with information about your environment and how to duplicate the bug.

The MySQL team follows the bug-tracking system very closely and usually gets to work on a bug report within just a few hours.

Support Options

A chapter on troubleshooting wouldn't be complete without mentioning support options. Each organization has different needs, and you have a wide spectrum of options when you're looking for support for your MySQL installation. What matches your needs will depend on what assistance you require and when you require it.

Here are some support options:

Mailing lists: If you have some expertise with MySQL, and your troubleshooting priorities allow you time to search and post, you can get a lot of information and help from the MySQL mailing lists. The collective group of people who participate have a great deal of expertise, and response time is typically pretty good (provided you have good manners). Even if you have a critical problem that is happening in real time, it's still worth trying out a mailing list to get help exploring the issue and formulating a strategy to resolve it. There are several MySQL mailing lists. Unless you have a specific question about a particular piece of MySQL that has its own mailing list, the general user mailing list is the place to go. For a list of all of MySQL mailing lists, along with the list archives and instructions for subscription, visit http://lists.mysql.com/.

Consultants: If you are running an instance of MySQL, but don't have the time, interest, or ability to resolve a problem, a consultant may be the right person to step in. A web search for "MySQL consultant" brings up hundreds of links leading to people who have experience with MySQL and are looking for opportunities to apply their knowledge and experience.

Help from MySQL AB: If you are looking for MySQL expertise, why not turn to the folks who are building the database? MySQL AB offers several consulting packages, including a one-day rapid response service for urgent needs (a certified consultant will work with you on troubleshooting, performance, architecture, or any of your MySQL needs). Another option from MySQL AB is the MySQL Network (http://www.mysql.com/network/), a service that gives you access to production support and MySQL developers to help solve your unique issues. The MySQL Network also provides certified releases of the MySQL database.

Summary

Troubleshooting a database server can be a stressful experience, especially if the problem is occurring in your production environment and affecting the availability of your application. A good database administrator is familiar with the details of MySQL and knows exactly what to do when a situation arises. This includes having a thorough knowledge of how to use the troubleshooting tools and where to look for answers.

We spent a significant portion of the chapter discussing the various tools and logs that are the foundation for dealing with specific problems. We then went through a number of different common problems and gave details on possible causes and solutions. Our goal was to provide some detailed information, as well as to show you examples of the methodology for working through problems.

As you combine the knowledge of MySQL administration with the honing of your real-time problem-solving skills, you will become more capable of surviving a problem in your database without unnecessary stress and wasted time. This, in turn, will please the users of your database, as well as your manager, customers, and clients.

CHAPTER 21

■ ■ ■

MySQL Data Dictionary

In this chapter, we'll be taking a closer look at a feature of MySQL 5 that's receiving considerable attention. As of version 5.0.2, the INFORMATION_SCHEMA virtual database is available, which offers a standardized way of reading meta information about the database server and its schemas. In this chapter, we'll examine what exactly the INFORMATION_SCHEMA data store is, how you can use it, and what information is contained inside it.

Before we go further, we want to discuss a few terms used in this chapter. The discussion of a database server's *meta* information commonly involves the following terms:

- *metadata*

- *data dictionary* or *system catalog*

- INFORMATION_SCHEMA

The definition of *metadata* is simply data *about* other data. Metadata describes or summarizes another piece of data. Examples of metadata include the number of rows in a table, the type of index structure used on a set of columns, or the statement used to create a stored procedure. Each of these pieces of data describes another piece of data or structure.

All major database vendors have a repository, or container, for metadata, but different database vendors refer to this repository differently. The two most common terms, however, are *data dictionary* and *system catalog*. We consider them synonymous, but when referring to the metadata repository, we'll use the term data dictionary.

The term INFORMATION_SCHEMA describes the ANSI standard interface to the database server's metadata. The INFORMATION_SCHEMA is *not* an actual schema (database), but the data contained inside this *virtual* database can be accessed just like any other database on the server. In this way, the INFORMATION_SCHEMA interface acts as a standardizing component for accessing information about the database server and its actual schema. The "tables" inside this virtual database aren't tables at all, but rather table-like data that is pulled from a variety of sources, including the underlying mysql system database, and the MySQL server system variables and counters.

In this way, the INFORMATION_SCHEMA tables are more like views than tables. If you're coming from a Microsoft SQL Server background, you'll recognize this concept, as the INFORMATION_SCHEMA supported by Microsoft SQL Server are views that pull actual data from the Microsoft SQL Server system tables, such as sys_objects and sys_indexes. INFORMATION_SCHEMA views are read-only, partly because the data contained in the INFORMATION_SCHEMA views isn't contained in a single location, but instead pulled from the storage areas noted earlier.

In this chapter, we'll be looking at the following topics related to the new INFORMATION_ SCHEMA feature of MySQL 5:

- Benefits of a standardized interface
- The INFORMATION_SCHEMA views
- Examples of usage

Benefits of a Standardized Interface

Before we get into the specific tables that comprise the MySQL Data Dictionary, we want you to understand why the data dictionary has been added as a feature to the MySQL 5 source code. For those of you without much experience with MySQL's SHOW commands, the transition to using the INFORMATION_SCHEMA database might take some getting used to, but we highly recommend taking the time to do so.

There are three main advantages to the INFORMATION_SCHEMA interface versus the SHOW commands:

- Adherence to standards
- Using SELECT to retrieve metadata
- More information than SHOW commands

Adherence to Standards

MySQL's SHOW commands are proprietary and not standards-compliant. By contrast, the INFORMATION_SCHEMA interface is a standard outlined by ANSI/ISO as part of the SQL-99 and SQL:2003 standards.

One advantage to complying with these standards is that applications that rely on querying for metadata—for example, a monitoring application—can be written in a portable fashion. The databases supporting INFORMATION_SCHEMA views are MySQL, Microsoft SQL Server, and, to some extent, IBM's DB2 database. Hopefully, in the future, all major database vendors will move to full compliance, and application code can be truly vendor-agnostic. Having metadata queries written for the INFORMATION_SCHEMA interface is a proactive stance for future portability needs.

To adhere completely to the SQL standard, MySQL's implementation of the INFORMATION_ SCHEMA shows columns for which MySQL has no equivalent data. For these columns—for instance, the INFORMATION_SCHEMA.TABLES.TABLE_CATALOG column—MySQL simply displays a NULL value, because MySQL has no concept of a database "catalog." In addition, MySQL displays certain additional data pieces in the INFORMATION_SCHEMA output where MySQL stores nonstandard or extension information. This is done to provide complete equivalency to the MySQL SHOW commands. We'll detail later where the MySQL implementation diverges from the ANSI standard.

Using SELECT to Retrieve Metadata

Perhaps the best reason to use the INFORMATION_SCHEMA views is that you can access metadata through your standard SQL SELECT statements. Instead of various SHOW commands—such as SHOW TABLES, SHOW FULL COLUMNS, and so on—you access the data through the old familiar SELECT statement.

This means you'll have to learn the INFORMATION_SCHEMA views, to ensure you know where to look for information. However, the advantage to using SELECT here is that you don't have to learn any new syntax to read information from the INFORMATION_SCHEMA. You can use the various joins you learned in Chapter 7 to present views of related metadata in a way that was impossible before. Because the INFORMATION_SCHEMA is accessible through standard SQL statements, you can operate on the data sets returned from a query on the INFORMATION_SCHEMA tables as you would any other SQL statement. This makes it easy to construct complex SELECT statements that use the information in the INFORMATION_SCHEMA views like any other table in your other databases.

More Information than SHOW Commands

As you'll see in the following section, the INFORMATION_SCHEMA offers you more detailed information than equivalent SHOW commands. In some cases, a single SELECT statement against the INFORMATION_SCHEMA views can output more than what multiple SHOW commands could provide.

■**Note** To use the INFORMATION_SCHEMA views, the user must be granted privileges on the object *that the view represents.* Therefore, although no special privilege is needed to issue a SELECT against the INFORMATION_SCHEMA, the results of certain SELECTs on the metadata repository depend on which schema, tables, or columns the user has been granted access to.

The INFORMATION_SCHEMA Views

In this section, we cover each of the views available under the INFORMATION_SCHEMA, and outline which columns returned from the view equate to the prior SHOW command, if one existed. We use simple examples in this section to highlight the information available from the following INFORMATION_SCHEMA views:

- INFORMATION_SCHEMA.SCHEMATA

- INFORMATION_SCHEMA.TABLES

- INFORMATION_SCHEMA.TABLE_CONSTRAINTS

- INFORMATION_SCHEMA.COLUMNS

- INFORMATION_SCHEMA.KEY_COLUMN_USAGE

- INFORMATION_SCHEMA.STATISTICS

- INFORMATION_SCHEMA.ROUTINES

- INFORMATION_SCHEMA.VIEWS

- INFORMATION_SCHEMA.CHARACTER_SETS

- INFORMATION_SCHEMA.COLLATIONS

- INFORMATION_SCHEMA.COLLATION_CHARACTER_SET_APPLICABILITY

- `INFORMATION_SCHEMA.SCHEMA_PRIVILEGES`

- `INFORMATION_SCHEMA.USER_PRIVILEGES`

- `INFORMATION_SCHEMA.TABLE_PRIVILEGES`

- `INFORMATION_SCHEMA.COLUMN_PRIVILEGES`

■**Note** Plans are under way to add more views to `INFORMATION_SCHEMA`. Notably, the following views are planned for release: `TRIGGERS`, `PARAMETERS`, and `REFERENTIAL_CONSTRAINTS`. As we go to press, details about these views are still limited. Check the MySQL documentation for the latest `INFORMATION_SCHEMA` view lists: `http://dev.mysql.com/doc/mysql/en/information-schema-tables.html`.

It's worth noting again here that the results displayed from the `INFORMATION_SCHEMA` views are specific to the user logged in. That means that only schemata, tables, or columns to which the user has been granted access appear in the resultsets.

In the following subsections, for each `INFORMATION_SCHEMA` view, we show you the `DESCRIBE` of the view, a simple `SELECT` on the view, then in a bulleted list, we define what each of the output columns contains. For each section, you'll see a note block detailing which `SHOW` commands, if any, correspond to the new `INFORMATION_SCHEMA` view.

Instead of arranging the views in alphabetical order, we've ordered them in groups that most closely relate to one another. For instance, we've grouped the privileges views together and the character set and collation views together. This order will help give you an idea of the relationship of the view data.

In the following sections, fields that are *not* part of the ANSI standard appear in *italics* to denote that the column is a MySQL-specific data element. These fields have been left in the `INFORMATION_SCHEMA` outputs as an extension to allow equivalent output to some `SHOW` commands. If you're attempting to create cross-platform portable SQL code, please be aware of these extension fields.

■**Note** Two quick notes before we get into the views. First, some of the following examples were issued against the `test.http_auth` table created and used in Chapter 6. If you get an empty resultset for some of the examples, either follow along in the reading, or refer to Chapter 6 for creation of the `http_auth` table in the `test` database.

Second, depending on your operating system and version of MySQL, you may notice slight differences in some of the output. Notably, depending on the version of MySQL you use, a `VARCHAR(4096)` column displayed in results in this chapter may appear as `VARCHAR(4095)`, or in a Windows environment, `VARCHAR(512)`. These are minor discrepancies, and as the data dictionary features of MySQL 5 are an evolving work, these data types may have changed by the time we go to print.

INFORMATION_SCHEMA.SCHEMATA

The SCHEMATA view shows information about the databases on the server. Listing 21-1 shows the columns displayed by the view.

Listing 21-1. *INFORMATION_SCHEMA.SCHEMATA*

```
mysql> DESCRIBE INFORMATION_SCHEMA.SCHEMATA;
+----------------------------+---------------+------+-----+---------+-------+
| Field                      | Type          | Null | Key | Default | Extra |
+----------------------------+---------------+------+-----+---------+-------+
| CATALOG_NAME               | varchar(4096) | YES  |     | NULL    |       |
| SCHEMA_NAME                | varchar(64)   | NO   |     |         |       |
| DEFAULT_CHARACTER_SET_NAME | varchar(64)   | NO   |     |         |       |
| SQL_PATH                   | varchar(4096) | YES  |     | NULL    |       |
+----------------------------+---------------+------+-----+---------+-------+
4 rows in set (0.04 sec)

mysql> SELECT * FROM INFORMATION_SCHEMA.SCHEMATA;
+--------------+--------------------+----------------------------+----------+
| CATALOG_NAME | SCHEMA_NAME        | DEFAULT_CHARACTER_SET_NAME | SQL_PATH |
+--------------+--------------------+----------------------------+----------+
| NULL         | information_schema | utf8                       | NULL     |
| NULL         | mysql              | latin1                     | NULL     |
| NULL         | test               | latin1                     | NULL     |
+--------------+--------------------+----------------------------+----------+
3 rows in set (0.02 sec)
```

The fields contained in INFORMATION_SCHEMA.SCHEMATA are as follows:

- CATALOG_NAME: This field will always be NULL, as MySQL doesn't have any concept of a catalog. It's provided to maintain the ANSI standard output.

- SCHEMA_NAME: This is the name of the database.

- DEFAULT_CHARACTER_SET_NAME: This is the name of the default character set for the database. We discuss the INFORMATION_SCHEMA.CHARACTER_SETS view later in the chapter.

- SQL_PATH: This field will always be NULL. MySQL doesn't use this value to "find" the files associated with the database. It's included for compatibility with the ANSI standard.

Although the SCHEMATA view isn't the most useful of the INFORMATION_SCHEMA views, it does contain the database's default character set, while the corresponding SHOW DATABASES command doesn't.

■**Note** The SHOW DATABASES command is the closest command to SELECT * FROM INFORMATION_SCHEMA.SCHEMATA.

INFORMATION_SCHEMA.TABLES

The INFORMATION_SCHEMA.TABLES view stores information about the database tables on the server. Listing 21-2 shows the DESCRIBE and a simple SELECT from the view.

Listing 21-2. *INFORMATION_SCHEMA.TABLES*

```
mysql> DESCRIBE INFORMATION_SCHEMA.TABLES;
+-----------------+---------------+------+-----+---------+-------+
| Field           | Type          | Null | Key | Default | Extra |
+-----------------+---------------+------+-----+---------+-------+
| TABLE_CATALOG   | varchar(4096) | YES  |     | NULL    |       |
| TABLE_SCHEMA    | varchar(64)   | NO   |     |         |       |
| TABLE_NAME      | varchar(64)   | NO   |     |         |       |
| TABLE_TYPE      | varchar(64)   | NO   |     |         |       |
| ENGINE          | varchar(64)   | YES  |     | NULL    |       |
| VERSION         | bigint(21)    | YES  |     | NULL    |       |
| ROW_FORMAT      | varchar(10)   | YES  |     | NULL    |       |
| TABLE_ROWS      | bigint(21)    | YES  |     | NULL    |       |
| AVG_ROW_LENGTH  | bigint(21)    | YES  |     | NULL    |       |
| DATA_LENGTH     | bigint(21)    | YES  |     | NULL    |       |
| MAX_DATA_LENGTH | bigint(21)    | YES  |     | NULL    |       |
| INDEX_LENGTH    | bigint(21)    | YES  |     | NULL    |       |
| DATA_FREE       | bigint(21)    | YES  |     | NULL    |       |
| AUTO_INCREMENT  | bigint(21)    | YES  |     | NULL    |       |
| CREATE_TIME     | datetime      | YES  |     | NULL    |       |
| UPDATE_TIME     | datetime      | YES  |     | NULL    |       |
| CHECK_TIME      | datetime      | YES  |     | NULL    |       |
| TABLE_COLLATION | varchar(64)   | YES  |     | NULL    |       |
| CHECKSUM        | bigint(21)    | YES  |     | NULL    |       |
| CREATE_OPTIONS  | varchar(255)  | YES  |     | NULL    |       |
| TABLE_COMMENT   | varchar(80)   | NO   |     |         |       |
+-----------------+---------------+------+-----+---------+-------+
21 rows in set (0.01 sec)

mysql> SELECT * FROM INFORMATION_SCHEMA.TABLES
    -> WHERE TABLE_SCHEMA = 'test' AND TABLE_NAME = 'http_auth' \G
*************************** 1. row ***************************
  TABLE_CATALOG: NULL
   TABLE_SCHEMA: test
     TABLE_NAME: http_auth
     TABLE_TYPE: BASE TABLE
         ENGINE: MyISAM
        VERSION: 9
     ROW_FORMAT: Fixed
     TABLE_ROWS: 90000
 AVG_ROW_LENGTH: 59
    DATA_LENGTH: 5310000
```

```
   MAX_DATA_LENGTH: 253403070463
      INDEX_LENGTH: 3716096
         DATA_FREE: 0
    AUTO_INCREMENT: NULL
       CREATE_TIME: 2005-03-08 23:25:28
       UPDATE_TIME: 2005-03-08 23:29:38
        CHECK_TIME: NULL
   TABLE_COLLATION: latin1_swedish_ci
          CHECKSUM: NULL
    CREATE_OPTIONS:
     TABLE_COMMENT:
1 row in set (0.00 sec)
```

The fields contained in INFORMATION_SCHEMA.TABLES are as follows:

- TABLE_CATALOG: Again, will always be NULL. Shown for compatibility purposes.

- TABLE_SCHEMA: The name of the database to which this table belongs.

- TABLE_NAME: The name of the table.

- TABLE_TYPE: Either BASE TABLE, TEMPORARY, or VIEW. Those entries having a VIEW value also appear in INFORMATION_SCHEMA.VIEWS. More details about this view come later in the chapter.

- *ENGINE*: The storage engine handling this table's data.

- *VERSION*: The internal versioning of the table's .frm file. Indicates how many times the table's definition has changed.

- *ROW_FORMAT*: Either FIXED, COMPRESSED, or DYNAMIC. Indicates the format of table rows. See Chapter 5 for more details on the difference between the row formats.

- *TABLE_ROWS*: Shows the number of rows in a table.

- *AVG_ROW_LENGTH*: Shows the average length, in bytes, of the table's rows.

- *DATA_LENGTH*: Shows the total length, in bytes, of the table's data.

- *MAX_DATA_LENGTH*: Shows the maximum storage length, in bytes, that the table's data can consume.

- *INDEX_LENGTH*: Shows the total length, in bytes, of the table's indexes.

- *DATA_FREE*: Shows the number of bytes that have been allocated to the table's data, but that haven't yet been filled with table data.

- *AUTO_INCREMENT*: Shows the *next* integer number to be used on the table's AUTO_INCREMENT column, or NULL if no such sequence is used on the table.

- *CREATE_TIME*: Timestamp of the table's initial creation.

- *UPDATE_TIME*: Timestamp of the last ALTER TABLE command on this table. If there have been no ALTER TABLE commands, then shows the same timestamp as CREATE_TIME.

- *CHECK_TIME*: Timestamp of the last time a table check was performed on the table, or NULL if the table has never been checked for consistency.

- *TABLE_COLLATION*: Shows the table's default character set and collation combination. See INFORMATION_SCHEMA.COLLATION_CHARACTER_SET_APPLICABILITY for more details.

- *CHECKSUM*: Internal live checksum for the table, or NULL if none is available.

- *CREATE_OPTIONS*: Shows any options used at table creation, or nothing if none has been used.

- *TABLE_COMMENT*: Shows any comment used during table creation.

Clearly, the INFORMATION_SCHEMA.TABLES view has a wealth of useful information about the database tables on your MySQL server. The vast majority of the columns, as you may well have noticed, are extension fields that MySQL has included to provide compatibility with the SHOW TABLE STATUS command.

■**Note** The SHOW TABLE STATUS command displays most of the information that a SELECT * FROM ➡ INFORMATION_SCHEMA.TABLES would output.

INFORMATION_SCHEMA.TABLE_CONSTRAINTS

The INFORMATION_SCHEMA.TABLE_CONSTRAINTS view shows columns related to all tables for which a constraining index exists. Listing 21-3 shows a DESCRIBE and a simple SELECT from this view.

Listing 21-3. *INFORMATION_SCHEMA.TABLE_CONSTRAINTS*

```
mysql> DESCRIBE INFORMATION_SCHEMA.TABLE_CONSTRAINTS;
+-------------------+--------------+------+-----+---------+-------+
| Field             | Type         | Null | Key | Default | Extra |
+-------------------+--------------+------+-----+---------+-------+
| CONSTRAINT_CATALOG | varchar(4096) | YES |     | NULL    |       |
| CONSTRAINT_SCHEMA  | varchar(64)  | NO   |     |         |       |
| CONSTRAINT_NAME    | varchar(64)  | NO   |     |         |       |
| TABLE_SCHEMA       | varchar(64)  | NO   |     |         |       |
| TABLE_NAME         | varchar(64)  | NO   |     |         |       |
| CONSTRAINT_TYPE    | varchar(64)  | NO   |     |         |       |
+-------------------+--------------+------+-----+---------+-------+
6 rows in set (0.01 sec)
```

```
mysql> SELECT * FROM INFORMATION_SCHEMA.TABLE_CONSTRAINTS
    -> WHERE CONSTRAINT_SCHEMA = 'test' \G
*************************** 1. row ***************************
CONSTRAINT_CATALOG: NULL
 CONSTRAINT_SCHEMA: test
   CONSTRAINT_NAME: PRIMARY
      TABLE_SCHEMA: test
        TABLE_NAME: http_auth
   CONSTRAINT_TYPE: PRIMARY KEY
*************************** 2. row ***************************
CONSTRAINT_CATALOG: NULL
 CONSTRAINT_SCHEMA: test
   CONSTRAINT_NAME: PRIMARY
      TABLE_SCHEMA: test
        TABLE_NAME: http_auth_idb
   CONSTRAINT_TYPE: PRIMARY KEY
2 rows in set (0.31 sec)
```

The fields contained in INFORMATION_SCHEMA.TABLE_CONSTRAINTS are as follows:

- CONSTRAINT_CATALOG: Again, always NULL.

- CONSTRAINT_SCHEMA: Name of the database in which the table constraint (index) resides. This is always the same as the value of TABLE_SCHEMA.

- CONSTRAINT_NAME: Name of the constraint.

- TABLE_SCHEMA: Name of the database for the table on which the index is built.

- TABLE_NAME: Name of the table on which the index is built.

- CONSTRAINT_TYPE: Either PRIMARY KEY, FOREIGN KEY, or UNIQUE, depending on what engine is handling the table, and how the key was referenced in a CREATE TABLE statement. In the future, MyISAM tables will fully support FOREIGN KEY constraints. Currently, you only see FOREIGN KEY pop up when an InnoDB table is referenced during create time.

Tip The SHOW INDEX command most closely resembles the output from INFORMATION_SCHEMA. TABLE_CONSTRAINTS. The CONSTRAINT_TYPE column contains similar information to the KEY_NAME column returned by SHOW INDEX for entries with a NON_UNIQUE value of 0.

INFORMATION_SCHEMA.COLUMNS

The INFORMATION_SCHEMA.COLUMNS view shows detailed information about the columns contained in the server's database tables. Listing 21-4 shows a DESCRIBE and a simple SELECT from the view.

Listing 21-4. *INFORMATION_SCHEMA.COLUMNS*

```
mysql> DESCRIBE INFORMATION_SCHEMA.COLUMNS;
+--------------------------+---------------+------+-----+---------+-------+
| Field                    | Type          | Null | Key | Default | Extra |
+--------------------------+---------------+------+-----+---------+-------+
| TABLE_CATALOG            | varchar(4096) | YES  |     | NULL    |       |
| TABLE_SCHEMA             | varchar(64)   | NO   |     |         |       |
| TABLE_NAME               | varchar(64)   | NO   |     |         |       |
| COLUMN_NAME              | varchar(64)   | NO   |     |         |       |
| ORDINAL_POSITION         | bigint(21)    | NO   |     | 0       |       |
| COLUMN_DEFAULT           | varchar(64)   | YES  |     | NULL    |       |
| IS_NULLABLE              | varchar(3)    | NO   |     |         |       |
| DATA_TYPE                | varchar(64)   | NO   |     |         |       |
| CHARACTER_MAXIMUM_LENGTH | bigint(21)    | NO   |     | 0       |       |
| CHARACTER_OCTET_LENGTH   | bigint(21)    | NO   |     | 0       |       |
| NUMERIC_PRECISION        | bigint(21)    | YES  |     | NULL    |       |
| NUMERIC_SCALE            | bigint(21)    | YES  |     | NULL    |       |
| CHARACTER_SET_NAME       | varchar(64)   | YES  |     | NULL    |       |
| COLLATION_NAME           | varchar(64)   | YES  |     | NULL    |       |
| COLUMN_TYPE              | longtext      | NO   |     |         |       |
| COLUMN_KEY               | varchar(3)    | NO   |     |         |       |
| EXTRA                    | varchar(20)   | NO   |     |         |       |
| PRIVILEGES               | varchar(80)   | NO   |     |         |       |
| COLUMN_COMMENT           | varchar(255)  | NO   |     |         |       |
+--------------------------+---------------+------+-----+---------+-------+
19 rows in set (0.00 sec)

mysql> SELECT * FROM INFORMATION_SCHEMA.COLUMNS
    -> WHERE TABLE_SCHEMA = 'test' AND TABLE_NAME = 'http_auth' \G
*************************** 1. row ***************************
           TABLE_CATALOG: NULL
            TABLE_SCHEMA: test
              TABLE_NAME: http_auth
             COLUMN_NAME: username
        ORDINAL_POSITION: 1
          COLUMN_DEFAULT:
             IS_NULLABLE: NO
               DATA_TYPE: char
CHARACTER_MAXIMUM_LENGTH: 25
  CHARACTER_OCTET_LENGTH: 25
```

```
          NUMERIC_PRECISION: NULL
              NUMERIC_SCALE: NULL
         CHARACTER_SET_NAME: latin1
            COLLATION_NAME: latin1_swedish_ci
                COLUMN_TYPE: char(25)
                 COLUMN_KEY: PRI
                      EXTRA:
                  PRIVILEGES: select,insert,update,references
             COLUMN_COMMENT:
… omitted
*************************** 4. row ***************************
              TABLE_CATALOG: NULL
               TABLE_SCHEMA: test
                 TABLE_NAME: http_auth
                COLUMN_NAME: gid
            ORDINAL_POSITION: 4
             COLUMN_DEFAULT: 0
                IS_NULLABLE: NO
                  DATA_TYPE: int
   CHARACTER_MAXIMUM_LENGTH: 11
     CHARACTER_OCTET_LENGTH: 11
          NUMERIC_PRECISION: 11
              NUMERIC_SCALE: 0
         CHARACTER_SET_NAME: NULL
            COLLATION_NAME: NULL
                COLUMN_TYPE: int(11)
                 COLUMN_KEY:
                      EXTRA:
                  PRIVILEGES: select,insert,update,references
             COLUMN_COMMENT:
4 rows in set (0.01 sec)
```

The fields contained in INFORMATION_SCHEMA.COLUMNS are as follows:

- TABLE_CATALOG: Again, always NULL.

- TABLE_SCHEMA: Name of the database.

- TABLE_NAME: Name of the database table or view.

- COLUMN_NAME: Name of the column.

- ORDINAL_POSITION: Starting with 1, position of a column in the table.

- COLUMN_DEFAULT: Default value for a column in the table.

- IS_NULLABLE: Either YES or NO, describing whether the column allows for NULL values.

- DATA_TYPE: Shows only the data type keyword, not the entire field definition, for the column.

- CHARACTER_MAXIMUM_LENGTH: Shows the maximum number of characters that the field may contain.

- CHARACTER_OCTET_LENGTH: Shows the maximum length of the field in octets.

- NUMERIC_PRECISION: Shows the precision of numeric fields, or NULL if a non-numeric field type.

- NUMERIC_SCALE: Shows the scale of numeric fields, or NULL if a non-numeric field type.

- CHARACTER_SET_NAME: Shows the character field character set, or NULL if a noncharacter field type. See the section "INFORMATION_SCHEMA.CHARACTER_SETS."

- COLLATION_NAME: Shows the character field collation set, or NULL if a noncharacter field type. See the section "INFORMATION_SCHEMA.COLLATIONS."

- *COLUMN_TYPE*: Shows the full field definition for the column.

- *COLUMN_KEY*: Shows any of PRI, UNI, MUL, or blank. PRI appears when the column is part of a PRIMARY KEY. UNI appears when the column is part of a UNIQUE INDEX. MUL appears when the column is part of an index that allows for duplicates. Blank appears for all other columns.

- *EXTRA*: Shows any extra information about the column that MySQL stores; for instance, the AUTO_INCREMENT keyword.

- *PRIVILEGES*: Shows a list of privileges available to the current user for this column.

- *COLUMN_COMMENT*: Shows the comment used during table creation.

Note The SHOW FULL COLUMNS command is the closest equivalent to a SELECT * FROM INFORMATION_ SCHEMA.COLUMNS WHERE TABLE_NAME = 'table_name'.

The COLUMNS view has a wealth of information that doesn't appear in the SHOW FULL ➡ COLUMNS output. The most useful part of the view output is that you get a normalized output for numeric precision and scale, the data type, and the ordinal position of the column within the table. This means you can avoid scripts that must parse out the non-normalized SHOW COLUMNS output. You'll see an example of this usage later in the chapter.

INFORMATION_SCHEMA.KEY_COLUMN_USAGE

The INFORMATION_SCHEMA.KEY_COLUMN_USAGE view details information about the columns used in a table's indexes or constraints. Listing 21-5 shows an output from DESCRIBE and a simple SELECT from the view.

Listing 21-5. *INFORMATION_SCHEMA.KEY_COLUMN_USAGE*

```
mysql> DESCRIBE INFORMATION_SCHEMA.KEY_COLUMN_USAGE;
+-----------------------------+---------------+------+-----+---------+-------+
| Field                       | Type          | Null | Key | Default | Extra |
+-----------------------------+---------------+------+-----+---------+-------+
| CONSTRAINT_CATALOG          | varchar(4096) | YES  |     | NULL    |       |
| CONSTRAINT_SCHEMA           | varchar(64)   | NO   |     |         |       |
| CONSTRAINT_NAME             | varchar(64)   | NO   |     |         |       |
| TABLE_CATALOG               | varchar(4096) | YES  |     | NULL    |       |
| TABLE_SCHEMA                | varchar(64)   | NO   |     |         |       |
| TABLE_NAME                  | varchar(64)   | NO   |     |         |       |
| COLUMN_NAME                 | varchar(64)   | NO   |     |         |       |
| ORDINAL_POSITION            | bigint(10)    | NO   |     | 0       |       |
| POSITION_IN_UNIQUE_CONSTRAINT | bigint(10)  | YES  |     | NULL    |       |
+-----------------------------+---------------+------+-----+---------+-------+
9 rows in set (0.00 sec)

mysql> SELECT * FROM INFORMATION_SCHEMA.KEY_COLUMN_USAGE
    -> WHERE TABLE_SCHEMA = 'test' AND TABLE_NAME = 'http_auth' \G
*************************** 1. row ***************************
           CONSTRAINT_CATALOG: NULL
            CONSTRAINT_SCHEMA: test
              CONSTRAINT_NAME: PRIMARY
                TABLE_CATALOG: NULL
                 TABLE_SCHEMA: test
                   TABLE_NAME: http_auth
                  COLUMN_NAME: username
             ORDINAL_POSITION: 1
POSITION_IN_UNIQUE_CONSTRAINT: NULL
1 row in set (0.00 sec)
```

The fields contained in INFORMATION_SCHEMA.KEY_COLUMN_USAGE are as follows:

- CONSTRAINT_CATALOG: Always NULL.

- CONSTRAINT_SCHEMA: Name of the database containing the constraint.

- CONSTRAINT_NAME: Name of the constraint.

- TABLE_CATALOG: Always NULL.

- TABLE_SCHEMA: Name of the database containing the table in which the constraint can be found. Is always the same value as CONSTRAINT_SCHEMA.

- TABLE_NAME: Name of the table on which the constraint or index operates.

- COLUMN_NAME: Name of the column in the constraint.

- ORDINAL_POSITION: Position of the column within the index or constraint, starting at the number 1.

- POSITION_IN_UNIQUE_CONSTRAINT: Either NULL, or the position of the column in a referenced FOREIGN KEY constraint that happens to be a UNIQUE INDEX.

The KEY_COLUMN_USAGE data is useful for identifying column positioning in constraints on tables. There's no equivalent SHOW command that returns the same information.

INFORMATION_SCHEMA.STATISTICS

The INFORMATION_SCHEMA.STATISTICS view displays information regarding the indexes operating on the server's tables or views. Listing 21-6 shows a DESCRIBE and a simple SELECT from the view.

Listing 21-6. *INFORMATION_SCHEMA.STATISTICS*

```
mysql> DESCRIBE INFORMATION_SCHEMA.STATISTICS;
+---------------+---------------+------+-----+---------+-------+
| Field         | Type          | Null | Key | Default | Extra |
+---------------+---------------+------+-----+---------+-------+
| TABLE_CATALOG | varchar(4096) | YES  |     | NULL    |       |
| TABLE_SCHEMA  | varchar(64)   | NO   |     |         |       |
| TABLE_NAME    | varchar(64)   | NO   |     |         |       |
| NON_UNIQUE    | bigint(1)     | NO   |     | 0       |       |
| INDEX_SCHEMA  | varchar(64)   | NO   |     |         |       |
| INDEX_NAME    | varchar(64)   | NO   |     |         |       |
| SEQ_IN_INDEX  | bigint(2)     | NO   |     | 0       |       |
| COLUMN_NAME   | varchar(64)   | NO   |     |         |       |
| COLLATION     | varchar(1)    | YES  |     | NULL    |       |
| CARDINALITY   | bigint(21)    | YES  |     | NULL    |       |
| SUB_PART      | bigint(3)     | YES  |     | NULL    |       |
| PACKED        | varchar(10)   | YES  |     | NULL    |       |
| NULLABLE      | varchar(3)    | NO   |     |         |       |
| INDEX_TYPE    | varchar(16)   | NO   |     |         |       |
| COMMENT       | varchar(16)   | YES  |     | NULL    |       |
+---------------+---------------+------+-----+---------+-------+
15 rows in set (0.00 sec)

mysql> SELECT * FROM INFORMATION_SCHEMA.STATISTICS
    -> WHERE TABLE_SCHEMA = 'test' AND TABLE_NAME = 'http_auth' \G
*************************** 1. row ***************************
TABLE_CATALOG: NULL
 TABLE_SCHEMA: test
   TABLE_NAME: http_auth
   NON_UNIQUE: 0
 INDEX_SCHEMA: test
```

```
    INDEX_NAME: PRIMARY
  SEQ_IN_INDEX: 1
   COLUMN_NAME: username
     COLLATION: A
   CARDINALITY: 90000
      SUB_PART: NULL
        PACKED: NULL
      NULLABLE:
    INDEX_TYPE: BTREE
       COMMENT:
1 row in set (0.00 sec)
```

The fields contained in `INFORMATION_SCHEMA.STATISTICS` are as follows:

- `TABLE_CATALOG`: Always `NULL`.

- `TABLE_SCHEMA`: Name of the database in which the table resides.

- `TABLE_NAME`: Name of the table on which the index operates.

- `NON_UNIQUE`: Either 0 or 1. Indicates whether the index can contain duplicate values. Note that `NON_UNIQUE` returns a numeric Boolean representation, as opposed to `YES` or `NO`.

- `INDEX_SCHEMA`: Name of the database in which the index is housed. It's always the same as `TABLE_SCHEMA`.

- `INDEX_NAME`: Name of the index within the schema.

- `SEQ_IN_INDEX`: Shows the position of this column within the index key, starting at position 1.

- `COLUMN_NAME`: Name of the column in the index key.

- `COLLATION`: The column's collation. Will either be A for an ascending index order, or `NULL` for descending.

- `CARDINALITY`: The number of unique values contained in this column for this index key.

- `SUB_PART`: If a prefix on a character field was used in the creation of the index, `SUB_PART` will show the number of characters that the index column uses; otherwise `NULL`.

- `PACKED`: Either 0, 1, or `DEFAULT` depending on whether the index is packed. See Chapter 5 for more information about MyISAM key packing.

- `NULLABLE`: Either `YES` or `NO`, indicating whether the column can contain `NULL` values.

- `INDEX_TYPE`: Any of `BTREE`, `RTREE`, `HASH`, or `FULLTEXT`.

- `COMMENT`: Any comment used during creation of the index; otherwise blank.

The `STATISTICS` view has a wealth of information about the columns used in your indexes. We'll be using this table in the following examples to get a feel for the selectivity of your indexes, so stay tuned.

> ■**Note** The SHOW INDEX command most closely resembles the output from a SELECT * FROM ➥
> INFORMATION_SCHEMA.STATISTICS WHERE TABLE_NAME = 'table_name';.

INFORMATION_SCHEMA.ROUTINES

The INFORMATION_SCHEMA.ROUTINES view details information about the stored procedures and user-defined functions created on your system. Listing 21-7 shows the output of DESCRIBE and a simple SELECT on the view.

Listing 21-7. *INFORMATION_SCHEMA.ROUTINES*

```
mysql> DESCRIBE INFORMATION_SCHEMA.ROUTINES;
+--------------------+---------------+------+-----+---------------------+-------+
| Field              | Type          | Null | Key | Default             | Extra |
+--------------------+---------------+------+-----+---------------------+-------+
| SPECIFIC_NAME      | varchar(64)   | NO   |     |                     |       |
| ROUTINE_CATALOG    | varchar(4096) | YES  |     | NULL                |       |
| ROUTINE_SCHEMA     | varchar(64)   | NO   |     |                     |       |
| ROUTINE_NAME       | varchar(64)   | NO   |     |                     |       |
| ROUTINE_TYPE       | varchar(9)    | NO   |     |                     |       |
| DTD_IDENTIFIER     | varchar(64)   | YES  |     | NULL                |       |
| ROUTINE_BODY       | varchar(8)    | NO   |     |                     |       |
| ROUTINE_DEFINITION | longtext      | NO   |     |                     |       |
| EXTERNAL_NAME      | varchar(64)   | YES  |     | NULL                |       |
| EXTERNAL_LANGUAGE  | varchar(64)   | YES  |     | NULL                |       |
| PARAMETER_STYLE    | varchar(8)    | NO   |     |                     |       |
| IS_DETERMINISTIC   | varchar(3)    | NO   |     |                     |       |
| SQL_DATA_ACCESS    | varchar(64)   | NO   |     |                     |       |
| SQL_PATH           | varchar(64)   | YES  |     | NULL                |       |
| SECURITY_TYPE      | varchar(7)    | NO   |     |                     |       |
| CREATED            | datetime      | NO   |     | 0000-00-00 00:00:00 |       |
| LAST_ALTERED       | datetime      | NO   |     | 0000-00-00 00:00:00 |       |
| SQL_MODE           | longtext      | NO   |     |                     |       |
| ROUTINE_COMMENT    | varchar(64)   | NO   |     |                     |       |
| DEFINER            | varchar(77)   | NO   |     |                     |       |
+--------------------+---------------+------+-----+---------------------+-------+
20 rows in set (0.01 sec)

mysql> SELECT * FROM INFORMATION_SCHEMA.ROUTINES \G
*************************** 1. row ***************************
    SPECIFIC_NAME: test_proc1
  ROUTINE_CATALOG: NULL
   ROUTINE_SCHEMA: test
     ROUTINE_NAME: test_proc1
     ROUTINE_TYPE: PROCEDURE
```

```
       DTD_IDENTIFIER: NULL
         ROUTINE_BODY: SQL
   ROUTINE_DEFINITION: BEGIN
SELECT COUNT(*) INTO param1 FROM http_auth;
END
        EXTERNAL_NAME: NULL
    EXTERNAL_LANGUAGE: NULL
      PARAMETER_STYLE: SQL
     IS_DETERMINISTIC: NO
      SQL_DATA_ACCESS: CONTAINS SQL
             SQL_PATH: NULL
        SECURITY_TYPE: DEFINER
              CREATED: 2005-04-10 13:21:58
         LAST_ALTERED: 2005-04-10 13:21:58
             SQL_MODE:
      ROUTINE_COMMENT:
              DEFINER: root@localhost
1 row in set (0.00 sec)
```

The listing shows a simple test procedure we've created in the test schema for illustration purposes. If you're unfamiliar with stored procedures, please refer to Chapter 9.

The fields contained in INFORMATION_SCHEMA.ROUTINES are as follows:

- SPECIFIC_NAME: The name of the stored procedure or function.

- ROUTINE_CATALOG: Always NULL.

- ROUTINE_SCHEMA: The name of the database to which the procedure is tied.

- ROUTINE_NAME: Same as SPECIFIC_NAME.

- ROUTINE_TYPE: Either PROCEDURE or FUNCTION.

- DTD_IDENTIFIER: For functions, returns the complete data type definition of the function, otherwise NULL for procedures.

- ROUTINE_BODY: Shows the language in which the procedure is written. Currently, only the value SQL appears, but in future versions of MySQL, other extension languages may be used to write procedures.

- ROUTINE_DEFINITION: For procedures, shows either the whole procedure definition, or for long procedures, a truncated part of the definition.

- EXTERNAL_NAME: Always NULL, because all stored procedures in MySQL are kept internal to the database.

- EXTERNAL_LANGUAGE: Again, always NULL.

- PARAMETER_STYLE: Currently, only the value SQL appears for this column.

- IS_DETERMINISTIC: Either YES or NO. Shows whether the stored procedure or function will return the same value for the same passed input parameters.

- SQL_DATA_ACCESS: Any of NO SQL, CONTAINS SQL, READS SQL DATA, or MODIFIES SQL DATA. See Chapter 9 for an explanation of these various values.

- SQL_PATH: Always NULL.

- SECURITY_TYPE: Either DEFINER or INVOKER, depending on what type of security model was used during creation. Again, for more information check out Chapter 9.

- CREATED: Timestamp of when the procedure or function was created.

- LAST_ALTERED: Timestamp of the last alteration to the procedure or function.

- *SQL_MODE*: Shows the sql_mode server variable setting that was in effect at the time the procedure was created. This is done to ensure that the procedure is always run under the same mode as when it was created.

- *ROUTINE_COMMENT*: Any comment issued at procedure creation time.

- *DEFINER*: User who created the procedure in user@host format.

There's no SHOW command equivalent for the data contained in INFORMATION_SCHEMA. ROUTINES. However, the mysql.proc system table contains all the information available in the view.

INFORMATION_SCHEMA.VIEWS

The INFORMATION_SCHEMA.VIEWS view details information about the views created on the server. Listing 21-8 shows a DESCRIBE and a simple SELECT displaying a test view created for illustration purposes. For more information on views, check out Chapter 10.

Listing 21-8. *INFORMATION_SCHEMA.VIEWS*

```
mysql> DESCRIBE INFORMATION_SCHEMA.VIEWS;
+-----------------+---------------+------+-----+---------+-------+
| Field           | Type          | Null | Key | Default | Extra |
+-----------------+---------------+------+-----+---------+-------+
| TABLE_CATALOG   | varchar(4096) | YES  |     | NULL    |       |
| TABLE_SCHEMA    | varchar(64)   | NO   |     |         |       |
| TABLE_NAME      | varchar(64)   | NO   |     |         |       |
| VIEW_DEFINITION | longtext      | NO   |     |         |       |
| CHECK_OPTION    | varchar(8)    | NO   |     |         |       |
| IS_UPDATABLE    | varchar(3)    | NO   |     |         |       |
+-----------------+---------------+------+-----+---------+-------+
6 rows in set (0.00 sec)

mysql> SELECT * FROM INFORMATION_SCHEMA.VIEWS \G;
*************************** 1. row ***************************
  TABLE_CATALOG: NULL
   TABLE_SCHEMA: test
     TABLE_NAME: UserPass
VIEW_DEFINITION: select `test`.`http_auth`.`username` AS `username`, \
`test`.`http_auth`.`pass` AS `pass` from `test`.`http_auth`
   CHECK_OPTION: NONE
   IS_UPDATABLE: YES
1 row in set (0.04 sec)
```

The fields contained in INFORMATION_SCHEMA.VIEWS are as follows:

- TABLE_CATALOG: Always NULL.

- TABLE_SCHEMA: Database on which the view operates.

- TABLE_NAME: Name of the view.

- VIEW_DEFINITION: Complete definition of the view.

- CHECK_OPTION: Either NONE, LOCAL, or CASCADE, depending on the value of the WITH CHECK ➥ OPTION done during view creation. See Chapter 10 for details.

- IS_UPDATABLE: Either YES or NO, depending on whether the view supports updating.

As you can see, Listing 21-8 shows a simple view, called UserPass, in the test schema, which simply outputs the username and password columns from the http_auth table. The INFORMATION_SCHEMA.VIEWS view provides useful information about whether the view is updatable and its checking options. There is no equivalent SHOW command, though the mysql.views system table stores all the basic information displayed here.

INFORMATION_SCHEMA.CHARACTER_SETS

The INFORMATION_SCHEMA.CHARACTER_SETS view shows the available character sets on the database server. Listing 21-9 shows a DESCRIBE and limited SELECT on the view.

Listing 21-9. *INFORMATION_SCHEMA.CHARACTER_SETS*

```
mysql> DESCRIBE INFORMATION_SCHEMA.CHARACTER_SETS;
+----------------------+-------------+------+-----+---------+-------+
| Field                | Type        | Null | Key | Default | Extra |
+----------------------+-------------+------+-----+---------+-------+
| CHARACTER_SET_NAME   | varchar(64) | NO   |     |         |       |
| DEFAULT_COLLATE_NAME | varchar(64) | NO   |     |         |       |
| DESCRIPTION          | varchar(60) | NO   |     |         |       |
| MAXLEN               | bigint(3)   | NO   |     | 0       |       |
+----------------------+-------------+------+-----+---------+-------+
4 rows in set (0.00 sec)

mysql> SELECT * FROM INFORMATION_SCHEMA.CHARACTER_SETS LIMIT 5;
+--------------------+----------------------+--------------------------+--------+
| CHARACTER_SET_NAME | DEFAULT_COLLATE_NAME | DESCRIPTION              | MAXLEN |
+--------------------+----------------------+--------------------------+--------+
| dec8               | dec8_swedish_ci      | DEC West European        |      1 |
| cp850              | cp850_general_ci     | DOS West European        |      1 |
| hp8                | hp8_english_ci       | HP West European         |      1 |
| koi8r              | koi8r_general_ci     | KOI8-R Relcom Russian    |      1 |
| latin1             | latin1_swedish_ci    | ISO 8859-1 West European |      1 |
+--------------------+----------------------+--------------------------+--------+
5 rows in set (0.00 sec)
```

The fields contained in INFORMATION_SCHEMA.CHARACTER_SETS are as follows:

- CHARACTER_SET_NAME: Name of the character set.
- DEFAULT_COLLATION_NAME: Name of the default collation for this character set. See the following section, "INFORMATION_SCHEMA.COLLATIONS."
- *DESCRIPTION*: Description of the character set.
- *MAXLEN*: Shows the number of bytes used to store a single character in the set.

This view isn't the most useful in the world, but the extension field MAXLEN can come in handy when you want to get a list of character sets needing more than 1 byte to store characters.

■**Note** The SHOW CHARACTER SET command contains equivalent information to the INFORMATION_SCHEMA.CHARACTER_SETS view.

INFORMATION_SCHEMA.COLLATIONS

The INFORMATION_SCHEMA.COLLATIONS view lists the collations available to the current user. Listing 21-10 shows a DESCRIBE and a simple SELECT from the view.

Listing 21-10. *INFORMATION_SCHEMA.COLLATIONS*

```
mysql> DESCRIBE INFORMATION_SCHEMA.COLLATIONS;
+--------------------+-------------+------+-----+---------+-------+
| Field              | Type        | Null | Key | Default | Extra |
+--------------------+-------------+------+-----+---------+-------+
| COLLATION_NAME     | varchar(64) | NO   |     |         |       |
| CHARACTER_SET_NAME | varchar(64) | NO   |     |         |       |
| ID                 | bigint(11)  | NO   |     | 0       |       |
| IS_DEFAULT         | varchar(3)  | NO   |     |         |       |
| IS_COMPILED        | varchar(3)  | NO   |     |         |       |
| SORTLEN            | bigint(3)   | NO   |     | 0       |       |
+--------------------+-------------+------+-----+---------+-------+
6 rows in set (0.00 sec)

mysql> SELECT * FROM INFORMATION_SCHEMA.COLLATIONS LIMIT 5;
+------------------+--------------------+----+------------+-------------+---------+
| COLLATION_NAME   | CHARACTER_SET_NAME | ID | IS_DEFAULT | IS_COMPILED | SORTLEN |
+------------------+--------------------+----+------------+-------------+---------+
| dec8_swedish_ci  | dec8               |  3 | Yes        |             |       0 |
| dec8_bin         | dec8               | 69 |            |             |       0 |
| cp850_general_ci | cp850              |  4 | Yes        |             |       0 |
| cp850_bin        | cp850              | 80 |            |             |       0 |
| hp8_english_ci   | hp8                |  6 | Yes        |             |       0 |
+------------------+--------------------+----+------------+-------------+---------+
5 rows in set (0.00 sec)
```

The fields contained in `INFORMATION_SCHEMA.COLLATIONS` are as follows:

- `COLLATION_NAME`: Name of the collation.

- `CHARACTER_SET_NAME`: Name of the character set to which the collation applies.

- *ID*: A numeric identifier for the collation.

- *IS_DEFAULT*: Either YES or NO, indicating whether this collation is the server default for this character set.

- *IS_COMPILED*: Either YES or blank. Indicates whether the server has been compiled with this collation.

- *SORTLEN*: Shows the number of bytes needed in memory to perform sorting on the collation.

■**Note** The SHOW COLLATIONS command is most equivalent to a SELECT * FROM INFORMATION_ SCHEMA.COLLATIONS.

INFORMATION_SCHEMA.COLLATION_CHARACTER_SET_APPLICABILITY

The `INFORMATION_SCHEMA.COLLATION_CHARACTER_SET_APPLICABILITY` view shows the relation between character sets and collations. Listing 21-11 shows a `DESCRIBE` and a simple `SELECT` from the view.

Listing 21-11. *INFORMATION_SCHEMA.COLLATION_CHARACTER_SET_APPLICABILITY*

```
mysql> DESCRIBE INFORMATION_SCHEMA.COLLATION_CHARACTER_SET_APPLICABILITY;
+--------------------+-------------+------+-----+---------+-------+
| Field              | Type        | Null | Key | Default | Extra |
+--------------------+-------------+------+-----+---------+-------+
| COLLATION_NAME     | varchar(64) | NO   |     |         |       |
| CHARACTER_SET_NAME | varchar(64) | NO   |     |         |       |
+--------------------+-------------+------+-----+---------+-------+
2 rows in set (0.01 sec)

mysql> SELECT * FROM INFORMATION_SCHEMA.COLLATION_CHARACTER_SET_APPLICABILITY
    -> LIMIT 5;
+------------------+--------------------+
| COLLATION_NAME   | CHARACTER_SET_NAME |
+------------------+--------------------+
| dec8_swedish_ci  | dec8               |
| dec8_bin         | dec8               |
| cp850_general_ci | cp850              |
| cp850_bin        | cp850              |
| hp8_english_ci   | hp8                |
+------------------+--------------------+
5 rows in set (0.00 sec)
```

This view isn't terribly useful, and merely represents the first two columns of the `INFORMATION_SCHEMA.COLLATIONS` view.

INFORMATION_SCHEMA.SCHEMA_PRIVILEGES

The `INFORMATION_SCHEMA.SCHEMA_PRIVILEGES` table houses the database privileges on the server. This view is *not* part of the ANSI standard, and is provided so that a common interface can be used to gather information from the `mysql.db` system table for privileges associated with the database. Because MySQL tracks a separate level of permission at the database level, this view was added as a complement to the `TABLE_PRIVILEGES` and `COLUMN_PRIVILEGES` standard views. Listing 21-12 shows a `DESCRIBE` and a simple `SELECT` from the view.

Listing 21-12. *INFORMATION_SCHEMA.SCHEMA_PRIVILEGES*

```
mysql> DESCRIBE INFORMATION_SCHEMA.SCHEMA_PRIVILEGES;
+----------------+---------------+------+-----+---------+-------+
| Field          | Type          | Null | Key | Default | Extra |
+----------------+---------------+------+-----+---------+-------+
| GRANTEE        | varchar(81)   | NO   |     |         |       |
| TABLE_CATALOG  | varchar(4096) | YES  |     | NULL    |       |
| TABLE_SCHEMA   | varchar(64)   | NO   |     |         |       |
| PRIVILEGE_TYPE | varchar(64)   | NO   |     |         |       |
| IS_GRANTABLE   | varchar(3)    | NO   |     |         |       |
+----------------+---------------+------+-----+---------+-------+
5 rows in set (0.00 sec)

mysql> SELECT * FROM INFORMATION_SCHEMA.SCHEMA_PRIVILEGES LIMIT 5;
+---------+---------------+--------------+----------------+--------------+
| GRANTEE | TABLE_CATALOG | TABLE_SCHEMA | PRIVILEGE_TYPE | IS_GRANTABLE |
+---------+---------------+--------------+----------------+--------------+
| ''@'%'  | NULL          | test         | SELECT         | NO           |
| ''@'%'  | NULL          | test         | INSERT         | NO           |
| ''@'%'  | NULL          | test         | UPDATE         | NO           |
| ''@'%'  | NULL          | test         | DELETE         | NO           |
| ''@'%'  | NULL          | test         | CREATE         | NO           |
+---------+---------------+--------------+----------------+--------------+
5 rows in set (0.01 sec)
```

The fields contained in `INFORMATION_SCHEMA.SCHEMA_PRIVILEGES` are as follows:

- *GRANTEE*: Shows the `'user'@'host'` format for the user having this database access.

- *TABLE_CATALOG*: Always `NULL`.

- *TABLE_SCHEMA*: Shows the database for which the user has been granted access.

- *PRIVILEGE_TYPE*: Any of the standard privileges on a MySQL system dealing with database-level permissions.

- *IS_GRANTABLE*: Either `YES` or `NO`. Indicates whether the `WITH GRANT OPTION` was used in assigning access permissions.

The advantage of using this view over the `mysql.db` system table is that the SCHEMA_
PRIVILEGES view shows a *normalized* version of the grant information, with each privilege
provided in a separate row entry. However, unfortunately the User and Host columns of the
`mysql.db` table are combined in the view as the GRANTEE column. There's no equivalent SHOW
command for this operation.

INFORMATION_SCHEMA.USER_PRIVILEGES

Like the previous view, INFORMATION_SCHEMA.USER_PRIVILEGES is not part of the ANSI standard.
It shows information pertaining to the *global* privileges of the system users. Listing 21-13
shows a DESCRIBE and a simple SELECT from the view.

Listing 21-13. *INFORMATION_SCHEMA.USER_PRIVILEGES*

```
mysql> DESCRIBE INFORMATION_SCHEMA.USER_PRIVILEGES;
+----------------+---------------+------+-----+---------+-------+
| Field          | Type          | Null | Key | Default | Extra |
+----------------+---------------+------+-----+---------+-------+
| GRANTEE        | varchar(81)   | NO   |     |         |       |
| TABLE_CATALOG  | varchar(4096) | YES  |     | NULL    |       |
| PRIVILEGE_TYPE | varchar(64)   | NO   |     |         |       |
| IS_GRANTABLE   | varchar(3)    | NO   |     |         |       |
+----------------+---------------+------+-----+---------+-------+
4 rows in set (0.00 sec)

mysql> SELECT * FROM INFORMATION_SCHEMA.USER_PRIVILEGES LIMIT 5;
+--------------------+---------------+----------------+--------------+
| GRANTEE            | TABLE_CATALOG | PRIVILEGE_TYPE | IS_GRANTABLE |
+--------------------+---------------+----------------+--------------+
| 'root'@'localhost' | NULL          | SELECT         | YES          |
| 'root'@'localhost' | NULL          | INSERT         | YES          |
| 'root'@'localhost' | NULL          | UPDATE         | YES          |
| 'root'@'localhost' | NULL          | DELETE         | YES          |
| 'root'@'localhost' | NULL          | CREATE         | YES          |
+--------------------+---------------+----------------+--------------+
5 rows in set (0.00 sec)
```

The fields contained in INFORMATION_SCHEMA.USER_PRIVILEGES are as follows:

- *GRANTEE*: Again, the 'user'@'host' format for the privileged user.

- *TABLE_CATALOG*: Always NULL.

- *PRIVILEGE_TYPE*: Any of the MySQL standard global privilege types.

- *IS_GRANTABLE*: Either YES or NO. Was this user given the right to assign similar privileges
  using the WITH GRANT OPTION during creation?

Again, the advantage here is that privileges are normalized to appear as
entries. There's no SHOW command equivalent, but the information appearing
comes from the mysql.user system table, which stores the information in a d
normalized layout.

INFORMATION_SCHEMA.TABLE_PRIVILEGES

The INFORMATION_SCHEMA.TABLE_PRIVILEGES view *is* an ANSI standard view. It displays information about the user's table-level MySQL privileges. Listing 21-14 shows a DESCRIBE and a simple
SELECT for a mock user having limited access to the http_auth table in the test schema.

Listing 21-14. *INFORMATION_SCHEMA.TABLE_PRIVILEGES*

```
mysql> DESCRIBE INFORMATION_SCHEMA.TABLE_PRIVILEGES;
+----------------+---------------+------+-----+---------+-------+
| Field          | Type          | Null | Key | Default | Extra |
+----------------+---------------+------+-----+---------+-------+
| GRANTEE        | varchar(81)   | NO   |     |         |       |
| TABLE_CATALOG  | varchar(4096) | YES  |     | NULL    |       |
| TABLE_SCHEMA   | varchar(64)   | NO   |     |         |       |
| TABLE_NAME     | varchar(64)   | NO   |     |         |       |
| PRIVILEGE_TYPE | varchar(64)   | NO   |     |         |       |
| IS_GRANTABLE   | varchar(3)    | NO   |     |         |       |
+----------------+---------------+------+-----+---------+-------+
6 rows in set (0.00 sec)

mysql> SELECT * FROM INFORMATION_SCHEMA.TABLE_PRIVILEGES
    -> LIMIT 2 \G
*************************** 1. row ***************************
       GRANTEE: 'mkruck'@'localhost'
 TABLE_CATALOG: NULL
  TABLE_SCHEMA: ToyStore
    TABLE_NAME: Customer
PRIVILEGE_TYPE: SELECT
  IS_GRANTABLE: NO
*************************** 2. row ***************************
       GRANTEE: 'mkruck'@'localhost'
 TABLE_CATALOG: NULL
  TABLE_SCHEMA: ToyStore
    TABLE_NAME: Customer
PRIVILEGE_TYPE: INSERT
  IS_GRANTABLE: NO
2 rows in set (0.00 sec)
```

The fields contained in INFORMATION_SCHEMA.TABLE_PRIVILEGES are as follows:

- GRANTEE: Again, the user in a 'user'@'host' format.

- TABLE_CATALOG: Always NULL.

- TABLE_SCHEMA: Name of the database housing the table.

- TABLE_NAME: Name of the table.

- PRIVILEGE_TYPE: Any of the MySQL table-level privileges available to the user.

- IS_GRANTABLE: Either YES or NO, depending on whether the WITH GRANT OPTION was used in assignment of privileges.

Like the previous privilege views, there's no equivalent SHOW command. The view represents a normalized perspective of the mysql.tables_priv system table, and is a combination of results returned by SHOW GRANTS and SHOW FULL COLUMNS.

INFORMATION_SCHEMA.COLUMN_PRIVILEGES

Finally, the INFORMATION_SCHEMA.COLUMN_PRIVILEGES view is an ANSI standard view that shows grant information at the column level. Listing 21-15 shows a DESCRIBE and a simple SELECT from the view.

Listing 21-15. *INFORMATION_SCHEMA.COLUMN_PRIVILEGES*

```
mysql> DESCRIBE INFORMATION_SCHEMA.COLUMN_PRIVILEGES;
+----------------+---------------+------+-----+---------+-------+
| Field          | Type          | Null | Key | Default | Extra |
+----------------+---------------+------+-----+---------+-------+
| GRANTEE        | varchar(81)   | NO   |     |         |       |
| TABLE_CATALOG  | varchar(4096) | YES  |     | NULL    |       |
| TABLE_SCHEMA   | varchar(64)   | NO   |     |         |       |
| TABLE_NAME     | varchar(64)   | NO   |     |         |       |
| COLUMN_NAME    | varchar(64)   | NO   |     |         |       |
| PRIVILEGE_TYPE | varchar(64)   | NO   |     |         |       |
| IS_GRANTABLE   | varchar(3)    | NO   |     |         |       |
+----------------+---------------+------+-----+---------+-------+
7 rows in set (0.00 sec)

mysql> SELECT * FROM INFORMATION_SCHEMA.COLUMN_PRIVILEGES \G
*************************** 1. row ***************************
      GRANTEE: 'test_user2'@'localhost'
 TABLE_CATALOG: NULL
  TABLE_SCHEMA: test
    TABLE_NAME: http_auth
   COLUMN_NAME: uid
PRIVILEGE_TYPE: UPDATE
  IS_GRANTABLE: NO
*************************** 2. row ***************************
      GRANTEE: 'test_user2'@'localhost'
 TABLE_CATALOG: NULL
  TABLE_SCHEMA: test
    TABLE_NAME: http_auth
```

```
    COLUMN_NAME: username
PRIVILEGE_TYPE: UPDATE
  IS_GRANTABLE: NO
2 rows in set (0.00 sec)
```

The fields contained in INFORMATION_SCHEMA.COLUMN_PRIVILEGES are as follows:

- GRANTEE: The user in 'user'@'host' format.

- TABLE_CATALOG: Always NULL.

- TABLE_SCHEMA: Name of the database housing the table.

- TABLE_NAME: Name of the table.

- COLUMN_NAME: Name of the column.

- PRIVILEGE_TYPE: Any of the MySQL column-level privileges available to the user.

- IS_GRANTABLE: Either YES or NO, depending on whether the WITH GRANT OPTION was used in assignment of privileges.

Again, the results from the view show a mixed combination of the results from SHOW GRANTS and SHOW FULL COLUMNS, but in a normalized output. Internally, the view is pulling from the mysql.columns_priv system table.

Usage Examples

Now that you're familiar with the INFORMATION_SCHEMA views, we're going to take you a step further than simple SELECTs, and create some examples that should highlight the power and flexibility of this new interface. We'll work through the following examples:

- How to gather selectivity numbers on indexes

- How to summarize table sizes by engine

Example 1: Gathering Selectivity Numbers on Indexes

In the first part of the book, you learned about the importance of knowing the selectivity of your indexes, and you should understand how a low selectivity may lead to poor performance of certain queries using your indexes. In this example, we'll create a SQL script that looks at the INFORMATION_SCHEMA views and outputs the selectivity numbers for each of your indexes.

The goal of our script is as follows:

- Limit results only to indexes with a selectivity lower than 1.0. Index selectivity of 1.0 means that the index is unique. We're not interested in identifying unique indexes, as they're generally not performance problems.

- Sort the results based on the lowest selectivity to the highest. Remember, the selectivity of an index can be viewed as the number of unique values in the index divided by the total number of entries in the index.

Listing 21-16 shows our script.

Listing 21-16. *ShowIndexSelectivity.sql*

```
SELECT
    t.TABLE_SCHEMA
    , t.TABLE_NAME
    , s.INDEX_NAME
    , s.COLUMN_NAME
    , s.SEQ_IN_INDEX
    , (
        SELECT MAX(SEQ_IN_INDEX)
        FROM INFORMATION_SCHEMA.STATISTICS s2
        WHERE s.TABLE_SCHEMA = s2.TABLE_SCHEMA
        AND s.TABLE_NAME = s2.TABLE_NAME
        AND s.INDEX_NAME = s2.INDEX_NAME
    ) AS "COLS_IN_INDEX"
    , s.CARDINALITY AS "CARD"
    , t.TABLE_ROWS AS "ROWS"
    , ROUND(((s.CARDINALITY / IFNULL(t.TABLE_ROWS, 0.01)) * 100), 2) AS "SEL %"
FROM INFORMATION_SCHEMA.STATISTICS s
    INNER JOIN INFORMATION_SCHEMA.TABLES t
    ON s.TABLE_SCHEMA = t.TABLE_SCHEMA
    AND s.TABLE_NAME = t.TABLE_NAME
WHERE t.TABLE_SCHEMA != 'mysql'
    AND t.TABLE_ROWS > 10
    AND s.CARDINALITY IS NOT NULL
    AND (s.CARDINALITY / IFNULL(t.TABLE_ROWS, 0.01)) < 1.00
ORDER BY t.TABLE_SCHEMA, t.TABLE_NAME, s.INDEX_NAME, "SEL %" \G
```

Here we see the true power of the INFORMATION_SCHEMA interface. This would have been impossible to do with a single SQL SELECT before. Instead, to get the same information, we would have had to use a scripting language to make multiple calls to SHOW INDEX and SHOW ➥ TABLE STATUS, combining the results into a table format. In the ShowIndexSelectivity script, we use a correlated scalar subquery to find the total number of columns in the index (see Chapter 8). We then join the STATISTICS and TABLES views to get all the information we need, and use a calculated column to output the selectivity percentage for the Index part.

Listing 21-17 shows the output of our script when run against a small sample database containing some Job (as in Career) data tables.

Listing 21-17. *Output from ShowIndexSelectivity*

```
mysql> source ShowIndexSelectivity.sql
*************************** 1. row ***************************
 TABLE_SCHEMA: jobs
   TABLE_NAME: Job
   INDEX_NAME: EmployerExpiresOn
  COLUMN_NAME: Employer
 SEQ_IN_INDEX: 1
COLS_IN_INDEX: 2
```

```
                 CARD: 31
                 ROWS: 56895
                SEL %: 0.05
*************************** 2. row ***************************
  TABLE_SCHEMA: jobs
    TABLE_NAME: Job
    INDEX_NAME: EmployerExpiresOn
   COLUMN_NAME: ExpiresOn
  SEQ_IN_INDEX: 2
 COLS_IN_INDEX: 2
          CARD: 49
          ROWS: 56895
         SEL %: 0.09
*************************** 3. row ***************************
  TABLE_SCHEMA: jobs
    TABLE_NAME: Job
    INDEX_NAME: ExpiresOnLocation
   COLUMN_NAME: Location
  SEQ_IN_INDEX: 2
 COLS_IN_INDEX: 2
          CARD: 28447
          ROWS: 56895
         SEL %: 50.00
*************************** 4. row ***************************
  TABLE_SCHEMA: jobs
    TABLE_NAME: Job
    INDEX_NAME: ExpiresOnLocation
   COLUMN_NAME: ExpiresOn
  SEQ_IN_INDEX: 1
 COLS_IN_INDEX: 2
          CARD: 38
          ROWS: 56895
         SEL %: 0.07
... omitted
*************************** 13. row ***************************
  TABLE_SCHEMA: jobs
    TABLE_NAME: EmployerRegion
    INDEX_NAME: PRIMARY
   COLUMN_NAME: Employer
  SEQ_IN_INDEX: 1
 COLS_IN_INDEX: 2
          CARD: 9
          ROWS: 495
         SEL %: 1.82
*************************** 14. row ***************************
  TABLE_SCHEMA: jobs
    TABLE_NAME: JobSeekerJob
```

```
    INDEX_NAME: PRIMARY
   COLUMN_NAME: JobSeeker
  SEQ_IN_INDEX: 1
 COLS_IN_INDEX: 3
          CARD: 7687
          ROWS: 23062
         SEL %: 33.33
14 rows in set (0.47 sec)
```

■**Tip** In Listing 21-17, you see an example of using the MySQL client `source` command, which simply takes a filename parameter and executes the SQL source in the file.

It's important to recognize here that the `STATISTICS.CARDINALITY` field contains the number of unique entries for *the current column and all columns in the index of a lower ordinal position*. This means that the value returned for the second column in a three-part index includes the total number of unique *tuples*, or entries, for all combinations of the first and second index part. This is tracked in this way because you can only use an index if all parts of the index to the left of the current column are used in a `WHERE` or `ON` condition.

In the preceding results, what have we identified for the `Job` table? It seems that the `EmployerExpiresOn` index, which is a two-part index comprised of the `Employer` and `ExpiresOn` columns of the `Job` table, has extremely low selectivity for *both* parts of the index keys. This query has shown us an index that, more than likely, the optimizer won't use, because the distribution of values is so sparse.

Example 2: Summarizing Table Sizes by Engine

In our second example, we want to display a report that does the following:

- Summarizes the total size, in megabytes, of all our database tables, grouped by storage engine.

- Shows a running total size. We'll use our knowledge of running totals from Chapter 8.

Listing 21-18 shows the `EngineStorageSummary.sql` script.

Listing 21-18. *EngineStorageSummary.sql*

```
SELECT
   t1.ENGINE
 , t1.SIZE_IN_MB / (1024 * 1024) AS "ENGINE MB"
 , SUM(t2.SIZE_IN_MB) / (1024 * 1024) AS "Total MB"
 FROM
 (
  SELECT ENGINE, SUM(DATA_LENGTH) AS "SIZE_IN_MB"
  FROM INFORMATION_SCHEMA.TABLES
  WHERE ENGINE IS NOT NULL
```

```
  GROUP BY ENGINE
  ) as t1
  INNER JOIN
  (
   SELECT ENGINE, SUM(DATA_LENGTH) AS "SIZE_IN_MB"
    FROM INFORMATION_SCHEMA.TABLES
    WHERE ENGINE IS NOT NULL
    GROUP BY ENGINE
  ) as t2
   ON t1.ENGINE >= t2.ENGINE
GROUP BY t1.ENGINE;
```

Here, we've demonstrated the use of running sum calculations by joining two identical derived tables using the >= operator. The outermost SELECT statement simply divides the sum and the running sum by the (1024 * 1024) constant to produce the storage needed in terms of megabytes. Listing 21-19 shows the result on our test system.

Listing 21-19. *Results of EngineStorageSummary.sql*

```
mysql> source EngineStorageSummary.sql
+--------+-----------+----------+
| ENGINE | ENGINE MB | Total MB |
+--------+-----------+----------+
| InnoDB | 4.51563   | 4.51563  |
| MEMORY | 0.00000   | 4.51563  |
| MyISAM | 23.55081  | 28.06643 |
+--------+-----------+----------+
3 rows in set (0.10 sec)
```

Note that the MEMORY engine doesn't take up any storage space; everything is in RAM.

Although these are simple examples of what can be done with the INFORMATION_SCHEMA views, we hope they illustrate the power and flexibility of this new standards interface.

Summary

In this final chapter, you've learned about one of the newest features of the MySQL 5 server: INFORMATION_SCHEMA. You were introduced to some of the advantages of using this virtual database for reviewing metadata about your database objects, most notably the benefits of standardization and the ability to use SELECT to view metadata. We detailed the fields available in each of the views in INFORMATION_SCHEMA. Afterwards, we demonstrated how valuable the virtual database interface can be through two examples that wouldn't previously have been possible in a single SELECT statement.

Because this is a new feature, be sure to check http://www.mysql.com in case new columns or views become available. We hope that you'll take some time to experiment with the INFORMATION_SCHEMA views, and create some of your own scripts summarizing the metadata stored in MySQL.

Index

forums.apress.com